Handbook of Cross-Cultural Psychology

METHODOLOGY

VOLUME 2

EDITED BY

Harry C. Triandis
University of Illinois at Urbana-Champaign, USA

John W. Berry
Queens University, Kingston, Ontario, Canada

ALLYN AND BACON, INC.
Boston   London   Sydney   Toronto

Library of Congress Cataloging in Publication Data

Main entry under title:

Handbook of cross-cultural psychology.

    Includes bibliographies and index.
    CONTENTS: v. 1. Triandis, H. C. and Lambert, W. W.,
editor. Perspectives.—v. 2. Triandis, H. C. and Berry,
J. W., editors. Methodology.—v. 3. Triandis, H. C.
and Lonner, W. Basic processes.— [etc.]
    1. Ethnopsychology—Collected works. I. Triandis,
Harry Charalambos, 1926—
GN502.H36   155.8   79-15905
ISBN 0-205-06498-1 (v. 2)

Printed in the United States of America.

Contents

Volume 3. BASIC PROCESSES

Volume 4.   DEVELOPMENTAL PSYCHOLOGY   (in press)

Preface

Cross-cultural psychology has been expanding in the past twenty years[1] to the point that there is now a need for a source book more advanced than a textbook and more focused than the periodical literature. This is the first handbook of cross-cultural psychology. It is an attempt to assemble in one place the key findings of cross-cultural psychologists. In addition to serving the needs of graduate instruction, the *Handbook* will be useful to advanced undergraduates and to professional social and behavioral scientists.

This *Handbook* will do more than summarize the state of cross-cultural psychology in the 1970s. It should provide a bridge that will allow more traffic in the direction of a new kind of psychology. One of the key facts about psychology is that most of the psychologists who have ever lived and who are now living can be found in the United States. About 50,000 psychologists live in the United States and several thousand more graduate each year. The rest of the world has only about 20 percent of the psychologists that are now or have ever been alive. Moreover, psychology as a science is so overwhelmingly the product of German, French, British, Russian, and North American efforts that it is fair to consider it an entirely European-based enterprise (with American culture considered the child of European culture). Yet, science aspires to be universal. Cross-cultural psychologists try to discover laws that will be stable over time and across cultures, but the data base excludes the great majority of mankind who live in Asia and the Southern Hemisphere. Are so-called "psychological laws" really universal? Are theories merely parochial generalizations, based on ethnocentric constructions of reality? This *Handbook* assembles reports of the methods, procedures, and findings that ultimately will give definitive answers to such questions, answers that are crucial for the development of psychology. If psychology must be changed to understand the behavior and experience of the majority of mankind, then this is a fact of profound importance. If not, it is still good to know that no changes are needed. The reality probably lies between these two extremes, and different psychological laws can be held as "true" with varying degrees of confidence.

We engage in cross-cultural psychology for many reasons, which are enumerated in the Introduction to Volume 1. Volume 1 examines the field in broad perspective and examines how it relates to some other fields. Volume 2 focuses on methodology, since the cross-cultural enterprise poses formidable methodological difficulties. The remaining volumes concentrate on basic psychological processes such as learning, motivation, and perception (Volume 3); developmental processes (Volume 4); social psychological (Volume 5); and psychopathological (Volume 6) phenomena.

One key policy decision for a handbook is whether to cover the material exhaustively, saying a word or two about every study, or in depth, saying rather more about a few key studies. Our decision for greater depth resulted in incomplete coverage. However, much of the work in cross-cultural psychology is methodologically weak. Rather than attacking such studies, we decided to de-emphasize them in favor of those studies that are methodologically defensible. However, this was not a decision that was applicable to all the methodologically weak areas. In some areas of cross-cultural psychology, there has been so *much* weak work that any student starting to work on related problems is likely to find dozens of studies and hence get the impression that this is a respectable area of inquiry. In such cases we could not ignore the weak studies. But while we had to quote them and criticize them, we could not sacrifice much space in this effort. For instance, most of the work using versions of the prisoner dilemma game in different cultures results in uninterpretable findings. In Volume 5 Leon Mann and Gergen, Morse, and Gergen discuss this work and show why it is weak.

Some work was left out simply because space limitations did not allow complete coverage. Other work was omitted on the grounds that it really is not cross-cultural psychology, and may more appropriately be included in comparative sociology, cultural anthropology, or some other field. Some of these decisions are inevitably arbitrary. Obviously, a *Handbook* like this one is likely to *define* the field, both by what it includes and by what it excludes. We are distinctly uncomfortable about some of the exclusions. For instance, our coverage of Freudian, neopsychoanalytic, and related cross-cultural studies is extremely limited. However, other theoretical systems, such as a "liberated cognitive behaviorism" (Triandis, 1977) will encompass the insights derived from this tradition. We have very little discussion of ethnoscience, ethnomusicology, and ethnolinguistics; we believe these materials now belong to other neighboring disciplines. It is of course obvious that this judgment may be wrong. A revision of this *Handbook*, which may be necessary in a decade or two, could well give a central position to one of these topics.

In writing this *Handbook* we have been very much aware of the probability that psychologists from non-European-derived cultures will find it among the most useful books that they may obtain from European-derived cultures. Much of what psychologists teach in their own cultures is based on studies done with subjects from European-derived cultures. They cannot be sure that such information is culture-general. This *Handbook* faces this question and could become a companion volume of any European-derived psychology book. Since many psychologists do not have English as their first language, we have tried to keep the language as concise as possible. If the style appears telegraphic at times, it is intentional.

We allowed the authors of the chapters considerable freedom in expressing themselves. We felt that an international enterprise such as this *Handbook*, should not impose narrow, possibly ethnocentric standards. Thus, authors have been allowed to use the style and spelling that is more appropriate in their own country. English now exists in many versions; the language of Scotland is not identical to Indian English. Rather than obliterate such differences with a heavy editorial hand, we have preserved them.

Volume 1 includes background material that any serious student of cross-cultural psychology would want to know. It examines the history, the major theoretical frameworks, and the relationship between cross-cultural psychology and some other closely related disciplines.

Volume 2 concentrates on methodological problems. Cross-cultural psychology has all the methodological problems of research done by psychologists in a homogeneous culture, plus additional ones that arise because it is cross-cultural. The authors describe the particular technique and emphasize the special difficulties—the particular methodological dilemmas that one faces in cross-cultural work—stressing those strategies developed to deal with those dilemmas. For example, since the reader is assumed to know about experimental methods, the chapters on experiments deal only with special concerns of cross-cultural psychologists doing experiments.

Volume 3 focuses on basic psychological processes—perception, learning, motivation, and so on. Here we tried to give the experimental psychologists who investigate such processes a chance to expand their perspective. We focused on what appears to be universal, but also emphasized ways in which cultural factors may intrude and change some of the processes.

Volume 4 examines developmental perspectives. Some of the key areas discussed are the development of language, personality, and cognition. Since the major effort in the past twenty years in cross-cultural developmental psychology has been on testing aspects of Piaget's theoretical system, a major focus is on this topic.

Volume 5 deals with cross-cultural social psychology. It examines the major traditional topics—attitudes, values, groups, social change—and some of the newer topics—environmental psychology and organizational psychology.

Volume 6, the last one, is of greatest interest to clinical psychologists or psychiatrists. The focus is on variations of psychopathology, on methods of clinical work, as well as on the cultural and family antecedents of psychopathology.

Our expectation is that the committed student of cross-cultural psychology will want to own all six volumes. However, in this age of specialization and high costs we know that many will buy only Volume 1 plus one other. Finally, certain specialists will want a single volume to enlarge their perspective on their own discipline, by examining the related cross-cultural work. These different patterns of acquisition produce a serious policy problem concerning coverage. A key theory or key cross-cultural finding may have to be mentioned in each volume for those who purchase only one volume, which may create considerable overlap across volumes. However, the authors have cross-referenced chapters in other volumes. Also, we have allowed minimum coverage of a particular topic that has been covered extensively in another volume, so that purchasers of only one volume will acquire some superficial familiarity with that topic.

In some cases, the topics are sufficiently large and diffuse that coverage by two different authors does not result in redundancy. When this was the case, I simply sent copies of the relevant sections of other chapters to these authors and asked them, when revising, to be fully aware of coverage in other chapters.

The idea to publish a *Handbook of Cross-Cultural Psychology* originated with Jack Peters of Allyn and Bacon, Inc. He asked me at the 1972 meetings of the American Psychological Association, in Hawaii, whether I would be interested in editing such a handbook. The idea appealed to me, but I was not sure of the need. We wrote to a sample of distinguished psychologists for their opinions. They were almost unanimous in thinking that such a handbook would be worth publishing. At the conference on "The Interface between Culture and Learning," held by the East-West Center, in Hawaii, in January 1973 we asked a distinguished, international sample of cross-cultural psychologists for their opinion. They were also supportive. By the summer of 1973 a first outline of a handbook was available, but it also became very clear that I alone could not handle the editing. The handbook should reflect all of psychology; I was not competent to deal with such a vast subject. Hence the idea emerged of having several Associate Editors, who would cover different aspects of the topic.

The Society for Cross-Cultural Research, at its 1975 Chicago meetings, heard a symposium in which G. Kelly, G. Guthrie, W. Lambert, J. Tapp, W. Goodenough, H. Barry, R. Naroll, and I presented our ideas about the shape of the *Handbook,* and we heard criticism from both anthropologists and psychologists in the audience about our plans.

In January 1976 we were fortunate to be able to hold a conference sponsored by the East-West Center, Hawaii, in which about two-thirds of the chapters were thoroughly discussed. We are most grateful to the Center for this support. The East-West Center held a course for post-doctoral level, young social scientists from Asia, the Pacific, and the United States, using the drafts of the *Handbook* chapters as a textbook. Richard Brislin, Stephen Bochner, and George Guthrie were the faculty. Fifteen outstanding young social scientists[2] were thus able to give us feedback from the point of view of the consumer, but even more important, they pointed out statements that may have been ethnocentric, incorrect, confusing, and outdated.

From the very beginning, we were committed to producing a handbook with authors from every continent. This was not possible. However, the *Handbook* includes chapters by authors from nine countries. To avoid as much ethnocentrism as possible, I appointed a board of twenty Regional Editors. These editors were asked to supply abstracts of publications not generally available in European and North American libraries. These abstracts were sent to those chapter authors who might find them useful. Thus, we increased the chapter authors' exposure to the non-English international literature. By summer 1975, fourteen of these twenty Regional Editors had supplied abstracts listed by cultural region. They were:

Africa

R. Ogbonna Ohuche (University of Liberia, Monrovia, Liberia)
The late M. O. Okonji (University of Lagos, Nigeria)
Christopher Orpen (University of Cape Town, South Africa)
Robert Serpell (University of Zambia, Lusaka, Zambia)

Circum-Mediterranean

Yehuda Amir (Bar-Ilan University, Israel)
Terry Prothro (American University, Beirut, Lebanon)

East-Eurasia

S. Anandalakshmy (Lady Irwin College, New Delhi, India)
John L. M. Dawson (University of Hong Kong)
Wong Fong Tong (Jamaah Nazir Sekolah, Kuala Lumpur, Malaysia)
S. M. Hafeez Zaidi (University of Karachi, Pakistan)

Insular Pacific
Subhas Chandra (University of South Pacific, Fiji)

South America

Eduardo Almeida (Mexico City)
Gerardo Marin (Universidad de los Andes, Bogotá, Colombia)
Jose Miguel Salazar (Universidad Central de Venezuela, Caracas, Venezuela)

It should be mentioned that with such an international group of authors, chapters required particularly skillful editing of the style so that all chapters would be excellent not only in content but in language. My wife, Pola, and Doris S. Bartle supplied this expertise and were among those who contributed to the realization of a truly international undertaking.

A number of colleagues functioned as special reviewers for individual chapters. Thanks are due to S. M. Berger, Charles Eriksen, Lucia French, Lloyd Humphreys, and Fred Lehman for their critical comments. In addition, the final version of each volume was read by a scholar, and I would also like to acknowledge their valuable suggestions and comments: Volume 1, Daniel Katz; Volume 2, Uriel Foa; Volume 3, Lee Sechrest; Volume 4, Barbara Lloyd and Sylvia Scribner; Volume 5, Albert Pepitone; and Volume 6, Ihsan Al-Issa.

Harry C. Triandis

NOTES

1. Documentation of this point would include noting that several journals (the *International Journal of Psychology*, the *Journal of Social Psychology* and the *Journal of Cross-Cultural Psychology*) publish almost exclusively cross-cultural papers; there is a *Newsletter*, first published in 1967, that is largely concerned with this area; there are *Directories* of the membership of cross-cultural psychologists, first published by Berry in the *International Journal of Psychology* in 1969, then revised and extended and published as a booklet by Berry and Lonner (1970) and Berry, Lonner, and Leroux (1973); and finally, there is the International Association for Cross-Cultural Psychology, which has held meetings in Hong Kong (1972), Kingston, Canada (1974), Tilburg, Holland (1976), Munich, West Germany (1978), which now has a membership of about 350 active researchers from about fifty countries. Psychology has been an international enterprise for almost a century, and the Union of Scientific Psychology, and the International Association of Applied Psychology have been meeting every two or so years, since the turn of the century. But the emphasis on collecting *comparable* data in several cultures is relatively new, and has expanded particularly after the mid 1960s. A number of regional international organizations, such as the Interamerican Society of Psychology, and the Mediterranean Society of Psychology, have become active in the last twenty years.

2. Listed by country the participants were:
   Australia: Brian Bishop (Perth, Institute of Technology), Margaret M. Brandl (Darwin, Department of Education), Betty A. Drinkwater (Townsville, James Cook University), Michael P. O'Driscoll (Adelaide, Flinders University).
   Fiji: Lavenia Kaurasi (Suva, Malhala High School)
   Indonesia: Suwarsih Warnaen (Jakarta, University of Indonesia)
   Japan: Yuriko Oshimo (University of Tokyo) and Toshio Osako (Tokyo, Sophia University)
   Pakistan: Sabeeha Hafeez (Karachi University), Abdul Haque (Hyderabad, University of Sind)

Philippines: Liwayway N. Angeles (Rizal, Teacher Education)
Thailand: Jirawat Wongswadiwat (Chaingmai University)
United States: Angela B. Ginorio (New York, Fordham University), Howard Higginbotham (University of Hawaii), Caroline F. Keating (Syracuse University), and James M. Orvik (Fairbanks, University of Alaska)

At the conference, the following authors and editors, in addition to Brislin, Bochner, and Guthrie, were also present: Altman, Barry, Berry, Ciborowski, Davidson, Deregowski, Draguns, Heron, Holtzman, Hsu, Jahoda, Kiineberg, Lambert, Longabaugh, Lonner, R. and R. Munroe, Michik, Pareek, Price-Williams, Prince, Sanua, Sutton-Smith, E. Thompson, Tseng, Triandis, Warwick, Zavalloni.

Biographical Statements

HARRY C. TRIANDIS, the General Editor, was born in Greece, in 1926. During childhood he received several cross-cultural influences: German and French governesses, French and Italian high school years. After three years of engineering studies at the Polytechnic Institute of Athens, he attended McGill University in Montreal, Canada, where he graduated in Engineering. He worked in industry for three years, during which he obtained a master's degree from the University of Toronto. But engineering was not as interesting to him as studying people. He returned to McGill to learn basic psychology, and studied with Wallace E. Lambert and Don Hebb. From there he went to Cornell University, where he studied with W. W. Lambert, W. F. Whyte, T. A. Ryan, Alexander Leighton, and others. From Cornell in 1958 he went to the University of Illinois, where he is now Professor of Psychology. He conducted cross-cultural studies in Greece, Germany, Japan, and India, and worked in collaboration with black psychologists on the perceptions of the social environment among blacks and whites. His books include *Attitude and Attitude Change* (1971), *The Analysis of Subjective Culture* (1972), *Variations in Black and White Perceptions of the Social Environment* (1975), and *Interpersonal Behavior* (1977). He was Chairman of the Society of Experimental Social Psychology (1973–74), President of the International Association of Cross-Cultural Psychology (1974–76), President of the Society for the Psychological Study of Social Issues (1975–76), President of the Society of Personality and Social Psychology (1976–77), and Vice-President of the Interamerican Society of Psychology (1975–77).

JOHN W. BERRY was born in Montreal, in 1939. He grew up in rural Quebec, completed high school in Montreal, and then spent three years working as a merchant seaman. He graduated from Sir George Williams University (Montreal) in 1963, and obtained a Ph.D. from the University of Edinburgh in 1966. His research has been directed toward the study of the development of behaviour in differing ecological and cultural settings, toward the psychological effects of acculturation and the study of intergroup attitudes and relations. He has conducted field studies in Arctic Canada (Eskimo, Cree) and the mid-north (Ojibway, Carrier and Tsimshian), in Africa (the Temne of Sierra Leone and the Pygmy of the Central African Republic), in Australia (the Arunta, the Koongangi, and the Illawara) and in New Guinea (the highland Telefol and the coastal Motu). His books include *Social Psychology: The Canadian Context* (edited with G. J. S. Wilde, 1972), *Culture and Cognition* (edited with P. Dasen, 1974), *Applied Cross-Cultural Psychology* (edited with W. Lonner, 1975), *Multiculturalism and Ethnic Attitudes in Canada* (with R. Kalin and D. Taylor, 1976), and *Ecology of Cognitive Style: Comparative Studies in Cultural and Psychological Adaptation* (1976).

WARD H. GOODENOUGH was born in Cambridge, Mass. in 1919. Most of his early childhood was spent in England and Germany, and he was bilingual in English and German at the time of his return to New Haven, Conn. where he resided until 1948. He attended Groton School, took his A.B. in Scandinavian languages and literature at Cornell University in 1940, and his Ph.D. in anthropology at Yale University in 1949. From 1941 to 1946 he was first an infantryman, then a field worker in attitude and opinion research for the Research Branch of the Information and Education Division of the War Department, including seven months in Italy, and finally a civilian case analyst for the Corrections Branch of the Adjutant General's Office. After one year as an instructor at the University of Wisconsin, he joined the anthropology faculty at the University of Pennsylvania, where he became professor in 1962 and department chairman in 1976. He has done ethnographic research in Micronesia (Truk, 1947 and 1964-65; Gilbert Islands, 1951), and Papua, New Guinea (1951 and 1954). His books and monographs include *Property, Kin, and Community on Truk* (1951), *Cooperation in Change* (1963), *Description and Comparison in Cultural Anthropology* (1970), *Culture, Language and Society* (1971), and an edited volume *Explorations in Cultural Anthropology* (1964). He has been editor of the *American Anthropologist* (1966–70), President of the American Ethnological Society (1962), President of the Society for Applied Anthropology (1964), Vice President and Chairman of Section H in the American Association for the Advancement of Science (1971), a Director of the same organization (1972–75), and Chairman of the Board, Human Relations Area Files, Inc. (1971). He is a member of the National Academy of Sciences, the American Philosophical Society, and the American Academy of Arts and Sciences.

RICHARD LONGABAUGH received his A.B. from Dartmouth College, in 1957, with a psychology major and minor in sociology and anthropology. He received an M.A. from Harvard University in 1958. He enrolled in the doctoral program in Human Development at Harvard directed by John W. M. Whiting. This program focused on developmental psychology, personality, and psychological anthropology. It was in this setting that he first became exposed to cross-cultural research. His doctoral dissertation involved the systematic behavioral observations of black mothers and their children, first- and second-generation descendents from the southern United States on the island of Barbados. During this period he also became involved with the analysis of the observational data collected from the Six Cultures study. Concomitantly he began observational studies of psychiatric patients diagnosed as schizophrenic who were living in a long-term hospital residential setting. After a year's postdoctoral research he went to Cornell University to teach social psychology. In 1966 he moved to Harvard Medical School and McLean Hospital where he initiated further observational research involving hospitalized populations of psychiatric patients. His research with psychiatric populations broadened to include methodologies other than systematic behavioral observations. However, his interests in this methodology, especially as applied to the study of social behavior remained paramount. In 1971 he was at the University of California at San Francisco's Langley Porter Neuropsychiatric Unit. Following this he accepted a position at Brown University, as Associate Professor of Medical Science and at Butler Hospital as Director of Evaluation and Research. Throughout this period he has continued his study of the use of systematic behavioral observations in naturalistic settings and has benefited greatly from collaboration with colleagues of other disciplines: anthropology, psychiatry, sociology and the information sciences, as well as from stimulation from other cross-cultural researchers. His continuing studies of psychiatric patients have provided interesting similarities and contrast to his work with nondeviant populations from other cultures.

UDAI PAREEK was born in India in 1925. After taking a Master's degree in psychology from Calcutta University and a Bachelor's degree in education from Agra University and another Master's in philosophy, he taught educational psychology in Teachers Training Institutes. He spent a year in 1952–53 in the University of Rome for cross-cultural research in personality using some projective techniques. Then he went to Delhi University for his doctoral work in psychology. He worked in the field of education. With Stephen M. Corey he worked in designing programmes of action research in India. In 1962 he travelled for six months to the United States for specialised work in laboratory training and group dynamics. He worked with Mathew Miles and Kenneth Benne. After returning to India he worked in agriculture and then in small industry. He worked with Rolf Lynton in designing laboratory training programmes in India, and coauthored with him *Training for Development*. With Willis Griffin he worked on the process of change in education and coauthored with him *The Process of Planned Change in Education*. From 1966–68 he taught psychology at the University of North Carolina at Chapel Hill, and was a member of the Carolina Population Center. He was elected an Associate and later a Fellow of the National Training Laboratories. He worked as a trainer with several American and cross-national groups in the United States, and with a group of industrial executives in Egypt. On returning to India, he worked in the field of health, took an administrative role in a university, and joined the Indian Institute of Management at Ahmedabad, where he is currently teaching, doing research, and consulting in institution building and organisation development areas—currently a consultant to WHO, UNESCO, and UNIDO for research and development projects in Asian countries. He has edited three volumes of *Directory of Behavioural Sciences in India*, and has written several books. He has been President of the Andhra Pradesh Psychological Association, and Delhi Branch of the Indian Psychological Association. He has been on the editorial boards of several journals, including *Journal of Cross-Cultural Psychology, Psychologia, Administrative Science Quarterly*, and *Organization and Administrative Science*. He is Chairman of the Policy Board of Behavioural Science Center (India) and of the Board of Learning Systems.

T. VENKATESWARA RAO was born in India in 1946. After taking his Bachelor's degree in science from Andhra University, and another Bachelor's degree in education from Regional College of Education, Mysore, he took his Master's in psychology from Osmania University, Hyderabad. He taught psychology at Andhra University for a few months and then joined the faculty of National Institute of Health Administration and Education, New Delhi. During this period he also worked for his Ph.D. on the impact of the medical college environment on students of different regions and was awarded his Doctorate by Sardar Patel University. In 1971, he joined the University of Udaipur to open the Department of Psychology along with Professor Udai Pareek. He taught psychology there for a couple of years and then joined Indian Institute of Management, Ahmedabad. He worked with Professor David C. McClelland at Harvard University during the summer of 1975 on developing a maturity scale for students and adults. At the Indian Institute of Management he is a member of Educational Systems Group and Population Project Unit and Public Systems Group. He has been working in the area of influencing rural people for family planning and for entrepreneurial activities in two different regions of India. He also did research on changing teacher behaviour in a metropolitan city. He has several research publications in both Indian and foreign journals. He is the Associate Editor of *Indian Psychological Abstracts* and the *Indian Behavioural Sciences Abstracts* and is a life member of the Indian Psychological Association and the Indian Association for Programmed Learning. He has coauthored the following books: *Handbook of psychological and social instruments* (Samasti publications, Baroda); *Behavioural sciences research in family planning* (Tata-McGraw-Hill); and *Institution building in education and research* (in press). His recent publication is "Doctors in Making" (Sahitya Mudranalaya, Ahmedabad).

S. H. IRVINE is Professor of Educational Research at Brock University. His first landfall in Africa was in 1969 and since then he has pursued, through some dozen field trips over the past decade, cross-cultural research in abilities during appointments at Bristol University, Educational

Testing Service (as U.S. Public Health Service Visiting Scholar, 1967–68) and the University of Western Ontario. Books include *Human Behaviour in Africa* and *Cultural Adaptation Within Modern Africa*. Other interests are ability theory and the occupational psychology of teaching. Honours include Fellowships of both the British Psychological Society and the Eugenics Society of Great Britain.

WILLIAM K. CARROLL studied sociology and psychology at Brock University where he was awarded the Vice-Chancellor's medal for outstanding academic achievement in 1975. He is now a graduate student at York University, Toronto, with interests in personal construct theory and open-systems analysis.

WAYNE H. HOLTZMAN was born in Chicago, Illinois in 1923. After completing his undergraduate work in chemistry at Northwestern University and serving several years in the Navy, he entered graduate work at Northwestern, receiving his master's degree in experimental psychology in 1947. His doctoral work in psychology and statistics was completed at Stanford University in 1949, after which he accepted a position at the University of Texas where he has been a professor of psychology ever since. In 1955, he received a faculty research fellowship from the Social Science Research Council that led to a major research program on perception and personality. From 1955–64, he was associate director of the Hogg Foundation for Mental Health in charge of their research program at the University of Texas. 1962–63 was spent as a fellow at the Center for Advanced Study in the Behavioral Sciences in Stanford, California. From 1964–70, he served as dean of the College of Education, and since 1970, he has been president of the Hogg Foundation. His interest in cross-cultural studies began in 1955 when he served as chairman of the Organizing Committee for the Third Interamerican Congress of Psychology. In 1966, he was elected president of the Interamerican Society of Psychology, and since 1972, he has served as Secretary-General of the International Union of Psychological Science. Among his many articles and books are a number dealing with projective techniques and cross-cultural psychology, the most recent of which is *Personality Development in Two Cultures* (1975) written in collaboration with Rogelio Diaz-Guerrero, Jon Swartz, and others. Other recent books include *Inkblot Perception and Personality* (1961); *Tomorrow's Parents* (1965); *The Peace Corps in Brazil* (1966); and *Computer-Assisted Instruction, Testing and Guidance* (1971). He also served as president of the Division of Evaluation and Measurement of the American Psychological Association in 1969–70.

TOM CIBOROWSKI was born in a Polish neighborhood in New York City. In the home, on the street, and in the local elementary school, the language of communication was Polish. This caused some difficulty and cultural shock when his family moved to southern California. His undergraduate degrees were in mathematics and physics, and for a time, he worked in the missile industry as an associate engineer. But studying people proved more fascinating than manipulating abstract symbols. He received the Ph.D. in psychology under Michael Cole at the University of California at Irvine in 1971. After a postdoctoral year at the Rockefeller University he assumed a faculty position at the University of Hawaii. Under Michael Cole's guidance he conducted research in West Africa (on several occasions) and in lower Yucatan. At present he is engaged in a research program with Douglass Price-Williams that focuses on rural Hawaiian children.

ELIZABETH BROWN has a B.A. degree with a major in psychology and a minor in anthropology/sociology from the University of Connecticut, and an M.S. degree in psychology from the Florida State University. She is at present a candidate for the Ph.D. degree in clinical psychology at the Florida State University and is completing the clinical internship requirement for the degree at the Palo Alto Veterans Administration Hospital in Palo Alto, California. Her areas of interest include research methodology, program evaluation, prevention of psychopathology, and consumer satisfaction in mental health services.

LEE SECHREST received his Ph.D. in psychology from the Ohio State University with a specialty in clinical psychology. He is now Professor of Psychology at Florida State University. He taught previously at Northwestern University and Pennsylvania State University. His interest in cross-cultural psychology goes back to the early 1960s when he had a fellowship that allowed him to travel extensively in Asia and Europe and to do field work on psychopathology in the Philippines. Subsequently he spent one year at the East-West Center (1965–66) and an additional year doing field work in the Philippines (1968–69). While at Northwestern, Sechrest was Associate Director, and later Director, of the Council for Intersocietal Studies. During that period of time he became involved in the development of a research center of Cali, Colombia, which has evolved into the "Fundacion de Investigaciones de Ecologia Humana" and that has completed a major study of the effects of early nutritional and educational interventions with young barrio children. Sechrest has also done field work in Pakistan. He has developed a strong interest in research methodology and considers that his major focus at present. Among his other publications are *Unobtrusive Measures, Psychology and Human Problems, The Nature and Study of Psychology*, and *Psychological Foundations of Education*, all coauthored with present and former colleagues.

STEPHEN BOCHNER received a B.A. from the University of Sydney, an M.A. from the University of Hawaii, and the Ph.D. from the University of New South Wales, where he is now a Senior Lecturer in Psychology. His teaching specialties are social and cross-cultural psychology. He has held research and teaching posts at Rutgers University, the University of Hawaii, and at the East-West Center, and has had field experience in Asia, Central Australia, and the United States. He is coeditor of *Overseas Students in Australia* (1972), and of *Cross-Cultural Perspectives on Learning* (1975), and has served on the editorial board of the *Journal of Cross-Cultural Psychology* since its inception in 1970. He conducts research in the general area of culture learning, and has a special interest in the methodology of unobtrusive experiments.

RICHARD W. BRISLIN was born in Barre, Vermont and lived in New England until his family moved to Alaska, where he graduated from high school. He accompanied his family on its next move to Guam, and he received a B.A. degree there in English and American literature. Guam provided extensive cross-cultural experience since other students came there from various Pacific islands (especially Palau, Truk, Ponape, and the Marshalls) to pursue a higher education. He received his Ph.D. from the Pennsylvania State University, with a dissertation involving a trip back to Guam to study translation problems. He is now a research associate at the Culture Learning Institute, East-West Center in Honolulu, Hawaii where he continues his interests in cross-cultural methodology and social psychology. He is director of a yearly program, "Cross-cultural research for behavioral and social scientists" that attracts approximately twenty participants each year from Asia, the Pacific, and North America. He is coauthor or editor of four books: *Cross-Cultural Research Methods* (1973); *Cross-Cultural Perspectives on Learning* (1975); *Cross-Cultural Orientation Programs* (1976); and *Translation, Applications and Research* (1976). Since 1973 he has edited a yearly volume, *Topics in Culture Learning.*

HERBERT BARRY III was born in New York City in 1930. His introduction to cross-cultural research was a Senior Honors Thesis in 1952 at Harvard College. He rated samples of art objects in each of thirty societies and found that cultural differences in art style corresponded with some cultural differences in child training practices, measured by his advisor, John W. M. Whiting. For the next nine years, as a graduate student and then Post-Doctoral Fellow in Psychology at Yale University, he tested learning theories and subsequently drug effects in rats, while working part-time with Irvin L. Child and Margaret K. Bacon on a study of child training and then alcohol consumption in a sample of more than one hundred societies. Since 1963 he has been at the University of Pittsburgh, where he is Professor of Pharmacology in the School of Pharmacy with an adjunct appointment as Professor of Anthropology. He directed a Summer Institute in Cross-Cultural Research in 1965 and 1966 and participated in cross-cultural research projects with George P. Murdock (supported by a grant from NSF) and with Alice Schlegel (supported by a grant from NIMH). He was President of the Society for Cross-Cultural Research 1973–74 and is a Fellow of the American Psychological Association, American Anthropological Association, and American Association for the Advancement of Science.

RAOUL NAROLL was born in Canada in 1920. He grew up in southern California and attended UCLA. He served in the U.S. Army in Hawaii and in Germany during World War II. After the war he returned to UCLA and received the Ph.D. in history in 1953. He was a Fellow at the Center for Advanced Study in the Behavioral Sciences at Stanford during 1954–55, and then went to Washington, D.C., where he wrote country background studies for the Washington branch of the Human Relations Area Files. In 1956 he did field work in the Austrian Tyrol. In 1957 he returned to California, and taught anthropology at California State University, Northridge, until 1962. While at Northridge he worked on cross-cultural methodology and on the War, Stress, and Culture research project, a cross-cultural study of fifty-eight societies. In 1962 he joined the faculty of Northwestern University with joint appointments in anthropology, sociology, and political science. While at Northwestern he continued to work on cross-cultural methodology and finished a cross-historical study of military deterrence. In 1965–66 he did field work in Greece, Switzerland, and Belgium. Since 1967 he has been professor of anthropology at the State University of New York, Buffalo, and since 1973, president of the Human Relations Area Files. His books include: *Data Quality Control* (1962); *A Handbook of Method in Cultural Anthropology* (editor, with Ronald Cohen, 1970, 1973); *Main Currents in Cultural Anthropology* (editor, with Frada Naroll, 1973); and *Military Deterrence in History* (with Vern Bullough and Frada Naroll 1974). He is Editor of *Behavior Science Research*. For the past several years he has been working on a book called the *Human Situation*.

GARY L. MICHIK began his cross-cultural interests as an undergraduate participant in the Education Abroad Program of the University of California, spending a year at the University of Norway studying psychology and anthropology. After completing his B.A. with a double major in psychology and anthropology, he went on to obtain an M.S. in psychology under the supervision of Dr. Walter Lonner at Western Washington State College. His studies at Western convinced him of the overriding importance of culture in psychological research so he went on to study anthropology at the State University of New York at Buffalo, working with Raoul

Naroll, Marvin Opler, Terrence Tatje, and others. He is presently employed by the Human Relations Area Files as a research methodologist and continues to work toward his Ph.D. in anthropology, specializing in psychological anthropology and cross-cultural research methodology.

FRADA NAROLL was born in California in 1918. She attended UCLA, where she received the M.A. degree in 1940. She taught from 1944 to 1955, and then began collaboration with Raoul Naroll in his research and writing. She did field work with him in the Austrian Tyrol in 1956 and in Greece, Switzerland and Belgium in 1965–66. She has done a cross-cultural study: "Position of Women in Childbirth: A Study in Data Quality Control," *American Journal of Obstetrics and Gynecology* 82:943–54 (with Forrest H. Howard and Raoul Naroll); and she has assisted on War, Stress, and Culture research as well as on the cross-historical study of military deterrence. Since 1973 she has been assistant to Raoul Naroll, president, Human Relations Area Files. Her books include: *Main Currents in Cultural Anthropology* (editor, with Raoul Naroll, 1973); and *Military Deterrence in History* (with Vern Bullough and Raoul Naroll, 1974).

1

Introduction to *Methodology*

J.W. Berry

Contents

The Method of Cross-Cultural Psychology

Most areas of psychological enquiry are defined by their *content*; however, cross-cultural psychology is defined primarily by its *method* (e.g., Lijphart, 1971). Thus it is to our methodology that we must turn in order to seek our identity as a discipline, and it is in the strength of our methodology that we must root ourselves.

We are not alone in this situation, for as Teune (1975) has pointed out, a number of common issues run right across what, in ordinary circumstances, would be distinctive and separate social sciences. However, in sociology, anthropology, economics, political studies, and psychology there is currently a sharing of concern for the "comparative method" and how it can be exploited in the interests of each discipline.[1] Note that an implicit

1

identity is made between the use of the term *cross-cultural* in psychology and the term *comparative* in the other disciplines. Were it not for the historical accident that *comparative* became identified in psychology exclusively with phylogenetic comparison (leaving no room for ontogenetic or cultural group comparison), the term might still be employed identically across all of these disciplines. Nevertheless, the tradition of comparative research in these other disciplines can provide a well-needed basis for our own cross-cultural comparisons.

Historically, cross-cultural comparison in anthropology became an important methodological tool with Tylor's presentation (1889) of a paper on the development of social institutions. The approach was not used for nearly fifty years (Whiting, 1968) until it was revived by Murdock in 1937. Two thousand years before, the classical scholars had used the basic comparative framework in pursuing their interests in cultural origins and stages of development (Nisbet, 1971, p. 95).

In psychology, the earliest use of cross-cultural comparison is often traced to W. H. R. Rivers (1901, 1905) who conducted field work in New Guinea and in India. At the same time Wundt was developing a comprehensive comparative study of "folk psychology" in ten volumes; this was later published in English in a single volume (1916).

The comparative method, it has been argued (e.g., Campbell & Stanley, 1963, p. 176), is the core of the scientific method: without comparison, differences, similarities, co-variation, and cause cannot be observed or inferred. And so it is in a restricted usage that the comparative method has acquired its cross-cultural overtones. Essentially the method involves comparing *two or more naturally occurring* cases which *differ substantially.*

Campbell (1961) and Campbell and Naroll (1972) have argued that "a comparison of a single pair of natural objects is nearly uninterpretable" (p. 449). For any one interpretation of such a difference, rival alternatives can be advanced; a two-point comparison by itself provides no guidance toward the valid interpretation. However, Hsu (1972), among many others, has argued that such a rule applies to a pair of observations only if they are in isolation. If such observations are made in their "multidimensional contexts" (p. 266), there is rich supplementary information which may permit the elimination of alternatives.

Second, with respect to the nature of the phenomena, comparative studies are typically nonmanipulative in the sense that the situation has not been staged for the purposes of the research. This clearly distinguishes it from the *experimental* method. However, the selection of natural phenomena for comparison may constitute a quasi manipulation of some variables (Berry, 1976) and thus the comparative method may qualify as a quasi-experimental method (Campbell & Stanley, 1963). Edgerton (1974) views cross-cultural psychology as tied to "experimentation" while anthropological enquiry is devoted to "naturalism." However, his comments appear to be directed more toward data gathering techniques than toward the overall design or purpose of the studies. That is, the label "experimental" is more applicable to the intrusive, structured, and often psychometric nature of psychological research, rather than to its outright manipulation of independent cultural variables.

Third, the sweep of comparative studies is generally large, encompassing major variations in the variables. For example, to be cross-cultural a study usually employs nations or culture groups, rather than provinces or ethnic groups as points in the comparison. The point of such grandeur is not to satisfy a peculiar psychopathology of cross-cultural psychologists, but to "maximize the variance" available for study (LeVine, 1970; Eckensberger, 1972). Its opposite (to "minimize the variance") has been attempted by Berry and Annis (1974), and is equivalent in an experiment to reducing the experimental manipulation to a point where effects may no longer be observed.

These three features provide the hallmarks of a comparative or cross-cultural study. When applied specifically to psychological study, a number of definitions of the field have emerged. One of the earliest (Whiting, 1954; 1968) is not now (and perhaps never was) an accurate statement of either cross-cultural psychology or of its method:

> The cross-cultural method utilizes data collected by anthropologists concerning the customs and characteristics of various peoples throughout the world to test hypotheses concerning human behavior. (Whiting 1968, p. 693)

Such a definition limits the role of cross-cultural psychologists to that of secondhand data users; surely one discipline should not have all the field fun. This definition also limits the cross-cultural enterprise to the testing of hypotheses; the generation of new hypotheses, and the incorporation of new behaviours into old generalizations are all part of the goals of cross-cultural psychology.

In keeping with Whiting's definition, Hsu (1972, p. 3) argued that psychological anthropology (his term for the field of "culture and personality") is not concerned with individual differences, but with "natural group differences." Given this group-level analysis, it is not surprising to find Whiting content to employ data collected by anthropologists for use by psychologists. Although both disciplines are comparative, the units of comparison are groups or modal patterns in psychological anthropology, while the units are individuals, means, and variances in cross-cultural psychology.

Another early definition was proposed by Biesheuvel (1958). At the time, he referred specifically to the study of behaviour in Africa, but Poortinga (1971, p. 6) enlarged the terms of reference. For Biesheuvel, the enterprise involved gaining an understanding of the behaviour of other cultural groups in order to test the general validity of psychological hypotheses concerning human behaviour, and to establish which environmental factors exercise a significant effect on the development of psychological attributes. This was the first of the individually focused definitions to appear.

More recently, in quick succession, three definitions of the field were formulated by Eckensberger (1972); Triandis, Malpass, and Davidson (1972); and Brislin, Lonner, and Thorndike (1973):

> Cross-cultural research in psychology is the explicit, systematic comparison of psychological variables under different cultural conditions in order to specify the antecedents and processes that mediate the emergence of behaviour differences. (Eckensberger, 1972, p. 100)

> Cross-cultural psychology includes studies of subjects from two or more cultures, using equivalent methods of measurement, to determine the limits within which general psychological theories do hold, and the kinds of modifications of these theories that are needed to make them universal. (Triandis, Malpass, & Davidson, 1972, p. 1)

> Cross-cultural psychology is the empirical study of members of various culture groups who have had different experiences that lead to predictable and significant differences in behaviour. In the majority of such studies, the groups under study speak different languages and are governed by different political units. (Brislin, Lonner, & Thorndike, 1973, p. 5)

All three definitions cast cultural variables in the role of antecedent or independent variables, and individual behavioural variables in the role of dependent variables. With such a framework, the comparative method in psychology appears to be more devoted to a search for cause and effect relationships (or covariation, between two levels of variables—the cultural and the behavioural) than the search for worldwide generalizations about one level of variable (either cultural or individual). This question of goals will be taken up in the next section.

A second general observation is that by adopting the term *cross-cultural* to replace the more general term *comparative*, psychologists seem to have limited themselves unnecessarily to only cultural variables. But it is obvious that group comparisons must take into account other bases of group differences, such as their biological and ecological adaptations. For this reason Berry (1966, 1969, 1976), Dawson (1969, 1971), and Jahoda (1970) have all argued for the inclusion of ecological and biological variables as well as cultural variables in the comparative study of behavioural variation.

The Goals of Cross-Cultural Psychology

This section asks "Why do cross-cultural psychology?" A first answer is direct and uncomplicated: cross-cultural psychology seeks to comprehend the systematic covariation between cultural and behavioural variables. Included within the term *cultural* are ecological and societal variables, and within the term *behavioural* are inferred variables. Thus the purpose is to understand how two systems, at the levels of group- and individual-analyses, relate to each other. Ideally, of course, more than covariation is sought; under some conditions *causal* relations may be inferred as well.

A second goal that relates to the "large sweep" characteristic of the method is to bring the total range, the broad variability, and all the possible differences exhibited in human behaviour within the scope of psychological science (Berry & Dasen, 1974, p. 13). This goal was implied in many of the earlier definitions, and is perhaps the most popular and visible of the goals. It is the psychological equivalent to the search for "general statements about social phenomena" which was proposed by Przeworski and Teune (1970, p. 4) as the basic goal of comparison. The collecting of novel, exotic and exciting new data has always intrigued anthropologists; it has now captured the attention of cross-cultural psychologists as well.

This second goal is important for its own sake, for it ensures that all the possible data which are relevant to a question are brought forward. Paradoxically, its concern with *variability* serves yet another goal concerned with *uniformities* and *consistencies* across mankind. Only when all variation is present, can its underlying structure be detected; for with limited data, only partial structures may be discovered. Real universals, if indeed any exist (see Lonner in *Handbook*, Volume 1), can emerge only when all variability is available for analysis.

Finally, a less exciting, but necessary goal must always be attended to: to check the generality of our existing psychological knowledge, theory, laws, and propositions. This, indeed, is usually the first step in conducting cross-cultural research, but all too often it is also the last. Leaving it to the final position in this parade of goals will, hopefully, suggest its "limited" importance in the scale of the whole cross-cultural enterprise.

Some Advantages and Disadvantages of the Cross-Cultural Approach

A major advantage of the cross-cultural method is that it permits the pursuit of the essential goals of cross-cultural psychology. General (or universal) statements about systematic (or causal) relationships among variables can be asserted only on the basis of comparative analysis. If this is a desirable goal, then the method's usefulness in attaining it constitutes a major advantage. But this is a general advantage, composed of numerous smaller advantages, most of which are worthwhile in their own right.

One of these constituent advantages has been noted by Whiting (1968, p. 694) as the "increase in the range of variation of many variables." This contributes directly to the general search for universal statements, and Whiting's mention of it seems to be in service of this larger goal. However, a strictly methodological advantage is apparent as well. If cultures are viewed as independent variables, then increasing the range of variation constitutes a stronger quasi manipulation of the independent variables. Additionally, if cultures and behaviours are viewed as co-variates, the increased range enhances the likelihood of meaningful correlational analysis.

Another constituent advantage is that the method provides the only possibility for culturally decentering psychological science. There is no other methodology which could enable psychology to incorporate all the behavioural phenomena known to human beings in all their splendid variations. However, the method is not without its dangers. According to Nisbet (1971), the comparative method involves both ethnocentric and evolutionary assumptions; thus, societies may be ranged from "primitive" to "modern," with Western European and American cultures being the culmination of "progressive" change (Nisbet, 1971, pp. 95-97, passim). This view of the comparative method provides a warning to those scholars who wish to employ it; this warning is all the more necessary because many believe they are actually reducing the ethnocentrism in their discipline—that they are actually culturally decentering their scientific approach. However, Nisbet's view suggests that the method may be fraught with ethnocentric dangers which everyone should be aware of.

Finally, interests in applied psychology increasingly express the view that service to widely differing populations requires a psychology which is sensitive to their special needs (Jahoda, 1973; Berry & Lonner, 1975). Consistent with our previous point, only a cross-cultural psychology is capable of supplying the necessary basis for programmes in the service of diverse groups of people.

However, a number of criticisms may be levelled at the cross-cultural method, which if accepted, would constitute grave disadvantages for it. Within anthropology Köbben (1970, pp. 583-92) and Pelto (1970, p. 27) have outlined some of these criticisms, while Przeworski and Teune (1970) have explicated similar problems in political science. Following Köbben, three major problems are considered.

First, cross-cultural comparisons are alleged to produce generalizations which are trivial or tautological. The basic problem seems to be that in order to make any comparisons, the level of abstraction has to be high; and "the higher our level of abstraction the greater the danger that our generalizations are commonplace" (Kobben, 1970, p. 585). This issue is similar to that raised by Lonner (in *Handbook*, Volume 1) where he refers to the existence of "yawning truisms" and "faceless banalities."

A second allegation is that generalizations should be arrived at by thoroughly analyzing one society rather than a great number of societies. Leach (1961) has argued that comparison is not necessary to generalization, charging that "comparsion is a matter of butterfly collecting—of classification, of the arrangement of things according to their types and subtypes" (Leach, 1961, p. 2). On the contrary, Kobben argues that explanation, rather than classification is of primary concern (p. 585), and that generalizations which seek explanation are impossible without comparison (p. 586). Further, Kobben, while acknowledging some earlier over-simplified comparisons, documents pairs of instances where generalizations from single case studies are directly opposed to each other. Only by comparing a number of cases is a resolution of these oppositions likely to occur.

Finally, Kobben considers the allegation that "comparing elements from differing societies leads to inadmissible distortions of reality" (p. 584). This problem has contributed to the "Malinowskian Dilemma" (Goldschmidt, 1966, p. 8):

> Malinowski was most insistent that every culture be understood in its own terms, that every institution be seen as a product of the culture within which it developed. It follows from this that a cross-cultural comparison of institutions is essentially a false enterprise, for we are comparing incomparables.

A similar point of view was expressed by Durkheim (1912; 1960, p. 133): "social facts are functions of the social system of which they are a part; therefore they cannot be understood when they are detached." In answering this charge of isolation from context, Kobben points out that social scientists no longer take single traits out of their sociocultural setting, but instead complexes of traits are isolated and compared.

These advantages and disadvantages have been phrased primarily in terms of the debate in anthropology and political studies. Translation of these debates into a psychological framework has been provided by Berry (1969) and by Brislin, Lonner, and Thorndike (1973). Historically, the arguments for and against the cross-cultural method have been presented in terms of other disciplines. Henceforth, the specific issues—both problems and solutions—will be treated primarily in a psychological context.

Comparability and Equivalence

To compare two phenomena, they must share some feature in common; and to compare them to some advantage, they should usually differ on some feature. That is, it must be possible to place two phenomena on a single dimension in order to judge them validly in relation to each other; and for the comparative judgment to be of value they should not be identical in all respects. The first idea appears in various places in the literature of cross-cultural psychology. For example, Duijker and Frijda (1960, p. 138) and Frijda and Jahoda (1966, p. 115) have insisted that "comparison requires dimensional identity." In a similar vein, Campbell (1964, p. 325) has argued that only when a common underlying process exists can there be the possibility of interpreting differences in behaviour. When such dimensional identity or common underlying process is demonstrated, then comparability is established.

Such dimensional identity can be established by demonstrating an underlying *universal*, or by searching for *equivalences*. The existence of universals or equivalences, however, should not be taken as evidence for lack of variation. For the existence of variation or differences in a phenomenon is what makes comparison a worthwhile enterprise; if such differences were not to be found, then comparative enquiry would soon cease to be worthwhile.

These facts seem to be contradictory: to compare, there must be dimensional identity, universals, and equivalence; but to compare fruitfully, there must be *variation* in the observed phenomena. The resolution of this difficulty lies in the notion of *levels of analysis*: at one level, usually identified by structure or function, there can be identity; but at another level, usually identified by observable phenomena, there can still be wide variation. A similar distinction has been made by Poortinga (1975a) in terms of *attributes* of behaviour and the *repertoire* of actions which is at the disposal of a person; the former refers to underlying and unobservable processes, while the latter refers to the observable phenomena at the surface of the organism. To be a useful distinction, one must be able to operationalize both levels, starting with the first one: the deeper level at which dimensional identity may be sought.

There are two ways to demonstrate dimensional identity: one is by the adoption of *universals* from biology, linguistics, anthropology, or sociology; the other is by the empirical demonstration of *equivalence* in the data collected from two or more samples cross-culturally. The question of universals has been considered in detail by Lonner (in *Handbook*, Volume 1). From these sister disciplines it is possible to adopt universals which may be in the form "all human beings . . ." or "all human groups. . . ." For example, from biology, a list of primary needs; from anthropology, a list of common cultural components (language, tool use, myth, etc.); and from sociology, a set of functional prerequisites for social life (Aberle, Cohen, Davis, Levy, & Sutton, 1950) such as role differentiation, normative regulation of behaviour, and socialization may be adopted as universals. No known cultural group or individual lacks such common features; thus they may be termed universal, and as a result, they may be employed as common dimensions along which groups and individuals may vary and may be compared.

With respect to the notion of *equivalence,* the demonstration is not as simple. Berry and Dasen (1974) suggested that three kinds of equivalence could be demonstrated, each providing some evidence for dimensional identity: *functional, conceptual,* and *metric equivalence.*

First, *functional equivalence* exists when two or more behaviours (in two or more cultural systems) are related to functionally similar problems. This term has been coined simultaneously by Frijda and Jahoda (1966) and Goldschmidt (1966) to refer to the same notion and in pursuit of the same argument: "obviously if similar activities have different functions in different societies, their parameters cannot be used for comparative purposes" (Frijda & Jahoda, 1966, p. 116). In elaborating this position, Berry (1969, p. 122) has argued:

> Thus, functional equivalence of behaviour exists when the behaviour in question has developed in response to a problem shared by two or more social/cultural groups, even though the behaviour in one society does not appear to be related to its counterpart in another society. These functional equivalences must pre-exist as naturally occurring phenomena; they are discovered and cannot be created or manipulated by the cross-cultural psychologist. Without this equivalence, it is suggested, no valid cross-cultural behavioural comparisons may be made.

Turning to *conceptual equivalence,* Sears (1961) argued that the *meaning* of research materials (stimuli, concepts, etc.) or of behaviour must be equivalent before comparison is possible. Within anthropology, Tatje (1970) considered this problem in some detail, and within psychology, Price-Williams (1974) examined the issue with special emphasis upon categories. Essentially, both argue that the researcher must search for and discover the local meaning of concepts within the cognitive systems of the people and groups being compared. Only if common meaning is discovered, can comparison legitimately take place. Note that, as in the case of functional equivalence, conceptual equivalence is a precondition of comparison.

A number of attempts have been made to operationalize this requirement. One is through the use of forward and back translations of words, sentences, and test items to demonstrate *translation equivalence* (Brislin, 1970; Brislin, 1976b; Werner & Campbell, 1970). This technique usually involves an initial translation to a target language by one bilingual person, and a back translation to the original language by another; discrepancies will often indicate the presence of conceptual nonequivalence. Variations on this basic technique have been elaborated by Brislin, Lonner, and Thorndike (1973, Chapter 2).

A second approach to conceptual equivalence is semantic differential analyses (Osgood, 1965). For example, the meaning of a concept can be explored by having a respondent judge its position on a set of bipolar adjective scales. Excellent use of this technique has been made by Wober (1974) who explored the Kiganda concept of "intelligence" (*obugezi*), and its differences from the Western notion, represented both in psychological tests and common usage.

Third, the ethnoscience or cognitive tradition of anthropology has demonstrated that phenomena and experience are categorized in different ways in differing cultural groups (Tyler, 1969); even cannibals are known to divide their edible universe idiosyncratically (Keesing, 1973). This research approach seeks to discover, through linguistic analyses and object classification, how the world is organized in the cognitive systems of a group of people. If the divisions and structures of concepts and categories are different, then it may be argued that conceptual equivalence does not exist. However if they are substantially the same, then conceptual equivalence has been demonstrated, and comparability can be asserted.

A final type of equivalence has come to the fore in recent years: *metric equivalence* exists when the psychometric properties of two (or more) sets of data from two (or more) cultural groups exhibit essentially the same coherence or structure. Within this general approach, two lines of argument have developed. One, termed *subsystem validation* (Roberts & Sutton-Smith, 1962), requires that statistical relationships remain fairly constant among independent and dependent variables, no matter whether the variance available is used intraculturally or cross-culturally. In this version the basic argument is that covariation among variables should be stable, regardless of the source of the variation. A second requirement, one of increasing importance, is that statistical relationships among dependent variables should be patterned similarly in two or more cultural groups before comparisons are allowed. Essentially, the various forms of this argument are attempts to demonstrate *scalar equivalence* (Poortinga, 1975a, b; *Handbook* chapter by Irvine & Carroll in this volume). It may be demonstrated by similarity in correlation matrices (Poortinga, 1975) or by common factor structures (Irvine, 1966; Buss & Royce, 1975). In both cases, it requires behavioural measurements (observations, test data, etc.) to be structured in similar ways *within* groups before comparisons *across* groups are allowed. Unlike functional and conceptual equivalence, metric equivalence can usually be established only after the data have been collected and analyzed.

Once the three forms of equivalence are established and comparability is asserted, it may be possible to demonstrate *construct validation* across the cultural groups in the comparisons. Such demonstration, however, also requires theoretical argument and abstraction that require a further process of transcultural adaptation. Comparisons may be appropriate with only the demonstration of comparability; but interpretation demands construct validation as well.

In summary, comparability is a prerequisite for valid comparison; comparability may be attained either by adopting *universals* from other disciplines or by demonstrating the *equivalence* of psychological concepts and data across groups. It is necessary to keep track of two levels, both the local (single cultural) meaning, function, and structure, and the broader transcultural dimension or framework on which comparisons might be made.

Emics and Etics

In the previous section the various prerequisites for valid cross-cultural comparison were argued to exist at a relatively deep (structural or functional) level. At the same time it was noted that the existence of variation in phenomena initiates comparative enquiry; without such apparent differences, the comparative method would have no scientific value. A set of terms has been proposed which captures the essence of these two levels—*emic* and *etic*.

These two terms, initially proposed by Pike (1954/1966), are derived from the two special approaches in linguistics of phonemics and phonetics. Phonemics focuses on sounds which are employed within a single linguistic system; phonetics emphasizes more general or even universal aspects of language. By dropping the root (phon), the two suffixes (emics, etics) become terms which are applicable to this local versus universal distinction in any discipline. By analogy, emics apply in only a particular society; etics are culture-free or universal aspects of the world (or if not entirely universal, operate in more than one society). The following table, gleaned from Pike's (1966) comments, should exemplify the distinction:

Emic approach	*Etic approach*
studies behaviour from within the system	studies behaviour from a position outside the system
examines only one culture	examines many cultures, comparing them

Emic approach	Etic approach
structure discovered by the analyst	structure created by the analyst
criteria are relative to internal characteristics	criteria are considered absolute or universal

Akin to the emic description of culture or behaviour is Sturtevant's (1964) approach, which has been termed *ethnoscience*. The main proposition is that "study of a culture involves the discovery of native principles of classification and conceptualization and that the use of *a priori* definitions and conceptual models of cultural content is to be avoided" (p. 3), which is also a statement of Malinowski's point of view: "The final goal . . . is, briefly, to grasp the native's point of view . . . to realise his vision of his world" (Malinowski, 1922, p. 25). Both of these approaches—the ethnoscientific and the Malinowskian (and the idiographic or clinical)—are attempts to produce internal descriptions of behaviour, and correspond to the emic type of analysis.

In contrast, the *etic* approach is characterized by the presence of universals in a sytem. When these universals are assumed they have been termed *imposed etic* (Berry, 1969, p. 124) or *pseudo etic* (Triandis, Malpass, & Davidson, 1972, p. 6). In such cases, these etics are usually only Euroamerican emics, imposed blindly and even ethnocentrically on a set of phenomena which occur in other cultural systems (for example "intelligence" or "personality" tests). On the other hand a true etic is one which emerges from the phenomena; it is empirically derived from the common features of the phenomena. Such an etic has been termed a *derived etic* by Berry (1969, p. 124).

Our major problem is how to describe behaviour in terms which are meaningful to members of a particular culture (an emic approach) while at the same time to compare validly behaviour in that culture with behaviour in another or all other cultures (the etic aim). The proposed solution (Berry, 1969, p. 124) involves the initial application of extant hypotheses concerning behaviour. A research problem must be tackled from some point of view; the conventional one has been termed an imposed etic approach. The researcher must recognize the culturally specific (perhaps even ethnocentric) origins of our approach, and deliberately remain open to new and even contrary kinds of data variation. If he enters into the behaviour system of another culture, knowing that his point of entry (imposed etic) is probably only a poor approximation to an understanding of behaviour in that system, then the first major hurdle is passed. Modification of external categories must be made in the direction of the behavioural system under study; eventually a truly emic description of behaviour within that culture will be achieved. That is, an emic description can be made by progressively altering the imposed etic until it matches a purely emic point of view; if this can be done without destroying the etic character of the entry categories, then the next step can be taken. If some of the etic is left, it is possible to note the categories or concepts that are shared by the behaviour system previously known and the one just understood emically. Now a derived etic that is valid for making comparisons between two behaviour settings can be set up; thus the problem of obtaining a descriptive framework which is valid for comparing behaviour across behaviour settings has been resolved. This new derived etic can then be transported to another behaviour setting (again as an imposed etic), be modified emically, and thence form the basis of a new derived etic which is valid in three behaviour settings. When all systems which may be compared (limited by the initial functional equivalence requirement) have been included, then a universal for that particular behaviour will be achieved.

A further concept has been proposed by Naroll (1971; Naroll, Michik, & Naroll, *Handbook*, Chapter 12, this volume), that of *theorics*. For Naroll, "theoric concepts are those used by social scientists to *explain* variations in human behaviour" (1971, p. 7). They represent an even higher level of abstraction than etics (see the earlier discussion of construct validation); etics in turn are more abstract than emics. Thus emics are local concepts employed by a people to classify their environment; etics are pan-cultural concepts employed by social scientists to analyse the emic phenomena; and theorics are theoretical concepts employed by social scientists to interpret and account for emic variation and etic constancies.

Both emics and etics are essential levels of analysis in cross-cultural psychology: without etics, comparisons lack a frame; without emics, comparisons lack meat. In the originator's terms "emic and etic data do not constitute a rigid dichotomy of bits of data, but often present the same data from two points of view" (Pike, 1966).

Finally, the approach to cross-cultural comparison which employs the emic and etic terminology is not without its critics. Recently, Jahoda (1977) criticised the distinction and the terms, for being too abstract and beyond the actual reach of cross-cultural researchers. Whatever the future of these terms in the discourse of cross-cultural psychology, it should be clear that the very name "cross-cultural" implies at least two points of view: being "cultural" requires a point of view similar to that of the emic, and "cross" requires a perspective akin to the etic.

Sampling Questions

As in all social sciences, questions of sampling are rooted in questions of purpose. An earlier section outlined a number of goals for cross-cultural psychology; this section proposes sampling strategies parallel to these goals.

A first goal was presented in terms of the "systematic co-variation (or cause) between cultural and behavioural variables." Within the confines of this goal, it is important only to sample cultures and behaviours which display sufficient variation to allow an examination of the systematic relationships between them. The second goal was then presented in terms of "universal generalizations." This broader purpose requires that sampling take into account not only the *range*, but also the *representativeness* of the cultures and behaviours.

Thus two general sampling strategies may be proposed: the first selects contrasting observations on one or more variables to assert covariation, and perhaps cause, but does not depend upon representativeness; the second employs the comparative method to assert universal generalizations, and depends upon representativeness.

For both of these sampling strategies, sampling usually takes place from four phenomena. In the first strategy, these four make sense when presented as pairs: cultures and individuals; stimuli and responses. That is, the first goal and sampling strategy seeks to discover systematic relationships between aspects of cultures and aspects of individuals on the one hand, and between stimuli and responses on the other. For the second goal, however, all four phenomena must be representatively sampled in their own right, without regard for relationships among them.

The largest amount of literature on cross-cultural sampling is about which *cultures* to select; it is primarily concerned with the second strategy—that of seeking generalizations. In Chapter 12 (this volume), Naroll et al. outline the dimensions of "holocultural" studies, those which seek generalizations which may characterize the whole world. Unquestionably such studies require cultural groups in the sample which represent all known cultural groups. Additionally, these cultures should be independent of each other, so that each cultural variable is represented in the sample only in its correct proportion to its natural occurrence. The existence in a sample of cultures of two groups which are related to each other has been termed "Galton's Problem." These questions of acquiring a representative sample of independent cultures are discussed fully in Chapter 12 and in Naroll (1970) and Driver and Chaney (1970).

In contrast, the selection of a sample of cultures to acquire an adequate range of variation in a variable of interest has received much less attention. While many researchers have employed this method (e.g., Segall, Campbell, & Herskovits, 1966; Berry, 1966, 1976), the methodological discussion of it has been minimal. In one reference, Eckensberger (1972, p. 105) argued that

> Since the aim of cross-cultural research is to determine the influence of 'cultural conditions' on behaviour (in our terms 'systematic co-variation or cause') in time, the samples to be compared must not be representative of

their corresponding 'cultural groups'; they need only represent the single 'cultural variables' in question in various degrees.

In a similar vein Berry (1976) has argued that the choice of cultural groups may constitute a "quasi-manipulation by selection" of the independent variable. Thus in this second strategy, worldwide representativeness is not all-important; what is essential is that the cultures selected represent the values required of the cultural variables in order to examine covariation or cause.

In the second focus—*individuals*—virtually parallel arguments can be made. On the one hand if individuals are to represent their culture (or at other levels, if individuals are to represent their community and, in turn, the community is to represent the culture) then representativeness is definitely required. That is, the sample should mirror the population. On the other hand, if individuals are being selected because they represent some variable of interest, then their representativeness of some population is not important.

In some respects, the sampling of individuals in cross-cultural research does not differ from sampling of individuals in noncomparative studies. Standard techniques may be employed: for example a *random* sample of a community may be drawn from a list of the complete population; or a *stratified* sample (perhaps stratified by age and sex) may better allow the data analysis to pursue special questions of interest (such as age and sex differences). Further, it is also important to extract standard identifying information of a biographical and demographic nature (Brislin & Baumgardner, 1971).

In the past few years increasing attention has been paid to some special features of sampling individuals in diverse national or cultural settings (see, e.g., O'Barr, Spain, & Tessler, 1973 for sampling problems in Africa; Frey, 1970 and Scheuch, 1968 for issues confronting political science; Warwick & Lininger, 1975, for sociology; and Honigmann, 1970, for sampling in ethnographic fieldwork). This literature should be examined by those wishing technical details. Beyond some problems which are outlined by Goodenough (*Handbook*, Chapter 2, this volume) it is perhaps necessary only to point out the limitations of two common assumptions made in sampling.

The first assumption is that everyone "counts"; in some societies, not everyone counts as equally as they do in the relatively egalitarian milieu where the traditional sampling strategies have been developed. For example in highly stratified populations, some extremely low status strata or social groupings are beyond communication with outsiders. But even if they do supply information, their data cannot be considered, in any additive way, along with the rest of the population.

A second assumption is that a fairly standard ratio of sample to population is required. But since the internal diversity varies from society to society, such sampling ratios may have to be drastically altered. Homogeneous populations may require only a small sample, while heterogeneous societies will require a much larger one.

The sampling of *stimuli* is a topic about which little has been written explicitly. However, it is likely that most cross-cultural researchers would agree that debates about the "cultural fairness" of tests can be easily translated into questions of the representativeness of the stimuli which are presented to individuals. One explicit reference to this form of the issue is by Goodenough (1936, p. 5) who asserted that we must "be sure that the test items from which the total trait is to be judged are representative and valid samples of the ability in question, as it is displayed within the particular culture with which we are concerned." By this criterion, stimuli (test items, questions, tasks) are fair, only if they correspond to stimulus variables existing in the individual's milieu. An extensive discussion of the criteria for selecting suitable stimuli can be found in Triandis, Vassiliou, and Nassiakou (1968). Thus, the argument for representativeness of stimuli is similar to that made for representativeness of cultures and individuals; general statements depend upon these arguments.

In contrast, nonrepresentative stimuli have an accepted place in psychological research (e.g., nonsense syllables in classical memory studies), and they have been considered of potential value by Frijda and Jahoda (1966, p. 118):

> In the discussion so far the aim of "fairness" to all cultures has been tacitly accepted, but it may itself be questioned and viewed as a problem of the sociology of knowledge. Following an era when western superiority was unthinkingly taken for granted, have we, as social scientists, perhaps fallen into a different trap by our declared purpose that we must be "fair" to everybody? The notion of "fairness" looks suspiciously as though there were an underlying feeling that, given appropriate measures, cultural differences ought to disappear. This of course is a deliberate overstatement, designed to raise the question whether there is not perhaps an unduly exclusive emphasis on the so-called "culture-fair" or "culture-appropriate" tests. A good deal can be said in favour of the alternative strategy of using the same test in various cultures and attempting to tease out the causes of such differences as are found, or even of looking for tests which maximize cultural differences, as was done in a study by Berry (1966). The optimal strategy will depend on one's goals.

Finally we turn to the sampling of *responses*. In the present discussion responses should be understood in broad terms, ranging all the way from an eye blink to the development of a complex behaviour or skill. We have already argued that thorough *emic* analyses are an essential stage in the course of cross-cultural research; this analysis should provide the researcher with the population of responses and behaviours which can be detected in a given cultural system. From the "fairness" or "representativeness" point of view, Wober (1969) has argued that we should not be asking "how well can *they* do *our* tricks," but rather "how well can we measure how *they* do *their* tricks?" Implied here is that only by observing what is actually present can psychologists obtain data which are representative of the behaviour and skills of people in a particular culture; continually attempting to sample what is not there is of no value to either party.

In contrast to this established point of view, reconsider the value (expressed above by Frijda and Jahoda, 1966) of both presenting novel stimuli and checking for novel behaviour. Such a strategy approximates Biesheuvel's (1972) concept of *adaptability*, which refers to the need for all human organisms to adapt to their surroundings and to adjust to changes in them; in essence it is concerned with an individual's potentiality to meet *new* demands. What is suggested, then, is that there is a role for new situations, ones outside the normal daily experience of an individual; without sampling from such stimuli and provoked responses, we may never find out what individuals *might* do. However, with such an approach, some control has to be exercised over the relative degree of novelty of the new tasks; in our earlier terms, an imposed etic may not be equally "imposing" for all cultural groups.

Measurement

It is a commitment to measurement as much as the use of experimental procedures that distinguishes cross-cultural psychology from anthropology and psychological anthropology. If measurement sets us apart, then measurement should be a major concern of those wishing to develop the enterprise. However, it is safe to say that questions of measurement have arisen only incidentally in most cross-cultural research. Only recently have studies been conducted which are explicitly devoted to it.

The basic problem is validity—how do we know we are actually measuring what we think we are measuring? At least three validity issues have been considered in the cross-cultural literature: biases, communication, and validation techniques.

A classic statement of the bias problem has been advanced by Campbell in various forms and at various times (Campbell, 1961, 1970; Campbell & Naroll, 1972; Brewer & Campbell, 1976). Basic to all these presentations is the argument that observations or measures of phenomena in culture B by a scientist from culture A are "inherently ambiguous" (Campbell, 1970, p. 70); the observations or measures may be a function of the real phenomena in culture B or a function of the observer bias derived from culture A. Ideally, a single research study should be conducted four times, twice in culture B (once with an observer from culture A and once with one from culture *B*), and twice in culture *A* (with observer sources the same). Only then would it be possible to tease out the relative contributions to the data from the "real phenomena" and from "observer bias."

At the level of individual measurement, this strategy is well known in psychology in the use of a multitrait multimeasure approach:

> With a single observation at hand, it is impossible to separate the subjective and the objective component. When, however, observations through separate instruments and separate vantage points can be matched as reflecting "the same" objects, then it is possible to separate out the components in the data due to observer (instrument) and observed. It turns out that this disentangling process requires both multiple observers (methods) and multiple, dissimilar objects of study. (Campbell, 1970, p. 70)

Actual comparative use of either the "cultural" or "individual" versions of the multimeasurement matrix is very limited. At the level of cultural groups, Brewer and Campbell (1976) have approximated the technique on their study of reciprocal intergroup stereotypes in East Africa. At the level of individual measurement, Triandis and Vassiliou (Chapter 9 in Triandis, Vassiliou, Vassiliou, Tanaka, & Shanmugam, 1972) have shown that such multimeasurement of attitudes and mutual stereotypes held by Greeks and Americans exhibits consistencies that in turn permit the valid interpretation of differences.

A second validity issue has also been discussed by Campbell (Campbell, 1964; Segall, Campbell, & Herskovits, 1966, Chapter 7). In essence Campbell asked how cross-cultural researchers can be sure that the task that is communicated is the task that is responded to, or "On what grounds does an experimenter decide whether an unexpected recording (response) is a new phenomenon or an instrumentation error?" (Campbell, 1964, p. 317). His answer is to provide "comprehension checks" which are composed of stimuli which almost certainly evoke no variation in response cross-culturally. Actual test items can then be built upon the established communication of the task, and any observed cross-cultural variation in response can be taken as an indicator of valid behavioural differences. In their classical illusion studies, Segall, Campbell, and Herskovits (1966) were able to follow their own advice, but it has not been as simple for others who have dealt with more complicated behaviours and more subtle measures. However, it is possible to construct and employ these checks with such measures (see, e.g., Triandis, Feldman, Weldon, & Harvey, 1975). Hopefully future studies will attend to these requirements with more care.

Finally, many researchers have proposed various concepts and techniques which may be useful for the cross-cultural worker in his search for validity. Construct validity may be examined cross-culturally by checking correlation matrix similarity, or by estimating factor structure and individual test loading constancy from culture to culture (Poortinga, 1975; Irvine & Carroll, Chapter 14). Furthermore, two recent papers have proposed solutions to problems of validity cross-culturally (Irwin, Klein, Engle, Yarbrough, & Nerlove, 1977; Davidson, Jaccard, Triandis, Morales, & Diaz-Guerrero, 1976).

In the first of these, Irwin et al. proposed three types of validity based upon the now-familiar *imposed etic, emic,* and *derived etic* distinctions of Berry (1969). Imposed etic validity is established by correctly predicting an outcome in culture *B* on the basis of a theory, construct, or test imposed from culture *A*. Emic validity is established when correct predictions of behaviour in a culture are made on the basis of the investigator's understanding of that culture's own conceptual system: "if in fact the investigator is validly measuring constructs that correspond to indigenous units of organizing the world, he should be able to predict the outcomes of these judgments on the basis of his behavioural measurements" (Irwin et al., 1977). Finally, derived etic validity can be established only after imposed etic and emic validities have been proved, and it resides in this intersection; that is, derived etic validity, which is appropriate for valid cross-cultural comparison, must be based upon the known validity in two or more cultural systems. The proposal of these three forms of validity constitutes an important advance in cross-cultural methodology, because it attempts to operationalize concepts which were largely considered as "ideals," as important goals, but difficult to attain in actual practice.

A further operationalization of the emic and etic concepts by Davidson et al. (1976) has also advanced cross-cultural methodology. In their view, the problem of measuring behaviour in different cultural settings is one of first "generating the emic content of the etic construct" (p. 3). Such content can then be employed for the development of appropriate test materials; measurements taken with these materials would have, in the terms of Irwin et al. (1977), "derived etic validity" since they would have grown out of both etic and emic analyses.

Beyond these three special problems of cross-cultural bias, communication, and validity, there are all the usual measurement problems encountered in single cultural research, such as response styles, social desirability, the use of full scale ranges, and demand characteristics. In one study (Triandis & Triandis, 1962) cultural differences in a number of attitude and personality variables disappeared when acquiescence was statistically controlled. In the same study, extreme checking style (Soueif, 1958) on a semantic differential scale was also examined; however in this case, controlling for style did not appreciably affect the differences between cultures. It would be useful if generalizations were available to guide the researcher, such as "acquiescence tends to be high in cultures of type *A*" or "a limited use of a scale range should be watched for in cultures of type *B*," but this information simply does not exist. At best, researchers should be sensitive to the possibility that there may be interactions between cultural variables and measurement problems which could make cross-cultural differences very difficult to interpret.

Outline of Chapters

At the outset, it was discovered that most chapters contained a number of common themes, such as the nature of the comparative method, or a discussion of the emic and etic strategy. This introduction has attempted to glean these themes and provide a single statement of them for the whole volume. For this reason, then, readers should consider this introduction as a part of each chapter. And to a similar extent each chapter should be read as a part of the methodology volume as a whole, rather than as individual or isolated statements.

The eleven chapters which follow have been set in a sequence which begins with ethnographic and field techniques (entry into the field and observations) and ends with the treatment of archival materials (oral and written records and ethnographic reports). In between the chapters are devoted to the more traditional methods of general psychology (interviewing, testing, and experimentation).

In the second chapter, Goodenough provides an initiation into fieldwork and its particular problems. Writing from an anthropological point of view, he outlines most of the basic issues that psychologists in the field should attend to. From the definition of the people in a culture, and their established interrelationships, to a specification of environment and resources, to an inventory of their common activities, and then to their world view, Goodenough takes a rapid excursion through the essentials of field investigation. He then discusses the practical problems of field living and field data handling and provides an overview of some of the ethical concerns facing field workers. (See also Warwick chapter in Volume 1.)

Direct observation of behaviour under natural conditions is one of the traditional tools of field studies. In the third chapter, Longabaugh overviews this technique. Since few comprehensive treatments of this topic exist, considerable detail is provided on what to look for, where to look for it, how to look at it, and how to deal with it once you have it. This chapter, along with Bochner's on unobtrusive methods later in this volume, makes a clear methodological thrust away from the "experimentalism" of conventional psychological enquiry and toward the "naturalism" of traditional anthropological research.

The survey interview is another traditional tool used in field studies. In the chapter by Pareek and Rao, emphasis is placed upon those aspects which are characteristic of the comparative use of such instruments, particularly those which arise in their use with more traditional peoples. A number of topics are considered, including comparability, cultural factors in interview and response style, and a further look at ethical questions.

Perhaps the most common method in the history of cross-cultural work has been the one of tests with samples of individuals drawn from disparate populations. In psychology (particularly in educational and industrial psychology) ability and related measures have occupied a central position for many years. In psychological anthropology ("culture and personality") the emphasis has been more on the use of personality measures, particularly of the projective kind. The chapters by Irvine and Carroll, and by Holtzman present critical overviews of these two traditions of testing.

In the first of the two, Irvine and Carroll classify most of the research into five major assessment traditions and evaluate each in turn. Attention is then directed toward the core problem of construct validity in the cross-cultural use of tests. In the second, Holtzman also classifies the major research traditions, particularly variations on the Inkblot, Thematic Apperception, Association and Completion, and Expressive techniques. He then also turns his attention to the key problem areas in the cross-cultural use of such tests.

In contrast to the use of tests, manipulative experiments have rarely been employed cross-culturally. In the chapter by Brown and Sechrest, both this previous lack and some opportunities for future experimental development are discussed. However, the numerous difficulties which confront cross-cultural experimentation are also examined, so that invalid experimentation might be avoided.

One experimental approach which has been effectively used in recent years is that of "experimental anthropology," developed by Cole (see Cole, Gay, Glick, & Sharp, 1971). Rather than reviewing and criticising the approach, the chapter by Ciborowski presents its basic idea—that the cultural context, the situation, can be experimented with in order to tease out the cultural elements which may account for the observed variations in test performance (see also the chapter by Price-Williams in Volume 3).

The methods discussed by Bochner in the chapter on Unobtrusive Measures has already been compared with the use of systematic behavioural observation. However, some element of experimentation is present since the situation, although usually natural in appearance, can often be controlled and manipulated. In one sense such a method attains the best of both worlds, avoiding both the reactions to intrusive experimentation and testing, and the lack of control in pure observational methods. However, as Bochner points out, there are ethical and other problems which must be ironed out before such an approach can be widely used cross-culturally.

The chapter by Brislin provides a neat transition between the previous chapter and the two subsequent ones on the use of ethnographic archives.

In Brislin's discussion of the use of oral and written materials, there are elements of both unobtrusive yet systematic analyses of human behaviour and human products. Over and above this, however, is the important treatment of issues of translation and equivalence.

Following the sequence, the chapter by Barry, and the one by Naroll, Michik, and Naroll, focus on the systematic analysis of archives produced by anthropologists. Unlike the "natural" products of oral and written traditions treated by Brislin, these two chapters examine the resources available to psychologists in the thousands of cultural studies accumulated in the Human Relations Area Files. The chapter by Barry is essentially descriptive of the Files and their potential use in cross-cultural psychological research. The tone is informative and practical, with an emphasis upon their historical development, their structure, their samples, and codes. Complementing this emphasis is a concern for the method of large scale cultural (or holocultural) studies in the Naroll et al. chapter. Such issues as statistical control, sample independence, culture unit definition, and causal inference constitute their major concerns.

In all eleven chapters, an effort has been made to focus specifically on those features of a method which are characteristic of its psychological use across cultures. For example, the basic methods of interviewing, testing and experimentation, are not covered. Rather, it is assumed that standard works on psychological methods are available and have been mastered. It is hoped that these chapters will prove to be valuable supplements to the more conventional treatments of the methodological issues.

With such a variety of methods available, the question often arises concerning which is "the best." Such a question betrays two assumptions which are questionable: one is that a *single* method is to be chosen to the exclusion of all others; and a second is that one method is *superior*, in some absolute sense, to all others.

The position espoused here is that the appropriate method depends upon both the question being asked and the cultural group in which it is studied; there is no methodological superiority inherent in any one strategy. Furthermore, many cross-cultural studies require a triangulation of methods (e.g., Rohner, 1975) to deal with a particular issue; the use of a single method may leave empirical and eventually theoretical gaps which will be difficult to plug.

Considering methodological appropriateness further, it is possible to argue that some research questions call for a particular approach while others preclude it. For example, the use of surveys and interviews with a cultural group which is characteristically reticent would be next to impossible, while observational and unobtrusive techniques would be quite suitable. Studies which demand a large pool of homogeneous participants that can be randomly assigned to different experimental conditions cannot be conducted in small-scale societies; however, intensive ethnographic field work, combined with repeated test measures could deliver very valuable information in such settings. Thus there are some very real psychological, demographic, and cultural variables (as well as ethical and political ones, see the chapter by Warwick in Volume 1) which render some methods more suitable than others, depending upon the situation.

Turning to the issue of multimethod approaches, it can be argued that the more kinds of information available, the more sure we can be of our findings. In cross-cultural psychology, particularly, it is important to obtain cross-validating evidence using ethnographic and observational techniques that will exhibit consistency with, for example, test results. If there is contradiction between these cultural and test sources, then the problem must be resolved, perhaps with the use of yet another method. Moreover, ethnographic and archival methods may be important in the selection of field sites, in the development of hypotheses, and in the interpretation of data eventually collected by interviewing or testing with field samples. Thus it is clear that a combination of methods may not only increase empirical coverage, but also become indispensable to developing a more complete theory. Reliance upon a single (cultural or psychological) method, takes psychologists only halfway toward their goals.

Note

1. See, for example, Brislin, 1976a; Brislin, Lonner, and Thorndike, 1973; Holt and Turner, 1970; Marsh, 1967; Naroll and Cohen, 1970; Przeworski and Teune, 1970; Rokkan, 1968; Triandis, 1976; Warwick and Osherson, 1973; Malpass, 1977; and Sheehan, 1976.

References

ABERLE, D. F., COHEN, A. K., DAVIS, A. K., LEVY, M. J., & SUTTON, F. X. The functional prerequisites of a society. *Ethics*, 1950, *60*, 100–11.

BERRY, J. W. Temne and Eskimo perceptual skills. *International Journal of Psychology*, 1966, *1*, 207–29.

————. On cross-cultural comparability. *International Journal of Psychology*, 1969, *4*, 119–28.

————. *Human ecology and cognitive style: comparative studies in cultural and psychological adaptation*. Beverly Hills: Sage/Halsted, 1976.

BERRY, J. W., & ANNIS, R. C. Ecology, culture, and psychological differentiation. *International Journal of Psychology*, 1974, *9*, 173–93.

BERRY, J. W., & DASEN, P. (Eds.), Introduction to *Culture and cognition*. London: Methuen, 1974.

BERRY, J. W., & LONNER, W. J. (Eds.), *Applied cross-cultural psychology.* Amsterdam: Swets and Zeitlinger, 1975.

BIESHEUVEL, S. Adaptability: its measurements and determinants. In L. J. Cronbach & P. Drenth (Eds.), *Mental tests and cultural adaptation.* The Hague: Mouton, 1972, pp. 47–62.

————. Objectives and methods of African psychological research. *Journal of Social Psychology,* 1958, 47, 161–68.

BREWER, M. B., & CAMPBELL, D. T. *Ethnocentrism and intergroup attitudes: East African evidence.* Beverly Hills: Sage/Halsted, 1976.

BRISLIN, R. Back translation for cross-cultural research. *Journal of Cross-Cultural Psychology,* 1970, 1, 185–216.

————. Comparative research methodology: cross-cultural studies. *International Journal of Psychology,* 1976a, 11, 215–29.

BRISLIN, R. (Ed.), *Translation: applications and research.* New York: Wiley-Halsted, 1976b.

BRISLIN, R., & BAUMGARDNER, S. Non random sampling of individuals in cross-cultural research. *Journal of Cross-Cultural Psychology,* 1971, 2, 397–400.

BRISLIN, R., LONNER, W. J., & THORNDIKE, R. *Cross-cultural research methods.* New York: Wiley, 1973.

BUSS, A., & ROYCE, J. B. Detecting cross-cultural commonalities and differences: intergroup factor analyses. *Psychological Bulletin,* 1975, 82, 128–36.

CAMPBELL, D. T. The mutual methodological relevance of anthropology and psychology. In F. L. K. Hsu (Ed.), *Psychological anthropology.* Homewood, Ill.: Dorsey, 1961.

————. Distinguishing differences of perception from failures of communication in cross-cultural studies. In F. S. C. Northrop & H. H. Livingston (Eds.), *Cross-cultural understanding.* New York: Harper & Row, 1964, pp. 308–336.

————. Natural selection as an epistemological model. In R. Naroll & R. Cohen (Eds.), *A handbook of method in cultural anthropology.* New York: Natural History Press, 1970, pp. 51–85.

CAMPBELL, D. T., & FISKE, D. W. Convergent and discriminant validation by the multitrait—multimethod matrix. *Psychological Bulletin,* 1959, 56, 81–105.

CAMPBELL, D. T., & NAROLL, R. The mutual methodological relevance of anthropology and psychology. In F. L. K. Hsu (Ed.), *Psychological anthropology,* 2nd Ed. Cambridge, Mass.: Schenkman, 1972, pp. 435–68.

CAMPBELL, D. T., & STANLEY, J. C. *Experimental and quasi-experimental designs for research.* Chicago: Rand McNally, 1966.

COLE, M., GAY, J., GLICK, J., & SHARP, D. *The cultural context of learning and thinking.* New York: Basic Books, 1971.

DAVIDSON, A., JACCARD, J., TRIANDIS, H. C., MORALES, M., & DIAZ-GUERRERO, R. Cross-cultural model testing: toward a solution of the etic-emic dilemma. *International Journal of Psychology,* 1976, 11, 1–13.

DAWSON, J. L. M. Theoretical and research bases of biosocial psychology. *University of Hong Kong Gazette,* 1969, 16, 1–10.

————. Theory and research in cross-cultural psychology. *Bulletin of the British Psychological Society,* 1971, 24, 291–306.

DRIVER, H. E., & CHANEY, R. P. Cross-cultural sampling and Galton's problem. In

R. Naroll & R. Cohen (Eds.), *Handbook of method in cultural anthropology*. New York: Natural History Press, 1970, pp. 990–1003.

DURKHEIM, E. *Les formes elementaires de la vie religieuse*, 4th ed. Paris: Presses Universitaires de France, 1960.

DUIJKER, H. C. J., & FRIJDA, N. H. *National character and national stereotypes*. Amsterdam: Noord-Hollandse, 1960.

ECKENSBERGER, L. The necessity of a theory for applied cross-cultural research. In L. J. C. Cronbach & P. J. D. Drenth (Eds.), *Mental tests and cultural adaptation*. The Hague: Mouton, 1972, pp. 99–107.

EDGERTON, R. B. Cross-cultural psychology and psychological anthropology: one paradigm or two. *Reviews in Anthropology*, 1974, *1*, 52–65.

FREY, F. W. Cross-cultural survey research in political science. In R. T. Holt & J. E. Turner (Eds.), *The methodology of comparative research*. New York: Free Press, 1970, pp. 173–294.

FRIJDA, N. H., & JAHODA, G. On the scope and methods of cross-cultural research. *International Journal of Psychology*, 1966, *1*, 110–27.

GOLDSCHMIDT, W. *Comparative functionalism*. Berkeley: University of California Press, 1966.

GOODENOUGH, F. The measurement of mental functions in primitive groups. *American Anthropologist*, 1936, *38*, 1–11.

HOLT, R. T., & TURNER, J. E. (Eds.), *The methodology of comparative research*. New York: Free Press, 1970.

HONIGMANN, J. J. Sampling in ethnographic fieldwork. In R. Naroll & R. Cohen (Eds.), *A handbook of method in cultural anthropology*. New York: Natural History Press, 1970, pp. 266–81.

HSU, F. L. K. (Ed.), *Psychological anthropology*, 2nd. Ed. Cambridge, Mass.: Schenkman, 1972.

IRVINE, S. H. Towards a rationale for testing attainments and abilities in Africa. *British Journal of Educational Psychology*, 1966, *36*, 24–32.

IRWIN, M., KLEIN, R., ENGLE, P., YARBROUGH, C., & NERLOVE, S. The problem of establishing validity in cross-cultural measurements. *Annals of the New York Academy of Sciences*, 1977, *285*, 308–25.

JAHODA, G. A cross-cultural perspective in psychology. *The Advancement of Science*, 1970, *27*, 1–14.

———. Psychology and the developing countries: do they need each other? *International Social Science Journal*, 1973, *25*, 461–74.

———. In pursuit of the emic-etic distinction: can we ever capture it? In Y. Poortinga (Ed.), *Basic problems in cross-cultural psychology*. Amsterdam: Swets and Zeitlinger, 1977.

KEESING, R. M. Kwara ae ethno glottochronology: procedures used by Malaita cannibals for determining percentages of shared cognates. *American Anthropologist*, 1973, *75*, 1282–89.

KÖBBEN, A. Comparativists and non-comparativists in anthropology. In R. Naroll & R. Cohen (Eds.), *A handbook of method in cultural anthropology*. New York: Natural History Press, 1970, pp. 581–96.

LEACH, E. R. *Rethinking anthropology*. London: University of London, Athlone Press, 1961.

LEVINE, R. A. Cross-cultural study in child psychology. In P. H. Mussen (Ed.),

Carmichael's manual of child psychology, Vol. 2. New York: Wiley, 1970, pp. 559–612.

LIJPHART, A. Comparative politics and the comparative method. *American Political Science Review*, 1971, 65, 682–93.

———. The comparable-cases strategy in comparative research. *Comparative Political Studies*, 1975, 8, 158–77.

MALPASS, R. Theory and method in cross-cultural psychology. *American Psychologist*, 1977, 32.

MARSH, R. M. *Comparative sociology.* New York: Harcourt, Brace and World, 1967.

MURDOCK, G. P. Correlations of matrilineal and patrilineal institutions. In G. P. Murdock (Ed.), *Studies in the science of society.* New Haven: Yale University Press, 1937, pp. 445–70.

NAROLL, R. Cross-cultural sampling. In R. Naroll & R. Cohen (Eds.), *A handbook of method in cultural anthropology.* New York: Natural History Press, 1970, pp. 889–926.

———. Conceptualizing the problem, as seen by an anthropologist. Paper presented at American Political Science Association Annual Meeting. Chicago, 1971.

NISBET, R. Ethnocentrism and the comparative method. In A. R. Desai (Ed.), *Essays on modernization of underdeveloped societies*, Vol. 1. Bombay: Thacker, 1971, pp. 95–114.

O'BARR, W., SPAIN, D. H., & TESSLER, M. A. (Eds.), *Survey research in Africa.* Evanston: Northwestern University Press, 1973.

OSGOOD, C. Cross-cultural comparability in attitude measurement via multilingual semantic differentials. In I. Steiner & M. Fishbein (Eds.), *Current studies in social psychology.* Chicago: Holt, Rinehart and Winston, 1965.

PELTO, P. *Anthropological research: the structure of inquiry.* New York: Harper & Row, 1970.

PIKE, R. *Language in relation to a united theory of the structure of human behavior.* Glendale: Summer Institute of Linguistics, 1954, and The Hague: Mouton, 1966.

POORTINGA, Y. Cross-cultural comparison of maximum performance tests: some methodological aspects and some experiments with simple auditory and visual stimuli. *Psychologia Africana Monograph Supplement*, 1971, 6, 1–100.

———. Limitations on international comparison of psychological data. *Nederlands Tijdschrift voor de Psychologie*, 1975a, 30, 23–39.

———. Some implications of three different approaches to intercultural comparison. In J. W. Berry & W. J. Lonner (Eds.), *Applied cross-cultural psychology.* Amsterdam: Swets and Zeitlinger, 1975b, pp. 329–32.

PRICE-WILLIAMS, D. Psychological experiment and anthropology: the problem of categories. *Ethos*, 1974, 2, 95–114.

PRZEWORSKI, A., & TEUNE, H. *The logic of comparative social inquiry.* New York: Wiley, 1970.

RIVERS, W. H. R. Introduction and vision. In A. C. Haddon (Ed.), *Report of the Cambridge Anthropological Expedition to the Torres Straits*, Vol. II. Cambridge: Cambridge University Press, 1901.

———. Observations on the senses of the Todas. *British Journal of Psychology*, 1905, 1, 321–96.

ROBERTS, J., & SUTTON-SMITH, B. Child training and game involvement. *Ethnology*, 1962, *1*, 166–85.

ROHNER, R. *They love me, they love me not*. New Haven: HRAF Press, 1975.

ROKKAN, S. (Ed.), *Comparative research across cultures and nations*. The Hague: Mouton, 1968.

SCHEUCH, E. K. The cross-cultural use of sample surveys: problems of comparability. In S. Rokkan (Ed.), *Comparative research across cultures and nations*. The Hague: Mouton, 1968, pp. 176–209.

SEARS, R. R. Transcultural variables and conceptual equivalence. In B. Kaplan (Ed.), *Studying personality cross-culturally*. New York: Row, Peterson, 1961, pp. 445–55.

SECHREST, L. Experiments in the field. In R. Naroll & R. Cohen (Eds.), *A handbook of method in cultural anthropology*. New York: Natural History Press, 1970, pp. 196–209.

SEGALL, M., CAMPBELL, D. T., & HERSKOVITS, M. J. *The influence of culture on visual perception*. Indianapolis: Bobbs-Merrill, 1966.

SHEEHAN, P. W. The methodology of cross-cultural psychology. In G. E. Kearney & D. W. McElwain (Eds.), *Aboriginal cognition*. Canberra: Australian Institute of Aboriginal Studies, 1976.

SMELSER, N. J. The methodology of comparative analysis. In D. Warwick & S. Osherson (Eds.), *Comparative research methods*. Englewood Cliffs, N.J.: Prentice-Hall, 1973, pp. 42–86.

SOUEIF, M. I. Extreme response sets as a measure of intolerance of ambiguity. *British Journal of Psychology*, 1958, *49*, 329–33.

STURTEVANT, W. C. Studies in ethnoscience. In A. K. Romney & R. D'Andrade (Eds.), *Transcultural studies in cognition. American Anthropologist*, 1964, *66*, 99–131 (special issue).

TATJE, T. A. Problems of concept definition for comparative studies. In R. Naroll & R. Cohen (Eds.), *A handbook of methods in cultural anthropology*. New York: Natural History Press, 1970, pp. 689–706.

TEUNE, H. Comparative research, experimental design and the comparative method. *Comparative Political Studies*, 1975, *8*, 195–99.

TRIANDIS, H. C. (Ed.), Methodological problems of comparative research. *International Journal of Psychology*, 1976, *11*, No. 3 (special issue).

TRIANDIS, H. C., VASSILIOU, V., VASSILIOU, G., TANAKA, Y., & SHANMUGAM, A. V. *The analysis of subjective culture*. New York: Wiley, 1972.

TRIANDIS, H. C., FELDMAN, J. M., WELDON, D. E., & HARVEY, W. M. Ecosystem distrust and the hard-to-employ. *Journal of Applied Psychology*, 1975, *60*, 44–56.

TRIANDIS, H. C., MALPASS, R. S., & DAVIDSON, A. Cross-cultural psychology. *Biennial Review of Anthropology*, 1972.

TRIANDIS, H. C., & TRIANDIS, L. M. A cross-cultural study of social distance. *Psychological Monographs*, 1962, *76*, 21, whole no. 540.

TRIANDIS, H. C., VASSILIOU, V., & NASSIAKOU, M. Three cross-cultural studies of subjective culture. *Journal of Personality and Social Psychology*, Monograph Supplement, 1968, *8*, 4 part 2.

TYLER, S. (Ed.), *Cognitive anthropology*. New York: Holt, Rinehart and Winston, 1969.

TYLOR, E. B. On a method of investigating the development of institutions, applied to laws of marriage and descent. *Journal of the Anthropological Institute of Great Britain and Ireland*, 1889, *18*, 245–69.

WARWICK, D., & LININGER, C. A. *The sample survey: theory and practice.* New York: McGraw-Hill, 1975.

WARWICK, D. P., & OSHERSON, S. (Eds.), *Comparative research methods.* Toronto: Prentice-Hall, 1973.

WHITING, J. W. M. Methods and problems in cross-cultural research. In G. Lindzey & E. Aronson (Eds.), *Handbook of social psychology*, Vol. 2. Reading, Mass.: Addison-Wesley, 1968, pp. 693–728.

WOBER, M. Distinguishing centri-cultural from cross-cultural tests and research. *Perceptual Motor Skills*, 1969, *28*, 488.

———. Towards an understanding of the Kiganda concept of intelligence. In J. W. Berry & P. R. Dasen (Eds.), *Culture and cognition.* London: Methuen, 1974, pp. 261–80.

WUNDT, W. *Elements of folk psychology.* London: Allen & Unwin, 1916.

2

Ethnographic Field Techniques

Ward H. Goodenough

Contents

Abstract

Ethnographic field work aims to describe a society's culture. That is, it describes what people must have learned in order to participate acceptably in most of the activities of that society. It also describes how members of a society deal with one another. To do this requires that the observer isolate, inventory, and categorize the people, things, and events to which the people in a given society respond. This can be done by tracing the way categories of people, things, and events are distributed on a variety of dimensions. Analyses of these distributions make possible precise formulations of cultural expectations as rules of conduct and as principles governing group memberships, ritual performances, and all manner of decisions in the conduct of local affairs. To keep on top of what the field worker is learning it is necessary to analyze the collected material, write it up, and store and retrieve data in the field. The intensive learning required of the field worker and the separation it necessitates from emotionally rewarding and accustomed relationships tend to make ethnographic field work a profound emotional experience. Problems of professional conduct and ethics are best understood in terms of respecting others as one would have others respect oneself.

Introduction

Excellent accounts of ethnographic fieldwork and related matters have been published in recent years. Especially useful are the numerous contributions in Naroll and Cohen (1970) and the review by Pelto and Pelto (1973).[1] With those works as background, this discussion will be confined to the nature of the ethnographic enterprise insofar as its goal is to learn and describe a people's culture, the kinds of data and data handling that this goal requires, and some of the emotional and ethical problems that are likely to confront the fieldworker.

The acts of scientific observation and recording involve some categorization of inputs to them by the sensing equipment, whether that equipment is the human nervous system or some other sensing device. With human observers the categorization of inputs is usually much cruder than is possible within the limitations of the nervous system. All kinds of observed events are treated as if they were identical, even when people get down to what they consider minutiae. The criteria by which observations are basically categorized and then further aggregated as data of record may or may not be appropriate to the subsequent uses to which those data are put. The problem of relating the criteria to the subsequent data uses is complicated by the habits and predispositions of observers. These habits lead observers to make their observations and aggregations consistently in terms of certain criteria, but not in terms of others. What are assumed to be the empirical facts often rest on unquestioned habits of observation that may ignore what is more relevant to the problem under study. Since questions are phrased in terms of concepts built up from observations, it is often difficult to get leverage on why the models and theories of behavior prove inadequate.

This fundamental problem of how to categorize and aggregate observations into data appropriate to the problems at hand and how to overcome observer bias is present in all the empirical sciences, whether it is recognized or not. Often, failure to recognize it does not matter for practical purposes of the moment. In behavioural science, failure to recognize it becomes serious when people's behavior is understood as their responses to events going on around them; for to do so, how they are classifying those events must somehow be accounted for. To do this may require the observers to aggregate their observations in accordance with discriminations they have never learned to make or criteria that they never used. This problem has been a major concern of descriptive linguistics since early in this century and recently has become an important concern in descriptive ethnography. It is by no means the only concern of ethnography, but it is necessarily a central one.

The problem of linking the responses other people make to events going on around them is not peculiar to behavioral science. It is equally the problem of every human being as he tries to learn how to anticipate the behavior of others and how to meet their expectations (at least insofar as he wants to). Becoming enculturated is successfully solving this problem. To understand just how people do this is crucial for behavioral theory as well as for ethnographic method. Without such understanding there can be no acceptable theory of significant symbols, of shared meanings, or of cultures as systems of such symbols and meanings.

In the normal course of enculturation, people learn to anticipate the responses and to meet the expectations of others unself-consciously and without close attention to *how* they do it. The processes remain largely subjective. To make these processes objects of scientific study requires that behavioral scientists do the following things:

1. They must self-consciously undertake to learn about the expectations of others.
2. They must make as careful a record as possible of what they seem to be learning as they go.
3. They must seek through introspection to discern and objectify the cognitive operations by which they feel they are learning it.
4. They must try to describe what they have learned in a manner that will allow others to know as precisely as possible what they, too, must learn if they are to learn the same thing.

Whether scientists have learned adequately the expectations of others can be established only through their ability to meet those expectations, and through their capacity to describe their findings in a way that allows someone else, using the description as his guide, to meet those same expectations.

The problem of ethnographic research may be treated in relation to two major tasks. One, as just indicated, pertains to describing the criteria people under study use to discriminate among things and how they respond to them and assign them meaning, including everything in their physical, behavioral, and social environments. This is the task of cultural description. The other task is to describe these same environments and the effects of people's behavior on them, not in terms of how the people perceive them, but in terms appropriate to the questions under investigation.

Environment includes much more than physical surroundings. Very important is the human environment that people form for one another. The kind of emotional climate people live in, for example, is sustained by the effect of their actions on one another. The complicated influences of environment on culture and culture on environment cannot be studied unless there are instruments for measuring and describing the environment that are independent of how the local people perceive and respond to it. Thus, environmental description takes us into many disciplines, encompassing the entire range of physical, biological, behavioral, and social sciences. But the environment concerns ethnographers primarily as it is formulated in the local culture and is affected by the culturally mediated behavior of the local people. The local culture is, therefore, the central subject matter of reference for most environmental investigations that are most often undertaken by anthropologists and other behavioral scientists. The following, therefore, will focus on the description of cultures.

When one goes into a strange community, what is manifested on the surface consists of people, physical arrangements (houses, roads, etc.), activities, and talk. Ethnography necessarily begins with these four things, seeking to learn (a) who the people are, and in what terms they perceive one another and their relationships; (b) what the physical arrangements mean to the people, and how people would like to maintain them; (c) what the activities are about, how they fit in with other undertakings and what principles govern them; and (d) how to talk the language and what people talk about. All of these things are, of course, interrelated, so that what one learns about any one of them helps to clarify others. Field study proceeds on all fronts at more or less the same time, immediate attention shifting from one to another and back again. For each, however, there are at least some systematic procedures.

Who Is Who?

Basic to ethnography is the cast of characters. Much of a group's culture concerns the ordering of people into systems of relationships. Every human group necessarily has understandings regarding who takes precedence over whom in the gratification of wants. It also has understandings about the contexts in which these precedences apply. These understandings require that people be sorted conceptually into kinds, that they be given different social identities, and that these identities be assigned rights and duties to one another with respect to matters of interest to them. Classifications of people by sex, age, marital condition, parenthood, task

being performed, and skill occur everywhere; other classifications according to such things as personality, rank, social class, ethnic group, occupation, and political office are widespread.

It is useful to distinguish between social and personal identities in analyzing the cultural ordering of human relationships. Any category of self
that makes a difference in how one's right and/or duties distribute to
others is a kind of social identity; whereas any category of self that affects
behavior or attitudes apart from rights and/or duties is a kind of personal
identity. Thus employers have certain rights and obligations vis-a-vis their
employees and both are regarded by others in their society as justly ag-
grieved if their rights in the relationship are not honored. Sticklers will
insist on all their rights, whereas people who are easygoing will not. The
rights are the same in either case, but the style of operation in relation to
them is quite different. The terms employer and employee designate
kinds of social identity, as do the terms male, female, adult, minor, husband, wife, father, and mother in American culture. The terms stickler
and easygoing designate kinds of personal identity, as do the terms marti-
net, crook, liar, cheat, smooth operator, and generous person in American
culture.

It is important to note that cultural classifications of kinds of personal
identity, of personality traits, and of insanity or socially pathological behavior, all acquire their meaning largely from how people behave in relation to their rights and duties in their various social-identity relationships,
as has been noted by Caughey (personal communication). The same act is
understood as generous or stingy depending on the obligations of the particular social-identity relationship in which it occurs. An observer cannot
grasp the characterological meaning of actions until he has mastered the
system of social-identity relationships and the rights and duties that provide the framework for expectations within them.

Systematic investigations of these and other aspects of social organization require a house-by-house census, listing everyone by name (or
names), their marital conditions, their locally assigned age category (and
also actual age, if possible), and their kinship and other social connections
to one another. If the community under study is too large to make an exhaustive census possible, then a complete census should be made of those
segments of it that are selected for intensive study. An *n*th-person sample
is of little use, except as a beginning point for inquiry, because it fails to
reveal the ways people are linked to one another. See Honigmann (1970)
for a discussion of sampling in ethnographic fieldwork.

To the census should be added genealogies, which should be collected
as fully as local knowledge permits. In some societies, people customarily
keep genealogies in great depths; in others, they do not. Genealogies
should not be confused with records of biological kinship. A genealogy is
a record of a chain of marital ties and parent-child links as these ties and

links are recognized in the society under study. To be a spouse or a parent is to have a culturally defined identity. Sexual rights and biological reproduction are always relevant in some way to the definition of these identities and provide the constants needed to equate them cross-culturally, but how they are applicable differs from culture to culture. Thus in one society a socially significant father may be whoever is recognized as the child's biological genitor, while in another society he is whoever is recognized as the husband of the socially significant mother. Genealogies, therefore, provide a record of criss-crossing kinship networks in terms of marriage and parenthood as defined in the culture under study. These social ties of marriage and parenthood are the primitive ones for kinship study. Their ramifications produce the structural properties of genealogical space. These properties are used by people in different ways to define the categories of kin relationships into which that space is culturally partitioned and that are verbally represented by kinship terms.

Collecting genealogies helps provide access to unusual cases relating to marriage and parenthood that are likely to be most revealing of underlying cultural principles. But genealogies are useful for much more. Present arrangements in a community are largely the product of events and transactions that have taken place in the past, involving people who are no longer alive. To the extent that people make a point of remembering their ancestors and predecessors, these ancestors remain socially significant persons of reference in their affairs. The genealogical record is, therefore, an indispensable inventory of a community's population of currently significant persons. A useful review of the "genealogical method" has been provided by Hackenberg (1973).

Making inventories, such as censuses and genealogies, is a basic procedure of field research. For every kind of social identity, one should get a list of all the people in one's census and genealogies (when appropriate) who have that kind of identity. A list should be compiled of every other kind of social identity with which any one identity can be in meaningful (socially grammatical) relationship. An inventory should also be made of the specific kinds of actions that are obligatory or forbidden in one or more identity relationships including a record of how each obligation or prohibition is distributed in the various identity relationships. It is from such information that status systems can be constructed (Goodenough, 1965; Keesing, 1970a). For every identity relationship, it is useful to have a list of those in the census who stand to one another in that relationship: who is in what kin category to whom, who is friend to whom, who is patron to whom, client to whom, and so on.

Obviously, it cannot be done all at once, but it is important to take every opportunity to add to the inventories of kinds of identity and relationship and to find how these additions are distributed in the population. Each new distribution should be examined against the distributions already collected, with an eye to possible lines of inquiry with informants. It is by such procedures that it becomes possible to formulate acceptable models of a society's cultural principles that govern the ordering of social relationships.

A frequent misconception among the inexperienced is that ethnographic fieldwork consists of sitting down with local informants and asking them to explain the cultural principles they operate with. Ethnographers do not neglect this line of inquiry, but they find that for most topics of inquiry their informants are unable to give well-thought out expositions of just how things work. They know the principles of etiquette, for example, just as they know the grammatical principles of their language, but they have as much trouble explaining the former in systematic fashion as they do the latter. People teach children by articulating specific dos and don'ts in relation to concrete situations and examples as they arise in the course of everyday life. From these many concrete situations, individuals extrapolate for themselves a subjective feel for the cultural principles, a process that Sapir called "unconscious patterning" (Sapir, 1927). The strategy of ethnography requires ethnographers to find ways of maximizing their encounters, either vicariously or first-hand with the kinds of concrete situations that provide examples of what it is they want to learn. Informants explain the concrete examples, and out of these many explanations come the ethnographer's extrapolations of cultural principles. Censuses, genealogies, and inventories generally, provide a means for maximizing a wide variety of such encounters with concrete examples.

For example, consider social identities that are based on membership in groups: families, kin groups, work groups, local or residential groups, voluntary societies, ritual groups, and so on. As lists are compiled of all present and past memberships of everyone in the census and genealogies, questions will arise about why particular individuals became members or ceased being members. As ethnographers go from case to case, a pattern of reasons will begin to emerge, and they will be able to formulate principles governing membership and eligibility for membership. Here and there, however, there will be memberships that are inconsistent with these apparent principles. Close inquiry into these exceptional cases is likely to lead to a deeper understanding of how memberships work and may result in considerable revision of what had appeared at first to be the apparent principles.

How censuses are drawn up, genealogies laid out, and lists compiled affects what are likely to be seen as patterns in the data. Genealogies, especially, are a problem; they ramify such that it becomes necessary to find some convenient way of collecting them. The most convenient approach is to draft them by local groups or descent groups (if they exist), and to use some system (numerical or alpha-numerical) for quickly identifying the various groups. Thus all the past and present members of a lineage may be put together in the same genealogical chart along with their spouses (after whose names will appear the code for their own lineage memberships). Such a way of compiling is handy for record-keeping purposes, but it has its drawbacks. Keeping genealogies by patrilineal lineages, for example, makes readily apparent patrilineal relationships and any patterns of marital exchange between the patrilineal lineages, but it obscures patterns that follow other principles. It may be necessary to redraw genealogical charts several times according to different criteria in order to perceive all the patterns inherent in the data. Computerization of genealogies can be especially helpful in this regard.

In addition to the living and the dead, the socially significant cast of characters may include spirits and ghosts, as illustrated by Hallowell (1955, pp. 172–182). How these are classified, the contexts in which they are socially or behaviorally accounted for, the powers they possess, and their rights and duties as social beings are also things to be recorded. The common ethnocentric approach that calls spirits and ghosts the supernatural can prevent understanding the phenomenal world of the people studied (Frake, 1964). Careful inventorying and cross-inventorying in the various ways suggested here can be a helpful corrective.

What Is Where?

In addition to the cast of characters are the setting and the props—all of the nonhuman features of the environment, that the people under study respond to in some way. They have their ways of categorizing these things; they believe them to have various kinds of properties and uses; and they value them relative to one another. The enjoyment and use of these things is the subject matter of rights and duties in property relationships.

As these observations imply, here too is almost endless subject matter for inventorying. Take, for example, that most important resource: land (Lundsgaarde, 1974). Is it divided into named tracts, divisions, and subdivisions? If so, what are their names and where are they located on the map? Just as basic as genealogies and censuses are maps (however rough) that show the various tracts and divisions, the kinds of holdings within them, and who holds them. It is important to record the location of all valuable resources, whether they are privately owned or are public goods, such as water, mineral deposits, and so on.

It is also useful to compile a list of all the different kinds of manufactured objects. A census of such objects by household can be very revealing (Kay, 1964; LeBar, 1964). How these objects, land, and other property holdings are distributed among individuals and groups should be inventoried, as well as how these holdings have been transferred in the past from former owners in the genealogies. Also to be recorded are the specific rights and duties people can have with respect to each different kind of object of ownership. Each distinctive cluster of rights thus revealed constitutes a kind of entitlement in the local property system.

An important part of any property system is the rights people have in other people as objects of value or in the services others can provide. The rights of parents over their children or of employers over their employees, and vice versa, are not ordinarily thought of as forms of property; but as kinds of entitlement that is precisely what they are. These rights differ in significant ways from one culture to another, as do the kinds of transactions (such as adoption) to which they are subject (Carroll, 1970). It is as important to see how rights distribute among different categories of *persons* as it is to see how they distribute among different categories of *things*. Also subject to rights are the practice of skills, the performance of dances and ceremonies, the telling of stories, the initiation of various kinds of undertaking, the wearing of certain costumes, and even the public use of certain forms of speaking. Rules of etiquette define the immunities from liberties to their persons that people can expect, as well as the forms of recognition that are their due.

For each kind of entitlement, it is useful to have an inventory indicating which individuals and groups hold title to each kind of subject matter, and also which individuals and groups formerly held them, as far back as is remembered. It is also important to know what kinds of transactions any particular entitlement is subject to. Is it transferable in whole or in part, and, if so, under what circumstances and in how many different ways? A record should be compiled of the past transactions, since it provides a basis for inquiry into the kinds of transactions possible and into the values attaching to them. It is likely to bring out trends, both linear and cyclical, in the distribution of property rights.

Similar inventories should be made of past places of residence, something an ordinary house-to-house census does not reveal. Such information brings out patterns in changing domestic arrangements in the course of individual lives; it also reveals the developmental cycle of households, and other local groups. Here again, explanations of specific residence decisions will show what the public justifications for them are and what the public values are about residence.

What Is Doing?

Thus far the discussion has dealt with recording what people understand to be the properties of their phenomenal world: including people, spirits and ghosts, things, the ways in which people and things are believed to interact, and the ways in which these possible actions are ordered and regulated. The emphasis has been on how people, things, and behaviours are categorized and how the various categories are considered to be appropriately distributed with respect to one another. Yet to be considered are the things that an ethnographer observes. For excellent treatments of observation in ethnographic field research, see the accounts by Whiting, Child, and Lambert (1968) and by Whiting and Whiting (1970).

A natural unit of observation is what we commonly refer to as an activity. An activity is any intentional action or coordinated grouping of actions that is aimed at affecting existing arrangements in the phenomenal world in some way. The arrangements to be affected may be material, social, or psychological. The purpose may be instrumental and aimed at accomplishing something needed to further some other purpose, or it may be an end in itself. Irreducible minima of purposeful action and ultimate versus instrumental ends, need not be considered in the initial ordering of observations.

Observation alone is insufficient for identifying activities. All that can be observed is a lot of action, not what people are really up to, unless the kinds of activities in which they engage, what they involve, and how they are organized are already known. Observing people with spears and goggles in the waters off a Pacific Island, one may surmise that they are engaged in fishing, but the surmise rests on a prior acquaintance with spears and goggles as instruments used for fishing. Observation is inevitably coupled, therefore, with the age-old questions: "What is happening?" "What are they doing?" The answers, in other societies as well as in our own, often imply the end in view: "They are making a boat;" "They are mending thatch;" "They are preparing dinner;" "They are taking a rest." Often, too, another kind of answer refers to the particular means among alternatives for accomplishing recognized purposes: "They are lighting a stove;" "They are using a wedge." Uninitiated observers who are still not satisfied with the first kind of answer follow it up with: "Then, what are they doing *that* for?" They follow up the second kind of answer with: "Why?" As these follow-up questions reveal, people make sense out of one another's behavior to the extent that they can relate it to an intended consequence. Every activity has some intended consequence. Behaviour is judged as rational, it appears to help achieve a desired purpose. The apparent universality of this human trait serves ethnographers well, enabling them to sort observed behavioural events, as they contribute to specific activities.

Many activities are highly routine whereas others are ad hoc affairs. Routine or not, activities necessarily are initiated in relation to occasions that justify pursuing their purposes; they follow procedures, use resources, have a locale, involve particular kinds of people organized in particular ways, and have unintended as well as their intended consequences.

A checklist of things to bear in mind when recording activities must include the following as features of activities.

1. Purposes: (a) stated goals and their justifications; (b) other gratifications accruing to participants.
2. Procedures: (a) operations performed; (b) media used, including raw materials; (c) instruments and tools employed; (d) skills involved.
3. Time and space requirements: (a) time required for each operation; (b) time as affected by numbers of participants and their skills; (c) minimum and maximum time requirements; (d) space requirements such as work areas and storage facilities.
4. Personnel requirements: (a) minimal and optimal division of tasks; (b) minimal and optimal number of persons for each; (c) specialists, if any.
5. Social organization: (a) categories of personnel; (b) rights, duties, privileges, and powers and their allocation; (c) management and direction; (d) sanctions; (e) permanence of organization (ad hoc or standing groups).
6. Occasions for performance: (a) occasions when mandatory, permitted, and prohibited; (b) processes that initiate activity; (c) locus of privilege, power, or duty to initiate; (d) relation of initiator's role to director's role; (e) availability of media, instruments, and personnel.

Some ordering of activities is necessary. The requirements of some important activities may limit the ways in which other purposes can be conveniently accomplished. To optimize the accomplishment of their many conflicting purposes, people mutually adjust their various activities. They let the same standing groups be responsible for more than one activity, use the same principles of social organization from one to another, and develop multipurpose tool kits, for example. On the other hand, they keep some activities in a complementary relationship, allocating different raw materials to different activities and substituting other materials if necessary, thus paving the way for and developing different kinds of specialists. Some activities are instrumentally linked to others; others are partially fused to take advantage of common requirements—the occasion for performing one activity becomes the occasion for performing another. Such ordering of activities underlies the development of fixed institutionalized arrangements in societies (Goodenough, 1963). At the same time, it provides the systematic links through which change has its ramifying effects no matter where the change begins—in the physical environment, the social environment, or customary practices. Pelto (1973) and Sharp (1952) provide well-analyzed examples.

Recurring patterns in the allocation of rights and duties, the priorities assigned to the occasions for performing various activities, and the things that are said in public to justify undertaking the activities, provide important information needed to understand a society's public values (as distinct from the private sentiments of its members).

Because activities are purpose oriented, they have outcomes, which in any specific instance may be consistent with their purposes. The performance of an activity usually results in a number of different outcomes. Functional analysis is largely concerned with the gamut of common outcomes of the performance of specific routines. A given activity functions to provide emotional release for specific tensions, to give expression to specific emotional concerns, to reinforce specific public values, to maintain particular networks of social relationships and obligations, to provide particular necessities of physical existence, and so on. Such analysis relates to the ecology of customary routines.

Because activities have intended outcomes and because their various components involve resources and their use, the cultural organization of activities is like programs or recipes. Obviously, the programs are not unvarying routines, except when activities become highly ritualized. They allow, rather, for various alternatives, depending upon the availability of specific resources, tools, skills, and personnel, as well as the particular combinations of purposes that are intended as outcomes. The program for a wedding intended to take care of minimal obligations to the community and the couple's kin will differ from one intended to enhance the social standing of those responsible for staging it. Any particular performance involves selection of alternative routines. Of special concern is the selection of available subroutines calculated to achieve a particular combination of purposes, according to their priorities for that occasion.

From this point of view, the cultural organization of activities is productively viewed within the framework of decision making (Quinn, 1975); its description can be effectively approached with conceptual tools developed in cybernetics, computer programming, and operational analysis. Examples in the published literature involve the use of flow diagrams that indicate culturally possible outcomes at the output end and begin with a given triggering event at the input. All the decision points that are culturally significant are indicated in between, in appropriate order. All of the different pathways leading to outcomes constitute routines or subroutines. Examples and further discussion of such analyses are provided, among others, by Keesing (1970, 1971) and Geoghegan (1971).

Flow diagramming provides economy and precision of ethnographic presentation; it is a valuable tool in ethnographic research when used in the field to organize what investigators know about the organization of activities. If they cannot diagram the pathways from triggering events to known outcomes they discover that they have not yet achieved closure on the subject. They can also pinpoint the gaps in their information. Thus, flow diagramming provides a check on the extent to which investigators have exhausted a line of inquiry into the cultural organization of activities.

Once many activities have been diagrammed, investigators have available something akin to the recipes in a cookbook. These provide the materials for further distributional analyses from which more general cultural principles can be formulated. Since, like the cooking of recipes, cultural routines use the same set of resources (tools, operations, kinds of social group, and principles of social organization) over and over again in different combinations, it is now possible to see which combinations occur and which combinations would not make sense if they did occur, or would even be regarded as taboo. The procedures in such analyses are similar to those used by linguists in the analysis of syntactic structures, whereby various syntactic classes are isolated and rules governing their ordering are derived. These procedures are also like those developed in industry to break down operations into various component steps in order to maximize efficiency. This kind of analysis is only beginning to be developed in ethnographic research, but it appears to offer exciting prospects for behavioral and cultural science in the long run. The case method approach to the ethnographic study of law, reviewed by Epstein (1967), provides a subject of inquiry, for example, where its application should be especially fruitful.

What's on People's Minds?

To see activities organized in terms of the accomplishment of human purposes inevitably brings human motivation into the explanation of customs and institutions and into the theory of cultural and social change. Functional interpretations also make assumptions about human motives and priorities, implicitly if not explicitly. Students of culture and personality, as the subject used to be called, stressed the effect of institutional practices on the structuring of chronic anxieties and preoccupations that in turn affected the shaping of other customary practices and beliefs. Ethnography has as one of its tasks obtaining evidence about chronic concerns, cravings, anxieties, and personal aspirations for the self—things that tend to preoccupy the members of every community a great deal of the time.

While many of these concerns have an important effect on the conduct of human activities, they are not in themselves the explicit considerations that provide publicly acceptable reasons for performing those activities. The man in American society who "makes a religion out of his business," for example, is using an area of activity ostensibly for practical purposes to manage his private but dominating emotional concerns. Often there is a wide discrepancy between the publicly stated reasons for doing things and the private satisfactions people get out of doing them—satisfactions that give the activity far more value for them than its ostensible purposes. Religious rituals are obvious examples. To join with others in worshipping God is not in itself sufficiently rewarding for many who regularly attend church on Sunday. To understand the investment people have in their customary practices and beliefs requires data and analysis that go far beyond the bland and safe answers people give to those who would pry into their motives.

Several kinds of data are useful in this regard; each kind can be obtained and analyzed independently of the others, making it possible to use one as a check on the conclusions derived from another.

One kind of data derives from the use of projective tests, such as the Rorschach and Thematic Apperception Tests. They will not be discussed here, but it should be noted that the analysis of such test results by Gladwin and Sarason (1951) proved enlightening later in explaining the value for Truk's people of their pre-Christian religious practices as well as some more recent pastimes that many seem strongly attracted to (Goodenough, 1974).

Various kinds of ethnographic data can also provide patterned syndromes that indicate underlying preoccupations.

The things that teenagers spend much of their time talking about with one another indicate their major interests and concerns. That middle class American mothers with young children spend much of their social visiting hours with one another talking about their children and matters of child care and child health clearly indicates a major focus of their concern. Witness the fact that books on child care are best sellers.

In literate societies the profitable topics of popular literature, such as western stories, detective stories, and science fiction, are indicative of the preoccupations of those who regularly read them. Indeed their standardized plots are like those of morality plays, giving expression to things that are problems in the actual lives of many people. Similarly among peoples without written literature, the stock figures and standard plot motifs in the stories they tell—e.g., bumbling older brother, clever younger brother, and their encounters with cannibalistic ghosts in some Micronesian societies—are symptomatic of preoccupying problems arising from the way social relationships are culturally structured in those societies. The kinds of moving pictures that happen to be popular are symptomatic also.

Especially indicative are the ways that people modify the rituals and stories they have taken from others. The liberties taken with borrowed stories and rituals are not usually haphazard but indicative of what makes them more interesting and satisfying to the borrowers.

Apart from the things people are concerned about and preoccupied with are the things that make up their view of their world. To get at their worldview—their cognitive map—and describe it is a major ethnographic challenge. It requires finding out what criteria people use to classify their experiences of things and events, and then discovering the propositions about the relationships among these things that they accept as true. The theoretical issues in the study of beliefs have been ably summarized and discussed by Black (1973). For the ethnographers it is clear that language is the major means of access to the world view of others. Indeed, it is through language learning that human beings acquire this kind of understanding of one another, to the extent that it is possible to acquire it at all.

A question often arises about the use of interpreters in ethnographic fieldwork. For many problems of ethnography, such as taking censuses and getting genealogies, it is possible to work through interpreters. There is nothing culturally subtle about enumerating people, however difficult it may be under some field conditions to count them. But for most ethnographic purposes working only through interpreters is unsatisfactory. Years ago, Bronislaw Malinowski (1935) demonstrated the enormous difference that learning the local language makes in ethnography. It has been demonstrated repeatedly ever since.

Ethnographers really have no choice. They must do what all humans have always had to do in order to learn how their fellows perceive and understand things: learn the language they use to express those perceptions and understandings and be with them in the various contexts of daily living in which they do so.

But ethnographers must do more than that. They must learn self-consciously. They must make a record of what they think they are learning from day to day as they are trying to learn it. They must record why they know what they think they know as they go along. When they think they understand something, they must ask themselves just what it is they understand and try to make their intuitive knowledge explicit to themselves. In this way they not only contribute to the growing corpus of data, they also help to objectify the processes by which cultural learning takes place and thus help to develop explicit and rigorous methods of ethnography.

Much of ethnography involves descriptive semantics. Methodological progress has been slow. An important beginning was made by Malinowski (1935: vol. 2). Since the 1950s, anthropologists have begun to use contrastive analysis, developed in structural linguistics, as an approach to descriptive semantics (Berlin, Breedlove, & Raven, 1974; Conklin, 1955; Goodenough 1956; Goodenough, 1967; Pospisil, 1964, 1965a, 1965b). Many problems remain before descriptive semantics can be regarded as a fully developed ethnographic tool, but it is clear that its continued development is essential for rigorous cultural description.

Storage and Retrieval of Data
in the Field

A common mistake in field work is to keep notes and observations solely in the form of a diary or journal until the field work is finished. While a diary or journal is indispensable, it is poor practice to have it as the only form of record keeping. When the ethnographers go home to analyze their data, they find that they must spend as much time sorting and classifying as they spent in the field. Only after that can they begin to work the data up. They then discover that their notes are full repetitions of the same information on some matters and woefully inadequate on others, whose importance they only now appreciate after they begin the task of pulling things together in a coherent account. It is essential for ethnographers to be on top of their data or to be able to get on top of it quickly at all times, including the time they are in the field.

To do this requires taking time out every day if possible, to write up the current work. This effort reveals the gaps in information and primes the investigators for what needs to be looked into further. It is also helpful to have some kind of indexing system, such as that in the Human Relations Area Files' *Outline of Culture Materials* (Murdock, 1950) or a suitable modification of it. By classifying data according to this system as the daily writing is done and by then filing copies under each of the index headings, ethnographers will be able quickly to retrieve information accumulated about any particular topic. Classifying and filing by topic allows taking a day at periodic intervals to put the material together and provides time to write a rough draft of what will eventually be a section of the research report. Then the original notes for the rough draft can be filed chronologically to serve as a journal.

Inevitably, ethnographers pick up incidental information about other subjects, some of which they will consider more seriously later. Classifying as they go, enables them to see readily what they have already learned about these other topics when they get to them. Having such material readily available, also helps provide ethnographers with new initiatives in their work. A common difficulty in field work occurs when the investigators achieve a premature or false closure and discover they are unable to think of any further line of inquiry. Finding ways to get more deeply involved in local activities helps, as does consulting topical outlines and guides to field work such as those provided by Murdock (1950), and the Royal Anthropological Institute (1951). Being able to consult those peripheral topics on which data has been incidentally accumulating is also helpful.

The necessity of keeping a record of photographs, faithfully indicating by film number and frame number the content of each photograph including the names of the people in it, goes without saying. It is dismaying to discover how quickly the names of people and the precise occasions on which pictures were taken are forgotten. Useful discussions of the uses of still photography in field work are provided by Collier (1967) and Mead (1970).

Many people doing field work for the first time regard tape recorders as handy time savers. Tape recordings are clearly useful to have for matters where an exact record of what has been said is important. But they are no time saver; if ethnographers fail to transcribe them and translate them while they are in the field, they are likely to find that they are unable to do so satisfactorily when they get home, even if they have achieved a fair degree of fluency in the local language. Experience shows that it is prudent to allow a week's work in the field for every hour of narrative on tape.

Clearly, efficient field work requires careful targeting of data collection, and it requires analyzing data, at least in a preliminary way, and writing them up as one goes along in a form that will make them readily usable in the course of subsequent data gathering. Competing for the ethnographers' time are all those interesting and important things going on in the community that they hate to miss. But it is impossible to keep up with everything. It is important to find a balance between observation and data gathering on the one hand and classification, processing, and analysis on the other, a balance that is most appropriate to their research objectives and to the kind of data that they require.

Field Work as an Experience

Good field work is necessarily an intense learning experience. It is likely to be an intense emotional one as well. It is almost inevitably so when ethnographers are undergoing their first exposure to the society, language, and culture under investigation. In order to learn, they must immerse themselves in dealings with people they can learn from. Such immersion requires cutting themselves off, at least for major portions of their time, from those people who will not contribute to their work. One learns a language faster from people with whom one does not already share a common language. Similarly, one learns a local culture faster from people who have not learned to get around in the researcher's own home society. Plunging into a situation where one is so completely ignorant can be emotionally difficult, and people are said to suffer from "culture shock" when they find themselves unable to cope with that kind of stress. Where motivation to learn is high, as is presumably the case with ethnographers, it carries an investigator through the early stress. But the stress is nonetheless real.

What should ethnographers do, for example, when a local acquaintance nudges them and tells them to say something to someone in words they do not understand? Is the acquaintance being helpful or is he having fun at their expense? Or is he trying to get them into trouble? Suppose the ethnographers say what he told them to say, and suppose that the listeners laugh. Are they laughing at them or at something else in the situation that they know nothing about? It may be that they are simply laughing at the other person's surprise at being addressed colloquially in his own language by people he assumed knew no word of it. Or they may be simply serving as a pawn in some horseplay between two people who have a joking relationship. However innocent the situation may actually be, ethnographers are likely to be angry at being put into it. A local acquaintance can have no real appreciation of how thoroughly he or she has shattered the dignity the ethnographers had been struggling to preserve in the face of so many uncertainties. If one does not know how to respond when someone brings him or her a present, it can be a crisis. When, after several weeks of such daily crises, one finds oneself sitting with local people in the evening, straining to catch a word here and there of what they are saying, as they talk animatedly to one another, every now and then glancing at one and laughing, then, indeed, one is likely to feel abused and persecuted. Ethnographers need confidence in themselves and faith in the fundamental good will of the local people to keep a healthy perspective on their predicament. They who cannot laugh at themselves are most vulnerable.

As time goes on, ethnographers learn to communicate and how to deal with gifts and the other things that gave them so much concern at first; they begin to establish on-going relationships with people. By this time new emotional needs begin to arise.

All people derive essential emotional nourishment from the relationships in which they regularly take part. It is in these relationships that they share their experiences, receive love and attention, find themselves being important to others, and get continual confirmation of their worth as persons. Only with such ongoing nourishment can people remain emotionally whole. The field situation that is most conducive to intense learning is one that effectively cuts researchers off from the relationships in which they have been getting this nourishment. They have to live off emotional fat, so to speak, at a time when they are subjected to the stresses derived from their ignorance and their consequent social and cultural disorientation. Their motivation to learn the local language and culture derives enormous impetus from their need to establish meaningful and emotionally sustaining relationships. But their emotional fat inevitably gets used up, and as it does, their needs become more pressing. They are likely to find themselves paying less attention to ethnography and more attention to

fulfilling their needs. Revealing expressions of these problems are provided by Bowen (1954) and Malinowski (1967). For further discussion, see
Mead (1970) and Goodenough (1963, pp. 401–406).

Attempts to solve these problems may take various directions such as
retreating into escape literature or into alcohol. Instead of retreating, ethnographers may seek to establish relationships with local people that
serve as substitutes for those that have been most important in filling their
needs in the past. Here the problem is that their need is most likely to be
matched by a corresponding need on the part of the misfits and marginal
members of the local community for a relationship with them. It is easy to
be drawn to people with whom a close association jeopardizes the working relations ethnographers need with other members of the community.
In any event, the nature of their need is likely to lead them to seek particular kinds of relationships. Commonly sought are the intimate heterosexual
relationship of a man and woman, a dependency relationship on someone
as a father figure, or a nurturing relationship with someone as adopted
child. It is inevitable that ethnographers will invest a great deal in the relationship they develop with someone as their principal informant, as is illustrated in some of the accounts compiled by Casagrande (1960).

After an extended and successful period of field work, ethnographers
return home. They have had a profound learning and emotional experience that will forever be a significant part of who they are. Back home they
find they cannot share it with their relatives and friends, who can, of
course, have no feeling for it at all. Anthropologists who have had such
experiences, especially those who have worked in the same parts of the
world, gravitate to one another at professional meetings. Indeed, meetings
of the American Anthropological Association share some of the characteristics of a war veterans' organization, in which people commune together
over their drinks, reliving their experiences with an understanding and
appreciative fellowship, recounting to one another things that happened
to them in the field that they feel unable to tell anyone else.

But what about taking one's family into the field situation? It helps
solve a number of the problems indicated above, but it has its own poten-
tials for difficulty. Spouses are likely to find their relationship being re-
structured by the local people in terms of local behavioral expectations
and in ways that seriously cramp a husband and wife's habitual style with
each other. If the professional interest of one provides a high motivation to
learn the local language and to relate well with local people, while a lack
of such commitment provides low motivation in the other, they may find
themselves reacting very differently to the field situation, and with growing tension and strain in their relationship. To the extent that they can
freely and sympathetically communicate their feelings to each other and
are committed to sharing their experience they will deal successfully with
the problems that arise. Having a spouse and children in the field, while it

has advantages, also serves to divide the attention of the ethnographer, and thus dilute the intensity of his involvement in the ethnographic process. But as with everything, doing ethnography requires striking an optimal balance between competing professional and other life requirements. Ethnographers must work out their own balance.

Professional Conduct and Ethics in Field Work

Some of the problems having to do with field work as an emotional experience are relevant to standards of professional conduct by the investigators as members of both the scientific and the human communities. Ethnographers' efforts to use the local community and its members as a means of gratifying their own emotional needs may lead them to overstep the bounds of appropriate behavior. But what are the standards of professional conduct?

They can be summarized simply as the things that follow from the basic principle that investigators owe all of the people with whom they deal, both as scientists and as human beings, the kind of respect for them and their humanity that they would like others to show them. As scientists, it is their responsibility to strive to understand everyone as fellow human beings, warts and all. It is not their mission as scientists to try to reform them. As sympathetic fellow humans, they will try to be helpful, but they are not there to take sides in others' political battles. They cannot afford the arrogant luxury of assuming that as representatives of western civilization they know better than the local inhabitants do how they should arrange their lives or even how they should deal with practical problems confronting them. On the other hand investigators cannot remain so aloof as to look upon the local people as objects of investigation or experimental subjects. Rather, they are fellow humans whom they wish to get to know. Without such an attitude of respect for and acceptance of the local people's own humanity ethnographers cannot do the kind of cultural learning that they are there to do. The "golden rule" is the practical necessity for ethnographic research.

But what if respecting the local people in this way means not getting certain kinds of data that the research objectives call for? There is only one possible answer: abandon those research objectives until ways can be found to implement them in a manner consistent with standards of mutual decency and respect. There are many other things that can be profitably investigated in the meantime. Researchers who in the interest of getting the data they want do things that make subsequent field workers unwelcome and objects of suspicion have been derelict in their professional obligations to their fellow scientists. They have exhibited contempt for their colleagues as well as for the local people.

The more specific dos and don'ts in the codes of ethics developed by the Society for Applied Anthropology and the American Psychological Association follow logically from the general principle. Field workers have to honor the ethical principles of the host community in which they work as well as those of their home communities, for example. They have to be honest about their research objectives and their sponsorship. They must not deceive the local people regarding the intent or intended uses of their research. They must consider the impact of the conduct of the research on the people under study and do all they can to insure against what the people will regard as significant negative effects.

Similar consideration applies to publication of research results. What is published is certain to be read by members of the community studied and by people who are in a position to use what is published for good or ill. Preserving the anonymity of the community and the individuals in it may well be a matter of utmost importance. What can be published and the way it can be published is often directly related to the extent to which such anonymity is both necessary and possible. There is also the necessity to honor privileged communications about professional, trade, or family secrets. If the investigators are instructed in specialized knowledge that is not to be made available to people generally, for example, then they cannot publish it, at least not in a form that betrays the trust that was placed in them.

Apart from more obvious considerations of this kind, field research inevitably provides information about a community that is likely to be regarded as demeaning by its members. One must always ask oneself whether publication of such information is necessary or really serves any useful purpose. Often, it is not so much the facts themselves that are demeaning as the way they are presented. One can describe the contents of house yards, for example, without referring to them as "litter."

Especially problematical is the language used to describe the results of psychological tests or to delineate national character, the prevailing emotional climate, or the foci of emotional concern. The difficulty is that the words for such things in the investigator's language, even in its technical jargons, are usually value laden and judgmental in their connotations. English psychological language, for example, has developed largely in clinical contexts in relation to what have been regarded pathologies. Its use simply to describe certain recurring patterns of behavior in a population is likely to have connotations of pathology that outrage the members of that population. Here, obviously, is a matter where great care must be taken.

Another way in which it is easy to give offense, especially for Americans, is in regard to etiquette. Americans tend to value egalitarianism in social relations and to assume that treating others in an egalitarian manner is a sure way to build rapport. The temptation is to equate informality and a disregard for social ceremonial with egalitarianism. True egalitarianism, on the contrary, sees the etiquette systems of others as worthy of the respect that one expects to have accorded to one's own. Every system of etiquette includes "common courtesies" of one kind or another that define the immunities people can expect to enjoy in their dealings with one another. To disregard such courtesies is to take liberties with their persons, and to take liberties, however culturally defined, is to show disrespect. It is necessary, therefore, to beware lest one's own cultural habits regarding social relations lead one to act in ways that are offensive to others. A newcomer makes mistakes, of course. Mistakes are usually forgiven those who show an interest in learning how to avoid making them in the future. Where there is true respect for others, such willingness will be evident.

Nowhere are the outsiders' good will and attitude of respect more severely tested, than in regard to food and matters of hygiene. In all societies people have definite ideas about what is and is not fit for human consumption and what is and is not fit for human physical contact. By deprecating the food that members of the host community eat, field workers insult them; for the implication is clear that people who eat what field workers regard as unfit for human consumption must be less than fully human. It can be difficult not to give offense in this regard. Field workers are usually offered food as a gesture of friendship and hospitality, and it is sometimes in a form that from their point of view is either unappetizing or unhealthy. Whether they are in a position to decline the offer or not, they must try to keep their feelings to themselves. A nose wrinkled in disgust can betray an attitude that will be resented. How important this can be is demonstrated by the intensity of feeling often revealed to anthropologists in response to their willingness to eat local food and share food with the local people. The people's experience of Europeans and Americans has been such that they expect negative attitudes from them towards their food. Over and over again, it comes out that it is one of the things they most resent in their dealings with Europeans and Americans: the implication that what they eat is unfit and that what they prepare is dirty.

Field workers who have taken up residence in the community under study are likely to be looked upon by its members as a resource to be exploited. They are people from whom to borrow money; they can intercede with government authorities; they can be called upon for transportation or for medicines. As a result, field workers are likely to find themselves asked to spend considerable time, effort, and money helping people to get what they want at the expense of their own work. They should accept this as a part of the price they must pay in return for the local people's cooperation. Ethnographers must also find ways, appropriate to local custom, to keep themselves from being overly taxed in this manner. But the relationship they establish is inevitably one that calls for reciprocity on their part. How they can make themselves useful consistent with their research objectives deserves their serious attention.

People in the host community are likely to be concerned about how they will benefit not only from field workers' presence but from their research as well. Concern with benefits from the research itself is increasingly being expressed by government officials in the countries in which it is conducted. European and American field workers are often expected to contribute in some way to local or national educational institutions by teaching or providing research training for people in the host country. Cooperation in these ways can be very useful in providing visible evidence of the field worker's respect for the people of the host country and for their interests.

These considerations bear directly on the matter of professional conduct as it relates to getting established in the field setting. It would be out of order for social scientists to go to a university campus to study it as a community without clearing their project first with the president of the university, its deans, department heads, and other appropriate officials. They would also need to enlist the cooperation of the faculty and students by explaining to them the nature of their project, perhaps in a news story to the campus paper as well as in other ways. The investigators would want to learn who were the important opinion leaders among the faculty and students and keep them informed about the course of their work. In this way the social scientists would show their recognition of and respect for these leaders' positions in the university community, whether these positions were official or unofficial. The investigators would want to learn from these leaders, moreover, in what ways their project might be helpful to the university community and in what ways it might be adjusted to make it of greatest benefit to the community.

The same procedures are proper wherever field work is done. One does not get a permit from a national government, for example, and then not pay appropriate respect to the local officials. How to do all these things properly, however, and how to approach unofficial leaders can be a problem. It is often helpful to have a local contact who can provide introductions and act as a mediator in these matters. Here, as in matters of etiquette more generally, a fieldworker inevitably makes mistakes, but they are usually salvageable if he is genuinely concerned about correcting them.

At every point, it is essential to tell the truth about research objectives and procedures. It follows, of course, that it is necessary to have research objectives and procedures that one can tell the truth about. Objectives that must be concealed from people reflect the attitude that others are objects to be manipulated or are lesser beings to be patronized. The truth will be revealed in the end when the study results are published. It is better that

things be made as clear as possible from the beginning. This is often difficult to do, especially if the research problem requires a background in social or behavioral science before it can be understood. But there is nothing
esoteric about what field workers have to learn in the field: the language
and culture of the local people; things they must learn first, regardless of
anything else they may hope to do. Once they make significant progress,
field workers will learn better how to communicate their other research
interests.

Leaving the field setting also calls for appropriate courtesy calls on officials, with thanks for the help they may have given and the courtesies
they may have extended. Too often, one hears unfavorable comments
about previous field workers who simply packed up and went home without checking in with anyone. When they leave the field, moreover, ethnographers take with them continuing obligations. At the least these
obligations include such things as sending back copies of photographs
they have taken and, eventually, copies of their published reports. Beyond
that, they are likely to have established some enduring relationships of a
kind that may long continue to obligate them financially as well as in other
ways. The field and the people in it will have become a part of their social
world with all that that may imply both in terms of the local culture and in
terms of the field workers' own.

Again, the principle that underlies problems of ethics is respecting the
humanity of others as one would have others respect one's own. If field
workers genuinely feel such respect for others, they are not likely to get
into serious trouble. But if they do not feel such respect, then no matter
how scrupulously they follow the letter of the written codes of professional ethics, or follow the recommended procedures of field work manuals, they will betray themselves all along the line in the little things, such
as food and etiquette. They will be less patient than they should be, more
grudging in responding to the demands made upon them, and less likely
to think about the effect of their actions on others, including the field
workers who come after them and who will be prejudged accordingly.

Note

1. Reference should also be made to Pelto (1970), Williams (1967), Goldstein
   (1964), Junker (1960), and to the accounts in Freilich (1970), Epstein (1967), and
   Jongmans and Gutkind (1967).

References

BERLIN, B., BREEDLOVE, D. E., & RAVEN, P. H. *Principles of tzeltal plant classification.*
New York: Academic Press, 1974.

BLACK, M. B. Belief systems. In J. J. Honigmann (Ed.), *Handbook of social and cultural anthropology.* Chicago: Rand McNally, 1973, pp. 509–77.

BOWEN, E. S. *Return to laughter.* New York: Harper & Brothers, 1954.

CARROLL, V. (Ed.), *Adoption in Eastern Oceania.* Honolulu: University of Hawaii Press, 1970.

CASAGRANDE, J. B. *In the company of man.* New York: Harper & Brothers, 1960.

COLLIER, J. *Visual anthropology: photography as a recording method.* New York: Holt, Rinehart and Winston, 1967.

CONKLIN, H. C. Hanunóo color categories. *Southwestern Journal of Anthropology,* 1955, *11,* 339–44.

EPSTEIN, A. L. (Ed.), *The craft of social anthropology.* London: Tavistock, 1967.

EPSTEIN, A. L. The case method in the field of law. In A. L. Epstein (Ed.), *The craft of social anthropology.* London: Tavistock, 1967, pp. 205–30.

FRAKE, C. O. A structural description of Subanun "religious behavior." In W. H. Goodenough (Ed.), *Explorations in cultural anthropology.* New York: McGraw-Hill, 1964, pp. 111–29.

FREILICH, M. (Ed.), *Marginal natives: anthropologists at work.* New York: Harper & Row, 1970.

GEOGHEGAN, W. H. Information processing systems in culture. In P. Kay (Ed.), *Explorations in mathematical anthropology.* Cambridge, Mass.: MIT Press, 1971, pp. 3–35.

GLADWIN, T., & SARASON, S. B. *Truk: man in paradise.* Viking Fund Publications in Anthropology No. 20. New York: Wenner-Gren Foundation for Anthropological Research, 1951.

GOLDSTEIN, K. S. *A guide for fieldworkers in folklore.* Hatboro, Pa.: Folklore Associates, 1964.

GOODENOUGH, W. H. Componential analysis and the study of meaning. *Language,* 1956, *32,* 195–216.

———. *Cooperation in change.* New York: Russell Sage Foundation, 1963.

———. Rethinking "status" and "role": toward a general model of the cultural organization of social relationships. In *The relevance of models for social anthropology.* ASA Monographs 1. London: Tavistock, 1965, pp. 1–24.

———. Componential analysis. *Science,* 1967, *156,* 1203–09.

———. Toward an anthropologically useful definition of religion. In A. W. Eister (Ed.), *Changing perspectives in the scientific study of religion.* New York: Wiley, 1974, pp. 165–84.

HACKENBERG, R. A. Genealogical method in social anthropology: the foundations of structural demography. In J. J. Honigmann (Ed.), *Handbook of social and cultural anthropology.* Chicago: Rand McNally, 1973, pp. 289–325.

HALLOWELL, A. I. *Culture and experience.* Philadelphia: University of Pennsylvania Press, 1955.

HONIGMANN, J. J. Sampling in ethnographic field work. In R. Naroll & R. Cohen (Eds.), *A handbook of method in cultural anthropology.* New York: Natural History Press, 1970, pp. 266–81.

JONGMANS, D. G., & GUTKIND, P. (Eds.), *Anthropologists in the field.* New York: Humanities Press, 1967.

JUNKER, B. H. *Fieldwork: an introduction to the social sciences.* Chicago: University of Chicago Press, 1960.

KAY, P. A Guttman scale model of Tahitian consumer behavior. *Southwestern Journal of Anthropology,* 1964, 20, 160–67.

————. Taxonomy and semantic contrast. *Language,* 1971, 47, 866–87.

KEESING, R. M. Toward a model of role analysis. In R. Naroll & R. Cohen (Eds.), *A handbook of method in cultural anthropology.* New York: Natural History Press, 1970a, pp. 423–53.

————. Kwaio fosterage. *American Anthropologist,* 1970b, 72, 991–1019.

————. Formalization and the construction of ethnographies. In P. Kay (Ed.), *Explorations in mathematical anthropology.* Cambridge, Mass.: MIT Press, 1971, pp. 36–49.

LEBAR, F. M. A household survey of economic goods on Romonum Island, Truk. In W. H. Goodenough (Ed.), *Explorations in cultural anthropology.* New York: McGraw-Hill, 1964, pp. 335–49.

LUNDSGAARDE, H. P. (Ed.), *Land tenure in Oceania.* ASAO Monograph No. 2. Honolulu: University of Hawaii Press, 1974.

MALINOWSKI, B. *Coral gardens and their magic.* London: Allen & Unwin, 1935. (Reprinted 1965, Bloomington: Indiana University Press.)

————. *A diary in the strict sense of the term.* New York: Harcourt Brace and World, 1967.

MEAD, M. The art and technology of field work. In R. Naroll & R. Cohen (Eds.), *A handbook of method in cultural anthropology.* New York: Natural History Press, 1970, pp. 246–65.

MURDOCK, G. P. *Outline of cultural materials,* 4th rev. ed. Behavior Science Outlines No. 1. New Haven: Human Relations Area Files, 1950.

NAROLL, R., & COHEN, R. (Eds.), *A handbook of method in cultural anthropology.* New York: Natural History Press, 1970.

PELTO, P. J. *Anthropological research: the structure of inquiry.* New York: Harper & Row, 1970.

————. *The snowmobile revolution: technology and social change in the Arctic.* Menlo Park: Cummings, 1973.

PELTO, P.J., & PELTO, G. H. Ethnography: the fieldwork enterprise. In J. J. Honigmann (Ed.), *Handbook of social and cultural anthropology.* Chicago: Rand McNally, 1973, pp. 241–88.

POSPISIL, L. Law and societal structure among the Nunanmiut Eskimo. In W. H. Goodenough (Ed.), *Explorations in cultural anthropology.* New York: McGraw-Hill, 1964, pp. 395–431.

————. A formal analysis of substantive law: Kapauku Papuan laws of inheritance. In L. Nader (Ed.), *The ethnography of law. American Anthropologist,* 1965a, 67 (no. 6, pt. 2), 166–85.

————. A formal analysis of substantive law: Kapauku Papuan laws of land tenure. In E. A. Hammel (Ed.), *Formal semantic analysis. American Anthropologist,* 1965b, 67 (no. 5, pt. 2), 186–214.

QUINN, N. Decision models of social structure. *American Ethnologist,* 1975, 2, 19–45.

ROYAL ANTHROPOLOGICAL INSTITUTE. *Notes and queries on anthropology,* 6th ed. London: Routledge, 1951.

SAPIR, E. The unconscious patterning of behavior in society. In E. S. Dummer (Ed.), *The unconscious: a symposium.* New York: Knopf, 1927, pp. 114–42.

SHARP, L. Steel axes for stone age Australians. In E. H. Spicer (Ed.), *Human problems in technological change: a casebook.* New York: Russell Sage Foundation, 1952, pp. 69–81.

WHITING, J. W. M., CHILD, I. L., & LAMBERT, W. W. *Field guide for the study of socialization.* New York: Wiley, 1968.

WHITING, B., & WHITING, J. Methods for observing and recording behavior. In R. Naroll & R. Cohen (Eds.), *A handbook of method in cultural anthropology.* New York: Natural History Press, 1970, pp. 282–315.

WILLIAMS, T. R. *Field methods in the study of culture.* New York: Holt, Rinehart and Winston, 1967.

3

The Systematic Observation of Behavior in Naturalistic Settings[1]

Richard Longabaugh

Contents

Abstract

In this chapter the use of systematic behavioral observations in naturalistic settings is examined. Conditions under which an observational methodology should be and should not be used are indicated. This is followed by a review of the sequence of decisions and operations involved in study implementation: selecting the phenomena for study, data collection, systems for data recording and coding. In conceptualizing the phenomena of study a differentiation is made between the "how" of behavior as opposed to the "what." A second major emphasis is on defining the boundaries of a unit of study and how with modern technology, traditional boundaries of units can be modified. The section on data collection focuses on sampling strategies for: cultures, people, settings, and behavior. It concludes with a typology for categorizing what kind of event sampling is being used. Systems for data recording are contrasted along two dimensions: selective versus all-inclusive description and behavioral replicas versus transformations. Then specific recording strategies are critiqued. Distortion occurring at the phenomena-recorder intersect is assessed. Systems for categorizing behavior are contrasted along several dimensions. Problems in the cross-cultural application of coding systems are addressed and alternative solutions considered. Distortions occurring at the recording-coding intersect are examined. In the section on data analysis, three characteristic problems of observational study are focused upon: the number of behavioral categories, the distribution of behavioral frequencies, and small samples. The issue of whether to use behavioral rates or proportions in data analysis is then addressed as are the advantages and disadvantages of each, particularly in cross-cultural settings. Lastly, an important research question which is especially tractable to observational methodology is examined: the analysis of interactional sequences. It is pointed out that this is an extremely important area of study which traditionally has been neglected. However, recent advances in information statistics and computer methodology now provide valuable ways of studying this topic. The chapter concludes by drawing attention to both the great value to be gained by measuring behavior in its natural settings across cultures and by reemphasizing the difficulty apparent in using this methodology.

Introduction

Systematic observation of behavior in natural settings is a method of study which has a long history (Darwin, 1872). It has not been a frequently used method (Wright, 1960) and there are many difficulties involved in its application. However, the spirit underlying this *Handbook of Cross-Cultural Psychology* is consistent with the objective of systematically studying behavior in the context of its natural occurrence. The same forces underlying the desire to develop a pan-cultural psychology are also giving this methodology a renewed impetus. For this reason it is important that cross-cultural researchers come to an understanding about (1) when to use systematic behavioral observations, (2) how to use them, (3) how to avoid repeating the mistakes that have been made when this methodology was used within culturally bound western psychology, and (4) how to anticipate the particular pitfalls which will be encountered when this methodology is applied cross-culturally. This chapter is devoted to a discussion of these issues.

A Definition of the Method of Systematic Observations of
Naturalistic Behavior

As with any other methodological technique, varying descriptions have been attached to what is meant by systematic behavioral observations.

What these terms typically imply is that a person is trained to become an instrument for recording and/or classifying the behavior of other people, as he/she directly observes them as they go about the business of conducting their every day lives. This human recorder-coder is trained to use a sufficiently explicit set of rules concerning when, how, and what to observe, and record and classify so that another human recorder-coder, given the same set of rules, can substantially replicate the data produced by the first observer. The emphasis is on "naturalistic observations," that is, observations made of other persons (or animals, e.g., DeVore, 1965) in their natural environment.

Traditionally excluded have been methods which involve laboratory studies (i.e., researcher-produced "nonnatural environments"), experimental manipulations (i.e., experimentally induced stimuli to which to respond), self-report techniques (self-observation), behavior not available to external observers (e.g., thoughts or feelings) and behavioral events which are not observable by the human recorder without significant aid of instrumentation. However, because of modification and elaboration many of these traditionally excluded methods can now be used, and, in fact, some of the innovative aspects of current work is in these areas. Therefore, for the purpose of what will be covered in this chapter, the method of systematic observations of naturalistic behavior is defined as follows: it is a methodology which involves the recording of overt behavior as it occurs in its natural setting. The recording of behavioral phenomena, its unitization and classification are conducted by a person trained to function as a scientific instrument. The objective of this training is to ensure that the conversion from phenomena to information concerning interrelationships among abstracted units from these phenomena can be repeated using other persons trained in a similar manner. This data collection and analysis may be performed by a human being without the aid of significant artifacts, but preferably will proceed with the assistance of all of the instrumentation currently available to an investigator.

Only four elements are preserved by this definition: (1) overt behavior must be recorded as it occurs, or very shortly thereafter, (2) the data processing must be guided by a set of rules that ensure that it is replicable, (3) the behavior under study must occur in a natural habitat, and (4) a human being is required somewhere in the data processing to convert observations into quantitative information. These broader criteria are designed to take into account recent innovations which may add to the scientific understanding of behavior.

Differentiation of Systematic Observations of Natural
Behavior from Other Methodologies

The observational metholology explicated in this chapter is quantitative in character. Field observation that ordinarily yields qualitative rather than quantitative data is beyond the purview of this chapter. Such techniques which are frequently included under the rubric of "participant observation" are critiqued elsewhere (McCall & Simmons, 1969; Goodenough's chapter). Although it is not possible now, in the future it may be possible to subsume several related methodologies within the same structure.

Self-Report and Behavioral Observation

An actor may also be the observer. When a study participant is also used as the recording mechanism, the significant factor in the data collection is whether or not public events are being recorded which can be reliably recorded by an outside observer. For instance, if thoughts are being recorded, these cannot be noted by an outside observer. If, however, the frequency of cigarette smoking is recorded during a period of time, this can, under certain conditions, be independently verified. Several behavioral analysts are currently engaged in determining the potential and limits in self-recording (see Kanfer, 1970; Nelson & McReynolds, 1971; Simkins, 1971a, 1971b).

Systematic Behavioral Observations and Content Analysis

The technique that most closely overlaps systematic behavioral observation is content analysis. Content analysis has to do with the unitization and classification of the verbal content of recorded communication. Where systematic behavioral observations have focused exclusively on verbal communication and the content of the communication is recorded in isomorphic relation to the communication that occurred, then the two methods would be identical. However, systematic behavioral observations often focus on more than verbal content and the recorder-observer often does not attempt to replicate exactly the verbal content of messages sent. Most characteristically, the recorder-observer is the instrument of data recording and not the object or phenomenon to be studied.

Investigation employing systematic behavioral observations can benefit greatly from a study of the methodology of content analysis, as many techniques from this methodology can be readily applied to the unitization, categorization, and analysis of observable data.

Criteria for Deciding When the Behavioral Observational
Method Should Be Used

As has been noted elsewhere (Gellert, 1955; Wright, 1960) the use of systematic behavioral observations had an early popularity, but has since
been employed only in a small percentage of studies (Hutt & Hutt, 1974).
Recently there appears to be renewed interest in this methodology (see
Willems & Raush, 1969), partly due to increasing dissatisfaction with
others (e.g., Yarrow, Campbell, & Burton, 1968). The reasons for infrequent use in the past have been the modest yield produced (benefits
derived) by studies employing this method, while the costs involved have
been large in comparison with most other methodological tools available
to an investigator (Gellert, 1955; Weick, 1967; Hutt & Hutt, 1974). The
overall cost effectiveness of the method has been low compared with alternative methodologies.

Costs. Costs apparent in observational studies include the time, the
monetary costs, and psychological costs. When observational studies are
carried out across cultures these costs are multiplied (Longabaugh, 1977).
To cite two extreme cases of cost in time: (1) the Six Cultures study
(Whiting & Whiting, 1975) took twenty years to complete; (2) the first
sentence of Scheflen's preface to his book *Communicational Structure* is instructive regarding his research: "The major effort of ten years of my
career has been the analysis of this thirty minute transaction and the publication of the method and results" (Scheflen, 1973, xi). The benefits
gained from each of these studies have been monumental. Yet, clearly, the
costs have been great.

   Given the large cost factor, it is especially important that the investigator be sure he/she has chosen the most effective methodology before
he/she embarks upon an observational study of behavior in its natural
settings. Gump and Kounin (1959–60) have discussed occasions in which
observational studies are and are not preferred. Before observational studies are undertaken at least three conditions should be met: (1) the phenomena of interest should be readily observable by an outside observer
(without the aid of recording instrumentation, unless the use of such instrumentation is practically feasible), e.g., molar social behavior; (2) a
human observer acting as a recording and encoding instrument provides
the best data source available (superior to self-report, cultural or material
artifacts, native informants, or data collected solely by instruments devised for the purpose); and (3) that the amount of control of the phenomenon necessary to answer the research question posed is not greater than
can be provided in naturalistic studies. With methodological advances in
the use of statistics to control for sources of variance and in determining

the direction of causation, the requirement of experimental control is less crucial than formerly. A fourth consideration, which may dictate that naturalistic observational studies become a more popular methodology than they have been, is the advent of stringent controls put upon research with human subjects, causing the researcher to employ less obtrusive methods for studying people. (See Warwick in Volume 1 and Bochner in this volume.)

In summary, while the costs of observational studies may be large, there are certain conditions under which it is clearly the preferred (and on occasion the only feasible) methodology. For example, this is most likely to be the case when a researcher is interested in describing and interrelating molar social behavior as it occurs in its natural habitat or when a person's competency or mastery of his environment is the focus.

What is to be learned from a given observational study is, of course, a highly selective matter. While the selective process is obvious, its implications for the results and conclusions that may be derived from the study often are not. Choices are made at four points which narrow down and determine the nature of the study: (1) the phenomenon to be studied, (2) the method of recording the phenomenon, (3) the categorization of the (recorded) phenomenon, and (4) the analytic tools used to manipulate the categorization of the phenomenon. Transformational operations connect each of these four levels: (a) from phenomena to record, (b) from record to variable construction, and (c) from variables to concluding analysis.

Following is an examination of the alternative strategies available at each of these four decision points in order to present the options available and the consequences of particular options chosen.

The Phenomena to Be Studied

Research Aim

The first way in which the investigator circumscribes his/her study is by deciding what to study. Is the primary purpose of the study *description, hypothesis formulation,* or *hypothesis testing?* (Weick, 1967). At the description level, an investigator might be interested in finding out how children use their time in a given culture that had not yet been systematically studied (Barker & Wright, 1955; Whiting, Child, & Lambert, 1966). This kind of aim would imply a very broad approach, where a general description of behavior would be used to describe as much as goes on as can be reasonably attended to. Where the aim is hypothesis formulation, the investigator is apt to have in mind a much narrower range of phenomena from which to collect data. The most selective strategy is involved when the investigator is testing a hypothesis. Perhaps a relationship has been found between a child's physical distance from home and performance level on an intellective task requiring spatial ability in one culture (Munroe & Munroe, 1971a); the aim is to test whether this relationship also holds true in another culture (Nerlove, Munroe, & Munroe, 1971). In such a case, the investigator has already developed highly selective variables to measure his constructs and to develop functionally equivalent measures for the other culture in which the generality of the finding is to be tested. Or, depending upon the variables, the same measures may be applicable without modification in other cultures.

Depending on the degree of specificity of the investigator's study aims, observational methodologies will tend to diverge. Most cross-cultural studies seem to involve questions at all three levels and as a consequence data are collected at all three levels of specificity. Such studies are ideal in the present phase of cross-cultural observational work as all three aims are much in demand.

The Components of Content

In a handbook of cross-cultural psychology, it can be assumed that *people's behavior* will be at least a part of the content of the investigator's focus. Furthermore, the methodology described in this chapter focuses on *observable* behaviors.

Here the focus is limited to social behavior: behavior that, if it occurs in the presence of another person, has the capacity to act as a stimulus for the other person. This defining limit is of little import, except conceptually. Any behavior that an observer is going to be able to record falls within this definition. Any behavior that does not is not the subject matter for systematic behavioral observation. While this focus may appear to exclude nonsocial, person-environment interaction, in practice it does not. Most nonsocial molar behavior is observable and as such will fall within the boundaries offered. Thus, a child's mastery of the physical environment is a legitimate focus for an observational study, as observation of this mastery acts as a stimulus for the observer's behavior (of recording). However, whether or not an investigator has conceptualized determinants of the behavior as including their social effects is important because this can have a marked impact on the conclusions. Ekman has shown that disregard for social factors affecting "display rules" for facial expression of emotion has led earlier investigators to conclude that there were no universal facial expressions conveying particular emotions. In contrast, his own cross-cultural research supports the universality of facial expression for certain emotions. However, Ekman first had to control for culturally determined display rules (Ekman, Friesen, & Ellsworth, 1972; Ekman, 1973).

In order to classify the phenomena under study it is necessary to identify and characterize not only the behavior but also the study population and the settings in which the behavior is to be observed. Especially in cross-cultural research it is apparent that behavior is meaningless outside of the context of its occurrence (Barker & Gump, 1964; Barker & Schoggen, 1973). Therefore, considerations of the phenomena chosen for study will be discussed under two headings: "behavior" and "the context for behavior."

Behavior.   The study of social behavior can be grouped roughly into two major foci: the study of *what* and the study of *how.*

The study of "what" is the study of what it is actors communicate to one another: both what is intended and encoded and what is received or decoded. The study of "how" is the study of how the content is expressed. Traditionally these two foci have not always been clearly separated. Early coding systems often mixed together the "what" with the "how." However, recent debate over what should be the legitimate behavioral unit for analysis has begun to crystallize this distinction. The debate between the psychological ecologists and the ethologists is a case in point. The psychological ecologist espouses a molar behavior unit which includes the social context of the behavior and the actors' intention (Barker, 1968; Wright, 1967). The ethologist, on the other hand, explicitly excludes judgments of intention and consciously limits the observer to the description and classification of actions of specific muscle groups, and espouses a more molecular unit, the ethogram (Hutt & Hutt, 1974, p. 15).

The investigator who is focusing upon *what* is communicated or expressed makes an informed judgment based upon the knowledge of the shared meanings cultural participants attach to symbols. The coder may systematically, unsystematically, or even unconsciously make use of the cues providing information as to how the communication is being encoded (i.e., with what). In contrast, the investigator who focuses on how behavior is enacted eschews inference in judgments as to what is communicated. This question is temporarily bypassed in pursuit of relating the behavioral enactment empirically to the surrounding context, which includes other behavioral enactments of the person or of other people. The behaviors may also be related to other variables, such as actor, target, relationship, or environmental characteristics. In any case, the attempt is made to avoid judgment of intention in the behavioral description, although "intention" may be used in interpreting the findings.

Both perspectives are making inroads on the traditional domains of the other. On the one hand as "hardnosed experimentalists" go into the field as "applied behavioral analysts" they find themselves relying less upon physical things, muscle pattern definitions of their behavioral operants, and more on the symbolic significance of the behavior to be modified, e.g., appropriate and inappropriate (Gelfand, Gelfand, & Dobson, 1967) or "deviant" versus "nondeviant" (Patterson, Ray, Shaw, & Cobb, 1969). On the other hand investigators of behavior in natural settings find a new breed emerging in their midst. This new cohort of researchers is attempting to forego the temptation to take undue advantage of the fact that they have inside knowledge of the nature of the organism—homo sapiens—that they are studying. Instead, they are attempting to break down complex sequences of behavior into their specific components and develop objective and reliable measures of such components (Charlesworth & Spiker, 1975; Hutt & Hutt, 1974).

For the foreseeable future both approaches will continue in tandem. Far in the future it may all come together. Meanwhile a cadre of investigators will continue to focus exclusively on the "what," other investigators will break down the "how" into its component parts, and still others will try to establish the connections between the two.

a. The "How" of Behavior. The focus on the "how" of behavior has been segmented primarily into (1) language and paralanguage, and (2) body expression and movement. Within each of these general areas specializations are developing. The study of vocal behavior has quickly developed into the specialty of linguistics (plus psycholinguistics and sociolinguistics) which has become a highly technical area of study (pitch, range, resonance, articulation control, and vocal control) and vocalizations not having language structure such as laughing, crying, grunting, yawning, and speech nonfluencies (such as hesitations, differentiated by length, type, and location) (Duncan, 1969).

The study of movement is being approached from two perspectives. The ethologists are attempting to develop an ethogram, a complete catalog of human behavior (Hutt & Hutt, 1974). For instance, McGrew has developed a glossary of 111 motor patterns of four-year-old nursery school children (Hutt & Hutt, 1974, pp. 210–18). These patterns consist of behaviors such as "look," "cry," "shake head," "hit," "remove," "rub," etc. From a different orientation for the past twenty years Birdwhistell has pioneered the attempt to develop a kinesic classification of body movement and facial expression (Birdwhistell, 1970; Dittman, 1971). Scheflen has deepened this perspective (Scheflen, 1973; 1975).

A more segmented approach is being provided by psychologists who are focusing on particular areas and kinds of body movements: (1) locomotive behavior and interpersonal distance, (2) body posture and orientation, (3) head orientation, (4) facial expressions, and (5) eye contact and visual gaze.

Hall (1959, 1963) and Sommer (1969, 1974) have been studying the relationship of the *physical distance* between people to the characteristics of the participants, their relationship, the setting, and their culture.

Physical locomotion has become a variable of interest for cross-cultural studies, where distances traveled have been related to spatial ability (Munroe & Munroe, 1971a; Nerlove, Munroe, & Munroe, 1971).

Posture and body orientation toward others has been related to the status of the participants and their attitudes toward one another (Mehrabian, 1968, 1969).

Facial expression and eye contact have received the most attention. In a multifaceted investigation of the expression of emotion, Ekman, Friesen, and Ellsworth (1972) were able to conclude that there are universally recognized facial expressions for certain emotions (Ekman, 1972, 1973) in contrast to the assertions of earlier investigators (LaBarre, 1947; Birdwhistell, 1970). *Eye contact* in its amount and timing has been found to relate to characteristics of actor and settings (Duncan, 1969; Exline, 1962a, 1962b, 1963; Exline & Winters, 1965; Exline & Long, 1965; Exline, Gray, & Schuette 1965). Other research has begun to relate cross-modality co-variations. For example, Kendon (1967) has been able to relate eye contact and visual orientation to speaker-listener variables. Besides vocal and motor behavior (including tactile approach, Frank, 1957; Hall, 1966), olfactory and heat production remain two other channels for communication. However, these are not likely to occupy a central focus for research in social behavior.

An interesting discussion about describing "the how of behavior" is provided by Wright (1967, especially pp. 12–14).

Most of the research done on the "how" has not yet been subjected to cross-cultural validation; moreover, much of the within-culture research cited above has been carried out in laboratory situations. Thus cross-cultural systematic observation of the "how" of behavior in nature is an area of study which is just beginning.

b. Focus on "what" is communicated.   Is the person offering help, suggesting responsibly, reprimanding, seeking dominance, acting sociably, seeking attention, offering support, touching (seeking physical contact), seeking help, assaulting sociably, assaulting, or aggressing symbolically? These are the twelve categories of behavior employed in the analysis of children's behavior observed in the Six Cultures study (Whiting & Whiting, 1975). This pioneer study has served as a prototype for subsequent cross-cultural studies of children's social behavior (Seymour, 1971; Weisner, 1974). The particular value of this conception for describing the "what" is that it has already been used to characterize children's social behavior in several different cultures, thus providing a baseline against which behavior of children from other cultures can be compared. However, it is just one example of a great number of category systems that characterize the content of communication (see Simon & Boyer, 1967, 1970 where seventy-nine different observation systems are presented). Some systems focus on

particular kinds of behavior, while others attempt to classify all social behavior. In a subsequent section (coding systems) the relationship between
behavior and coding systems will be examined in detail. Such codes rely
primarily upon being privy to the symbolic meaning of behavior. The behavior may be viewed in terms of what it communicates to the observer
about the state of the actor, sometimes despite himself (Goffman, 1958)
and/or it may be viewed in terms of what the actor intends to communicate to the recipient. Usually these two bits of information are commensurate (Longabaugh, 1970b) but if they are not, the investigator must be clear
as to which is his focus of interest.

In addition to the "how" and "what" of behavior, other elements
of the phenomena which must be taken into consideration in developing
the unit for study are "who" in relation to whom or what, in what setting,
and within what spatial-temporal boundaries. All of these elements must be
enumerated to clearly define the phenomena under study.

Actors, Targets, and Settings

In early observational studies of behavior, a major focus was a description
of the differences in people's behavior, and the attempt to relate these differences to other characteristics of the actors. Observations were typically
carried out in one setting. Consequently, the effects of the setting upon the
behavior were unknown and generally unaddressed. Furthermore, the
target for the behavior observed was either a single person, e.g., a child's
mother, or multiple others (e.g., all of a child's classmates) and therefore
too numerous to take into account in the analysis. Consequently, generalizations would refer to psychological differences among individuals, with
little attention to the possible effects of setting or targets in accounting for
these observed differences. More recent studies, especially by the ecological psychologists, have documented that setting can have a powerful effect
upon behavior, both in terms of constraints upon, and opportunities for
behavioral expression (e.g., Barker, 1951, 1963a; Barker & Gump, 1964;
Barker & Schoggen, 1973; Gump, Schoggen, & Redl, 1957; Insel & Moos,
1974; Mischel, 1968). Similarly the effect of the target person to whom the
actor is relating was recognized as an obvious source of variance (e.g.,
Gellert, 1962; Thompson, 1960). For these reasons targets and settings, as
well as actors, must be well specified in defining the unit for study.

Here a classification system begun by Lambert (1960, pp. 862–63) will
be completed. This classification demonstrates that the nature of the investigator's unit of study will differ markedly, depending upon his enumeration of these three elements. Three levels of characterization can
apply to each element.

First the investigator may identify the actor uniquely, in the sense that the actor is not replaceable, without altering the conclusions of the study. Such investigations are case history studies of individual personalities, and more recently, single case study designs (Hersen & Barlow, 1976). Second, the actor may be identified by characteristics which can be pan-culturally applied to individuals, e.g., "girls, ages 5–9," "persons scoring high on a self-report test of assertiveness," or "mothers." In such cases the unit to be studied is persons having such characteristics (perhaps versus another group having other characteristics, e.g., "boys, ages 5–9," "persons scoring low on an assertiveness test," "fathers"). This is the predominant kind of study. Third, the actor may be unidentified. This is an unusual kind of study where the focus may either be on the setting (i.e., what kinds of behaviors are evoked by a setting, irrespective of who enacts them, e.g., Barker & Gump, 1964; Barker & Schoggen, 1973) or may be a study of recipients of behavior (what kinds of behavioral stimuli are individuals presented with, irrespective of their origin, e.g., Olson & Wilkinson, 1932).

What has been less clear from the literature is that the same three levels of enumeration also apply to targets and settings. A target of behavior may be uniquely identified (e.g., Fred Smith), or be partially classified (an adult, male teacher), or left unidentified and unclassified. Similarly, settings may be uniquely identified (e.g., "Apple Valley Mall"), partially classified (e.g., "drug stores" or "beaches"), or unidentified and unclassified. Because of the variable and sometimes overwhelming effects of targets and settings on behaviors, researchers of behavior in naturalistic settings cannot let any of these elements go unidentified. To do so is to render the results of study ambiguous. Rather, the optimal strategy is to identify each element uniquely and then, depending upon the purposes of study, to characterize all three elements by those properties believed to be the potentially important sources of variability. By such a strategy the unit of study is clearly identified. Unique identification of each element permits subsequent reclassification of the elements. This procedure would be desirable if considerable variability was observed within an element which had been assumed to be homogeneous.

All combinations of the three levels of classification of each of these three elements generate a typology of twenty-seven types of generalizations about the same phenomenal unit of study: three levels of actor identification (unique identification, identification by categorization and therefore partially replaceable, and no identification) multiplied by three levels of target identification, multiplied by three levels of setting identification. It is most important to be clear about the level of generalization being offered. Failure to do so will result in unnecessary confusion regarding apparently contradictory findings, which in reality are simply not comparable.

The cross-cultural researcher should be especially careful that the study design reflects the level of specificity or generality of the research question to be answered. When a researcher becomes unable to return to the settings in which the data were collected, adequate description of the unit of study is imperative, and generalizations appropriate to the level of specificity provided by the data are critical.

Environment in which the behavior occurs.   The environment in which behavior occurs has been described from one of three perspectives. First is the physical description in terms of objects and terrain: the physical environment. This environment stands without regard to the actors who inhabit it. For the ethologist it is a given which may provide explanations concerning the evolution of the species (Blurton-Jones, 1972); for the psychocultural researcher the physical environment interacts with populations creating history, giving rise to maintenance systems which produce a child's learning environment (Whiting & Whiting, 1975). For the ecological psychologist the physical environment in interaction with people gives rise to the settings (Barker, 1968).

Second, the environment can be described in terms of its relation to an actor. Here the significant aspects of the environment are identified for the actor (the persons' situation) by an empirical determination of covariation between respondent behavior and environmental precedents and consequents. By such identifications the applied behavior analyst determines the stimuli and reinforcers for the individual's operant behaviors (e.g., Bijou & Baer, 1961; Reynolds, 1968; Skinner, 1953).

The third way in which the environment has been described is through the shared meaning attached to a locale by its inhabitants. Regardless of who is in the setting, the setting has the same identity, e.g., Johnson's corner drug store, or Mrs. Smith's first grade classroom. This is the environment of the ecological psychologists (e.g., Barker, 1968; Barker & Schoggen, 1973; Barker & Wright, 1955).

In cross-cultural studies each of the three environments has been either assumed or found to be a significant variable (e.g., Munroe & Munroe, 1971a, 1971b; Barker & Schoggen, 1973; Whiting & Whiting, 1975.)

a. Spatial-temporal boundaries of the phenomenal unit.   The phenomena under study occur in space and time. The investigator offers generalizations which are intended to be independent of the particular temporal and spatial loci in which the phenomena occurred (i.e., if the same conditions were present in another time-space frame, the same interrelationship would be found). In specifying the spatial-temporal boundaries of the unit of study one of two choices can be made: the boundary can be defined in terms of intervals of time and measures of distance; or, the characteristics of the phenomenon itself may be used for establishing its boundaries. In this case the temporal-spatial size of the unit is likely to vary.

When properties of the unit are used for defining boundaries, two types of properties may be used: physical thing, matter-energy properties (when the "how" of behavior is the focus), and/or the symbolic meaning of information conveyed (when the "what" of behavior is the focus).

Temporal boundaries of units.   Behavioral events seem to have their own variable temporal boundaries, which differentiate their beginning and ending from what precedes and follows them. These phenomenal boundaries tend to be delineated by changes in movement (particularly when the description focuses on the "how," the matter-energy transformation itself, e.g., Hutt & Hutt, 1974, pp. 30–32) and a lack of sequential dependency or predictability (particularly when the description focuses on information and symbol, or the "what"). In this case a full knowledge of the cultural manners of behavior can be approximated only by members of the culture studied. If temporal behavior boundaries are not defined in terms of such phenomenal indicators, then preselected time intervals are used for setting boundaries, e.g., millisecond snapshots of temporal happenings, ten-second intervals, one-minute intervals, five-minute intervals, hourly intervals. These units may themselves be temporally adjacent or separated by fixed intervals of time. Each temporal interval is then characterized according to the investigator's behavioral classification system which is independent of the time frame.

Depending upon whether the temporal length of the unit employed is defined by fixed or phenomenal boundaries, the substantive conclusions of a study may be substantially altered (Hayes, Meltzer, & Wolf, 1970).

Spatial boundaries of units.   Spatial boundaries are explicitly fixed in defining the unit much less frequently than is the case for temporal boundaries. Most typically, spatial boundaries are defined in terms of *mass-energy concentrations*, e.g., a part of a person's body, like the face (Ekman, 1972), the hands (Connolly & Elliott, 1972), the person's whole body, or a physical setting which people occupy (e.g., a classroom). Alternatively, such units are defined in terms of their *symbolic meaning* (informational properties), e.g., smiling, greeting (Kendon & Ferber, 1973), "the dinner setting," "the playground," the "water hole" (e.g., Barker & Wright, 1955; Barker & Schoggen, 1973).

Fixed spatial boundaries might be used to study an individual's or a group's locomotion. In such cases the area would be marked off into equal intervals and the identity and frequency of people moving into this territory could be observed and recorded.

b. Spatial-temporal extensions of the unit boundaries.   In early study of naturalistic behaviors, the defined unit of study was the actor's behavior. Little

attention was paid to the interrelationship of these behaviors to their spatial-temporal surroundings. However, the search for variables outside of
the organism which control behavior in its natural settings has led to an
increasingly explicit concern with environmental stimuli and consequences of behavior. More complex units have been developed which extend beyond single action units. Applied to the study of social behavior,
these increasingly complex spatial-temporal units have been defined. In
order of increasing complexity they are: (1) the interact (an initiating act
and its interpersonal outcome), (2) a double-interact (the instigating act,
the response, and the subsequent act), (3) an interactional sequence (chain
of interpersonal exchanges, preceded and followed by an apparent discon-
tinuity in topic or theme), and (4) an interpersonal contact (an unbroken
chain of interpersonal exchanges preceded and followed by an absence of
social interaction among the participants).

When the surrounding environment is taken into account, temporally
adjacent events come into focus. In applied behavioral analyses operant
behaviors are related to subsequent environmental events in order to determine reinforcers for the operant class (behavior effect). The paradigm is
broadened on the temporally precedent side to determine environmental
stimuli for the response class (stimulus → response). The unit is elaborated further to the s→ r→ s paradigm by the inclusion of environmental
stimulus→ behavioral response→ environmental effect.

The ecological psychologists have lengthened this unit to a "behavioral episode" which includes a behavioral intention which may be sustained over a long sequence of unbroken or broken chains of events
(Wright, 1967). They have also lengthened environmental stimuli by the
development of *environmental force units.* An environmental force unit is any
action in a person's environment directed at that person, with a goal or
end state for that person specified or implied, and recognized as such by
that person (Schoggen, 1963; Schoggen & Schoggen, 1968). Environmental
force units, like behavioral episodes, may involve long chains of events. In
such extensions the primary enlargement is in the temporal dimension;
however, such extensions often include behavior of other people, resulting
in a spatial extension.

Spatial extensions have been generated to include areas much larger
than the boundaries of a single person, relationship, or group. The purpose has been to study the effects of *settings-for-behavior* on behavior. In
such cases it is the setting which is primarily the unit to be generalized
about, rather than individuals within the setting. Barker and Schoggen
(1973) have used towns and behavior settings in their cross-cultural research. Barker and Barker have discussed such behavioral units in cross-
cultural research (1961).

Another instance in which the spatial unit has been extended is in the
work of investigators of context (e.g., Scheflen, 1973). Such investigators

often take the position that the unit for study is the *relationship-in-its-setting*. Therefore, the simultaneously occurring behaviors of the participants in the physical environment is the unit to be described. Such investigators often reject what they see as the oversimplification of the stimulus-response-stimulus paradigm (e.g., Scheflen, 1973, pp. 5–6). Rather, it is maintained that the simultaneously occurring elements of behavioral phenomena are best understood in larger, holistic units (Scheflen, 1973). (Of course, more sensitive recording instruments can tag these simultaneous events in time, and thereby put them into their temporal sequence). This controversy reflects investigator orientations more than the properties of the phenomena under study. An alternative framework which subsumes both perspectives is one which takes into account the fact that each actor's behavior is a continuous source of feedback for the actor as well as for every other observer. People are all actors and consumers of their own and others' behavior all the time.

A behavioral unit which explicitly expands both the temporal and spatial boundaries is one which looks at relational units across temporal sequence, i.e., behavior in the A:B relationship at time one, followed by behavior in the A:B relationship at time two, etc.

c. Spatial-temporal contractions of unit boundaries.   While conceptualization of the behavioral units of study has expanded to transcend individuals, the developing technology for recording behavior has provided the ability to differentiate units much smaller than those historically available to the human eye and ear. Now video and audio equipment can be used to slow down and even stop and "freeze" the behavioral units for detailed examination and classification. This technology has enabled researchers to get a much more reliable and accurate description of vocal and motor behavioral events (e.g., Pittinger, Hackett, & Danchy, 1960; Birdwhistell, 1952, 1970; Scheflen, 1973). This slowing down of the behavior by using recording instruments opens up the possibility for studying previously unavailable behaviors (due to the rapidity of their occurrence) which possibly occur at a subliminal level of detection but still serve as social cues. It is also possible that behavioral units will be identified which have no social stimulus value but may be sensitive indicators of intra-organismic events.

Data Collection

This section moves from a consideration of the phenomena to be studied to strategies for collecting data about them. There are three major strategies: (1) sampling strategies, (2) systems for data recording, and (3) coding systems.

Sampling Strategies

Prior to recording and categorizing the phenomena, a decision must be made concerning their sampling: who, where, and when? Who and how many people will provide the sample population? In what situations or settings will their behavior be observed? When will the behavior be observed?

The Sample Population

If people did not affect one another, the behavior of each person would be totally independent of the behavior of every other person; population sampling could simply be a random sample. However, people do affect one another as they come into direct or indirect contact. Often it is precisely these interpersonal effects which are the focus of study. People living in direct contact with one another are certainly not independent cases for study. People within the same subculture or culture are not totally independent of one another either because they do share these common cultural effects. In cross-cultural study the question is whether a given relationship between variables will be obtained across cultures (irrespective of people) and across people (irrespective of their cultural membership). Thus, there are two competing criteria for optimum selection of the population sample. As many cultures as possible should be sampled, and a sufficiently large number of people within each culture should be sampled to ensure adequate representation for generalizations. Given the finiteness of staff, time, and resources available in undertaking a cross-cultural study, it is essential that cultures and people within a culture be chosen wisely. The model provided by Whiting, Child, & Lambert (1966) provides an excellent example of how to go about this task.

Sampling cultures.   Before choosing cultures for study, all available information about the variables and their dispersion within each culture should be consulted. Much of this information can be collected from the Human Relations Area Files (Chapter 11 of this volume) and ethnographies available for the culture. As much of this know-how is reported in Chapter 12, it will not be discussed further. The investigator should be alerted to specific cultural factors which may mitigate or preclude his study. For example, if studying parent-child interaction within the home is the objective, do not choose a culture in which children are sent out of the home when a visitor arrives! It is probably obvious (but painful) that at least three cultures should be included to test the adequacy of a pan-cultural generalization. But even three data points are not really adequate for most investigations. The practical impact of this fact is that collaborative ventures among researchers are highly desirable, and often a sine qua non. However, it is reasonable to study two cultures in studies that are in the hypothesis-formulation phase, and even one culture in a descriptive study. The idea of developing on-going field stations in various areas of the world is one of the most promising in facilitating an adequate sample of representative cultures (Barker, 1969; Clignet, Lambert, LeVine, Prothro, Whiting, & Whiting, 1974). The availability of such stations for cross-cultural studies will greatly reduce costs and other barriers to such studies.

Population selection within cultures.   People within the same culture are directly or indirectly affected by one another. *Direct* effects can be equated with genetic transmission and with direct interpersonal interaction. *Indirect* can be equated with being derivative members of the same gene pool or the same culturally shared symbols.

Rather than drawing a random sample of people from the culture, various strategies for drawing stratified samples have been employed. The difficulties of drawing random samples in most cultures are insurmountable. Furthermore, because of the complexity of observational studies it is better to define the sample in terms of carefully selected characteristics. In practice, subjects have generally been selected by a combination of practical and theoretical criteria (e.g., Seymour, 1971, Chapter 5). In addition to displaying the behavior that interests the investigator, people have to be available for study; both in terms of their accessibility and their willingness to cooperate in the study (often upper-class persons will be inaccessible). The theoretical criteria applied will depend upon the variables of interest for study. In cross-cultural studies, age, sex, socioeconomic stratum, rural versus urban locale, ethnic membership, and same primary sampling unit are frequently applied sampling criteria. Once the population universe to be generalized about has been defined, it may be possible to randomly sample people or families within this defined population. However, especially in widely dispersed cultures, the number of people available for study is quite small, and not readily accessible for observation. Particularly when the investigator is an alien the task of getting to know people well enough to invite them to participate in the study is time consuming.

The Six Cultures study (Whiting, Child, & Lambert, 1966, Chapter 6), relied upon defined Primary Sampling Units within each of the six cultures, and focused on children of two age ranges (3–5) and (7–11) in equal numbers for each sex. The number to be included from each cultural Primary Sampling Unit was six young boys and six young girls; six older boys and six older girls: twenty-four children in all. Even this size sample taxed observers to the limit. Yet by most standards, such a sample is minimal. More recent studies have included more people per defined population but at the expense of limiting the study to one (other) or two (other) cultures (Seymour, 1971; Weisner, 1974). It seems clear that the validity of their results must rest upon cumulative findings across such studies.

Setting Sampling

It should be clear that disregarding the setting for behavioral observation is likely to render the study results ambiguous. Because of the largely unknown or unmeasured effects of setting on particular categories of behavior, observed differences in behavior may be mistakenly attributed to differences in the populations sampled, rather than to differences in the behavioral settings encountered, or to interactions between the two. Therefore, it is imperative that the settings for behavior be described, measured, and whenever possible, controlled for, or systematically varied.

Barker and his associates have found that culturally defined settings have compelling effects on behavior (Barker & Gump, 1964; Barker & Schoggen, 1973) as have others (Magnusson, 1971). The physical attributes of the setting also set constraints upon what behaviors can be enacted (Gump, Schoggen, & Redl, 1957).

A culturally defined setting can be given a single characterization. School in England can be equated with school in the United States. Once equated, then differences in the physical attributes of the two school settings (e.g., size of school) can be related to differences in the behavior observed in the two settings (Barker & Schoggen, 1973).

Many physically defined properties of settings can be measured, such as square footage within a room, number of rooms in a house, distance from water, annual rainfall, etc. Some of these attributes obviously affect the ways in which the setting will be used (Gump, Schoggen, & Redl, 1957) as well as how people will behave within it (e.g., Smith & Connolly, 1972; Sommer, 1969, 1974). So, in addition to determining the cultural definition of the setting, it is highly desirable to assess the most prominent aspects of the physical environment. In the present conceptualization, calendar and clock time are considered to be elements of the setting. The time of day the observation is to occur will often indicate much about what kind of activities will be going on, e.g., at 3:00 A.M. local time, the most likely behavior will be sleeping.

While one setting may be physically and culturally equivalent to another, individuals in this setting are likely to perceive and experience the setting differently. Much of the difference may be attributed to the socially defined roles they occupy in the setting (e.g., *baby* versus *baby sitter*). Thus, the situation of different individuals within a setting, and the different occasions within the same setting may differ. Insofar as such differences can be tagged as part of socially defined roles, the investigator may wish to study such role related differences or control for them.

If the focus of study is social behavior, then the identity and characteristics of the other person or persons to whom behavior is directed may affect the individual's behavior (e.g., Whiting & Whiting, 1975, Chapter 7). Thus all of these sources of setting variance must be either controlled or measured. Which sources of variance investigators will choose to control, as opposed to allow to vary, and measure, will depend upon their research questions. However, unless the expected differences are very large, it is wise to control for most of these sources of variance and allow other variables to take on only a few values. Recommended strategies are to limit settings to be studied to a very small number, e.g., two or three which are carefully selected on the basis of their relevance to the research questions; or to limit the study to one setting. Because occupants are unlikely to change a setting much over a short period of time, settings can be characterized as fairly stable.

The more variable elements of a setting are likely to be the people present, to whom and from whom behavior is directed, and the behavioral instigations and responses from such people. Depending upon the purposes of the study, setting sampling may be limited to occurrences when the critical persons are present, or even more specifically to instances when these critical people direct an instigational act toward the person under observation, e.g., when a father scolds a child for spilling food. The more elements in a setting that are controlled for, the less ambiguous the result will be. However, a longer period of time will be necessary to collect the data because of the greater infrequency of the concurrent presence of all of the critical setting elements. If the investigator is a native of the culture, it will be considerably easier to identify when these situations will occur and how to gain access to them.

One hypothesis, which uses differential exposure to settings, is that settings increase the rates of some behaviors and decrease the rates of others. Therefore, a person exposed to a particular setting more often than another person will develop a greater habit strength for this behavior, and will emit this behavior more frequently in new settings than would other people. Such generalization effects "are implicit" in many studies of socialization and have been tested with some confirmation (Whiting & Whiting, 1975, pp. 160–173). However, depending upon the behavior studied, a setting may not affect its likelihood of occurrence, or the behavior may be setting-specific. Another hypothesis is that suppression of behavior in one highly frequented setting results in its displacement to an increased behavioral rate in another setting (e.g., children whose hostile impulses are heavily suppressed at home may show frequent aggression in play settings with peers).

The main conclusion is that behavioral variables have unknown relations to setting variables. Each relationship must be empirically determined. Meanwhile, generalizations regarding findings must be couched carefully to avoid overly inclusive generalizations.

The study of behavior in naturalistic settings will be greatly facilitated when a typology of settings can be developed and researched. The work of Barker and his associates is a landmark step in this direction (Barker & Wright, 1955; Barker & Gump, 1964; Barker & Schoggen, 1973). It is now clear that settings greatly affect behavior. Further work in the study of settings must be a first priority if cross-cultural studies of naturalistic behaviors are to increase the knowledge of human behavior.

Behavior Sampling

Historically, behavior sampling has focused upon the issue of whether the period of observation was to be determined by continuous observation, time sampling, or event recording. An example of continuous observation is when the total course of psychotherapy is recorded and scanned for the occurrence and context of criterion behavior. If less than the total period of the phenomenon's occurrence is to be selected from, then the strategy followed has been either to sample arbitrarily by using a method of time sampling, or to begin recording when the event occurs. Time sampling has many variations. It has three parameters: (1) whether the schedule for sampling is fixed or variable, (2) the duration of the interval of time in which the event is observed, and (3) the duration of the interval of time between periods of observation. If the time schedule is fixed, the recording recurs at equal intervals and continues for equal intervals, e.g., observe for five minutes, rest for five minutes, then repeat the sequence. If the schedule is variable, the sampling may be randomly determined: periods of observation would vary over a range of time intervals as would the periods between observation. In practice, no observation schedule has been totally randomly determined. A partially fixed observation schedule is typical. In this instance the period of observation is set at a constant, e.g., ten minutes, but the interval of time between observations is allowed to vary, subject to certain constraints (for example, no child should be observed twice in the same day, or twice within the same setting on the same day). Fixed recording schedules are also typical. When the schedule is fixed both the period of observation and the interval between observations is specified in advance. The period of observation may be very short, e.g., one-tenth second snapshot, and the interval between observations long, e.g., once a month. Alternatively, the period of recording might be very long, e.g., an hour, and the intervals between observation periods short, e.g., fifteen minutes. Usually the observation period will be considerably shorter than the intervals between observation periods. Length of the observation period depends upon many considerations, including the frequency of occurrence of the behavior, its variability, the complexity of the observational task, observer fatigue, whether recording can be done without an observer's presence, etc. Intervals between observation periods vary depending upon considerations such as the number of people to be observed, investigator time allocated for data collection, whether the criterion behavior is thought to be cyclical, or likely to change rapidly, and observer considerations such as the time involved in getting to observation sites, etc. Useful discussions regarding time sampling methods can be found in Arrington (1939, 1943), Hutt and Hutt (1974), and Wright (1960).

Event recording, the historical alternative to time sampling techniques, consists of recording being initiated coterminously with, or immediately following the occurrence of the criterion event (Hutt & Hutt, 1974; Wright, 1960). In this strategy an observer is stationed in a setting where the event is likely to occur and begins recording when the event begins, e.g., what happens when a baby starts crying? How long does the crying go on? What may have instigated the crying? How long is it before a caretaker attends to the crying infant (e.g., Munroe & Munroe, 1973)? Time sampling and event recording methods don't necessarily produce equivalent measures of behavior. Thus decisions about what kind of behavior sampling to use are not trivial (Munroe & Munroe, 1973; Hayes, Meltzer, & Wolf, 1970). Moreover, as Chapple has noted (1970b) if behavior has a temporal structure, then time sampling lessens the chances of seeing that structure.

Event Sampling

In retrospect, sampling techniques have been described primarily in terms of their juxtaposition to the behavior under study. In fact decisions concerning setting and subject sampling have also been involved in determining behavior sampling strategies. However, such decisions have been implicit, rather than separately addressed and conceptualized as part of the event sampling strategy. What is needed is a separate and then combined consideration of all three components of the event to be sampled: persons, settings, and behaviors. Such a typology is offered in Table 3-1. The point of the typology is that sampling strategies may fix the component of the event or allow it to vary.

Independent of this typology is the decision regarding the length of observation periods, the interval between observations and whether these two intervals are to vary or must be fixed (columns 5 and 6 of the table). Obviously, the longer the period of observation, the greater the opportunity for the criterion event to occur. In practice, the length of observation periods and their frequency will be related to the presumed frequency and periodicity of the events.

In the first horizontal row of the table, the strategy is to predetermine

Table 3-1. Event Sampling Strategies.

Suggested Nomenclature	People	Environment Setting	Behavior	Duration of Observation	Intervals between Observation
1. Predetermined event sampling	fixed	fixed	fixed	fixed / variable	fixed/variable fixed/variable
2. Predetermined person/setting sampling	fixed	fixed	variable	fixed / variable	fixed/variable fixed/variable
3. Predetermined person sampling	fixed	variable	variable	fixed / variable	fixed/variable fixed/variable
4. Predetermined setting and behavior sampling	variable	fixed	fixed	fixed / variable	fixed/variable fixed/variable
5. Predetermined setting sampling	variable	fixed	variable	fixed / variable	fixed/variable fixed/variable
6. Predetermined behavior sampling	variable	variable	fixed	fixed / variable	fixed/variable fixed/variable
7. Null	variable	variable	variable	fixed / variable	fixed/variable fixed/variable

the person or persons to be studied as a representative sample of a specified population. The environmental setting is also fixed and is considered to be a representative sample of specified settings. The behavior to be recorded is also predetermined, and is considered to be representative of behaviors so characterized. In this sampling condition, recording commences when all three predetermined criteria are met, e.g., a preselected person has entered a preselected setting, and a preselected behavior is occurring. Under these conditions and only these conditions, recording of the event occurs. For example, in the Munroe study (1973) their event sampling consisted of predetermined infants being observed in a partially specified setting (two mornings, two afternoons, apparently in the infant's home setting). The sample observation period was intended to be one hour, but was shortened if the infant fell asleep. One behavior designated for event sampling was the infant's crying behavior while awake. If and when the infant commenced to cry during the one-hour observation period, various characteristics of the event were recorded. Among them: number of seconds which elapsed from the onset of the cry until the caretaker responded to the infant, the identity of caretaker responding, the nature of the caretaker's response, and the time elapsed from the caretaker's response to the cessation of the cry. Measures from this technique consist primarily of the duration of these events.

In the second horizontal row of the table both setting and people are predetermined, while behavior is allowed to vary. Two conditions have to be present for the recording to commence: (1) a specified person must be present in a (2) specified setting. For example, in the Schoggens' study (1976) of the home lives of three-year-olds, twenty-four children in their fourth year of life were selected as a sample from three populations. Eight children each were from low-income/low-education urban homes, low-income/low-education rural homes, and middle-income/high-education urban homes. The observational setting had three criteria: (1) it was a setting in which either eating or free-play took place, and (2) it was inside or outside of, but close by, the child's home, and (3) the mother had to be present as at least a potential agent (for relating to the child). The observer went to the home on the average of twice a week. As soon as she would observe that the situation conditions were being met she would begin recording the event, and would continue until the situation conditions were no longer met. Records varied in length, covering periods of time ranging from ten to forty-seven minutes. From the carefully kept logs it is possible to note that no recordings were made earlier than 7:35 A.M. or later than 7:03 P.M. With this kind of sampling strategy, rates of occurrence of particular behavior and their characterization can be generated.

In the third horizontal row of the table only the sample people are predetermined; settings and behaviors may vary. Ecological studies of primates often follow this form. A particular troupe is selected for observation. It is then followed as it travels across settings, and behavioral events are recorded during specified periods of observation. In studies of homo sapiens this sampling strategy has been used rarely. One exception was provided by Barker and associates who observed and recorded the behavior of and happenings to sixteen predesignated children as they went from setting to setting throughout the course of a day. *One Boy's Day* describes one of these sixteen children (Barker, 1951).

In the fourth horizontal row of the table the strategy is to preselect the setting and the behavior, and allow people to vary. Dawe (1934) carried out such a study when she observed quarreling behavior of preschool children in the playground. She stationed herself at one setting and observed. When a quarrel occurred she recorded all the details of the quarrel. It was not necessary for a predetermined child to be involved for her to start recording. Quarrels involving any children in the playground were included in the collection and data analysis.

The fifth sampling strategy focuses on the much needed study of environments for behavior. In this methodology only the environmental setting is predetermined. People entering the environment and the behavior which occurs there are recorded and analyzed. While this was not the precise methodology employed, the rationale behind the study of the camp milieu and its immediate effect by Gump, Sutton-Smith, and Redl (n.d.) and Gump, Schoggen, and Redl (1957) could have used this sampling strategy. A study by Updegraff and Herbert (1933) which varied play materials and observed differences in young children's behavior also falls within this design. A more recent cross-cultural study by Weisner (1974) fixed both setting and child in the sampling strategy. In data analysis the behaviors of individual children were summed together; thus, the data analysis operation resulted in a sampling strategy which could have been preselected for settings only. Studies of the use of space are most apt to use this sampling strategy (Sommer, 1969, 1974).

The sixth strategy tends to be problematical as an observational strategy since only the behavior is preselected (e.g., Kendon and Ferber, 1973).

The last possible strategy is a null category. Neither persons, settings, nor behavior are fixed. The observer randomly selects a place and time to observe, and begins recording whatever events occur. Barker and Schoggen make reference to a related sampling strategy when they describe large scale units, the largest consisting of film which would record

> human behavior over the whole of man's existence. A frame is exposed every year, compressing 35,000 years into about six hours of viewing. [The film] . . . shows the expansion and contraction of population centers . . . and large scale environmental changes such as the . . . contraction of forests. . . . (Barker & Schoggen, 1973, p. 13)

However, even in this strategy the planet Earth was preselected as the environment to be sampled.

Since research to date has indicated that the sampling procedure can affect research conclusions, it is extremely important that sampling strategies be completely enumerated. Historically, lack of appreciation for the significant impact of setting on behavior has resulted in insufficient attention to this variable.

Systems for Data Recording

Systems for behavior recording differ in many ways. Two central ways in which they differ are: (1) the extent to which the record is intended to be a complete description of the behavior which occurs versus a selective, partial description, and (2) the extent to which the recording echoes the phenomenon and serves more as an index of theoretical constructs under study. By combining these two dimensions, a four-fold table is generated which is useful in differentiating the major methods of data recording: (1) all-inclusive replicas of the phenomena, (2) selective replicas of the behavioral phenomena, (3) all-inclusive transformational systems, and (4) selective transformational systems.

Representation of the Phenomena

To what extent does the recording mechanism maintain the phenomenon in a form which is close to a replica of it? Audio and video recordings attempt to retain the phenomenon in a close correspondence with the original event. So does specimen record narrative reporting (Wright, 1967) and the ethologist's ethogram (Hutt & Hutt, 1974). In contrast, preset coding systems where the observer records the behavior in categorized form as it occurs involve a transformation away from the raw data toward partial or total operational indicators of the theoretical constructs to be measured. The coded material cannot be translated back into a replica of the phenomena. This is true also with summary trait ratings where on the basis of long periods of observation the observer rates the individuals on rating scales devised to measure the theoretical constructs under study (Wright, 1960). The inherent problems of summary trait ratings are fully documented by D'Andrade (1974). Intermediate cases along this continuum of replica to transformation are the recording procedures of the interaction chronograph (Chapple, 1940a, 1940b, 1949, 1953, 1970a, 1970b) and the interactional language narrative recordings used by Baldwin and Baldwin

Table 3-2. A Two-Dimensional Scheme for Characterizing Recording Mechanisms.

		Behavioral Description	
		All Inclusive — — — — — — —+— — — — — — — Selective	
Replica		Two Channel Simultaneous Audio & Video Tape Recording	Audio Recording Video Recording
		Ethogram	
		Specimen Record	
Representation of the Phenomena		Interaction Language	Interaction Chronograph
		Narrative Recording	
		Resource-Process Coding	
		Preset Coding Systems	
Transformation			Summary Trait Ratings

(1969) where the observer is provided with a restricted vocabulary and a simple grammatical structure for vocally recording the happenings as they occur.

One variable which will affect the amount of transformation to be performed during data recording is the distance of the theoretical construct from the behavioral phenomenon. If the investigation is totally atheoretical and empirical the investigator will wish to maintain the record as close as possible to the phenomenon. There is no distance to travel to get to theoretical constructs. On the other hand if the theoretical constructs are phenomenologically distant and not readily apparent in the behavior studied, it will be necessary to abstract the information which is indicative of these theoretical constructs. However, even with considerable distance from behavior to construct an investigator will not necessarily attempt to decrease the distance through the behavioral record. Transformation may be reserved for a subsequent categorization of the record.

To the extent that the theoretical constructs guiding the study rely upon symbols which can be interpreted only by a human decoder, there will be a necessary distance between behavior and construct. Spanning this distance will be error variance. In contrast, constructs which are defined in physical-thing language will be easier to measure and will tend to be more reliable. The burden on these constructs is in demonstrating their external validity.

Selective versus all-inclusive behavioral descriptions.   While all investigators recognize that it is not possible to make a complete record of all of the organism's behavior, many strive to approach this ideal, maintaining that for most practical purposes the records they make can be used as if they were complete. The ecological psychologist has long maintained that the specimen record accomplishes this (Barker & Wright, 1955). Their records have been criticized by ethologists and others as being too inferential and therefore subject to considerable observer error (Hutt & Hutt, 1974). The ethologist's own records also attempt all-inclusive descriptions of behavior as it is reflected in motor patterns, but these descriptions are not likely to be all-inclusive either. However, they approach the ideal. Ironically two recording methods which should come closest to an all-inclusive record of behavior do not. Video-taped and audio-taped records are limited to only one channel for encoding behavior: video records can record motor behavior and body position; audio records can record vocal behavior and its dimensions. But humans express themselves through *both* motor and vocal behavior. Thus, in order to approach an all-inclusive record, audio and video recording must be done jointly. Even then good replicas are hard to capture. Investigators with focused objectives in mind often develop techniques for recording only some behavior. The audio tape recording is used for analysis of vocal, verbal, and linguistic behavior. The video tape recording is used for studies of body movement and posturing. Chapple's interaction chronograph (1940a, 1970b) is used for recording only the activity and inactivity in a person's behavior. Similarly, recording-by-coding mechanisms frequently focus on classification of certain properties of preselected on-going behavior (e.g., Longabaugh, 1963b; Longabaugh & Eldred, 1970). Trait ratings (Wright, 1960) also fall into this category. The scale ratings are the behavioral recording.

Behavioral replicas versus transformations.   Applied to cross-cultural investigation, the preservation of the behavior in replica form, whether it be all-inclusive or selective, appears to make more sense than transformational recording systems. The advantage of the transformational record is that it enables the investigator to collect considerably more data relevant to his focus per man hours of observation than is possible by separate recording and categorizing operations. However, in cross-cultural research the cost "of transition" in getting from the point of the study inception to the point of data collection is considerable. The infrequency of cross-cultural observational studies testifies to their tremendous difficulty. Therefore the cross-cultural researcher is under some obligation to the scientific community to collect records of behavior which can be made available to other researchers.

While a library of such replica records of behavior should be developed and nourished, one should not make the mistake of assuming that the existence of such a library will be a panacea for cross-cultural observational studies. Investigators' interests and research designs are sufficiently different that it will be a long time before even more than a fragmentary library can be built. Ecological psychologists have long been advocates of constructing such a library of specimen records (Barker, 1969). After twenty-five years of building, this library is still a small one, and only infrequently used by researchers outside this orientation. However, as recording technology improves, the usefulness of such archives will also increase.

Recording Mechanisms and Instruments

People express themselves primarily through gross movement and vocalization. Recordings of human expression therefore focus on movement and sound. The human observer primarily *sees* movement and *hears* vocalizations. Insofar as the behavioral recording is to be provided solely by the human observer, visual and auditory sensory apparatus will be the primary channels used to decode the information. Because organismic movement and position is the study focus, the investigator must use the observer in a way to maximize visual capacity. Insofar as vocalization is the study focus the observer's auditory capacity should be maximized. Studies which focus on both movement and vocalization must make maximal use of both the visual and auditory capacities of the observer.

Instruments may be used to enhance the capacity of the investigator to record either vocal or motor patterns of behavior. Table 3–3 classifies recording techniques on the basis of what kind of behavior is being recorded and the extent to which mechanical aides are used in recording the behavior under study. This latter dimension includes at one extreme recording mechanisms which are preset and then not further controlled or guided by the observer (e.g., a fixed camera in place). A mix which makes greater use of the observer is provided in Column 2 where the recording is carried out primarily by instruments, but this recording is guided and controlled by the human observer (Collier, 1969). Video taping guided by a cameraman and directed microphones would be examples. A third category switches the emphasis to rely primarily upon the observer as the recording apparatus, facilitated by use of instrumental aides. A dictated-and-audio-taped observer narrative is such an example. The last two categories rely solely on the observer as the recording mechanism, where no significant instrumentation is used. The observer-written narrative is an

Table 3–3. A Two-Dimensional Classification of Recording Techniques.

Recording Mechanism and Instrumentation / Mode of Expression	(1) nonguided recording through instrumentation	(2) observer-guided recording by instrumentation	(3) observer recording with instrumental aides	(4) observer recording without instrumental aides	(5) observer coding on the spot transformational recording
motor behavior only	fixed camera fixed video tape	guided camera guided video tape zoom lens	audio taped narrative	written protocol ethograms	checklists and code forms
vocal behavior only	stationed audio tape recording bone head microphones	worn radio transmitter with observer control	audio taped narrative court stenographer	written protocol using shorthand	checklists and code forms
motor and vocal behavior	audio and fixed combined video recording	observer-monitored audio-and-video-taped recording	two channel observer LANAL II interaction language interaction chronograph	written narrative specimen records	checklists and code forms

example of a replica. Observer check lists and code forms are examples of recording by coding-on-the-spot.

In using any of the recording techniques described below the investigator must give first consideration to how a chosen technique could be used within the culture to be studied. People of some cultures might well experience particular kinds of recording mechanisms as intrusive or aversive in other ways. People in other cultures might experience the same techniques as unobtrusive or as increasing the value or importance of participating in the study. Thus in selecting any recording technique the investigator must pay particular attention to its likely effects upon study subjects, and to how the recording technique will be introduced to these study participants.

Recording of motor behavior. Use of motion picture and video tape (Columns 1 and 2). The most faithful replica recording of motor behavior would ordinarily be that provided by film or video taping. Such cinematographic records can be permanent and provide a two-dimensional record which involves minimal distortion. With motion pictures the activity can be replayed at a more leisurely speed; with video taping the activity can be played over and over again. Advantages are apparent in that the data record is available for verification of findings, also behavior which ordinarily is too fast or too complex to be seen and recorded by human observer(s) can be slowed down and made accessible to reliable characterization. Such instances may be when (a) the action is so fast that it is not possible to record all that is required by other methods; (b) where actions are so complex that observer attention is focused on certain components at the expense of others, (c) where behavioral changes are so subtle that delineation between one act and another is otherwise too difficult, (d) where sequential changes in fairly complex behaviors are the subject of study, or (e) where it is necessary that specific parameters of belief or complex events be measured precisely (Hutt & Hutt, 1974, pp. 97–98). Motion pictures are preferable to video taping for detailed analysis. Video taping is more likely to be preferred when the recording needs to be less obtrusive. In such instances discreetly positioned video cameras fitted with wide-angle lenses can be monitored at a distance by an operator. In their study of human greetings, Kendon and Ferber (1973) used both motion picture and video cameras.

The disadvantages of video tape and motion pictures are less apparent, but significant. The time spent in replay and analysis is considerable. If no editing has been performed (Table 3-3, Column 1) then the viewer may be faced with large portions of empty or irrelevant recording. Since cameras view from only one direction, only "one side" of the behavior can be viewed. If actors move outside the camera's range, the behavior is lost. If the camera is fixed, it is often not possible to determine the focus of the subject's attention. Observer-guided cameras (Column 2) require sophisticated camera men who are also following a predetermined set of rules for sampling the behavior under study.

The most remarkable characteristic of studies involving film and video-taped records of motor behavior is their restriction of temporal focus. Very short segments of film may provide the total sample for the behavior under study. For example Duncan (1969, p. 124) reports that Condon and Ogsten (1966, 1967a, 1967b), spent "many months" intensively examining a five-second strip of sound film. Less extreme examples are provided by Birdwhistell who reports an analysis/recording time ratio of 95:1 (1952). Kendon and Ferber (1973), in their analysis of greetings, rely on film from three recorded situations, but primarily upon the greetings observed at one birthday party. Even when an investigator collects a large sample of video records, a sampling of such records eventually is resorted to because of the inordinate time involved in coding the video record at the level of detail decided upon.

In cross-cultural studies video recordings have particular value because of the increased difficulty in getting such records, in making the protocols available for independent verification of findings, and for use by other scholars. However, the added difficulties in obtaining such records in the field may be incommensurate with the gain. Recorder obtrusiveness is a special problem. (In one study of squirrel monkeys, however, the observer was found to be more intrusive than a video tape: Candland, Dresdale, Leiphart, & Johnson, 1972). Other problems include: getting the instrumentation to the field, bringing special video equipment that can be used in the observational setting (where's the plug?), and preserving tapes that require proper temperature and humidity controls. A particularly significant problem is added by a recommendation made in a later section (on "coding") that data be partially analyzed in the field. Therefore, it is suggested that most cross-cultural studies of motor behavior should involve video taping for at least a small sample of the total recording period whenever this is possible.

An entirely different kind of instrument for recording human movement is an electrical system for automatically recording the number and location of footsteps across a floor, called a hodometer (Bechtel, 1967). This imaginative device can be used only in prepared settings, however, making it less useful to the cross-cultural researcher.

Recording of motor behavior by the observer with and without the use of instrumental aide (Columns 3 and 4). If motor behavior is the focus of study, it is extremely important that the observer sees what is happening. The recording task must be simplified through such solutions as alternating "observer" intervals with "recording" intervals. The spacing of these tasks should depend upon the frequency and duration of the behavior and the complexities of the observing and recording tasks. The disadvantages of this procedure are that the temporal sequence is not preserved (see "data analysis") and the behavioral units recorded often will not be coterminous with the "observe" intervals, resulting in either unintelligible units or variable observation time intervals.

Another solution is to have the observer make only brief or shorthand notes, which can be completed later, relying on notes and memory. This procedure was followed in the Six Cultures study (Whiting, Child, & Lambert, 1966) and in most of the studies involving the use of specimen records (Barker & Wright, 1955; Wright, 1967). The disadvantages of this method are that some "looking time" is sacrificed for "recording time," and that the delay in completing the recording brings with it distortions in memory and gaps in recall (D'Andrade, 1974). The primary advantage is that it is a relatively unobtrusive method of recording.

When recording is primarily based on the human observer it is desirable to make use of whatever instrumental aides are available and feasible. Schoggen (1964) used a "steno mask," a small, shielded microphone which permits the observer to talk his observations into a battery driven, portable tape recorder, while continually maintaining the visual field. This method sacrifices neither observation nor recording and is highly recommended. While the introduction of the mask increases the obtrusiveness of the observer, it also effectively removes one as a target for interaction while observing. Subjects under study know that the observer is "working." However, the "on-off" feature of the mask also tips off subjects as to when "official recording" is taking place. This knowledge coupled with the prominence of the mask may make subjects more self-conscious about their behavior and thus increase their "reactivity" (see below).

Where recording by coding is the procedure (Column 5) and simple codes and/or few categories of behavior are being recorded, various kinds of mechanical counter devices are available (Hutt & Hutt, 1974). While maintaining visual field the observer can press a few keys to count and categorize on-going behavioral events. While event recorders have traditionally been stationary these recording mechanisms are increasingly being constructed for portable use. One such device has been marketed under the brand name Data-Myte. Such devices do not have the capacity for permitting the equivalent of an unrestricted narrative account of the behavior. Their use is limited to situations where behavior will be coded on the spot.

Recording vocal behavior. Audio tape recordings (Columns 1 and 2).   In small, fixed, and bounded settings the ceiling and/or microphone and audio tape recorder has been the standard laboratory mechanism for recording vocal behavior. A recent alternative microphone, particularly useful for tracking speaker sounds, is a bone-conducting head microphone (Hayes & Meltzer,

1967). A typical setting has been the psychotherapy hour. As with video taping, use of this method has tended to condense the periods of study. The Pittinger, Hackett, and Danchy detailed multifaceted study of the first five minutes of one therapy interview is an extreme example (1960). Where the complete course of psychotherapy sessions has been taped researchers have been forced to select a subset of all the tapes for analysis, because they had collected more data than they had time to analyze.

In some recent investigations wireless microphones have been developed and used for recording behaviors in more naturalistic settings (e.g., Soskin & John, 1963; Hargreaves & Starkweather, 1963; Johnson, Christenson, & Bellamy (n.d.); Hargreaves & Starkweather, 1965; Hargreaves & Blacker, 1967; Purcell & Brady, 1966). Such instruments may significantly affect some person's behavior (Moos, 1968). Alternatively the sound recording laboratory has been made into a more naturalistic setting and people have been brought into this setting to live (Hayes & Cobb, n.d.).

As with video taping of motor behavior the primary danger in audio taping of vocal behavior is being overwhelmed by the data collected. Eventually, the investigator is likely to sample the total data available. Moreover, unless tapes are played back and coded shortly after the event they tend to become unintelligible to the observer with increasing lapses of time. If the coder has not also been present when the audio tape was made, significant segments of the vocal behavior may never be intelligible. If there are more than two people talking it becomes difficult to distinguish the voices. Another disadvantage is that the investigator may feel secure that all the data are on record, and is therefore less apt to analyze it while still in the field and in a good position to collect more data should this prove necessary.

The coder may be unable to categorize much of the vocal content, if the vocal behavior is not in his native language without the cues provided by visual context. (Unlike motion pictures or video taping, a slowing down of audio tape speed does not permit a clearer account of what is happening.) Repeated replay can make vocal happenings more intelligible; also speech subtleties likely to be missed by the human observer are preserved. Thus if vocal behavior is the study focus, it is highly desirable to make sound recordings whenever feasible. However, for most studies it is recommended that such recordings be used only as supplements to a human observer's recording or coding on the spot.

Recording of vocal behavior. Observer recording with or without the use of instrumentation (Column 3 and 4). If an observer is going to rely solely upon a narrative record for data collection, it is necessary to keep recording periods short enough so that events can be kept up with and recorded accurately. Again this suggests a shorthand, approaching transformational coding. With vocal behavior the observer does not have the same interference as when recording motor behavior: it is not necessary to maintain a visual field. The behavior can be listened to while the recorder writes, permitting longer observation periods. However, if characterization of the behavior is dependent upon verbal equivalents such as head-nods and other gestures then maintenance of visual field is still important.

Motor and vocal behavior. If the behavioral focus is both motor and vocal then it is possible to combine audio taping with video taping on multitrack tapes. This quasi-ideal, multidimensional approach generally requires a stationary setting to which the subjects are likely to come. However, as equipment becomes more compact and portable the researcher can go to the subjects.

a. Observer recording without instrumental aids (Column 4). The specimen record of the ecological psychologist provides the classical example of this methodology (Barker & Wright, 1955). Wright provides ample description of this methodology elsewhere (Wright, 1967). Aspects of this methodology were adopted for the Six Cultures study. The details of the adapted techniques are reported in Whiting, Child, and Lambert (1966), and Whiting and Whiting (1975).

The advantages of recording without instrumental aids are that this method can be used in any setting, is relatively unobtrusive, makes maximum use of the fact that the observer has inside knowledge of his object of study—people, the records developed may be used again by other researchers, and such records tend to provide a rich description of the setting and behavior observed. The disadvantages are those mentioned in preceding sections for narrative protocols. Such records are not totally objective in description. Because they are free narrative it is very difficult to ascertain recorder reliability, and when such reliabilities are estimated they tend to be lower than those achieved from less inferential recording systems. Their scientific status is elusive.

The ethological approach also ordinarily involves observer recording without use of significant instrumentation. The method is at its best when the focus is on simple behavior patterns such as nonverbal behavior. Studies of infants and young children exemplify this methodology (Blurton-Jones, 1967, 1972; Eibl-Eibesfeldt, 1967; Hutt & Hutt, 1974; McGrew, 1972; Smith, 1975). However, application to verbal and complex cognitive behaviors are almost never dealt with, and few rigorous studies of adult behavior have been carried out (Charlesworth & Spiker, 1975, p. 166).

b. Observer recording with instrumental aids (Column 3). The Interaction Chronograph, developed by E. D. Chapple (1940a, 1940b, 1970a, 1970b), is an example of this methodology. The observer has the task of recording whether persons are active (vocally and/or physically) or inactive. As long as a person is judged to be active a key is pressed. When the person becomes silent the observer releases the key. The recording apparatus records the duration and frequency of the activity and inactivity of each of the people observed. Numerous measures of interaction are generated from this simple selective recording. Measures of tempo, latency, and dominance arise out of the relationship between behaviors of the two actors observed (Chapple, 1940b). While Chapple has used this recording methodology primarily in conjunction with a standardized interview situation (1953), he and other investigators (1940a) have applied it to situations where neither person's behavior was programmed (Kendon, 1963; Matarazzo, 1964) and in naturalistic settings (Matarazzo, 1964; Longabaugh, 1962). The shortcoming of the Interaction Chronograph is that it has not been related sufficiently to other measures of social behavior of interest to behavioral scientists. (Exceptions are Longabaugh, 1963a; Matarazzo, Phillips, & Matarazzo, 1963; Phillips, Matarazzo, Matarazzo, & Saslow, 1961.) A second difficulty is that other researchers with the same general interest have employed more sophisticated technology for recording similar behavioral phenomena, but have found that the units generated by these techniques are not isomorphic with those of Chapple (Hargreaves & Starkweather, 1959; Hayes, Meltzer, & Wolf, 1970). Therefore, the generality of the findings stemming from this method of recording is uncertain. A third limitation for many investigators is that their interest in behavior is focused on more content than can be provided by this technique. However, at least one experimental study (Hayes, Meltzer, & Bouma, 1968; Hayes, Meltzer, & Lundberg, 1968) suggests that the activity pattern conveys implications for content meaning.

c. Observer-guided recording by instrumentation coupled with observer recording with instrumental aids (Columns 2 and 3).   An increasingly popular technique for recording motor and vocal behavior simultaneously is a two-channel audio tape recorder that records the vocal behavior of the subjects on one channel and observer dictation of his own observations of the accompanying motor behaviors on the other (Baldwin & Baldwin, 1973). Such a procedure has several intrinsic advantages: (1) it requires an observer's presence, thus ensuring first-hand familiarity with the behavior; (2) observer commentary on motor behavior provides a helpful context for interpreting the vocal behavior; (3) the recording of the vocal behavior relieves the observer of making a complete and accurate record of that aspect of the behavior; (4) hearing the vocal behavior enables the observer to put the motor behavior into its vocal context; (5) visual contact with the phenomena can be maintained because it need not be broken for recording purposes; and (6) the temporal contiguity of the two behavioral modalities tends to be preserved for contextual and sequential analyses. The prime disadvantage of this method is that it tends to be restricted to small, fixed settings inhabited by only two or three people. Other disadvantages are: increased obtrusiveness, possible contamination of observer reporting of motor behavior by hearing the verbal behavior, and a doubling of data to be analyzed, thus resulting in a decrease in the temporal scope of behavior to be studied.

Using this recording mechanism Baldwin and Baldwin (1973) achieved a significant breakthrough by coupling this procedure with a computer program for coding and counting the behavior units, thus vastly reducing the time necessary for data analysis (Baldwin & Ward, 1973). Their procedure is as follows. Mothers with a single child are observed in a standard play setting. The mother is given the task of relating to the child as she would at home if she had a free half-hour. A two-channel audio tape is made. On one channel the (primarily vocal) sounds of mother and child are recorded. On the other channel the observer records the goings on, out of hearing of mother and child. Observations are recorded with a restricted language that involves a restricted vocabulary and simple sentence structure, both learned as part of the observer's training. After the observation session, the observer report is reconstructed and transcribed, using the subjects' sound channel to supplement the observers record. The reconstruction is performed in a manner that is compatible with the computer program in two ways: (1) the syntax is organized so that the computer program will be able to identify and categorize the components of the observer's sentences, and (2) the computer program has a dictionary which has been generated from past descriptions of behavior in this setting that defines each word in terms of a number of features. The restricted language is then processed by the computer program which provides a line-by-line printout of the sequence of occurrence of the behavior. The program also prints out words recorded which are not presently in the dictionary and sentences which were not codable. Preserved on the tape is the transcript of the session which can then be subjected to word counts, attribute counts, and sentence attribute counts. For example, the computer program will count the number of times the mother made a behavioral request of the child and how many times the child complied (Baldwin & Baldwin, 1969). By enlisting the computer's help in categorizing the behavior, a large component of coding time has been eliminated. As a coder, the computer will code in a totally consistent way— coding the same descriptive sentences the same way 100 percent of the time. With coder reliability 100 percent, only observer reliability needs to be a continuing concern. The use of a restricted language greatly facilitates intercoder reliability studies and increases the actual reliability coefficients.

The disadvantage of this procedure has been the limited applicability of the recording-coding procedure to one fixed setting. However, it is now being applied in other settings and three person settings (Baldwin, Baldwin, & Cole, 1976). Further development of the methodology will undoubtedly result in its application to cross-cultural studies. The restricted nature of the language will facilitate translation into the different languages of other cultures (see "coding"). Thus these developments set the stage for a most significant advance in systematic observational studies.

Subject-Recorder Distortion

In the process of behavior recording two kinds of distortions of the phenomena are likely to occur: (1) because people are aware that they are being studied, they are likely to modify their behavior. This phenomenon is referred to as *subject reactivity*; and (2) because observers are not perfect recording instruments, observer error and biases will emerge, leading to observer unreliability.

Subject reactivity.   When people know that they are being observed they may modify their behavior, resulting in an unrepresentative picture of how they behave. This likelihood has long worried researchers but until recently the problem had not been systematically studied. Observers dispatched to the field were given suggestions as to how to make themselves unobtrusive. However, often the mere arrival of an observer was sufficient to radically alter on-going activities (Whiting, Lambert, & Child, 1966; Munroe & Munroe, 1973). In cross-cultural studies, reactivity can be increased by factors such as differences between researcher and subjects, and differences in language, manners, and customs.

Through cumulative experience field observers have developed strategies for minimizing their disruption of on-going activities (Munroe & Munroe, 1973; Seymour, 1971). Sometimes long periods of observation (Soskin & John, 1963) or other saturation techniques have been used, under the assumption that subjects would eventually ignore the presence of the observer because of the more pressing concerns of daily living. While such techniques have reduced people's obvious reactivity to observation, the question of more subtle reactivity still remains.

Within the past few years researchers, mainly in the applied behavior analysis field, have begun to question and research the conditions under which reactivity will occur. Johnson and Bolstad (1973) propose five sources of reactivity: (1) conspicuousness of the observer (physically present observers produce more reactivity than microphones unaccompanied by observer); (2) individual differences of the subjects (e.g., young children may be less reactive than older children); (3) personal attributes of the observer; (4) rationale for observation (more explanation leads to less reactivity than less explanation); and (5) observees' bias to meet their own needs or the perceived needs of the investigator. Reactivity is controlled either by noting increasing stability of behavior with subsequent exposure to observers, or by comparing the effects of various levels of obtrusiveness in the observation procedure and examining for co-varying differences in the dependent variable. In cross-cultural investigations reactivity is likely to be great, or at least highly variable, depending upon cultures as well as the situational variables noted above by Johnson and Bolstad. Thus, an effort must be made to minimize such effects and to assess their magnitude.

A recent technique that appears to minimize reactivity combines un-obtrusiveness with the opportunity for continuous recording. The child wears a radio transmitter throughout waking hours. No observer is present. The transmitter broadcasts to a receive-record apparatus in the home which can be activated by an internal timer at predetermined, random times or by an otherwise selected timer. Because the subjects do not know when data are being collected, they are less likely to behave reactively (Johnson, Christenson, & Bellamy, n.d.). While the usefulness of this method in other cultures has not yet been tested, the possibilities are there.

Recording Reliability

When instruments are used to make replica records, errors resulting from the process of recording will occur, but tend not to be significant. However, when a person is used as the recording instrument, errors in the decoding-encoding procedure may be considerable. Once unitization and categorization have occurred the numbers generated can be compared to assess coding reliabilities. However, when a narrative is generated to produce a replica record it cannot easily be compared with other narratives of the same phenomena, because the data are qualitative rather than quantitative. Equivalencies are difficult to determine. Despite the possibility of significant observer error, researchers using specimen records have had to by-pass direct studies of recorder reliabilities (Wright, 1967).

Some ethologists had been quick to criticize the subjectivity of the ecologist's specimen records. "It is thus clear by now that the ecologists have abandoned any attempt at objective description. . . ." (Hutt & Hutt, 1974, p. 24). However, in their own work ethologists are apt to take reliability issues lightly.

> Practical experience, usually in the field, of both good and bad observers, is one of the factors predisposing ethologists to skepticism over too great a reliance on inter-observer reliability as a way of evaluating the reality of items to be recorded. The rare bird that flies past (and which they collect the next day) is made no less real by the fact that ten other observers didn't notice it or couldn't identify it. (Blurton-Jones, 1972, p. 12)

Thus, there appears to be a convergence in attitude about reliabilities between these otherwise very different perspectives.

Reliability studies of narrative records can be carried out indirectly.

The procedure would be to have two narratives constructed independently of the same event across a sample of subjects and events. Each narrative would be coded separately, using whatever category or rating system is appropriate to the aims of the study. Summary scores could then be compared for each protocol. Furthermore, the two sets of data could be used to establish convergent validity. This procedure is feasible in cross-cultural settings where two recorders are available.

There is an increasing possibility that the restricted language narratives of the Baldwins could be directly compared by the same procedure. Two observers separately prepare narratives which are independently reconstructed and then fed into the computer. The computer output for the separate LANAL II interaction language sentences could be compared by percentage of agreements, both at the word feature level, and by complete sentences. In summary, it would appear that narrative specimen records can be subjected to more systematic reliability assessments than they have to date. This is as possible in cross-cultural studies as in within-culture studies.

A last word on recording techniques. This chapter has been entitled "Systematic Observations of Behavior in Naturalistic Situations." The observations are made by a human observer, often with the aid of instrumentation. The human observer is a fallible recording instrument, not intrinsically suited for accurate and unselective reproduction of objective events. Rather, a person's nature is programmed to be highly selective in encoding, storage, and decoding of information. For this reason the human observer should be supplemented and at times supplanted as a *recording* instrument by emergent technology, as much as is possible and feasible. This would free the investigator to do what a human is better equipped to do—transformation of matter-energy into information which can be used to clarify human nature and the human condition. Hopefully, a future chapter covering this same subject matter will be entitled "Systematic Recording and Analysis of Behavior in Naturalistic Settings."

Coding Systems

Whether simultaneous with the behavior or later from a replica record, the behavior must be transformed into the variables of interest to the researcher, resulting in a further narrowing and selective abstraction of the behavior under study. The first step of this transformation is the unitization and assignment of properties to the units. Depending upon whether the unit is a predetermined time interval or is defined by phenomenal boundaries, its unitization and characterization may be either a sequential or a simultaneous process. If a fixed time interval defines the unit then its characterization will occur after the unit has begun and prior to its completion. If the behavioral unit is defined in terms of its intrinsic properties then unitization and assignment of attributes will take place simultaneously after the temporal completion of the unit. Depending upon which of these two unitizing strategies is used, the subsequent classification procedure and the assumptions underlying the variables will be different.

1. Time Intervals as Units

A time interval may be used to define a unit of observation in which case the coder counts the events, characterized by the attributes of interest that occur within the time interval. Using this rule, a single time interval may be characterized by the presence of O to N separate attributes. However the temporal sequence of the occurrence of these attributes within the unit will be lost. Also, if the attribute appears more than once during the interval this information will be lost. An alternative rule which the coder might operate under is: characterize as present the first, and only the first, of the events with the desired attribute to appear within the time unit. However, this will result in a failure to detect events with other attributes. Still another rule might be: if more than one attribute occurs during a given time interval, and it is not possible to record all as present during the interval (because of lack of time) then use a priority list for determining which to classify: attribute A before B, B before C, etc. This procedure, too, will result in a distortion of the frequency of actual occurrence of behavioral attributes.

This procedure of unitizing by equal interval time units, despite a certain sense of cleanliness and perhaps a simplification of the coder's task, is not recommended. (Unfortunately, it has become a rather frequently used procedure.) The distortions created in the resulting picture of the data are considerable. Perhaps an exception is where the time interval of the unit is shorter than the time it takes to be enacted, and only one attribute is being studied. Here the attribute would be noted as either present or absent, and the duration of the attribute's presence and absence across time units could be measured. (However, in this condition investigators have sometimes provided for a "no-record" break between observations, thus losing this bit of information.)

2. Behavioral Boundaries as Units

The alternative strategy of defining units by the intrinsic properties of the behaviors' boundaries will usually result in more information being gained from the behavioral stream. Historically, one disadvantage of this method is that while the duration of a unit is variable, this duration has generally been unmeasured and therefore unknown. Some attributes might occur many times more often than others, but occupy considerably less time (and energy). One person might offer support fifteen times, each offer taking only a second's duration. Another person might give help only once, but the help might take hours (or years) to complete.

However, when coding is done from frozen replicas of the behavior which preserve time markers, the coder can also measure the duration of each behavioral attribute manifested. Therefore, this strategy no longer needs to be a shortcoming of this kind of coding procedure.

A second limitation of unitizing by properties intrinsic to the attribute has been the difficulty of the task posed for the coder because of the relatively short temporal duration of many behavioral attributes combined with pressure on the coder to accurately measure the presence of them all. This has resulted in reduced coder reliabilities. But, with frozen records this kind of temporal pressure is removed from the coder and he can slow down the action or replay it as needed. Particularly in combination with the use of replica records of behavior, this strategy of unitizing by intrinsic properties of the behavior is a superior coding procedure.

Coding systems vary along a large number of other dimensions. Some of the important ways in which they differ will be described.

Theoretical Base and Empirical Base

Some category systems have been developed simply out of prior observation of the behavior. Many of the category systems of the ethologists have developed in such fashion. Here the code capitalizes on the behavioral changes apparent as one watches behavior. Sometimes these changes may be more readily apparent (e.g., the positioning of two persons vis-à-vis one another, Hall, 1963, 1966); sometimes they become apparent only after separate detailed examination of the same phenomenon (e.g., Birdwhistell, 1952, 1970; Ekman, Friesen, & Ellsworth, 1972; Scheflen, 1973). The closer the apparent similarity between the coded behavior and the raw behavior, the greater the face validity of the categories, and the easier the coder's task.

Codes also differ in the extent to which they are derived from theoretical constructs. An investigator may start with a theory or theoretical orientation and then look at the behavior to develop ways of categorizing it which will, at least partially, operationalize the theoretical constructs. Resource process coding is an example. Starting from resource theory (Burton & Whiting, 1961) and social exchange theory (Homans, 1961) categories were developed to attempt to measure the social exchange process (Longabaugh, 1963b). The advantage of this approach is that the theory directs the analysis, and whatever validity is obtained strengthens the theory as well as the observational categories. A disadvantage is that the categories developed may be poor or uneven measures of the constructs, as well as less than obvious descriptions of the empirical phenomena.

It might seem that the closer the categories are to the empirical phenomena the more distant they are from the theoretical constructs and vice versa. While there is a tendency for these two forces to pull the categories in opposite directions, it is not necessary that this happen. If the internal consistency and external validity of the theory is held constant (the latter of which, of course, is unknown until after research has been completed), the closer the categories represent both theory and behavior, and the better the category system. Where the theoretical constructs themselves are close to the phenomena the categories can represent both the theoretical concepts and the phenomena as well. Where the theoretical constructs are very unlike the phenomena the categories will either be distant from the constructs (making these linkages tenuous) or distant from the phenomena (thus necessitating considerable inference and low reliability).

Breadth and Detail of Coverage

Two other dimensions along which category systems differ and that tend to be negatively related to one another are *breadth of coverage* and *detail of coverage*. Codes which make subtle differentiation within one aspect of behavior tend to ignore other large segments of behavior, e.g., Birdwhistell's kinesic code which examines gesturing in detail but ignores verbal behavior (1952). On the other hand, codes which attempt to be all inclusive, also tend not to categorize the behavior in detail. The Interaction Chronograph is a case in point (Chapple, 1940a, 1970a). If the person's behavior is categorized continuously, however, the classification is limited to the categories of "active and inactive." The reasons why codes tend not to do both reside in the limitations in data collection and analysis. If an observer is coding on the spot he cannot both classify everything and make minute differentiations among the phenomena at the same time. This is also true if the observer merely records, as in specimen records (Wright, 1967). It is possible to do both well only with frozen replicas that can be studied at the coder's pace rather than at the temporal pace of the happening. Even here, the question remains as to how much time a coder can devote to a given segment of recorded behavior.

An example of a code which tends toward both all-inclusiveness (of social behavior) and detailed categorization of these events was the original Six Cultures code (Whiting & Whiting, 1975, Appendix B). The elegance of the code could not be sustained by the relative paucity of the amount of observations made. With its breadth and detail the code admitted to the possibility of 630 unique categorizations of the central act. However, only 20,000 units were coded, and of these almost half were nonsociable behaviors which were omitted from the analysis. The primary analysis was carried out on a collapsed and condensed eleven category code.

Related to the issue of breadth and depth is the variability in the number of categories available in a code. In principle a category system which is highly differentiated provides a more comprehensive (depth × breadth) characterization of the behavior. However, highly detailed codes also tax the coder, resulting in increasing coder unreliability. With a large, unwieldy code, two coders may find two different coding solutions for classifying the same behavior. Also, the more categories a code has, given even an equal frequency of attribute occurrence (which *never* happens) and mutual exclusiveness, the less data are available for analysis of any single attribute. When frequencies get too low, meaningful analysis is usually impossible.

If a comprehensive code is viewed as necessary or highly desirable by an investigator then two recommendations are made: (1) coding should be done after the fact of recording, so that the coder can have the time to do the code justice by methodically going through the coding rules; (2) in order to ensure sufficient observations for analysis the code should be hierarchically structured. This means that the categories should be related to one another in such a way that if there are insufficient frequencies of observations at one level of specificity, the investigator has predetermined rules for lumping categories together to pursue analysis at a more general level of classification.

Categories should also be mutually exclusive of one another. The definitions of each category should not overlap a definition of another category if they are to be compared with one another at any time. Mutual exclusiveness can be obtained in two ways. First, the categories may be defined in such a way that their meanings are mutually exclusive and the coding rule is that a single segment of behavior can be classified in only one category. This is the usual way in which mutual exclusiveness of categories is maintained. A second way is defining the categories so that the attributes that each refers to is phenomenally distinct from all others, but a single temporal segment of behavior may be categorized using more than one of these mutually exclusive attributes, e.g., a single segment of behavior may reflect both supportiveness and behavioral direction. Each attribute can be counted as present during the segment. This multiattribution approach allows for the simultaneous or overlapping occurrence of more than one kind of behavior within the same time interval. If the code is highly inferential this multiclassification procedure allows for the possibility that the same concrete behavior may be manifesting more than one attribute that the code is addressed to classify. Mutual exclusiveness of category attribution is maintained while allowing multiple assignment of attributes to behavior.

Inference

An important way in which codes differ is in terms of the amount and kind of inference the coder needs to make in order to classify the behavior. This is a classical issue in psychology (e.g., Tolman versus Skinner) and has been a continuing issue among those who have used systematic behavioral observations. On the one hand are those who insist that inference must be virtually left out of coding (e.g., the ethologists). On the other hand are those who believe that most of what the behavior is really about will be missed, unless the coders make such inferences (e.g., Barker & Schoggen, 1973).

Essentially, a "no" (minimal) inference code is one in which a physical thing, matter-energy language, is used to describe and characterize the behavior. It has to do with matter and its movement and continuation through space and time. The ethologists and the pure behavioralists generally adopt this perspective. The critical test to determine inference is the extent to which the human observer-coder can be replaced by instrumentation without loss of information. Stated differently, to what extent is the coder required to take advantage of the fact that he is a socialized human being, sharing a common culture, in order to characterize the behavior? In terms of the data of "hard science" the matter-energy proponents have the more secure scientific base. In principle, sooner or later, everything must be describable in terms of matter-energy transpositions. Physical-thing language has more objectivity about it. The cues upon which judgments are made are more readily identifiable and the resulting reliability among and within observer-coders will generally be higher. Moreover, to the extent to which categories are defined by physical-thing language, cross-cultural studies are made more easily. Observers and coders do not need recourse to the culturally shared meanings of symbols. On the other hand, while all phenomena should in principle be reducible to physical-thing language, presently for all practical purposes much of human behavior is not. Such a reduction could make the data unwieldly, at best, and probably irrelevant to the central purposes of many investigations.

The major type of inference that investigators make is with regard to the intention or purpose of the behavior. What is the actor trying to accomplish? Researchers of this persuasion believe that unless the intention of the behavior can be summarized, the behavior will remain unintelligible. Barker's example of trying to make sense of the behavior of individual baseball players without knowing the rules of the game is a good example of this kind of perspective (Barker & Schoggen, 1973).

Codes which require inferences regarding intention are more difficult to develop, harder to use, more subject to sources of observer error, generally characterized by lower reliabilities, and more suspect of observer, coder, and investigator biases and distortions. Moreover, such codes are exceedingly difficult to use in cross-cultural research (see below). There-fore the use of such codes requires considerable justification. The primary justification is that the critical aspect of behavior would otherwise be in-accessible to study. Positions regarding the use of inferences are some-what related to the kind of behavior being studied and the kind of relationships the investigator is attempting to test. When (a) the person as a whole is focused upon, (b) the major question is how much people relate to others, and (c) the behavioral units are relatively molar, then the inves-tigator is likely to use inference (e.g., Baldwin & Baldwin, 1973; Barker & Wright, 1955; Longabaugh, 1963b, 1966, 1970; Whiting, Lambert, & Child, 1966; Wright, 1967). When (a) particular parts of the organism are focused upon, (b) particular action sequences are the focus, especially locomotion or movement, rather than vocal or verbal behavior, and (c) when the in-vestigator is attempting to determine the functional significance of the be-havior for the organism, then the code is less likely to use inference (e.g., Birdwhistell, 1952; Blurton-Jones, 1972; Connolly & Elliot, 1972; Hayes & Cobb, n.d.; Hutt & Hutt, 1974; Kendon & Ferber, 1973). The most frequent type of inference the code tried to capture was that of actor intent. Varia-tions have included behavioral effect (Bales, 1950), the significance of the behavior for the relationship (Longabaugh, 1963b), or its cultural meaning (Glad & Glad, 1963). All such judgments require intersubjective con-sensus. Intersubjective agreement requires that all evaluators have re-course to the same data. There are only two means for people to understand one another: one is their common genetic heritage, in so far as they share one. Such a common heritage suggests that people will respond in similar ways to similar environmental and organismic events: that is, "human nature." But just similar response tendencies are not sufficient to enable them to infer one another's intentions. Also needed is a common culture to enable people to interpret one another's behavior and anticipate how others will respond to them, thus enabling interhuman communica-tion. To the extent to which people use the same set of symbols to derive meaning, they can successfully send and interpret messages. Even within the same culture persons have only partial access to shared meaning and an imperfect understanding of what they have access to. When several ob-servers are asked to categorize a particular unit of behavior, the greater the number of observers, the less the average agreement obtained. Each per-son has access to a part of this shared meaning that is interpreted in the context of prior experience. As the number of observers increases, the meaning shared by all remains at best constant. Meanwhile the compo-nent of meaning shared by fewer than all observers increases as does the idiosyncratic meaning unique to each observer. Using this framework, judgments concerning actor intention, effect of behavior on target, mean-ing of the act for the relationship, and cultural meaning are all drawn from this cultural pool. Veridical judgments regarding actor intention require that *actor* and *observer* share the same symbols; veridical judgments regarding the effect of the behavior require that *observer* and *target* share the same symbols; veridical judgments concerning the meaning of the behavior for the relationship require that *actor*, *target*, and *observer* share the same symbol. Veridical judgment concerning the cultural significance of the behavior requires that *observer*, *actor*, *target*, and *most* other *cultural participants* (in principle) agree upon the meaning of the symbol. Some kinds of behavior will meet these criteria better than others. In particular, those behaviors which are most heavily relied upon by cultural participants for communication will most easily meet the test.

But what happens if the investigator is from outside of the (sub-) culture and doesn't have ready access to these shared meanings? This is most typically the case in cross-cultural studies of behavior in naturalistic settings. In such cases, recording-coding procedures must meet a cultural equivalency test.

Cross-cultural equivalency test. To date, cross-cultural researchers using systematic behavioral observations have been "winging it." Typical methods have included the researcher learning the language of the culture prior to arrival, and then immersing himself in the culture to learn about it. Once he feels confident in his access to these shared meanings, the code is applied to the behavior and the data are collected. A bilingual assistant may be enlisted to use the code to collect data. Or, if sufficiently conversant with the language, the researcher may train a monolingual in the use of the code. Once coder reliability is considered achieved the formal data collection process begins. A second method is used when the investigator is a native of the culture to be investigated. The researcher is bilingual, typically coming to a Western community for advanced training, then returning home to conduct the study with a translated version of an English theory and code. The researcher collects the data and/or trains monolingual assistants in the code in order to collect the data.

Neither of these methods is really satisfactory. There is no evidence that such procedures generate culturally equivalent data.

Back translation. For questionnaire data, Brislin describes a methodology to produce and demonstrate cultural equivalence (Brislin, Chapter 10 in this volume; Whiting, Child, & Lambert, 1966). The gist of this method is that it should be possible to translate a questionnaire from language *A* to language *B*; then have a second person translate the questionnaire from *B* to *A*. If there were no change or loss of meaning, this procedure would demonstrate a cross-cultural equivalence, which should then be tested against criterion measures in order to show equivalent performance in response to the alternative forms. Applying this methodology of back translation to behavioral categorization, the following ideal is proposed. Step 1:

The investigator develops a coding system that can be used within one's own culture with asymptomatic reliability and validity. Step 2: If the researcher is bilingual, the code is rewritten in the language to be applied to the culture to be studied. If the researcher is not bilingual then a first bilingual associate is found to translate the code into the language of the second culture. Step 3: A second bilingual translates the code back into the original language. Step 4: At this point the investigator and first bilingual compare the two codes and note where changes in meaning have occurred. The translations are reworked making changes in both the original language version as well as the language to which the code was translated. Step 5: The second bilingual again translates "blind" from the second language to the first. Step 6: This procedure is continued until the prior and subsequent versions of the original language code are judged comparable. (The same equivalency test can be carried out with a prior and subsequent version of the code in the second language.) Step 7: Once code equivalency has been established then "performance procedures" should be carried out.

The point of the performance criterion is to demonstrate that either form of the code should yield identical classifications when applied to categorization of behavior in either of the cultures for which it has been developed. Thus, two independent coders, using versions A and B of the code, should be able to agree in classifying behavior in culture A and B using the two respective codes. The behaviors classified could be either prepared specifically for testing the coders or could be protocols of behavior in the natural settings. Four coders would be better than two coders, so that intercoder agreement using the same code version could be compared with intercoder agreement using the different versions of the code. Where between-code-agreement was equal to within-code-agreement the effect of the code would be judged nil. However, if the within-code-agreement was greater than the between-code-agreement this would suggest that the codes still had substantial nonequivalencies. Further work would need to be done. In this case redundancies should be increased and language and sentence difficulty should be decreased. Testing procedures should be continued until equivalency in meaning and performance is demonstrated.

The procedure outlined above may be an ideal to strive toward in trying to demonstrate cross-cultural meaning for a code. However, if such equivalence is not demonstrated in some way, the results of the study will lose their force, particularly where cultural differences are claimed. Such differences may be due to the nonequivalence of the coding procedures in the different cultures.

In attempting code translation it may be found that culture B has no language for characterizing some behavioral attributes. Or it may be found that culture B has a much more detailed way of characterizing certain behavioral attributes. In such instances it is likely that true cultural differences exist. The task then becomes one of documentation. The procedure is to develop a null class where the missing behavioral attribute is a subset of a more general category of behavior which is present in both cultures. Language would then be available for describing the superordinate class as well as the criteria which separate the adjacent behavioral attributes from those which are missing within the specific culture.

Coding and Coder Errors

A code should be detailed enough to provide a characterization sufficient to the interests of the investigator. However, the simpler the code, the easier it will be to train coders to use it and the more reliable the data will be that are gathered. If a code is more complex than a coder can handle it may be possible to divide the characterization process into independent components and have separate coders code these independent attributes. This diversification of coder task may also be desirable when the investigator wishes to determine empirically the association of attributes which may otherwise be hard to measure within a single code. The emphasis on coder accuracy and reliability will work as a constraint against an overly ambitious coding system. The coder's task is to translate complex input into a simpler output language (Campbell, 1958). Weick (1967) reviews many of the more prominent sources of coder error. Assuming a real difference between the behaviors under investigation in a cross-cultural study most coder errors are likely to distort the results in the direction of greater differences between cultures than actually exist.

In training coders it is good practice to expose them to the rationale behind the code (its context). Once familiarity with the code itself is attained, coders should be trained initially by using prepared records which clearly illustrate different behavioral categories. As they achieve criterion, then they can be given more complex tasks that move closer in their simulation to the actual coder task. Initial coding tasks may be very brief, with subsequent sessions involving more time. However at each stage of the training, time should be given to detailed discussion and clarification of apparent ambiguities in the phenomena, the code, and the phenomena-code-intersect. If possible, prior to the completion of training it would be desirable to give coders a coding experience which is more difficult than those which they would ordinarily encounter. Such an experience, in addition to providing some necessary overtraining, would also give them the experience to know when they are "in over their heads."

In cross-cultural studies the question of training to criterion is more difficult. Assuming the code has already met the test of cross-cultural equivalence it is still necessary to train coders so that they are interchangeable in their use of it. But, in fact, coder training may not be possible until the investigator is in the field and finds participants of the culture for coders. Such coders are likely to be the sole source of data for their own culture. In such instances coder effects will be confounded with cultural effects, with no possibility of disentangling the two. For this reason it is recommended that at least one coder from each culture be used to categorize the records of both his own culture and every other culture in the sample. Then coder variance can be separated from cultural variance. However, there are numerous practical difficulties in having coders from each culture code records from all cultures. If the coders are not multilingual, and the coding involves verbal behavior, then each record must, prior to coding, be translated into the language of the coder. Records or coders must be transported to one another so that coding can proceed.

A much less elegant solution is to have coders from one culture do the coding of the records from all cultures. In this instance it is likely that they will generate higher category frequencies from the records of their own culture, because of their greater sensitivity to the behavior subtleties involved. In such a case the resulting data would be highly suspect in any between-culture data analysis. Within-culture data analyses would presumably not be affected by this bias. In the Six Cultures study (Whiting & Whiting, 1975) it was necessary to use proportion scores in across-culture comparisons because of different behavioral rates noted for some of the cultures. Because observers were confounded with cultures it was impossible to disentangle observer effects from culture effects. However, use of proportion scores doesn't necessarily solve the problem either, because there is evidence that different kinds of social behaviors are differentially related to overall rate of social behavior (Longabaugh, 1966). If true differences exist between rates of social behavior in different cultures, then resort to proportion scores in the analysis cannot reveal these differences.

A compromise strategy would be to have each coder code records from two cultures and each culture have at least two coders. In this way coder and cultural variance could be separately assessed.

Coder Reliability

Coder reliabilities are used in three phases of study: in code development, in coder training, and in assessing coder reliability during actual data collection. When a code is in the developmental phase, the categories need to be tested for their ability to differentiate behavior. Reliability studies in this phase are likely to be informal and ad hoc. Along with comparing coders' classifications of individual units, the investigator is likely to compute unreliability among pairs of categories to determine to what extent the two categories are separate from one another. To the extent that pairs of categories are not sufficiently separable from one another their definitions and descriptive features need further clarification. If sufficient separation cannot be obtained, then the categories may be collapsed or omitted.

Once a code has been developed to completion, an investigator may well want to undertake reliability studies to determine the optimum discriminability the categories can generate. Less than perfect discriminability under optimum conditions indicates inherent continuing ambiguities in the coding procedure. This does not necessarily mean that the study should not go on to the next phase or that the code should be discarded. But such a reliability study will indicate the maximum discriminability the code can produce. Depending upon other considerations such as the anticipated size of differences between groups, and other known sources of error variance, reliability coefficients will be a useful guide to the fruitfulness of the proposed study.

Once a code has been perfected the next task is to train coders to criterion so that it will be possible to know when each should begin participation in actual data collection. By computing reliabilities between coders at various stages of their training, coders who are most and least in agreement with everybody else can be detected. By inference, coders with lowest average agreements are those most in need of further training. However the majority view is not necessarily the correct view. A better procedure is to compare each coder with an established criterion coding if it can be made available. Comparison with this "true standard" will give a purer measure of coder proficiency during training. If several criterion codings can be produced, then by computing agreement with the criterion across several comparison sessions a coder's asymptotic competency can be estimated. It is then possible to determine how long it will take to reach asymptote, and to what extent the projected asymptote will approach criterion. This procedure will allow poor coders to be selected out early, prior to a complete investment in them.

After coders are ready to begin data classification, it is still necessary to compute coder reliabilities subsequently to determine average level of performance. This is clear from recent studies of observer performance which have demonstrated the presence of "instrument decay" (Campbell & Stanley, 1966) through the course of data collection. The accuracy of the human observer declines because of forgetting, new learning, fatigue, decreased motivation and other factors. If "end of training" reliability agreements are relied upon to estimate the accuracy of subsequent data collection, the estimate will be too high (Reid, 1970).

Spot checks where observers know that their coding will be compared with a criterion improves the performance when the comparison is made—but not at other times (Taplin & Reid, 1973). If observers know with whom their coding is to be compared, obtained reliabilities with the identified calibrating agent will be higher than with an unidentified assessor (Kent, 1974). If observers are paired with one another over time they will produce modifications in their interpretations of a behavioral code in order to effect higher reliability with each other. However, reliabilities with other observers using the same code will be lower. This has been called *consensual observer drift* (O'Leary & Kent, 1973). If observers are informed of experimenter hypotheses they are likely to generate data in support of the hypotheses despite the fact that there are no real differences. The better defined the code, the lesser the effect (Kass & O'Leary, 1970)—the more inferential the judgments required, the greater the effect (Kent, 1974).

Still another kind of drift is one that Nydegger has called *ipsative drift* (Nydegger, 1976). Through this process the observer comes to expect certain behaviors of the person studied based on knowledge gained through previous observation. When coding involves some inference this may lead the coder to interpret subsequent behaviors according to the expectation. For example, a child who was observed as "aggressive" in an earlier observation may have his behavior coded as aggressive in a subsequent observation, because the observer expects him to act aggressively. A more conscientious observer may become aware of this tendency, overcompensate, and try especially hard not to infer that the child's behavior was aggressive. This may lead to an underreporting of the behavioral intention. Ipsative drift may also be one of the important variables that leads summary ratings of behavior to show closer interrelationships to one another than correlations based on the frequency of acts. This latter subject has been discussed in detail elsewhere by D'Andrade (1974).

The cumulative implications of these studies for observations in cross-cultural settings are rather devastating. One observer, who has committed a significant period of time to a study, is in the field alone for a long period of time repeatedly observing the same sample of persons. Perhaps the first observer has trained a second observer. An increasingly idiosyncratic application of the code develops through observer drift. The first and second observers carry out reliability assessments from time to time. If one observer is an assistant, the assistant may match the coding on such occasions to maximize possible coder agreement. The two coders discuss their differences and develop new interpretations to facilitate subsequent reliability with the result that consensual observer drift increases. If the observers have knowledge of the investigator's hypotheses and if the code is inferential, as is likely in a cross-cultural application, data collected may be skewed in the direction of the hypothesis. While high reliabilities may be obtained, if either of the coders were compared surreptitiously with other trained observers using the code, the comparability of data would likely be vastly reduced.

Strong precautionary steps must be taken to minimize these sources of observer decay. Replica records must be made, at least on a sample basis. Calibration coding should be done on a random basis either surreptitiously, or after the first coding has been completed. Ideally, more than one calibrator should be involved. Such calibrations should be numerous. Codes should be minimally inferential and the coding task made simple. If inferential coding is necessary then replica recordings of a significant portion of the data should be collected by coders who are unaware of the hypothesis. The coding of the replica sample subset of the data should be compared with the remainder of the data to determine the amount of consistency between the two sets. If such measures cannot be made, then the verifiability of the findings will remain in doubt.

The specific statistics to be used in reliability comparisons depend on the nature of the code, the observed category frequencies, and related matters. Johnson and Bolstad provide a full review of many of these matters (1973) while Guilford (1965) may be consulted for determining appropriate statistics.

Data Analysis

The last transformation operation, again involving considerable selectivity, is relating the data collected to the original aims of the study by data analysis and interpretation. Data analysis has not ordinarily been included as a part of prior reviews on systematic behavioral observations. However, there are a few recurrent problems in analysis of observational data. These occur primarily in the phase of internal data analysis, rather than in relation to external criteria.

Three interrelated characteristics of observational studies are often apparent at the beginning of data analysis: (1) the number of behavioral categories is often very large, (2) the distribution of observed frequencies of behavior across categories is highly skewed and for most categories the frequencies are disappointingly low, and (3) the small number of people in the sample combined with the many behavioral targets in the multiple settings in which the observations were made make the sensitivity or the stability of the data suspect.

The Number of Categories of Behavior

Even if there are sufficient frequencies of each behavior category, the number of behavior categories alone often presents a problem. There is an embarrassment of riches, in that there is too much to look at, and often too many perspectives from which to approach the data. Investigators' responses to this situation may be to (1) analyze one part of the data in depth, ignoring the rest of it, or (2) do a superficial analysis of all of the data. As a consequence the yield from observational studies has often been disappointing.

To prevent being overwhelmed by the data, the investigator typically looks to data reduction techniques. This response is often paradoxical in that one of the reasons for undertaking a study of behavior in nature is a desire to preserve the complexity of the behavior. The coming of the computer and the sophistication of multivariate statistics have increased the capacity to analyze data, but they have also increased aspirations. Consequently, researchers have often been left with a false sense of security that the computer and available statistical technology will take care of these problems.

Cluster and factor analysis are the most frequently used data reduction techniques. In using such techniques one assumes that behaviors that tend to co-vary are redundant measures of the same underlying process. Given a melange of behavioral indicators, clustering/factoring techniques seek to find groups or combinations of indicators that co-vary systematically: one may then infer that each group of indicators represents some major underlying influence plus minor influences affecting the individual indicators. Attention is then focused on the major influences represented by the factors or groups of indicators. Assuming that such data reduction is desirable, there are several pitfalls along the way. If some of the behavioral categories are not well represented by sufficient frequencies the correlation matrix may be unreliable. An analysis may produce a set of indicators, some or all of which may not be interpretable, or may be quite dissimilar to prior expectations.

Several advances have been made in factor analytic techniques. For example, Humphreys and Ilgen (1969) has developed a method for determining the number of factors which should be extracted from a given matrix with a specified number of variables and number of observations per variable. However the conclusiveness of this procedure assumes: (1) a homogeneous population (that is, the correlations among the subjects are the same for all people), (2) multivariate normality, and (3) linear relations among the variables. (Nonlinear relations among the variables can lead to a solution with a greater number of dimensions.) Still to be decided are questions such as whether (and how) the data should be transformed, what variables should be included, whether to factor the co-variance or the correlation matrix, what rotations are most appropriate, etc.

One cannot have confidence in the outcome of a large complex study unless the results have been replicated by cross-validation. Unfortunately it may be necessary to use all the data in the initial analysis, making cross-validation impossible and reducing the value of the results. If a second or third culture is used to carry out a replication, and the results are comparable, fine. But if the results obtained are dissimilar, are these differences attributable to cross-cultural differences, or to the idiosyncrasies of the data reduction process (e.g., Overall, 1964)? Recourse to other methodologies in search of a convergence seems necessary.

On the other hand it does make sense to examine the interrelationships among behavioral categories before attempting to relate each separate behavior category to external variables. If certain categories are closely interrelated it is redundant to relate each separately to the external criterion. Where a large number of categories has been used, variable reduction seems reasonable. In such instances a preexisting theoretical scheme for combination of behavior categories is helpful in guiding data reduction procedures.

One aspect of correlation not yet addressed is: correlated with what? Usually, one thinks of an "r-r" matrix where each kind of behavior an individual enacts is correlated with other kinds of behaviors the person enacts, across individuals. But two other models are "s-r" and "r-s" associations. In the "s-r" model the question is asked: Are certain responses associated with one another in that they share a likelihood of being responses to certain stimuli but not others? For example, running away, assaulting, and crying may all be likely responses to receiving an assault from another child. Similarly a behavior may be associated with other behaviors on the basis of similarity of response it evokes. For example, an act of help, a statement of approval, and a responsible suggestion may all increase the probability of an appreciative response. Careful thinking about possible interdependencies in the data can lead to ways of simplifying the data analysis.

Distribution of Behavioral Frequencies

When a graph is drawn of the frequency distribution of categorized behavior and the categories are arranged along the horizontal axis in rank order of frequency (where the most frequently occurring category is positioned next to the origin) and the actual frequencies are scaled along the vertical axis, a general finding in social science data emerges: the resulting curve has a concave shape. There is a rapid drop from the first to the second ranked category, with successively smaller drops occurring as rank decreases (D'Andrade, 1974). For most observational studies, a few behavioral categories will have large frequencies, while most categories will have fairly low frequencies. Low frequency category occurrence has emerged as a problem in cross-cultural studies. When frequencies are too low to yield stable measures of behavior (within or across settings and targets) for individuals in the sample, one procedure used is to treat all individuals within the data cell as a single data case by lumping the separate frequencies together (e.g., Seymour, 1971). This is an inadvisable practice because it cannot be determined to what extent one or two individuals may have been responsible for any between-group (or cells) differences obtained. Another frequently used procedure is to group behavioral categories which have low and unstable frequencies of occurrence. Often, before data collection an investigator will justify using a large number of categories by saying that if the frequency of occurrence is too low, such categories can be intercorrelated with others and then lumped with those with which they correlate. This, too, is inadvisable because if a category's frequency is so low that it is unstable, any correlations that it demonstrates with other categories may be spurious, and the lumping may confound categories which have no real relation to one another. Thus it is recommended that category systems be hierarchically organized so that more specific categories are theoretical subsets of more general categories. Then if it is necessary to combine categories because of low frequencies there is a theoretical rationale for doing so. If the grouped categories show more stability than their subsets this adds some justification for the lumping procedure.

Rather than having to resort to all of these data-saving maneuvers after the completion of data collection, the recommended procedure is to code, count, and compute the stability of behavioral acts while still in the field and prior to the completion of data collection. (It is recommended that the counting and computing procedure be carried out by a person other than the coder, to safeguard against contamination through feedback.) Stability measures can be computed by test-retest, odd-even correlation, or other procedures for testing behavioral consistency. By doing both odd-even and test-retest reliabilities one can get a picture of the extent to which inadequate sampling versus real behavioral change (resulting from maturation, learning, etc.) is responsible for the lack of behavioral stability. If instability can be attributed to inadequate sampling, then the solution is to collect more data. If instability is being affected by behavioral change, this suggests that the rate of data collection is too slow and should be increased.

The observed concaveness of a rank-frequency graph of an investigator's categorized behavior might lead to the conclusion that the low frequency categories should be omitted from the study. However, this may be a premature conclusion. Low frequency behaviors should not be ignored simply because of their rare occurrence. Some may be much more informative than their more frequently occurring neighbors (e.g., murders are much less frequent than nonmurderous assaults, yet understanding the former may be more important to survival).

In terms of information theory, events which occur less often carry more information than frequently occurring events (e.g., Garner, 1962). It has been proposed (Longabaugh, 1973) that social behaviors which occur infrequently have greater risk attached to them than behaviors which occur more frequently. In the Six Cultures study (Whiting & Whiting,

1975), the two behaviors which were observed to occur least frequently in the eleven category system were "assaults" and "touches." In contrast, behaviors occurring most frequently were "acts sociably" and "insults." Both of the low frequency behaviors require that people be close enough to touch one another (a highly vulnerable distance) whereas the two latter categories can be enacted at a much safer distance. When a behavior has a low frequency of occurrence the technique used to study it may have to be modified. Individual case analysis of such occurrences may be a more appropriate method of gaining understanding than quantitative analysis, except with very large data bases. (Methods of recording may also need to be altered for adequate description of such events. In-depth descriptions should gain greater emphasis at the expense of in-breadth description.)

Small Samples

Observational studies of behavior in naturalistic settings, especially cross-cultural studies, often involve small samples. Two consequences are readily apparent. First, true differences must be very large to be detected, which suggests that such cross-cultural studies with their high costs are risky ventures. Second, because of the large number of behavioral categories and other variables measured it is very likely that there will be many more variables than individuals in the study, with the result that data reduction procedures become more important but also more difficult. Where measures approach and even exceed individuals in the sample, then "significant results" are of dubious value. The probability of obtaining differences of a given magnitude by chance alone increases rapidly with the number of variables studied. Other than increasing sample sizes and decreasing the number of variables per investigation, no easy solutions are apparent. One important way of strengthening the credibility of obtained findings is by demonstration that a given relationship obtains both within and between several distinct cultures. Such a strategy has long been advocated by Whiting, Lambert, and Child (1966).

Given these three characteristic problems of naturalistic studies of behavior: (1) a large number of behavioral categories, (2) low frequencies of most behaviors observed, and (3) small sample sizes, it is apparent why such studies often have small or questionable yield. The deck is stacked against finding true differences and when observed differences are noted it is often not possible to determine which are spurious, and which reflect real differences. The difficulty of isolating true differences is magnified by the fact that natural settings haven't received sufficient study so that their effects upon behavior may be unexpected and very different from what would be anticipated from a laboratory study (see Barker, 1969). When puzzling findings and expected findings occur in a context in which it is virtually certain that some of the obtained relationships have occurred "by chance," the puzzling relationships are those that are likely to be deemphasized and cast aside as spurious. However, in-depth study of such surprising relationships may yield a greater gain in knowledge.

Behavior Scores: Rates versus Proportions

One dilemma often confronting an investigator of behavior in naturalistic settings is whether to use as the behavioral variable a "rate" or a "proportion" score. A behavioral rate is computed by dividing the frequency of the behavior's occurrence by the period of observation to yield a rate of occurrence per time unit, e.g., .10 acts per minute or six acts per hour. The latter expression of rate per hour is ordinarily much easier to interpret and get the feel of than is a rate per minute. However, rate per minute or per five minutes have ordinarily been used. In a proportion score the frequency of a given kind of behavior is divided by the total frequency of behavior enacted by the sample person. This score removes the variability created by different activity levels of different individuals and instead answers the question: Given that individual *I* is going to do something (where the "something" is defined by the total set of code categories) what is the probability that he is going to do *X*? Both indices have merit and are useful indicators of behavior (Longabaugh, 1966). However they may yield very different perspectives on the behavior and have different mensurable properties. These issues have been addressed by Jones (1972) in a highly illuminating paper. Proportion scores are interdependent, technically called ipsative, i.e., the higher an individual's score on any one measure, the lower the individual's score on the sum of the other measures. Thus when comparisons of proportion scores are made across individuals, an individual's ranking on one measure will be affected by his ranking on other measures. Depending upon the constraints imposed upon the behavior by the code, interpretations of the data may be misleading (Jones, 1972). In many situations, rates may be the more useful measure. However in at least one cross-cultural study (Whiting & Whiting, 1975) the use of behavioral rates was not useful. Preliminary analysis indicated that the behavioral rates of children in one culture was far below that of children in other cultures, and rates in two cultures seemed to be quite high. It was possible that this was a true difference between the children in these different cultures. If this were so then it would simply be concluded that the children in the low frequency culture did less social behavior of any and all kinds than children in any of the other cultures. Such a finding might have strong implications for a theory concerned with the antecedents and/or consequences of social behavior. (However, further between-culture analysis of differences in the rates of different kinds of social behavior would be redundant.) The researchers also noted that the coded frequencies of behaviors were related to the length of the recorded specimen record: longer records had more coded social behaviors. This could be due to the fact that more social behavior produced longer records, or that more detailed records resulted in more categorizations of behavior. Further study revealed that the different field of observers tended to produce records of different average length, regardless of what was going on. This led the investigators to conclude that the differences in social behavior rates were primarily a function of the observers rather than of the children. On this basis the decision was made to ignore differences in behavioral rates and instead to use proportion scores in the data analysis. The resulting validity of the approach used justified this decision. However, the question remains as to what kind of a picture would have emerged if rates had been used to complete the analysis.

In a different context a single protocol describing the behavior of one child was categorized using four different coding systems: environmental force units (Schoggen & Schoggen, 1976) a modified Six Culture code (Whiting & Whiting, 1975), interaction language (Baldwin & Baldwin, 1969), and resource process coding (Longabaugh, 1970a); each code utilized a behavioral unit of a different level of molecularity. The number of units generated by the four codes differed markedly: 56, 78, 104, 168. Yet when comparisons were made between initiated and received acts among various child-other dyads, identical data were generated at an ordinal level of measurement and converging information was apparent at the interval level. This led to the conclusion that the four codes were interchangeable in terms of measuring relative amounts of interaction. Where the content of the codes was overlapping, here too there was evidence of convergence in the profiles generated (Longabaugh, 1972). One implication suggested by this comparison is that different category systems focusing on the same areas of behavior will yield similar results, particularly when the scaling procedure involves fewer assumptions about the properties of the behavior observed. The encouraging aspect of these results is that it may be possible to aggregate findings across different studies using different coding systems. To the extent that this is possible, not all cross-cultural studies would have to use the same coding system as long as they used the same standardized recording mechanisms.

Sequence Analysis

This last section focuses on one area where the method of systematic observations in naturalistic settings could be used to considerable advantage. This is in the study of interpersonal interaction in naturalistic settings (and by implication, also in the study of any man-environment interactional sequence). Interpersonal behavior is an interactive process. On-going behaviors are affected by what has preceded them, and they in turn affect what is to follow. *Where* in a sequence a given behavior occurs will affect the meaning it has for the participants. Only by using a method of data recording which preserves behaviors in this chronological sequence is it possible to study interpersonal interaction in detail and develop a body of knowledge about it. In the study of behavior in its natural settings, systematic behavioral observations are unique in their ability to preserve these happenings in their sequence of occurrence. But in order to take advantage of this capacity it is necessary that data be analyzed the way it occurred and was recorded: in its chronological sequence. Until recently the study of interaction sequences has been severely limited by the costs of such analyses and by the lack of appropriate statistics for assessing potential relationships. But the development of the computer with its data storage, retrieval, and computational capacities has made the study of interaction sequences feasible. The development of applied mathematics suitable to the study of interactional behaviors has also become a reality (Abelson, 1967; Garner, 1962).

In 1965 Raush reported a study of the interaction sequences of children in a natural setting. In that year Altmann also reported a study of the behaviors of rhesus monkeys, using comparable mathematical techniques (Altmann, 1965). These efforts demonstrated the use of two methods of investigating interaction sequences: multivariate informational analyses and transitional probability models. These seminal papers have provoked a number of subsequent investigations (e.g., Bobbitt, Gourevitch, Milker, & Jensen, 1969; Charfield, 1970; Jaffe & Feldstein, 1970; Longabaugh, 1969a, 1969b; 1973a, 1973b; Sackett, 1976; Wolf, 1967). These methods enable an investigator to determine the extent and locus of dependency of the behavior on the surrounding behaviors and events, e.g., to what extent can the behavior be predicted from knowledge of the prior act by the actor, by the other person, and/or by the combination of the two (Longabaugh, 1969b)?

The value of applying these tools to behavioral sequences is still to be fully exploited. Problems generic to observational studies of behavior, such as inadequate data bases, are magnified (Longabaugh, 1973a). However, these tools give promise of greatly aiding in the description and understanding of behavior observed in its natural setting. It is therefore recommended that investigators of behavior in cross-cultural settings examine the applicability of such tools to their own research questions.

Conclusion

Inasmuch as a primary reason for the focus of this *Handbook* is the desire to broaden the knowledge of human behavior through a cross-cultural perspective, the direct study of human behavior in all of the cultural, physical, and social contexts in which it occurs becomes an extremely important element in this broadened scientific perspective. Direct measurement of this behavior by the method of systematic behavioral observations would seem to be a first priority of the day. However, this methodological approach carries numerous liabilities. The human observer as a recorder is a weak link in the process. A person is not easily converted into a sensitive and reliable recording instrument. It is for this reason that various safeguards must be built in to ensure the reliability and validity of the data. Also partly for this reason, instrumentation is recommended wherever possible to ease the task of making systematic behavioral observations.

There are two conclusions to this chapter: (1) Direct measurement of human behavior in settings of its natural occurrence must be a high priority of a transcultural science of human behavior; (2) But, this is a very difficult methodology to use, and its most difficult application is probably in cross-cultural field studies, exactly the point where it is most needed.

Note

1. I would like to thank the following people for their most constructive critiques of earlier drafts of this manuscript:

Linwayway Angeles	Corrine Nydegger
Alfred Baldwin	Maxine Schoggen
Margaret Brandl	Phil Schoggen
Donald Hayes	Robert Stout
William Lambert	Suwarsih Warnaen

I would also like to thank all the participants of "Cross-Cultural Research for Behavioral and Social Scientists Project" held at the East-West Culture Center for their helpful response to an earlier draft of the paper. Of course, the responsibility for the final project remains my own. I would also like to thank the Grant Foundation for helping to make possible my review of observational methods.

References

ABELSON, R. P. Mathematical social psychology. In L. Berkowitz, (Ed.), *Advances in social psychology*, Vol. 3. New York: Academic Press, 1967.

AINSWORTH, M. *Infancy in Uganda*. Baltimore: Johns Hopkins University Press, 1967.

ALTMANN, S. A. Sociobiology of Rhesus II: Stochastics of social communication. *Journal of Theoretical Biology*, 1965, 8, 490–522.

ARGYLE, M. & KENDON, A. The experimental analysis of social performance. In L. Berkowitz (Ed.), *Advances in social psychology*, Vol. 3. New York: Academic Press, 1967.

ARRINGTON, R. E. Time sampling studies of child behavior. *Psychological Mongraphs*, 1939, *51*, 2.

———. Time sampling studies of social behavior: a critical review of techniques and results with research suggestions. *Psychological Bulletin*, 1943, *40*, 81–124.

BALDWIN, A. L., & BALDWIN, C. P., A description of interactional language. Paper presented at the Conference on the Analysis of Interactions in Naturalistic Situations, Cornell Center for Early Education, 1969.

———. The study of mother-child interaction. *American Scientist*, 1973, *61*, 714–21.

BALDWIN, A. L., BALDWIN, C. P., & COLE, R. E. Interaction patterns in families in which one parent has been mentally ill. Paper presented at American Psychological Association Meeting, Washington, D.C., December 1976.

BALDWIN, A. L., & WARD, P. Computerized coding of observers' narration of interpersonal interaction. Paper presented to Society for Research in Child Development, March 1973.

BALES, R. F. *Interaction process analysis*. Cambridge, Mass.: Addison-Wesley, 1950.

BARKER, R. *One boy's day*. New York: Harper & Row, 1951.

———. *The stream of behavior*. New York: Appleton-Century-Crofts, 1963a.

———. On the nature of the environment. Kurt Lewin Memorial Award Address, *Journal of Social Issues*, 1963b, *19*, 17–38.

———. *Ecological psychology: concepts and methods for studying the environment of human behavior*. Stanford: Stanford University Press, 1968.

———. Wanted: an eco-behavioral science. In E. P. Willems & H. L. Raush (Eds.), *Naturalistic viewpoints in psychological research*. New York: Holt, Rinehart and Winston, 1969.

BARKER, R., & BARKER, L. S. Behavior units for the comparative study of culture. In B. Kaplan (Ed.), *Studying personality cross-culturally*. New York: Harper & Row, 1961, 457–76.

BARKER, R., & GUMP, P. V. *Big school, small school*. Stanford: Stanford University Press, 1964.

BARKER, R., & SCHOGGEN, P. *Qualities of community life*. San Francisco: Jossey-Bass, 1973.

BARKER, R., & WRIGHT, H. F. Psychological ecology and the problem of psychosocial development. *Child Development*, 1949, *20*, 131–43.

———. *Midwest and its children: the psychological ecology of an American town*. New York: Harper & Row, 1955.

BECHTEL, R. A. The study of man's human movement and architecture. *Transaction*, 1967, *1*, 53–56.

BERNAL, M. E., GIBSON, D. M., WILLIAMS, D. E., & PESSES, D. I. A device for recording automatic audio tape recording. *Journal of Applied Behavior Analysis*, 1971, *4*, 151–56.

BIJOU, S. W., & BAER, D. M. *Child development, vol. I: a systematic and empirical theory*. New York: Appleton, 1961.

BIRDWHISTELL, R. L. *Introduction to kinesics*. Louisville: University of Louisville Press, 1952.

————. *Kinesics and context.* Philadelphia: University of Pennsylvania Press, 1970.

BLURTON-JONES, N. An ethological study of some aspects of children in nursery school. In D. Morris (Ed.), *Primate ethology.* London: Weidenfeld & Nicholson, 1967.

————. Characteristics of ethological studies of human behavior. In N. Blurton-Jones (Ed.), *Ethological studies of child behavior.* Cambridge: University Press, 1972.

BOBBITT, R. A., GOUREVITCH, V. P., MILKER, L. E., & JENSEN, G. D. Dynamics of social interactive behavior: a computerized procedure for analyzing trends, patterns and sequences. *Psychological Bulletin,* 1969, *71,* 110–21.

BRISLIN, R., LONNER, W. J., & THORNDIKE, R. M. *Cross-cultural research methods.* New York: Wiley, 1973.

BURTON, R. V., & WHITING, J. W. M. The absent father and cross-sex identity. *Merrill-Palmer Quarterly of Behavior and Development,* 1961, *7,* 85–95.

CAMPBELL, D. T. Systematic error on the part of human links in communication systems. *Information and Control,* 1958, *1,* 334–69.

CAMPBELL, D. T., & STANLEY, J. C. *Experimental and quasi-experimental designs for research.* Chicago: Rand McNally, 1966.

CANDLAND, D. K., DRESDALE, L., LEIPHART, J., & JOHNSON, C. Videotape as a replacement for the human observer in studies of nonhuman primate behavior. *Behavioral Research Methods and Instruments,* 1972, *4,* 24–26.

CHAPPLE, E. D. Measuring human relations: an introduction to the study of the interaction of individuals. *Genetic Psychology Monograph,* 1940a, *22,* 3–147.

————. Personality differences as described by invariant properties of individuals in interaction. Proceedings of the National Academy of Sciences, 1940b, *26,* 10–16.

————. The interaction chronograph: its evolution and present application. American Management Association, 1949.

————. The standard experimental (stress) interview as used in interaction chronograph investigations. *Human Organization,* 1953, *12,* 23–32.

————. Experimental production of transients in human interaction. *Nature,* 1970a, *228,* 630–33.

————. *Culture and biological man.* New York: Holt, Rinehart and Winston, 1970b.

CHARLESWORTH, W. P., & SPIKER, D. An ethological approach to observation in learning settings. In R. A. Weinberg & F. H. Wood (Eds.), *Observation of pupils and teachers in mainstream and special education settings: alternative strategies.* Minnesota: Leadership Training Institute Special Edition, 1975.

CHARFIELD, C. Analyzing sequence of behavioral events. *Journal of Theoretical Biology,* 1970, *29,* 427–45.

CLIGNET, R., LAMBERT, W., LEVINE, R., PROTHRO, E. T., WHITING, B., & WHITING, J. A strategy for facilitating comparative studies in child rearing and development. Cross-National Conference on Childhood and Adolescence, February, 1974.

COLLIER, J. *Visual anthropology.* New York: Holt, Rinehart and Winston, 1969.

CONDON, W. S., & OGSTON, W. Sound film analysis of normal and pathological behavior patterns. *Journal of Nervous and Mental Diseases,* 1966, *143,* 338–46.

———. A method of studying animal behavior. *Journal of Auditory Research*, 1967a, *1*, 359–65.

———. A segmentation of behavior. *Journal of Psychiatric Research*, 1967b, *5*, 221–35.

CONNOLLY, K., & ELLIOTT, J. The evolution and ontogeny of hand function. In N. Blurton-Jones (Ed.), *Ethological studies of child behavior*. Cambridge: University Press, 1972.

D'ANDRADE, R. G. Memory and the assessment of behavior. In H. M. Blalock, Jr. (Ed.), *Measurement in the social sciences: theories and strategies*. Chicago: Aldine, 1974.

DARWIN, D. *Expressions of the emotions in man and animals*. London: Murray, 1872.

DAWE, H. C. An analysis of two hundred quarrels of preschool children. *Child Development*, 1934, *5*, 139–57.

DEVORE, I. *Primate behavior: field studies of monkeys and apes*. New York: Holt, Rinehart and Winston, 1965.

DITTMAN, A. Book review of R. Birdwhistell *Kinesics and context. Psychiatry*, 1971, *34*, 334–42.

DUNCAN, S. Nonverbal communication. *Psychological Bulletin*, 1969, *72*, 118–37.

EIBL-EIBESFELDT, I. Concepts of ethology and their significance in the study of human behavior. In E. H. Hess & H. L. Rheingold (Eds.), *Early behavior: comparative and developmental approaches*. New York: Wiley, 1967.

EKMAN, P. Universals and cultural differences in facial expressions of emotion. In J. K. Cole (Ed.), *Nebraska symposium on motivation, 1971*. Lincoln: University of Nebraska Press, 1972.

———. Cross-cultural studies of facial expression. In Paul Ekman (Ed.), *Darwin and facial expressions: a century of research in review*. New York: Academic Press, 1973.

EKMAN, P., & FRIESEN, W. The repertoire of nonverbal behavior: categories, origins, usage, and coding. *Semiotics*, 1969, *1*, 49–98.

EKMAN, P., FRIESEN, W., & ELLSWORTH, R. *Emotion in the human face: guidelines for research and an integration of findings*. New York: Pergamon Press, 1972.

EKMAN, P., FRIESEN, W., & TOMPKINS, S. S. Facial affect scoring technique: a first validity study. *Semiotics*, 1971, *3*, 37–38.

EKMAN, P., SORENSON, E. R., & FRIESEN, W. F., Pan-cultural elements in facial displays of emotion. *Science*, 1969, *164*, 86–88.

EXLINE, R. V. Need affiliation and initial communication behavior in problem-solving groups characterized by low interpersonal visibility. *Psychological Reports*, 1962a, *10*, 79–89.

———. Effects of need for affiliation, sex, and the sight of others upon initial communications in problem-solving groups. *Journal of Personality*, 1962b, *30*, 541–56.

———. Explorations in the process of person perception: visual interaction in relation to competition, sex, and need for affiliation. *Journal of Personality*, 1963, *31*, 1–20.

EXLINE, R. V., GRAY, D., & SCHUETTE, D. Visual behavior in a dyad as affected by interview content and sex of respondent. *Journal of Personality and Social Psychology*, 1965, *1*, 201–209.

EXLINE, R., & WINTERS, L. C. Affective relations and mutual glances in dyads. In S. S. Tompkins & C. E. Izard (Eds.), *Affect, cognition, and personality*. New York: Springer, 1965.

EXLINE, R., & LONG, B. H. An application of psychological scaling methods to content analysis: use of empirically derived criterion weights to improve intercoder reliability. *Journal of Applied Psychology*, 1965, 49, 142–149.

FLANDERS, N. A. *Teacher influence, pupil attitudes and achievement*. Monograph, U. S. Office of Education, 1965.

FRANK, R. L. Tactile communication. *Genetic Psychology Monographs*, 1957, 56, 209–55.

GARNER, W. R. *Uncertainty and structure as psychological concepts*. New York: Wiley, 1962.

GELFAND, D. M., GELFAND, L., & DOBSON, W. P. Unprogrammed reinforcement of patient behavior in a mental hospital. *Behavior Research and Therapy*, 1967, 5, 201–207.

GELLERT, E. Systematic observation: a method in child study. *Harvard Educational Review*, 1955, 25, 179–95.

————. The effect of changes in group composition on the dominant behavior of young children. *British Journal of Sociology, Clinical Psychology*, 1962, 1, 168–81.

GLAD, D. D., & GLAD, V. *Interpersonality synopsis*. New York: Libra Press, 1963.

GOFFMAN, E. *The presentation of self in everyday life*. Edinburgh: University of Edinburgh, Social Science Research Center, 1958.

GUILFORD, J. P. *Fundamental statistics in psychology and education*. New York: McGraw-Hill, 1965.

GUMP, P. Intra-setting analysis: the third grade classroom as a special but instructive case. In E. P. Willems & H. Raush, *Naturalistic viewpoints in psychological research*. New York: Holt, Rinehart and Winston, 1969.

————. Operating environments in open and traditional schools. *School Review*, August 1974, 84, 4.

GUMP, P., SUTTON-SMITH, B., & REDL, F. Influence of camp activities upon campers behavior. (n.d.)

GUMP, P. V., & KOUNIN, J. S. Issues raised by ecological and "classical" research effects. *Merrill-Palmer Quarterly*, 1959–60, 6, 145–52.

GUMP, P., SCHOGGEN, P., & REDL, F. The camp milieu and its immediate effect. *Journal of Social Issues*, 1957, 13, 40–46.

HALL, E. T. *The silent language*. Garden City, N. Y.: Doubleday, 1959.

————. A system for the notation of proxemic behavior. *American Anthropologist*, 1963, 65, 1001–26.

————. *The hidden dimension*. Garden City, N. Y.: Doubleday, 1966.

HARGREAVES, W. A., & BLACKER, K. H. A dynamic approach to descriptive psychiatry. *Archives of General Psychiatry*, 1967, 16, 390–98.

HARGREAVES, W. A., & STARKWEATHER, J. Collection of temporal data with the duration tabulator. *Journal of the Experimental Analysis of Behavior*, 1959, 2, 179–83.

————. Recognition of speaker identity. *Language and Speech*, 1963, 6, 63–67.

————. Voice quality in depression. *Journal of Abnormal Psychology*. 1965, 70, 218–20.

HAYES, D. P., & COBB, L. Ultradian periodicity in human social interaction. Mimeograph (n.d.)

HAYES, D. P., & MELTZER, L. Apparatus: bone-conducting microphones. *American Journal of Psychology*, 1967, *80*, 619.

HAYES, D. P., MELTZER, L., & BOUMA, G. D. Activity as a determinant of interpersonal perception. Proceedings of the 76th Annual Convention, American Psychological Association, 1968a, 417–18.

HAYES, D. P., MELTZER, L., & LUNDBERG, S. Information distribution, interdependence, and activity levels. *Sociometry*, 1968b, *31*, 162–179.

HAYES, D. P., MELTZER, L., & WOLF, G. Substantive conclusions are dependent upon techniques of measurement. *Behavioral Science*, 1970, *15*, 3, 265–68.

HERSEN, M., & BARLOW, D. H. *Single case experimental designs: strategies for studying behavior change.* New York: Pergamon Press, 1976.

HOMANS, G. *Elementary social behavior.* New York: Harcourt, Brace and World, 1961.

HUMPHREYS, L. G., & ILGEN, D. R. Note on a criterion for the number of common factors. *Educational and Psychological Measurement*, 1969, *29*, 571–78.

HUTT, S. J., & HUTT, C. H. *Direct observation and measurement of behavior.* Springfield, Ill.: Thomas, 1974.

INSEL, P., & MOOS, R. Psychological environments; expanding the scope of human ecology. *American Psychologist*, 1974, *29*, 179–88.

JAFFE, J., & FELDSTEIN, S. *Rhythms and dialogue.* New York: Academic Press, 1970.

JOHNSON, S. M., & BOLSTAD, O. D. Methodological issues in naturalistic observation: some problems and solutions for field research. In L. A. Hamerlynck, L. C. Handy & E. J. Nash (Eds.), *Behavior change: methodology, concepts and practice.* Champaign, Ill.: Research Press, 1973, pp. 7–67.

————. A comparison of audio recorded behavior with observers present or absent. *Journal of Applied Behavioral Analysis*, 1975, *8*, 181–85.

JOHNSON, S. M., CHRISTENSON, A., & BELLAMY, G. Evaluation of family intervention through unobtrusive audio-recording: experiences in bugging children. Psychology Clinic, University of Oregon. Mimeograph, (n.d.)

JONES, R. P. Behavioral observation and frequency data: problems in scoring, analysis and interpretation. In Proceedings of the Fourth Baniff International Conference on Behavior Modification, 1972.

KANFER, F. H. Self-monitoring: methodological limitations and clinical applications. *Journal of Consulting and Clinical Psychology*, 1970, *35*, 2, 148–52.

KASS, R. E., & O'LEARY, K. D. The effects of observer bias on field-experimental settings. Paper presented at a symposium, Behavior Analysis in Education. University of Kansas, April 1970.

KENDON, A. Some functions of gaze-direction in social interaction. *Acta Psychologicia*, 1967, *26*, 22–63.

————. Temporal aspects of the social performance in two-person encounters. Doctoral dissertation, Oxford, 1963.

KENDON, A., & FERBER, A. A description of some human greetings. In R. P. Michael & J. H. Cook (Eds.), *Comparative ecology and behavior of primates.* London: Academic Press, 1973.

KENT, R. N., DIAMENT, C., DIETZ, A., & O'LEARY, K. D. Observational recordings of child behavior obtained via observation mirror, closed circuit television, and in vivo. (Unpublished paper).

———. Expectation biases in observational evaluation of therapeutic change. *Journal of Consulting and Clinical Psychology*, 1974, 42, 6, 774–80.

LABARRE, W. The cultural basis of emotions and gestures. *Journal of Personality*, 1947, 16, 49–68.

LAMBERT, W. W. Interpersonal behavior. In P. H. Mussen (Ed.), *Methods in child development*. New York: Wiley, 1960.

LIPINSKI, D., & NELSON, R. Problems in the use of naturalistic observation as a means of behavioral assessment. *Behavior Therapy*, 1974, 5, 341–51.

LONGABAUGH, R. The description of mother-child interaction. Doctoral dissertation, Harvard University, 1962.

———. A comparison of two ways of coding observed mother-child interaction. Paper presented at Eastern Psychological Association, New York, April 1963a.

———. A category system for coding interpersonal behavior as social exchange. *Sociometry*, 1963b, 26, 319–44.

———. The structure of interpersonal behavior. *Sociometry*, 1966, 29, 4.

———. Uncertainty in mothers and their children's acceptances and rejections. Paper presented at Eastern Psychological Association, Philadelphia, Pa., April 1969.

———. A working paper: coding interaction as social exchange. A modified perspective. In A. Simon & G. Boyer (Eds.), *Mirrors for behavior*. Philadelphia: Center for the Study of Teaching, Temple University, 1970, Vol. X, 53.3.

———. Level II analysis: an empirical comparison of four codes. Presented at Conference on Naturalistic Observations, Cornell University, June 1971.

———. Uncertainty analysis of interaction sequences. Paper presented at Mathematical Social Science Board Conference on Human Behavior Observations, October 1973, Monroeville, Pa.

———. The cost benefits of cross-cultural behavioral observations. Unpublished manuscript, 1977.

LONGABAUGH, R., & ELDRED, S. A resource process coding manual. In A. Simon & G. Boyer (Eds.) *Mirrors for behavior*. Philadelphia: Center for the Study of Teaching, Temple University, 1970, Vol X, 53.3.

LONGABAUGH, R., & HAYES-ROTH, F. An approach to the sequential analysis of interpersonal interaction. Paper presented at Conference on the Analysis of Interactions in Naturalistic Situations, Cornell Center for Early Education, 1969.

———. Interactional uncertainty and premorbid asocial adjustment of schizophrenics. Proceedings 81st Convention, American Psychological Association. 1973, 471–72.

MAGNUSSON, D. An analysis of situational dimensions. *Perceptual and Motor Skills*, 1971, 32, 851–67.

MATARAZZO, J. D., PHILLIPS, J. S., & MATARAZZO, R. G. Interview content and interviewee speech durations. *Journal of Clinical Psychology*, 1963, 19, 463–72.

MATARAZZO, J. D. Speech durations of astronaut and ground communicator. *Science*, 1964, 143, 148–50.

McCall, G. J., & Simmons, J. L. *Issues in participant observation: a text and reader.* Reading, Mass.: Addison-Wesley, 1969.

McGrew, W. C. *An ethological study of children's behavior.* New York: Academic Press, 1972.

Mehrabian, A. Relationship of attitude to seated posture, orientation, and distance. *Journal of Personality and Social Psychology,* 1968, *10,* 26–30.

————. Significance of posture and position in the communication of attitude and status relationship. *Psychological Bulletin,* 1969, *71,* 359–72.

Miller, D. R. The study of social relationships: situation identity and social interaction. In S. Koch (Ed.), *Psychology: a study of a science.* New York: McGraw-Hill, 1963, pp. 639–737.

Mischel, W. *Personality and assessment.* New York: Wiley, 1968.

Moos, R. H. Behavioral effects of being observed: reaction to a wireless radio transmitter. *Journal of Consulting and Clinical Psychology,* 1968, *32,* 4, 383–88.

Munroe, R. L., & Munroe, R. H. Effect of environmental experience on spatial ability in an East African Society. *Journal of Social Psychology,* 1971a, *83,* 15–22.

————. Household density and infant care in an East African society. *Journal of Social Psychology,* 1971b, *83,* 3–13.

————. Differential predictions based on time sampling versus event sampling behavior observations. Paper presented at Mathematical Social Science Board Conference on Human Behavior Observations. October 1973, Monroeville, Pa.

Nelson, C. M., & McReynolds, W. T. Self-recording and control of behavior: a reply to Simkins. *Behavior Therapy,* 1971, *2,* 594–97.

Nerlove, S. A., Munroe, R. H., & Munroe, R. L. Effect of environmental experience on spatial ability: a replication. *Journal of Social Psychology,* 1971, *84,* 3–10.

Nydegger, C. Personal communication, 1976.

O'Leary, K. D., & Kent, R. N. Behavior modification for social action: research tactics and problems. In L. A. Hamerlynck, L. C. Handy, & E. J. Nash (Eds.), *Behavior change: methodology, concepts and practice.* Champaign, Ill.: Research Press, 1973.

Olson, W. C., & Wilkinson, N. H. The measurement of child behavior in terms of its social stimulus value. *Journal of Experimental Education,* 1932, *1,* 92–95.

Overall, J. E. Note on the scientific status of factors. *Psychological Bulletin,* 1964, *61,* 270–76.

Patterson, G. R., Ray, R. S., Shaw, D. A., & Cobb, J. A. *Manual for coding family interaction,* sixth revision. Chicago: University of Chicago Press, 1969.

Phillips, J. S., Matarazzo, R. G., Matarazzo, J. D., & Saslow, G. Relationships between descriptive content and interaction behavior in interviews. *Journal of Consulting Psychology,* 1961, *25,* 260–66.

Pittinger, R. E., Hackett, C. F., & Danchy, J. J. *The first five minutes.* Ithaca, N.Y.: Paul Mertineau, 1960.

Purcell, K., & Brady, K. Adaptation to the invasion of privacy: monitoring with a miniature radio transmitter. *Merrill-Palmer Quarterly,* 1966, *12,* 242–54.

Raush, H. Interaction sequences. *Journal of Personality and Social Psychology,* 1965, *3,* 487–99.

REID, J. B. Reliability assessment of observation data: a possible methodological problem. *Child Development,* 1970, *41,* 1143–50.

REYNOLDS, G. S. *A primer of operant conditioning.* Glenville, Ill.: Scott, Foresman, 1968.

ROMANCZYK, R. G., KENT, R. N., DIAMENT, C., & O'LEARY, K. D. Measuring the reliability of observational data: a reactive process. *Journal of Applied Behavioral Analysis,* 1973, *6,* 175–84.

SACKETT, G. P. A nonparametric lag sequential analysis for studying dependency among responses in observational scoring systems. Unpublished manuscript, 1976.

SCHEFLEN, A. E. *Communicational structure: analysis of a psychotherapy transaction.* Bloomington, Ind.: Indiana University Press, 1973.

———. *How behavior means.* New York: Aronson, 1975.

SCHOGGEN, P. Environmental forces in the everyday lives of children. In R. G. Barker (Ed.), *The stream of behavior.* New York: Appleton-Century-Crofts, 1963.

———. Mechanical aids for making specimen records of behavior. *Child Development,* 1964, *35,* 985–88.

———. Ecological psychology and mental retardation. Paper presented at Conference on the Application of Observational/Ethological Methods in the Study of Mental Retardation. Washington, D. C., June 1976.

SCHOGGEN, M., & SCHOGGEN, P. Environmental forces in the home lives of three-year-old children in three population subgroups. JSAS Catalog of Selected Documents in Psychology, Winter, 1976, (in press).

SCHOGGEN, P., & SCHOGGEN, M. Behavioral units in observational research. Paper presented at American Psychological Association, San Francisco, California, 1968.

SEYMOUR, S. Patterns of child rearing in a changing Indian town: sources and expressions of dependence and independence. Unpublished doctoral dissertation, Harvard University, 1971.

———. Caste/class and child-rearing in a changing Indian town. Paper presented at the 70th Annual Meeting of the American Anthropological Association, New York, 1971.

SIMKINS, L. The reliability of self-recorded behaviors. *Behavior Therapy,* 1971a, *2,* 83–87.

———. A rejoinder to Nelson and McReynolds on the self-recording of behavior. *Behavior Therapy,* 1971b, *2,* 598–601.

SIMON, A., & BOYER, E. G. *Mirrors for behavior: an anthology of observation instruments,* Vol. I-VI. Philadelphia, Pa.: Research for Better Schools, Inc., 1967.

———. *Mirrors for behavior: an anthology of observation instruments,* Vol. XII-XIV. Philadelphia, Pa.: Research for Better Schools, Inc., 1970.

SKINNER, B. F. *Science and human behavior.* New York: Macmillan, 1953.

SMITH, P. K., & CONNOLLY, K. Patterns of play and social interaction in pre-school children. In N. Blurton-Jones (Ed.), *Ethological studies of child behavior.* Cambridge: University Press, 1972, pp. 65–95.

SMITH, P. K. Ethological methods. In B. M. Foss (Ed.), *New perspectives in child development.* London: Penguin, 1975.

SOMMER, R. Studies in personal space. *Sociometry,* 1959, *22,* 247–60.

————. Leadership and group geography. *Sociometry,* 1961, *24,* 99–110.

————. Further studies in small group ecology. *Sociometry,* 1965, *28,* 337–48.

————. Small group ecology. *Psychological Bulletin,* 1967, *67,* 145–52.

————. *Personal space: the behavioral basis of design.* Englewood Cliffs, N. J.: Prentice-Hall, 1969.

————. *Tight spaces: hard architecture and how to humanize it.* Englewood Cliffs, N. J.: Prentice-Hall, 1974.

SOSKIN, W. F., & JOHN, V. P. The study of spontaneous talk. In R. Barker (Ed.), *Streams of behavior.* New York: Appleton-Century-Crofts, 1963.

TAPLIN, P. S., & REID, J. B. Effects of instructional set and experimenter influence on observer reliability. *Child Development,* 1973, *44,* 547–54.

THOMPSON, G. G. Children's groups. In P. H. Mussen (Ed)., *Handbook of research methods in child development.* New York: Wiley, 1960, pp. 821–53.

UPDEGRAFF, R., & HERBERT, E. An experimental study of the social behavior stimulated in young children by certain play materials. *Journal of Genetic Psychology,* 1933, *42,* 372–90.

WARD, P. LANAL II, a computer system for the programmable content analysis of language. Unpublished paper, Cornell University, 1971.

WEICK, K. E. Systematic observational methods. In G. Lindsey & E. Aronson (Eds.), *Handbook of social psychology,* Vol II. Reading, Mass.: Addison-Wesley, 1967.

WEISNER, T. S. Urban-rural differences in social behaviors of Kenya children. Paper presented at the American Anthropological Association, Mexico City, November 1974.

WHITING, B. B., & WHITING, J. W. M. in collaboration with R. Longabaugh. *Children of six cultures: a psycho-cultural analysis.* Cambridge, Mass.: Harvard University Press, 1975.

WHITING, J. W. M. Methods and problems in cross-cultural research. In G. Lindsey & E. Aronson (Eds.), *Handbook of social psychology,* 2nd ed., Vol. II. Research Methods. Reading, Mass.: Addison-Wesley, 1968, pp. 693–728.

WHITING, J. W. M., CHILD, I. L., & LAMBERT, W. W. *Field guide for a study of socialization: six cultures series,* Vol. I. New York: Wiley, 1966.

WILLEMS, E. P. Planning a rationale for naturalistic research. In E. P. Willems & H. L. Raush (Eds.), *Naturalistic viewpoints in psychological research.* New York: Holt, Rinehart and Winston, 1969.

WILLEMS, E. P., & RAUSH, H. L. *Naturalistic viewpoints in psychological research.* New York: Holt, Rinehart and Winston, 1969.

WOLF, G. An experimental and mathematical analysis of dyadic, sequential, cooperative behavior. Doctoral dissertation, Cornell University, 1967.

WRIGHT, H. F. Observation child study. In P. H. Musson (Ed.), *Handbook of research methods in child development.* New York: Wiley, 1960.

————. *Recording and analyzing child behavior.* New York: Harper & Row, 1967.

YARROW, M. R., CAMPBELL, J. D., & BURTON, R. V. *Child rearing: an inquiry into research methods.* San Francisco: Jossey-Bass, 1968.

4

Cross-Cultural Surveys
and Interviewing

Udai Pareek
and
T. Venkateswara Rao

Contents

Abstract

Cross-cultural surveys are widely used. The many problems in the use of surveys and interviewing for cross-cultural purposes should be properly understood by the investigators. The two main problems in the use of surveys are those of comparability and proper sampling design (including sampling and nonsampling errors). Some ethical questions are also involved in survey research. Surveys use either questionnaires (if mail surveys are used) or interviews (if the surveys are done by field investigators). The main aspects of preparation of questionnaires are discussed in this chapter.

The interview is a form of communication with the specific purpose of obtaining information from the respondents. A paradigm of this process will be presented and discussed which takes into account the factors affecting coding of message (questions asked by the interviewer) and decoding of the message (understanding of the questions by the respondent). The answer given by the respondent is also understood in a particular way by the interviewer and thus influences his future questions. This paradigm suggests how one may make the interview a more effective and satisfying procedure. The factors influencing social disclosure by the respondent and those which the interviewer can use in building rapport are also discussed. Other factors such as the preparation of the schedule, question and response structure, sequencing of items, coding responses, and scaling of data are also discussed.

A new concept—*authenticity* (different from reliability and validity)—is proposed. Authenticity is the capability of the interviewer to get unbiased and genuine responses from the respondent. Four sets of factors influence authenticity and they are discussed in detail. They are: 1) interviewer-related factors (interviewer affiliation, interviewer image, respondent-interviewer distance, respondent relevance, and interviewer bias), 2) interview and its setting (the setting, thematic relevance, thematic sensitivity, cultural relevance, social desirability, capacity to reach depth, length, and structure), 3) respondent related factors (private-public opinion gap, omniscience syndrome, previous experience, saturation, and response-set), 4) cultural factors (courtesy norm, reticence, and game playing norm). Also discussed are suggestions on how to deal with these factors and various methods of dealing with the respondents' answers. The final section focuses on the interviewer—his selection and training. The preparation of the manual for interviewing and coding of responses is important and this can be used both for the training and supervision of interviewers.

Introduction

The present chapter is not intended to be a comprehensive treatment of surveying and interviewing methodology. Very good accounts on survey methodology are available elsewhere (Back & Stycos, 1959; Converse, 1964; Duncan, 1973; Frey, 1970; Hyman, 1954; Kish, 1965; Mitchell, 1968;

Population Council, 1970; Selltiz, Jahoda, Deutsch, & Cook, 1959; Srivastava, 1971; Stycos, 1960; United Nations, 1964; 1971; Young, 1966; Warwick & Liniger, 1975). Accounts on interviewing, which will be discussed later, are also available. Cross-cultural surveys and interviewing, however, have some special problems which will be the focus of this chapter.

Interviewing as a methodology has been used both for social surveys and for other purposes. Interviewing will be treated as a part of social surveys and as a technique for cross-cultural research. In addition to the use of interviews in selection, counseling, and therapy, the interview as a research technique has been used by both psychologists and anthropologists. In both cases the interview has been used for in-depth analysis. The use of interviews as a technique, as discussed here, is concerned with research on individual differences and general patterns of behaviour, attitudes, opinion, etc., and is not used for the in-depth study of a single individual case or for the analysis of cultural processes only. Therefore, the interview as used by clinical psychologists or anthropologists is not discussed in this chapter.

The distinction between structured and unstructured interviews is an important dimension of survey research. This discussion will deal briefly with the unstructured interview, but will focus mainly on the structured interview.

Survey research and interviews have been very widely used in cross-cultural research. With the emergence of international programmes in the fields of agriculture, family planning, nutrition and health, and community development, the use of cross-cultural surveys has increased tremendously. Thus surveys are being used widely in preindustrial and semiliterate cultures.

Whiting (1968) has cited a large number of studies on child rearing practices in different cultures. Weiner (1974) reported a survey on unemployment. Freedman (1974a, 1974b) has given several examples of community level sample surveys of fertility. Questionnaires have been developed for African, Korean, Indian, and Turkish samples. Some classical single country survey research includes surveys of industrial absenteeism (Katz & Hyman, 1949), public opinion about the atom bomb (Cottrell & Eberhart, 1947), opinion on commercial radio (Lazarsfeld & Field, 1946), the authoritarian personality (Adorno, Frenkel-Brunswik, Levinson, & Sanford, 1950), sexual behaviour (Kinsey, Pomeroy, & Martin, 1948), attitudes towards homosexuality (Levitt & Klassen, 1974), class-consciousness (Centers, 1949), and changing attitudes towards the police (Carte, 1973). Although these surveys were conducted in single countries, subcultural differences were discussed, and they provide good examples of both the topics and the nature of survey research. These surveys were done on large samples using questionnaires. Some of the classic studies in social psychology used these techniques. Typical of these are the studies of Bogardus (1928) on ethnic social distance, of Katz and Allport (1932) on social attitudes among college students, and of White on attitudes towards public employment (see Murphy, Murphy, & Newcomb, 1937).

Some Issues in Designing Survey Research

Brislin, Lonner, and Thorndike (1973) have outlined different types of studies undertaken by cross-cultural psychologists that meet the criteria suggested by Triandis, Malpass, and Davidson (1971). Survey interviews have been used to: (a) test and establish the generalizability of theories and concepts in cultures apart from those in which they were developed; and (b) to pursue studies of subjective culture, such as those of Triandis, Vassiliou, Vassiliou, Tanaka, and Shanmugam (1972) who investigated certain aspects of human cognitive behaviour in different cultural contexts. Interviews may be used as supplementary instruments in cross-cultural experiments. For example, if experiments on conformity, learning, or social perception are replicated in different cultures, postexperimental interviews may be conducted to gain insight into the results of cross-cultural variations.

Survey research may be defined as a "method (or the products thereof) for systematically obtaining specific information from a relatively large number of individuals ordinarily through questioning" (Frey, 1970). Of all the research methodologies survey research is probably the most commonly used in cross-cultural research.

Comparability

One crucial problem in cross-cultural surveys and interviews is to make them meaningful to the cultures in which they are conducted, as well as ensuring their comparability and hence appropriateness for cross-cultural comparison. Unless interview schedules are culture-specific, they may not be able to elicit valid and authentic data. Each culture has its own way of cutting the pie of experience, traditions, customs, and norms. An interview schedule should include culture-specific items. The questions asked, the words used in asking questions should appear natural for the particular setting. However, in order to compare findings across cultures, the information should be functionally equivalent (see Berry's discussion of equivalence in the introduction to this volume). This would mean that the instruments have to be made equivalent, which is a difficult task.

The comparability of any phenomenon in cross-cultural research has been and remains a major methodological problem. Arguments have been advanced that every culture should be understood in its own terms, and that institutions and behaviour must be seen as products of the culture they developed in. Such arguments may be interpreted to mean that cross-cultural comparison of institutions or behaviour is not possible, for we are comparing incomparables (Goldschmidt, 1966). However, just as Kluckhohn (1953) and Goldschmidt (1966) have offered resolutions to this dilemma for anthropological studies, Berry (1969) has suggested a three-step procedure for studies which include cross-cultural comparisons of behaviour. He suggested that: (1) Aspects of behaviour occurring in differing behavioural settings may be compared only when they can be shown to be *functionally equivalent*. The concept of functional equivalence means that the behaviours in question are solutions to the panhuman, recurrent problems of behaviour across cultures. Thus, functional equivalence of behaviour exists when the behaviour in question has developed in response to a problem shared by two or more social/cultural groups, even though the behaviour in one society may be superficially quite different from the behaviour in another society. (2) When aspects of behaviour occurring in differing behaviour settings are *functionally equivalent*, then a comparative descriptive framework, valid for both behaviour settings, can be generated from an *internal* description of behaviour within each setting. (3) Only when *both* these conditions are met, may an attempt be made to construct and apply *instruments* to gauge behaviour in these two settings. This attempt must also satisfy the criterion that the instruments are *conceptually equivalent* for the individuals in the two settings. Berry (1969) cites examples of this approach and deals with this topic extensively, including a historical perspective. This dilemma of understanding behaviour from a cultural perspective versus a cross-cultural perspective has been discussed also by Brislin et al. (1973, pp. 24–29).

Warwick and Osherson (1973) have discussed conceptual equivalence, equivalence of measurement, and linguistic equivalence as important issues in cross-cultural research. Under conceptual equivalence, they mention universality, specificity, definability, comparability, and identifiability as important problems in cross-cultural research. While some concepts are experienced universally in some cultures, they are specific in some other cultures. The satisfactory definition of variables with the same meaning is difficult to establish. Similarly, the concepts and definitions of variables like socioeconomic status, mental deficiency, abnormality, etc. are difficult to make equivalent in meaning in different cultures. As far as equivalence of measurement is concerned, Warwick and Osherson (1973) mention researchability, comparability of contexts, comparability of response, and comparability of reliability and validity as the main problems. Linguistic equivalence has been dealt with in detail by Deutscher (1973) and Anderson (1973). They discuss the problem of translation as a general part of linguistic equivalence.

Przeworski and Teune (1973) suggest that the problem of equivalence in cross-cultural research can be solved by assuming that (a) indicators of similar variables are manifested in different ways in different populations, and (b) the influence of a third, or intervening, variable can be taken into account in the analysis of cross-cultural research. They suggest that cross-national measures should be composed of a set of cross-national etic indicators and a set of nation-specific emic indicators. By combining these, a scale can be obtained which will provide reliable and valid measurement of the same phenomenon in various countries. In that case, the measurement is identical to the extent to which the operations furnish homogeneous indices for all countries; measurements for specific countries are equivalent to the extent to which the specific (emic) measures are well related to the identical (etic) measures. Some functional equivalence models, including a *domain generality* model, are discussed by Scott (1968).

Survey Design

The design of survey research depends on its purpose. As already stated, survey research could be used for generalisation of findings, cross-cultural comparison, intra-cultural comparison over time, intensive study of some variables, action planning, etc. Some good accounts of research designs are available (Selltiz et al, 1959; Young, 1966; Duncan, 1973 for fertility surveys, etc.).

Important decisions must be made initially to achieve the goals of the research. Often the specific purpose of the survey may imply the basic conceptual framework that is most appropriate for the objectives of the study. An excellent example of a well thought out framework for cross-national research with clear-cut objectives, sampling, etc., is provided by the World Fertility Surveys of the International Statistical Institute (Duncan, 1973).

Once adopted, the conceptual framework should indicate the variables to be measured. As detailed understanding of the operational nature of the variables may be necessary, the interrelationships among the variables being studied may have to be examined. This will result in a functional conceptual model with which the investigator begins. After the first test of this model it may be modified.

Survey research is not merely a collection of information, comparable to census work. Survey research is capable of answering new and interesting social psychological questions across cultures. Survey research, therefore, should be preceded by a thorough understanding of the conceptual framework of the investigator. It is often useful to prepare a detailed statement of the various concepts used in the investigation, and an outline of the conceptual framework and interrelationships among variables expected from existing theories. The objectives of the study will often specify research strategies and narrow the range of choices. For example, if the purpose of the research is to study cultural constraints to entrepreneurship among the rural elite of developing countries, the sampling design might include only those rural elite groups which have demonstrated low/high entrepreneurial activities. The study may then include comparisons on the hypothesised cultural dimensions, which account for the difference in activities. Similarly, in fertility surveys covering different cultures, it could be decided, depending on the purpose and scope of the research, to cover all the women in a specified group or married women only.

An important dimension of survey design is the extent of coverage. There may be a conflict between coverage and the quality of the research. There may be both the need and temptation to have large samples as well as to include many variables. However, the limited time available for the interviews may impose constraints on such extensive interviewing. If the coverage is too vast, either in terms of the sample, or of people, or of variables, the investigator and the quality may suffer. This leads to the issue of sampling.

Sampling

Designing survey research involves a complicated network of trade-offs which must be weighed during the strategy formulation stage (Duncan, 1973). Financial considerations involved in determining sample size have already been discussed by several writers (Askensay, 1966; Bonilla, 1964; Campbell, 1968; Frey, 1970; Almond & Verba, 1963). The analysis of the fertility surveys in several countries brought out by the International Statistical Institute (Duncan, 1973) points to the influences of other issues on the sampling design. The Institute's analysis has revealed that the survey type, method, region of the survey, the agency sponsoring the survey, geographic coverage, and questionnaire content influence the sampling design. For example, demographic surveys had sample questionnaires and larger size samples than KAP (Knowledge, Attitude, and Practice) studies; single-round or multiround survey type influenced the sample size; and KAP studies were generally single-round and retrospective.

In addition to the books dealing with sampling techniques, some excellent accounts discuss sampling as a part of the survey (Kish, 1965; Daly, 1969). Warwick and Lininger (1975) have dealt with the problem of sampling as a part of survey research, including cross-cultural problems. This is probably the first book to summarise the Michigan approach to survey research with a cross-cultural emphasis.

The problem of sampling in surveys relates to sampling of (a) the research areas, (b) cultures, (c) individuals within a culture, and (d) indicators for the variables being studied. The problem of sampling becomes especially important as the attrition rate of a sample survey may be high. Adequate representation of a population may require stratification, and the basis for stratification (e.g., status of the individuals) must be determined so as to maximize representativeness.

Naroll, Michik, and Naroll (Chapter 12 in this volume) discuss the sampling of cultures in that chapter. When sampling individuals for survey research, sampling frames may be useful. A sampling frame is a device, in the form of a list, which helps increase representativeness of the sample, with respect to a population. Electoral rolls, records of people obtained from local village administrators, may provide such sampling frames. Almond and Verba (1963) used a *repetitive-concurrent* approach in sampling. The sampling procedures were prepared and used independently by a local research agency in each of the five nations which participated in the study. The main question in such studies is the comparability of the sampling frames. "A sample fulfilling stratified multi-stage probability requirements in most of the design can lose its probability aspect in the last stage—the choice of individuals or households from the sample frame" (Warwick & Osherson, 1973, p. 37). Even after the decision about the sampling frame, the important problem is the procedure used for choosing the respondents or households. Regarding the respondents it is necessary to ensure that the various strata of the population being studied are represented in the sample. This can be done in some cases by selecting a pure random sample, but in most cases, a carefully stratified random sample may be more useful. While deciding the sample size, the attrition rate, that is, the loss of returns, should be kept in view.

A number of biases occur in sampling. Usually, for the sake of convenience, the rural areas included in samples are adjacent to larger metropolitan towns, and most research has concentrated in such "rural areas" (Pareek & Rao, 1974c). It is doubtful that such rural areas are representative of all rural areas. Furthermore, as Mitchell (1973) points out, when sampling resources are not adequate and funds are limited, quota sampling is often employed. Quota sampling procedures are generally poor because biases are uncontrolled. For example, only the most accessible individuals of a given type may be interviewed, and they may fill the quota, although they do not represent the type.

Errors

It is useful to distinguish sampling from nonsampling errors. Sampling errors occur when the investigators use (a) easily accessible samples (or samples of people who respond mainly to please the investigator), (b) small samples, (c) samples from special groups with which the researcher is familiar and so on. In such cases, observations may not be representative of the universe under study. For example, in large countries like India intranational cultural differences are so vast that any sample selected from a specific geographic region cannot be used to make generalisations about the whole country.

Under such conditions, the investigator is bound to increase his sample size and coverage. However, such attempts to reduce sampling errors might increase costs and the probability of nonsampling errors. Nonsampling errors that might increase include reductions in reliability, validity, and the authenticity of responses; or, increases in interviewer variation, and in the need for linguistic comparisons.

Minimizing sampling errors calls for strategies like increased sample size, careful stratification, and minimal clustering. Decreasing nonsampling errors requires using a relatively expensive multiround survey method or more training, interviewing and supervising the interviewers.

It is possible to reduce the magnitude of the overall survey error by trading off a measurable amount of sampling variance for better control of the other error components. Sponsors must be convinced that it is worth the additional cost. In discussing some of the principles of statistical surveys and possible sources of error in measurement, Daly (1969) points out that a properly designed sample survey can be depended on to yield results which will not differ by more than a small amount from the results of a complete canvas, using essentially the same data collection and processing methods. But Bershad and Tepping (1969) pointed out that many problems of design and analysis of surveys remain unresolved. For example, there is a need for a theoretical model of survey systems. It is imperative to take into account in an interdependent set of decisions the design of the sample, errors introduced by the respondents and interviewers, the organizational structure of the collecting system, the devices used for recording responses, the coding, editing, and the uses to which survey results are put. Such a model is needed to guide the design of a total survey system to substitute the present intuitive approach that results in suboptimization of important parts of the design.

Among the important problems are: (a) underenumeration, (b) estimating the total error of survey results, and (c) estimating the components of the total error.

One way to reduce error margin is to employ multiple methods for investigation (see Berry's Introduction). Although this may be expensive, the payoff is considerable.

Some Ethical Questions

Cross-cultural research poses some ethical questions. There is a growing concern among psychologists and other social scientists about the ethical aspects of research and other professional work. Most discussions on ethics in psychology relate to therapy and counseling, and the manipulation of human subjects in social psychological experiments. Rosenthal and Rosnow (1975) have summarised the discussion of ethical questions with regard to those who volunteer for experiments and social investigations.

One question that deserves attention is related to collaboration in research. In many cases people from two or more cultures collaborate in a cross-cultural investigation. The general approach so far has been for a social scientist from an economically developed country to come with financial resources and a complete research design. Frequently, the research design is used also in several other (usually developing) countries, and data are collected and analysed for generalisations and comparisons. In such an arrangement the role of the social scientists from the developed country is more dominant, and the collaborators from developing countries merely act as data collectors, although they may have a share in analysing their data from their own cultures, in preparing papers, and other publications. This arrangement is unsatisfactory, because it tends to be degrading to the social scientists from both developed and developing countries. An arrangement of a genuine collaboration should be worked out, and contributions from all those who are involved in collaborating in a particular research should be obtained from the beginning (from the stage of research conceptualisation). Fortunately, more recent research efforts have been much more collaborative, in the true sense. However, this question needs to be considered when planning research.

The attitudes of investigators towards the culture they are studying and its people needs some attention. It is unethical to treat respondents as *mere subjects*. Frequently, investigators from both inside and outside that culture treat the respondents as "ignorant" and "incapable of understanding" and assume that they are incapable of active participation in the investigation. Such an attitude is likely to produce biases. The obtained response may confirm the expectations but their validity may be low. Thus it is good methodology as well as good ethics to treat the respondents as responsible human beings. This requires that the investigators explain to them the crucial aspects of the investigation, and that participation reflects informed consent.

The question of secrecy deserves special attention. It has been alleged that in some cases, outside investigators have done studies without the knowledge of people in particular cultures. The respondents have a right to know the purpose of the research and how the research results will be used. Accusations of the use of data collected for subversive purposes may have some basis. Such practices make the work of legitimate researchers very difficult. This is the most serious ethical question in cross-cultural research. Social scientists who collect secret information under the guise of cross-cultural research are totally unethical.

The use of methods in which some variables are studied on the pretext of studying something else, raises some serious ethical questions. Even when such a method is used as an unobtrusive technique, this may jeopardise future investigations.

Unethical practices also include methods of baiting the respondents. False promises may be made, or, an impression may be created that the investigators come from influential organizations which can provide some material benefits to the respondents. In some cases money may be distributed to respondents for getting information. If the respondents are compensated for the time spent in answering questions, and if this is clearly stated, it may be acceptable. However, if some favours are given only to get the information from the respondents, this raises an ethical question.

In some studies, it is important for the investigator to give feedback to the respondents on the results obtained and the conclusions drawn from the research. This may not be possible in all cases. However, it is desirable that the investigator go back to the community and share the results of the study, and if possible, discuss their implications. A good principle is that the community should obtain something of value in exchange for its participation in the study.

Survey Instruments

An integral and important part of survey research and design is the development of the instruments, questionnaires, or interview schedules. Questionnaire designing is discussed later in this chapter. Details of other methodologies have been discussed in other chapters of the *Handbook.* However, it may be pointed out here that many agencies and researchers have been developing, adapting, standardising, and compiling questionnaires, attitude scales, etc. that are useful for research in different countries. Although cross-culturally standardised instruments are few in number, instruments to measure the same variables are available in different countries. For example, the fertility surveys compiled for various countries by Baum, Dopkowski, Duncan, & Gardner (1974a, 1974c, 1974d), Baum, Katheen, Duncan, & Gardiner (1974b), and Caldwell (1973, 1974) present information about various surveys and survey questionnaires which are available for different regions of the world. Several survey instruments compiled and published by the Institute of Social Research at Michigan (Robinson & Shaver, 1969) are being widely used all over the world. Similarly, a recent handbook of social science research instruments, developed and standardised in India (Pareek & Rao, 1974a) has given information about and has reproduced several survey instruments on attitudes, beliefs, and stereotypes developed and standardised in India for use in areas such as agriculture, family planning, industry, health, and education.

Wiseman (1972) points out that the selection of a data collection technique in surveys is generally based on four criteria: cost, completion time, response rate, and response bias. Typically, more weight is placed on the first three factors and, as a result, adequate attention has not been given to response bias. In his study comparing the data obtained through a mailed questionnaire, telephone interviews, and personal interviews, Wiseman (1972) found that the responses obtained depended upon the method used to collect data. Biases elicited by each method of investigation should be considered at the time of designing the survey. Problems of reliability and authenticity will be discussed in a later part of this chapter.

The large-scale use of survey methodology and the heavy demand on survey researchers for quick and large-scale studies has resulted, unfortunately, in too many cases of inadequate measurement of the psychological dimensions. One example of this is provided by the KAP (Knowledge, Attitude, and Practice) studies in family planning. Innumerable KAP studies have been conducted in various countries of the world. For example, in India alone, there are at least a thousand studies as revealed in a recent survey (Pareek & Rao, 1974c). The items included in the KAP schedules do not measure attitude; the knowledge items are also weak. Thus, the information collected through KAP surveys is of hardly any scientific use. Similarly, several survey schedules contain *one* or *two* items that are said to measure achievement motivation or other psychological variables. Unfortunately such attempts are increasing. On the basis of such studies, erroneous generalisations are being published. It is extremely important that attention be given to this problem. It is urgent to develop guidelines for the construction of schedules which will do justice to the psychological dimensions under investigation.

Interviews and questionnaires are the main tools used in survey research. Since in most third world cultures, interviews are more widely used, this method will be discussed more extensively. However, survey research may be used in conjunction with other techniques for data collection, such as observations, or unobtrusive measures. As Berry pointed out in his Introduction, the use of multiple methods increases the validity of research.

Questionnaires

Questionnaires are used in mail surveys and studies done in educational settings. It is the most widely used instrument for data collection. The questionnaire is used both to collect data and to measure specific variables. A questionnaire could be (a) sent by mail, (b) administered personally by an investigator (if the respondent's level of education permits him to answer questions), or (c) filled out by the investigator himself on the basis of the information provided by the respondents at the time of the interview.

A questionnaire can either be the only instrument or it can supplement an interview. If the sample is very large, and people can read, understand, and answer questions, questionnaires may be a good method of collecting data. Some studies have reported comparisons of questionnaires and interviews. Most of these studies find no differences between questionnaires and interviews. (Moore & Cook-Hubbard, 1975; Krohne, Waldo, & Chiricos, 1974). Brown (1974) used five different types of anonymous questionnaires as well as panel interviews on two samples. No differences were found in the responses elicited from these various methods. It may, therefore, be concluded that questionnaires or interviews may be preferred depending on the purpose of the research and the kind of sample being used in the study.

Questionnaires can vary from completely unstandardized to well standardized. We shall not discuss the techniques of preparing standardized scales, since the procedures are the same in all cultures. Scales can be built into the questionnaires being prepared for a specific purpose. Sinclair (1975) discussed the special nature of a questionnaire as a tool of data collection. A good account of the questionnaire as a method for survey research is available in Oppenheim (1966).

In general, questionnaires should not be too long. Sheth and Roscoe (1975) did not find any difference in response when the length was changed from four pages to six pages in an American sample. However, very long questionnaires tend to discourage the respondents from answering the questionnaire, and their motivation to answer carefully the whole questionnaire may become too low. In a questionnaire, unlike in an interview, there is no possibility of having personal probes. Therefore, preparation of the questionnaire requires much more attention. The question should be simple and unambiguous. They should be worded in the language which is understood by the respondents for whom it is meant. The questions should be short and clear. It is essential to pretest the questions with populations similar to the final sample. It may be useful to have precoded answers, for example, in the form of a multiple choice. Stevens

(1974–75) tested whether precoding had any effect on the responses and the return of questionnaires. He found little effect of precoding and has concluded that the advantages of precoding outweigh the disadvantages. Precoding of questionnaires may help in the final coding of data.

Before constructing a questionnaire, it is necessary to be clear about the purpose of the research and to have a list of dimensions on which information is sought. It is useful to construct different sets of questions for each dimension, and to pretest the sets before the final questionnaire is composed. The purpose of pretesting the questions may be to see which types of questions elicit better information in the particular culture in which the study is made. In some cases, more structured questions with multiple choices may be suited, while in other settings, questions requiring free responses may elicit more information from the respondents. The usual steps followed in the construction of instruments should also be followed in the case of questionnaires—collection of items, testing the reliability and validity of the various items, testing the effectiveness of the various forms in which questions are asked, preparing the first draft of the questionnaire, pretesting it with a small sample for reliability and validity, revising it, and determining its final form. During pretesting, both the types of questions and the sequencing of these questions should be examined. Schuman (1973) discussed the use of a random probe as a technique for evaluating the validity of closed questions.

If a questionnaire uses scaled categories of responses, it is necessary to do the scaling separately in each of the cultures, since the items may have different scale values in each culture (Triandis, Davis, & Takezawa, 1965). Schriesheim and Schriesheim (1974) tested the level of measurement provided by the five most frequently used response categories (Always, Often, Occasionally, Seldom, and Never). Drawing on previous research concerning the frequency meanings of these adverbs, they tested on two groups whether the distances between the adverbs were reasonably equal (using a frequency estimation procedure). Results indicated that equal intervals between the adverbs were approached, but not achieved. However, a second study using Thurstone Case III pair comparisons of complete ranks showed that a different response category set (Always, Very often, About as often as not, Seldom, and Never) provided reasonable interval measurement. A third study (using a frequency estimation procedure) generally supported the results of the Thurstone Case III method for the new category set.

While pretesting the questionnaire, sequence effects should be checked. For example, the positioning of open ended and multiple choice questions may produce differences in the amount of information obtained in different cultures. Johnson, Sieveking, and Clanton (1974) in two studies done with black and white Americans found that placing open ended questions at both the beginning and end of a predominantly multiple-choice questionnaire elicited more responses than did the multiple-choice questions without the open ended questions. They also found that when the positionings in the beginning and at the end were compared, the one at the beginning elicited more discrete ideas. This finding was true in the case of both the groups and also for different topics and questionnaire lengths.

One of the main problems in mail samples using questionnaires is that of low response rate. It has been reported that the responses seldom exceed 80 percent, usually are between 40 percent and 60 percent (Oppenheim 1966), and even in the case of social scientists in one developing country, the response to a questionnaire was as low as 17 percent (Kumar & Pareek, 1966). Although methods of determining nonresponse bias and weighting for nonresponse in survey research have been suggested (Fuller 1974; Mandell, 1974), it is necessary to ensure high response rates. It may be useful to study in each culture who fails to respond and why. There may be several reasons for nonresponse. In one case it was suggested that nonresponse may be related to the intelligence of the respondents (Macek & Miles, 1975). Nonresponse may be due to a lack of appeal of the questionnaire to the respondents, either because the questionnaire appears irrelevant to their interests, or because the respondents are too busy and get the questionnaire at a wrong time. Extensive pretesting of the questionnaire, both for its perceived relevance to the respondents and other factors, such as length, may be useful.

Several methods have been suggested for improving the rate of return of mail surveys. It has been suggested that the amount of personalisation may be increased (Carpenter, 1975). Cox, Anderson, and Fulcher (1974) found that personalised covering letters had significant positive effects on response rate, while follow-up reminders did not have the effect even when they were personalised. In other words, it seems that the initial personalisation of mail questionnaires is more effective. Matteson (1974) also found significantly more return rate to a semipersonal letter than to a formal letter. Eisinger, Janicki, Stevenson, and Thompson (1974) have suggested the use of registered mail, sending advance postcards, and rewards for return as some ways of ensuring a better return rate. Blumberg, Fuller, and Hare (1974) have similarly made suggestions including guaranteed return postage, appealing format of covering letter, prestige of the sponsor, length of the questionnaire, and premiums or gifts for the return of questionnaire. Different procedures may have differential appeals in different cultures. Hansley (1974) has proposed a novelty hypothesis as an appeal for higher rates of return. It was found that use of multicolored commemorative postage increased the rate of return. In a study of the response of the members of a professional organisation, Matteson (1974) found higher return of a coloured questionnaire compared to a plain white paper questionnaire.

Hinrichs (1975) conducted three studies investigating differences in response rate to mail surveys. Study 1 contrasted response rates for four surveys sent to about 5,000 respondents, representing all members of two populations, with rates for four similar surveys sent to about 2,000 respondents, representing systematic samples of two comparable populations. Study 2 contrasted rates of response in three populations of about 2,000 respondents who received a follow-up reminder with the rates of three populations of about 3,500 respondents who received no follow-up. Study 3 contrasted rates of response of about 2,500 respondents—half receiving a postcard requesting an immediate participation commitment and half receiving no postcard. A significantly greater response was found with both follow-ups and precommitted participation on postcards.

Those who have studied the problem of low response rate have also suggested a good follow-up procedure to ensure higher returns. Roscoe, Lang, and Sheth (1975) using two questionnaires in eight different geographical areas found that a telephone reminder was the best overall follow-up procedure. Similarly, Sheth and Roscoe (1975) found telephone reminders were the best follow-up method. A mailed reminder was found to be the next best, and telephone reminders without prior alert gave the poorest results. Anderson and Berdie (1975) used various kinds of follow-up letters— humourous and whimsical, and hand written and typed label address letters. They found that different groups responded more to the formal letters whereas faculty members and research assistants responded more to humourous and whimsical letters. Undergraduate students responded to humourous letters and hand-addressed labels. They have concluded that different techniques are more effective with different groups, suggesting the need for pretests to determine the best technique.

All the studies cited here are from American or Western cultures. They suggest that it is necessary to pretest such methods to determine the appeal of questionnaires and survey research procedures in third world countries.

Interviewing as a Research Method

In an extensive review of the studies on interviewing, Cannel and Kahn (1968) defined the research interview as a two-person conversation; it is initiated by the interviewer for the specific purpose of obtaining research-relevant information and focussed by him on the content specified by research objectives of systematic description, prediction, or explanation. The role of the interviewer is to initiate the conversation, to introduce each topic through specific questions, to decide when the conversation on a topic has satisfied the research objectives, and to record the information provided. Interviews can be used for any purpose. Census interviews, public opinion surveys, and attitude surveys are some examples. Many good accounts of the interview as a research technique are available (Cannel & Kahn, 1968; Hyman, 1975; Kahn & Cannel, 1957; Richardson, Dohrenwend, & Klein, 1965).

A Paradigm of the Interview

The interview is a form of communication with the specific purpose of obtaining information from the respondent. The interviewer sends a message by means of a question, which is decoded by the respondent, who, in turn, sends back a message in the form of an answer which is then decoded by the interviewer. In this act of communication, the background factors of the interviewer and the respondent work as filters for the coding and decoding of messages. However, this act of communication is complicated by several other variables. The dynamics of the communication process in an interview is shown in Figure 4-1. As shown in the figure, eight different factors are involved in the process. Many of these factors will be explained in more detail in a later section.

1. *Interviewer's background:*   The process of the interview starts with the interviewer, who has his own background of sex, race, culture, biases, and attitude towards the respondent, e.g., whether he considers the respondent to be ignorant or knowledgeable. The interviewer's background influences not only the kinds of questions he frames but also the way in which he conducts the interview and poses the questions. Sometimes the

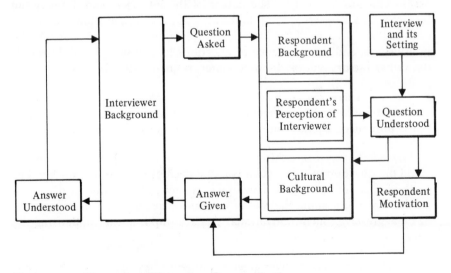

Figure 4-1.   Dynamics of Interview Communication.

nonverbal cues he gives to the respondent communicate more than his verbal behaviour.

2. *Question asked:*   The interviewer frames questions, phrases them in the respondent's language and then communicates with the respondent. Both the content and the language of the interviewer are as important as his total behaviour.

3. *Respondent's relevant background:*
   a. *Respondent's background:*   As in the case of the interviewer, background factors are also important in the case of the respondent. These include (besides his age, sex, race, culture, education, etc.) his general behaviour, e.g., how well he is able to communicate his real opinions verbally; whether he is eager to answer, or is bored with such interviews; whether he is aware of his strengths as well as of his limitations, etc.
   b. *Respondent's perception of the interviewer:*   The respondent's image of the interviewer is important in influencing his attitude towards the interview. The question of interviewer affiliation will be elaborated later in this chapter.
   c. *Cultural background:*   Some culture-specific attitudes may influence the perception of the interviewer's questions. The respondent's perception of the question will be influenced by norms prevailing in his culture, e.g., the norm of giving replies which the respondent thinks the interviewer anticipates or the norm of not responding to direct questions, or the norm of playing games with the interviewer.

4. *Interview and its setting:*   The nature of the interview and the way the interview is set up are quite important. Even more significant are factors such as the relevance of the interview to the topic and to the people being interviewed, and the avoidance of questions loaded with social desirability. Other factors will be discussed later in greater detail.

5. *Questions understood:*   The question is understood, i.e., is given a particular meaning by the respondent, who not only receives verbal messages but is influenced by the context in which the question is asked.

6. *Respondent motivation:*   After the respondent has perceived and understood the question in a particular way, he decides how he will answer. His motivational framework is developed. He may, for example, decide to play it safe and assume the role of a pleasant respondent, or play games, or be aggressive. Such motivational sets are important in influencing the answers.

7. *Answer given:*   The answer given is influenced by the respondent's motivation as well as by the various background factors. The answer not only

contains a message which is verbalised, but various nonverbal cues can also serve as messages to indicate the communication he or she would like to convey to the interviewer. For example, the respondent may communicate his pleasantness by his enthusiasm, or his boredom by looking at his watch, or his cynicism or indifference by his sneers.

8. *The answer understood:* The interviewer, equipped with his background factors, receives some messages sent by the respondent, loses some messages, and distorts others. Finally (and hopefully) he interprets the answers in a particular way and understands them. This understanding in turn, may influence his attitude either positively or negatively, and will, therefore, influence the next question he asks.

Therefore, as shown in Figure 4–1, the interview becomes a circular process of communication in which the various factors, indicated above, play an important role. An understanding of this model of the dynamics of interview communication may help the interviewer appreciate and understand the variables which are likely to influence the effectiveness of an interview.

Reschka (1971) sees the interview as a transactional process and a language game that is preconditioned by the total structure formed by language, culture, and the social system of the respondent. In addition, the interviewer tends to structure the conversation according to his background, previous experiences and information, the subject matter to be investigated, his own personality and emotional make-up, etc. Different interviewers not only show different behaviour, but also elicit different results from the same respondents. Reschka (1971), after an examination of the interview processes in United States and German settings, concluded that a complete standardization of the interview is impossible due to the variety of intervening factors in the interviewing process. Even if it were attempted, it would lead to an artificial situation which would be detrimental to the accuracy of the data.

Structured and Unstructured Interviews

The interview as the main methodology in cross-cultural research may be preferable because in many cultures (a) people may not be sufficiently literate to answer a questionnaire, (b) the motivation to complete the questionnaire may be low, (c) many new phenomena may be observed and insights gained by talking to people in the field rather than by means of a structured questionnaire, (d) answering questions in an interview situation may be easier as the interviewer establishes a relationship with the respondent. Different types of interviews may be used in cross-cultural research. One classification system used is that of distinguishing between structured and unstructured interviews.

Unstructured interviews are characterised by flexibility in both the number and nature of questions which fall within the limits of the topic under investigation. Unstructured interviews can be useful for exploratory purposes and for collecting preliminary information. The unstructured interview is generally guided by a topic or a set of topics around which the conversation between the interviewer and the respondent takes place. The interviewer does not have with him a set of predetermined questions which will limit the extent and pattern of the conversation and thereby structure the response patterns. The interviewer establishes rapport, explains the purpose of the interview, and begins by asking questions which lead to an evolving conversation.

The unstructured interview has several advantages over the structured one. Being flexible it permits the interviewer to change the language, the form of questioning, and the way of interpreting the question if it is not understood. Unstructured interviews permit the interviewer to become creative. In the structured interview, the interviewer asks questions which are prepared beforehand. Thus the scope of probing deeply and the opportunity to develop a meaningful and creative relationship with the respondent is very limited. In certain situations, such as in sensitive areas such as sex and family planning, unstructured interviews are more useful.

The unstructured interview makes possible a better understanding of the dynamics of certain phenomena. For example, in interviewing people on social prejudice, an unstructured interview may elucidate the extent of prejudice shown and the subtle ways which transmit such prejudices within a given culture.

The unstructured interview is also helpful when it is necessary to probe into the answers. This may apply particularly to search in the area of attitudes, stereotypes, and prejudice. Similarly, investigations in the area of clinical behaviour in the culture may require in-depth interviews; unstructured interviews, therefore, may be the preferred alternative.

The unstructured interview may also be helpful in some cultural settings, especially in cultures where the norms prevent authentic replies to structured questions. For example, in some cultures, people hesitate to express their opinions in a direct way. In such cases, structured interviews may fail to get authentic answers. An unstructured interview may allow the interviewer flexibility in establishing a relationship of trust with the respondent so that he can explore ways of eliciting authentic replies.

While the unstructured interview has many advantages, it also has its limitations. For large scale investigations involving many interviewers, the unstructured interview may not be helpful since interviewer biases may influence the results. Generalizations based on such responses may, therefore, not be valid. The structured interview has this main advantage:

it can be used for a large sample and for purposes of comparative studies. Data collected through unstructured interviews are often not conducive to quantitative analysis. Both kinds of interviews have a role and can be meaningfully used to supplement one another.

The effectiveness of the structured interview may increase if the interviewer is trained to use his discretion and, in exceptional cases, to ask questions which exceed the limits set by the structured questionnaire. An open ended interview in which the information is not collected strictly according to a fixed order, has been found to increase the information-processing competence of the interview (Johns, 1975). By building on these advantages of the unstructured interview, the structured interview may become more effective.

Structured and unstructured interviews are helpful for various purposes. Table 4–1 lists various purposes for which either or both types of interviews are useful.

The most frequently used method is the structured interview. A structured interview is typically conducted according to a schedule. The amount of structure in the schedule might vary from an open ended projective question to a set of questions with items that have been carefully scaled (Edwards, 1957).

Structured interviews impose certain requirements on the interviewers. In view of the importance of structured interviews in cross-cultural research, some of the procedural requirements for such interviews are outlined below.

The Interviewing Process

Self-Disclosure in Interview

The main purpose of the interview is to collect reliable, valid and authentic data. The interview technique may vary according to the needs of the research. However, one important aspect to be considered is the self-disclosure by the respondent. Self-disclosure may be higher in situations ensuring the confidentiality of the information given. Wilson and Rosen (1975) found more self-disclosure by army personnel to a civilian particularly under conditions of anonymity. Research reported so far does not suggest any influence of the respondent's personality on his self-disclosure, e.g., extraversion-introversion (Becker & Munz, 1975), or interpersonal trust (McAllister & Kiesler, 1975) did not show any effects. The greatest influence on self-disclosure seems to be derived from the interviewer; specifically, interviewer personality. Weight (1974) found interviewers with higher internal locus of control generally more effective than externals in eliciting positive self-reference, and they were significantly

Table 4-1.   Usefulness of Structured and Unstructured Interviews for Various Purposes.

Purpose	Type of Interview
1. Generalization	Structured
2. Cross-cultural comparison	Structured
3. Intracultural comparison	Structured
4. Intensive study	Both
5. Action planning	Both
6. Theory testing	Both
7. Supplementing other instruments	Both
8. Programme impact	Both
9. Choose the appropriate sample	Unstructured
10. Pretesting	Unstructured

more confident about the quality of their relationship with the respondents.

In general, it seems that self-disclosure on the part of the interviewer elicits disclosure by the respondent. Nasanchuk (1973) found that interviewers using a mutual disclosure technique (where both the interviewer and respondent ask and answer questions) elicited significantly higher levels of self-disclosure from respondents than the interviewers using direct questioning. In another study, Turoezi (1973) found that a disclosing interviewer elicited significantly more disclosures from the respondents than did a nondisclosing interviewer. Davis and Sloan (1974) found that respondent disclosure was strongly facilitated by disclosure on the part of the interviewer, and was sustained at a high level only if the interviewer continued to disclose. Mann and Murphy (1975) similarly found that disclosure by the interviewer initiates reciprocity of disclosure and creates more positive reactions to the interview. However, they did not find any differences in two types of interviewer self-disclosure [prior to the interview (modeling) or after the interview (reinforcement)]. McGuire, Thelen, and Amolsch (1975) used video taped instructions for the interview in which modeling of self-disclosure was used, and they found that the respondent's disclosure increased as a function of the length of modeling. These various studies suggest the need to pay attention to the interviewer's introduction of the subject of interview, in which modeling of self-disclosure can be built. It seems that self-disclosure on the part of the interviewer establishes more effective rapport with the respondent.

Rapport Building

It is important that the interviewer establish rapport with the respondent in the beginning of the interview. The preliminary questions in the interview schedule, therefore, should establish such a rapport. The preliminary part of the interview may also emphasize the importance of the subject under study and the importance of the role of the respondent. In this way, the respondent may feel that, by answering questions, he is contributing to a significant research project. This may help to establish the authenticity of the data. It is equally important for the interviewer to listen to the respondents.

Some respondents are very vocal and eager, and insist on talking about several things in response to a single question. Such cathartic responses may provide authentic data and some insights. However, they are likely to distract, to take the discussion away from the main topic, and thus prolong the interview. The interviewer has to deal with them skillfully. When scales are used, it is better to check back with the respondent rather than to record the cathartic response.

The experienced interviewer often learns how to avoid the monotony of interviewing. He learns, for instance, to skip certain questions and to change the sequencing of questions by judging the answers which are being given. The interview should not be mechanical; the pattern established in the schedule need not be followed rigidly. The schedule is important and all the answers should be recorded. However, the sequencing can be changed; the main purpose of the interview should be to code genuine responses and to help the respondent express his frank opinions.

A common problem in rural cultures is the cathartic phenomenon mentioned above. Sometimes the interviewer may be overwhelmed with responses, and he or she may not know how to handle them. Some interviewers infer responses from such cathartic talk and fill in the schedule. While this may work well with unstructured interviews, such inferences are misleading unless the interviewers are certain about the authenticity of the respondents' messages.

Some rural respondents assume a very casual attitude and leave it to the interviewer to fill in the schedule. After a cathartic discussion the respondents have the tendency to make statements such as "I have already told you in the beginning, I agree with the statement." If the interviewer asks: "To what extent?", the respondent might reply "To any extent," or "To what extent I don't know; you write whatever you think is proper." They may thus inveigle the interviewer into distorting the interpretation of their responses.

The interviewer should also be sensitive to topics on which the respondent may not like further probing. Kaplan, Firestone, Degnore, and Moore (1974) found that interviewer attractiveness decreased with the intimacy of questions.

Back and Stycos (1959) have suggested several techniques for building rapport: expanding on the project's purpose, catharsis, encouraging identification, praise and flattery, and so on.

Preparation of the Schedule

In preparing the interview schedule the size of the schedule, the language abilities of the respondent, and the nature of the problem under investigation have to be carefully considered. Based on the experience of interviewers in the field, an optimum duration of the interview should be worked out. Usually interviews should not exceed ninety minutes. Longer interviews are likely to create boredom in both the respondents and the interviewers, and thus affect responses and their interpretation. The size of the schedule should be kept as short as possible. Sometimes it may be necessary to include questions that are not used in the final analysis but for the purposes of establishing rapport, to provide logical continuity to other questions, to maintain the interest of the interviewee and to terminate the interview in a mutually satisfying way. Such questions, however, tend to prolong the interview unduly and should be included only after careful weighing of the purpose they serve vis-à-vis the time they consume.

Sequencing

Another aspect of the interview that requires careful attention, is the sequencing of questions. The advantages of privacy, which are available to the respondent in a questionnaire (mailed, or otherwise), are not available to him in a face-to-face, structured interview. Eliciting reliable responses on matters of privacy and of taboos requires extra skill and effort on the part of the interviewer. Ensuring cooperation, helping the respondent to overcome inhibitions, and to give reliable responses places extra responsibility on the interviewer, a responsibility that the usual field investigator does not have.

One important aspect of interview management is the sequencing of the questions. Questions which are likely to pose some threat to the respondent, or those which are likely to be considered suspect, should not be asked at the beginning of the interview. Even questions relating to the socioeconomic status of the individual, or information about personality are likely to be threatening to certain respondents; such questions should be asked at the end of the interview rather than at the beginning. Sensitive questions should be postponed and asked only after rapport has been established. For example, in cultures where talking about death is taboo, information about the dead, etc. should be asked only at the end of the interview. Sequencing also requires some other considerations, such as logically linking questions. Clancy (1971) discussed several problems of sequencing questions, as well as positional effects, and problems of fatigue. Campbell and Joiner (1973) have suggested some techniques to take care of the social desirability of responses.

Question and Response Structure

Structuring the questions also requires attention. The interview schedule should be prepared in stages. In the first stage, the schedule can be tentatively prepared on the basis of the interviewer's knowledge and experience. However, this should be pretested in the field, and responses from some of the respondents should be analysed to see if the questions in the interview schedule require change. When sensitive topics are to be discussed it may be useful for the interviewer in the pretesting phase to ask the respondents whether these questions cause embarrassment, whether the respondent finds it difficult to answer these questions honestly, whether the questions are too complicated, vague, etc. This kind of pretesting may help modify the questions. Sometimes it may be useful for the interviewer to listen to responses that have already been collected in the field. Tape recorded responses can be analysed and may also modify the interviewing patterns. Kahn and Cannell (1957) have given examples of some medical practitioners who, after listening to the taped interviews they have conducted, were amazed at the ineptness of their questions. The interviewer may sometimes be surprised to discover the unintended consequences of some questions.

Pretesting may also involve obtaining information which concerns the length of the interview, the sequencing of questions, the reaction of the respondents, and the way rapport is established with the respondents.

The structured interview has certain advantages: the various responses can be precoded; the respondents answer the same questions. This helps to quantify the data and to ensure the uniformity of data collection. In order to precode the answers, it is useful to do some field work and to explore the possible response categories for each question. On the basis of a preliminary interview, various categories for precoding answers can be developed. Categories developed on the basis of field work, rather than on desk work alone, make the interviewing process easier and reduce certain methodological problems. An unstructured interview may be used for developing coding categories, and these categories can subsequently be tested in the field. Precoding, of course, will have to be done according to the requirements of data analysis.

Scaling

An interview can use certain structured techniques, such as scaling. For this purpose, the various scales to be included should first be standardized. For example, the methods of pair comparison, or successive intervals scaling (Edwards, 1957), or the semantic differential may be used in the interview schedule. In fact, most of the scales which are commonly used for collecting data can be incorporated in the interview schedule. However, the use of scaling methods as aids in cross-cultural interviews requires separate scaling in each culture to ensure the respondent's comparable understanding of the distance between the choices in a question. For example, when one uses a five-point scale or a Semantic Differential, it is necessary to ensure that the respondents have comparable understandings of the scale distances in each culture. If such an understanding is not shared, cross-cultural comparisons cannot be made. An example of using different scaling techniques in cross-cultural interviews can be found in Pareek and Rao (1974b).

Data from Interviews

The construction of an interview schedule should be accompanied by a response coding sheet. Construction of the coding sheet helps to clarify the methodology for framing the questions, and to facilitate the analysis at later stages. Frequencies and scale scores will be two types of data. The response coding sheet should provide space for the total scale scores. The data obtained from interviews may be classified under different categories.

Coding Responses

Some doubt that interviewers can code the data effectively while interviewing. However, Bauman and Chase (1974) have found interviewer coding as efficient as office coding. Cantril's (1966) self-anchoring technique is a good example of systematic coding of open-ended interview data. This technique measures hopes, fears, and the respondent's level of aspiration.

A higher order of coding might fulfil the requirements of ordinal scale measurement. In designing the response coding sheets, the possibility of the direct transfer of data from the response sheets to computer cards might be kept in mind. This may help save time. If the scales are not cross-culturally comparable, different coding systems may have to be developed for each culture. Even in cases where they are comparable in item content, the scaling may be different. These points have to be kept in mind while coding. Lee Pui-Leung (1969) has discussed in detail the use of correlational and multivariate statistics for survey research. After an examination of various statistical methods like multiple R, canonical and nonparametric tests, factor analytic techniques, etc., Lee Pui-Leung (1969) finds a contingency table approach to be the most appropriate for survey research. He points out the danger of using strong models with weak data and stresses the need for using statistical models where the assumption can be maximally approximated.

It is advisable to code the data on the response code sheets as soon as the questions are answered. With training and practice, the interviewer can learn to code simultaneously with the interview. Postinterview coding can lead to biases because of incorrect recall of the responses. If coding on a separate sheet creates problems, coding could be done on the schedule itself, or the schedule could be designed to eliminate this problem. Coding on the spot also ensures a correct understanding of what the respondent truly means. For more details on coding procedure see Holsti (1968).

Reliability, Validity, and Authenticity

The schedule of a structured interview needs to be tested for its reliability, validity, and accuracy or authenticity. Well-known methods are available for establishing reliability (both internal consistency and test-retest reliability) and validity. Stebbins (1972) discusses the issues of objectivity and rapport in an interview setting. He points out that, unless the interviewer and the respondent are sufficiently in rapport to permit further interaction, a true interview does not take place. However, once interaction in the interview setting begins, a number of interpersonal relationship-generating mechanisms become apparent. Pernanen (1974) suggests the use of an unobtrusive measure like yearly rate of alcohol as a validity criterion for alcohol comsumption. Stebbins (1972) concluded that validity in this type of interview is increased not by pursuing objectivity, but by pursuing subjectivity.

Oscar (1970a) examined, by means of a reinterview (interviewing a second time) technique, the reliability of responses that were obtained through the use of a structured interview schedule. He studied a depressed population, for which the formal survey is sometimes held to be inappropriate. Marginal distributions for groups of subjects proved to be highly reliable, but individual responses were apparently random. For individual data, open questions were more reliable than closed questions, and there was a decline in reliability proportionate to the length of the interview. Boruch and Creager (1972) suggest it is desirable to assess the stability of item response over time as an index of reliability.

A new concept of accuracy or authenticity is important in connection with structured interviews. One of the problems of structured interviews is that it is difficult to know whether the responses to the various questions are genuine or biased. Neither validity nor reliability guarantee authenticity. While validity is an internal property of the instrument reflecting whether the instrument really measures what it is supposed to measure, authenticity depends on various factors other than the research instrument. It is the total capability to get unbiased and genuine responses from the respondent. It is necessary to test the authenticity of the responses. This can be done in the pretest. After the preparation of the interview schedule, the respondents can be asked to indicate the extent to which they were able to give frank and authentic answers and the extent to which their genuine answers were inhibited. The schedule can be improved, if the factors which inhibit answers are noted.

Even when the same standardized interview schedule is used, in different cultures it is important to establish authenticity of the responses in each culture. Cultural factors which influence authenticity may differ.

Besides cultural factors, various other factors contribute to the lack of authenticity of an interview schedule. Care taken to control these factors will improve the quality of the interview schedule. Specifically, factors that have been found to influence the authenticity of responses can be grouped under four categories (Brislin et al., 1973): interviewer-related, interview-related, respondent-related, and cultural factors. These are presented in Table 4-2.

Interviewer-Related Factors

Several factors related to the interviewer may influence the responses. Some of these are as follows:

1. Interviewer affiliation: The organization with which the interviewer is affiliated may create bias. If the interviewer is seen as coming from a highly prestigious organisation, well known for its quality of work and for the genuine help it provides, the respondent is likely to take the interview

Table 4-2.   Factors Affecting Interview Authenticity.

A. *Interviewer Background*
  1. Interviewer affiliation
  2. Interviewer image
  3. Respondent-interviewer distance
  4. Respondent relevance
  5. Interviewer bias

B. *Interview and its setting*
  1. Setting
  2. Thematic relevance
  3. Thematic sensitivity
  4. Cultural relevance
  5. Social desirability
  6. Capacity to reach depth
  7. Length
  8. Structure

C. *Respondent Background*
  1. Private-public opinion gap
  2. Omniscience syndrome
  3. Previous experience
  4. Saturation
  5. Response set

D. *Cultural Background*
  1. Courtesy norm
  2. Reticence
  3. Game playing norm

more seriously, and his answers may be more authentic than if the interviewer is affiliated with less desirable organisations. If the interviewer is seen as coming from a suspicious or unknown organisation, the attitude of the respondent may be very negative. In a multicultural study, the responses might be noncomparable if the sponsoring agency is perceived noncomparably in different countries.

Atkin and Chaffe (1972) have studied the influence of the interviewer affiliation on the respondent's orientation. When certain respondents were informed that the interviewer was a member of the fire-fighters' union, the respondents expressed disapproval of fire-fighters' strikes. However, they attempted to ingratiate themselves with the interviewer by giving favourable opinions of fire-fighters in general. In the second study, parents were prone to give extreme responses to a question about possible governmental control of violence on TV. This occurred when they thought that the interviewer represented a governmental body which might exercise such a control on the media. However, survey sponsorship is not always important (Fhaner & Hane, 1974).

2. *Interviewer image:*   The image the respondent has of the interviewer influences his responses. Brislin et al. (1973) have used the word *rudeness* to indicate the perception of the interviewer as an interrupter of the respondent's activities. If the interviewer is seen negatively, as a spy, an interrupter, or as an undesirable government agent, the attitude of the respondent is likely to be negative (Bonilla, 1964). The interviewer needs to create a favourable image by establishing rapport with the respondents by means of a proper introduction of the subject and by clarifying the relevance of the research. Jahoda (1968) and Stycos (1960) have reported some strategies for dealing with this problem.

3. *Respondent-interviewer distance:*   From his study on interviewer effects on responses in a less developed country, Oscar (1970a) concludes that the higher the trust between the interviewer and the respondent, the higher the reliability, and presumably the authenticity of the response; this is the case whether the trust is based on racial origin or group membership. In his study, response consistency increased with time when the interviewers were similar to the respondents. Interviewers may have a different background from the respondents in terms of sex, race, socioeconomic status, rural-urban background. Brislin et al. (1973) mention *status difference bias* and *racial difference bias*. If the respondents are sensitive to a particular aspect of the interviewer's background, care should be taken to select interviewers who will not cause problems. For example, in some countries, in interviewing women on matters of sex and family planning it is necessary to use women interviewers; otherwise, the respondents may refuse to be interviewed.

Schuman and Converse (1971) examined recent evidence on racial effects in interviewing on both racial and nonracial topics. They examined such effects by age, education, and several other background variables. They also provided some evidence on which responses are distorted: those given to white or to black interviewers. Questions dealing with militant protest and hostility to whites showed the greatest sensitivity to interviewer effects. Reports of racial discrimination, poor living conditions, and personal background showed little interviewer influence. This brings out clearly the fact that the interviewer effects vary according to the topics of investigation. Using four Vietnamese interviewers posing as South Vietnamese, Thai, or Japanese, Chau and Sager (1975) found that interviewer's nationality can influence the responses, but the influence was not predictable.

Rangonetti (1970) investigated the effects of the interviewer's sex on responses given to controversial questions. A sample of Cornell male freshmen was asked a controversial question concerning patterns of sexual intercourse. This question was posed in three different survey situations: a group administered questionnaire, a male interviewer, and a female interviewer. Though other noncontroversial items employed in the study showed no significant differences by survey techniques, the personal interview revealed significantly higher estimates of patterns of sexual intercourse than the group administered questionnaire. There were no significant effects attributable to the sex of the interviewer.

In another study, on premarital intercourse (Zehner, 1970), answers of male respondents were unaffected by the sex of the interviewer; but female respondents, when being interviewed by another female, were significantly more inhibited. A further analysis of the results from an earlier study indicated that young adults became inhibited on sex matters when interviewed by the opposite sex. In this study, explicit reference to sexual behavior in the same sex interview situations appeared most conducive to eliciting the most "moral" and inhibited responses from female respondents. The absence of a parallel effect among men is attributed to the lack of similar "moral" expectations about mens' behavior by society.

Mendras (1969) has outlined the difficulties posed in survey interviews by the differences in background between interviewers from the city and rural samples. Mendras suggests methods for establishing contact and for interviewing rural samples. In England Giles and Chavasse (1975) found that the dress of the interviewer more than the interviewer's status affected the information provided by the respondent.

4. *Respondent relevance:* Unless the interviewer is able to make the respondent feel that he is important and that his opinions are valuable to the interviewer, the responses may lack authenticity. If the interviewer assumes that the respondent is disinterested and his responses are irrele-

vant, this attitude can be communicated through various nonverbal cues, and may influence the respondent's replies.

Often respondents may not be aware of the meaning of research and its implications. Fein (1971) suggests that the interviewer should be concerned that the respondent may not understand that his or her answers are going to be used for research purposes only, and thus be unwilling to discuss intimate issues. Sufficient explanation of how the information is to be used can overcome this difficulty.

5. *Interviewer bias:*   Inadequately trained interviewers may communicate their own opinions to the respondent during the interview, thus influencing the responses. In some survey interviews in India, interviewers who had negative attitudes toward family planning extracted more anticontraception material from the respondents than actually existed. The problem of interviewer bias has been explored by several researchers (Bonilla, 1964; Jahoda, 1968; Stycos, 1960; Converse, 1964; Cannell & Kahn, 1968; Mitchell, 1968; Keesing & Keesing, 1956; Frey, 1970; Weiner, 1964; Edwards, 1957; Gordon, 1968; Werner & Campbell, 1970).

Interview and Its Setting

Several variables in relation to the interview are important. Some of these are discussed below:

1. *The setting:*   The place where the interview is conducted is important. If the interview is conducted in a public place, the responses are likely to be affected. On the other hand, in a private setting a professional aura may overwhelm the respondent.

Lutynska's study (1970) of sociological interviews describes four categories of settings: (1) respondent's private residence, (2) respondent's place of work, (3) café, restaurant, or similar public place, and (4) park, street, garden, yard, village green, etc. The first two are usually well known to the respondent but unknown to the interviewer; the third and the fourth may be considered "neutral" since they are usually known or unknown to both interviewer and respondents. In a study of 3,568 interviews conducted mostly in private homes (78 percent), the place of work (17 percent), or public settings, the influence of the place of work on the interviewers and that of the place of the interview on the respondents' replies was explored. Some bias could be traced to the impressions which the interviewer received from a respondent's home. The respondents' replies also varied, depending upon the locale of the interview. The respondent's role may reflect the locale of the interview. For example, in the home, the role of father or head of the family may be salient, while at work, the role of employee may be most salient. The people's behavior varied according to their roles while replying to the interviewer, as well as the subject matter. But the most unbiased replies were found in the home and at the place of work.

The presence of other people very often constitutes an important factor in the interview situation. In some cultures, but not in other cultures, the presence of a third person may be a distracting factor. Mitchell (1973) estimates that in developed countries about 50 percent of the interviews are conducted in the presence of third parties, whereas in many areas of the developing countries almost all interviews are conducted in the presence of others. Lutynska (1969) has observed that the presence of a third person in interviews is almost unavoidable in Poland because of social, cultural, and housing conditions. Since third parties can influence the interview outcome, the percentage of interviews which take place in the presence of a third person should be reported in all investigations. In investigations carried out among the intelligentsia in the city of Lodz, the percentage amounted to 27.4, while in the case of a population sample studied in a small town the percentage reached over 60 percent. The mean number of third persons participating in the interviews was 1.6. The respondents were most frequently in the presence of members of their family (spouse or children). In small towns, neighbours, acquaintances or friends took an active part in the conversation. The respondent's social milieu, his occupation, education, and his dwelling place determine the extent of third person participation. It was also found that the third persons most frequently took part in the conversation when the questions concerned social and family topics. The analysis shows that in general, the influence of third persons on the respondent's answers was not significant.

Results of interviews with Arab rural samples, during which an American professor was present, showed that the presence of an outsider did not lead to bias (Sutcliffe, 1974). However, Podmore, Chaney, and Golder (1975) found that in Hong Kong, the presence of parents significantly affected the responses of teenagers to two of eleven questions. Back and Stycos (1959), based on their experience in cross-cultural research, have suggested several methods that may be employed by interviewers in dealing with the "others" intruding during the interview sessions: diverting and sidetracking the "outsider" (especially children), freezing the outsider (making the atmosphere cold and unresponsive for him), satisfying the outsiders' curiosity, role-educating the outsider (frankly discussing with them the bias effect of their presence), and getting the respondents to expel the outsider. Another way to overcome this problem is to use teams of interviewers, who "saturate the village" (Mitchell, 1973). A long stay of such interviewers in the local community may help to reduce curiosity.

2. *Thematic relevance:*   If the interview is seen as relevant to a respondent's interests, the responses are likely to be authentic. However, if the topic is

seen as irrelevant to the respondents' problems, they may not take much interest in the interview. Therefore, it may be necessary to emphasize the relevance of the interview through initial rapport-building exchanges.

Interview schedules have to be equivalent. However, if the variables of an investigation are etic, they can be operationalised with quite different emic items. If the same schedules are used, translation of the schedules into several languages may be necessary. Translation itself poses methodological problems (see Chapter 10 in this volume by Brislin). Hymes (1970) suggests that social scientists should do linguistic pretests before interviewing. Besides translation reliabilities, inter-interviewer reliability needs to be established.

3. Thematic sensitivity: In certain cultures some questions are highly sensitive or taboo and they are likely to embarrass the respondents. For example, in some cultures, responses to questions about sexual behavior are likely to embarrass the respondents and the answers may not be authentic. Similarly, in other cultures, answers to questions on political attitudes may not be authentic, if the respondents fear that their answers are likely to cause problems for them.

4. Cultural relevance: The interviewer should take into account the special cultural characteristics, traditions, customs, and norms of the group he is investigating. The language used in the interview should reflect the interviewer's acquaintance with cultural norms. In many cases, word usage makes a pronounced difference in creating the proper climate for communication. This is particularly important in sensitive areas, such as sex. Knowledge of local terms used for sex organs, copulation, menstruation, etc., can help make the interview culture-relevant.

5. Social desirability: Respondents tend to prefer to give socially desirable answers; there is also a tendency among respondents to disagree with socially undesirable answers, in which case the responses may not be authentic (Weiss, 1975). It may be useful to match questions on social desirability, although it may be difficult to establish social desirability norms (Orwick, 1972).

6. Capacity to reach depth: The questions that elicit answers only at a superficial level may not do justice to topics that require depth. In some cases, the interview schedule has to be carefully examined to see if a sufficient number of "depth questions" has been included.

7. Length: The length of the interview schedule can affect authenticity. If an interview in a single sitting goes beyond ninety minutes, fatigue may result in less authentic responses.

8. Structure: As mentioned above, the way the interview schedules is prepared and the sequencing of the items can influence authenticity.

Respondent-Related Factors

1. *Private-public opinion gap:*   One major problem with authenticity is the gap between the expressed and private opinions of the respondent. Slomezynski (1969) has examined two issues: (1) to what extent answers given to the interviewer are consistent with the respondent's everyday life statement on the same subject, and (2) to what degree the answers are consistent with the respondent's actual convictions at the time of the interview. Respondents consisted of a group of forty people who had secondary education and held managerial or independent posts or were members of learned professions. The first interview consisted of a structured questionnaire administered by a trained interviewer. Several days later, Slomezynski, who knew the respondents, had a private talk with each one. The aim of these private talks was to discover private opinions on the very same problems which were the subject of the questionnaire and also to collect information on the respondent's sincere evaluation of the statements he made during the official interview. The investigation confirmed the hypothesis that the opinions disclosed in the interview were more consistent with the official line of state policy than the opinions expressed by the respondents who spoke privately as members of small, informal social groups. Distortions resulted as a rule in inconsistencies with private opinions. This was caused partly by a sense of uncertainty about the use that would be made of the information elicited during the interview.

2. *Omniscience syndrome:*   Some respondents tend to believe that they can answer any question. Brislin et al. (1973) have referred to this bias. Unless the interviewer is sensitive to this bias, he may get answers which are not authentic.

3. *Previous experience:*   The previous experience of the respondent with interviews may influence his attitude towards the interview. In one survey Roloff and Mathias (1971) interviewed in depth twenty-six respondents who had refused a previous interview. They found that the first contact with the interviewer (written or oral) was decisive. None of the respondents who had participated long enough to hear the first question refused to continue the interview.

4. *Saturation:*   Members of communities in which too many investigations have taken place are likely to become so accustomed to being interviewed that they may answer questions in a superficial, routine way. In

some cases, communities located near a metropolitan area may be subject to overstudy simply because of their accessibility. People in those communities may become saturated with such frequent visits. Before deciding on the sampling design it is desirable to ascertain whether such saturation has occurred in particular areas.

5. *Response sets:*   Kolson and Green (1970) have pointed out a number of response-set biases—the tendency to gamble, extreme checking style, and acquiescence response set. Political socialization research has revealed that American children, almost universally, evaluate nearly all political constructs in highly positive terms. A study designed to test the effect of response sets upon the validity of children's response to fixed-alternative survey questions revealed that, when uncertain about the content of the item, children are likely to gamble, agree with a question no matter what the topic or give a positive evaluation of any concept. This tendency on the part of children to express positive attitudes toward unfamiliar political objects makes fixed-alternative questions invalid. Since lack of some cognitive skills is associated with childhood, researchers are cautioned to scrutinize the cognitive requirements of questionnaire items.

Cultural Factors

Cultural factors are very important in ensuring authenticity in the interview. If people in a culture have not been exposed to interviews, their responses may not be authentic if the usual interview technique is used. In such cases, good anthropological observations should supplement the interviews.

Katriak (1971) notes the role of culture on the effectiveness of survey research. Among significant factors operating in the interview situation are a sample's degree of acquaintance with sociological research and its social function. The validity of findings obtained in interviews cannot be mechanically transferred from one sociocultural area to another. For example, an analysis of a Slovak sample revealed that a great majority had a positive attitude toward sociological research and considered it to be socially significant.

Subcultural differences may exist in a given country, and different groups might have varying orientations requiring different approaches to interviewing. It is necessary for the interviewer to be sensitive to such differences. Gostkowski (1970) found several such problems in interviewing different categories of social groups in Poland. In his study, student interviewers who used a "personal favour approach" were found to be the most successful. Problems of interviewing special groups of respondents have been discussed by Pelka Slugocka (1969) and Gostkowski (1970).

1. *Courtesy norm:* In some cultures the respondents tend to give answers which they think could please or satisfy the interviewer. If the interview is not seen as particularly relevant to their own lives and problems, people in conforming cultures are likely to be influenced by this norm. It has been the experience of the authors of this chapter that in rural India the courtesy bias can be reduced if the interviewer's dress and appearance is similar to that of villagers. Sometimes the distance is further decreased by accepting their hospitality (tea, bidi) rather than refusing it when the respondents keep insisting.

2. *Reticence:* In some cultures, such as the Japanese or the Chinese residing in Malaysia, people do not talk much (Brislin et al., 1973) or are slow to give responses. This may result in unauthentic responses. Weiner (1964) suggests ways of dealing with this problem. These include opening the conversation in the vernacular, using abbreviations and nicknames. Insight and spontaneity of the interviewer are important in this respect (Mitchell, 1968). In some cultures people are constrained by their inability to articulate their own impressions, feelings, and actions. For example, Doob (1961) points out such difficulties with Africans, who were perfectly willing to provide information but were simply unable to express themselves due to their lack of experience with the interview situation. The interviewer needs to be sensitive to such problems.

3. *Game playing norm:* In some cultures, people may enjoy playing games with the strangers by giving unauthentic answers, and enjoy leading the stranger astray. Brislin et al. (1973) call it the "sucker bias." If local people are employed as interviewers, this factor can be controlled, to some extent. In some cultures the norm is to lie to a stranger. In India such game playing is common when the sex of the interviewer is different or when he is perceived as threatening (e.g., representing the income tax department).

Coder Reliability

Interviews have the special problem of coding the responses, which raises the question of coder reliability.

Crittenden and Hill (1971) point out that while there is considerable literature devoted to the process of coding interview data, the empirical investigation of coding errors has been limited. They report a study of the performance of ninety-seven coders employed to code responses to twenty-two interview items. Measures of intercoder reliability and validity were developed. Data from McGee (1971) were used. The item intercoder reliability levels found were ominously low. While a minimum acceptable level of .90 for intercoder reliability was specified, only nine of the twenty-two items qualified as reliable. These low levels of reliability suggest that certain coding tasks may be characterised by an unacceptably high degree of measurement error. When the coding task involves both a search procedure and an evaluative judgment, measurement error is particularly pronounced. The findings suggest that coding requires special investigation to reduce such errors. In general, guidelines must be developed for coding and special reliability checks made in each culture.

The Respondents

The respondent is an important partner in the interview process. It may be useful for the interviewer to check whether the respondent understands the terms he is using. One frequent problem concerns technical terms which the interviewer may need to use in the interview.

Another important consideration is the sampling of the interviewees (see Berry's Introduction). Still another problem is that some respondents are more frank than others. In one field situation, for instance, one of the authors realised that some members of a particular family were more frank than other members. Interviewers should be informed of such biases and interview persons who are most likely to give genuine responses. However, interviewers should be careful not to select respondents in ways causing sampling biases.

Another context in which proper understanding of the respondent becomes important concerns his perceptions of the interviewer. Respondent reactions to interviewers are often similar to their reactions to strangers. As explained elsewhere in this chapter, such reactions can bias the responses. Interviewers need to be sensitive to this problem.

In some cultures and indeed even within the same culture in some groups, strangers are mistrusted. For example, small businessmen tend to regard a stranger, who comes for nonbusiness purposes, as a tax officer, or a government agent. Similarly, foreign interviewers might be perceived as secret agents. Often, foreign sponsored projects may arouse suspicion. Such stereotypes in a given culture need to be studied before any research is undertaken.

Respondent Resistance

Interviews in some cases may raise particular expectations among the respondents. For example, surveys done in some parts of India, in industrial settings, elicit particular expectations. Certain questions, such as: "What do you think of working conditions here?" "How satisfied are you with your job?" may lead some respondents to ask "Are you going to suggest to the management to increase our salaries?" "Are you a government man, sent to control private management?" "Are you a management man sent to identify disloyal workers?" It is obvious that such suspicions may lead to resistance to the interview.

In some cases, mass resistance to surveys and interviews may occur. Josephson (1970) discussed the problem of public resistance to survey research. A large scale survey of adolescent health in Harlem in 1967, sponsored by Columbia University, elicited considerable protest and included a demonstration with signs "We need hospitals not surveys." The survey was linked by militant blacks to a number of other activities in which Columbia University was engaged. After the protests it was decided to alter the objectives and procedure of the study, but to continue with it. Specifically, almost all items dealing with deviant behaviour were omitted. In addition, an ad hoc advisory committee was formed to facilitate community participation in the project. With these modifications, about 700 interviews with adolescents (twelve to seventeen years of age) were completed (completion rate 80 percent). Cooperation in the medical examination phase of the project was equally high. The area of drug use among Harlem adolescents was not investigated, though this was a major health problem which created wide concern. This was part of the cost of continuing the project. Several lessons can be drawn from the protest against this project. Prospective interviewers must be more carefully screened as they may initiate controversies or may bring them to the surface. More care should be taken about the content of the interview. Researchers should obtain a greater degree of community participation in planning their project. Resistance to surveys is not necessarily unhealthy. Community residents may view research as a mechanism of control and exploitation, particularly regarding studies of "deviant" behaviour. Questions are raised regarding the real importance of survey research in relation to the needs of the community studied. Survey researchers' usefulness to communities and study populations is still uncertain and they must codify their relationships with informants. A code of ethics, similar to the codes of physicians or lawyers, needs to be developed.

The Interviewer

The interviewer is certainly of critical importance in the interview. The sex of the interviewer may be a crucial factor. In some cultures, men and women may like to be interviewed only by members of their own sex. In a study conducted at the Planning Research and Action Institute, Lucknow, India, the sex of the interviewer (who was a social worker) was found to be critical in eliciting cooperation and responses related to family planning.

Hyman (1975) has reviewed recent studies to show that bias introduced by the interviewer is so small as to be practically negligible. Nevertheless, it is necessary to ensure that the interviewer is able to understand the reactive nature of the interview so that he may be careful in not influencing respondent behaviour. Krant and John (1973) have reported, on the basis of an interview of 104 respondents of Italian descent, that the process of interviewing in a survey did increase the probability of the respondents' voting in an election.

Interviewer Personality

The personality of the interviewer is also an important factor. Richardson et al. (1965) have reported that the most competent and experienced field workers held stronger value judgments, as reflected in the TAT. They state: "the effective interviewer enjoys people, seeks friendly relations with them, and has insight in the complex of relationships among widely varying types of people. He is a persistent evaluator and judge of himself and others, and he possesses considerable latent hostility" (Richardson et al., 1965, p. 356). Weight (1974) found internal locus of control correlated with the effectiveness of interviewers. These findings and suggestions are based mainly on studies done in the USA. Similar studies are needed in other cultures.

The interviewer's education, appearance, and style are also important factors. Unless the interviewer is well acquainted with the various topics of the interview, he is not likely to be effective. For example, interviewers working in rural parts of India encounter questions from respondents who are seeking guidance on various issues. Respondents are often eager to share their problems and perceive the educated interviewer as a source of help. This is specially so because many people identify an educated man as a specialist in everything. If the interviewer cannot be helpful in giving information and guidance, the authenticity of the responses may be affected. It may also be embarrassing for the interviewer, since he is encroaching upon the respondent's time without being able to give something in return.

The commitment of the interviewer is another crucial factor. In several field studies done in India, it was found that when the interviewer lacks commitment, he is likely to communicate this to his respondents and may not succeed in getting authentic answers. The interviewer should also be trained to be patient and not get annoyed with answers which do not coincide with his expectations.

The dress, mannerisms, and language of the interviewer are likely to have an effect on the responses. For instance, if he appears like an officer with a suit, necktie, and long side burns, he might create a distance between himself and a villager. In general, people tend to disclose personal matters when they confide in strangers. However, in cultures where strangers are not trusted, local investigators should be identified and trained. A significant problem that often arises in cross-cultural research is the working condition of the interviewers. When trained and well-educated interviewers have to be hired for interviewing rural respondents, many organisational issues arise. Generally, trained interviewers are available in urban areas, and they do not like to stay for long periods in rural areas. It is important to sustain their interest in rural people and provide them with proper working conditions.

Selection of Interviewers

The following are some guidelines to be kept in mind in selecting interviewers.

1. Interviewers should be selected from different cultures so as to minimize interviewer biasing of the interview process. For example when much subcultural variation is anticipated in a culture under study, interviewers who can be effective in all of these or in each subculture separately, should be selected.
2. When interviewer effects on data cannot be controlled, the dimensions which are likely to be affected should be studied.
3. As far as possible the interviewers selected and respondents should have similar backgrounds.
4. When interviewers and respondents of known dissimilar backgrounds are used it is desirable to study the effect of this variable on responses.

Cultural familiarity: Familiarity with the cultural aspects of a community is necessary. In addition, the interviewer must know the cultural norms of the people to be interviewed and establish acceptable channels of communication. It may be advisable for the principal investigator to live in the culture/community under study before hiring interviewers (Weiner, 1964).

Specific qualification: Although it is difficult to specify any general rules in terms of the specific background qualifications of people who would be good interviewers, some evidence is available. Girard (1963) and Hanna and Hanna (1966) have suggested that interviewers should be from the same groups (status, race, etc.) as the respondents. Much depends upon the nature of the phenomena under investigation, the culture being investigated, and the depth of insight required.

Armstrong (undated) and Frey (1970) have offered a few selection guidelines on the basis of their experience in India and Turkey.

1. Middle class and middle aged married women constitute a good group of potential interviewers.

2. Underemployed white collar workers, from the middle class and about thirty to forty-five years of age, tend to inject their own biases into an interview.

3. Underemployed younger men and women, twenty to thirty years of age, have low motivation for the hard work demanded of an interviewer.

4. Underemployed postgraduates, graduates, and former social science students have low motivation, feel superior, and shirk responsibility.

These generalisations are culture-specific. However, similar suggestions are available for other cultures. For example, Hoffman (1963) offers comparable suggestions on the basis of his research in West Africa.

It is possible to identify some psychological skills that are helpful for successful interviewers. For example, "interpersonal sensitivity" seems to be one such skill which has been found to be characteristic of successful interviewers (Cannell & Kahn, 1968). Cross-cultural tests are now available to measure such sensitivity (for example, the nonverbal sensitivity tests which are being developed by Rosenthal) and further validation of these measures for interviewer selection should be undertaken.

Training Interviewers

In view of the complexity of the issues involved in cross-cultural research in general and the interviewing dynamics outlined so far, it becomes evident that the training of interviewers needs special attention. Traditional training programmes have, unfortunately, concentrated only on the theoretical background on the process of interviewing. More emphasis on the internal dynamics and problems of cross-cultural research, such as those raised in this chapter, would help interviewers develop a good technique. The following dimensions are suggested for this training:

1. Understanding the subculture of the respondents.

2. Understanding the dialect of the respondents (i.e., the connotations of words used even though the interviewer may speak the same language).

3. Understanding the phenomena to be studied, and how the data will be handled. (Unless the interviewer knows how the data is going to be handled, he may not look for the significant aspects required for analysis.)

4. Establishing rapport.

5. Asking questions.

6. Sensitivity to response biases.

7. Communicating neutrality and avoiding biases.

8. Sensitivity to cultural effects and differences in behaviour, and to phenomena that are likely to be distorted in cross-cultural comparisons.

9. Flexibility in interviewing, so that the interviewer can change, within permissible limits, the order, structure, etc. of the questions, to get authentic answers.
10. Recording responses without distracting the respondents' attention and without disrupting the natural course of the interview.

Frey (1970) has outlined the training programme he supervised in Turkey. The training included lectures on the purpose of the research and the nature of the survey instrument, and modeling procedures with trainees observing an experienced researcher complete a questionnaire with a respondent. The trainees subsequently practised on each other, with constructive feedback from the faculty. They then, in turn, interviewed a friend, an accessible stranger, and others in a full-fledged field test.

In the classroom, interview conversations could be recorded for a critique by prospective interviewers. At the Indian Institute of Management, Ahmedabad, a study examined the effects of the nature of family planning worker-client transactions on the acceptance of family planning. The interviewers were required to observe the transactions between family planning workers and members of a rural community; they were required to interview the clients before and after these interactions. Thus, interviewers required skills for observing, coding, interviewing, and listening. Their training for these roles included observing each other in operation, recording their own transactions, tape recording worker-client transactions, developing a coding system, and providing a critique of the total process. The critique helped to locate several problems which may affect the quality of interviews. A similar strategy was used by Pareek and Rao (1971) in a simplified way when they trained observers to code classroom interactions of teachers.

The use of feedback is helpful in the training of interviewers. The first few interviews can be taped and brought back to the classroom, and a group can produce a critique of the interviews. Feedback strategy could be used through "microinterviews" and through "role-play-interviews." Microinterviews are experimental in nature; the researcher participates in the role of interviewer depicting one of the several stages of the interview, followed by a critique. Also useful are role-reversal interviews, in which each interviewer plays the role of a respondent, in a classroom setting, and that is followed by a critique.

Role playing can be used to deal with special problems and biases, such as the respondent trying to influence the interviewer, or win support for his point of view. Hafeez (1977) used a training program for interviewers in the slum areas of Karachi involving two modeling sessions, one before the interviewers were sent out into the field for the pretest and another after they had had field experience. In the first modeling session, the interviewers role-played the role of respondents, and received a critique from the research director. The second modeling session provided the respondents opportunity to reexamine their style of asking questions and of recording responses, taking account of the actual field experiences they had had.

As Brislin et al. (1973) have observed, even poorly qualified candidates can be improved by means of properly designed training that meets the needs of a specific project. Brislin et al. (1973) have dealt with the topic of training interviewers for cross-cultural research. Two of their suggestions follow: training should include instructions on how to handle all foreseeable problems, and interviewers should be given a knowledge test. They recommend the manual developed by the Institut National de la Statistique et des Etudes Economiques (INSEE), for its interviewers in West Africa. It may be useful to develop similar manuals for other cultures. This manual gives detailed instructions on the nature of initial contacts in the community where interviews will be conducted, on cultural norms of reticence, courtesy, game playing, etc., and other details on conducting the interview.

A manual may be helpful both for the training and the guidance of interviewers. It is desirable that the manual lay down the main procedures of interviewing, and it should draw attention to specific problems that are likely to confront an interviewer in a particular culture. The manual should be prepared on the basis of experience interviewing people from that culture, and on the preliminary experience of interviewing people on the specific topic.

Two kinds of manuals are usually developed for interviewing. There are general manuals which discuss the techniques of interviewing and various general questions which the interviewer has to keep in mind while collecting data in a sample survey. One good example of such a manual is that by Cannell, Lawson, and Hausser (1975). The manual describes the interviewing procedure, the coding procedure, and its use in training and supervising interviewers. The other type of manual is specific to the research problem and is prepared specifically for ensuring that the interviewers have a similar approach to the problem. Many details which are specific to asking questions on that problem are dealt with in such a manual. The Survey Research Centre at Michigan (1972) developed a training manual for interviewers. Similar manuals and books are available and some of them are appropriate for interviewers on specific topics. For example, for cross-cultural research on population, the Population Council (1970), Seltzer (1973), United Nations (1964, 1970, 1971), Back and Stycos (1959), Bogue (1970), Campbell and Joiner (1973), and Mauldin (1967) have published very useful material. A manual for coders (Muehl, 1973) can be of general use in training interviewers. Such manuals developed for different cultures will be helpful to local interviewers as well as to research coordinators.

The importance of nonverbal cues needs to be stressed in cross-cultural research. The interviewer should both pick up nonverbal cues from the respondents to understand their reaction and be aware of what nonverbal cues he is giving. In each cultural context, these have to be carefully studied. The interviewers should be trained to understand such cues. McClintock and Hunt (1975) have discussed significant cues indicating unpleasant involvement and deception on the part of the respondents. Deception responses were marked by a decrease in smiling, and an increase in self-manipulation and postural shifts. Eye contact and gazing may have a great cultural variation in their effect. In western cultures, gazing has not been found to have any effect on the respondents; in fact, non gazers were rated as less attractive (Kleinke, Staneski, & Berger, 1975). In various other cultures, gazing creates a relationship of dominance. Similarly, the postural changes of the interviewer may have significant cues for the respondents. A Japanese study (Bond & Shiraishi, 1974) found that Japanese females showed greater sensitivity than males to postural manipulation. Forward leaning (20°) rather than backward leaning made the interviewers appear more polite and more flexible. This was so both for male and female respondents, but was stronger for the females.

Conclusion

Sample surveys and interviewing are most extensively used in cross-cultural research.

The most important problems in cross-cultural survey research are those of comparability: comparing the results obtained from the surveys within cultures, as well as generalising these results across cultures, sampling design, and utilising appropriate research methods in survey research. Various ways of minimising sampling and nonsampling errors need attention in cross-cultural studies and several new creative methods are needed to solve these problems. The development and standardization of questionnaires deserves special attention.

Interviewing will continue to be the most used research method, since in several cultures people are not literate enough to answer mail questionnaires, and such questionnaires are alien to these cultures. In addition to paying attention to the questions of reliability and validity of interviews, the crucial problem in interviewing is that of authenticity, i.e., capability of the interview to get the genuine responses from the respondents. This problem has been extensively discussed in the present chapter. Several factors related to the interviewer, to the respondent, to the culture of the respondent, and to the interview itself have been discussed in detail. Various ways can be found to manage these factors and thereby increase the authenticity of interviewing in cross-cultural settings. Research workers should increasingly publish their experiences and should share both the experiences of success and failure in dealing with problems of authenticity. Such experiences may help in developing training programmes for interviewers as well as manuals which may be used both for training purposes and for the supervision of interviewers.

References

ADORNO, T. W., FRENKEL-BRUNSWIK, E., LEVINSON, D. J., & SANFORD, R. N. *The authoritarian personality.* New York: Harper's, 1950.

ALMOND, C., & VERBA, S. *The civic culture: political attitudes and democracy in five nations.* Princeton: Princeton University Press, 1963.

ARMSTRONG, L. Technical survey difficulties in India. Cited in F. Frey, Cross-cultural survey research in political science. In R. Holt & J. Turner (Eds.), *The methodology of comparative research.* New York: Free Press, 1970, 173–294.

ANDERSON, J. F., & BERDIE, D. R. Effects on response rates of formal and informal questionnaire follow-up techniques. *Journal of Applied Psychology,* 1975, *60,* 255–57.

ANDERSON, R. B. W. On the comparability of meaningful stimuli in cross-cultural research. In P. P. Warwick & S. Osherson (Eds.), *Comparative research methods.* Englewood Cliffs, N.J.: Prentice-Hall, 1973, pp. 149–62.

ASKENASY, A. The multinational comparative research corporation. *American Behavioural Scientist,* 1966, *10,* 4.

ATKIN, C., & CHAFFEE, S. H. Instrumental response strategies in opinion interviews. *Public Opinion Quarterly,* 1972, *36,* 69–79.

BACK, K. W., & STYCOS, J. M. *The survey under unusual conditions.* Ithaca, N.Y.: The Society for Applied Anthropology, Cornell University, 1959.

BAUM, S., DOPKOWSKI, K., DUNCAN, W. G., & GARDINER, P. *The world fertility survey inventory: major fertility and related surveys conducted in Asia, 1960–1973.* International Statistical Institute, World Fertility Survey Occasional Papers, April 1974a, No. 3.

————. *The world fertility survey inventory: major fertility and related surveys conducted in Latin America, 1960–1973.* International Statistical Institute, World Fertility Survey Occasional papers, April 1974c, No. 5.

————. *The world fertility survey inventory: major fertility and related surveys conducted in Europe, North America and Australia, 1960–1973.* International Statistical Institute, World Fertility Survey Occasional Papers, April 1974d, No. 6.

BAUM, S., KATHEEN, D., DUNCAN, W. G., & GARDINER, P. *The world fertility survey inventory: major fertility and related surveys conducted in Africa, 1960–1973.* International Statistical Institute, World Fertility Survey Occasional Papers, April 1974b, No. 4.

BAUMAN, K. E., & CHASE, C. L. Interviewers as coders of occupation. *Public Opinion Quarterly*, 1974, *38117*, 107–12.

BECKER, J. F., & MUNZ, D. C. Extraversion and reciprocation of interviewer disclosures. *Journal of Consulting and Clinical Psychology*, 1975, *43*, 593.

BERRY, J. W. On cross-cultural comparability. *International Journal of Psychology*, 1969, *4*, 119–28.

BERRY, J. W., & ANNIS, R. C. Ecology, culture and psychological differentiation. *International Journal of Psychology*, 1974, *9*, 173–93.

BERSHAD, M. A., & TEPPING, B. J. The development of household sample surveys. *Journal of the American Statistical Association*, 1969, *64*, 1134–40.

BLUMBERG, H. H., FULLER, C., & HARE, A. P. Response rates in postal surveys. *Public Opinion Quarterly*, 1974, *38*, 113–23.

BOGUE, D. T. A model interview for fertility research and family planning evaluation. In *Family Planning Research and Evaluation Manual*. Chicago: University of Chicago, 1970.

BOND, M. H., & SHIRAISHI, D. The effect of body lean and status of an interviewer on the nonverbal behavior of Japanese interviewees. *International Journal of Psychology*, 1974, *9*, 117–25.

BONILLA, F. Survey techniques. In R. Ward (Ed.), *Studying politics abroad*. Boston: Little, Brown, 1964, pp. 134–52.

BORUCH, R. F., & CREAGER, J. A. Measurement error in social and educational survey research. *ACE Research Reports*, 1972, *7*, 62.

BRISLIN, R. W., LONNER, W. J., & THORNDIKE, R. M. *Cross-cultural research methods*. New York: Wiley, 1973.

BROWN, G. H. Drug usage rates in relation to method of data acquisition. *HumRRO Technical Report*, 1974, No. 74–20, p. 46.

CALDWELL, J. C. *The world fertility survey: problems and possibilities*. International Statistical Institute, World Fertility Survey Occasional Papers, November 1973, No. 2.

———. *The study of fertility and fertility change in tropical Africa*. International Statistical Institute, World Fertility Survey Occasional Papers, May 1974, No. 7.

CAMPBELL, C., & JOINER, B. L. How to get the answer without being sure you have asked the question. *American Statistician*, 1973, *27*, 229–31.

CAMPBELL, D. T. A cooperative multinational opinion sample exchange. *Journal of Social Issues*, 1968, *24*, 245–58.

CANNELL, C. F., & KAHN, R. L. Interviewing. In G. Lindzey & E. Aronson (Eds.), *Handbook of social psychology*, Vol. 2. Reading, Mass.: Addison-Wesley, 1968, pp. 526–95.

CANNELL, C. F., LAWSON, S. A., & HAUSSER, D. L. *A technique for evaluating interviewer performance: a manual for coding and analyzing interviewer behavior from tape recordings of household interviews*. Ann Arbor, Mich.: Institute for Social Research, 1975.

CANTRIL, H. *The pattern of human concerns*. New Brunswick, N.J.: Rutgers University Press, 1966.

CARPENTER, E. H. Personalizing mail surveys: a replication and reassessment. *Public Opinion Quarterly*, 1975, *38*, 614–20.

CARTE, G. E. Changes in public attitude toward the police: a comparison of 1938 and 1971 surveys. *Journal of Police Science and Administration*, 1973, *1*, 182–200.

CENTERS, R. *The psychology of social classes.* Princeton: Princeton University Press, 1949.

CHAU, Thi Hue, & SAGER, E. B. Interviewer's nationality and outcome of the survey. *Perceptual and Motor Skills,* 1975, *40,* 907–13.

CLANCY, K. J. Positional effects in shared-cost surveys. *Public Opinion Quarterly,* 1971, *33,* 258–65.

CONVERSE, P. New dimensions of meaning for cross-section sample surveys in politics. *International Social Science Journal,* 1964, *16,* 19–34.

COTTRELL, L. S., & EBERHART, S. *Public reaction to the atomic bomb and world affairs.* Ithaca, N.Y.: Cornell University Press, 1947.

COX, E. P., ANDERSON, W. T., & FULCHER, D. G. Reappraising mail survey response rates. *Journal of Marketing Research,* 1974, *11,* 413–17.

CRITTENDEN, K. S., & HILL, R. J. Coding reliability and validity of interview data. *American Sociological Review,* 1971, *36,* 1073–80.

DALY, J. F. Some basic principles of statistical surveys. *Journal of American Statistical Association,* 1969, *64,* 1129–34.

DAVIS, J. D., & SLOAN, M. L. The basis of interviewee matching of interviewer self-disclosure. *British Journal of Social and Clinical Psychology,* 1974, *13,* 359–67.

DEUTSCHER, I. Asking questions cross-culturally: some problems of linguistic comparability. In D. P. Warwick & S. Osherson (Eds.), *Comparative research methods.* Englewood Cliffs, N.J.: Prentice-Hall, 1973, pp. 163–203.

DOOB, L. W. *Communication in Africa, a search for boundaries.* New Haven: Yale University Press, 1961.

DUNCAN, W. G. The nature and content of fertility surveys conducted throughout the world since 1960. International Statistical Institute World Fertility Survey, Occasional Papers, October 1973, No. 1.

EDWARDS, A. *The social desirability variable in personality assessment and research.* New York: Dryden, 1957.

EISINGER, R. A., JANICKI, W. P., STEVENSON, R. L., & THOMPSON, W. L. Increasing returns in international mail surveys. *Public Opinion Quarterly,* 1974, *38,* 124–30.

FEIN, E. Inter-city interviewing: some perspectives. *Public Opinion Survey Quarterly,* 1970–71, *34,* 625–29.

FHANER, G., & HANE, M. Seat belts: contextual factors and bias of reported use. *Journal of Safety Research,* 1974, *6,* 166–70.

FREEDMAN, R. *Community-level data in fertility surveys.* International Statistical Institute World Fertility Survey Occasional Papers, May 1974a, No. 8.

————. *Examples of community-level questionnaires from sample surveys about fertility.* International Statistical Institute. World Fertility Survey Occasional Papers, May 1974b, No. 9.

FREY, F. Cross-cultural survey research in political science. In R. Holt & J. Turner (Eds.), *The methodology of comparative research.* New York: Free Press, 1970, pp. 173–264.

FULLER, C. H. Weighting to adjust for survey nonresponse. *Public Opinion Quarterly,* 1974, *38,* 239–46.

GATTON, M. J., & TYLER, J. D. Nonverbal interview behavior and dependency. *Journal of Social Psychology,* 1974, *93,* 303–04.

GILES, H., & CHAVASSE, W. Communication length as a function of dress style and social status. *Perceptual and Motor Skills*, 1975, *40*, 961–62.

GIRAD, A. Introduction. *International Social Science Journal*, 1963, *15*, 7–20.

GOLDSCHMIDT, W. *Comparative functionalism.* Berkeley: University of California Press, 1966.

GORDON, L. W. Comments on "cross-cultural equivalence of personality measures." *Journal of Social Psychology*, 1968, *75*, 11–19.

GOSTKOWSKI, Z. Special categories of respondents and their attitude towards interviews and fill-in questionnaires in Poland. *Polish Sociological Bulletin*, 1970, *2*, 107–14.

HAFEEZ, S. Voluntary organizations as agents of planned slum change. In R. G. Wirsing (Ed.), *Coping with urbanization: problems and policies of urban development in Pakistan.* Spring, 1977, (to be published).

HANNA, W., & HANNA, J. The problem of ethnicity and factionalism in Africa: survey research. *Public Opinion Quarterly*, 1966, *30*, 290–94.

HANSLEY, W. E. Increasing response rates by choice of postage stamps. *Public Opinion Quarterly*, 1974, *38*, 280–83.

HINRICHS, J. R. Effects of sampling, follow-up letters, and commitment to participation on mail attitude survey response. *Journal of Applied Psychology*, 1975, *60*, 249–51.

HOFFMAN, M. Research on opinions and attitudes in West Africa. *International Social Science Journal*, 1963, *15*, 59–69.

HOLSTI, O. R. Content analysis. In G. Lindzey & E. Aronson (Eds.), *Handbook of social psychology*, Vol. 2. Reading, Mass.: Addison-Wesley, 1968, pp. 596–692.

HYMES, D. Linguistic aspects of comparative political research. In R. Holt & J. Turner (Eds.), *The methodology of comparative research.* New York: Free Press, 1970, pp. 295–341.

HYMAN, H. H. *Survey design and analysis.* Glencoe: Free Press, 1954.

————. *Interviewing in social research.* Chicago, Ill.: University of Chicago Press, 1975.

JAHODA, G. Some research problems in African education. *Journal of Social Issues*, 1968, *24*, 161–75.

JOHNS, G. Effects on information order and frequency of applicant evaluation upon linear information-processing competence of interviewers. *Journal of Applied Psychology*, 1975, *60*, 427–33.

JOHNSON, W. R., SIEVEKING, N. A., & CLANTON, E. S. Effects of alternative positioning of open-ended questions in multiple-choice questionnaires. *Journal of Applied Psychology*, 1974, *59*, 776–78.

JOSEPHSON, E. Resistance to community surveys. *Social Problems*, 1970, *18*, 117–29.

KAHN, R. L., & CANNEL, C. F. *The dynamics of interviewing: theory, techniques and cases.* New York: Wiley, 1957.

KAPLAN, K. J., FIRESTONE, I. J., DEGNORE, R., & MOORE, M. Gradients of attraction as a function of disclosure probe intimacy and setting formality: on distinguishing attitude oscillation from attitude change—study one. *Journal of Personality and Social Psychology*, 1974, *30*, 638–46.

KATRIAK, M. Nocktore Otazky Applikacie interview a nasich podmienkach (Some problems of applying the interview in our conditions). *Sociolicky Casopis*, 1971, *8*, 463–71.

KATZ, D., & HYMAN, H. Industrial morale and public opinion methods. *International Journal of Opinion Attitude Research*, 1949, *1*, 13–20.

KEESING, F., & KEESING, H. *Elite communication in Samoa: a study of leadership.* Stanford: Stanford University Press, 1956.

KINSEY, A. C., POMEROY, W. G., & MARTIN, C. E. *Sexual behaviour in the human male.* Philadelphia: Saunders, 1948.

KISH, L. *Survey sampling.* New York: Wiley, 1965.

KLEINKE, C. L., STANESKI, R. A., & BERGER, D. E. Evaluation of an interviewer as a function of interviewer gaze, reinforcement of subject gaze, and interviewer attractiveness. *Journal of Personality and Social Psychology*, 1975, *31*, 115–22.

KLUCKHOHN, C. Universal categories of culture. In A. L. Kroeber (Ed.), *Anthropology today.* Chicago: University of Chicago Press, 1953, pp. 507–23.

KOLSON, K. L., & GREEN, J. J. Response set bias and political socialization research. *Social Science Quarterly*, 1970, *51*, 527–38.

KORMEN, W., & VAN RAVESTEIJN, L. (Influence of the presence of others in the answering of interview questions.) *Sociologische Gids*, 1968, *15*, 87–91.

KRANT, R. E., & JOHN, B. M. How being interviewed affects voting: an experiment. *Public Opinion Quarterly*, 1973, *37*, 398–406.

KROHNE, M., WALDO, G. P., & CHIRICOS, T. G. Self-reported delinquency: a comparison of structured interviews and self administered checklists. *Journal of Criminal Law and Criminology*, 1974, *65*, 545–53.

KUMAR, V. K., & PAREEK, U. Response behaviour of behavioural scientists. *Interdiscipline*, 1966, *3*, 75–80.

LAZARSFELD, P. F., & FIELD, H. *The people look at radio.* Chapel Hill: University of North Carolina Press, 1946.

LEE, R. P. The use of correlational statistics in social survey research. *Chung Chi Journal*, 1969, *9*, 66–71.

LEVITT, E. E., & KLASSEN, A. D. Public attitudes towards homosexuality. *Journal of Homosexuality*, 1974, *1*, 29–43.

LONDON, I. D. Interviewing in sinology: observations on methods and fundamental concepts. *Psychological Reports*, 1975, *36*, 683–91.

LUTYNSKA, K. The place of interviewing in Polish sociological research and its influence on the results obtained. *Polish Sociological Bulletin*, 1970, *2*, 121–29.

———. Third person in sociological interviews and their influence on the respondents' replies. *Polish Sociological Bulletin*, 1969, *20*, 139–45.

MACEK, A. J., & MILES, G. H. IQ score and mailed questionnaire response. *Journal of Applied Psychology*, 1975, *60*, 258–59.

MANDELL, L. When to weight: determining nonresponse bias in survey data. *Public Opinion Quarterly*, 1974, *38*, 247–52.

MANN, B., & MURPHY, K. C. Timing of self-disclosure, reciprocity of self-disclosure, and reactions to an initial interview. *Journal of Counseling Psychology*, 1975, *22*, 304–08.

MATTESON, M. T. Type of transmittal letter and questionnaire colour as two variables influencing response rates in a mail survey. *Journal of Applied Psychology,* 1974, *59,* 535–36.

MAULDIN, W. P. (Ed.), *Selected questionnaires on knowledge, attitudes and practice of family planning.* New York: Population Council, Demographic Division, 1967.

McALLISTER, A., & KIESLER, D. J. Interview disclosure as a function of interpersonal trust, task modeling and interviewer self-disclosure. *Journal of Consulting and Clinical Psychology,* 1975, *43,* 428.

McCLINTOCK, C. C., & HUNT, R. G. Nonverbal indicators of affect and deception in an interview setting. *Journal of Applied Social Psychology,* 1975, *5,* 54–67.

McGEE, R. *The academic tenus: the private college and its faculty.* San Francisco: Jossey-Bass, 1971.

McGUIRE, D., THELEN, M. H., & AMOLSCH, T. Interview self-disclosure as a function of length of modeling and descriptive instructions. *Journal of Consulting and Clinical Psychology,* 1975, *43,* 356–62.

MENDRAS, H. Problems of enquiries in rural communities. *Sociologia Sela,* 1969, *7,* 23–24, 41–52.

MITCHELL, R. E. Survey materials collected in the developing countries: obstacles in comparisons. In S. Rokkan (Ed.), *Comparative research across cultures and nations.* The Hague: Mouton, 1968, 210–39.

————. Survey materials collected in the developing countries: sampling, measurement, and interviewing obstacles to intra- and inter-national comparisons. In P. Warwick & S. Osherson (Eds.), *Comparative research methods.* Englewood Cliffs, N.J.: Prentice-Hall, 1973, pp. 204–26.

MOORE, D. S., & COOK-HUBBARD, K. Comparison of methods for evaluating patient response to nursing care. *Nursing Research,* 1975, *24,* 202–04.

MUEHL, D. (Ed.), *A manual for coders,* 2nd ed. Ann Arbor, Mich.: Institute of Social Research, University of Michigan, 1973.

MURPHY, G., MURPHY, L., & NEWCOMB, T. M. *Experimental social psychology.* New York: Harpers, 1937.

NASANCHUK, M. F. The comparative effects on different methods of interviewing on self-disclosing behaviour. *Dissertation Abstracts,* 1973, April 10 (33).

OLSON, G. K. The effects of interviewer self-disclosing and reinforcing behaviour upon subject self-disclosure. *Dissertation Abstracts,* 1973, May 11 (33), 6096-A.

OPPENHEIM, A. N. *Questionnaire design and attitude measurement.* New York: Basic Books, 1966.

ORWICK, J. M. Social desirability for the individual, his group and society. *Multivariate Behavioral Research,* 1972, *7,* 3–32.

OSCAR, A. J. Reliability of survey techniques in Highland Peru. *Rural Sociology,* 1970a, *35,* 500–11.

————. Interviewer effect on survey response in an Andean estate. *International Journal of Comparative Sociology,* 1970b, *11,* 208–19.

PAREEK, U., & RAO, T. V. *Handbook of psychological and social research instruments.* Baroda: Samashti, 1974a.

————. Structured interviews and FRM acceptability. Paper presented at WHO Task Force meeting on FRM Acceptability. Geneva, May 11–23, 1974b.

————. *A status study of population research in India: behavioural science*. New Delhi: Tata McGraw-Hill, 1974c.

————. *Motivation training for mental health*. New Delhi: National Institute of Health Administration and Education, ICMR Project Report, 1971.

PELKA SLUGOCKA, M. D. Conducting interviews with prisoners in penal settlements. *Polish Sociological Bulletin*, 1969, *20*, 146–53.

PERNANEN, K. Validity of survey data on alcohol use. In R. J. Gibbons et al. (Eds.), *Research advances in alcohol and drug problems: I*. New York: Wiley, 1974.

PODMORE, D., CHANEY, D., & GOLDER, P. Third parties in the interview situation: evidence from Hong Kong. *Journal of Social Psychology*, 1975, *95*, 227–31.

POPULATION COUNCIL. *A manual for surveys of fertility and family: knowledge, attitude and practice*. New York: Population Council, Demographic Division, 1970.

PRAI, L. *Male workers and IUCD*. Lucknow, India: Planning Research and Action Institute, Mimeographed, 1967.

PREZEWORSKI, A., & TEUNE, H. Equivalence in cross-cultural research. In D. P. Warwick & S. Osherson (Eds.), *Comparative research methods*. Englewood Cliffs, N. J.: Prentice-Hall, 1973, pp. 119–37.

RAGONETTI, T. J. A social psychology of survey techniques: an examination of the influence of personal confrontation and interviewer's sex upon survey results. *Cornell Journal of Social Relations*, 1970, *5*, 41–50.

RESCHKA, W. The interview as a verbal international process. *Kochner Zeitschriftfuer Soziologic and Social-Psychologie*, 1971, *23*, 745–60.

RICHARDSON, S. A., DOHRENWEND, B. S., & KLEIN, D. *Interviewing: its forms and functions*. New York: Basic Books, 1965.

ROBINSON, J. P., & SHAVER, P. R. *Measures of social psychological attitudes*. Ann Arbor, Mich.: Institute for Social Research, University of Michigan, 1969.

ROLOFF, E. K., & MATHIAS, V. The search for sociology of interview refusers: remarks on a gap in the literature. *KAI*, 1971, *1*, 22–28 (Ger).

ROSCOE, A. M., LANG, D., & SHETH, J. N. Follow-up methods, questionnaire length, and market differences in mail surveys. *Journal of Marketing*, 1975, *39*, 20–27.

ROSENTHAL, R., & ROSNOW, R. L. *The volunteer subject*. New York: Wiley, 1975.

SCHUMAN, H. The random probe: a technique for evaluating the validity of closed questions. In D. P. Warwick & S. Osherson (Eds.), *Comparative research methods*. Englewood Cliffs, N.J.: Prentice-Hall, 1973, pp. 138–48.

SCHUMAN, H., & CONVERSE, J. The effects of black and white interviewers on black responses in 1968. *Public Opinion Quarterly*, 1971, *35*, 44–68.

SCHRIESHEIM, C., & SCHRIESHEIM, J. Development and empirical verification of new response categories to increase the validity of multiple response alternative questionnaires. *Educational and Psychological Measurement*, 1974, *34*, 877–84.

SCOTT, W. A. Attitude measurement. In G. Lindzey & E. Aronson (Eds.), *Handbook of social psychology*. Reading, Mass.: Addison-Wesley, 1968.

SELLTIZ, C., JAHODA, M., DEUTSCH, M., & COOK, S. W. *Research methods in social relations*. New York: Holt, Rinehart and Winston, 1959.

SELTZER, W. *Demographic data collection*. New York: Population Council, Occasional Papers, 1973.

SHETH, J. N., & ROSCOE, A. M. Impact of questionnaire length, follow-up methods, and geographical location on response rates to a mail survey. *Journal of Applied Psychology,* 1975, *60,* 252–54.

SINCLAIR, M. A. Questionnaire design. *Applied Ergonomics,* 1975, *6,* 73–80.

SLOMEZYNSKI, K. M. Conditions of interview: their impact upon statements of respondents. *Polish Sociological Bulletin,* 1969, *20,* 125–35.

SRIVASTAVA, S. S. *Survey research technique.* Allahabad: Chaitanaya Publishing House, 1971.

STEBBINS, R. A. The unstructured research interview as incipient interpersonal relationship. *Sociology and Social Research,* 1972, *56,* 164–79.

STEVENS, R. E. Does precoding mail questionnaires affect response rates? *Public Opinion Quarterly,* 1974–75, *38,* 621–22.

STYCOS, J. Sample surveys for social science in underdeveloped areas. In R. Adams & J. Preisa (Eds.), *Human organization research.* Homewood, Ill.: Dorsey Press, 1960, 375–88.

SURVEY RESEARCH CENTRE. *Interviewer's manual.* Ann Arbor, Mich.: Institute for Social Research, University of Michigan, 1969.

SUTCLIFFE, C. R. Eliminating the biasing effect of social distance in cross-cultural survey research projects. *Journal of Social Psychology,* 1974, *94(1),* 141–42.

TRIANDIS, H. C., DAVIS, E. E., & TAKEZAWA, S. I. Some determinants of social distance among American, German and Japanese students. *Journal of Personality and Social Psychology,* 1965, *2,* 540–51.

TRIANDIS, H. C., MALPASS, R., & DAVIDSON, A. Cross-cultural psychology. *Biennial Review of Anthropology,* Palo Alto: Annual Reviews, Inc., 1971.

TRIANDIS, H. C., VASSILIOU, V., VASSILIOU, G., TANAKA, Y., & SHANMUGAM, A. V. *The analysis of subjective culture.* New York: Wiley, 1972.

TUROEZI, J. C. The effects of interviewer evaluation statements and self disclosing behaviour of interviews. *Dissertation Abstracts,* 1973, *11,* 5990–A.

UNITED NATIONS. *Variables and questionnaire for comparative fertility surveys.* Population Studies No. 45, UN, ESA, New York, 1970.

UNITED NATIONS. *Methodology of demographic sample surveys.* Report of the Interregional Workshop on Methodology of Demographic Sample Surveys, Copenhagen, Denmark, 1969. Statistical Papers, Ser. M. No. 51, UN, ESA, Statistical Office of the UN, New York, 1971.

UNITED NATIONS. *Handbook of household surveys.* New York: Ser. F, No. 10, UN, ESA, Statistical Office of the UN, 1964.

WARWICK, D. P., & OSHERSON, S. Comparative analysis in the social sciences. In D. P. Warwick and S. Osherson (Eds.), *Comparative research methods.* Englewood Cliffs, N.J.: Prentice-Hall, 1973, pp. 3–41.

WARWICK, D. P., & LININGER, C. *The sample survey: theory and practice.* New York: McGraw-Hill, 1975.

WEIGHT, D. G. Interviewer's laws of control and conditioning of interviewer's self-reference statements. *Psychological Reports,* 1974, *35,* 1307–16.

WEINER, M. Political interviewing. In R. Ward (Ed.), *Studying politics abroad.* Boston: Little, Brown, 1964, 103–33.

WEINER, R. S. Consequences of a self-survey by a Belfast community. *Journal of Social Psychology,* 1974, *93,* 197–201.

WEISS, R. W. Effect of social-desirability set in responding to questionnaire on ethnic stereotypes. *Psychological Reports*, 1975, *36*(1), 247–52.

WERNER, O., & CAMPBELL, D. Translating, working through interpreters and the problem of decentering. In R. Naroll & R. Cohen (Eds.), *A handbook of method in cultural anthropology*. New York: Natural History Press, 1970, pp. 398–420.

WHITING, J. W. M. Methods and problems in cross-cultural research. In G. Lindzey & E. Aronson (Eds.), *Handbook of social psychology*, Vol. 2. Reading, Mass.: Addison-Wesley, 1968, pp. 693–728.

WILSON, T. R., & ROSEN, T. H. Self-disclosure on army surveys: survey procedures and respondent beliefs related to candidness. *HumPRO Technical Report*, 1975, No. 75-2, p. 65.

WISEMAN, F. Methodological bias in public opinion surveys. *Public Opinion Quarterly*, 1972, *36*, 105–08.

YOUNG, P. V. *Scientific social surveys and research*. Englewood Cliffs, N.J.: Prentice-Hall, 1966.

ZEHNER, R. B. Sex effects in the interviewing of young adults. *Sociological Focus*, 1970, *3*, 75–84.

5

Testing and Assessment across Cultures: Issues in Methodology and Theory

Sid H. Irvine

and

William K. Carroll

Contents

Abstract

The central issue is the interpretation of test scores across cultures. From an assertion that it is possible to define the *construct-referenced* or *descriptive meanings* of test scores, the chapter develops its argument by first outlining the main assessment traditions in cross-cultural testing and experimentation. Each has its own methodological strengths and weaknesses. Key case studies in cross-cultural measurement provide an historical focus for procedures devised to stabilize sources of true-score variance and to reduce error-variance or unwanted, systematic variance. Problems of stimulus identity and equivalence are outlined by investigating item-analysis and attempts to validate test presentation methods and to explore test content. Factor analysis provides stable construct dimensions for *classifying subjects* within and across cultures. Used in this fashion, factor scores may act as treatment variables for experimental research. Psychometric checks and balances, which are necessary before group comparisons may be made on either tests or factor scores, are indicated as a way to achieve perfection. Finally, the chapter touches on attitude and personality methodology that is fraught with psychometric problems of the same nature as those that hamper test research. The whole self-report methodology field is summed up in an argument for the systematic extension of the Campbell-Fiske paradigm for construct validity to include *culture-syntonic* measures of the trait wherever *culture-alien* tests are used or adapted for use. Promising procedures for inclusion in such designs are presented and evaluated. Each of the assessment traditions contributes positively to the pursuit of construct validity, provided it is checked by methods appropriate to the other schools of enquiry.

Issues and Approaches

Introduction and Overview

Self-report tests of achievement, aptitude, and personality have been used, in cultures other than those on which they were standardized, for almost as long as the history of mass testing itself. Moreover, such practices have, until the last ten years, disregarded the distinction between operational use (*criterion-referenced meaning*) and comparative use (*construct-referenced meaning*) of the test scores generated. In one of the early British summations on intelligence testing (Knight, 1943), for example, various group mean IQ results from the American forces Alpha and Beta tests used in the First World War as screening devices are ranked by declared ethnic origin. More recently Jencks (1972, p. 113) revived similar data to ask whether gains or losses in average test scores from one generation to the next can be interpreted scientifically. Both these exercises invoke construct-referenced meaning for cross-cultural test results. Few experimenters are at ease when confronted by the problems of comparing meanings of test scores across cultures. Since 1960, the use of tests by psychometricians working in test-alien cultures (cultures alien to the test in its original standard form) has seldom been unqualified. Comparisons resulting from the application of tests in alien cultures have evoked criticism and aroused controversy, even downright hostility. Much of the recent debate over interethnic testing seemed ideological rather than scientific. Polemics have taken precedence over plausible rival hypotheses; simplistic interpretations of results, in which ethnicity assumes a pivotal causal position, have tended to make matters worse. However, controversy is not new to psychometricians. Whenever inferences have been made from group means about the aptitudes and processes of mankind (e.g., Fick, 1939) *scientific* rebuttals based on construct definition (Biesheuvel, 1943), have survived. The original work has inevitably provided the heuristic stimulus to further research. It is in this spirit that one has to approach the controversies of the late sixties.

Hence, some dismay might well be registered by psychologists perceiving the *weltanschaung* of Cole and Scribner (1974, pp. 171 ff.) and Scribner (1975) who advance this position: "There is simply no way to evaluate the sources of variation when aborigines do not respond to an IQ test in the same way Cambridge undergraduates do" (Cole & Scribner, 1974, p. 173). Again, two pages on, they proceed in this fashion:

> In a very important sense we do not know what they [intelligence tests] measure. . . . So long as IQ tests are treated solely in terms of their ability to predict a child's school performance [*criterion-referenced meaning*], arguments about the nature of the test need not arise. But as soon as we ask, what do IQ tests really measure? [*construct-referenced meaning*], we enter an area of seemingly endless arguments and ambiguity. (p. 175)

Can this be the sum of half a century of psychometric effort and theory? Cole and Scribner put the case for a view that knowledge of anthropology and linguistics, experimental finesse, and a belief in the universality of process[1] in mankind will produce results when psychometric approaches apparently have failed. Indeed their counsels are to be heeded, but "the testing movement," as Scribner (1975) somewhat pejoratively describes it, cannot be written off—indeed, neither can any other serious *scientific* attempt at investigating cognition across cultures.

Debate about testing across cultures must first center around its scientific credentials. Cross-cultural testing, far from offering no assistance in bringing about a theory of intellect, is indeed a scientific enterprise of some credibility, offering heuristic possibilities that single experiments cannot. This chapter attempts to answer the question that Scribner and Cole raise—"What scientific advances have been and can be made through testing across cultures, apart from a welcome critique of testing itself?" Several issues will be considered. Germane to these issues is, of course, knowledge of the various schools of cognitive inquiry, each of which is theory laden. The first section of the chapter deals with various present-day schools of assessment and their interrelationships. Particularly, psychometric, Piagetian, field differentiation, and anthropological cognition positions are outlined. They are supplemented by references to cognitive information processing studies that today offer a *rapprochement* among some of the traditional enterprises. The advantages and disadvantages of each approach are shown. With that outline complete, a proposition is then advanced about the nature of test-data collection across cultures. Various aspects of the problems surrounding this proposition are illustrated by going to the origins of mass testing and uncovering what advances have been made by recent studies. Particularly, the operational advances of cross-cultural testing are stated with reference to case studies. Attention is given to the progress made to define the meanings of test scores and to establish the limits of methods of comparing and clarifying them. A brief glance at attitude and personality assessment, in the context of self-report materials, records modest advances and highlights unsolved areas of method and theory. A reprise of the themes of the chapter, in terms of construct validation theory, marks its conclusion. The whole chapter argues that, while psychometric checks based on existing theory are often sufficient to prevent extravagant claims for results, only systematic attempts at construct validation will advance the discipline.

Assessment Traditions and their Scientific Status

Psychometric approaches (PSM). While theories of personality have been far more numerous than theories of ability, diversity has not brought predictions based on personality tests anywhere near the accuracy achieved by tests of mental abilities. Psychometric test results have been used to classify people by economic status, occupational level, sex, ethnic background, type of school attended, and so on. These predictions are "strong" scientifically since the tests predict success or failure, or classify people accurately according to other variables that are not tests. On the other hand, arguments about what the tests test, or what dimensions are occupied by the true score variance of the tests continue. Briefly, psychometricians were and probably still are disposed either to hierarchical and correlated factor theories of abilities, with g as a determinant construct, following Spearman, Burt, Vernon, and Cattell; or to relatively uncorrelated factor theories, in which no single ability determines any other, following Thurstone and Guilford. Tests have been based on theories of correlated or uncorrelated factors; and they have reflected these theories in their construction. For example, Jensen's recent, and controversial studies (1969, 1971a, 1973a, 1973b, 1973c, 1974a, 1974b, 1974c), are empirical attempts to assign levels of abilities (implying hierarchy) to limited cognitive domains. His constructs have not led him to any new measures of intelligence. Instead he has selected from those tests already available a number of measures that imply hierarchy in their construction. Consequently Jensen's work, in its present state, represents no major theoretical advance across cultures. It is, rather, a variant of the correlated factor tradition.

Unlike the claims for prediction and classification, the positions of the various "schools" of psychometrics cannot be resolved by the empiricism most commonly used in the past. Whatever the investigator's theoretical stance, his methods have usually encompassed the use of relative scales of measurement, in which the data are the summations of products of assumed mental acts (item answers). Correlations are the products of deviations from the groupings of these relative scales that have been factor analyzed. The constructs derived from factor analysis are usually, and paradoxically, named after examining the *stimuli* (test items), and conjecturing about the *processes* that have produced the *products* (item answers). It is the products that are de facto the basis for calculation of the correlation matrices. Little in the way of verification of the accuracy of an *isolated* guess about a factor is possible. In this area some critics have been particularly forthright, and undeniably correct (Horn, 1967; Carroll, 1973; Hunt, Frost, & Lunneborg, 1973; Estes, 1974), about the weaknesses of factor analysis *by itself*, as a construct validity process. In a cross-cultural context Irvine and Sanders (1972) have pointed to the same logical weaknesses and suggested correctives. On the other hand, the scientific paradigms necessary for construct validation of test scores are available (Campbell & Fiske, 1959; Cronbach, 1972, p. 421). Much of the current debate about test score meanings could be resolved by stricter application of existing procedures.

Piagetian approaches (PGT).   Although there have been recent signs of convergence (Lunzer, 1972; DeVries, 1974; Wilkinson, 1974), Piagetian and psychometric (PSM) theories and practices have diverged. Most students in introductory classes on testing can point out that Piagetian workers test individual children with a few standard clinical measures, while PSM testers require many subjects and many tests to stabilize correlations and assay the many cognitive constructs that factor analysis has suggested. This apparently superficial observation conceals the more fundamental difference between PSM relative scales and PGT absolute stages of cognitive development. Piagetian theory is more like the logic of sets or more Bayesian, than PSM measurement, which takes the mean point and moments about the mean as the logical extension of a scientific method in which individuals are differentiated relative to one another. Moments around an average have no place in PGT measurement. The procedures devised by Piaget and his coworkers illustrate the progression of individuals through certain organismic states that are irreversible, and therefore, absolute. These changes involve processes called conservation, dissociation, spatial representation, imagining, classification, inclusion and intersection of classes, and elementary and formal logic. Certain clinical procedures have been devised to estimate the progression of the individual through these inexorable organic shifts. There are not many of these mental-organic changes, four at most, and adolescence brings refinement of skills within the grasp of all, once formal operations are possible. Not many tests are needed to chart individual progress; those that are available consistently show that progression through the various stages of growth is accompanied by predicted performance changes that are generally consistent with Piaget's description of these stages. For example, children who conserve matter, mass, and volume can be distinguished consistently from those who do not by their performance in tasks involving everyday materials such as beakers, clay, and water. Psychometric methods would attack the problem of demonstrating growth by comparing *group* means over time using the "same" set of tests, and assessing the significance of differences among an array of means derived from correlated scores.

Although PGT and PSM approaches to measurement hardly seem to share the same universe of scientific discourse, nevertheless, they share the same scientific paradoxes. Both approaches assign to the products of mental interaction with given stimuli underlying processes that are necessary *logical* assumptions, but whose psychological validity has to be demonstrated. Construct validation of Piagetian ability has seldom been attempted with non-Piagetian tasks; when it was, results were variable and seldom conclusive. Attempts have been made to verify developmental stages as transcultural universals. In general, the stages are robust, but the elasticity of the concrete-operational stage puzzles many researchers (Heron & Dowel, 1974). Again, when conservers are contrasted with non-conservers the classification obtained by *Piagetian* procedures has not been verified by *other* mental tests used across cultures (Heron, 1971, 1974; Heron & Dowel, 1973). Piagetian theory can be generalized because similar tasks classify children into the same stages consistently. It has been difficult to establish that children thus classified can be differentiated by different (non-Piagetian) kinds of measures. Convergent validity through predicting performance changes in PSM or cognitive information processing tasks to accompany classification into distinct Piagetian stages would be a welcome advance. Some of the implications of this lack of convergent validity have been elegantly described by Heron (1974). On the other hand, few plausible rival hypotheses for Piagetian organismic-stage theory have emerged, so that this research has not been marked by, nor has it required (unlike PSM theories), the inclusion of discriminant validity procedures.

Field differentiation (FDI). Of importance to cross-cultural psychology (Witkin & Berry, 1975) is the concept of field differentiation, which experimenters have operationalized with the *Rod and Frame Test* (RFT) or mutants of the *Embedded Figures Test* (EFT). It is important to remember that use of EFT measures puts the experimenter under the constraint of psychometric methods of construct validation. A recent bibliography published by Witkin, Dyk, Faterson, Goodenough, and Karp (1973-1974) lists no fewer than 1,508 references; most of them include variants of one or the other of these measures. His cross-cultural colleagues use field differentiation theory extensively and have linked it with the seminal work of Barry, Child, and Bacon (1959) on child rearing and socialization practices. This, in itself, is an extension of Kardiner's hypothesis that culturally specific personality structures are the product of culturally specific modes of child rearing (Crijns, 1966). Disciples of Witkin and Berry have extrapolated the Kardiner concept to perception and to other mental events. In so doing they have posited an ecological determinism as a corrective to the Freudian version of determinism employed by Kardiner and his followers.

FDI theory has not been short of controversy or hypotheses about what is measured by the *Rod and Frame Test* (RFT) and the *Embedded Figures Test* (EFT). As both of these key measures may be regarded as psychometric-relative scales in which individuals are assessed relative to the mean of a group, debate about the assigning of construct-referenced meaning has been sustained. This is consistent with the logic of relative measurements, which requires convergent and discriminant validity studies. Some researchers have attempted discriminant validity studies (Vernon, 1972) and have concluded that "... it is doubtful whether different versions of the same test measure the same thing, and whether they do not also involve general intelligence" (Vernon, 1972, p. 386). Others have been even more skeptical. "*Embedded Figures* correlates so strongly with *Block Design* and *Matrices* as to suggest to me that what Witkin calls 'field differentiation' is nothing but *g* and he offers no evidence to dispel this criticism" (Cronbach, 1972, p. 422). Some studies have continued the debate into the realm of personality, arguing that *California Personality Inventory Scale* correlations with RFT measures are much lower when intelligence test and spatial relations test scores are co-varied with *Rod and Frame Test* scores. On the other hand, if critics regard general intelligence as operationally defined by the Wechsler scales, then the results of Goodenough and Karp (1961) show that the verbal components of the Wechsler do not load on the same factor as FDI markers. The success of EFT measures in predicting differences in food accumulation habits and social structures in preliterate society is also a strong scientific paradigm. But the methodological problem remains. What do the RFT, and more crucially the EFT, really measure?

Witkin's operationalization of the concept through EFT and RFT measures has fostered studies of convergent validity, but has lacked correlational verification of the discriminant validity of his concept. Hence the construct validity of field differentiation theory is defined and limited by the observation that different methods assess the same trait. The suggestions by Vernon and Cronbach that other traits may be measured operationally in the EFT and RFT measures themselves, have not been satisfactorily refuted. It will take multivariate cross-cultural studies in conjunction with experimental studies to resolve the doubts that exist. Such studies, however, are rarely planned and even more rarely executed. Hence, although cross-cultural work has enabled FDI theory to extend its claim to convergent validity by means of the ecological framework used by Berry (1976) and derived from the work of anthropologists, without the rigorous application of psychometric logic to the problem of construct validation, field differentiation theory will be plagued with rival plausible hypotheses about what its instruments measure.

Anthropological cognition (ANC). Significant cross-cultural *experimental* work has been accomplished by Deregowski (1968a, 1986b, 1970), Deregowski and Munro (1974), Cole, Gay, and Glick (1968a, 1968b), Price-Williams (1962), and Segall, Campbell, and Herskovits (1963, 1966). All of these researchers work in carefully controlled settings, using analysis of variance rather than correlations. Although they share this procedural heritage, they can be differentiated into two camps: those who seek generality through the same set of stimuli; and those who use different stimuli from one culture to another, thereby seeking conceptual generalities. For the latter group the stimuli may be different, but they assert that the basic dynamics of the structure are under control (Cole, Gay & Glick, 1968a). For example, one can persuasively argue that clustering in verbal recall is comparable across languages only when there are conceptually comparable sets of verbal stimuli that permit clustering. Logic demands that these conceptual sets must first be established in different languages (Scribner, 1974). Food, for example, may be a suitable concept for clustering in Western societies through words like chicken, steak, French fries, salad, ice cream. Many tasks used by experimental psychologists can be performed better if the subject clusters the words on lists he is memorizing, learning, or recalling. But in Chishona, a Central African Bantu language, the words might well be *sadza* (grits is the equivalent), *nyama* (meat), plus several edible plants used in the relish or gravy that have no equivalent English translation. The Western list, when translated, might have the expected conceptual and taxonomic properties for sophisticated Shona subjects, but the back translated Shona food list would probably be nonclusterable as food among non-Africans.

Jensen's (1973b) experiment in white and black clustering of the "same" stimuli does not, for example, offer verification of the conceptual generality (and by implication, psychological equivalence) of his "identical stimulus" lists of free-recall items for black and white children. They *could* be equivalent, but it is not certain. Hence, a rival hypothesis is possible. The debate will continue, but it is constrained, or should be, by the scientific point at issue. The anthropological contribution to the study of verbal learning across cultures is well taken, or should be, by psychologists venturing experiments in this area in cultures other than their own.

Invariably, the challenge to experimental work is to verify any claim to or assumption of stimulus generality or "phenomenal identity" (Straus, 1969) since a demonstration of some sort of "dimensional identity" is prerequisite to valid cross-cultural comparison (Berry, 1969). Even when Cole et al. (1968a) presented random and ordered dots to Kpelle and American groups, they concluded that this relatively simple experiment gave rise to the hypothesis of a "nontrivial cultural difference" in information ordering. Again, Scribner's (1974) work on categorization shows remarkably dissimilar "maps" of hierarchical complexity for bush villagers and high school students in recalling clustered objects. The task of remembering the objects was a different one for each sample. Explanations other than the consistent application of a verbal category among high school students could have been formulated had one been able to *predict* categorization by entirely different methods. It is reasonable to suggest the inclusion of a number of performance scales of ability in such a context. That they exist, and function well for illiterates (Ord, 1971), is evident. The Scribner study, however, did not have, nor did it seek, samples on whom multivariate analysis could be performed as a way of isolating individual differences from the error terms. Consequently, the meaning of a single dependent variable, even in anthropological approaches, is no more verifiable in isolation from other variables than the result of one psychometric test given in two different cultures. Herein lies the real nature of the gap between sociological/anthropological approaches to cognition and psychological approaches based on tests. That gap can be bridged given knowledge of both traditions and samples in other cultures sophisticated enough to be able to test in a variety of methods. Indeed, Cole et al. (1968b) admit that the ANC approach requires multitrait, multimethod support. In fact, Cronbach's criticism of PSM methods cross-culturally is just as apposite for experimenters dipped in anthropological and linguistic solutions. If the reader substitutes *task* or *experiment* for *test* in this quotation the point will become clear:

> The typical cross-cultural study compares groups on a single test. Such research will take on far greater significance if the future investigator carries along additional tests to represent the various rival interpretations for the test of central interest. Evidence on the convergence or divergence of these several indicators will raise the study from the descriptive one to one that can be given a theoretical interpretation. (Cronbach, 1972, p. 422)

Cognitive information processing (CIP).   Although cognitive information processing theory is relatively new, and has yet to make a contribution to cross-cultural research, recent work indicates that CIP may bring about major changes in cross-cultural testing. Accordingly, a short account of CIP theory is relevant. One particular model of CIP has been argued eloquently by Hunt, Frost and Lunneborg (1973) as a means of devising PSM measures that are theory-based. Essentially, it depends on a model of cognition that is process-oriented. According to CIP, information from the outside world is sensed, coded, perceived, stored, and integrated with the inner world of previous relevant experience that has been personally constructed for each individual. The methods used by CIP scientists are laboratory based and experimentally controlled. However, like FDI theorists, Hunt and his coworkers are using the procedure and methods of another school, namely the psychometric approach, to predict for their theory. They are using PSM tests as meaningful classifiers of subjects (Hunt, Lunneborg, & Lewis, 1974), and attempting predictions from their model of cognition to the results derived from another means of classification. They have met with encouraging initial success. Previous pioneer work (Allison, 1960; Bunderson, 1964) on transfer, has also been encouraging, but from different theoretical positions. Unfortunately, its technical demands are so fierce that few have followed up available research avenues. Berry, it will be remembered, also used PSM tests to quantify predicted differences in intellectual functioning in societies characterized by their food accumulation and social structure. Both CIP and FDI approaches rely partly on the meaning of test scores, but intracultural assumptions about test score meaning are easier to justify than cross-cultural assumptions at the moment. Moreover, FDI still has a rival theory ("*g*") embedded in its field of instruments.

Recent work by Carroll (1974), based on the model by Hunt et al. (1973), begins with a detailed, computer assisted, subjective analysis of cognitive processes that may underlie responses to psychological tests. The analysis concerns precisely what the test taker is doing when responding to a test. The examination of the situation includes coding the necessary activities according to the kind of *stimulus materials*. For example, one has to decide whether *S* responds to one or two words; one or two pictures; if the response requires retrieval of information from short, intermediate, or long term memory; if the contents of the stimulus are lines, maps, letters, words, semantics, etc. One must also indicate what kind of response is required; for example, select response from presented alternatives; produce one correct answer; produce as many responses as possible; produce a specified number of words, make a spoken response. One must state *the criterion of acceptability* of any response, such as identity, similarity, and semantic opposition. One specifies *the task structure*, such as stimuli presented on one occasion and response made on another occasion. Kinds of *operations and strategies* are required; for example, number of operations; types of operations such as identify, retrieve, name; perform serial operations; record intermediate result; imagine; judge stimulus with respect to a specified characteristic, and so on. One must also know if the operation is specified in the instructions; how dependent the performance is upon this operation; and what kind of memory is involved in the operation.

Thus, each test can be checked against a list of task specifications, and characterized by a number of fundamental cognitive processes. The system is designed to handle 1,920 types of stimuli, 672 types of responses, and over a million kinds of operations; thus, theoretically it can give a different characterization to each of about 2×10^{12} psychological tests—a much larger number than people are ever likely to invent. In spite of the richness of the system, however, it is not clear that it can reflect all the differences in performance that might be observed across cultures. For example, it is not clear where differences in the extent of use of *context* in responding to a task will be represented in the system. Nevertheless, Carroll's (1974) paper, by showing how basic cognitive processes can be found in different factor analytically determined test types, promises to provide a bridge between the CIP and PSM scientists and to allow a much clearer understanding of cultural differences in the performance of psychological tests. Particularly, it offers a framework for strong discriminant validity and convergent validity studies among all the other approaches listed in this section. Above all, it will force test users to reexamine their assumptions, within an exacting task-analytic structure, about what tests are testing.

The Cross-Cultural Balance Sheet

The previous history of all these models (except the rather new CIP model), particularly the PSM and FDI models, has been marked by considerable controversy whenever the operational measures of the constructs have been transported across cultures with the accompanying assumption of psychological equivalence. What is the scientific verdict on such enterprises? And what issues have been raised by them?

Recent evaluative comparisons of test scores have usually involved two or perhaps three different ethnic groups, e.g., Lesser, Fifer, and Clark (1965), Stodolsky and Lesser (1967), Jensen (1971a), Marjoribanks (1972). Such comparisons have been based on mean differences derived from raw test scores; on mean differences derived from factor scores in PSM research; or, on comparisons of regression line slopes (Jensen, 1973c). Such group comparisons involving derivations from the moments about the means of test scores, have been considered both problematic and scientifically challenging by many scientists. Specific methodological and dispassionate criticisms against the Lesser/Jensen kind of PSM comparisons have been made in Irvine and Sanders (1972) and in Biesheuvel (1972). A handy summary of the logical restrictions on cross-cultural comparison is available in Cronbach and Drenth (1972, pp. 479–482). The verdict is that comparisons are seldom defensible, and the issues are, correctly, the methods used to obtain the results. Later in the chapter a set of procedures for cross-cultural comparison is outlined, more as an indication of the assumptions that underlie such comparisons, but always in the hope that the suggested procedures will be observed.

In PGT research (Dasen, 1972a, 1972b; Heron & Simonson, 1969; DeLacey, 1970; Cowley & Murray, 1962) the data for comparison have been a head count of subjects actually achieving success in the prescribed tasks across cultures. Although the Piagetian processes are more absolute than relative, comparisons of numbers in the various stages still beg the question of construct congruence. FDI theorists are still relying heavily on PSM methodologies for comparison between sexes or ethnic groups (Berry, 1974b). As for the ANC approach, in spite of the careful disclaimers within the rationale of Cole et al. (1968a), the proposition that the combination of multimethod and multiculture experimental design procedures is required is not evident either in the operational definition of Scribner's experiment (1974) or in the consistent rejection of PSM procedures as a means of defining the meaning of measures in relation to others (Cole & Scribner, 1974; Scribner, 1975). Anthropological cognition has, then, made consistent predictions about behaviour in different language groups and in high and low food accumulation groups (a strong scientific procedure), but has avoided multivariate analysis of the measures used. In fact, there has been no synthetic attempt to validate constructs involving experimental tasks as well as psychometric tests that satisfy the strong model for equivalence posited by Irvine and Sanders (1972). Recent work by MacArthur (1973, 1974), however, claims partial attempts at cross-cultural synthesis of PSM and PGT (although PGT work is unpublished), but without within-culture conceptual validation of constructs. MacArthur has certainly ventured more than many; his results are consistent, but his interpretations are cautious, constrained by his theoretical stance and factor analytic models. Methodological constraints on the interpretation of results, however, are endemic in the cross-cultural field. Some of the reasons for this are made apparent in the next section.

Not all anthropological cognition can be criticized because the use of one chosen or preferred method to the exclusion of other methods is insufficient to lend meaning to a construct. In recent years the most painstaking study involving measures of brain waves (EEG recordings), cognitive tasks of a clinical-experimental nature, and psychometric test adaptations, has come from Reuning and Wortley (1973) in their monograph *Psychological Studies of the Bushmen*. The authors described five expeditions to the Kalahari desert and results from administering various measures to a people with a low authoritarian, low food accumulation society. According to the authors, the Kalahari subjects found disembedding an almost impossible task (p. 48). On tasks requiring size-constancy they performed well, in keeping with studies that find good performance on this skill part of a *field-dependent* perceptual style. Although the study needs an agricultural referent, the findings need reconciliation with the ecological adaptation theory of Berry (1974b, 1976), which demands that Bushmen evidence field-independent perceptual responses. The results of Reuning and Wortley's report are also qualified by the knowledge that sample sizes vary for individual correlation coefficients. Nevertheless, their major conclusion remains that correlations among psychometric tests, cognitive tasks, and physiological measures applied to illiterate subjects will not always result in undifferentiated general factors that are almost impossible to define, and bedevil comparison. Second, the unmistakable *methodological conclusion* is that when psychometric tests and cognitive tasks are applied together, they differentiate groups more sharply than either one of them can alone. Lastly, when the EEG measures (from a different branch of psychology) are related to the other measures, they provide *prima facie* evidence for Reuning's view that personality functions should be regarded as part of the wide range of individual differences in test and task performance.

Thus far, we have noted some of the scientific limitations of each approach to the measurement of cognition. The essential problems of construct validation have been stated for each approach. The testing tradition will, of course, come under much more detailed scrutiny than all the others. Later, the implications of cognitive information processing (CIP) approaches will be discussed in more detail. But in view of the dearth of material from non-Euro-North American cultures, this approach cannot be discussed as a cross-cultural procedure. By implication, however, it offers to PSM methodology the construct validity framework that factor analytic techniques so far have been unable to provide.

The application of methods from the various traditions across cultures can be summarized by saying that all approaches to cross-cultural assessment contain scientific limitations; some are weaker than others because the validity of the constructs they posit has been assumed rather than demonstrated; and no consistent method of data collection has emerged. Each approach has had its own methodology, resulting in a fragmented effort in pursuit of a theory of data collection.

From Past Methods to
Present Progress

A Central Proposition

Scientific observation is necessarily theory-laden; rationalism and empiricism interact to produce scientific explanation (cf. Hempel, 1965; Popper, 1961, for extensive treatments). In short, observation implies theory, and the use of psychological tests implies some kind of prior theorizing, either explicit or implicit. Scientists and philosophers of science have long recognized this eventuality as a mixed blessing that has two salient consequences. First, in the *short term*, it dictates that any particular scientific observation is subject to various biases arising from the researcher's theoretical perspective, e.g., experimenter effects or observer bias. Influenced is not only the choice of the problem to be investigated, but also the method of investigation itself. Since a concerted effort at the study of cross-cultural psychological phenomena has been a relatively recent development in the social sciences, many of the characteristics of cross-cultural research may be shown to include methodological biases which are short-term consequences of the proposition stated above. The previous section of this chapter was written to demonstrate this point of view. A full discussion for *African* psychological research can be found in Irvine, Sanders, and Klingelhofer (1973, pp. vii–xxvi), and Wober (1975). Even so, cross-cultural researchers have increasingly been learning from their methodological (and theoretical) mistakes; indeed, the cross-cultural field is a particularly viable arena for exposing latent, often ethnocentric flaws in theory and methods (Berry & Dasen, 1974, pp. 16–20).

The prospect of steady theory and method development brings up the more positive consequence of our central proposition. In the *long term* it is possible to produce a rationale for data collection and instrumentation; that is, dialectically to employ theory and methods in a complementary fashion so that the process of observation and measurement is transformed from its initial status to a theoretically explicable process. Instead of relying solely on the establishment of concurrent criterion and content validity for a test of personality or ability, while ignoring the test-taking process as a psychological phenomenon which needs explanation, it is possible to develop instruments directly from established theories of human psychological functioning.

In the strict sense, this amounts to the construct validation of psychological tests (Cronbach & Meehl, 1955; Loevinger, 1957; Hunt et al., 1973). In discussing the prospects for cross-cultural paper and pencil testing, and in making suggestions for the future, this favourable long-term consequence of our central proposition will be especially stressed. It will be argued that in order to have valid cross-cultural paper and pencil research that can be generalized, it is imperative to have a rationale for data collection based on the general conceptual framework from which hypotheses are developed. For a useful treatment of this issue in the context of cross-cultural applied research see also Eckensberger (1972). By analogy, the onus on other traditions to show how their procedures contribute to a consistent universe of discourse about data collection across cultures is just as strong. Despite Cole and Scribner's view, other directions should not be dismissed as unproductive. Rather, unity in learning from all their methodologies should be sought. Indeed this chapter demonstrates how such a unity might be achieved. However, in order to find out where PSM methodology seems to be headed, the nature of the short-run successes and failures must first be examined. In doing so we shall discover that the methods of psychometric construct validation, if correctly applied, are often effective, but also that improvement is still possible.

Past Methods: Large-Scale Cross-Cultural Testing

Ord (1972) has provided a comprehensive review of advances and improvements in occupational and educational assessment across cultures. The reader will discover that Ord's statement is definitive and that close reading of it is required for a full description of the endeavour in Africa, India, and the Pacific. Other standard texts for the student of cross-cultural assessment include Ingenkamp (1969), Ord (1971), Triandis (1972), Cronbach and Drenth (1972), Lloyd (1972), Brislin, Lonner, and Thorndike (1973), and Berry and Dasen (1974). Instead of summarizing points of view already expressed admirably elsewhere, this discussion will expose more fully the vein of the present argument by illustrating key issues in a historical context. All of these are concerned with establishing valid procedures of data collection in the long run. The painful transition from short-run error to long-term theory will be illustrated. Two interdependent issues face us: (1) communicating with subjects, and (2) the meaning of test scores. Test instructions, indeed, can be seen as an independent variable whose manipulation will alter outcomes, and hence interpretations of test scores. Careful use of test instructions can lend insight into the meanings of test scores themselves. However, uncontrolled experimentation with the independent variable, allied with different theories of test construction, can multiply the possibility of confusion in interpreting the dependent variable (the test score).

Present progress: the seven principles. As one reflects on fifteen years of cross-cultural test application, one searches for a dramatic incident or highlight that will illustrate at once the relevance of history in both stating and helping to solve problems in (a) the methods of presenting tests, and in (b) the interpretations of test scores. Already mentioned were testing practices that were outcomes either of hierarchical or "g" based theories or of orthogonal and uncorrelated factor theories. Does history record the confluence of such traditions across cultures—and with what results? Perhaps one such incident occurred in 1963 in Lusaka when representatives from the Paul Schwarz (AIR/AID) test team in Nigeria and from Biesheuvel's National Institute for Personnel Research (N.I.P.R.) team met in Zambia to discuss the inclusion of their tests in the forthcoming Mental Ability Survey (MacArthur, Irvine, & Brimble, 1964). Subsequently, tests from both suppliers were used; hence the study contained tests with two entirely different theories of test construction embedded in them. The AIR/AID tests were assumed to be uncorrelated (see especially Schwarz, 1961, p. 69); and the N.I.P.R. tests were essentially correlated. Yet, as the independent test construction teams were to find, basic test theory was then secondary to the common priority of explaining test-taking and answer-recording procedures fully to subjects prior to testing. This was considered a vital step in reducing unwanted variance in testing just-literate, but test-alien groups. The first steps towards a rationale for data collection were implicit in the operationalization of such procedures. They became explicit only when large-scale enterprises (Vernon, 1961; Schwarz, 1963; Irvine, 1964b, 1965, 1966; Silvey, 1963) were completed and the principles were synthesized. The principles are as follows:*

1. Every test response must be learned. No assumption should be made about a person's ability to respond in the manner required by the test. Both test materials and methods of recording answers must be fully understood.

2. Often, in other cultures, the instruction not to turn back to previous tests is bewildering and distressing to the people taking the test. Hence, omnibus test booklets are undesirable. Each test should be separate from every other and should be accompanied by its own instructions.

3. Instructions should be oral, not written, since the ability to read instructions is not part of the test situation. Flexible visual aids should demonstrate each type of test item and response, preferably by building up the components through the use of plastigraph or flannelgraph techniques that allow cut-outs to be stuck to boards so that a large class can see.

4. If translations for test instructions are necessary, these should not be literal. They should be idiomatic expressions of the intent of the test demonstrator, who ideally should be from the same ethnic group as those taking the test. This will reduce the possibility of extraneous motivational influences on test scores.

5. Supervised practice for each test is essential to make certain that test instructions have been understood.

* Reproduced by permission from Irvine, 1973, pp. 462–63.

6. Familiar test material should be given first, so that early attempts at recording answers in a certain way are the only unfamiliar element. As recording answers becomes more automatic, unusual or abstract materials can be presented.

7. The climate of testing must be as convivial and dramatic and enjoyable as possible. Fully trained testers should employ every strategy to make the situation positively reinforcing and cheerful.

These seven principles, representing a painstaking reinvention of the wheel by field workers isolated from each other, are a summation of many independent discoveries. Today they can, and indeed should, be seen as a *basis for experimental manipulation of test conditions in test-alien groups.*[2] Each one of the principles is capable of experimental manipulation, so that what the tests test can be explored systematically by multivariate procedures. This procedure will be explained later.

However, before turning to that, one has to bring out another memory of Zambia that is important. The testing in the 1960s was largely carried out on school children. The seven principles have their roots in an earlier tradition that began by testing adults. How did they come about, and what do they offer? By exploring and understanding this earlier tradition, that of large-scale adult performance testing, we shall also demonstrate how the rigour of psychometrics itself generates plausible rival hypotheses concerning the meanings of test scores. And this, apart from a theory of communicating with test-alien subjects, is the second major problem.

Three Case Studies of Early Methods

A short time prior to the AIR/AID and N.I.P.R. meeting in Lusaka there was uncovered from the Library of the Institute for Social Research in Zambia, a now historic (although still unpublished) document, then almost twenty years old. It was a final report of a British Army Personnel and Selection Unit prepared by Macdonald (1945) and his associates. The report describes how a testing team had, with the cessation of hostilities in the Middle East, set about testing thousands of African soldiers with the aim of devising tests that would predict performance in the many skills that were required to maintain operational efficiency in the armed services of those days. The report confirms what each test-user in nonwestern cultures had to discover for himself in the 1960s. First, one had to communicate precisely with one's subjects. Second, given a criterion demanding intellective processes, tests could be devised operationally to predict to that criterion, regardless of the theory latent in such tests. These conclusions are hindsight, however, and they were certainly not as evident to workers in the 1960s as they are now. In short, the discovery of the Macdonald report, while paper and pencil tests were being tried out operationally on large samples in Central Africa, demonstrated that the history of large-scale assessment across cultures is obligatory scientific reading. Without it, one will traverse the same ground again.

Hence, for the purposes of illustrating key areas of progress, in the collection and interpretation of data, three major studies on illiterates have been chosen as benchmarks. First, Macdonald's; second, Ord's Pacific studies stretching over a decade, culminating in a standard reference work (Ord, 1971); and lastly, Biesheuvel's (1952, 1954) accounts of the construction of the N.I.P.R. General Adaptability Battery (GAB). The reasons for this selection are, briefly, that each study underlines certain basic principles of data collection; that each attempted more than operational interpretation of the test scores by analyzing the intercorrelations of tests; and finally, two of them, the Biesheuvel and Ord studies, have proved to have heuristic value. They have led to work in the late sixties and early seventies and they have bridged the gap between early and recent technologies. As the heuristic value of fundamental research is probably its best claim to survival, it is worth noting before proceeding with the case studies that the original Biesheuvel GAB has been carefully rescrutinized by Grant (1969, 1972) and Grant and Schepers (1969). In his research on this test battery, Grant has, indeed, very closely approximated a hard-line model (Irvine & Sanders, 1972) of construct congruence for comparison of test scores across cultures. In the Pacific, Ord's tests have been used many times (Bennett & Chandra, 1974; R. St. George, 1972; A. St. George, 1974). The St. Georges have completed an important new series of experiments that used Ord's work in test development (St. George & St. George, 1974). Their subjects span the developmental range from school entry to Form 3 on Cook Island. In these systematic studies, by Grant and the St. Georges, some of the methodologies used by the earlier testers have been refined; the lessons learned by the pioneers of mass testing have been put to good use; but other questions remain unresearched and unresolved. This will be demonstrated after discovering what the mass testers of preliterates themselves contributed to a theory of data collection, what questions they answered, and what questions remained for others to answer. Throughout is a consciousness of demonstrating directly or obliquely, short-run biases, methodological trial and error, and occasionally success. The seven cross-cultural testing principles were not produced without field work; their history goes back thirty years.

On examining the case-studies of Macdonald, Ord, and Biesheuvel, one will see that a clear rationale for test administration and test construction was not always present in the beginning. However, one should not confuse knowledge and understanding of the origins of cross-cultural data collection through the application of tests with a knowledge of its present state. These early studies reveal (a) the interdependence of test administration and meaning, and (b) the need for independent verification of the construct meaning. Second generation studies, on the other hand, tend to highlight the quests for more certainty in the interpretation of test scores once the problems of test administration were solved.

Next the chapter will address the aims, methods, results, and interpretation of results observed in the work of large-scale testers of illiterate populations in other cultures.

Macdonald's Askaris.   First, in terms of its date of origin, is Macdonald's work. He begins by stating three goals: (a) devising tests that would discriminate among African soldiers; (b) validating these tests by comparing results with proficiency ratings; and (c) constructing and validating tests to show how these can be applied for military, educational, and industrial requirements. Macdonald assumed man's psychic unity, and proceeded as if preliterate and semiliterate African soldiers could, for military purposes, be screened by the same types of tests used on Euro-North Americans, provided that the tests were carefully field tested and restandardized to maximize the probability of stimulus generality that was the basic condition of test administration at that time. For his choice of tasks, he simply "made a fairly intensive study of the previous research work of civilian psychologists and of the technical staff of the Personnel Selection Staff in Middle East Command" (Macdonald, 1945, p. 5). Macdonald and his team devised standardized versions of fifteen tests, only two of which demanded minimal literacy and numeration, and all of which required the subjects to remember and follow instructions which were presented orally in Swahili. One should understand that the subjects were drawn from various East African tribes, and that Swahili was the common language. The report provides a tribal breakdown. Each test was submitted to item analysis and the final battery was factor analyzed. Subsets of tests were also analyzed. This analysis provides the opportunity for discussion of the construct-meanings of the test scores apart from their criterion correlations. Proficiency ratings for 1,384 men were obtained. The "minimum literacy in English test" was the best single predictor. Multiple correlations were attempted by the method of pivotal condensation. The following tests were regarded as the most promising: a variant of the 1938 Raven's matrices called the *African Matrix Test;* a *Screwboard Dexterity Test;* a *Physical Agility Test* involving the transfer of rings from fixed positions to other positions some distance away, in sequence and at speed; basic *English* comprehension; a figural analogies performance test called *Fourth Corner Test;* and a *Block Design Test.* This grouping yielded a multiple R in the region of .35 with the criterion of supervisor's proficiency rating, whose unreliability is unquestioned. Looking back on it, this 1944 achievement, in terms of scope, size, and potential value for applied cross-cultural psychology, has yet to be surpassed.

Examination of the report also shows that Macdonald followed a British testing tradition. His measures carried with them an assumption about the nature of man's intellect. Not only that, but his centroid factor analysis, following the Burt method, was biased toward producing general factors. Far from being critical, however, the reader should remember that the hand calculated centroid was all that was available to Macdonald at that time. Simple structure and objective rotation methods were many years away. It is hardly surprising, then, that his analysis shows one general factor plus two others. Reasoning, manual dexterity, and physical quickness or speed appear to be the main latent dimensions of the battery.

Ord's Pacific Island tests.   Ord's experience with the Pacific Island Regiment (PIR) tests was almost identical. His early principles (Ord, 1971, pp. 20 ff.) can be explained in terms of the need to communicate the task easily. Such tasks were to have no variance associated with the dexterity required to perform them, nor, as far as possible, with the differing cultural heritage of the recruits. Finally, test security demanded that the content could not be passed on in kinship groups having oral traditions. With these requirements, Ord began with subtests of the *Stanford-Binet*, and versions of the *Knox Cube Text*, *Alexander's Passalong Test*, *Bead Chain Copying*, and the *Draw-a-Man Test*. He reported that any test requiring interpretation of figural or symbolic material, or needing a pencil to encode a response, had to be rejected. Hence the battery was determined by what could be communicated to illiterates, and was based on the assumption that Pacific Islanders could learn skills necessary to maintain a modern army. Both Ord and Macdonald assumed the psychic unity of mankind.

Whereas the major impacts of Macdonald's report are the revelation it provides for later field workers—something akin to what Scott's feelings might have been if he had realized that Ammundsen had indeed reached the Pole first but had expired on arrival—it also provides an object lesson in painstaking solid application of psychometric principles to operational tests. Ord's work illustrates another aspect. Working virtually in isolation, Ord found he had to replicate the methods of test presentation advocated by Macdonald that were unknown to him at that time. Ord left explicit instructions for stimulus generalization in a narrow band of tests. Moreover, wherever they have been used, serviceable validities have resulted; workers following Ord have found his data-collection methods robust, and his analyses to be further substantiated. Both studies underline the unassailable operational success of the methods used in these early large-scale group testing studies. What the tests mean in terms of their interpretation as constructs remains to be settled.

Biesheuvel's General Adaptability Battery (GAB).   Finally, Biesheuvel's General Adaptability Battery (GAB) has been used with unschooled populations to the satisfaction of heavy industry, not only in South Africa, but in other countries where the same mining companies have had the problems of selecting from a large number of applicants with little or no schooling. The characteristics of the tests are straightforward and the GAB consists of two speed classification tests, one of which uses nuts, bolts, screws, and washers for classification. The other uses coded metal discs to be sorted according to a visible code. A *Cube Construction Test* and a *Tripod Assembly Test* constitute the other measures. Good predictive validities have resulted from the use of the GAB in employee selection. Revisions of the battery have taken place over the years and it has now been replaced by another group of tests, to which Grant's (1969) work contributed greatly.

All three studies showed that communication could be established with illiterate groups; that satisfactory and predictive validities of performance in industrial settings were possible; and that, operationally, the testing procedures were sound. Each case study discovered its own testing principles, that were markedly similar although differing in detail. Such replication of procedures makes an oblique statement about what factors control true score variance. The seven principles were the long-term gain of such promising beginnings. As pointed out earlier, however, methods of communicating with subjects and the meanings of the test scores were not isolated from each other. Given successful communication with illiterates what did these test scores mean?

Constructs across cultures: the beginnings.   Biesheuvel assumed that most of the variance among individuals could be accounted for by a general factor; hence, the name *General Adaptability* given to the test battery. Unlike Ord and Macdonald who used an *implicit* general factor theory Biesheuvel constructed his test from a firm and *explicit* general factor position. Biesheuvel explicitly asserted that the structure of mankind's abilities implies unity in a hierarchical organization. Macdonald's, Ord's, and Biesheuvel's work dramatize one of the central debates in cross-cultural research. The question that arises is whether or not the structure of intellect that derives from factor analysis is a function of the sampling of test materials themselves or a function of the structure of man's abilities. Probably the answer is somewhere between these two extremes. Moreover, variations in experimenter bias, population parameters, and instrumentation will also contribute to what a particular factor analysis means. For a glimpse of the dangers, consult Carroll (1972, p. 323). Without taking sides in the great debate, it is thus possible to point out to those who see general factors as merely a consequence of man's mental structure itself, that a rival hypothesis is almost always plausible. Macdonald, Ord, and Biesheuvel all gave an extremely restricted range of mental tests to illiterates, and this may be the reason for the structure obtained. Because of the problems of communication, limits were set on what could or could not be assessed. Range was restricted by communication; and test meaning and communication procedures are interdependent. Yet, without assuming process-similarity behind the test products, testing in such circumstances would be a logical non sequitur.

Constructs: another universe of discourse.   However, when one reflects on the tests used with illiterates, one realizes that one *must* assume that a great many processes are going on inside the heads of the people who are being tested. Processes of short-term and middle-term memory, of classification, of storage of information, of retrieval of information, and of performing operations on pieces of information retrieved from storage are palpably involved. Introspective examination of the measures of Macdonald, Ord, and Biesheuvel also suggest visualization, transformation, and synthesis (for example, building single tiles or blocks into prescribed patterns); one could, in fact, reanalyse these early, basic tests by Carroll's (1974) method or from the point of view of Hunt et al. (1973), and find out just how much the early testers were taking for granted.

Hunt (1971) provocatively asked: "What kind of computer is man?" We could well ask the same question of the Macdonald, Biesheuvel, and Ord work. "What kind of computer was illiterate man shown to be?" Is he different in kind, or only in degree from literate man? Yet conventional factor analyses, reported by Macdonald, Ord, and Biesheuvel, produce global constructs that seem inadequate to encompass the diversity of demands made on illiterate subjects. With so many different operations clearly evident from a subjective analysis of the tasks demanded of the thousands of subjects tested by virtually the same procedures, and with tests emanating from the same general intelligence tradition, why is it that only general factors, or general plus minor deviations occur? The question is all the more potent when one recalls that the Reuning and Wortley (1973) study among the Bushmen failed to produce the all-powerful general factor.

Macdonald, Ord, and Biesheuvel, one might argue, did indeed have a battery. Their instruments constituted not only batteries of tests in the traditional psychometric sense, but "batteries" of cognitive processes implicit in individual test items, many of which include highly specific mental processes such as those just described. But these specific processes were embedded within the gross vehicle of these performance tests. It is not only possible that they cancelled each other out or acted randomly, but according to the Spearman-Burt theory, they did just that. Only if the specific processes cancel each other out can a general factor be the consequence. This general factor would seem to be the ability to perform rapidly a number of short-term memory operations in sequence according to remembered, stored, or implied information or strategies. The general factor could well be a simple blurring of many processes in tests that in themselves seem simple, but contain many implicit operations that are only globally assessed by the very blunt method of giving one or zero to a required global response that is by no means psychologically simple.

Undoubtedly the work of Hunt (1973) and his associates has suggested to us that psychometricians may indeed have been attacking the structure of intellect on a very broad front with blunt instruments. That they have not all but destroyed it is perhaps a function of the strictness of the discipline imposed by psychometricians on themselves. One may harbour a strong suspicion that *Raven's Matrices* behaves like a "g" test because it demands so many different specific processes, and the specifics do cancel each other out, producing a general factor. Evidence for this supposition simply comes from the fact that "g" tests do correlate with more homogeneous tests whose short-term memory operations are more evident. They correlate less well with long-term memory verbal tests. This discussion then, leads us to a third viewpoint that couches the debate between process and test-content sampling in these terms. How far then, are general factors artifacts of very imprecise instruments interacting with various basic mental processes for which adequate measuring instruments are only now being developed? It seems, indeed, that the reexamination of the case studies of Macdonald, Ord, and Biesheuvel has posed that question.

By implication, the methods of cross-cultural testing and of data gathering can never be the same again. Now there are the seven principles, some basic propositions for and the means of experimental variation of methods of giving tests across cultures. One such example has been presented, and many more are possible. Such research was not feasible in the pioneering days. Also available are the critique and the instrumentation of cognitive information processing (CIP) theorists to apply to traditional psychometric test theory. The Campbell-Fiske (1959) paper will not be denied. The discussion of the second generation paper and pencil studies will illustrate what methods have already moved on.

Second Generation Testing—A Decade of Progress

In considering second generation paper and pencil studies, and their methodological implications, this discussion first follows some present day extensions of the work of Biesheuvel and Ord, most of which use paper and pencil measures. Have present day studies produced any appreciable shift *in method or approach?* The evidence shows scientific advances over early work.

First, Biesheuvel's GAB has undergone extensive revision, as a consequence of Grant's (1969) work. The GAB has been revised, and scientists look on results from it in a different light, as some recent findings with the revised GAB clearly show. The annual report of the National Institute for Personnel Research (N.I.P.R., 1974) in Johannesburg deserves particular attention because it shows that the linear descendant of the GAB, now the Classification Test Battery (CTB), has been subjected to a quasi-experimental trial. It is now seen as a *learning task*, as well as a psychometric test. One group of mine workers was exposed to the battery five times at regular three-month intervals over a year. Another group took it four times following an initial six-month interval; the remaining test presentations were at three-month intervals. A third group had only three exposures, the second and third being nine and twelve months later. The fourth had only two exposures at a year's interval. Figure 5–1 shows the results. The report states (p. 11):

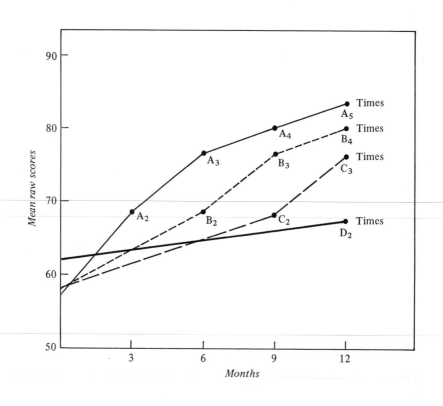

Figure 5–1. Means for Four Groups of African Mineworkers Tested at Different Intervals on Classification Test Battery. (NIPR 1974)

The results of the study show clearly that mining experience has a negligible effect upon test performance. Repeated exposure to the battery, on the other hand, has a marked effect, producing a classical learning curve. Some interesting points were that the greatest increase occurs between the first and the second exposure to the test battery and this is virtually the same magnitude whether the second exposure occurs 3, 6, 9 or 12 months after the first.

Clearly, this battery, as applied to the semiliterate respondents, is a learning *task* as well as an ability *test*. Given that mean differences exist for different conditions of exposure (Trial 1, 2, 3, 4, 5) how do the scores relate to other measures whose meanings are constant over time? Does structure change concomitantly with trials? What other learning measures relate to it? And in what way? To be sure, the questions are open ended, but the sophistication that would put a battery into a quasi-experimental design, capable of further multivariate analysis, was rare ten years ago, even in North American contexts. Today the tools that may be used to answer some, if not all of these questions, are available. See Allison (1960) and Bunderson (1964) for methodological insights into testing transfer and learning across cultures.

A painstaking cross-disciplinary approach, based on the studies with the early Biesheuvel GAB, is found in the work of Grant (1969). Again, this work is not well known since it has had only summary exposure in the literature (Grant, 1972). Grant conducted three experiments; the second constructed an urbanization scale. In his first experiment he included tests from the original GAB battery along with additional performance tests of implied spatial restructuring and synthesis. Significantly, he adopted one of Ord's tests that indicated a close literature review. The experiment showed that the previous single factor dominating performance scales among illiterates can be broken up by including different tests and using different rotational methods. It is possible to break up Macdonald's general factor, as Irvine (1969a) and Grant and Schepers (1969) independently discovered through reanalysis of the original data by different factorial methods. Having constructed an urbanization scale in the second experiment, *Grant then proceeded to use that scale and length of schooling as classification variables.* He then isolated four groups (rural literates, urban literates, rural illiterates, and urban illiterates) and tested them, using the same set of cognitive measures he developed in his first experiment. Grant then compared the four groups. By sophisticated factor analytic procedures, involving internal cross-checks on the comparability of the data matrices, he concluded that schooling affects not only mean levels of performance on tests, but also structure of intellect as implied in the correlation of various test measures. Had Grant (1969) simply argued differences in levels, as indicated by means, of the attainment of literates and illiterates he would have missed the point. From factor analytic data one can argue that the structure of intellect, as shown by the factors, is markedly altered (Grant,

1969, p. 275) by schooling. The differences in mean level performance might have the same predictive or operational function in relation to a single criterion of performance, but completely different construct definition (see Irvine, 1964a, 1970) depending on the structure implicit in the correlations of tests for each separate group. Grant explains the structure differences, with reference to Ferguson's (1954) theory of abilities, as clusters of overlearned skills.

In short, the heuristic impetus of the work by Biesheuvel and his colleagues has so far culminated in a carefully designed series of experiments that *begin* the study of the effects of schooling, urbanism, work experience, and learning within cognitive models. Known classifications were used to probe the meanings of tests. Without a multivariate design, in the context of acceptable scale definitions of literacy and urbanization, the effects of schooling and urbanization would undoubtedly have been confounded in Grant's study. A lot has been claimed for both constructs—schooling and urbanization—but Grant was one of the first to use the scientific windfalls of the cross-cultural setting (literate and illiterate subjects whose ages and levels of schooling were known, and degree of urbanization estimated by a well constructed scale) combined with psychometric procedures to make a start in the study of treatment variables. Although Cole and Scribner have claimed that one cannot make a coherent statement about test score meaning in literate and illiterate groups, the very value of the multivariate approach is that it does make such a statement possible. That universe of discourse, however, is not Piagetian; nor is it the discourse of anthropological cognition. Nevertheless, comparison of Grant's (1969) thesis and Scribner's (1974) paper is not as far fetched an exercise as it might seem. Although the studies are methodologically different, they are, surprisingly, in agreement. Scribner's results are a graphic example of the effects of schooling on recall using taxonomic categories. There are, however, no accompanying psychometric tests to control for individual differences in structure and level of cognitive functioning within each group. *Hence we cannot be certain that the same or different cognitive processes as defined by correlational analysis enter into the classification experiment for literates and illiterates.* Grant's work suggests that the cognitive structures may be different. Scribner's work does not indicate what the causes of such differences in taxonomic structuring are; they will remain unknown until they can be described and predicted more fully. Understanding would begin if it were known that different structures of intellect are reflected in the taxonomy. It can be surmised by extrapolating from Grant's work, but it cannot be proven until multivariate measures have been added to the experimental rigor of such studies. Had Scribner been open to the use of performance measures among illiterate and literate subjects, the gain of knowledge might have been worthwhile in itself, or indeed may have suggested further experimental trials. Reuning and Wortley's (1973) successes with the Bushmen can hardly be ignored.

This comparison of Grant's and Scribner's work enables us to assert that the split between anthropological and psychometric workers in cross-cultural psychology is really the same split that Cronbach described some years ago in psychology; namely, the split between experimental and psychometric traditions. Both Scribner and Grant used anthropological knowledge in order to structure their experiments. Grant used *macrocosmic* multivariate methods, while Scribner uses *microcosmic* experimental procedures [Lloyd's (1972) terms]. Individually, each points to the need for further study, but neither is complete. That realization is an important step forward. To sum up, Scribner's paper and Grant's thesis are apt examples of quests for certainty about psychological process. Grant's shows that searches for stimulus identity are not fruitless in multivariate contexts; Scribner's work, premised on conceptual equivalence, leaves questions that require greater assurance about the meaning of the stimuli than the conceptual experimental framework can supply. Methods used in the assessment of peoples across cultures have become more varied, but biases are hard to remove. In light of this, what assistance is now possible from psychometricians in the quest for a structure of intellect?

Stimulus generality. The St. George studies lead to a consideration of the important avenues of psychometric practice. The N.I.P.R. and Grant work illustrate both experimental design application and cross-disciplinary influence allied with advanced analysis techniques. In a sense these are external lessons from other disciplines, but indications are that PSM methodology has also searched within itself for solutions to the problem of test score meaning. The consistency of the results from empirical work carried out across cultures would not have been possible if the test administration procedures had not been robust. The work of the St. Georges (1974) further replicates the earlier operational findings of the 1960s and argues for the validity of test presentation procedures. First, good concurrent validities with performance scales can be found (p. 72). Second, factorial structures diverge from monolithic general factors as schooling increases (p. 135), and more kinds of tests are possible through release from the restrictions of illiteracy. Third, the constructs used in Western societies to describe the meaning of tests in well-schooled groups can be consistently applied to the results of tests administered. Without basically sound test administration procedures these findings could not be consistent, since error variance would randomize results. The methods of obtaining operationally valid test results across cultures are hardly in dispute now. What the individual items or tests signify has also been explored.

Item analysis across cultures.   Early in the 1960s work on item difficulties emerged as an important check on the method of test presentation. Testers were becoming concerned with bias in test results. Scientists in the United States at the Educational Testing Service were independently working on the problem of stimulus generality using an analysis of variance model. Campbell (1964), Cardall and Coffman (1964), Cleary and Hilton (1966), and Cleary (1966) all contributed to the review of several important issues in cross-cultural testing. Cardall and Coffman (1964) and Cleary (1966) concluded that an Item X Ethnic Group Interaction in an analysis of variance design that contrasted item variances across ethnic groups, would indicate *bias* in the test. Item difficulty correlations across ethnic groups, if significantly different from those within ethnic groups, would give an Item X Ethnic Group Interaction in analysis of variance of individual items. Irvine (1964a, p. 181–90) independently adopted a correlational approach. He considered that item difficulties would give a clue as to whether the test was validly and reliably presented.

> *A test presentation* becomes valid when original item difficulties are produced consistently with equivalent populations by one tester. It has reliability over and above validity when the difficulty values are reproduced consistently by any tester. . . . If one wishes to check whether or not a test score is valid for a group, valid that is in the sense of being equatable in meaning with the original standardization of the test, one can, it seems, correlate item difficulties as a means of checking this. (p. 190)

Recent studies, apart from the St. George work, that have been sensitive to differences in item difficulties include Poortinga (1971), Angoff and Sharon (1972), and, most recently, Jensen (1974b). Jensen, incidentally, in the evidence he produces, presents a firm case for presentation of the *Peabody Picture Vocabulary Test* and the *Coloured Progressive Matrices* to Anglo, Mexican, and black groups in California. He prefers to debate the question of "bias" in this context, but it seems that he is making a case for valid presentation and reduction of error variance. The case for psychological equivalence through comparing item difficulties is still assumptive.

The correlation and analysis of variance of item difficulties assumes that items may be difficult in different cultures for different reasons and should be difficult in the same cultures for the same reasons. Hypothetically, however, it is possible to conceive of a test whose ascending difficulty of items on, for example, arithmetical operations was predicated on invariance in the culture of verbal comprehension of these items. In another culture verbal comprehension of the same items could be the main barrier. It could also be possible that the level of difficulty of arithmetic operations per item in culture *A* was exactly the same as the level of difficulty of verbal comprehension per item in culture B. If there were no multivariate design to compare the correlations of different tests with the same test used in both cultures, however, there would be no way to uncover this possible, although unlikely, circumstance. Intercorrelations with other tests would show whether or not the meanings of the "same" test given in two different cultures were different.

Hence, correlation of item difficulties for the same test across cultures is simply an early prophylaxis of endowing a summation of correct responses to an imported test with the same meaning as a similar summation might have in the exporting culture. Irvine and Sanders (1972) particularly advocate calculating item difficulties for at least two groups in each culture and comparing within-group and across-group correlations to find out if the cross-correlations belong to a different population of correlations than do the within-group correlations. Given enough samples on the same test across cultures it is possible to factor analyze item indices or to conduct analyses of variance if the indices have been constructed on completely independent samples. If, in culture A a problem arithmetic test correlated well with other arithmetic tests but less well with language tests, but in culture B the opposite held, we would conclude that close correlation of item difficulties in the arithmetic test across cultures was an artifact of test construction. The chances are slim, but they are there, and it is better to check. If, on the other hand, item difficulties are totally dissimilar across cultures, it is difficult to conceive of a case where the constructs assessed by the test could be held to be identical. To sum up, where there are no significant differences in the cross- and within-culture item difficulty correlations, one can be almost certain that the true score variances are similar in kind and amount. If doubt exists, a multivariate check is necessary. When there are significant differences, one can be as certain, if not more so, that the true score variances in the test are somewhat different from each other, although they could have some true-score variance in common. Precisely what that would consist of could not be answered without further analysis. There are, however, many possible checks on test data within traditional test theory. Application of them can improve interpretation of data greatly by reducing the probability of incautious pronouncements.

Traditional and other item models.   Traditional testing theory, from which most of these studies originate, has its challengers and critics, not only across cultures but within cultures. The Rasch (1966) model of item analysis has been suggested as an alternative to so-called "circular" theories of test construction. Significantly, the time lag between suggesting this approach in one culture and operationalizing it in other cultures is shortening. Hence it does seem important that when a theory originates in western cultures, experienced cross-cultural psychologists should replicate or attempt to replicate the theories beyond the constraints of replication by willing Ph.D. students whose domicile is the North American laboratory. Strong methodological critiques of present day practices in test use across cultures are proposed by Eckensberger (1972) and Mellenbergh (1972). Few studies have checked as carefully and as commendably on individual differences in test item behaviour reflected in item characteristics as van der Flier's (1975). Mellenbergh (1972) operationalized the Rasch model (also suggested by Eckensberger) with Dutch and Indonesian children, only to find that it held neither for Dutch nor Indonesian children under the conditions of testing at that time. Mellenbergh's paper is, indeed, salutary for those who seek cross-cultural invariance of stimulus behaviour from a new theory requiring extensive within-culture trial in itself. One can be certain that the Rasch model will be tried out *alongside* traditional models as part of another *method* of looking at the same data. Just as different methods of factor analysis should be applied to the same correlation matrices to test for methodological bias, there is good justification for examining the same test protocols by different item analysis procedures.

Identical stimuli or equivalent processes. It must be apparent by now that there is no easy way of implementing a stimulus equivalence or "phenomenal identity" (Straus, 1969) approach to cross-cultural comparison. Practice which stresses the need for identical test conditions, and by implication identical stimuli, exists in the study of perception. The most obvious example is the Segall, Campbell, and Herskovits (1966) study of optical illusions. Here, the stimulus or test material *must* be phenomenally identical across cultures since it is a variable, as distinct from a means of inferring a variable. In the symbology of Woodworth's basic S-O-R model, only when one of the variables under investigation is an *S*, is the criterion of cross-cultural stimulus equivalence unequivocally applicable. In cases where *O* or *S-O* are involved, that is, where some cognitive attribute or process is inferred, the use of identical stimuli as a guiding principle of test construction may even be misleading. The cross-cultural research on the ability to classify provides a useful example of this problem. A number of researchers have employed tests of concept formation (e.g., Bruner, Olver, & Greenfield, 1966), as well as Piagetian cognitive abilities developed for use in Western cultures in studying non-Western peoples. In these exercises we have examples of adherence to a criterion of stimulus equivalence in studying cognitive functioning cross-culturally. Although findings from such research are often interpreted as indicative of greater simplicity and concreteness in non-Western modes of cognition, a plausible alternative interpretation of the data is that the physically standard instruments give rise to psychologically unequivalent test-taking phenomena. What was context-syntonic for Western subjects, who were much more familiar with the notion of testing itself, not to mention the material used in the tests, could have been context-alien for non-Western subjects. As a consequence, insistence on standard stimuli for all cultures has given way to insistence on equivalent experiences for all cultures. Proponents of the culture-syntonic approach, using basically modified materials (Okonji, 1971; Irwin & McLaughlin, 1970; Kellaghan, 1968; Cole & Gay, 1972· Price-Williams, 1962) have determined that familiar testing materials help to make manifest classificatory ability in test-alien groups that is similar to that demonstrated by Euramericans using culture-syntonic materials that are different from those used in other cultures. When familiarity with test materials is controlled, previously observed differences in classification among culturally different groups may diminish or disappear altogether. Which test materials are familiar or unfamiliar for subjects in the host culture can only be judged and hence controlled as a variable by gaining an understanding of the target culture. This is the lesson that anthropology has to teach psychometricians.

Many anthropological workers, on the other hand, hold that the sole means of ensuring that measurements gained from analogous instrumentation in differing cultures are "conceptually" (Sears, 1961; Straus, 1969) or "functionally" (Berry, 1969) equivalent is by understanding *the meaning and function* of test-taking in each culture. Stimulus equivalence using translated tests or subjects literate and fluent in English is by itself insufficient. Gordon and Kikuchi offer this comment on the use of American personality tests in cross-cultural research:

> Parallel instruments, consisting of identical or near identical items that fully and reliably measure a particular construct within two cultures, still may not provide sufficient data for making cross-cultural comparisons. Constructs, in any culture, do not stand alone. They bear particular relationships to other constructs for particular subgroups and these relationships help define the meaning of the construct as much as the items through which they are measured. (1966, p. 182)

This comment, of course, shows how difficult it is to make comparisons of any kind. Conceptual equivalence, without empirical demonstration that the construct is anchored similarly in the cultures under study, is difficult to interpret. In general psychometric work uncorrelated first-order factors can be interpreted only intuitively. Similarly, constructs that are without similar anchors can be interpreted only intuitively. If there is no empirical support for the transcultural portability of the "same stimuli" for conceptual equivalence in experimental studies, or an empirically validated rationale for *different* stimuli that offer convergent and discriminant validity across cultures (e.g., exact translation failing to convey meaning adequately), the experimental approach will have to rely on intuition to define what is being measured in the dependent variable.

A summation by Eckensberger (1972) carries over to the next section of this chapter that deals with traditional attempts at construct validation through factor analysis. The quotation provides a hint of a solution to the problem of construct validation.

> Carried to the extreme, the cross-cultural strategy, combined with designs of developmental psychology and experimental manipulation of cultural conditions (coaching, practice, test sophistication), in itself is to be interpreted as validating the instruments and theories of psychology: i.e., it is to be understood as part of construct validation. (pp. 105–106)

A theory of data collection is in fact a prerequisite for any reasonable and logical discussion of constructs across cultures. Nevertheless, once one has checked item difficulties in a cross-cultural test battery, and found that "different" stimuli produced identical sets of item statistics, one might be tempted to advance a claim for proceeding to factor analysis as a step towards theory construction. An assessment of the use of factor analysis in such theory construction will be discussed next.

Checks and Balances on Inference from Scores

Construct Validity Methods—Factor Analysis

In the long run, construct validation is the *only* thing. Factor analysis has been the major multivariate tool of users of paper and pencil tests across cultures. Few of those who have used paper and pencil tests have reified the constructs they have discovered in their correlation matrices. Yet, many reviewers and interpreters of these studies have not communicated the tentative nature of the findings that the field workers themselves advanced. Perhaps few will accept unequivocally factor analytic construct validation experiments across cultures when they are presented with a survey of broad, general analyses.

Generalized claims for construct validity arising from factor analysis of data matrices are usually a function of two kinds of sampling in cross-cultural research. To advance generalized claims one has first to demonstrate that the tests include an *adequate method and trait sampling* of what has to be measured. Second, the subjects themselves should be *representative of the population* or populations sampled. A third and necessary element in multivariate analysis is that *the size of the sample* must be sufficient to stabilize the correlations and/or regression equations. Fourth, structures should be invariant when subjected to a *number of factor analytic methods.*

Lastly, the invariance should *extend across many cultures.* For a multivariate analysis to be conclusive, large numbers are needed. Clearly, given an infinite number of variables and subjects, in an infinite number of populations to be compared by an infinite number of different factoring methods, similarity of factor loading profiles, factorial invariance, or construct congruence would be impressive empirical findings. Given the same invariance across a large number of *cultures* it would be even more impressive. As the number of cultures approached infinity, continued similarities of factor profiles in the face of such diversity would be conclusive to a theory that accounted for them. There would be, in the memorably clumsy, but immensely apt phrase of Segall, Campbell, and Herskovits (1966), "the background of non-discrepant fit!" (p. 213).

The ideal conditions for such studies will, of course, never be fulfilled; research workers know that. Instead, the tests, subjects, and cultures used in construct validation by multivariate methods are all *samples.* The trouble is that few writers seem to write as if they recognize this, and few interpreters seem to subject results from field studies to rigorous scrutiny for kinds of plausible rival hypotheses (e.g., sampling bias or test presentation nonvalidity). Some of the most prominent studies of cross-cultural factor analysis include Vandenberg (1959, 1967), Guthrie (1963), Irvine (1969b), Vernon (1969), and MacArthur (1973). As a study in many cultures Vernon's (1969) report is still unique, though severely limited as a factor-analytic model by virtue of its very small sample sizes, subjective methods of analysis, and the tendency of the author to overgeneralize from his findings. In terms of size and representativeness of samples Irvine's (1969) African results are satisfactory, yet the variables in that study are seriously restricted and the analysis is a post hoc one. Vandenberg's work extends over many tests and is replicated in Chinese-American and Spanish-American cultures. Vandenberg's rotation of various matrices to a target matrix, however, is held to be less defensible today than it was then. Guthrie's analysis shares a wide range of tests with Vandenberg's study and replicates Vandenberg's position, but it does not suffer from forced rotation of matrices to any prespecified pattern. Jensen (1971, 1973c) undertook large-scale studies and submitted his results to factor analysis in order to compare the patterns of correlations, based on several measures, across cultures. Further comparison may be made with earlier studies such as Grant (1969) and St. George (1974).

Various criticisms may be levelled at each of these studies; it is better to dispose of them initially and then to look at the positive gains. Table 5–1 summarizes the major qualifications that hedge these particular cross-cultural examples of factor analytic work.

The table headings list standard criticisms except for the check on item behaviour. The reasons for such a check have been explained in the

Table 5–1. Some Cross-Cultural Factor Analyses and Their Limitations (1959–1974).

Study		Two Groups Only	Restricted Variables	Restricted Educational Range	Small vs. Many	No Check on Item Difficulty	Intuitive Rotations	Post-Hoc Study
				LIMITATIONS OF STUDY				
VANDENBERG	1959	X		X	X	X		
VANDENBERG	1967	X		X	X	X		
GUTHRIE	1963			X	X	X		
IRVINE	1969		X	X		Partial		X
MacARTHUR	1973			X	X	X		
VERNON	1969			X	X	X		
GRANT	1969		X	Somewhat			X	
JENSEN	1973		X	X		Partial		
ST. GEORGE	1974		X	X	X			

214

previous section. These criticisms would now include the comparison of only two cultures, restricted samples of tests, small numbers of subjects in relation to the number of variables, samples restricted in educational range, no check on item characteristics, intuitive versus objective rotational procedures, post hoc analysis versus factor studies designed to test an experimental hypothesis. Each of the studies cited has faults, but it is interesting to note that the more recent studies commit fewer *unforced errors*. All studies have samples restricted to some degree by educational range. From a review of this work, most of which has had extensive quotation in the literature, the following conclusions emerge, despite the criticisms.

(1) *The various ability constructs are robust.* In spite of many factor analytic methods used independently by the investigators, they show the consistent clustering of test families across cultures for which similarity of interaction among groups of individuals and ordered sets of stimuli (tests) must be assumed. In this respect the results show gradual accumulation of evidence for factor invariance. They also confirm that test administration procedures are sound. Without such soundness factor patterns simply would not be consistent. Finally, *different tests* of the *same* ability have been analysed in different cultures, giving the same factor structure (Irvine, 1969a, p. 23). These tests were local school examinations constructed by different officials in different African states. Yet their factorial behaviour is remarkably stable. Because of these findings, there is a great deal of merit in regarding factors *operationally* as variables that have been found consistent across cultures particularly in the areas of verbal comprehension, arithmetic facility, perceptual speed, inductive reasoning, figural manipulation, and transformation in short-term memory (spatial reasoning), to name only the most consistent. As variables synthesised from tests, factors are often more consistent in their behaviour across cultures than the individual tests. Provided the factor analysis does not contain gross experimental errors, factor scores seem good variables for *classifying individuals within different cultures* on the same broad areas of competence. Thus classified by synthetic variables in whose true-score variance some confidence may be placed, subjects can then be subjected to experimental tasks to investigate whether or not the same experimental "laws" hold in culture X as they do in culture Y. One could, for example, find out whether high verbals in culture X behave in the same way as high verbals do in culture Y, using the procedures of Hunt, Lunneborg, and Lewis (1975). Factors used in this way are used profitably. Factor scores used to compare *levels* across cultures are back into the problem of proving that factor score X is exactly comparable in terms of proportions of true score variance as is factor score Y. That could well prove to be a systematically misleading and unprofitable enterprise.

(2) *The precise theoretical base of these clusters of interactions is, and always has*

been, a matter of some debate. The debate is almost as old as psychometrics itself. Some authors favour hierarchical constructs with strong, causal, global determinants such as *g* as ultimate explanations. Others favour uncorrelated constructs. Some point to invariant educational parameters as strong treatment effects (e.g., rigorous selection on nationwide examinations in developing countries) accounting for such factors. There is no resolution. But the resolution might come through another approach, which has been mentioned and will be discussed next. Meanwhile the consistency of the clusters of tests is unmistakable.

(3) *Others (particularly Carroll, 1974), strongly influenced by linguistic and computer applications to cognitive model building, offer a hope of resolution by suggesting that factors be investigated by alternative procedures.* That is, they describe factors in terms of assumed processes that can be measured *by another method.* That they can, to some extent, be measured by another method (see Hunt et al., 1973), is certain. In short, such approaches suggest how to strengthen the traditional psychometric tradition. When one reexamines (and only an intuitive examination has been attempted by the reviewers) some of the cross-cultural factor studies, it is possible to account for factor analytic results in terms of the broad division among tests relying on the contents of long-term memory store (all educational measures) but with different data bases (social studies, English comprehension, arithmetic): those relying on manipulation of material within the constraints of short-term and intermediate-term memory (e.g., most figural tests), and those that combine both long-term memory strategies and short-term memory operations (e.g. mental arithmetic). Hence it is one thing to attribute some differences in test performance to cultural variations in long-term memory stores. It is quite another thing to deny the existence of long- and short-term memory and operations as a construct in any culture. Simply to assess them as universal processes, however, is no help either. This last observation points to the need for more fine-grained analysis. Factors should be the variables used for preclassification of subjects in such fine-grained or microscopic studies. This quotation from Hunt et al. (1973, p. 119) may help cross-cultural psychologists. It points out the weakness and strength of traditional PSM work:

> In the most immediate future, then, the challenge to psychometrics will be that of bringing well-developed multivariate analytic tools to bear on the establishment of a measurement multidimensionality based upon a model of cognitive functioning. . . . We suggest that when extensive assessment is accomplished, the model parameters might be suitable for factorization.

The challenge is there, and the cross-disciplinary gap between anthropological cognition and the "testing movement" is not as wide as the gap within psychology itself, which Hunt and his associates attempt to close.

Just as test-based theories have something to learn from the theoretical contribution of cognitive information processing models, so, by implication, have other approaches to cognitive functioning across cultures.

A Checklist for Would-be Comparisons

The strong cross-cultural factorial similarities of PSM empiricists, then, are indicators that laboratory work can be carried out in other cultures using the ability construct as prima facie evidence of psychic unity. The clusters identified by correlation analysis seem sufficiently durable to enable laboratory experiments related to them in Euro-North American contexts to be carried out in conjunction with tried demonstrants of the construct in other cultures. For example, it would be entirely appropriate to use factor scores purporting to show individual differences in verbal skills in non-Western cultures to separate high verbal and low verbal groups for application of short-term memory (STM) tasks. If the results were identical across cultures one could conclude that high and low verbal subjects were both correctly identified by the factoring of PSM tests and that they obeyed the same set of experimental "laws." If not, and if the only uncertainty in the experiment were "the verbal factor," it could come under systematic scrutiny. However, the user has to justify his choice of measures, and intuition is hardly enough (see Lonner & Brislin, 1974, p. 382). Nor is a conviction that a process is universal, without defining precisely what is meant by process, and then operationalizing that definition by showing expected relationships in a multimethod, multitrait context. Hence cross-cultural comparisons based on factor analysis may have an important intermediate status. The constructs should not be seen as cultural and causal absolutes if they lack further theoretical verification by other assessment methods. They are constrained by the logic of constructs (see Royce, 1963; Irvine & Sanders, 1972), as well as by the errors in sampling that can confound interpretation.

A wide arc has been drawn around procedures of test administration and construct validity in first and second generation studies across cultures that maintain the thesis that psychometric procedures have an essential, but not unqualified, role in cognitive assessment. It now remains to set out a methodological rationale for the involvement of these procedures in experiments demanding that variables have a noncriterion or descriptive meaning. What can be distilled from (a) the previous discussion of different approaches to measurement, (b) a surviving strain of test-giving procedures, and (c) experiments with item indices and correlation matrices that show similarity in the face of much diversity?

It is possible to see that the early preliterate mass testing was limited by methodological and theoretical constraints. Paper and pencil testers, facing operational demands of the same kinds in the 1960s, provided a code of test application procedures that included the germs of a theory of intellect, since the procedures presuppose a learning model. Additionally, testers were becoming far more cautious about labeling the products of test scores in comparing means. They were searching for a rival plausible hypothesis for test results. In fact, the hard-line position was that the mean comparison of any pair of test scores, without several different kinds of checks, was indefensible. Hence if one were to put forward an experiential rationale for test data collection across cultures leading to comparisons across cultures, this would imply *descriptive* meaning, rather than *predictive* meaning, within cultures.

Experimental verification of many of the "methods" is still necessary, and all the lessons that have been learned in the past decade should be applied to the task. The check list would be long. A possible rationale, along with some supporting comments, is produced below since it follows from the discussions in the chapter so far.

(1) In the application of tests across cultures make certain that an adequate sampling of behaviours that have been overlearned in all cultures is represented. Study carefully school syllabi, curriculum guidelines, etc. for an operational definition of what has been or might have been overlearned in schools. Find out, from anthropological records, what intellectual games are played. As far as possible satisfy the Campbell-Fiske (1959) multitrait, multimethod constraints in the choice of tests used. Study closely the Straus (1969) paper on phenomenal identity and conceptual equivalence. In short, gain an insider's or participant observer's view of the target cultures.

(2) In group test application use vernacular presentation and local testers; but check for tester variation. Apply Irvine's seven principles of test presentation (pp. 196–197) to adapt methods to the local testing situation. Check to see if they hold up. Note particularly the difficulties subjects encountered. Ask them to tell the experimenters what these are, and have some subjects verbalize their test-taking strategies. Finalize testing procedures for each test after extensive field trials and then allow latitude to the trained testers.

(3) Make certain that complete item statistics exist for each measure used in any group comparison. Once the data is collected, first compare item statistics between the experimental (culture-alien) and control (culture-syntonic) groups for each measure. If these are dissimilar throughout, it would be unwise to proceed further with any group comparison of mean scores. If they are dissimilar for any one measure, discard it. Without such checks, phenomenal identity or stimulus generality could not even be assumed. If the check is satisfactory, then an argument for a presentation of the test has been made that is close to what one might expect in the culture of origin. But it is still only an assumption.

(4) If the item statistics are similar, proceed to examine the latent structure of the tests as shown by their intercorrelations. This must be done before means can be compared. Correlate all the test scores. Check the correlation matrices in the experimental group for correlations that exceed the 95 percent confidence limits of the control group correlations. If more than 5 percent of such correlations exist, further comparison may be dubious. It is assumed that in a distribution of a large number of pairs of correlations compared between two samples, 5 percent could exceed chance limits. Rank order the correlations among all possible pairings of variables for each of the samples. Calculate the rank order correlation coefficients. If these are not close to unity, discontinue. The absolute size of a coefficient is important, but the rank order of correlations is as important in factor analysis. If the rank orders of the correlations are decidedly different, it is unlikely that they will yield similar factors. If the variable size is too large, it may be simply less labour to factor analyze. If the variables are not too many, rank ordering and correlation may take less time than card punching.

(5) If these spot-checks show that the correlation matrices are similar, factor them by an objective method that is consistent for each matrix. Do not make the error of including all subsamples in a single factor analysis and then attempting to rotate each subsample to a target matrix in which the subsample has participated. Do not even pick a target matrix and rotate all matrices independently to that. Such procedures can introduce sophisticated experimental errors (Horn, 1967, 1973.). Factor each subsample separately. Before factoring try to ensure that there is one person in each sample for every correlation calculated. If the factors extracted account for all the extractable variance by being the same in number, if the proportions of variance are extracted by each factor, and if the correlations among all the factors extracted for the control and experimental groups are not significantly different for the groups to be compared, then some confidence can be placed in the supposition that tests and individuals have interacted, on the average, in the same fashion. In short, construct congruence could be assumed; but only, it should be noted, for the sample of measures used. It is always, alas, possible that these very constructs could correlate with other constructs not sampled by the tests in an entirely different way for each of the subsamples.

(6) If one then wishes to move from these checks to a comparison of mean levels of achievement within each test or factor score, one may proceed, it seems, at one's peril. Unequivocally, the comparison of means, outside criterion referent measurement, presupposes construct equivalence in all the groups under comparison. Analysis of variance with group classifications (social class, etc.) as a main effect is now feasible. But it should be underlined that factor analysis supports the assumption of similar interaction between stimuli and subjects. It does not prove it: it is not certain what constitutes proof of such an assumption. It seems much more sensible to use factor scores of dimensions that are consistently stable across cultures as a means of classifying different

ethnic groups along similar dimensions of intellectual functioning for the purposes of verifying laws of learning and laws of processing.

Hunt, Lunneborg, and Lewis (1975) have used psychometric variables to classify, in a general fashion, individuals as high or low verbal. Thereafter they uncovered by nonpsychometric methods several perceptual and process correlates of being high verbal. Among these are (a) the ability to recognize speedily a particular visual pattern as being a word, a letter; (b) the ability to retain in short-term memory information about the order of stimulus presentation; and (c) the ability to manipulate data rapidly in short-term memory (pp. 223–24). If information processing ability is "more basic," as Hunt et al. (p. 224) insist, than verbal aptitude, or indeed any other factorial composite, then one ought to be able to observe the *same* relationship between factorial composites and "more basic" abilities across cultures. It would seem that the psychic unity supposition would be upheld by this relationship. Psychic unity would be an assumption difficult to uphold, if the more basic abilities did not exert the same kind of influence on aptitudes in culture X as they did in culture Y. If the relationship between so-called basic abilities and factor scores was not identical then it would seem that the cultural variation in the factorial composite was more basic than the so-called basic abilities. Although semantic arguments about primary and secondary qualities should be avoided, the challenge to combine psychometric tests with cognitive tasks is there. Cross-cultural factor analysis suggests that the compound factor variable is a safer bet than a single test for separating "highs" from "lows" for experimental purposes. Hunt himself argues for reduced variance between CIP and PSM variables in non-American cultures. This should only be so, however, if there is more noise or error in the analysis. The structure should not be affected by lack of variance as much as by lack of consistent sources of variance. The series of checks advocated should reduce noise to a minimum, and high verbals in whatever language should show the same process abilities.

Few if any studies have met the schedule of recommended checks. Nor are many likely to, but the statement indicates where one can go wrong, or where rival hypotheses from mean differences may be generated. In spite of all the social opprobrium heaped on his work, Jensen, in a series of studies (1971, 1973a, 1973b, 1973c, 1974c), comes closest to satisfying all the various psychometric checks. But it should be stated that he has fulfilled some of the checks some of the time but not all of the checks all of the time. Poortinga (1971), Grant (1969), and St. George (1974) have likewise come commendably close. Jensen, however, has felt that his data were strong enough to maintain his unpopular theoretical stance. His scientific, as distinct from social, critics have been much more cautious when the assumptions of stimulus generality have not been met to their satisfaction.

Experienced users of psychological tests across cultures are well aware that for cross-cultural work involving comparisons, ordinary analysis of variance of test scores using one test on two samples is the most inappropriate method that could be applied. A handful of tests on three or more samples is better, but probably not enough (see Lesser, Fifer, & Clark, 1965; Stodolsky & Lesser, 1967). A critique of such procedures may be found in Irvine and Sanders (1972). An infinite number of tests with an infinite number of samples in an infinite number of cultures all satisfying the constraints outlined above would provide the background of "nondiscrepant fit" for true level comparisons. However, *level* as defined by means, and *structure* as defined by correlations in a sampling framework, are not separable, and we must turn now to a small scale practical demonstration of testing methodology, working in step with a single experimental procedure.

Testing Principles and Multivariate Practice: An Example

Given that life is short and art, or science across cultures, is a long affair, what experimental transformation of these recommended practices is possible? How is it possible to make a positive advance scientifically, after having discovered that the means are not comparable? This discovery, it will be readily understood, seldom offers an avenue of research in multivariate studies since there are seldom any variables that can be isolated for experimental control. What blend of experimental and multivariate method seems reasonable? One could begin with the most obvious problem, giving a single test under one set of positive, optimum culture-consonant conditions, and giving it under standard Western (culture-alien) conditions to samples from the same test-alien population. Assuming that previous analysis of item difficulties has assured valid and reliable stimulus presentation is not a new kind of exercise. Coaching experiments assuming psychological identity for two sets of test scores have been done on tests given in other cultures before, for example, the work of Lloyd and Pidgeon (1961), Silvey (1963), Jacobs (1963, 1964, 1966), and Roberts and Oppenheim (1966). We know, from these studies in particular and others like them, that mean increases on tests given under coaching conditions are to be expected. It is now suspected that motivational variance is introduced by ethnicity in conjunction with the language of test presentation.

None of this is very new, but the assumption that the meaning of a test is the same when test presentations are altered is now under attack. A most telling challenge to this assumption, when different motivational conditions have been experimentally induced, is provided by Hürsch (1972). Medley and Quirk (1974, p. 244) also find themselves intrigued by item X group interaction in a carefully crafted study. To tease out the complexities of this situation, no application of a single test is sufficient by itself. A test has meaning in relation to other tests or measures and its construct definition is obtained by relating the test with other tests and measures. This is the thrust of the multivariate method. It would not be appropriate to ask what the test score means without satisfying the strictures of such a method. How might one assert that different methods of test presentation achieve increases or nonincreases in score without changing the relationship of that score to other measures whose meaning remains constant? This is an interesting extension of Lord's (1965) elegant exposition of the paradox of group comparisons. Two conditions are necessary for resolution of the problem. First, the test can be administered using different methods. Test administration then becomes the independent variable. Previously shown was what happened to *Raven's Matrices* scores when race and language were manipulated as independent variables. Second, the test score results (the dependent variable) can be correlated with marker variables that have been administered under standard conditions. These procedures would enable the researchers to assess first whether a change of method increased or decreased a mean score. That, however, can be appropriate only if the meaning of the test as assessed by the marker variables remained unchanged. Hence, one must next relate those test scores to find out if the relationships between the marker variables and the tester's presentation method are constant when different methods of test administration are employed.

For example, Irvine (1964a) administered the *Standard Raven's Progressive Matrices* during field work in 1962, under uncoached and coached conditions, to five groups of children with eight years of education from schools in the same sector of Harare African township, Mashonaland. Fortunately, other tests and measures were given under identical conditions, thus providing marker variables. Mean differences in scores (see Table 5–2) favoured coached groups and variance was reduced under coached conditions. Had such scores been used in a summative and predictive way, the coached conditions would have been advantageous. Here, however, the concern is on possible variations in meaning or true-score variance of the dependent variable (*Raven's Matrices Score*) when the conditions of testing are altered. The correlations with marker variables given under identical conditions serve as indicators.

A population coefficient of correlation was first established with *Raven* and the other measures. Such a correlation, calculated on all 204 subjects, is somewhat clouded for comparison purposes, since each school group contributed to it. Nevertheless, that disadvantage is outweighed by the

Table 5–2.   Correlations of *Raven's Matrices* with Marker Tests, under Various Conditions of Administration to Shona Eight-Year Educated Children.

| Raven Conditions | Tests Given Same Conditions | | | | |
	Exams	M.A.L.	C.S.	Num.	S.9
All					
	45	56	49	52	46
Population Estimate	55–33	65–46	59–37	61–41	56–34
No Practice					
GP1	30*	43*	42	23*	31*
M25; SD11; N=89					
GP2	36	65	68*	54	41
Average No Practice	32*	55	56	40*	36
Practice					
GP3 A M27; SD8; N=40	53	78*	46	58	60*
GP4 B M30; SD7; N=49	47	38*	11*	55	52
GP5 A M27; SD8; N=39	66*	54	60*	69*	56
Average Practice	56*	59	46	61*	51

NOTES: For GP3 and GP5 means and SDs calculated together. Similarly for GPs 1 and 2. Details of this study found in Irvine, 1964a, pp. 68–79. Asterisked correlations beyond 95 percent limits of population estimate. Averages by *r* to *z* transformation.

knowledge that the correlation calculated over all five groups takes account of unintentional variation in testing conditions at the time. In short, the correlation thus calculated is the best population estimate available, since it accounts for variation in *all* the experimental conditions. Table 5–2 establishes the correlation of each of the marker tests with *Raven* under various coached and uncoached conditions. Average correlations for coached and uncoached conditions are also given. Briefly, it can be observed that when the correlations under specific experimental conditions are compared with the confidence-limit correlations of the population estimate, the correlation of *Raven* with educational aptitude tests (*School Examinations, Mental Alertness,* and the *Numerical Ability Test*) *increases* under coached conditions. On the other hand, the variations in *Raven* correlations with tests based on inductive reasoning operations are what one might expect from chance fluctuations. Therefore, in this particular experiment, the true-score variance *components* of *Raven* under different administration procedures are probably the same, although *the ratios* of the various components alter under different testing conditions. The variations in size of correlations for individual conditions are exaggerated by small numbers in the various groups, but Practice Condition *B* produced correlations that warrant more investigation.

The test procedures *themselves* now require study, since the results place them in a causal position, which is the point that was made early in this chapter. Further research would concentrate in that area. This example, of course, is imperfect in that other kinds of restrictions on the marker variables would have to be satisfied. To be fair, all the checks on method advocated above were not carried out on them. In 1962 they were not deemed relevant and the original protocols have long since disappeared. The marker variables would have to be shown to have intercorrelations among themselves that were not significantly different for the two separate samples; the item difficulties from school to school would have to be consistent, and so on. This particular example is not perfect. However, there *are* changes associated with different methods of communicating with respondents. Communication and test meaning are interdependent, and true-score variance is seldom unifactorial. Test administration variation has, of course, to be the agent of change in true-score variance. The interface of experimental rigour and multivariate analysis is not a circular, self-defeating maze.

The operational extension of these findings to decision making according to a criterion is simple. If any of these school achievement tests had been a criterion and *Raven's Matrices* the predictor, using *Raven's* scores for one group, as if they bore the same relationship to the criterion as they did in the other group, would have been problematic, since the regression slopes for the correlations would have been significantly different. The test's construct meaning can be made explicit only from the test's correlations with *many* other variables. Its criterion relationship depends only on its correlation with the criterion variable. But neither the total variance nor the proportions of variance accounted for by the test, when given under different conditions, would lead to the conclusion that it could be represented as "the same test," or more precisely the same psychological experience, for these two different samples. In short, conceptual equivalence cannot be assumed from these findings, since *phenomenal identity has not been preserved by the testing procedures*. Hence, although the circularity of construct validation and of psychometric testing across cultures has often been argued, it is possible to see that there are sufficient safeguards within the realm of traditional psychometrics to place constraints and cautions on the interpretation of data, and to advance significantly the quest for a theory of cognition. The solution lies in applying *both* experimental procedures and correlational analysis in the same experiment.

The implications of this example for manipulations of the independent variable in all contexts—correlational, experimental, anthropological, Piagetian, or field differentiation—either by treatments implicit in the groups themselves (e.g., literacy, urbanization, contents of long-term memory store) or by explicit changes in the stimulus, are fairly evident. Studies such as those reported above should incorporate standard checks before assertions are made about the possibility of generalizing stimuli and responses either within or across cultures. Remember the previous assertion that methods of administering instruments are often distinguished from general methodology. But, different *methods of giving a test* (external) can change its relationship to other tests, and different treatments (cf., Grant and Scribner) *within the subjects themselves* (internal) also can change test meaning. The average scores of different groups tested under different conditions, external and internal, are then not strictly comparable. The task remains to find which external or internal treatments matter. The significance of these findings should not be lost on people who may be tempted to take the meanings of test scores for granted, even within their own cultures. When tests are given *within* an ethnic group, and means and correlations are being compared, it seems that the test giver's first function is to search for a method to safeguard the assumption of conceptual equivalence by stabilizing test procedures. After that, he should place his measure firmly in a multivariate context.

Summary and Reprise

Before going on to give very brief opinions on methodological advances in cross-cultural paper and pencil personality assessment and attitude measurement, it is convenient to summarize the arguments so far. The chapter began by raising the issue of interpretation of test scores across cultures. It was asserted that test scores can be interpreted meaningfully, although they are indirect measures of constructs. Thereafter, psychometric, Piagetian, anthropological, field-differentiation, and cognitive information processing approaches to assessment were outlined. Each, by itself, was held to have methodological weaknesses. Then three key case studies in the development of methods of stabilizing true-score variance in tests were outlined. Problems of stimulus and psychological equivalence, and attempts to reconcile these, were presented. The role of factor analysis was defined as a means of reducing error variance so that individuals with high and low scores on any well-defined trait such as verbal ability, numerical facility, spatial or figural reasoning, and inductive reasoning, could be compared on other, nontest variables capable of more experimental control than tests. Factors may be seen as having intermediate status in any experimental paradigm. The psychometric checks and balances already available for those who wish to venture group comparisons were listed as a warning to the unwary. Finally, a short example was given of how it is possible to combine experimental constructs and correlational analysis.

The case for psychometric testing, far from being a weak one, is indeed very strong, since the checks of the discipline are many. If they are applied logically and rigorously, there is no need to be apologetic for the results. At the same time, weaknesses in dependent variable interpretation in all single variable experiments pervade all schools of assessment across cultures. The argument for multivariate marker analysis of the dependent variable is compelling.

A Rationale for Cross-Cultural Personality, Attitude, and Ability Measurement

Paradoxes and Possibilities

The whole complex phenomenon of personality assessment across cultures is clearly within the frame of reference of the use of paper and pencil inventories. *All that has been said about the use of psychometric techniques is directly applicable to all self-report personality questionnaires that base personality projections or profiles on the result of information supplied by the respondent.* However, a social paradox may encourage one endeavour and hinder the other. To assert that personality and life style differences vary among ethnic groups is not generally held as an unscientific position that denies the psychic unity of mankind. Instead, members of the group may laud it as a position that upholds the groups' claim to a separate identity. To hypothesize as, for example, Jensen has, that differences in levels and organization of abilities probably go together and vary within and across ethnic groups has been taken by many as a denial of that unity. Consequently, the very use of tests has been questioned. The inconsistency of holding the two positions simultaneously in different pigeon holes of the social-scientific communication system is obvious. There is as little, or as much, scientific support for the positive view that personalities and cultures vary together as there is for asserting that there are no co-varying differences in cognitive style or structure across cultures, or educational levels. In fact, to hold the first position is even more difficult, scientifically, than to hold the second, because theories, and consequently methods of personality research, are as diverse as the whole of psychology itself. Hence, although the quest for personality assessment across cultures may not be fraught with all the social opprobrium that greets assessment of abilities across cultures, it is even more complicated in that many different theoretical strands intertwine in the material presented in self-report tests and in other kinds of personality assessment. The risk of social censure may be smaller, but the risk of scientific opprobrium is greater. Having said this, one must logically urge caution in personality assessment across cultures, because of theoretical diversity and the small evidence of systematic gain from short-term failures.

Instead of reviewing the many attempts to reproduce factor profiles of personality traits across cultures, this discussion will draw attention to two studies that observe how the MMPI (*Minnesota Multiphasic Personality Inventory*) behaves when used to prediagnose schizophrenia among blacks and whites. These studies begin to show the required sensitivity to the use of diagnostic instruments across cultures. They mark the beginning of a search for refinement in their use. Davis, Beck, and Ryan (1973) and Davis and Jones (1974) showed that although the MMPI gives adequate diagnostic support in well-educated groups of blacks *and* whites in the United States, interactions of Race × Education × Diagnosis (schizophrenics versus nonschizophrenics) indicate that the scales in the MMPI show signs of conceptual nonequivalence for the two groups. The studies by Davis deserve careful scrutiny since they reveal clinical attempts to validate MMPI findings. The conclusion however is clear. The MMPI interacts differently with different ethnic groups when educational levels are not held constant; as a consequence the scale becomes unsuitable for use in clinical diagnosis unless one applies the knowledge gained from the Davis experiments. The quest for construct validation of the MMPI across cultures underscores that scale score meaning is capable of investigation *when more than one method of assessment is employed.* This method has to be recommended. Scale construction and clinical methods are both needed to advance cross-cultural appraisal. Much operationally valid cross-cultural personality assessment is clinical (Lambo, 1953, 1961; Prince, 1960, 1964), but theory formation has hardly begun. Consistent data-collection methods require interdisciplinary expertise that will not easily be gained through unqualified application of self-report questionnaires in English on different ethnic groups.

Attitudes and social change.   In order to give an impression of methodological progress, attention must be drawn to two themes: *race attitudes,* and *traditionalism-modernism.* The first example shows that the limits of traditional methodology in a well-defined construct—*race attitudes*—have been reached, and that new methods exist offering hope of experiments in equivalence. The second shows the construct *traditionalism-modernism* to be so challenged by rival interpretations and scales that discriminant validity studies are in order before cross-cultural work can proceed.

Early race attitude research in cultures other than North America can be exemplified by the work of Jahoda (1961) and Rogers and Frantz (1962). Both studies used traditional Likert methods to uncover dimensions of race attitudes. Rogers sought latent dimensions among his attitude statements, while Jahoda did not. A part replication of the Rogers and Frantz study (Irvine, 1974) showed that Rogers's factor analytic framework was substantially confirmed, although some collapsing of factors occurred. The analogy between construct definition in ability theory and attitude construct definition across cultures was pursued by Irvine and a case made for a stricter methodological frame for attitude studies, using the item-difficulty paradigm already described.

All of this work was undertaken within the realm of traditional attitude scale construct methodology, with the application of psychometric checks and balances. As in ability assessment across cultures, factor analysis showed consistent clusters of stimuli. The limits of the Likert correlational approach have been reached. New methods are in order. These have been identified in cross-cultural race attitude work by Jordan (1971a, 1971b, 1974) and Hamersma, Paige, and Jordan (1973). They have successfully applied Guttman's facet theory across cultures, including work in Africa, and covering many content areas. The theoretical basis of facet theory seems to be capable of producing robust scales, irrespective of culture, and often the possibility of (if all of the things can ever be equal!) comparison of attitude structure and magnitude. The coefficient of reproducibility of the scale within each culture effectively determines whether the scale has intracultural validity. Comparative validity, although still assumed, is more certain because of the systematic and a priori (Jordan, 1974) method of constructing items. Unlike the usual attitude scales, the structure is predetermined by a logical progression through hypothetical to real-life situations. Construct validity claims, although confined to the simplex correlational method that emerges as a *consequence* of Guttman's theory (1959, 1971), are impressive. Jordan's series of studies, handily referenced with a good bibliography in the 1974 paper (pp. 48–50), requires close attention from paper and pencil test users, since it presents one of the few cross-cultural attitude scale construction attempts to evolve from a theory of intergroup beliefs and action. Although this general approach is discussed in full in the last section of the chapter, it may be noted that as a universal theory of scale construction, Guttman's facet analysis permits culture-syntonic variations of items without sacrificing construct equivalence. As such it may escape the more general strictures of Sherif and Sherif (1967) referred to in the closing section. Preliminary results show that the method merits extended and serious trials across cultures. When the construct is well defined, methodological advance is possible. The other side of the coin is presented in studies of traditionalism-modernism.

A recent publication by Inkeles and Smith (1975) also concerned itself specifically with modernism. Has progress been as good as it seems? The very nature of modernity as advanced by Inkeles and Smith is, by their own admission, multivariate and complex. Consequently, claims from rival constructs have to be laboriously tested and evaluated. Armer's (1972) study of the traditionalism-modernism (T-M) dimension in the United States shows that T-M scales authored by various investigators, Inkeles and Smith among them, may be moderately equivalent, but they have no discriminant validity with respect to scales purporting to measure *anomie, alienation,* and *socioeconomic status.* Armer's subtitle, "a near myth," leaves serious doubts about the construct validity methods used by T-M proponents. Using T-M scales to predict cognitive style scores without discriminant validity checks as construct markers (which are themselves not subjected to discriminant validity checks) is hardly a procedure to be commended even within cultures. Yet it has been done across cultures (Dawson, 1967), and recently on a large scale (Jones, 1975).

Rival hypotheses, then, will accompany much self-report work in personality and attitude-belief investigation across cultures. Scientifically it is in no better or no worse shape than ability testing. Two brief exposures to personality inventory use and attitude-belief methodology across cultures indicate that we are not yet researching as well as we know how.

This choice of a biased sample of references may have distorted the picture. However, the problems of cross-cultural attitude and personality research are essentially short-run problems. The present indications of methodological bias and lack of theoretical referents will benefit from the application of procedures deemed appropriate for further research in cognition.

The final section of the chapter puts all three areas—attitude, personality, and ability measurement—into a general construct validity framework with some further suggestions.

Extending Construct Validity to Cross-Cultural Measurement

Cronbach and Meehl (1955), in their definitive discussion of construct validity, suggest that construct validation is involved whenever a test is to be interpreted as a measure of some attribute or quality which is not operationally defined (p. 282). This is the same point that was made in illustrating the mean-level-cognitive-structure paradox. When structure changes, comparisons of level are inappropriate. That is to say, whenever a theoretical inference is to be made from the empirical ground of data, the linkage between construct and instrumentation ought to be established. This chapter has suggested ground rules necessary to establish these links. Such a position carries with it the implication that "the investigation of a test's construct validity is not essentially different from the general scientific procedures for developing and confirming theories" (Cronbach & Meehl, 1955, p. 300). In a sense, however, the latter should logically precede the former. In order for a given test to have construct validity, the construct which it purports to measure must occupy a position in an empirically tenable theoretical framework or *nomological network* which is capable of explicitly predicting relationships among observables. Thus, in the case of the mercury thermometer as instrument and heat as construct, the construct originates as a vague observation that some objects feel hotter than others. Gradually, what Lord and Novick (1968) term empirical validities (e.g., concurrent or predictive validites) are established for the instrument, and eventually "a theoretical structure involving unobservable microevents—the kinetic theory—is worked out which explains the relation of mercury expansion to heat" (Cronbach & Meehl, 1955, p. 286). Theory and method have converged to yield a theory which explains the instrumentation. In the present context of cross-cultural paper and pencil testing, in as much as all such instruments presuppose and require some sort of cognitive functioning on the part of subjects, this eventuality translates to linking explicitly paper and pencil instruments with established theories of human cognitive functioning. The first part of this chapter gave examples of the converse, where use of tests was theory-implicit rather than theory-explicit. The latter part gives one of the few examples of theory-explicit construction based on Guttman's facet theory.

The implications of this general discussion for cross-cultural paper and pencil research in particular are clear. Cronbach and Meehl submit that "construct validity must be investigated whenever no criterion or universe of content is accepted as entirely adequate to define the quality to be measured" (1955, p. 282). In cross-cultural ventures, this situation is the rule, since specific denotative and connotative meanings of objects and behaviors may vary markedly. Hence, to reiterate an earlier point, the assumptions of stimulus equivalence or phenomenal identity are insufficient by themselves as basic principles in cross-cultural paper and pencil research. We do not mean to repudiate all of the voluminous research which has made use of Euro-North American instruments in other cultures. Often, particularly when the rigorous techniques for questionnaire wording and translation summarized by Brislin, Lonner, and Thorndike (1973) are employed, such imposed etic (Berry, 1969) investigations can be illuminating. Probably many cross-cultural investigations are more valuable than their critics will allow. In the long run, conceptual generality (Jones, 1966), conceptual equivalence (Sears, 1961), and psychological equivalence (Berry, 1969) predicated on the establishment of construct congruence (Irvine & Sanders, 1972), will emerge. Instruments constructed according to stated criteria ought to form the operational definition of cross-cultural research. Indeed, the concern for stimulus generality in tests involving cognitive processes is perhaps best viewed as a remnant of psychologists' early and understandable concern that the discipline be strictly empirical. This in turn led to the subsequent popularity of behaviorism as a theoretical perspective and of positivism, including operationism, as a philosophical stance. Operationism, in cross-cultural context, has become a somewhat restricted concept; the general conclusion among philosophers of science is that a scientific construct is not equivalent or reducible to its means of measurement. For example, one may measure temperature with a mercury thermometer for normal earth temperatures, but not for the temperature of the sun. Yet by having a theory that explains and even generates the means of measuring temperature in general, a fundamental higher-order explanation such as the kinetic theory, the equivalence of the concept of temperature across different research contexts is assured. Such conceptual equivalence, made possible by the advent of construct validity, is sorely needed in paper and pencil psychological testing, as the cross-cultural literature so well demonstrates. Three general areas of paper and pencil testing will be briefly reconsidered, namely attitude measurement, personality assessment, and ability testing, to demonstrate this point and suggest some possible improvements.

Attitudes.   A standard criticism of the methods used in constructing paper and pencil instruments for measuring attitudes is that they are based on mathematical models of scaling. Such models are not necessarily founded on basic principles of human psychological functioning. This criticism is ameliorated somewhat in Guttman's case but it is still, in general, justified. Triandis (1972) has demonstrated that some "insider's view" studies of subjective culture can be exempt from this criticism, which is explicitly stated by Sherif and Sherif as follows:

> In research practice the individual's attitude has been represented as a point on a scale derived by analogy from a physical model. Thus, an attitude has been represented as an arithmetic mean of acceptances (positive) and rejections (negative) as a point on an interval scale or a ratio scale with a zero point as in the measurement of temperature, as a point in two, three, or *n* dimensional space, or as a point on a cumulative scale as in the measurement of physical distance in Euclidean space. Too often the measurement model and the particular measurement itself have not been referred back to the phenomena they purported to measure. (1967, pp. 108–09)

Most cross-cultural studies of attitudes employ these kinds of scales, which, being predicated on models of physical measurement whose precise relationship to psychological functioning is unknown, have to prove construct validity. They cannot take construct validity for granted. And in this aspect they share the same problems as ability measures. Sherif and Hovland (1961) and Sherif, Sherif, and Nebergall (1965) have developed a definition of attitude and a technique for attitude measurement based upon established principles of psychophysical judgment. The *Own Categories Technique*, as it is called, represented an extension of principles of psychophysics to the issue of psychosocial judgment. The process of responding to a Sherif *Own Categories Scale* is itself explicable as an instance of psychosocial judgment in which a respondent constructs for himself a continuum of categories of statements in order of preference, respecting a given object. The Sherifian model of attitude measurement is derived from and claimed to be compatible with established principles of human psychological functioning. This compatibility is held to lend construct validity to the *Own Categories* method of attitude measurement. Sherif's approach removes the black box around the actual phenomenon of test taking, since the *process* of attitude measurement becomes itself interpretable as an instance of judgment. Its potential usefulness in cross-cultural research seems obvious, but, like all else, demands empirical verification. One may draw an analogy between using this approach in attitude measurement and the application of cognitive information processing procedures to the problems of construct definition in cognition.

Personality. In the area of personality research, most instruments can be classified into one of two categories: open-ended projective (e.g., the *TAT, Rosenzweig Picture-Frustration, Rorschach*), or closed-ended psychometric (e.g., *MMPI, Cattell 16 PF Test,* etc.). When employed across cultures all such tests may be applied either without modification, as in many studies using the Rorschach test, or adapted via back translation or some analogous procedure. In either case, the instruments can lack construct validity with the possible exception of the Rorschach which, instead, lacks reliability. There is generally no account of how the tests function psychologically in eliciting personality-relevant data. However, a cognitive theory of personality advanced by Kelly (1955) and its closely associated instrumentation (i.e., *The Role Construct Repertory Technique*) appear to offer some possibility of cross-cultural construct validity in personality research. Space does not permit an extensive treatment of the theory of personal constructs. Suffice it to say that the methodology used by personal construct researchers in assessing personality is directly derived from the theory and from established object-sorting techniques for the measurement of concept formation (Kelly, 1955). Hence, the phenomenon of test taking is explicable and is observable as an act of construing in itself, which is the basic conception of human experience in the theory. A study among the Xhosa of Africa by DuPreez and Ward (1970) shows the technique's usefulness in cross-cultural research, since it does not require literacy and therefore does not lead inexorably to biased samples of acculturated subjects. As self-report instruments, psychometric personality tests require literate and, accordingly, biased samples (e.g., Kline, 1967). *Both the Own Categories Attitude Measurement Techniques and the Role Construct Repertory Test allow for the presence of culture-syntonic content in the testing situation.* They are general methods, having some degree of a priori construct validity, not specific instruments. Hence they are potentially useful in cross-cultural research, as our argument for the extention of the Campbell-Fiske (1959) paradigm in the following section requires. The same logic was used by Osgood, May, and Miron (1975) and by Triandis (1972) in the development of instruments for the measurement of subjective culture.

Cognitive abilities. Like most attitude scales and personality inventories, tests of ability are typically based upon mathematical models of measurement rather than principles of psychological functioning (see explicitly Hunt et al., 1973 and Estes, 1974 for cogent arguments on this point). The replicable dimensions which emerge from factor analyses of such tests are interpreted as theoretical constructs (Royce, 1963). Psychometric tests of ability, at least in the West, tend to have good concurrent validity, and more often than not, fair predictive validity. A score on one test tends to be substantially correlated with a score on another test given at the same time or given some time in the future. However, as long as ability tests lack full construct validity the theoretical constructs signified by stable factors remain hypothetical or intermediate. A more serious scientific disclaimer is that they are insufficiently articulated as *models of cognitive process* to be replicated outside the factor analytic model. As well, there are the perennial questions of culture fairness and relativism. In short, the issue of comparing abilities cross-culturally by means of Western psychometric tests is highly contentious. This chapter goes as far as it can to establish limits and checks for this kind of endeavour. PSM factors have robustness and status as variables that will allow classification of subjects within and across cultures on similar dimensions of cognitive ability. Carroll (1974), in applying the cognitive information processing models of Hunt et al. (1973) and Newell (1974) to the realm of ability testing, provides a perspective which might yield a rational solution to the factor-analytic problems posed by cross-cultural ability assessment. Like the Osgood, Sherif, Triandis, Guttman, and Kelley methodologies, the information processing models allow culture-syntonic materials based on theory and anthropological sensitivity. As an alternative, the approach of Allison (1960) and Bunderson (1964) within factor analytic frameworks also has to be considered. In spite of technological complexities the learning parameters are replicable with culturally differing, but psychologically constant, stimuli.

In considering psychometric tests in relation to cognitive tasks, psychologists who do experiment and those who use multivariate methods of analysis together could remove theoretical lacunae in the construction of measures of intellect, and in supplying an explanation of it in terms of a more or less established model of cognitive processes. The possibility now exists for the development of cognitive-ability tests having construct validity. Moreover, we consider that such instruments would be valid for cross-cultural comparisons as long as factor structures continue to prove robust enough across cultures to permit classification of subjects. These three suggestions, as a reprise to the chapter, all point to the need for a culture-syntonic approach to cross-cultural instrumentation. Sherif et al. (1965) define attitude as establishing a subject-object relationship between a person and any socially or personally defined object. Kelly (1955) emphasizes that in measuring personality via the *Role Construct Repertory Test*, the researcher must have the subject construe events of relevance to him. The cognitive information processing framework implies the direction of attention to, among other things, the content of long-term memory and the specific learned programs and strategies for processing certain information. These approaches must logically assume, in the first place, that there will be cultural variation in particular content, but invariance in certain formal features of psychological functioning. Considered in isolation, they are problematic. Considered within the context of experimental and multivariate rigour, they diminish the gap between ethnocentrism and radical cultural relativism in cross-cultural research.

Conclusion

Generally, then, there ought to be an effort towards the development of methods of instrumentation having construct validity as tests of psychological functioning, as well as an increasingly syntonic approach to cross-cultural research. This does not suggest the invalidity of a researcher's initial use of an imposed etic framework in studying the people of a culture or cultures. Berry (1969) has persuasively argued that an important phase in a general procedure for cross-cultural comparison is the imposition of an etic framework. The point is that research employing an imposed etic theoretical framework ought not *concurrently* to impose a totally etic methodology. The risk thereby of ethnocentrism and self-fulfilling prophecy is greatly increased. Consequently, the multitrait multimethod paradigm of Campbell and Fiske is a logical result of this position that should be extended. *Convergent validity across cultures has to be demonstrated by the inclusion of measures constructed on the principle of stimulus identity along with measures supposed to guarantee conceptual equivalence.* This particular extension of convergent validity can be defined by comparing the resulting correlations. Agreement between the two different classes of measures would be a consummation. Disagreement, at this stage, would not lead to circularity of further work and methodology. The chapter suggests methods of experimentally determining the sources of noncongruence among measures.

Cross-cultural research has shown that the specific cognitive content of people having different ways of life will vary markedly. It does not matter whether this content is conceptualized as particular attitudinal objects, personal constructs, or long-term memory. Major variations will occur within cultures and across them. The goal of constructing a general science of man might best be furthered, in the context of paper and pencil testing, by recognizing this at the outset of research and theorizing, and by conducting such activities in terms of that recognition. However, the rejection of a single stimulus equivalence or conceptual equivalence model for cross-cultural test construction in favor of a criterion of stimulus and conceptual equivalence exemplars in the same experiment, also requires *that the instruments used cross-culturally have discriminant validity,* at least in the parent culture. Otherwise the analysis runs the risk of comparing only apples, while labeling them apples and oranges. As it is a young science, psychology does not have available a large number of instruments whose construct validities have been satisfactorily developed. Consequently, construct validity has generally not been satisfactorily determined for most psychological tests. In Kuhn's (1970) terms, a coherent paradigm directing both theory and methods, and therefore enabling construct validation, has not yet manifested itself. In the long term, however, it is clear that any nonbehavioristic, nonoperational attempt at cross-cultural comparison by way of paper and pencil instruments will have to come to terms, eventually, with the issue of construct validation. This, of course, does not mean that all past, present, or future research employing instruments lacking precisely defined construct validity (the vast majority of cross-cultural research) is useless or even ill advised. It indicates to all workers, independent of their disciplinary heritage, the direction in which cross-cultural paper and pencil methodology, and indeed other methodologies, might usefully move in the future.

Notes

1. If perception is not an absolute phenomenon across cultures (indeed it is not, on whatever side of the carpentered-world/pigmentation continuum the truth lies), and the long-term memory stores are a function of such perceptions, it is easy to accept the proposition that cognitive operations are *universal* but not that they are culturally identical. Operations cannot be dissociated from strategies embedded in the long-term memory stores, that are culturally programmed through language and ecological press.

2. One study in Mashonaland manipulated test conditions through the ethnicity of the tester and the language of instruction of the test. The experiment used *Raven's Progressive Matrices* as the dependent variable, standardized testing procedures, and back translated the instructions given verbally. The 2 × 2 study of ethnicity (black/white) of instructor language (Shona/English) with repeated measures on *Raven's Matrices* showed no main effects for ethnicity or language, but a pronounced trials effect and a significant ethnicity × language interaction. The simple conclusion is the *g* marker tests can be learned and that motivational influences affect test scores in a subtle fashion.

References

ALLISON, R. B. Learning parameters and human abilities. Technical Report, May 1960, Educational Testing Service and Princeton University, Contract Nonr 694(00)–NR151–113, Office of Naval Research.

ANGOFF, W. H., & SHARON, A. T. Patterns of test and item difficulty for six foreign language groups on the test of English as a foreign language. Research Bulletin, 72-2, Princeton, N.J.: Educational Testing Service, 1972.

ARMER, M., & SCHNAIBERG, A. Measuring individual modernity—a near myth. *American Sociological Review*, 1972, *37*, 301-16.

BARRY, H., CHILD, I., & BACON, M. The relation of child training to subsistence economy. *American Anthropologist*, 1959, *61*, 51-63.

BENNETT, M., & CHANDRA, S. Some ecological factors in individual test performance. In J. L. M. Dawson & W. J. Lonner (Eds.), *Readings in cross-cultural psychology*. Hong Kong: Hong Kong University Press, 1974, 185-89.

BERRY, J. W. On cross-cultural comparability. *International Journal of Psychology*, 1969, *4*, 119-28.

———. Radical cultural relativism and the concept of intelligence. In. J. W. Berry & P. R. Dasen (Eds.), *Culture and cognition: readings in cross-cultural psychology*. London: Methuen 1974a, 225-29.

———. Differentiation across cultures: cognitive style and affective style. In J. L. M. Dawson & W. J. Lonner (Eds.), *Readings in cross-cultural psychology*. Hong Kong: Hong Kong University Press, 1974b, 167-75.

———. *Human ecology and cognitive style: comparative studies in cultural and psychological adaptation*. Beverly Hills: Sage/Halsted, 1976.

BERRY, J. W., & DASEN, P. R. Introduction: history and method in the cross-cultural study of cognition. In J. W. Berry & P. R. Dasen (Eds.), *Culture and cognition: readings in cross-cultural psychology*. London: Methuen, 1974, 1-20.

BIESHEUVEL, S. *African intelligence*. Johannesburg: South African Institute of Race Relations, 1943.

———. The nature of intelligence: some practical implications of its measurement. *Psygram*, 1951, *1*, 78-80.

———. Personnel selection tests for Africans. *South African Journal of Science*, 1952, *49*(1), 3-12.

———. A technique for measuring the attitude of educated Africans. *Proceedings of the South African Psychological Association*, 1953, 4 13-20.

———. The measurement of occupational aptitudes in a multiracial society. *Occupational Psychology*, 1954, *24*, 4-5.

———. The measurement of African attitudes towards European ethical concepts, customs, laws and administration of justice. *Journal of the National Institute for Personnel Research*, 1955, *6*, 5-17.

———. Further studies on the measurement of attitudes towards Western ethical concepts. *Journal of the National Institute for Personnel Research*, 1959a, *7*, 141-55.

———. The development of personality in African cultures. Report of the C.C.T.A./C.S.A. Meeting of Specialists on the Basic Psychology of African and Madagascan populations. (Tananarive Conference, August 1959) Watergate House, London, 1959b. Annex I.

———. An examination of Jensen's theory concerning educability, heritability and population differences. *Psychologia Africana*, 1972, *14*, 87-94.

BRISLIN, R. W., LONNER, W. J., & THORNDIKE, R. M. *Cross-cultural research methods*. New York: Wiley, 1973.

BRUNER, J. S., OLVER, R. R., & GREENFIELD, P. M. *Studies in cognitive growth*. New York: Wiley, 1966.

BUNDERSON, C. V. Transfer functions and learning curves: the use of ability constructs in the study of human learning. Research Bulletin RB64–62, Princeton, N.J.: Educational Testing Service, 1964.

CAMPBELL, D. T., & FISKE, D. W. Convergent and discriminant validation by the multitrait-multimethod matrix. *Psychological Bulletin*, 1959, *56*, 81–105.

CAMPBELL, J. Testing of culturally different groups. Research Bulletin 64–34. Princeton, N.J.: Educational Testing Service, 1964.

CARDALL, C., & COFFMAN, W. E. A method for comparing the performance of different groups on the items in a test. Research Bulletin 64–61, Princeton, N.J.: Educational Testing Service, 1964.

CARROLL, J. B. Stalking the wayward factors. Review of *The analysis of intelligence* by J. P. Guilford & Ralph Hoepfner. New York: McGraw-Hill, 1971. *Contemporary Psychology*, 1972, *17*, 321–24.

————. Psychometric tests as cognitive tasks: a new structure of intellect. Research Bulletin 74–16. Princeton, N.J.: Educational Testing Service, 1974.

CHAPLIN, J. H. A note on Central African dream concepts. *Man*, 1958, *58*, 90–92.

CLEARY, T. A. Test bias: validity of the Scholastic Aptitude Test for Negro and white students in integrated colleges. Research Bulletin 66–31. Princeton, N.J.: Educational Testing Service, 1966.

CLEARY, T. A., & HILTON, T. L. An investigation of item bias. Research Bulletin 66–67. Princeton, N.J.: Educational Testing Service, 1966

COLE, M., & GAY, J. Culture and memory. *American Anthropologist*, 1972, *74*(5), 1066–84.

COLE, M., GAY, J., & GLICK, J. Reversal and non-reversal shifts among a West African tribal people. *Journal of Experimental Psychology*, 1968a, *76*, 323–24.

————. Some experimental studies of Kpelle quantitative behaviour. *Psychonomic Monographs Supplements*, 1968b, *2*(10), Whole No. 26. pp. 173–190.

COLE, M., & SCRIBNER, S. *Culture and thought.* New York: Wiley, 1974.

COWLEY, J. J., & MURRAY, M. M. Some aspects of the development of spatial concepts in Zulu children. *Journal of Social Research*, 1962, *13*, 1–18.

CRIJNS, A. G. J. African basic personality structure: a critical review of bibliographic sources and principal findings. *Gawein*, 1966, *14*, 239–48.

CRONBACH, L. J. Judging how well a test measures: new concepts and new analysis. In L. J. Cronbach & P. J. D. Drenth (Eds.), *Mental tests and cultural adaptation.* The Hague: Mouton, 1972, pp. 413–125.

CRONBACH, L. J., & DRENTH, P. J. D. (Eds.), *Mental tests and cultural adaptation.* The Hague: Mouton, 1972.

CRONBACH, L. J., & MEEHL, P. E. Construct validity in psychological tests. *Psychological Bulletin*, 1955, *52*, 281–302.

D'ANDRADE, E. M., DE GODOY ALVES, D., & FORD, J. A comparison of North American and Brazilian college students' personality profiles on the 16PF questionnaire. *International Journal of Psychology*, 1969, *4*, 55–82.

DASEN, P. R. Cross-cultural Piagetian research: a summary. *Journal of Cross-Cultural Psychology*, 1972a, *3*, 23–29.

————. The development of conservation in Aboriginal children: a replication study. *International Journal of Psychology*, 1972b, *7*, 75–85.

DAVIS, W. E., BECK, S. J., & RYAN, T. A. Race related and educationally related

MMPI profile difference among hospitalized schizophrenics. *Journal of Clinical Psychology*, 1973, 29, 478–79.

DAVIS, W. E., & JONES, M. H. Negro versus caucasian psychological test scores revisited. *Journal of Consulting and Clinical Psychology*, 1974, 42(5), 675–79.

DAWSON, J. L. M. Traditional versus western attitudes in West Africa: the construction, validation and application of a measuring device. *British Journal of Social and Clinical Psychology*, 1967, 6, 81–96.

DE LACEY, R. P. A cross-cultural study of classificatory ability in Australia. *Journal of Cross-Cultural Psychology*, 1970, I(4), 293–304.

DEREGOWSKI, J. Pictorial recognition in subjects from a relatively pictureless environment. *African Social Research*, 1968a, 5, 356–64.

———. Difficulties in pictorial depth perception in Africa. *British Journal of Psychology*, 1968b, 59, 195–204.

———. Effect of cultural value of time upon recall. *British Journal of Social and Clinical Psychology*, 1970, 9, 37–41.

DEREGOWSKI, J., & MUNRO, D. An analysis of "polyphasic picture perception." *Journal of Cross-Cultural Psychology*, 1974, 5, 329–43.

DE VRIES, R. Relationships among Piagetian, IQ and achievement assessments. *Child Development*, 1974, 45 746–56.

DOOB, L. W. Psychology. In R. A. Lysted (Ed.), *The African world: a survey of social research*. New York: Praeger, 1965, pp. 373–415.

DU PREEZ, P., & WARD, D. G. Personal constructs of modern and traditional Xhosa. *Journal of Social Psychology*, 1970, 82, 149–60.

ECKENSBERGER, L. H. The necessity of a theory for applied cross-cultural research. In L. J. Cronbach & P. J. D. Drenth (Eds.), *Mental tests and cultural adaptation*. The Hague: Mouton, 1972, pp. 99–107.

ESTES, W. K. Learning theory and intelligence. *American Psychologist*, 1974, 29, 740–49.

FERGUSON, G. A. On learning and human ability. *Canadian Journal of Psychology*, 1954, 8, 95–112.

FICK, M. L. *The educability of the South African native*. Research series No. 8, Pretoria: South African Council for Educational and Social Research, 1939.

GORDON, L. V., & KIKUCHI, A. American personality tests in cross-cultural research—a caution. *Journal of Social Psychology*, 1966, 69, 179–83.

GRANT, G. V. The organization of mental abilities of an African ethnic group in cultural transition. Unpublished doctoral dissertation. University of the Witwatersrand, Johannesburg, 1969.

———. The organization of intellectual abilities of an African ethnic group in cultural transition. In L. J. Cronbach & P. J. D. Drenth (Eds.), *Mental tests and cultural adaptation*. The Hague: Mouton, 1972, 391–400.

GRANT, G. V., & SCHEPERS, J. M. An exploratory factor analysis of five new cognitive tests for African mineworkers. *Psychologia Africana*, 1969, 12, 181–92.

GUTHRIE, G. M. Structure of abilities in a non-Western culture. *Journal of Educational Psychology*, 1963, 54, 94–103.

GUTTMAN, L. A structural theory for intergroup beliefs and action. *American Sociological Review*, 1959, 24, 318–28.

————. Measurement as structural theory. *Psychometrika*, 1971, *36*, 329–47.

HAMERSMA, R. J., PAIGE, J., & JORDAN, J. E. Construction of Guttman facet-designed cross-cultural attitude-behaviour scale toward racial-ethnic interaction. *Educational and Psychological Measurement*, 1973, *33*, 565–76.

HEMPEL, C. G. *Aspects of scientific explanation and other essays in the philosophy of science.* New York: Free Press, 1965.

HERON, A. Concrete operations, "g," and achievement in Zambian children. *Journal of Cross-Cultural Psychology*, 1971, *2*, 325–36.

————. Cultural determinants of concrete operational behaviour. In J. L. M. Dawson & W. J. Lonner (Eds.), *Readings in Cross-Cultural Psychology.* Hong Kong: Hong Kong University Press, 1974, pp. 94–101.

HERON, A., & DOWEL, W. The questionable unity of the concrete operations stage. *International Journal of Psychology*, 1974, *9*, 1–9.

————. Weight conservation and matrix-solving ability in Papuan children. *Journal of Cross-Cultural Psychology*, 1973, *4*, 207–19.

HERON, A., & SIMONSON, M. Weight conservation in Zambian children. *International Journal of Psychology*, 1969, *4*, 281–92.

HORN, J. L. On subjectivity in factor analysis. *Educational and Psychological Measurement*, 1967, *27*, 811–20.

HORN, J. L., & KNAPP, J. R. On the subjective character of the empirical base of Guilford's structure-of-intellect model. *Psychological Bulletin*, 1973, *80*, 33–43.

HUMPHREYS, L. G. Statistical definitions of test validity for minority groups. *Journal of Applied Psychology*, 1973, *58*, 1–4.

HUNT, E. What kind of computer is man? *Cognitive Psychology*, 1971, *2*, 57–98.

HUNT, E., FROST, N., & LUNNEBORG, C. Individual differences in cognition: a new approach to intelligence. In G. Bower (Ed.), *The psychology of motivation and learning*, Vol. 7, New York: Academic Press, 1973, pp. 87–121.

HUNT, E., LUNNEBORG, C., & LEWIS, J. What does it mean to be high verbal? *Cognitive Psychology*, 1975, *1*, 194–227.

HÜRSCH, L. Cultural influence on the development of number and flexibility-of-closure factors. In L. J. Cronbach & P. J. D. Drenth (Eds.), *Mental tests and cultural adaptation.* The Hague: Mouton, 1972, pp. 459–67.

INGENKAMP, K. H. *Developments in educational testing* (2 vols.). London: University of London Press, 1969.

INKELES, A., & SMITH, D. H. *Becoming modern.* Cambridge, Mass.: Harvard University Press, 1975.

IRVINE, S. H. A psychological study of selection problems at the end of primary schooling in Southern Rhodesia. Unpublished doctoral dissertation, University of London, 1964a.

————. Selection of Africans for post-primary education in Southern Rhodesia: pilot survey, June-July 1962. *Bulletin of the Inter-African Labour Institute*, 1964b, *11*, 69–93.

————. Adapting tests to the cultural setting: a comment. *Occupational Psychology*, 1965, *39*, 13–23.

————. Towards a rationale for testing attainments and abilities in Africa. *British Journal of Educational Psychology*, 1966, *36*, 24–32.

————. Factor analysis of African abilities and attainments: constructs across cultures. *Psychological Bulletin,* 1969a, *71,* 20–32.

————. Contributions of ability and attainment testing in Africa to a general theory of intellect. *Journal of Biosocial Science,* 1969b, *1,* 91–102.

————. Affect and construct: a cross-cultural check on theories of intelligence. *Journal of Social Psychology,* 1970, *80,* 23–30.

————. White attitudes towards blacks in Rhodesia: the implications of a replication for methodology and theory. In J. L. M. Dawson & W. J. Lonner (Eds.), *Readings in cross-cultural psychology.* Hong Kong: Hong Kong University Press, 1974, pp. 338–53.

————. Tests as inadvertent sources of discrimination in personnel decisions. In P. Watson (Ed.), *Psychology and race.* London: Penguin Books, 1973, pp. 453–66.

IRVINE, S. H., & SANDERS, J. T. Logic, language and method in construct identification across cultures. In L. J. Cronbach and P. J. D. Drenth (Eds.), *Mental tests and cultural adaptation.* The Hague: Mouton, 1972, 425–46.

IRVINE, S. H., & SANDERS, J. T., & KLINGELHOFER, E. L. *Human behaviour in Africa.* African Bibliographic Center, Special Bibliographic Series Vol. 8 No. 2, Westport, Conn.: Greenwood Press, 1973.

IRWIN, M. H., & McLAUGHLIN, D. H. Ability and preference in category sorting by Mano school children and adults. *Journal of Social Psychology,* 1970, *82,* 15–24.

JACOBS, P. I. Item difficulty and programmed learning. *Journal of Programmed Instruction,* 1963, *2*(2), 21–38.

————. Effects of coaching on the College Board English Composition Test. Research Bulletin 64–24. Princeton, N.J.: Educational Testing Service, 1964.

————. Programmed progressive matrices. Research Bulletin 66–7. Princeton, N.J.: Educational Testing Service, 1966.

JAHODA, G. A note on Ashanti names and their relationships to personality. *British Journal of Psychology,* 1954, *45,* 192–95.

————. *White man.* London: Oxford University Press, 1961.

————. Scientific training and the persistence of traditional beliefs among West African university students. *Nature,* 1968, *220,* 1356.

JENCKS, C. *Inequality.* New York: Basic Books, 1972.

JENSEN, A. R. How much can we boost IQ and scholastic achievement? *Harvard Educational Review,* 1969, *39,* 1–123.

————. Do schools cheat minority children? *Educational Research,* 1971a, *14,* 3–28.

————. A two-factor theory of familial mental retardation. In A. R. Jensen (Ed.), *Human Genetics.* Amsterdam: Excerpta Medica, 1971b, pp. 263–71.

————. Personality and scholastic achievement in three ethnic groups. *British Journal of Educational Psychology,* 1973a, *43,* 115–25.

————. Free recall of categorized and uncategorized tests: a test of the Jensen hypothesis. *Journal of Educational Psychology,* 1973b, *65,* 304–12.

————. Level I and Level II abilities in three ethnic groups. *American Educational Research Journal,* 1973c, *4,* 263–76.

————. Effect of race of examiner on the mental test of black and white pupils. *Journal of Educational Measurement,* 1974a, *11,* 1–14.

————. How biased are culture-loaded tests? *Genetic Psychology Monographs,* 1974b, *90,* 185–244.

————. Interaction of Level I and Level II abilities with race socio-economic status. *Journal of Educational Psychology*, 1974c, *66*, 99–111.

JONES, E. E. Conceptual generality and experimental strategy in social psychology (symposium). Methodological Problems of Social Psychology—Proceedings of the 18th International Congress of Psychology, 1966, *34*.

JONES, P. A. Modernization—relevant values and achievement of native and rural populations assessed within traditional and modern environments. A paper given at a Conference on Issues in Cross-Cultural Research, New York Academy of Sciences, New York, October 1975.

JORDAN, J. E. Attitude-behaviour research on physical-mental-social disability and racial ethnic differences. *Psychological Aspects of Disability*, 1971a, *18*(1), 5–26.

————. Construction of a Guttman facet-designed cross-cultural attitude-behaviour scale toward mental retardation. *American Journal of Mental Deficiency*, 1971b, *76*, 201–19.

————. Facet theory and cross-cultural research methodology. In J. L. M. Dawson & W. J. Lonner (Eds.), *Readings in cross-cultural psychology*. Hong Kong: Hong Kong University Press, 1974, pp. 39–50.

KELLAGHAN, T. Abstraction and categorization in African children. *International Journal of Psychology*, 1968, *3*, 115–20.

KELLY, G. A. *The psychology of personal constructs* (2 vols.). New York: W. W. Norton, 1955.

KLINE, P. The use of the Cattell 16 P. F. Test and Eysenck's E. P. I. with a literate population in Ghana. *British Journal of Social and Clinical Psychology*, 1967, *6*, 97–107.

KNIGHT, R. *Intelligence and intelligence test*. London: Methuen, 1943.

KUHN, T. *The structure of scientific revolutions*, 2nd ed. Chicago: University of Chicago Press, 1970.

LAMBO, T. A. The role of cultural factors in paranoid psychosis among the Yoruba tribe. *Journal of Mental Science*, 1955, *101*, 239–66.

————. A form of social psychiatry in Africa. *World Mental Health*, 1961, *13*, 190–203.

LEBLANC, M. La problematique d'adaptation du T.A.T. au Congo. *Zaire*, 1958, *12*, 339–48.

LEE, S. G. Social influences in Zulu dreaming. *Journal of Social Psychology*, 1958, *47*, 265–83.

LESSER, G. S., FIFER, G., & CLARK, D. H. Mental abilities of children from different social-class and cultural groups. *Child Development Monographs*, 1965, *30*(4), Whole No. 102.

LLOYD, B. *Perception and cognition: a cross-cultural perspective*. London: Penguin Books, 1972.

LLOYD, F., & PIDGEON, D. A. An investigation into the effects of coaching on non-verbal test material with European, Indian and African children. *British Journal of Educational Psychology*, 1961, *31*, 145–51.

LOEVINGER, J. Objective tests as instruments of psychological theory. *Psychological Reports*, 1957, *3*, 635–694 (Monograph Supplement No. 9).

LONNER, W. J., & BRISLIN, R. W. Methodological approaches to cross-cultural research. In J. L. M. Dawson & W. J. Lonner (Eds.), *Readings in cross-cultural psychology*. Hong Kong: Hong Kong University Press, 1974, 381–90.

LORD, F. A paradox in the interpretation of group comparisons. Research Bulletin 65–8. Princeton, N.J.: Educational Testing Service, 1965.

LORD, F. M., & NOVICK, M. R. *Statistical theories of mental test scores.* Reading, Mass.: Addison-Wesley, 1968.

LUNZER, E. A. An enquiry into the development of systematic thinking. In F. J. Mönks, W. W. Hartup, & J. de Wit (Eds.), *Determinants of behavioural development.* New York: Academic Press, 1972.

MACARTHUR, R. S. Some ability patterns: Central Eskimos and Nsenga Africans. *International Journal of Psychology,* 1973, *8,* 238–47.

———. Construct validity of three New Guinea performance scale sub-tests: Central Eskimos and Nsenga Africans. In J. L. M. Dawson & W. J. Lonner (Eds.), *Readings in cross-cultural psychology.* Hong Kong: Hong Kong University Press, 1974, pp. 51–60.

MACARTHUR, R. S., IRVINE, S. H., & BRIMBLE, A. R. *The Northern Rhodesia mental ability survey.* Lusaka, Zambia: Rhodes-Livingstone Institute, 1964.

MACDONALD, A. *Selection of African personnel.* Final report of the Selection of Personnel Technical and Research Unit, Middle East Force. London: Ministry of Defence Archives, 1945.

MAIRLOT, F. De quelques aspects de la psychologie profonde du Noir congolais. *Bulletin du Centre d'Etudes des Problemes Sociaux Indigenes,* 1956, *34,* 22–52.

MARJORIBANKS, K. Environment, social class, and mental abilities. *Journal of Educational Psychology,* 1972, *63,* 103–09.

MEDLEY, D. M., & QUIRK, T. J. The application of a factional design to the study of cultural bias in general culture items on the national teacher examination. *Journal of Educational Measurement,* 1974, *11*(4), 235–45.

MELLENBERGH, G. J. Applicability of the Rasch model in two cultures. In L. J. Cronbach & P. J. D. Drenth (Eds.), *Mental tests and cultural adaptation.* The Hague: Mouton, 1972, pp. 453–58.

MITCHELL, J. C. *The Kalela dance.* Rhodes-Livingstone Papers No. 27, Manchester: Manchester University Press, 1956.

NEWELL, A. Production systems of control processes. In W. G. Chase (Ed.), *Visual information processing.* New York: Academic Press, 1973, pp. 463–526.

N.I.P.R. ANNUAL REPORT. Johannesburg, National Institute for Personnel Research, 1974.

OKONJI, O. M. The effects of familiarity on classification. *Journal of Cross-Cultural Psychology,* 1971, *2,* 39–49.

ORD, I. G. *Mental tests for pre-literates.* London: Ginn, 1971.

———. Tests for educational and occupational selection in developing countries. *Occupational Psychology,* 1972, *46,* No. 3.

OSGOOD, C. E., MAY, W. H., & MIRON, M. S. *Cross-cultural universals of affective meaning.* Urbana: University of Illinois Press, 1975.

PEIFFER, E., PELAGE, S., & PELAGE, Mme. S. Quelques resultats obtenus au test de Rorschach, chez les Bamilekes du Cameroun. *Bulletin de l'Institut Francais d'Afrique Noire,* 1963, *25,* 454–57.

POORTINGA, Y. Cross-cultural comparison of maximum performance test: some methodological aspects and some experiments with simple auditory and visual stimuli. *Psychologia Africana Monograph Supplement* No. 6, 1971.

POPPER, K. R. *The logic of scientific discovery.* New York: Basic Books, 1961.

PRICE-WILLIAMS, D. Abstract and concrete modes of classification in a primitive society. *British Journal of Educational Psychology,* 1962, *32,* 50–61.

PRINCE, R. H. The "brain fag" syndrome in Nigerian students. *Journal of Mental Science,* 1960, *106,* 559–70.

———. Indigenous Yoruba psychiatry. In A. Kiev (Ed.), *Magic, faith, and healing, studies in primitive psychiatry today.* London: Collier-Macmillan, 1964, pp. 84–120.

RASCH, G. An individualistic approach to item analysis. In P. Lazarsfeld (Ed.), *Readings in mathematical social science.* Chicago: Science Research Associations, 1966, pp. 89–108.

REUNING, H., & WORTLEY, W. *Psychological studies of the Bushmen.* Johannesburg, South Africa: National Institute for Personnel Research, 1973.

ROBERTS, S. O., & OPPENHEIM, D. B. The effect of special instruction upon test performance of high school students in Tennessee. Research Bulletin 66–36, Princeton, N.J.: Educational Testing Service, 1966.

ROGERS, C. A., & FRANTZ, C. *Racial themes in southern Rhodesia.* New Haven: Yale University Press, 1962.

ROYCE, J. R. Factors as theoretical constructs. *American Psychologist,* 1963, *18,* 522–38.

SCHMIDT, F. L., BERNER, J. G., & HUNTER, J. E. Racial differences in validity of employment tests: reality or illusion? *Journal of Applied Psychology,* 1973, *58,* 5–9.

SCHWARZ, P. *Aptitude tests for use in the developing nations.* Pittsburgh: American Institutes for Research, 1961.

———. Adapting tests to the cultural setting. *Educational and Psychological Measurement,* 1963, *23,* 673–86.

SCRIBNER, S. Developmental aspects of free recall in West African society. *Cognitive Psychology,* 1974, *6,* 475–94.

———. Review of *Culture and cognition,* J. W. Berry & P. R. Dasen (Eds.). *Journal of Cross-Cultural Psychology,* 1975, *6,* 122–26.

SEARS, R. R. Transcultural variables and conceptual equivalence. In B. Kaplan (Ed.), *Studying personality cross-culturally.* Evanston, Ill.: Row, Peterson, 1961, 445–55.

SEGALL, M. H., CAMPBELL, D. T., & HERSKOVITS, M. J. Cultural differences in the perception of illusions. *Science,* 1963, *139,* 769–71.

———. *The influence of culture on visual perception.* New York: Bobbs-Merrill, 1966.

SHERIF, C. W., SHERIF, M., & NEBERGALL, R. E. *Attitude and attitude change. The social judgement-involvement approach.* Philadelphia: W. B. Saunders, 1965.

SHERIF, M., & HOVLAND, C. I. *Social judgment: assimilation and contrast effects in reaction to communication and attitude change.* New Haven: Yale University Press, 1961.

SHERIF, M., & SHERIF, C. W. Attitude as the individual's own categories: the social judgment-involvement approach to attitude and attitude change. In C. W. Sherif & M. Sherif (Eds.), *Attitude, ego-involvement, and change.* New York: Wiley, 1967, pp. 105–39.

SILVEY, J. Aptitude testing and educational selection in Africa. *Rhodes-Livingstone Journal,* 1963, *34,* 9–22.

ST. GEORGE, A. The Pacific infants performance scale: some preliminary and comparative New Zealand studies. Psychology research paper. University of Waikato, 1974.

ST. GEORGE, R. Tests of general cognitive ability for use with Maori and European children in New Zealand. In L. J. Cronbach & P. J. D. Drenth (Eds.), *Mental tests and cultural adaptation.* The Hague: Mouton, 1972, pp. 197–203.

ST. GEORGE, R., & ST. GEORGE, A. The measurement of cognitive abilities in the Cook Islands: a research report. A report to the interdepartmental Committee on Polynesian Research, Wellington, November 1974. Massey University, 1974 (pp. i–ix, 1–164).

STODOLSKY, S. S., & LESSER, G. S. Learning patterns in the disadvantaged. *Harvard Educational Review,* 1967, *37,* 546–93.

STRAUS, M. A. Phenomenal identity and conceptual equivalence of measurement in cross-national comparative research. *Journal of Marriage and the Family,* 1969, *31*(2), 233–39.

THOMAS, L. V. De l'usage de quelques tests projectifs pour la comprehension de la personnalite noire. *Bulletin de l'Institut Francais d'Afrique Noire,* 1959, *21* (Part 1–2, Serie B), 1–19.

TRIANDIS, H. C. *The analysis of subjective culture.* New York: Wiley, 1972.

VANDENBERG, S. G. The primary mental abilities of Chinese students: a comparative study of the stability of factor structure. *Annals of the New York Academy of Science,* 1959, *79,* 257–304.

———. The primary mental abilities of South American students: a second comparative study of the generality of a cognitive factor structure. *Multivariate Behavioural Research,* 1967, *2,* 175–89.

VAN DER FLIER, H. The comparability of individual test performances. *Nederland Tijdschrift voor de Psychologie,* 1975, *30,* 41–49.

VERNON, P. E. *Selection for secondary education in Jamaica.* Kingston: Government Printer, 1961.

———. *Intelligence and cultural environment.* London: Methuen, 1969.

———. The distinctiveness of field independence. *Journal of Personality,* 1972, *40,* 366–91.

WILKINSON, E. *Factors affecting cognitive behaviour of children in their first year of schooling.* Paper presented at 1973 meeting of the International Society for the Study of Behavioural Development. Unpublished manuscript, University of Glasgow, 1974.

WITKIN, H. A., DYK, R. B., FATERSON, H. F., GOODENOUGH, D. R., & KARP, S. A. *Field-dependence-independence and psychological differentiation.* Research Bulletin RB 73-62 and RB 74-42. Princeton, N.J.: Educational Testing Service, 1973–74.

WITKIN, H. A., & BERRY, J. W. Psychological differentiation in cross-cultural perspective. *Journal of Cross-Cultural Psychology,* 1975, *6,* 4–87.

WOBER, M. *Psychology in Africa.* London: Heinemann, 1975.

6

Projective Techniques

Wayne H. Holtzman

Contents

Abstract

An historical examination of the use of projective techniques in cross-cultural psychology is followed by the description of the Holtzman Inkblot Technique. Cross-cultural studies of inkblot perception are reviewed. The Thematic Apperception Test and its use in the assessment of achievement motivation in different cultures, the sentence completion and word association techniques, and other expressive techniques are critically examined. Methodological dilemmas in the use of projective techniques are stated and analyzed. Questions of whether or not to employ a projective technique in a particular cross-cultural study are also considered.

History and Concepts of Projective
Techniques

Prophets, soothsayers, and personologists for centuries have searched for the hidden meaning in what an individual reports seeing in clouds, inkblots, and other ambiguous stimuli. But it wasn't until 1895 that systematic efforts were made to develop a test of imagination based on these ideas. Unlike others before him, Alfred Binet was mainly interested in the measurement of individual differences in mental abilities. Seeing a large number and variety of different figures in a series of inkblots was interpreted as indicative of a lively visual imagination (Binet & Henri, 1896). Binet and his followers focused on the reaction time of each association to inkblots, the contents of consciousness, and the kinds of imagery produced.

Working from a different set of premises, in 1911 Hermann Rorschach started his famous experiments on inkblots that culminated in the publication of *Psychodiagnostik* in 1921. He stressed the importance of analyzing a person's mode of perception—whether the inkblot was interpreted as a whole or in part; whether the form, color, or shading of the inkblot was primarily responsible for evoking the response; and whether the person reported a static, lifeless percept, or one imbued with life and action. Rorschach was especially interested in a deeper understanding of mental illness and reported considerable success in the blind diagnosis of mental patients. Thousands of studies have since been published utilizing the same ten inkblots and much the same system of analysis that Rorschach used.

The term *projective method* was coined by L. K. Frank (1939) to encompass those indirect methods of personality assessment that involve a standardized procedure for eliciting a person's responses to ambiguous stimuli. Stemming largely from psychoanalytic theory, projective techniques can range all the way from free association in relatively unstructured situations to highly formalized, structured devices such as the Rorschach or Thematic Apperception Test. In any projective technique in which a person is given wide latitude to reveal himself, the particular sample of responses obtained is assumed to reflect significant aspects of the individual's personality, if only the examiner can find the key to its interpretation. Since the stimuli for eliciting responses are often chosen because they are ambiguous or inherently "meaningless," the specific perceptions and interpretations the individual makes must arise at least in part as a unique expression of the individual's personality. In short, the individual projects his personality into his response.

This assumption of a complex but direct relationship between an individual's personality and his responses when taking a projective test leads to three corollaries that are rarely made explicit: (a) belief that a test record is a sufficiently extensive sampling of the personality to warrant making judgments about it; (b) belief that the psychological determinants of the responses are basic and general; and (c) belief that projective techniques tap the durable essence of personality equally in different individuals across a wide range of ethnic, socioeconomic, and cultural variations (MacFarlane & Tuddenham, 1951). Most experienced users of projective techniques would argue that none of these three statements necessarily follows from the basic assumption underlying the projective method. They would insist that even the best of projective test protocols can reveal only a small fragment of the total personality, fraught with innumerable possibilities for misinterpretation. For this reason, projective techniques are usually used with a variety of other approaches when studying an individual personality. But in such clinical practice it is difficult to avoid falling into the dogmatic position of overinterpretation in an attempt to weave a consistent picture of the needs, fears, strivings, ego-defensive behavior, and inner resources that constitute the personality dynamics presumably reflected by the clinical techniques.

Methods for the assessment of personality can be ordered on a continuum according to the degree of structuring and control introduced. At one extreme are the completely qualitative, unstructured methods of psychoanalysis—free association in the presence of an analyst. At the other extreme are the highly structured paper and pencil tests which meet the standards of quantitative psychometric theory. As stated elsewhere (Holtzman, 1959), projective techniques generally fall somewhere between these two extremes. In most cases, an attempt has been made to preserve the qualitative, idiographic essence of the projective method while also looking for ways to categorize, quantify, and standardize the response variables underlying test behavior. For most clinical applications, the ideal projective technique would be one that covers a wide band of the continuum with a high degree of power throughout the range. The enduring appeal of the Rorschach inkblot method arises largely from its suitability for a wide range of individuals and from its broad-band, multidimensional nature that is amenable to intuitive clinical analysis as well as more objective treatment of signs and scores.

During the first twenty-five years after Rorschach's death in 1922, the use of his inkblots grew rapidly. Competing systems of scoring and analysis flourished in Europe and America. Concerned mainly with the psychodiagnosis of mental illness and personality disturbances, the Rorschach movement attracted a large following from psychiatrists, clinical psychologists, and a scattering of others, including cultural anthropologists who used the Rorschach in the study of culture and personality among nonliterate societies. The mainstream of academic psychology looked askance at the movement, criticizing its cultist character and lack of scientific discipline. World War II brought about a fusion of the Rorschach movement and psychology when hundreds of technicians were thrust into the role of psychodiagnostician and rapidly learned to use projective techniques for psychiatric screening and personality assessment within the armed forces. The growth of clinical psychology after the war led to a proliferation of projective techniques and thousands of empirical studies examining their value in countless situations. The number and variety of techniques put forward in the name of projective methods were almost without limit. Published handbooks and periodic reviews over the past twenty-five years provide a good introduction to the techniques that have been developed (Bell, 1948; Frank, 1948; Abt & Bellak, 1950; Anderson & Anderson, 1951; Lindzey, 1961; Gleser, 1963; Murstein, 1965; Fisher, 1967; Rabin, 1968; Molish, 1972; and Spain, 1972).

While clinical psychologists have been interested in projective techniques chiefly as instruments for improved psychodiagnosis and a deeper understanding of the individual personality, cultural anthropologists saw in projective methods a way of studying the relationships of culture and personality. In the earliest anthropological studies, only psychoanalytic psychology seemed to be sufficiently comprehensive to provide a bridge between field observations and theories of personality development that emerged from clinical studies. Testing the universality of Freudian concepts provided a major impetus for anthropologists studying exotic isolated cultures. The Rorschach inkblot test and later the Thematic Apperception Test were fully compatible with psychoanalytic psychology. The nonverbal, almost universal nature of the inkblot as a stimulus was an especially attractive feature when working across different cultures.

Early Cross-Cultural Applications

A. Irving Hallowell was one of the first and most ardent supporters of projective techniques, particularly the Rorschach, for cross-cultural studies of personality. As an anthropologist working with different American Indian cultures, Hallowell (1942, 1955) collected large numbers of Rorschach protocols that were then analyzed and compared with other information such as ratings of personal adjustment and degree of acculturation to the dominant white society. Hallowell's work led him to conclude that the Rorschach could be used effectively in cross-cultural studies of primitive people if a few changes were made in the method of test administration. Shortly thereafter, W. E. Henry (1947) reported a cross-cultural study on Hopi and Navaho children, using a modification of the Thematic Apperception Test (TAT). Henry compared the TAT, the Rorschach, a free-drawing test, and life histories for each child and concluded that, when properly modified, the TAT was a valid instrument for personality assessment in cross-cultural studies.

In spite of serious methodological flaws in these and other early cross-cultural studies, the use of projective techniques for personality assessment in diverse cultures grew rapidly during the 1950s. At the same time, growing criticism mounted and many of the earlier studies were strongly challenged. In 1961, Kaplan estimated that over 150 studies in seventy-five societies used projective techniques during the period 1949–60. In spite of his personal preference for such methods, Kaplan was forced to conclude that the positive values in projective techniques for cross-cultural studies of personality are very scant.

Gardner Lindzey's comprehensive review (1961) of projective techniques in cross-cultural research pointed out a number of serious weaknesses in all but a tiny handful of these studies. Among the modal flaws noted in his survey were the following: (1) all too frequently, personality inferences from the projective techniques were contaminated by knowledge of other important data concerning the individuals being assessed; (2) a full description of the circumstances under which the technique had been administered was typically lacking, making replication or synthesis impossible; (3) little attention was paid to situational factors that may have accounted for the responses obtained; (4) problems of sample comparability across cultures were usually ignored; (5) methods of scoring and interpretation developed on educated American and European subjects were often uncritically applied in markedly different cultures; and (6) average profiles were frequently presented as representative of modal personality for a culture while ignoring the wide individual differences actually obtained.

The lack of progress and the prevalence of major flaws Lindzey noted in his survey of anthropological studies employing projective techniques were reinforced by similar mounting criticism within psychology. With some notable exceptions, projective techniques and psychodiagnosis in general have declined markedly in the past fifteen years. As two past presidents of the Society for Projective Techniques and Personality Assessment recently pointed out (Hertz, 1970; Molish, 1972), the uncertain future of clinical psychology and changing attitudes toward projective methodologies indicate that projective methods no longer have the key position they once enjoyed in personality assessment. In spite of such pronouncements of relative decline, however, projective techniques continue to be widely used for clinical assessment of individual personality throughout the world. Reynolds and Sundberg's (1976) recent review indicates that the Rorschach continues to lead the list of all psychological tests in publications per year and is third in frequency of use. The Draw-a-Person Test and Thematic Apperception Test rank fifth and seventh, respectively. At the same time, the overall quality of psychometric refinement for these particular projective techniques was low, as independently judged by a group of psychologists, showing no relationship to frequency of usage or publications.

Following this brief introduction, a more detailed examination of characteristics of the leading projective techniques that are still in use, with particular reference to their applicability in cross-cultural research, will be presented. The most commonly used techniques for psychological research have remained unchanged in recent years. Most projective techniques can be classified into one of four categories: (a) the Rorschach and other inkblot methods; (b) thematic techniques and their variations; (c) completion techniques and word association; and (d) expressive and constructive techniques such as drawings, paintings, and structured play.

Rorschach and Holtzman Inkblot Techniques

The standard Rorschach test consists of ten symmetrical inkblots, five with various colors and five in black and white, that are shown to an individual one at a time. The subject is asked to tell the examiner what he sees in the blot while the examiner writes down his responses. After responding to each blot in a fixed order of presentation, the subject is then asked to look at each inkblot again. This time the examiner asks questions about where each percept was located and what characteristics of the blot seemed to determine the response. Usually the resulting protocol is then scored for location, determinants, and content, employing one of several systems for scoring and interpretation (Klopfer, Ainsworth, Klopfer, & Holt, 1954; Beck, 1961; and Exner, Jr., 1969). Sometimes intensive qualitative analysis is undertaken from a psychoanalytic point of view (Schafer, 1954), but such clinical approaches are rarely useful in cross-cultural research because of their subjectivity and the need for a psychoanalytically trained interpreter who is also thoroughly familiar with the cultures being studied. Minor variations in the Rorschach method have been developed, some with different inkblots (Zulliger, 1969; Kataguchi, 1970) and others with different instructions and methods of analysis (Harrower-Erickson & Steiner, 1945; Piotrowski, 1957; Zubin, Eron, & Schumer, 1965; and Schachtel, 1966), but with only limited success. None of these modifications has been used in any significant way for cross-cultural research.

The psychometric weaknesses in the Rorschach and the prominent role played by situational factors in determining a subject's response have greatly restricted the value of the Rorschach in cross-cultural research. Strong examiner-subject interaction, variations in style of inquiry, lack of an objective scoring system free of arbitrary conventions and showing high interscorer agreement, lack of satisfactory internal consistency or test-retest reliability, and questionable evidence with respect to validity of personality interpretations, are among the more serious weaknesses noted in the standard Rorschach (Holtzman, Thorpe, Swartz, & Heron, 1961; Zubin et al., 1965).

The Holtzman Inkblot Technique (HIT) was developed to overcome the psychometric weaknesses of the Rorschach while retaining the attractive features of the method (Holtzman et al., 1961). The HIT consists of two parallel forms, each containing forty-five matched inkblots of various colors, forms, and shading nuances, together with two trial blots common to both forms. The subject is asked to give only one response to each card rather than as many or few as he wishes, thereby overcoming a major problem in the scoring of the Rorschach. A simple, standardized inquiry immediately follows each response. Objective scoring criteria have yielded a number of scores similar to those in the Rorschach but with much higher reliability, better distribution characteristics, and clearer interpretability (Holtzman et al., 1961; Bock, Haggard, Holtzman, Beck, & Beck, 1963; Fischer & Spada, 1973). For the twenty-two standard HIT scores, interscorer agreement with trained scorers ranges from .89 to 1.00, with a median reliability coefficient of .98. Split-half reliability estimates for 18 of the scores, based on 1311 cases in fifteen samples ranging from young children to adult schizophrenics, ranged from .23 to .98 with a median of .79, the precise value of the coefficient varying according to the population and the score. Test-retest reliability after one year, using parallel forms of the HIT given to elementary school children, ranged from .28 to .75, with a median of .47. These reliability estimates are comparable to coefficients typically found with standard measures of cognitive and intellectual abilities. Such improved psychometric properties have been achieved without loss of the rich symbolic quality of projective responses for which the Rorschach has proved valuable in clinical work.

Initially, standardization data on twenty-two scores for the HIT were collected on 1,642 individuals from fifteen different American populations ranging from five-year-old children to adults and including schizophrenic, depressed, and mentally retarded persons. More recently, American norms for the individually administered version of the HIT have been published for emotionally disturbed children, juvenile delinquents, emotionally disturbed adolescents, adult neurotics, and alcoholics (Hill, 1972). Similar in many respects to various scores used for the Rorschach, the twenty-two standard scores for the HIT can be briefly defined as follows:

Reaction Time (RT). The time in seconds from the presentation of the inkblot to the beginning of the primary response.

Rejection (R). Score 1 when *S* returns inkblot to *E* without giving a scorable response; otherwise score 0.

Location (L). Tendency to break down blot into smaller fragments. Score 0 for use of whole blot, 1 for large area, and 2 for smaller area.

Space (S). Score 1 for true figure-ground reversals; otherwise, score 0.

Form Definiteness (FD). The definiteness of the form of the concept reported, regardless of the goodness of fit to the inkblot. A five-point scale with 0 for very vague and 4 for highly specific.

Form Appropriateness (FA). The goodness of fit of the form of the precept to the form of the inkblot. Score 0 for poor, 1 for fair, and 2 for good.

Color (C). The apparent primacy of color (including black, gray, or white) as a response-determinant. Score 0 for no use of color, 1 for use secondary to form (like Rorschach FC), 2 when used as primary determinant but some form present (like CF), and 3 when used as primary determinant with no form present (like C).

Shading (SH). The apparent primacy of shading as a response-determinant (texture, depth, or vista). Score 0 for no use of shading, 1 when used in secondary manner, and 2 when used as primary determinant with little or no form present.

Movement (M). The energy level of movement or potential movement ascribed to the percept, regardless of content. Score 0 for none, 1 for static potential, 2 for casual, 3 for dynamic, and 4 for violent movement.

Pathognomic Verbalization (V). Degree of autistic, bizarre thinking evident in the response as rated on a five-point scale. Score 0 where no pathology is present. The nine categories of V and the range of scoring weights for each is as follows: Fabulation, 1; Fabulized Combination, 2, 3, 4; Queer Response, 1, 2, 3; Incoherence, 4; Autistic Logic, 1, 2, 3, 4; Contamination, 2, 3, 4; Self Reference, 2, 3, 4; Deterioration Color, 2, 3, 4; Absurd Response, 3.

Integration (I). Score 1 for the organization of two or more adequately perceived blot elements into a larger whole; otherwise, score 0.

Human (H). Degree of human quality in the content of response. Score 0 for none, 1 for parts of humans, distortions, cartoons, and 2 for whole human beings or elaborated human faces.

Animal (A). Degree of animal quality in the content. Score 0 for none (including animal objects and microscopic life), 1 for animal parts, bugs, or insects, and 2 for whole animals.

Anatomy (At). Degree of "gutlike" quality in the content. Score 0 for none, 1 for bones, x-rays, or medical drawings, and 2 for visceral and crude anatomy.

Sex (Sx). Degree of sexual quality in the content. Score 0 for no sexual reference, 1 for socially-accepted sexual activity or expressions (buttocks, bust, kissing), and 2 for blatant sexual content (penis, vagina).

Abstract (Ab). Degree of abstract quality in the content. Score 0 for none, 1 for abstract elements along with other elements having form, and 2 for purely abstract content: ("Bright colors remind me of gaiety").

Anxiety (Ax). Signs of anxiety in the fantasy content as indicated by emotions and attitudes, expressive behavior, symbolism, or cultural stereotypes of fear. Score 0 for none, 1 for questionable or indirect signs, and 2 for overt or clearcut evidence.

Hostility (Hs). Signs of hostility in the fantasy content. Scored on a four-point scale ranging from 0 for none to 3 for direct, violent, interpersonal destruction.

Barrier (Br). Score 1 for reference to any protective covering, membrane, shell, or skin that might be symbolically related to the perception of body-image boundaries; otherwise, score 0.

Penetration (Pn). Score 1 for concept which might be symbolic of an individual's feeling that his body exterior is of little protective value and can be easily penetrated; otherwise, score 0.

Balance (B). Score 1 where there is overt concern for the symmetry-asymmetry feature of the inkblot; otherwise, score 0.

Popular (P). Each form contains twenty-five inkblots in which one or more popular percepts occur. "Popular" in the standardization studies, means that a percept had to occur at least 14 percent of the time among normal subjects. Score 1 for popular core concepts (or their precision alternatives) as listed in the scoring manual; otherwise, score 0.

Two standardized, group-administered versions of the HIT using colored slides have also been published, one with a special booklet for group administration (Swartz & Holtzman, 1963; Herron, 1963) and the other with a streamlined record form on which the subject merely writes a brief response and checks the amount of the blot used for the percept (Gorham, 1967). Among educated subjects the group method yields scores very similar to the individually administered version for eighteen of the twenty-two variables (Holtzman, Moseley, Reinehr, & Abbott, 1963).

A high-speed computer-scoring system has been developed for the group HIT using empirically derived dictionaries containing about 4000 words stored as a large table of scoring weights in the computer's memory (Moseley, Gorham, & Hill, 1963; Gorham, 1967; Gorham, 1970). Agreement between hand and computer scoring of the same protocols is surprisingly high in spite of the fact that syntax is taken into account only in a rudimentary way—above .80 for Rejection, Location, Movement, Human, Color, Form Definiteness, and Animal, and .50–.75 for Hostility, Popular, Anxiety, Anatomy, Shading, Penetration, Abstract, Sex, Barrier, and Integration. Equivalent dictionaries have been compiled in English, Spanish, and Portuguese to facilitate cross-cultural studies. Norms for the computer-scored HIT have been developed for eight United States populations, both normal and abnormal, and for university students in sixteen other countries—Argentina, Australia, Colombia, Denmark, Hong Kong,

Hungary, India, Japan, Lebanon, Mexico, Nigeria, Panama, Turkey, Venezuela, West Germany and Yugoslavia (Gorham, Moseley, & Holtzman, 1968). Protocols collected in native languages (except Spanish and English) were translated by bilingual collaborators and cross-checked before they were scored.

Cross-Cultural Studies of Inkblot Perception

Multivariate cross-cultural comparisons of group HIT scores have been reported for up to seventeen different nationalities totalling 2,643 individual cases (Gorham & Holtzman, 1972). The degree of similarity among these cultures was computed by using multiple-discriminant-function analysis to see how efficiently individuals could be classified as to culture on the basis of HIT scores alone. The method produced frequency data that can be arranged in a square matrix where the diagonal represents the correctly classified cases and the off-diagonal entries are cases incorrectly assigned to the other cultures. The Lebanese were most often misclassified as Turks (13 percent), college students in Hong Kong were frequently classified as Japanese (10 percent), and Americans were most often called Australians (12 percent), suggesting regional and ethnic clusters. When only the North and South American cultures were included in a separate analysis, misclassification was always greater for neighboring than distant countries; e.g., the Mexicans were most like the Americans, the Panamanians split between the Mexicans and Colombians, and the Venezuelans were most frequently misclassified as Colombians or Argentines (Moseley, 1967).

The most comprehensive cross-cultural study of inkblot perception and personality reported to date involved over 800 children in Mexico and the United States who were tested annually for six successive years, using the individually administered HIT and a large variety of other cognitive, perceptual, and personality tests (Holtzman, Diaz-Guerrero, & Swartz, 1975). Since the children were drawn equally from the first, fourth, and seventh grades at the start of the longitudinal study, data were eventually obtained on large numbers of children for all ages between six and seventeen. Correlational and factor-analytic studies of HIT variables by age and culture revealed the same five well-defined factors that have been reported in other studies: Factor 1—Integration, Movement, Human, Popular, and Form Definiteness; Factor 2—Color, Shading, and Form Definiteness (reversed); Factor 3—Pathognomic Verbalization, Anxiety, Hostility, and Movement; Factor 4—Location and Form Appropriateness; and Factor 5—Reaction Time, Rejection, and Animal (reversed).

On the basis of the defining variables and other independent studies of their validity (Hill, 1972; Holtzman, 1975), a high amount of Factor 1 is generally interpreted as indicative of well-organized ideational activity, good imaginative capacity, well-differentiated ego boundaries, and awareness of conventional concepts. Concerned with sensitivity to the stimulus qualities of the inkblots, Factor 2 is bipolar, a high score indicating overreactivity to the color or shading and a low score indicating primary concern with form alone, to the neglect of the more affect-laden color and shading. Although very high scores on Factor 3 usually indicate psychopathology and uncontrolled bizarreness, moderately high scores (as in the American children but not the Mexican) are more indicative of affective expressivity and loose imagination in fantasy. For this reason, Factors 1 and 3 are often positively correlated, especially in children. A high score on Factor 4 indicates perceptual differentiation coupled with a critical sense of good form. A high score on Factor 5 arises from an inability to see things in the inkblots or from an overly critical eye that leads to rejection.

While the HIT variables had the same meaning in the two cultures, the means differed markedly even when pairs of Mexican and American children were closely matched on age, sex, and socioeconomic status of their parents. The Mexican children gave slower response time to inkblots, showed less pathology, anxiety, hostility, and movement in their fantasy life, and integrated parts into a larger whole less often than did the American children. Together with other test data, observations and interview data, these results support the hypothesis that Americans tend to be more active than Mexicans in coping with the stresses of life. Similar results were obtained by Tamm (1967), who gave the HIT and other tests to first, fourth, and seventh graders in the bilingual American School of Mexico City. While the Mexican and American children showed no cross-cultural differences in any of the intelligence tests, the pattern of differences obtained for the HIT was identical to that found in the larger, longitudinal study.

These results generally indicate that the personality variables present in inkblot perception as measured by the HIT are rather basic and not as sensitive to situational factors as most other projective techniques (Holtzman, 1975). The method is particularly well suited for cross-cultural research because of its sensitivity to important aspects of personality that are likely to differ markedly across cultures and because of its wide applicability, ranging from young children to adults, from psychotic individuals to superior normals, from urban sophisticates to primitive New Guinean tribes (Leininger, 1966).

Thematic Apperception Test and
Its Variations

The second most frequently used projective technique is the Thematic Apperception Test (TAT) and its modifications. The standard version of the test consists of twenty pictures; the individual is asked to tell a story about each of them, using his imagination freely and focusing on what the figures in the pictures are thinking and feeling (Morgan & Murray, 1935). The series contains ten pictures used for all subjects plus a second ten drawn from twenty additional pictures according to the age and sex of the subject. The pictures cover a wide range of personal or interpersonal situations and vary in ambiguity or degree of structure, leaving plenty of room for the subject to project from fantasy his own needs, fears, and desires as he makes up a story.

Murray's (1943) original ideas for interpretation of the TAT involved translation and coding of story content into *needs* or inner states that can be expressed such as need for achievement (n Ach), need for affiliation (n Aff) or need for order (n Ord); into *presses* or inner states that involve a perception of some external force acting upon the individual; and into *thema* or condensed themes comprised of need-press combinations believed to represent motivational trends within the individual. Any psychodynamic theory of personality, particularly psychoanalysis, can be used as a basis for interpretation. A variety of other scoring systems have been developed as well as variations in method of administration (Clark, 1944; Tomkins, 1947; Aron, 1949; Eron, 1950; Bellak, 1954; Stein, 1955; Henry, 1956a, 1956b; Lindzey & Silverman, 1959; and Holt, 1961). These range from individual, semistructured interview methods of administration to multiple-choice group methods, from elaborate psychoanalytically based systems for interpreting unconscious, deep personality trends to detailed stimulus-oriented quantitative systems for classifying both the form and the content.

Reliability and validity are particularly difficult to establish for the TAT because of the free-response nature of the task, the high degree of interaction between situational factors and personality, the great difficulty in obtaining suitable independent criteria against which to validate inferences about unconscious aspects of personality, and the problems encountered in trying to develop meaningful, quantitative measures from stories (Murstein, 1963; Molish, 1972). No one has been able to solve these problems to anyone else's satisfaction. At the same time, the method has value when employed clinically in conjunction with other personal data, as in the case study of individuals (Henry & Farley, 1959). The TAT is best thought of as a clinical method for investigating personality rather than a test in the true sense of the word.

Many modifications of the TAT have been tried with varying degrees of success. Among the more interesting are the Blacky pictures with cartoonlike animals (Blum, 1968); the Children's Apperception Test and its variations (Bellak & Hurvich, 1966; Haworth, 1966); the Four Pictures Test (Lennep, 1951); the Object Relations Technique (Phillipson, 1955); the Michigan Pictures Test (Andrew, Hartwell, Hutt, & Walton, 1953); and the Make-a-Picture-Story Test (Shneidman, 1960). Recognition that pictures and story telling are highly culture-bound and strongly influenced by situational factors has led to countless adaptations of the TAT. Special forms of the TAT have been developed on an ad hoc basis for a wide variety of different cultures, ages, both sexes as well as homosexuals, and different occupational groups. While this rich diversity is testimony to the attractiveness of thematic methods for investigating personality, the proliferation of unstandardized methods makes it impossible to develop norms, to carry out repeated cross-cultural studies, or to build incrementally a strong empirical basis for the method.

The effective design and administration of picture stimuli techniques for particular cultures have been developed to a high degree by anthropologists who have found the methods useful for the study of culture and personality (Henry, 1956a, 1961; Sherwood, 1957; Goldschmidt & Edgerton, 1961; Caudill, 1962; Spindler & Spindler, 1965).

The use of such techniques to study attitudes, values, and role behavior as social and cultural phenomena rather than as expressions of individual personality has been particularly fruitful. As Edgerton (1970) pointed out, when thematic methods are used to examine social psychological and cultural questions rather than individual personality, the stimuli should be designed to maximize the dramatic impact of realism and should avoid the ambiguity characteristic of the TAT viewed as a projective technique.

The picture technique developed by Goldschmidt and Edgerton (1961) for the study of values among the Menomini Indians of Wisconsin is an excellent example of a specialized projective technique for investigating social and cultural phenomena rather than assessing individual personality. Their instrument consisted of a battery of twelve cards with realistic drawings involving Indians in various activities where conflicting values (traditional Menomini versus modern American) are deliberately elicited. Following an instruction card showing a father, mother, and son looking at a store window displaying a rack of guns alongside some house furniture, eleven test cards are shown to the subject one at a time. The interviewer first asks the subject to tell him what is happening in the scene, and then he asks what the various people are doing. For the instruction card, it is obvious that the man wants to buy a gun, the woman would like the furniture, and the boy is in the middle but looking at the gun rack. The test cards deal with such value conflicts as fishing versus work, group identification versus solitude, native religion versus Catholicism, consumer goods versus family welfare, family responsibility versus personal pleasure, moral attitudes toward sex, and generosity. Since the choice situation must be clear and realistic, the method requires redrawing for each cultural situation in which it is to be applied. It is particularly appropriate for studying the degree of acculturation among subgroups in any multiple society.

Assessment of Achievement Motivation

One of the more interesting cross-cultural uses of thematic methods has been the measurement of achievement motivation (n Ach) by McClelland and his followers (McClelland, Clark, Roby, & Atkinson, 1949; McClelland, Atkinson, Clark, & Lowell, 1953; McClelland, 1955; Atkinson, 1958; McClelland, 1961; Havighurst, Dubois, Csikszentmihalyi, & Doll, 1965; Angelini, 1966; LeVine & LeVine, 1966; McClelland & Winter, 1969; Atkinson & Raynor, 1974). Usually the method involves the presentation of four to six pictures designed to evoke achievement imagery which can then be scored by a standard method of content analysis. McClelland's original set of four pictures which have been widely used for the past twenty-five years consists of TAT Cards 7BM ("father" talking to "son") and 8BM (boy and surgical operation) and two pictures drawn especially for the purpose (two men in overalls looking or working at a machine; a young man looking into space seated before an open book). Any other set of pictures designed to elicit achievement imagery would probably work just as well as these four.

The scoring method developed by McClelland and his colleagues (McClelland et al., 1953; Atkinson, 1958) starts with a conception of (1) the person and his internal needs, anticipatory goal states, and affective states; (2) a perceived goal; (3) one or more perceived obstacles between the person and the goal which must be overcome; and (4) a nurturant press supplied by another person who provides support of some kind. The goal defines whether or not the various anticipations, affective states, and instrumental acts are achievement related. To be scored for achievement imagery, a story must meet at least one of three criteria: (1) competition with a standard of excellence, (2) a unique accomplishment, or (3) long-term involvement in working toward a goal. When achievement-related imagery is judged by these criteria to be present in the story, the scorer then classifies the imagery according to the following characteristics: generality of the need, instrumental acts, anticipatory goal response, press, substitution, and outcome. A single need achievement (nAch) score was originally obtained by assigning a weight of plus one to the seven characteristics found to increase under experimental achievement conditions and a weight of minus one to the two characteristics that decreased significantly in the experiment. Algebraically summing the positive and negative weights yielded a single nAch score for a given story that ranged from −2 to +7. Recent revisions of the scoring system have resulted in a new range of −1 to +11 per story (McClelland & Winter, 1969). Satisfactory scoring reliability (r of .80–.95) can be achieved by following the recommended training procedures. Test-retest reliabilities as high as .95 have been reported (McClelland et al., 1949).

The assessment of nAch by thematic apperception methods in cross-cultural studies has been stimulated further by the attempts of McClelland and Winter (1969) to develop and evaluate special training programs designed to raise achievement motivation among budding entrepreneurs in underdeveloped countries, particularly in India. Students in training sessions score their own stories to six pictures for nAch and then rewrite the stories at various times, trying to maximize their nAch scores. The increased associative network involving achievement imagery presumably helps the trainee to see ways he can increase his own achievement, and to become more enterprising and creative in trying to achieve specified goals. The work by Mehta (1975) illustrates the use of an adaptation of McClelland's method for measuring nAch among Indians. Test-retest reliabilities with a four-month interval for Mehta's six sketchy drawings are about .70 for ninth-graders. Only scanty evidence on validity is available. Comparative studies of nAch have also been reported by Gokulnathan and Mehta (1972) for tribal and nontribal Assamese secondary school students, but the results are difficult to interpret due to small numbers of cases and the presence of some confounded background variables. Still another variation of the Indian approach is reported by Dave and Krishnamurthy (1973), using a special four-picture series designed for farmers. While not differing in nAch, a control group of farmers who were refused small loans showed much more survival concern than concern with progress in their stories, while an experimental group who did receive loans showed about equal concern for the two outcomes.

These studies on measuring need achievement by thematic apperception methods illustrate a range of possibilities for adapting such techniques to the special requirements of investigators in different cultures. The fact that unique sets of pictures usually have to be developed and standardized for a given culture and situation severely limits the method for simultaneous use in two or more cultures, as would be required by most cross-cultural research designs. The low, often negligible, correlations obtained between nAch from TAT pictures and other measures of need achievement also raise serious questions about the convergent validity of the method, although the basic findings of McClelland, Atkinson, and others have held up fairly well (Fisher, 1967; Molish, 1972). Thematic methods of assessing n Ach remain an interesting approach to the measurement of an important personality characteristic that is often of special concern in cross-cultural studies.

Completion Techniques and Word Association

One of the earliest projective techniques (Jung, 1918) was the Word Association Test in which a person is presented orally with single words one at a time and asked to give as quickly as possible the first association that comes to mind. Variability of reaction time, content of associations, associative disturbances, generalized response sets, and linguistic properties of stimulus-response associations have been analyzed and used for inferring mental complexes, motives, and other aspects of personality (Rapaport, Schafer, & Gill, 1945; Moran, 1966). Word association techniques have declined in usage because of problems concerning response sets, changes in language, and limited value in personality assessment (Moran, 1966; Molish, 1972). Nevertheless several interesting cross-cultural applications have been recently reported dealing with the cognitive-linguistic aspects of word associations and idiomatic response sets characteristic of different age groups and cultures, rather than considering the word association test as a projective technique for assessment of personality (Moran & Nunez, 1967; Moran & Murakawa, 1968; Laosa, 1971; Holtzman et al., 1975).

Completion methods are more popular than association techniques among current investigators. Using a meaningful chain of words as an incomplete sentence instead of only one word, and asking the subject to complete the sentence rather than give only a single word as an immediate association, has been widely used as a projective technique. The typical sentence-completion test contains forty to fifty sentence stems such as "I like . . . , " "My greatest fear . . . , " and "I failed. . . . " Such sentence-completion tests have proven highly useful for assessing personal adjustment and emotional disorders (Symonds, 1949; Goldberg, 1965). In the commonly used Rotter Incomplete Sentences Blank (Rotter, Rafferty, & Schachtitz, 1949), interscorer agreement, split-half reliabilities, and validity coefficients using independent ratings of adjustment for college men and women are all high (Churchill & Crandall, 1955). Rotter's scoring method involves classifying all responses into three categories: positive (healthy), negative (unhealthy), and neutral, using scoring examples in a manual as a guide. Of all the techniques generally referred to as projective, the sentence-completion test is closest in form to the objective, paper and pencil questionnaires used for consciously held attitudes.

The sentence-completion method has been used extensively by Havighurst et al. (1965), and Peck, Havighurst, & Miller (1970) in cross-national studies of such dispositions as instrumental versus expressive orientation, autonomy versus dependence, need for achievement, and interest in heterosexual activity among teenagers in Argentina, Brazil, Great Britain Italy, Japan, Mexico, United States, West Germany, and Yugoslavia. V. ile satisfactory interscorer agreement can be obtained by following a manual, translating the test into different languages proves to be a severe problem. Different grammatical structures, word usages, and social customs concerning the expression of politeness or social status by language forms prove to be almost insurmountable problems in maintaining psychological equivalence of meaning across cultures (Manaster & Havighurst, 1972).

Still another interesting example of the sentence completion method in cross-cultural research is the work of Phillips (1966) on the Thai peasant personality and of Guthrie and Azores (1968) on the interpersonal behavior patterns of Filipinos. Starting with 144 items in two seventy-two-item forms, Phillips found twenty-nine items that were particularly revealing of personality characteristics common among the rice-growing peasants near Bangkok. Guthrie and Azores translated these items from the tonal Thai language to Tagalog as well as English. Difficult problems of translation arose due to difference in meaning, word order, tense, purposive verbs, sentence structure, and the frequent use of loan words from English in the responses of some individuals. Oral presentation of the sentence stems in Tagalog was used for rural peasants in four communities throughout the Philippines, making possible a closely matched comparison with Phillips' Thais. The concern was more with social norms, roles, values, and expressive emotions in the Thai and Filipino cultures than with the assessment of variations in individual personalities. As compared to the Thais, the Filipinos were more involved in status relationships, more interested in the exercise of personal power, more deeply involved in friendships, and more personally hurt when friends failed them. When dealing with tension-producing situations, the Filipinos tended to conceal their negative feelings by remaining calm or smiling while the Thais engaged in avoidance behavior. This cross-cultural comparison illustrates that the sentence completion method is not necessarily limited to literate societies but can also be given orally under standard conditions.

Story completion methods constitute still a third way in which association and completion techniques have been employed to study important aspects of personality as well as sociocultural attitudes and values. The typical approach is to state the beginning of a simple story, leaving the ending to be constructed by the subject. Usually the number of stories employed has to be very limited since each one takes some time to complete. For young children and illiterates, the technique is employed orally;

for older school children and educated adults, a group-administered paper and pencil method is usually employed. A comprehensive review of the method has been provided by Lansky (1968). Current usage has moved away from clinical applications and emphasizes structured stimuli designed specifically to test hypotheses concerning moral reasoning, values, and attitudes. Illustrative of these cross-cultural approaches are the international studies of Anderson and Anderson (1961), who coded story completions for honesty, responsibility, anxiety, and guilt as they related to attitudes of school children toward the teacher, and the Cross-National Coping Style and Achievement Study reported by Peck et al. (1970). Manaster and Havighurst (1972) point out the difficulties of resolving the language and cultural variations in these particular studies aside from the problems of validity.

Expressive Techniques

It is generally believed that certain aspects of a person's feelings, emotions, values, attitudes, and self-image often find expression in such creative activities as free-hand drawings, paintings, and even play. Such artistic productions are more likely to reveal significant features of an individual's personality when interpreted with a great deal of information about the person than when viewed in isolation.

The most commonly used expressive technique is some form of human figure drawing. The extent to which a human figure drawing can be considered a projection of one's self image has been debated for decades. The Draw-a-Person Test (Machover, 1949) assumes a direct relationship that can be interpreted clinically from a detailed analysis of body parts, clothing, shading, erasures, size, proportion, unusual features, and a myriad of other chracteristics. While this test appeals to the clinician when used in conjunction with other idiographic methods for the intensive study of a single individual, the research evidence on reliability and validity of the objectively scored Machover signs is devastating in its negative outcome (Swenson, 1957), although there is some value in global ratings (Swenson, 1968). In a major review of the clinical and projective uses of children's drawings, including some work in other cultures, Harris (1963) also concludes that there is little evidence to support the hypothesis that the human figure drawing is a drawing of the self, directly or indirectly, a conclusion confirmed by Molish (1972).

A more promising approach to the assessment of personality by human figure drawings is the scoring system devised by Koppitz (1968) for measuring emotional stability by the presence or absence of thirty emotional indicators or signs that significantly differentiated between children who were well adjusted and those who were psychiatric patients. Recently, this scoring system has been revalidated in a prediction study where the number of emotional indicators in the drawings of first-graders correlated significantly with independent ratings of maladjustment nine years later (Currie, Holtzman, & Swartz, 1974). In a large cross-cultural study using the Koppitz system for scoring the drawings of 276 matched pairs of lower-class children, from Guadalajara, Mexico and from a small industrial city in New York state, significant differences in the incidence of specific emotional indicators led Koppitz and Moreau (1968) to conclude that the American children tended to be more anxious, inadequate, resentful, and aggressive while the Mexican children showed more signs of timidity, immaturity, and concretist types of thinking.

Besides the assessment of individual personality, human figure drawings have been used in two other important ways: (1) to study cognitive development, and (2) to investigate values, sex roles and other sociocultural phenomena. The most definitive work on the use of human figure drawings for measurement of cognitive development is the revision and extension of the Goodenough Draw-a-Man Test by Harris (1963). Standardization of the Harris-Goodenough Scale involved validation of seventy-three items for scoring drawings of a man and seventy-one items for scoring drawings of a woman, using a carefully selected sample of 1,000 children representative of the general school-age population, five to sixteen years of age, in the United States. The complete technique involves asking a child to draw first a man, then a woman, and finally a picture of himself. In actual practice, some investigators prefer to ask the child first to draw a person and then to draw another person of the opposite sex, thereby permitting the examiner to note the chosen sex of the first-drawn figure as well as to score the records in the standard manner. Extensive cross-cultural and longitudinal comparisons of human figure drawings scored for cognitive development have been reported by Harris, 1963; Witkin, Price-Williams, Bertini, Christiansen, Oltman, Ramirez, and Van Meel, 1974; Laosa, Swartz, and Diaz-Guerrero, 1974; Holtzman et al., 1975; and others as discussed in more detail elsewhere in this *Handbook*.

Investigating aspects of culture as expressed in human figure drawings once again involves consideration of drawings as a projective technique rather than a test of cognition. The most extensive cross-cultural comparisons of children's drawings have been made by Dennis over a period of twenty-five years (1942, 1966a). His most recent studies involved the analysis of group values reflected in 2,550 drawings by boys in thirteen different countries that were collected on the Draw-a-Man Test. In another extended analysis of forty different groups, Dennis concluded that ability to draw a man provided an indirect index of modernization or culture change, as well as artistic background (Dennis, 1966b). Perceived sex-role differences have also been examined by analysis of degree of sexual differentiation in Filipino and American children's figure drawings (Rabin & Limuaco, 1959), by comparison of masculinity-femininity scores on the Franck Drawing Completion Test (Franck & Rosen, 1949) for Japanese, Caucasian-American, and Japanese-American high school students (Blane & Yamamoto, 1970).

Other media for personal expression can also be employed in projective techniques although very rarely have any been developed into methods that are suitable for cross-cultural studies. Clinical studies of young children have often employed dolls or toys in a semistructured play session (Buhler, 1951; Murphy, 1956; Lynn & Lynn, 1959), but little success has been achieved in standardizing such play methods in the form of a replicable technique that would have any value in cross-cultural investigations, although some attempts have been made (Kotaskova, 1971).

Methodological Dilemmas in the Use of Projective Techniques

Based upon psychoanalysis and related psychodynamic theories of personality, projective techniques were developed originally as a rebellion against the fragmentary, oversimplified approach of the early personality questionnaires. Projective techniques have proved especially well suited to the clinical, in-depth study of individual personality where the experience and intuitive skill of the interpreter is of utmost importance. Generally speaking, a technique that encourages projection also defies standardization with its fixed classifications and quantification of response variables. Too often what may have been an interesting projective technique for clinical analysis has been transformed into a more objective, replicable method of only trivial value, having lost its original projective qualities.

For the clinician who firmly believes that only an intensive, idiographic approach to the study of personality is worth pursuing, the problems of developing a cross-cultural psychology of personality are enormously difficult. And yet, at least one thoughtful anthropologist has advocated a return to psychoanalytic methods for the study of personality in different cultures, using bicultural analysts trained especially for this purpose (LeVine, 1973). While such methods might be useful to generate new insights and hypotheses when working with some cultures, the great expense of intensive clinical studies and the impossibility of standardization or replication make them unlikely choices for developing cross-cultural psychology.

As stated elsewhere (Holtzman, 1964, 1965, 1968), the main methodological dilemmas encountered in the use of projective techniques for cross-cultural studies are of two general kinds: (a) problems arising in any indirect, free-response approach to the measurement of personality; and (b) problems of special significance in cross-cultural research. These dilemmas are examined one at a time below.

Meaning of personality assessment.   The existence of many competing theories of personality and the limitless number and variety of ways in which people differ has led to an amazing proliferation of techniques, scores, trait definitions, and patterns of variables—both qualitative and quantitative—under the rubric of personality. Projective techniques suffer from this problem to an even greater extent than the more limited, trait-based inventories of personality that appear to have greater objectivity. Multiple levels of functioning may have to be measured simultaneously for even a single trait in order to achieve any understanding of personality. For example, at least four systems or levels of functioning have been studied with regard to hostility, though rarely at the same time: (a) hostility in both conscious fantasy and unconscious symbolism as revealed by thematic techniques or inkblots; (b) hostility measured as part of the inferred conscious self revealed in a self-report inventory; (c) hostility in the objectively observed self as in peer ratings; and (d) hostility as reflected in psychophysiological measures of emotional arousal. The manner in which these various levels of functioning interact is complex, differing from one person to the next and from one social situation to the next, complicating matters still further.

Systems of scoring and analysis.   Transforming a free-response projective protocol into meaningful, objective scores having good psychometric characteristics is a difficult, frequently impossible task. Too often, the coding and scoring of responses involves arbitrary conventions based on oversimplified, analogical reasoning. In techniques like the TAT and Rorschach that permit unlimited verbal productivity, the number of responses, the amount of verbiage, and the interaction of subject with examiner become overriding factors that can greatly distort any other personality measures, although they may be of interest in their own right. While satisfactory interscorer agreement can be achieved, especially if detailed (but often arbitrary) instructions are provided, internal-consistency reliability is another matter. Unless there is a sufficient number of independently presented stimuli as "items" or samples to achieve a fairly high degree of internal consistency for any derived scores, reliability of measurement with respect to individual personality remains in serious doubt. Change in personality or stability of measurement over time can only be investigated when parallel forms of the same technique are available or when the same technique can be given repeatedly without loss of meaning. Test-retest studies using projective techniques are usually of questionable value for this reason.

Situational and instrument factors. Projective techniques involve a special paradox. The freer the response elicited from a person in order to encourage projection of the personality, the more the method is subjected to the influence of extraneous factors that obscure the meaning of any derived scores. It is for this reason that many clinicians insist that only with a highly intuitive, idiographic approach where the clinician becomes a part of the instrument itself, can one preserve the projective nature of the task while also taking into account the situational and instrumental factors present. Many empirical investigations of projective techniques in recent years have demonstrated the pervasive influences of examiner, social context, and extraneous stimuli upon the responses of the subject. These confounding factors are particularly serious in cross-cultural research (Ciborowski, Chapter 7 in this volume).

Maintaining semantic equivalence across cultures. Most techniques rely upon verbal behavior for response and many use culture-bound stimuli such as pictures or words. Maintaining the equivalent meanings of these methods across cultures can be difficult, especially when the linguistic and cultural differences being studied vary markedly. Even an otherwise "meaningless" inkblot has culturally different connotations that obscure the meaning of personality interpretations unless they are taken into account. In techniques like the TAT, which involve a content analysis of verbal response, the language in which the response is given may be confounded with the way that the personality is expressed. In a study by Ervin (1964), sixty-four bilingual Frenchmen were given the TAT on two different occasions, once in French and once in English. The response content and associated personality variables shifted significantly from one language to the other in ways that had been predicted from knowledge of the French and English cultures. A bilingual individual's personality can appear different from language to language; there is no way in which language and personality can be completely separated in cross-cultural studies that employ different languages. The interactions of personality and culture (including language) must be addressed in any meaningful cross-cultural study (LeVine, 1973).

Delineation, measurement, and control of relevant cultural variables. Cross-cultural studies by definition involve the comparison of two or more cultures. Whether one is concerned with variation across a defined universe of cultures, with differences between only two selected cultures, or with subcultural variation in a single population, the sociocultural variables must be made explicit before appropriate instruments, including projective techniques, can be selected, adapted, or developed. As noted elsewhere in this *Handbook*, the delineation, measurement, and control of such cultural variables is difficult to achieve, regardless of the dependent measures of personality that are subsequently chosen. If such matters are not given serious attention *prior* to individual personality measurement, the resulting cross-cultural study may prove worthless. A more powerful research design can usually be developed by employing both cross-cultural and subcultural variation at the same time. For example, a cross-cultural study involving two or more urban societies can be greatly improved by including systematic variation of socioeconomic status, sex, and age—three subcultural variables that can usually be matched successfully across cultures. Interactions within and across cultures can then be investigated as well as the main cultural effects, greatly strengthening the power of any generalizations that are drawn.

Given the above methodological dilemmas, it is understandable why rigorous cross-cultural studies of personality are indeed rare, particularly when projective techniques have been employed. While numerous descriptive or impressionistic studies have been reported using projective techniques in different cultures, few of these lead to any valid cross-cultural findings. Those which have proved most successful are either specifically designed to test limited hypotheses about cultural differences or are restricted to fairly similar cultures where the same techniques are highly appropriate.

Some Questions to Consider in Deciding Whether or Not to Employ a Projective Technique in a Particular Cross-Cultural Study

The general idea underlying projective techniques is an intriguing one that has stimulated considerable research in the past fifty years. To be able to assess the inner feelings, wishes, anxieties, fantasies, values, and other deeper personality traits of an individual by the indirect method of eliciting projections onto ambiguous stimuli is an attractive possibility for the research investigator as well as the clinician. Compared to the simpler, direct methods involving questionnaires or inventories, projective techniques have the decided advantage of revealing information about an individual without his full awareness of what is being communicated. Consequently, many projective methods are difficult for the subject to fake or distort in order to disguise himself. Such nonverbal techniques as the use of inkblots to elicit imaginative responses have a wide range of standardized applicability across diverse cultures, an attractive feature in much cross-cultural research. In spite of the difficult methodological problems usually encountered in cross-cultural research with projective techniques, they merit serious consideration in any studies dealing with personality. Whether or not a particular technique can be suitably employed for such a study depends upon the answers to a number of practical questions; the more important ones are noted below.

How wide a range of different cultures and languages is to be studied simultaneously? If one is interested in studying subcultural variation or in making comparisons across cultures having the same language, most of the techniques described above can be considered. In working with fairly literate adolescents or adults across diverse cultures and languages, the semantic equivalence of the verbally based methods such as the Sentence Completion Test can probably be established by appropriate translation, back translation, and pilot testing. For most cultures, the drawing techniques and story telling methods are quite suitable although their equivalence cross-culturally speaking may be difficult to achieve. The inkblot techniques such as the Rorschach or the HIT have the widest range of applicability as standardized instruments.

Is it critical to assess individual differences in personality or are group (culture) trends sufficient? Most clinicians or investigators interested in personality assessment are concerned with individuals and their similarities and differences on selected personality attributes. With the exception of specialized methods for assessing value orientations as in the Goldschmidt-Edgerton picture technique, all of the projective methods reviewed herein were originally developed to study individual personalities. The kind of measurement required for individual reliability and validity is of a higher, more stringent order than the kind needed when only group trends are of interest. An instrument that may have unsatisfactory reliability for individual measurement can still be used effectively where differences in cultures or large groups are the main concern. The bipolar choice situations dealing with attitudes and cultural values in the Goldschmidt-Edgerton pictures and the use of only four to six rather than twenty or thirty TAT pictures for assessing n Ach in groups of individuals are examples of such applications.

What personality characteristics are of special interest? A major consideration in the selection of a projective technique is the kind and variety of personality attributes considered important to study. The inkblot methods provide the widest range of attributes that can be assessed by a single technique. With patterns of the twenty-two standardized inkblot scores on the HIT, for example, measures can be obtained dealing with creativity, imaginative capacity, ego strength and inner resources, sensitivity to external social stimuli, developmental maturity, degree of conventional socialization, anxiety and hostility, body image, coping style, emotional stability, mental obsessions or preoccupations, and bizarreness of thought processes. Where single traits such as need achievement or emotional adjustment are of interest, specialized techniques are more efficient. Many personality traits dealing with interpersonal behavior such as extroversion, shyness, or dominance are better measured by direct observation, peer group ratings, or self-report questionnaire than by projective techniques that generally deal with the deeper attributes of an individual that are not easily observable on the surface.

Is it essential to have equivalent quantitative measurement in two or more cultures?   Cross-cultural equivalence of meaning coupled with quantitative measurement is especially difficult to find in most projective techniques, particularly when the cultures are different. The HIT is superior to the Rorschach in this regard since it is less susceptible to examiner and situational influences, and since there is a sufficient number of inkblots (items) in the HIT to produce scores having good quantitative, psychometric characteristics in a wide variety of cultures. The Draw-a-Person Test is also likely to have a fairly wide range of cross-cultural equivalence, and Koppitz's scale of emotional stability looks promising as a quantitative score. Where language translation is not too difficult and literate subjects are employed, the Sentence Completion Test will retain a satisfactory degree of cross-cultural semantic equivalence while yielding one or more quantitative scores. The remaining projective techniques are less likely to be satisfactory in this respect. Thematic apperception methods, for example, are suitable only where approximate cross-cultural semantic equivalence and specialized scores such as nAch are desired, since the pictures usually have to be redrawn to fit different cultures and many general scoring systems are not quantitative. Of course, where only qualitative assessment is desired, other methods may be quite appropriate.

How much special training is required to administer, score, and interpret projective techniques?   In general, the more highly structured and standardized the technique, the easier it is to learn how to administer and score it. Of the various projective techniques mentioned, the Rorschach requires the greatest amount of specialized training under supervision of a competent instructor, while the Sentence Completion Test and the Draw-a-Person Test require the least. The TAT and the HIT can be easily mastered by self-instruction using available technical manuals and related training aids, although interpretation in the clinical sense of the word does usually require some supervised experience.

What is the likely cost in money, time, and effort to obtain the test results?   The specially developed inkblots in the HIT are the most expensive of the various techniques because there are forty-seven different inkblots in a set. The Rorschach and TAT also require the use of specially printed materials. For all three of these techniques, the initial cost is the primary one. Materials for most other projective techniques used in cross-cultural studies are inexpensive. The HIT, Rorschach, and TAT generally take forty to fifty minutes to administer. The HIT and Rorschach each take about thirty minutes to score while the TAT can range from twenty minutes to several hours, depending upon how elaborate the scoring system is. The sentence completion and word association methods can be administered and scored fairly rapidly in most cases. The Draw-a-Person Test usually takes only a few minutes to give and score. Most of the other specialized projective methods described earlier do not take a great deal of time and effort per individual, once the initial development and standardization has been achieved.

What are the ethical issues pertaining to the cross-cultural use of projective techniques?   Projective techniques share with other methods for personality assessment several characteristics that require careful attention to well-recognized ethical principles. As indirect, often disguised, approaches to the study of personality, projective methods may uncover sensitive, private information without the subject's full awareness of what is being revealed. Wherever there is any likelihood of such highly personal information being uncovered, the identity of the subject should be protected by coding and minor alteration of case material, thereby preserving the anonymity of the individual. Methodological issues concerning the reliability and validity of personality assessment by projective techniques pose serious problems for the use of an instrument developed in one culture as an assessment device in a very different culture unless previous research clearly indicates its appropriateness in the new situation. Such uncritical application in the new culture is scientifically unsound, and there is a possibility of potential harm to the subjects due to faulty interpretations. Excessive, unrealistic claims for the power of projective techniques should clearly be avoided. More general ethical considerations in the conduct of cross-cultural research have been presented elsewhere (Tapp, Kelman, Triandis, Wrightsman, & Coelho, 1974; also see Warwick's chapter in Volume 1 of this *Handbook*).

Summary and Conclusions

Projective techniques are indirect methods of assessment of personality by analyzing the responses of an individual to ambiguous stimuli presented in a standard manner. Stemming originally from clinical approaches based upon psychoanalytic theory, these techniques are specifically designed to elicit projections of inner thoughts, perceptions, fantasies, wishes, and anxieties. The relationship between inner personality and overt response to the projective technique is highly complex, usually requiring further analysis and clinical interpretation. Beginning with the Rorschach in some of the earliest studies of culture and personality, projective techniques have a long history of use and misuse in cross-cultural psychology.

Attempts to categorize, quantify, and standardize the response variables underlying projective test behavior have met with varying degrees of success. Although the Rorschach has proved to be somewhat refractory to such efforts, a new inkblot method, the Holtzman Inkblot Technique (HIT), yields twenty-two well-standardized scores having high reliability and demonstrated validity. The HIT scores are less subject to distortion by the examiner or situation than the Rorschach and have already been standardized in a number of different cultures throughout the world, making the HIT an attractive projective technique for cross-cultural studies.

Thematic apperception methods have also been widely used for personality assessment in different cultures. The most cross-cultural work has been done on the McClelland-Atkinson measures of need achievement because of strong interest in the relationship between motivation and achievement and how to influence them in many developing countries. Specialized thematic methods like the Goldschmidt-Edgerton picture technique for the study of values are useful for investigating social and cultural phenomena rather than assessing individual personalities.

Among the word association and completion techniques, the most commonly used is the sentence-completion method. A number of incomplete sentence stems are given to the subject who is asked to complete each sentence as rapidly as possible. As with other verbally based techniques, this method requires special care in translation and adaptation before it is suitable for cross-cultural use.

The fourth kind of projective method is comprised of expressive and constructive techniques such as drawings, paintings, and structured play. Very few of these methods are suitable for cross-cultural research although nearly all of them can be adapted to clinical uses in many different societies. The drawing of a human figure (Draw-a-Person Test) has been widely used to study cognitive and perceptual development in different cultures. But its use as a projective technique to reveal hidden aspects of the self is far more limited and questionable.

A number of methodological dilemmas continue to be serious problems in cross-cultural studies with projective techniques. The meaning of personality assessment may be questioned because of competing theories of personality, the almost limitless number and variety of ways in which people differ, the importance of the situation in which assessment takes place, and the different levels of functioning that may have to be measured simultaneously. Systems of scoring and analysis are often arbitrary and cumbersome, failing to yield measures of high psychometric quality. Situational and instrumental factors are particularly troublesome in many projective methods. Maintaining semantic equivalence across cultures and the problems in delineation, measurement, and control of relevant cultural variables are issues shared by projective techniques with all other cross-cultural methods in psychology.

A number of practical questions have also been posed and answered as they bear upon deciding whether or not to employ a projective technique in a particular cross-cultural study. These deal with (1) the range of cultures to be studied; (2) the question of assessing individual personality or group trends; (3) the choice of personality attributes to study; (4) the desirability of equivalent quantitative measurement in two or more cultures; (5) the requirements of special training to administer, score, and interpret projective techniques; (6) the costs in money, time, and effort to obtain test results; and (7) the question of ethical issues in the use of projective techniques for the cross-cultural study of personality.

References

ABT, L. E., & BELLAK, L. (Eds.), *Projective psychology: clinical approaches to the total personality.* New York: Knopf, 1950.

ANDERSON, H. H., & ANDERSON, G. L. (Eds.), *An introduction to projective techniques.* Englewood Cliffs, N.J.: Prentice-Hall, 1951.

————. Image of the teacher by adolescent children in seven countries. *American Journal of Orthopsychiatry.* 1961, *31*, 481–92.

ANDREW, G., HARTWELL, S. W., HUTT, M. L., & WALTON, R. E. *The Michigan picture test.* Chicago: Science Research Associates, 1953.

ANGELINI, A. L. Measuring the achievement motive in Brazil. *Journal of Social Psychology,* 1966, *68,* 35–40.

ARON, B. R. *A manual for analysis of the thematic apperception test.* Berkeley: Berg, 1949.

ATKINSON, J. W. (Ed.), *Motives in fantasy, action, and society.* New York: Van Nostrand, 1958.

ATKINSON, J. W., & RAYNOR, J. C. *Motivation and achievement.* New York: Halsted Press, 1974.

BECK, S. J., BECK, A. G., LEVITT, E. G., & MOLISH, H. B. *Rorschach's test, vol. I: basic processes*, 3rd ed. New York: Grune & Stratton, 1961.

BELL, J. E. *Projective techniques*. New York: Longmans, Green, 1948.

BELLAK, L. *The thematic apperception test and the children's apperception test in clinical use*. New York: Grune & Stratton, 1954.

BELLAK, L., & HURVICH, M. S. A human modification of the children's apperception test (CAT-H). *Journal of Projective Techniques and Personality Assessment*, 1966, *30*, 228–42.

BINET, A., & HENRI, V. La psychologie individuelle. *Année Psychologique*, 1895–96, *2*, 411–65.

BLANE, H. T., & YAMAMOTO, K. Sexual role identity among Japanese and Japanese-American high school students. *Journal of Cross-Cultural Psychology*, 1970, *1*, 345–54.

BLUM, C. S. Assessment of psychodynamic variables by the Blacky pictures. In P. McReynolds (Ed.), *Advances in psychological assessment*. Palo Alto: Science and Behavior Books, 1968.

BOCK, D. R., HAGGARD, E. A., HOLTZMAN, W. H., BECK, A. G., & BECK, S. J. *A comprehensive psychometric study of the Rorschach and Holtzman inkblot techniques*. Chapel Hill: Psychometric Laboratory, University of North Carolina, 1963.

BUHLER, C. The world test: a projective technique. *Journal of Child Psychiatry*, 1951, *2*, 4–23.

CAUDILL, W. Patterns of emotion in modern Japan. In R. J. Smith and R. K. Beardsley (Eds.), *Japanese culture: its development and characteristics*. New York: WGFAR Viking Fund Publications in Anthropology, 1962.

CHURCHILL, R., & CRANDALL, V. J. The reliability and validity of the Rotter incomplete sentences test. *Journal of Consulting Psychology*, 1955, *19*, 345–50.

CLARK, R. M. A method of administering and evaluating the thematic apperception test. *Genetic Psychology Monographs*, 1944, *30*, 3–55.

CURRIE, S. F., HOLTZMAN, W. H., & SWARTZ, J. D. Early indicators of personality traits viewed retrospectively. *Journal of School Psychology*, 1974, *12*, 51–59.

DAVE, P. N., & KRISHNAMURTHY, A. R. An investigation of motivational levels and risk-taking of small farmers of Mysore district. *Research Reports in Education*, 1973, *IV*, 55–77. (National Council of Educational Research and Training, New Delhi, India).

DENNIS, W. The performance of Hopi children on the Goodenough draw-a-man test. *Journal of Comparative Psychology*, 1942, *34*, 341–48.

————. *Group values through children's drawings*. New York: Wiley, 1966a.

————. Goodenough scores, art experience, and modernization. *Journal of Social Psychology*, 1966b, *68*, 211–28.

EDGERTON, R. B. Method in psychological anthropology. In R. Naroll & R. Cohen (Eds.), *A handbook of method in cultural anthropology*. New York: Natural History Press, 1970.

ERON, L. D. A normative study of the thematic apperception test. *Psychological Monographs*, 1950, *64* (Whole No. 315).

ERVIN, S. M. Language and TAT content in French-English bilinguals. *Journal of Abnormal and Social Psychology*, 1964, *68*, 500–07.

EXNER, J. E., Jr. *The Rorschach systems*. New York: Grune & Stratton, 1969.

FISCHER, G. H., & SPADA, H. *Die Psychometrische Grundlagen des Rorschachtests und der Holtzman Inkblot Technique.* Bern: Verlag Hans Huber, 1973.

FISHER, S. Projective methodologies. *Annual Review of Psychology,* 1967, *18,* 165–90.

FRANCK, K., & ROSEN, E. A projective test of masculinity-femininity. *Journal of Consulting Psychology,* 1949, *13,* 247–56.

FRANK, L. K. Projective methods for the study of personality. *Journal of Psychology,* 1939, *8,* 389–413.

———. *Projective methods.* Springfield, Ill.: Thomas, 1948.

GLESER, G. C. Projective methodologies. *Annual Review of Psychology,* 1963, *14,* 391–422.

GOKULNATHAN, P. P., & MEHTA, P. Achievement motive in tribal and nontribal Assamese secondary school adolescents. *Indian Educational Review,* 1972, *7,* 67–90.

GOLDBERG, P. A. A review of the sentence completion methods in personality assessment. In B. I. Murstein (Ed.), *Handbook of projective techniques.* New York: Basic Books, 1965.

GOLDSCHMIDT, W., & EDGERTON, R. B. A picture technique for the study of values. *American Anthropologist,* 1961, *63,* 26–45.

GORHAM, D. R. Validity and reliability studies of a computer-based scoring system for inkblot responses. *Journal of Consulting Psychology,* 1967, *31,* 65–70.

———. Cross-cultural research based on the Holtzman inkblot technique. *International Congress of the Rorschach and other Projective Techniques,* 1970, *7,* 158–64.

GORHAM, D. R., & HOLTZMAN, W. H. A computerized system of configural scoring and interpretation of the Holtzman inkblot technique for cross-cultural studies. *Abstract Guide, XX International Congress of Psychology.* Tokyo: Science Council of Japan, 1972.

GORHAM, D. R., MOSELEY, E. C., & HOLTZMAN, W. H. Norms for the computer-scored Holtzman inkblot technique. *Perceptual and Motor Skills Monograph Supplement,* 1968, *26,* 1279–1305.

GUTHRIE, G. M., & AZORES, F. M. Philippine interpersonal behavior patterns. In W. F. Bello & A. de Guzman II (Eds.), *Modernizations: its impact in the Philippines, III.* IPC Papers No. 6. Quezon City: Ateneo de Manila Press, 1968.

HALLOWELL, A. I. Acculturation processes and personality changes as indicated by the Rorschach technique. *Rorschach Research Exchange,* 1942, *6,* 42–50.

———. *Culture and experience.* Philadelphia: University of Pennsylvania Press, 1955.

HARRIS, D. B. *Children's drawings as measures of intellectual maturity.* New York: Harcourt, Brace and World, 1963.

HARROWER-ERICKSON, M., & STEINER, M. E. *Large scale Rorschach technique.* Springfield, Ill.: Thomas, 1945.

HAVIGHURST, R. J., DUBOIS, M. E., CSIKSZENTMIHALYI, M., & DOLL, R. *A cross-national study of Buenos Aires and Chicago adolescents.* Basel: Karger, 1965.

HAWORTH, M. R. *The CAT: facts about fantasy.* New York: Grune & Stratton, 1966.

HENRY, W. E. The thematic apperception technique in the study of culture-personality relations. *Genetic Psychology Monographs,* 1947, *35,* 3–135.

———. The thematic apperception technique in the study of group and cultural problems. In H. H. Anderson & G. L. Anderson (Eds.), *An introduction to projective techniques,* 2nd ed. Englewood Cliffs, N.J.: Prentice-Hall, 1956a.

————. *The analysis of fantasy: the thematic apperception technique in the study of personality.* New York: Wiley, 1956b.

————. Projective tests in cross-cultural research. In B. Kaplan (Ed.), *Studying personality cross-culturally.* Evanston, Ill.: Row, Peterson, 1961.

HENRY, W. E., & FARLEY, J. The validity of the thematic apperception test in the study of adolescent personality. *Psychological Monographs,* 1959, *73,* no. 17.

HERRON, E. W. Psychometric characteristics of a thirty-item version of the group method of the Holtzman inkblot technique. *Journal of Clinical Psychology,* 1963, *19,* 450–53.

HERTZ, M. R. Projective techniques in crisis. *Journal of Projective Techniques and Personality Assessment,* 1970, *34,* 449–67.

HILL, E. F. *The Holtzman inkblot technique.* San Francisco: Jossey-Bass, 1972.

HOLT, R. R. The nature of TAT stories as cognitive products: a psycho-analytic approach. In J. Kagan & G. Lesser (Eds.), *Contemporary issues in thematic apperception methods.* Springfield, Ill.: Thomas, 1961.

HOLTZMAN, W. H. Objective scoring of projective techniques. In B. M. Bass & I. A. Berg (Eds.), *Objective approaches to personality.* New York: Van Nostrand, 1959.

————. Recurring dilemmas in personality assessment. *Journal of Projective Techniques and Personality Assessment,* 1964, *28,* 144–50.

————. Cross-cultural research on personality development. *Human Development,* 1965, *8,* 65–86.

————. Cross-cultural studies in psychology. *International Journal of Psychology,* 1968, *3,* 83–91.

————. New developments in Holtzman inkblot technique. In P. McReynolds (Ed.), *Advances in psychological assessment,* Vol. 3. San Francisco: Jossey-Bass, 1975.

HOLTZMAN, W. H., DIAZ-GUERRERO, R., & SWARTZ, J. D. *Personality development in two cultures.* Austin: University of Texas Press, 1975.

HOLTZMAN, W. H., MOSELEY, M. C., REINEHR, R. C., & ABBOTT, E. Comparison of the group method and the standard individual version of the Holtzman inkblot technique. *Journal of Clinical Psychology,* 1963, *19,* 441–49.

HOLTZMAN, W. H., THORPE, J. S., SWARTZ, J. D., & HERRON, E. W. *Inkblot perception and personality.* Austin: University of Texas Press, 1961.

JUNG, C. G. *Studies in word-association.* London: Heinemann, 1918.

KAPLAN, B. Cross-cultural use of projective techniques. In F. L. K. Hsu (Ed.), *Psychological anthropology.* Homewood, Ill.: Dorsey Press, 1961.

KATAGUCHI, Y. *Psychopsy: manual for Ka-Ro inkblot test.* Tokyo: Kaneko Shobo, 1970.

KLOPFER, B., AINSWORTH, M. D., KLOPFER, W. G., & HOLT, R. R. *Developments in the Rorschach technique, vol. I, technique and theory.* Yonkers-on-Hudson, New York: World, 1954.

KOPPITZ, E. M. *Psychological evaluation of children's human figure drawings.* New York: Grune & Stratton, 1968.

KOPPITZ, E. M., & MOREAU, M. A comparison of emotional indicators on human figure drawings of children from Mexico and from the United States. *Revista Interamericana de Psicologia*, 1968, *2*, 41–48.

KOTASKOVA, J. Contribution to doll-play technique validation by comparison of English, Norwegian and Czech data. *Ceskoslovenska Psychologie*, 1971, *15*, 34–54.

LANSKY, L. M. Story completion methods. In A. I. Rabin (Ed.), *Projective techniques in personality measurement*. New York: Springer, 1968.

LAOSA, L. M. *Development of word association structures among school children of Mexico and the United States*. Ph.D. dissertation, University of Texas at Austin, 1971.

LAOSA, L. M., SWARTZ, J. D., & DIAZ-GUERRERO, R. Perceptual-cognitive and personality development of Mexican and Anglo-American children as measured by human figure drawings. *Developmental Psychology*, 1974, *10*(1), 131–39.

LEVINE, R. A. *Culture, behavior, and personality*. Chicago: Aldine, 1973.

LEVINE, R. A., & LEVINE, B. B. *Nyansongo: A Gusii community in Kenya*. New York: Wiley, 1966.

LEININGER, M. *Convergence and divergence of human behavior: an ethno-psychological study of two Gadsup villages in New Guinea*. Ph.D. dissertation. University of Washington, 1966.

LENNEP, D. J. The four-picture test. In H. H. Anderson & G. L. Anderson (Eds.), *An introduction to projective techniques*. Englewood Cliffs, N.J.: Prentice-Hall, 1951.

LINDZEY, G. *Projective techniques and cross-cultural research*. New York: Appleton-Century-Crofts, 1961.

LINDZEY, G., & SILVERMAN, M. Thematic apperception test: techniques of group administration, sex differences, and the role of verbal productivity. *Journal of Personality*, 1959, *27*, 311–23.

LYNN, D. B., & LYNN, R. The structured doll play test as a projective technique for use with children. *Journal of Projective Techniques*, 1959, *23*, 335–44.

MACFARLANE, J. W., & TUDDENHAM, R. D. Problems in the validation of projective techniques. In H. H. Anderson & G. L. Anderson (Eds.), *An introduction to projective techniques*. Englewood Cliffs, N.J.: Prentice-Hall, 1951.

MACHOVER, K. *Personality projection in the drawing of the human figure*. Springfield, Ill.: Thomas, 1949.

MANASTER, G. J., & HAVIGHURST, R. J. *Cross-national research: social-psychological methods and problems*. Boston: Houghton Mifflin, 1972.

MCCLELLAND, D. C. (Ed.), *Studies in motivation*. New York: Appleton-Century-Crofts, 1955.

———. *The achieving society*. Princeton: Van Nostrand, 1961.

MCCLELLAND, D. C., CLARK, R. A., ROBY, T. B., & ATKINSON, J. W. The effect of the need for achievement on thematic apperception. *Journal of Experimental Psychology*, 1949, *37*, 242–55.

MCCLELLAND, D. C., ATKINSON, J. W., CLARK, R. A., & LOWELL, E. L. *The achievement motive*. New York: Appleton-Century-Crofts, 1953.

MCCLELLAND, D. C., & WINTER, D. G. *Motivating economic achievement*. New York: Free Press, 1969.

MEHTA, P. Measuring achievement motivation. *Manas*, 1975, *22*, 1–8.

MOLISH, B. Projective methodologies. *Annual Review of Psychology*, 1972, 23, 577-614.

MORAN, L. J. Generality of word-association response sets. *Psychological Monographs*, 1966, 80, Whole No. 612.

MORAN, L. J., & MURAKAWA, N. Japanese and American association structures. *Journal of Verbal Learning and Verbal Behavior*, 1968, 7, 176-81.

MORAN, L. J., & NUNEZ, R. Cross-cultural similarities in association structures. *Revista Interamericana de Psicologia*, 1967, 1, 1-6.

MORGAN, C. D., & MURRAY, H. A. A method for investigating fantasies: the thematic apperception test. *Archives of Neurology and Psychiatry*, 1935, 34, 289-306.

MOSELEY, E. C. Multivariate comparisons of seven cultures: Argentina, Colombia (Bogota), Colombia (Cartegena), Mexico, Panama, United States, and Venezuela. In C. F. Hereford & L. Natalicio (Eds.), *Aportaciones de la Psicologia a la Investigacion Transcultural*. Mexico City: Trillas, 1967.

MOSELEY, E. C., GORHAM, D. R., & HILL, E. Computer scoring of inkblot perceptions. *Perceptual and Motor Skills*, 1963, 17, 498.

MURPHY, L. B. *Personality in young children: vol. I, methods for the study of personality in young children*. New York: Basic Books, 1956.

MURRAY, H. A. *Thematic apperception test manual*. Cambridge, Mass.: Harvard University Press, 1943.

MURSTEIN, B. I. *Theory and research in projective techniques (emphasizing the TAT)*. New York: Wiley, 1963.

————. *Handbook of projective techniques*. New York: Basic Books, 1965.

PECK, R., HAVIGHURST, R., & MILLER, K. (Eds.), *Coping styles and achievement: a cross-national study of children*. (Technical Report, Vol. I). University of Texas, Austin, 1970.

PHILLIPS, H. P. *Thai peasant personality*. Berkeley: University of California Press, 1966.

PHILLIPSON, H. *The object relations technique*. London: Tavistock, 1955.

PIOTROWSKI, Z. A. *Perceptanalysis*. New York: Macmillan, 1957.

RABIN, A. I. Culture components as a significant factor in child development: Kibbutz adolescents. *American Journal of Orthopsychiatry*, 1961, 31, 493-504.

RABIN, A. I. (Ed.), *Projective techniques in personality measurement*. New York: Springer, 1968.

RABIN, A. I., & LIMUACO, J. A. Sexual differentiation of American and Filipino children as reflected in the draw-a-person test. *Journal of Social Psychology*, 1959, 50, 207-11.

RAPAPORT, D., SCHAFER, R., & GILL, M. *Diagnostic psychological testing*, Vol. I. Chicago: Year Book Publishers, 1945.

REYNOLDS, W. M., & SUNDBERG, N. D. Recent research trends in testing. *Journal of Personality Assessment*, 1976, 40, 228-33.

RORSCHACH, H. *Psychodiagnostics: a diagnostic test based on perception*. New York: Grune & Stratton, 1942. (Originally published in 1921.)

ROTTER, J. B., RAFFERTY, J., & SCHACHTITZ, E. Validation of the Rotter incomplete sentences blank for college screening. *Journal of Consulting Psychology*, 1949, 13, 348-56.

SCHACHTEL, E. G. *Experiential foundations of Rorschach test.* New York: Basic Books, 1966.

SCHAFER, R. *Psychoanalytic interpretation in Rorschach testing.* New York: Grune & Stratton, 1954.

SHERWOOD, E. On the designing of TAT pictures, with special reference to a set for an African people assimilating Western culture. *Journal of Social Psychology,* 1957, *45,* 161–90.

SHNEIDMAN, E. S. The MAPS test with children. In A. I. Rabin & M. R. Haworth (Eds.), *Projective techniques with children.* New York: Grune & Stratton, 1960.

SPAIN, D. H. A supplementary bibliography on projective testing. In F. L. K. Hsu (Ed.), *Psychological anthropology,* 2nd ed. Cambridge, Mass.: Schenkman, 1972.

SPINDLER, G., & SPINDLER, L. The instrumental activities inventory: a technique for the study of the psychology of acculturation. *Southwestern Journal of Anthropology,* 1965, *21,* 1–23.

SWARTZ, J. D., & HOLTZMAN, W. H. Group method of administration for the Holtzman inkblot technique. *Journal of Clinical Psychology,* 1963, *19,* 433–41.

STEIN, M. I. *The thematic apperception test: an introductory manual for its clinical use with adults,* 2nd ed. Reading, Mass.: Addison-Wesley, 1955.

SWENSON, C. H., JR. Empirical evaluations of human figure drawings. *Psychological Bulletin,* 1957, *54,* 431–66.

————. Empirical evaluation of human figure drawings: 1957–1966. *Psychological Bulletin,* 1968, *70,* 20–44.

SYMONDS, P. M. *Adolescent fantasy: an investigation of the picture-story method of personality study.* New York: Columbia University Press, 1949.

TAMM, M. Resultados preliminares de un estudio transcultural y desarrollo de la personalidad de niños mexicanos y norteamericanos. In C. F. Hereford & L. Natalicio (Eds.), *Aportaciones de la Psicologia a la Investigacion Transcultural.* Mexico City: Trillas, 1967.

TAPP, J. L., KELMAN, H. C., TRIANDIS, H. C., WRIGHTSMAN, L. S., & COELHO, G. V. Continuing concerns in cross-cultural ethics: a report. *International Journal of Psychology,* 1974, *9,* 231–49.

TOMKINS, S. S. *The thematic apperception test: the theory and technique of interpretation.* New York: Grune & Stratton, 1947.

TRIANDIS, H. C., MALPASS, R. S., & DAVIDSON, A. R. Cross-cultural psychology. In B. J. Siegel (Ed.), *Biennial review of anthropology.* Stanford: Stanford University Press, 1971.

WITKIN, H. A., PRICE-WILLIAMS, D., BERTINI, M., CHRISTIANSEN, B., OLTMAN, P. K., RAMIREZ, M., & VAN MEEL, J. Social conformity and psychological differentiation. *International Journal of Psychology,* 1974, *9,* 11–29.

ZUBIN, J., ERON, L. D., & SCHUMER, F. *An experimental approach to projective techniques.* New York: Wiley, 1965.

ZULLIGER, H. *The Zulliger individual and group test.* New York: International Universities Press, 1959.

The Role of Context, Skill, and Transfer in Cross-Cultural Experimentation

Tom Ciborowski

Contents

Abstract

The present chapter focuses on a number of key variables in research methodology that are especially important to cross-cultural psychology. The variables discussed are experimental context and the role of transfer of cognitive skills from one domain to other domains. The discussion of these variables draws on cross-cultural and cross-subcultural evidence from the broad areas of speech and communication skills, memory skills, classification skills, and Piagetian cognitive skills. The major thrust of the chapter is that the importance of such variables as experimental context and transfer of cognitive skills needs to be strongly reemphasized in cross-cultural research methodology.

Introduction

It may be useful to indicate the dimensions and focus of the present chapter on experimentation in cross-cultural research. It is *not* intended to be a comprehensive review and analysis of the many strategies used in cross-cultural experimentation. A comprehensive exposition of experimentation in cross-cultural psychology can be found in Brislin, Lonner, and Thorndike (1973); Berry and Dasen (1974); or Sechrest (1970).

Cross-cultural experimentation has all the problems of experimentation in a single culture, plus additional difficulties. This chapter deals only with the additional problems.

This chapter is highly specific; its viewpoint is best exemplified by the extensive research of Michael Cole. However, this chapter should *not* be construed as a comprehensive and accurate reflection of Cole's theoretical position; it represents my interpretation of some of Cole's work and I apologize beforehand for whatever inaccuracies my interpretation contains. Sylvia Scribner's work has also greatly influenced this viewpoint on cross-cultural experimentation. This examination is pursued through a number of specific cross-cultural experiments which are cited as examples. Hence, the present chapter is pedagogic by way of repeated specific examples rather than by way of an extended theoretical exposition.

This chapter examines the role of some major variables in cross-cultural experimentation. Other investigators, for example, Cole, Gay, Glick and Sharp (1971a); Cole and Bruner (1971); Cole and Scribner (1974); and Scribner (1975); have concerned themselves with analyzing and underscoring the crucial importance of such variables as *context* and *skill* in cross-cultural experimentation. Despite their work, the role and importance of these variables need to be repeatedly stressed, since there are still a number of cross-cultural investigators who do not fully appreciate the importance of these variables.

For example, during a recent conference on Aboriginal cognition in Australia, a paper was presented dealing with the alleged linguistic skills of a group of Aboriginal children. The investigative tool used in the research was the widely used ITPA (Illinois Test of Psycholinguistic Abilities), but the use of such a tool as the ITPA to investigate the linguistic skills of a group of Aboriginal children was totally *inappropriate*. This example provides the springboard for a viewpoint on cross-cultural research to be elaborated in this chapter, starting with the work of the American linguist, William Labov.

Speech and Communication

Many investigators have recently examined the performance of economically disadvantaged English dialect (e.g., black English) speakers in a wide variety of tasks. It has generally been found that economically disadvantaged speakers do not perform as well in school and on standardized tests as their middle-class counterparts who speak standard English. Attempts to account for this finding led to two widely different points of view that were characterized as the *difference-deficit* controversy. It is important to note that both points of view agree that dialect speakers engage in verbal activity that is structurally different from standard English. For example, black English speakers frequently delete copulas in constructing sentences (e.g., "He going" instead of "He is going").

However, the *deficit* position held that dialect speakers, who displayed poor standard English verbal skills, suffered verbal and cultural deficiencies that resulted in social or cognitive liabilities (Bereiter & Engelmann, 1966; Deutsch, 1967). Supporters of this position held that poor school performance reflected a deficiency in the child and that intensive remedial programs were necessary to improve the standard English verbal skills of dialect speakers.

In direct opposition to the *deficit* point of view is the *difference* position, which held that although dialect speakers displayed poor standard English verbal skills, this did *not* mean that dialect speakers were verbally deprived (Labov, 1970; Ginsburg, 1972).

Labov (1970) argued that young ghetto-reared black children were *not* verbally deficient; they merely spoke a dialect of the English language that was *different* from what is commonly called Standard English (S.E.). Linguists and psycholinguists view Standard English as simply another dialect of the English language and it is in no way more structurally complex or linguistically more "sophisticated" than any other dialect. Recent research (Ciborowski & Choy, 1974) has supported Labov's *difference*.

The focus of this section is on particular methodological strategies that led Labov to advance his position. Many investigators observed that attempting to collect speech information from young ghetto-reared black children was not a simple task. The young children often remained silent, or when gently prompted, answered in terse monosyllables. Even when the investigator was a ghetto-reared black man, the young children still responded with terse monosyllables. It was this kind of evidence that led investigators such as Bereiter and Englemann (1966) and Deutsch (1967) to conclude that the young children were verbally deficient. But Labov carried the investigation a crucial step further.

Clarence Brown, a colleague of Labov, was a large (6'3") young black man who was completely familiar with life in the ghetto. Brown, like previous investigators, quickly found that just being alone with a young black child (Leon) did not elicit much speech output from the child. It was only when Brown changed the *context* of the testing situation that young Leon's speech output dramatically changed. Brown and Labov introduced the following changes:

1. Brought along Leon's best friend.
2. Brought along some potato chips and other food in order to alter the investigative context into something similar to a nonthreatening party.
3. Brown sat down on the floor with the children, thus reducing his height from an imposing 6'3" to approximately the same height as the children.
4. Introduced taboo words and topics into the conversation.

The effects of these changes were striking. Instead of speaking in guarded monosyllables, Leon burst forth in animated speech. This outcome, along with evidence from other sources, led Labov to argue strongly against a verbal deficit position. In fact, Labov (1970) went on to demonstrate that verbal skill was an integral and highly prized feature of ghetto life.

The work of Labov (1970) and his colleagues underscores the important dictum of Chomsky (1968) concerning the relation between performance and competence. Chomsky maintained that one cannot infer a person's underlying competence in a language from speech performance alone. Clearly, the kind of terse monosyllables of a young black child like Leon, have misled some psychologists into drawing inferences about Leon's competence in the English language.

A major problem still remains. How can researchers interpret or assess *performance*, either within a linguistic framework, or within a more general cross-cultural experimental framework? A useful starting point is to define *performance* and then supply a number of cross-cultural examples in support of that definition. Performance is here defined as particular behaviors emitted as a function of the subject's own interpretation of the specific *context* and demands of the experimental situation.

Explicit in the working definition is the idea that a subject in an experimental situation possesses a set of expectations about the situation, and may interpret the situation in a variety of ways. The experimenter's expectations may be quite different from those of the subject. Consider some examples in support of this view.

Experimental Examples

Glick (1968) was investigating classification behavior among traditional Kpelle tribesmen. The Kpelle are a large tribe of rice farmers living primarily in north-central Liberia, located on the west coast of Africa (see Cole et al., 1971a for more details). Glick was primarily interested in the particular attributes of objects that the Kpelle would use in classifying the objects. The experimental procedure was the standard one of presenting the subjects with an array of familiar objects and instructing the subjects to put together those objects that belong together. The instructions were a standard version of the typical Piagetian instructions used in classification studies. Glick found that most of the subjects did *not* make groupings based upon their common membership in a taxonomic category. Instead, the majority of the subjects made groupings based on either functional or perceptual relations among the items. Other investigators who obtained similar experimental results interpreted their findings as an indication of deficient conceptual thinking on the part of the subjects.

Glick (1968) however, pressed the investigation further. He first asked the subjects the reasons why they grouped the items in the way they did. Most of the subjects replied that the groupings they made were, in the Kpelle traditional sense (Kpelle custom and culture), the clever way to do it. Glick interpreted this reply as meaning that the subjects construed his instruction to group the items as a test of their cleverness; most importantly, a test of their cleverness according to the Kpelle culturally accepted view of the term. Acting on a hunch, Glick asked a subject to do the classification task as a *stupid* Kpelle person might do it. The result was dramatic. Under the new instructions, the subject produced a perfect taxonomic grouping!

Obviously, the subject possessed the cognitive skills to produce taxonomic groupings, the measure used by Western investigators to indicate intelligent conceptual thinking in classification tasks. Had Glick (1969) not followed up his hunch, his original results (using standard Piagetian instructions) could have been taken by some investigators as evidence of deficient thinking.

There have been many cross-cultural investigations of classification behavior using abstract objects such as triangles, circles, and squares that varied in color and size (see Cole & Scribner, 1974). The basic task consists of presenting all the stimuli to the subject and instructing the subject to form as many classifications as possible, that is, a hierarchy of classifications formed by a succession of smaller and smaller subsets. A number of investigators have suggested that the use of such stimuli is inappropriate with nonschooled subjects from nontechnological societies (see Biesheuvel, 1969; Deregowski & Serpell, 1971; Irwin & McLaughlin, 1970). Perhaps the best known studies relevant to this issue were conducted by Price-Williams (1961, 1962).

Price-Williams (1962) investigated classification behavior among the Tiv children of Nigeria. As his stimuli Price-Williams selected two categories—animals and plants that every Tiv child was completely familiar with. Price-Williams selected ten different kinds of animals, varying in color, size, edibility, etc. He used small plastic highly representational dolls for most of the animals (a real beetle and a real fish were used). For the plants, Price-Williams picked ten different kinds of plants that could be classified on the basis of edibility, size, etc. The first step of the experimental task consisted of asking the child to put together those objects that belonged together and to verbalize his reasons for doing so. After each grouping and verbalization the child was asked whether he could discover another way of grouping the objects. This procedure was followed until the child said that there were no other ways to group the objects. This investigation of nonabstract items showed that even the youngest children studied (approximately six years old) classified the objects. All the children reclassified the objects when instructed to do so; the youngest children found three to four different ways of grouping, while the eleven-year-olds found approximately six different ways.

Using the familiar items, Price-Williams (1962) found that the young Tiv children were as capable as European children in producing hierarchies of classifications, despite the fact that when presented with abstract shapes (triangles, circles, squares, etc.) the performance of these same Tiv children was woefully inferior to the performance of European children. By changing the stimuli from abstract unfamiliar material to concrete familiar material, and hence changing the very context of the experiment, Price-Williams obtained different kinds of performance from the Tiv children. We will return to this important aspect of cross-cultural investigations shortly.

Memory and Free-Recall

In Hawaii virtually every schoolchild possesses some degree of mastery of a dialect of the English language that is frequently referred to as Pidgin (or Hawaiian Islands Dialect). Pidgin is a major dialect of the English language and it shares many of the same features of other Creole variants of the English language (Carr, 1972). For example, copulas are frequently deleted and Standard English verbs are often replaced by expressive words. For example, instead of saying: "I did not do it" in Standard English; the comparable expression in Pidgin might be, "I lazy do it."

The Department of Education in Hawaii has recognized the important role of Pidgin and has instituted a number of innovative programs to deal with this educational problem (e.g., the Hawaii English Program, or HEP for short). Pidgin may be viewed as something of an educational problem because many young children in Hawaii, who speak solely in Pidgin, do not encounter Standard English (save for television) until they enter school. Upon entering school these children are immersed in a sea of Standard English, a dialect of the English language to which they have had very little (if any) exposure.

Unfortunately, despite the efforts of the Department of Education, there are a number of teachers who view a Pidgin speaking child, who allegedly possesses poor Standard English skills, as being verbally deficient. Some of these teachers feel that Pidgin speaking and verbalizing must be discouraged and *replaced* with Standard English speaking skills. They feel that until this is accomplished the child will not only be deficient verbally but perhaps cognitively as well. The situation is strongly reminiscent of the situation that Labov faced that was discussed earlier in this chapter (see Cazden, John, & Hymes, 1972).

Ciborowski and Choy (1974) sought to investigate both the Standard English and Pidgin verbal skills of a group of Hawaiian schoolchildren. The vehicle used to assess verbal skill was a free-recall task. A free-recall task was selected because it is quickly and easily administered and a wide cross-cultural literature using the task already exists (Cole et al., 1971a; Cole, Frankel, & Sharp, 1971b). Subjects were fifth-grade children attending a public school in Honolulu.

Two stories were written specifically for the experiment. Embedded within each story were eight familiar items that were later tested for recall. The stories were based on fifth-grade reading material and consultations with teachers and educational specialists. Although a free-recall task may not be the most sensitive measure of verbal skill, it is a reasonable assumption that verbal skill is intimately involved in first understanding the stories and then being able to recall their content. The stories were first written in Standard English and then "translated" into Pidgin.

There were two subject groups. According to teachers and school records one group possessed competent verbal skills in Standard English, but little if any skill in Pidgin. The second group allegedly possessed poor Standard English verbal skills but were highly skilled in speaking Pidgin. These two subject groups were then partitioned into four experimental groups. Half of the subjects in each group received the stories in Standard English and half in Pidgin English. The basic task consisted of reading the stories to each child and then asking the child to recall as many (as possible) of the (eight) embedded items in the stories. The number of items recalled was used as the primary measure of performance. The means are shown in Table 7-1.

As seen in Table 7-1, the recall scores were quite high when a subject received the stories in a dialect in which he or she was competent. More

Table 7-1.   Mean Number of Items Recalled as a Function of Dialect Skill and Dialect of the Stories.*

Dialect Skill	Dialect of Stories	
	Standard English	Pidgin
Standard English	7.3	5.5
Pidgin	6.8	7.2

* Current linguistic convention refers to both Standard English and Pidgin as dialects of the English Language.

important, however, an analysis of variance revealed a significant interaction between dialect skill and the dialect of the stories. The analysis revealed that the Pidgin speakers recalled significantly more items when the stories were presented in Standard English than the Standard English speakers who received the stories in Pidgin. Although both groups of subjects are clearly bidialectical, the striking finding is that the Pidgin speakers recalled a very high percentage of the items even when the stories were presented in Standard English. This happened despite the fact that according to teachers and school records, the Pidgin speakers were supposed to possess only *marginal* Standard English speaking skills.

Complete details on this study may be found in Ciborowski and Choy (1974). The major message of this study is a familiar one. That is, by changing the stimuli and hence context of a testing situation, or by moving away from a standardized test, subjects may display particular skills in which they allegedly are deficient.

One final example will be presented before turning to a general discussion of the relation between context and skill, and a discussion of the transfer of particular skills. The issue of transfer of skills is a central issue in education and in cross-cultural investigations.

In most free-recall studies the experimenter constructs a recall list by selecting, for example, four items from four different categories (e.g., animals, clothing, tools, and food) to produce a list of sixteen items. The items are then randomized five times to produce five different lists each containing the same items but in different orders. Typically, an experimental trial consists in reading the list to the subject and then asking the subject to recall as many items from the list as he can. This procedure is generally repeated five times using a differently ordered list each time.

One of the primary measures of performance in a free-recall task is the total number of items recalled. Another primary measure of performance is the degree of clustering by category of the items in the subject's recall protocol, that is, the degree to which the subject recalls the items from a particular category (say animals) before the subject recalls the items from a different category (say clothing), and so on. Clustering, in other words, could be called *recall by category*.

Arthur Jensen has hypothesized that there are two major levels of learning (Jensen & Fredericksen, 1973). Level I is characterized as simple rote learning while Level II is characterized as abstract conceptual learning. According to Jensen, one indication of Level II learning is the degree to which a subject demonstrates clustering in his recall protocol in a memory test. In Jensen's one published article on this issue, his subject groups consisted of black children and white children in the Oakland-Berkeley area of California. Jensen found little, if any, clustering in the recall protocols of the black children and suggested that they were displaying only Level I learning, and hence, by inference, were cognitively deficient. By contrast, the white children displayed clustering and hence Level II abilities. In a recent excellent paper, Scribner (1975) attacked Jensen's position in a variety of ways. One line of attack focused on the alleged relevance of the items in the recall list for the black children. That is, the items were selected from norms derived from primarily middle class white children and young adults.

Cole, Frankel, and Sharp (1971b) followed standardized free-recall procedures using familiar items and to their surprise found that the Kpelle showed extremely poor recall. Secondly, they found little, if any, evidence for clustering in the free-recall protocols. Even introducing real objects instead of using words produced no significant increase in total recall scores or in degree of clustering. Had Cole and his colleagues left the investigation at that point, it would have been yet another example of rural nontechnological subjects performing quite poorly in relation to their schooled counterparts living in a Western technological society. But Cole pushed the investigation further by introducing a number of innovative variations in the basic procedure and hence changing the context of the experimental situation.

One interesting innovation that Cole et al. introduced was to use a series of five chairs during the testing procedure. Each chair was associated with one of the five categories of items that comprised the recall items. Instead of reading a list of words, real objects were used. When an object (say a shirt) was presented it was simply held for a few moments over the chair that "represented" clothing. All the objects were presented in this way: an object from a particular category was held over the chair that "represented" that category. It is important to note that the subjects were *not* told that a particular chair "represented" a particular category, nor were subjects told beforehand what categories of objects would be presented. The results of this innovation were striking. Not only did overall recall increase dramatically, but the subjects displayed a high degree of clustering in their recall protocols!

Obviously, the subjects possessed the cognitive skills to recall extremely well and to display clustering—Jensen's measure of Level II learning. By varying the context of the testing procedure Cole et al. were able to demonstrate that rural Kpelle tribal children and adults possessed cognitive skills equivalent to subjects in Western technological societies.

Based on the work of Tenney (1975) and Nelson (1969), Cole and his colleagues collected lexical categories of items from lower class black children in New York City. An example of some of the categories that Franklin, Fulani, Henkind, and Cole (1975) collected were: soul food; dances; drugs; and recording artists. An interesting feature of many of the items collected was that these same items could also be found in standard collections of category norms (like Battig & Montague, 1964), but listed under a *different* category than the one supplied by the black children. For example, the category *drugs* elicited such items as smack, grass, and coke.

Franklin et al. constructed a number of free-recall lists in the standardized way but used the items collected from the black children. Using their specially elicited free-recall lists, they investigated the memory skills of this group of black children. The results were striking. All the subjects showed excellent recall and most important, displayed a high degree of clustering in their recall protocols. This happened despite the fact that when the recall of these same black children was tested using list items selected from standardized lists, the children showed quite poor performance.

Interestingly, when these lists, specially elicited from blacks, were administered to a group of middle and upper class white children in New York City, the white children did *not* display a degree of clustering comparable to the black children. By comparison, the white children showed quite poor clustering performance. Sardonically, one could possibly conclude that according to black standards, the white children who did not display adequate clustering were showing Jensen's Level I learning and hence were perhaps cognitively deficient. It is important to note that a number of investigators who are members of a majority group do not hesitate to make serious statements about the cognitive deficiencies of members from certain minority groups on this kind of inappropriate evidence.

There are a number of important messages concerning cross-cultural experimentation and education in general that can be drawn from these examples.

General Discussion

Recall the statement that it was completely inappropriate to administer a test such as the Illinois Test of Psycholinguistic Abilities to a group of Aboriginal children that led to a discussion of a rudimentary definition of performance. In that definition heavy emphasis was put upon the concept of experimental context. A number of examples demonstrating how a change in the context of an experiment can elicit allegedly missing skills on the part of the subjects being tested were cited.

It follows that in cross-cultural experimentation one should not view performance in a vacuum, but rather as the specific skills tapped by the specific context of the experimental situation. Although many authors have written about this issue, perhaps the classic statement was made by Campbell (1961):

> we who are interested in using such (cross-cultural) data for delineating processes rather than exhaustively describing single instances must accept this rule: *No comparison of a single pair of natural objects is interpretable.* . . . (p. 344)

Explicit in the above definition is the extreme difficulty in inferring and describing cognitive processes based on cross-cultural investigations. A sharp distinction must be drawn between cognitive skills and cognitive processes. Many researchers view the *universality* of basic cognitive processes as axiomatic. This view is hardly a new one and is frequently referred to as the doctrine of *psychic unity.* It holds that individuals from radically different societies and cultures all possess the same fundamental cognitive processes. If this is true, then the problem remains of how to explain why individuals from different cultures can exhibit such marked differences in "ability" when administered even simple experimental tasks.

One way of addressing the problem is to first stop assuming that the presence or absence of a basic cognitive process can be inferred from a single crucial experiment. Investigators should concentrate on isolating and manipulating cognitive skills; that is, cross-cultural investigation should focus on the cultural and contextual variables that would lead a subject to either use, or not use, some particular cognitive skill in an experiment. Consistent with this view, Cole and Scribner (1974) argue that

> . . . we are unlikely to find cultural differences in basic component cognitive processes. While we cannot completely rule out this possibility, there is no evidence, in any line of investigation that . . . any cultural group wholly lacks a basic process such as abstraction, or inferential reasoning, or categorization. (p. 193)

The earlier review of a wide variety of cross-cultural investigations demonstrated that tapping specific cultural and contextual variables can show a subject possesses a specific cognitive skill. This is not to say that all people are equally adept at utilizing some specific cognitive skill. It is possible that because of cultural and experiential variables one group of people may be better than another group of people in their use of some cognitive skill. But the potential *capacity* to use any cognitive skill is perhaps universally the same for all cultural groups.

The problem confronting cross-cultural investigations is the problem of determining the cultural, contextual, and experiential variables that give rise to the use or nonuse of some particular cognitive skill. A number of ways of dealing with this problem have already been suggested.

One way proposed by Cole et al. (1971a) is to *experiment* with the experiment, that is, to systematically vary the experimental procedure until equal levels of performance (or rather, skill) among populations that initially differed are achieved. As Scribner (1975) has written:

> Instead of carrying one fixed paradigm to many different cultures, the researcher works with many different variations of a single paradigm within one culture. (p. 316)

A second way of dealing with the problem is to search for the *naturally* occurring contexts in a culture that elicit particular skills. Armed with these naturally occurring contexts the investigator can then tailor a specific experimental paradigm to manipulate and test that skill. A number of examples of this approach can be cited.

Price-Williams and Ramirez (1969) undertook to investigate some conservation Piagetian tasks with a group of Mexican children whose fathers were potters by trade. It was assumed that the children would have a great deal of first-hand experience in estimating quantities of clay. The experimental task was the famous Piagetian investigation of conservation. That is, would a child realize and understand what remained the same (or was invariant) about some object or quantity when that object was transformed in some way? Piaget originally used plasticine clay and presented the child with two identical balls of clay. In one version of the conservation experiment, Piaget would flatten one of the balls into a sausage shape and then ask the child a remarkable question: "Do we still have two equal amounts of clay, or does one have more than the other?"

Children around four or five years old typically responded to this question as if it were a very sensible one and replied that the two quantities were no longer equal. Piaget would say that the child did not "conserve." That is, the child did not understand that the quantity of clay remained the same even though it was transformed. If the child responded by saying the two quantities were still the same and the child could logically justify the basis of his response, then Piaget would say that the child "conserved."

Price-Williams and Ramirez (1969) found that the Mexican children who had ample experience in manipulating clay conserved more *frequently* than children without such experience. This outcome underscores the importance of utilizing a naturally occurring context in performing an experiment. It clearly demonstrates the importance of experiential skill affecting a pattern of cognitive development that, according to strict Piagetian theory, is universal for all children regardless of their real life experiences (see Dasen, 1972; Cole & Scribner, 1974).

Greenfield (1972) sought to investigate a similar kind of naturally occurring context by focusing on the weaving skills of a group of Mexicans. The experimental question was whether a person who is extremely skilled in weaving an old standard pattern (over and over) could learn to weave a totally new pattern significantly faster than someone who was not skilled in weaving the old pattern. Cole (personal communication) has suggested a similar approach with Mayan hammock weavers. Cole observed that most Mayan hammocks are woven according to a few standard patterns. The same question could be posed: would a group of weavers that repeatedly weave a standard hammock pattern be able to learn a new pattern significantly faster than a group of subjects that were not skilled in weaving the old pattern?

Implicit in this discussion of the use of naturally occurring contexts is the important issue of the *transfer* of skills from one task to another task. Also involved is the crucial issue of the transfer of skills from one domain to a totally new or different domain. This issue will be discussed after discussing an on-going research project in Hawaii.

The experimental site is an isolated fishing village. According to reliable sources the village is the only one of its kind left in the entire state of Hawaii. The men of the village still fish in the same way that their ancestors fished centuries ago. To a degree, many of the old Hawaiian beliefs and customs are still in effect in the village today. The children of the village attend a regular Department of Education elementary school (located at a considerable distance from the village) and, on the average, their school performance is relatively poor. For example, reading and writing skills are substandard, according to *standardized* tests. One of the ultimate goals of the entire on-going research activity is to investigate and eventually propose an extensive program of procedures aimed at improving the overall school performance of the children. Price-Williams and Ciborowski are attempting to achieve this difficult goal by following a variety of research paradigms.

The major paradigm being followed is to first isolate and analyze the particular cognitive skills that the children already possess. Particular cognitive skills refer to specific skills, for example, perceptual, mnemonic, and inferential abilities, that are closely tied to the cultural and real-life experiences of the children. To achieve this end, an in-depth ethnographic and experimental investigation of the contextual and naturally occurring situations that elicit these skills is under way. Consider a specific example.

Many of the older children are already accomplished boatmen and fishermen. They are accustomed to going considerable distances (perhaps five miles) out to sea in what seem to be distressingly small outrigger canoes. Many times these older children must contend with waves and swells that are far larger than the canoe itself. More than simple brawn and daring are involved in not only staying afloat, but also fishing. It is likely that a number of specific perceptual and inferential cognitive skills are involved in this activity.

Once out at sea these older children must be able to detect and cope with strong currents in order to fish successfully. They must know, for example, how and when to throw out the correct *chum* (fish bait) in a particular current, and how to stay within that current and ahead of the fish, in order to catch a load of fish. Obviously, they must be able to estimate accurately the speed of the current, and the location (and speed) of the fish they hope to catch. This ability calls for specific complex perceptual and inferential cognitive skills. Because of space limitations the many other skills that are associated with fishing are not mentioned; for example: using nets; estimating how far down to drop a baited hook; how to land a 300–400 pound marlin or ahi (tuna) that is practically the same size as the canoe; etc.

After isolating and analyzing such specific cognitive skills as the ones briefly described above, ways to *transfer* or translate these skills are sought so that they may be tapped or elicited in the classroom setting. This is a crucial part of the research program. At present it is perplexing and frustrating to realize that the children possess specific cognitive skills such as inferential ability, yet fail to display this ability in the classroom. As a linguist once put it, how is it that some young black children do so poorly in school tasks yet as soon as they "hit" the streets they demonstrate complex cognitive skills? Ciborowski (1976) wrote about this point, but to date, there are no guaranteed ways of achieving transfer. However, the on-going research program will *have* specific recommendations in the near future (see Gallimore, Boggs, & Jordan, 1975).

A secondary effort of the on-going research program is to explore and to test the generalizability of a number of findings obtained by some major psychological and anthropological investigators. For example, they are presently engaged in investigating some of the findings of Jean Piaget. Again, the keystone of the investigation consists of exploring the contextual and experiential situations of naturally occurring events in which specific cognitive skills are elicited. One area of investigation focuses on the animistic beliefs of Hawaiian children and adults. Already completed research that is currently under analysis suggests that Piaget's stages of development in animistic thinking might have to be seriously modified for Hawaiian children.

Also under investigation are Piaget's (1969) experiments on children's understanding and conception of physical causality. Specifically, Piaget has delineated a fixed sequence of developmental stages in the child's understanding of water currents, tides, and the floating of boats, to name a few. Now in progress is the process of testing the generalizability of Piaget's findings with a group of young Hawaiian children that are known to possess an exhaustive experiential and naturally occurring exposure to such physical events as water currents and the floating of boats. Although it is very easy to speculate, it is suspected that the contextual and experiential variables may prove to be highly valuable in the Hawaiian children's understanding of physical causality.

A Brief Summing Up

To begin by addressing the general field of cross-cultural methodology, it can be argued that it is perhaps of little value to carry a specific experimental paradigm that was generated by a major theorist in one culture over to a large variety of other cultures. If this paradigm is to be fruitful, it *must* presuppose a great deal of vital information about these other cultures. That is, it presupposes how a theory generated in one culture can be applied to other cultures. Or as Cole and Scribner (1974) so aptly put it:

> By carrying such theories overseas without some awareness of their cultural roots and their very real limitations, even in the cultures in which they arose, carries with it the risk of experimental egocentrism—mistaking as universals the particular organizations of cognitive skills that have arisen in the historical circumstances of our own society, and interpreting their absence in other cultures as "deficiency." (p. 200)

In line with the above, even presupposing a substantial degree of information about a particular culture, a solitary experiment is perhaps of little value. As was discussed earlier, a fruitful alternative to the single-shot approach is to *experiment* with the experiment (see Cole et al., 1971a).

The writer has emphasized the importance of unearthing the contextual and experiential events that occur naturally and that can elicit specific cognitive skills. Unless an investigator pursues these often neglected aspects of cross-cultural methodology, he or she will be running a constant real *risk* of obtaining experimental results that show the subjects to be "deficient." As Cole and Scribner (1974) put it:

> Perhaps this risk may never be entirely overcome until psychological science in non-Western countries becomes further advanced and generates its own theories and research methods—which can be tested on us! (p. 200)

References

BATTIG, W., & MONTAGUE, W. Category norms for verbal items in 56 categories. *Journal of Experimental Psychology Monograph*, 1964, *80*, No. 3, 1–46.

BEREITER, C., & ENGELMANN, S. *Teaching disadvantaged children in the preschool.* Englewood Cliffs, N.J.: Prentice-Hall, 1966.

BERRY, J., & DASEN, P. *Culture and cognition: readings in cross-cultural psychology.* New York: Harper & Row, 1974.

BIESHEUVEL, S. Psychological tests and their application to non-European peoples. In D. R. Price-Williams (Ed.), *Cross-cultural studies.* Middlesex, England: Penguin Books, 1969.

BRISLIN, R., LONNER, W., & THORNDIKE, R. *Cross-cultural research methods.* New York: Wiley, 1973.

CAMPBELL, D. The mutual methodological relevance of anthropology and psychology. In F. L. K. Hsu (Ed.), *Psychological anthropology.* Homewood, Ill.: Dorsey Press, 1961, pp. 333–52.

CARR, E. *Da kine talk.* Honolulu: University of Hawaii Press, 1972.

CAZDEN, C., JOHN, V., & HYMES, D. (Eds.), *Functions of language in the classroom.* New York: Teachers College Press, 1972.

CHOMSKY, N. *Aspects of the theory of syntax.* Cambridge, Mass.: MIT Press, 1968.

CIBOROWSKI, T. Cultural and cognitive discontinuities of school and home: remedialism revisited. In D. W. McElwain & G. Kearney (Eds.), *Aboriginal cognition-prospect.* Canberra, Australia: Australian Institute of Aboriginal Studies, 1976, Chapter 7.

CIBOROWSKI, T., & CHOY, S. Nonstandard English and free recall: an exploratory study. *Journal of Cross-Cultural Psychology,* 1974, *5,* No. 3, 271–81.

COLE, M., GAY, J., GLICK, J., & SHARP, D. *The cultural context of learning and thinking.* New York: Basic Books, 1971a.

COLE, M., FRANKEL, F., & SHARP, D. The development of free recall learning in children. *Developmental Psychology,* 1971b, *4,* 109–23.

COLE, M., & BRUNER, J. Cultural differences and inferences about psychological processes. *American Psychologist,* 1971, *26,* No. 10, 867–76.

COLE, M., & SCRIBNER, S. *Culture and thought.* New York: Wiley, 1974.

DASEN, P. Cross-cultural Piagetian research: a summary. *Journal of Cross-Cultural Psychology,* 1972, *3,* 23–39.

DEREGOWSKI, J., & SERPELL, R. Performance on a sorting task with various modes of representation: a cross-cultural experiment. Human Development Research Unit, University of Zambia, Report No. 18, 1971.

DEUTSCH, M. *The disadvantaged child.* New York: Basic Books, 1967.

FRANKLIN, A., FULANI, L., HENKIND, E., & COLE, M. Ethnic group differences in organized recall. Unpublished manuscript, The Rockefeller University, 1975.

GALLIMORE, R., BOGGS, J., & JORDAN, C. *Culture, behavior, and education: a study of Hawaiian-Americans.* Beverly Hills, Calif.: Sage Press, 1975.

GINSBURG, H. *The myth of the disadvantaged child.* Englewood Cliffs, N.J.: Prentice-Hall, 1972.

GLICK, J. Cognitive style among the Kpelle. Paper read at annual meeting of the American Educational Research Association, Chicago, 1968.

GREENFIELD, P., & CHILDS, C. Weaving, color terms, and pattern representation: cultural influences and cognitive development among the Zinacantecos of Southern Mexico. Paper read at the International Conference of IACCP, Hong Kong, 1972.

IRWIN, H., & McLAUGHLIN, D. Ability and preference in category sorting of Mano schoolchildren and adults. *Journal of Social Psychology,* 1970, *82,* 15–24.

JENSEN, A., & FREDERICKSEN, J. Free recall of categorized and uncategorized lists. *Journal of Educational Psychology*, 1973, *65*, 304–12.

LABOV, W. The logic of nonstandard English. In F. Williams (Ed.), *Language and poverty*. Chicago: Markham, 1970.

NELSON, K. The organization of free recall by young children. *Journal of Experimental Child Psychology*, 1969, *8*, 284–95.

PIAGET, J. The child's conception of the world. Totowa, N.J.: Littlefield, Adams & Co., 1969.

PRICE-WILLIAMS, D. A study concerning concepts of conservation of quantities among primitive children. *Acta Psycologia*, 1961, *18*, 297–305.

————. Abstract and concrete modes of classification in a primitive society. *British Journal of Educational Psychology*, 1962, *32*, 50–61.

PRICE-WILLIAMS, D., GORDON, W., & RAMIREZ, M. Skill and conservation: a study of pottery-making children. *Developmental Psychology*, 1969, *1*, 769.

SCRIBNER S. Situating the experiment in cross-cultural research. In K. Riegel & J. Meacham (Eds.), *The developing individual in a changing world, Vol. 1, Historical and cultural issues*. The Hague: Mouton, 1975.

SCRIBNER, S., & COLE, M. Studies of subcultural variations in semantic memory: implications of cross-cultural research. Unpublished manuscript, The Rockefeller University, 1975.

SECHREST, L. Experiments in the field. In R. Naroll & R. Cohen (Eds.), *A handbook of method in cultural anthropology*. New York: Natural History Press, 1970, pp. 196–209.

TENNEY, Y. H. The child's conception of organization and recall. *Journal of Experimental Child Psychology*, 1975, *19*, 100–14.

8

Experiments in Cross-Cultural Research

*Elizabeth D. Brown
and Lee Sechrest*

Contents

Abstract

A number of threats to the validity of conclusions reached from cross-cultural experiments are examined, and methods for controlling such threats are reviewed. The use of theory to guide cross-cultural research is explored.

Introduction

Although the experimental method is unquestionably the strongest available to social scientists from the standpoint of permitting causal inferences, it is clearly underutilized in cross-cultural psychology (Sechrest, 1977a). At least in part, the underutilization of experimental methodology in cross-cultural studies may be attributable to a lack of understanding of the basic nature and purpose of cross-cultural research. Specifically, cross-cultural research is a methodology rather than a content field (Sechrest, 1977b). In doing cross-cultural research culture becomes, in effect, an independent variable used to account for findings on the dependent variable or outcome measure. In other words, one wishes to make a causal attribution involving culture. The problem is to do the research so that it is highly plausible that culture be accorded the status of a causal variable and relatively implausible that any other associated but irrelevant variable could have accounted for the observed results.

If culture is to be regarded as an independent variable, it will soon become evident that "culture" is what Campbell and Stanley (1963) labelled a "global X," i.e., an amorphous but complex treatment. It follows, then, that merely comparing performances of subjects across cultures will be minimally informative since there is no way of knowing just which of many facets of the cultures might account for performance differences. Cross-cultural research, to capitalize on its advantages as a method, will have to be carefully guided by theory, with cultures to be studied chosen deliberately to represent particular theoretical variables of interest (Sechrest, 1977b). Choosing cultures to study on the basis of expedience or adventitiousness will not permit researchers to obtain the maximum benefit that the otherwise illuminating method of cross-cultural study affords.

As detailed in earlier papers (Sechrest, 1977a; 1977b), cross-cultural study should begin with a theoretical proposition to be tested that makes explicit the cultural comparisons which are needed. Cross-cultural research is in no way different from other research in that it is directed toward the test of a hypothesis about the effect of one variable on another (or one set of variables on another set). There are a number of different reasons for using the cross-cultural method rather than some other to test hypotheses of interest, but essentially the reasons come down to the fact that comparisons across cultures may be made for relationships not easily studied by other research methodologies, e.g., laboratory studies or observations within a single culture. Once the theoretical proposition is clear, then the basis for choosing cultures to compare should be evident.

They would be chosen because they possess *specific* characteristics of interest and not simply because they seem satisfactorily different.

Tying cross-cultural research into theory also has implications for validity issues. The experimenter is unlikely to achieve an equal balance among the types of validity that are of concern in most experimental work; efforts to enhance one type of validity may have detrimental effects on another (Cook & Campbell, 1975). Therefore, hypotheses must be formed on the basis of theory, and research populations selected so as to have the best groups on which to test the hypotheses. In addition, priorities for validity emphasis must be set in order to maximize the effects being investigated.

The researcher who is interested in making causal statements will place internal validity first on a list of priorities, whether the research is to test theory or to study a program of a more applied nature. Experimental designs can effectively control threats to internal validity, but it is the true experiment—one employing both random assignment to conditions and having at least one control group—that usually permits the strongest inferences about causal relationships.

Experimental Design

Inclusion of a control group in an experimental design often permits the weakening of rival hypotheses and thereby increases the internal validity of a study. The strategy behind using controls is that if two groups are equal on some measure before the independent variable is manipulated (treatment), but they are no longer equal after the manipulation, then the treatment can usually be considered responsible for the change.

There is more to be recognized about control groups and the appropriate use of them than immediately strikes the senses; this is particularly true when experimental designs become more sophisticated and potentially more valuable. At present, the more common experiments in cross-cultural research are those that study only one culture. Some of these studies assume at least implicitly that the experiment will permit legitimate comparisons with another culture because the experiment is a replication of one already done. In still other research, the purpose is solely to illuminate some process within a given culture and not to make comparisons with other cultures.

However, as noted by Rohner (1977), one of the chief reasons for conducting cross-cultural work is to "test for the level of generality of a theory or proposition" (p. 6). This goal cannot be attained by relying on intracultural research. Even when studies are replications, other factors may interfere with testing the hypothesis of generality. As an example, Boruch and Gomez (1977) have recently related the difficulty of achieving a successful replication to a multiplicative phenomenon occurring from the interaction of measurement error and less than perfect reproduction of treatment conditions. Accordingly, if replications are difficult to produce, finding no significant results in a replication may be as much the result of the multiplicative phenomenon as evidence of the untenability of the hypothesis.

A third type of experiment is advocated—one that is rarely carried out, but perhaps the only kind with real value from the standpoint of permitting strong causal inferences: the true cross-cultural study which includes at least two cultures and in which at least one other factor in the design is manipulated by the experimenter and crossed with culture, i.e., each condition of the experimental manipulation is carried out in each culture. As will be discussed shortly, although culture itself can be viewed as an independent variable, it cannot be manipulated because individuals cannot be randomly assigned into a culture. Thus research focusing simply on comparisons of a dependent variable in two or more cultures can be expected to have a minimal impact on theory refinement since there is no experimental manipulation. An additional advantage with the true cross-cultural experiment is that it may be less difficult for investigators studying two or more cultures simultaneously to duplicate their own procedures than to replicate the work at a different period in time, or to reproduce someone else's procedure.

Internal Validity

When and if cross-cultural work does reach a more sophisticated level wherein the true cross-cultural experiment becomes predominant, the researcher will find other complications. Cook and Campbell (1975) have added several threats to internal validity to supplement the original list provided by Campbell and Stanley (1963). These additional threats cannot be reduced by the inclusion of a control group (as could the threats delineated by Campbell and Stanley); they are in fact the result of including a control group in the design. In studies that do not use a control group, there is no need to be concerned with such internal validity threats as diffusion or imitation of the treatment, compensatory equalization of treatment, resentful demoralization of respondents receiving less desirable treatments, and/or local history.

For example, *compensatory equalization of treatment*, one of the threats delineated by Cook and Campbell (1975), can cause the random assignment process to be subverted; those in executive positions might believe that the positive aspects that might be accrued from a treatment would be so great that it would be unfair to deprive the control group of treatment. It would, for instance, be very difficult to carry out an experimental study of nutritional supplementation in which some malnourished children were deliberately left untreated (e.g., McKay, McKay, & Sinisterra, 1973).

Another threat to internal validity could arise if the control group learns that another group is receiving a treatment. Extra effort then exerted to match or exceed the performances of the experimental group could introduce the problem of compensatory rivalry—the "John Henry effect." Resentful demoralization of respondents receiving less desirable treatments is yet another effect that researchers should be aware of and looking for: control groups may take umbrage because they are not being treated and may show their resentment by turning in a poorer performance than they might have ordinarily produced. In such instances, posttreatment differences between the experimental and control groups might be as attributable to the worsened control group performance as to the effect of treatment upon the experimental group.

Another threat to internal validity occurs when a treatment is of an informational nature and knowledge about it becomes widely diffused (spill-over effect). In such instances, control group outcome data may be influenced to the same degree as those of an experimental group. An example of the need to protect against and to study spill-over effects is provided by the Taichung, Taiwan (Freedman & Takeshita, 1965) study of the effects of publicity on acceptance of the intrauterine device for fertility control. The investigators wished ultimately to determine just how much spread (spill-over) of effect there had been from treated to untreated neighborhoods. In this study, since the treatment units were neighborhoods, it was possible that the informational content of the program could have spread. However, these investigators decided that, rather than trying to prevent spill-over effects altogether, they would try to measure them.

Controlling for Internal Validity Threats

There is not a great deal that can easily be done about some of these threats to internal validity, but the possibility of their having distorted outcome data should be investigated. One procedure that would be helpful in an investigation is to run a manipulation check on control group members, administrators, those delivering treatment, and so on, to determine if the integrity of the experiment was somehow affected.

Another of the internal validity threats outlined by Cook and Campbell (1975), *ambiguity about the direction of causal influence,* can cause interpretation problems even when there are no viable third hypotheses.

However, in this case the researcher is not confined to a passive explanatory role. Good experimental designs can eliminate the problem, for this threat to internal validity exists only when work is of a correlational or ex post facto nature; no causal statements can be made to explain data from such research. Therefore, the most productive cross-cultural research will be one that features manipulation of at least one independent variable in addition to being carried out in at least two cultures with near simultaneity.

Another threat to internal validity, *confounding from local history*, exists when data are collected simultaneously in large groups of people or when a treatment is delivered to large groups en masse; if some extraneous event occurring during common meeting times has a bearing on outcome measures, changes detected in subjects' performances may be due to these extraneous happenings rather than to the treatment. Here too, the researcher has safeguards: by running more and smaller groups, outcome data are not as imperiled. If differences within conditions are found, a manipulation check may suggest ideas for improvements in future research (Carlsmith, Ellsworth, & Aronson, 1976).

Other approaches to controlling possible confounding from local history can also be introduced. As an example, in an experimental study of alternative ways of eliciting blood donations, Sechrest, Fay, and Flores (1970) assigned large groups of Filipino ROTC cadets to recruitment conditions. There was no question that for any one group incidental but irrelevant factors such as wisecracking group members or an early volunteering and respected leader could affect results. Although conditions in this study did not permit any sort of manipulation check, replicating the experiment several times in different places produced evidence that one recruitment strategy was consistently better than the others.

Limitations on Internal Validity in
Cross-Cultural Work

Other limitations on experimental control may best be understood by examining the composition of such groups. Perhaps the most commonly cited description of these groups is that of the *nontreated controls*. In these cases, the control group is measured and then left alone until it is time to gather postmanipulation data. The reasoning behind the approach is straightforward: without contact (treatment), differences in performance are unlikely to occur unless they have been effected by one of the rival hypotheses falling under the general rubric of threats to internal validity. Therefore, changes in nontreated controls may be an indication that something has gone amiss and that any performance differences detected in data from the experimental group may be spurious.

However, it should be realized that, in actuality, an "untreated" control group is probably never achievable. Some change can and perhaps should be expected between premanipulation and postmanipulation measures, for people in untreated control groups do not live in a vacuum. It is sometimes just a question of how closely a naturally occurring (or simultaneously occurring) treatment can approximate the effects of the experimental treatment. The implications are that the stronger the experimental treatment becomes, the less the researcher has to worry about problems from rival treatments—an argument in favor of implementing treatments at a relatively strong level.

In some types of research, treatment may be crossed with culture when the primary question is whether there is an interaction between cultures and treatments. Again results may be misleading, because there can usually be no assurance that each treatment has been applied at an equal strength. For instance, if an investigator is trying to research attitude change and the treatment is varied content in an informational pamphlet, differences in outcome data might lead to the conclusion that what is effective in one culture is not in a second. Instead, what may be appearing in a significant culture-treatment interaction is a source of systematic error: if the quality of translation in the pamphlet differs between cultures, a significant culture-treatment interaction may merely be reflective of the differential quality of the printed materials. Translation problems are always present in cross-cultural research (Sechrest, Fay, & Zaidi, 1972) and have to be considered for both independent and dependent variables. In some instances it may be impossible simultaneously both to ensure that the translation has produced equivalence and to conclude that the cultures are in fact different.

Before concluding the discussion on the importance of internal validity in cross-cultural research, it may be helpful to pause briefly to examine culture as a variable. If it were possible to gather newborn infants systematically and ship them randomly to different cultures in which the maturation process would take place, culture would approach the status of an experimental variable. In reality, however, the possibilities of differing gene pools associated with cultures, as well as differences in prenatal and perinatal environments, prohibit any strong assumptions about assignments of infants to cultures as random procedure.

There is a second difficulty to be recognized: other variables, which are confounded with culture but are not inherent in it, may threaten a causal interpretation of cultural influences. For example, there are obviously cultural differences in the nutrition provided for children. If certain problem-solving tasks are completed less adequately by children from nutritionally deprived cultures, those inadequate performances should probably not be attributed to the culture itself.

Therefore, culture is usually a quasi-experimental variable that, when considered as a treatment, is particularly vulnerable to internal validity threats. For this reason, when culture is the only independent variable being investigated, the researcher has the task of seeking out the best methodology possible. Moreover, in many cases, it will be difficult to exert enough experimental control in just one study to clear up all ambiguity about causal interpretations; it may be necessary to conduct complementary studies, each designed to allay some internal validity concerns. The reader might recognize this approach as the *institutional cycle design*, perhaps better known as the "patched-up design" (Campbell & Stanley, 1963).

In establishing internal validity as the most important validity concern, considerable attention has been paid to alternative explanations that can rival ascriptions of causality. Such confounding is the result of flaws in the methodology of a study; if a methodologically impure experiment were replicated with the flaws corrected, presumably the problems of internal validity and the confounding would be ended.

Construct Validity

The issue of confounding is at least as closely related to construct validity, and it is to this topic that theory oriented researchers should next turn. Confounding problems in construct validity arise from difficulties in the labeling or conceptualization of causal attributions in generalizable terms (see Cook & Campbell, 1975). For instance, two flawlessly designed studies, using similar manipulations and yielding similar results, could each be cited by its investigator as support for a different theory. This should not be taken to mean that causal interpretations made at different levels of reduction are construct validity problems; it is not at all incompatible for one researcher to describe an outcome in behavioral terms, another researcher in cognitive terms, and still a third researcher in physiological terms. Each of these explanations might well coexist, and each might be equally beneficial in interpreting at the level at which it is aimed.

Of interest here are alternative explanations; one type may stem from different theoretical positions, as in the example cited above. This is where cross-cultural research fulfills a telic function in establishing the construct validity of a theory; widely accepted ideas may be disproved or approved when additional work is conducted in other cultures. As an example, Rohner (1977) has noted that Freud's mistake in theorizing the universality of the Oedipus complex resulted from his experience being limited to the Western culture. Had Freud had the same opportunity as Malinowski (1927) to work in the Trobriand Islands, he might have been able to separate the roles of mother's lover and child's disciplinarian, which are quite confounded in Western culture and separate in the Trobriands'. Cross-cultural research affords opportunities to study variables manifesting themselves in combinations and in ways not found within any one culture.

Cross-cultural research can, then, enhance our understanding of the constructs that we study by other means. Freud thought that the Oedipal problem arose from the child's attempts to resolve the conflict between his incestuous impulses toward his mother and the resultant hostility toward and fear of his father. Malinowski's work suggested that Freud's understanding of the nature of the treatment the child was exposed to was wrong. Recognition should also be given to the need for construct validity in individual experiments, and, in that context, construct validity becomes a means to an end. It is difficult to get from empirical findings to theory without a firm understanding of just what the critical constructs are; maximizing construct validity greatly facilitates correct interpretations of experiments. For instance, culture has already been construed in this chapter as a global X, a complex but amorphous treatment. Therefore, in order to gain an understanding of the critical underlying dimensions, it is often necessary to eliminate some of the confounds that are inherent in culture by experimental manipulation. A similar approach has been advocated by Whiting (1976) in her work on "unpackaging variables."

As an example of the manifestation of the confounded variable, imagine that some behavioral phenomenon were being attributed to a culture, say to that of the Philippines. Many factors associated with that culture might be a proximal cause for the behavior. How could the critical feature be identified? A conclusion that the nation's predominant religion was responsible for the outcome might be contested by other researchers arguing for an attribution to the country's Spanish heritage, to its peasant outlook, or perhaps even to some interaction of factors. (This, of course, is where Freud's work was in error; he mistook one aspect of Western culture for a cause, when, in fact, another aspect at the same level of reduction seems to have been responsible.)

It takes little imagination to move on from seeing culture as a global X to drawing analogies with other variables commonly of interest in experiments. If sociodemographic variables are being investigated, the same problems in ascribing cause exist as are found when culture is an independent variable. Such variables are merely surrogates: they mean little in and of themselves because they are really representing other unnamed variables. For instance, an effect may be attributed to differences in educational level between groups, but what may actually be affecting performance is some other variable associated with education, e.g., motivation, income, ability to delay gratification, and so on.

The situation does not usually become less complex even when variables are manipulated, for what appears on the surface to be a treatment may not be in fact. Often variables are not manipulated directly, but stimuli or treatments assumed to be directly related to the variables of interest are varied. Thus, while results supporting a hypothesis may be taken as an indication that something about the treatment did indeed produce performance changes, it may still not be at all clear just what aspect of the treatment or stimulus was responsible for the difference.

It should not be assumed that subject responses are any more easily interpreted than are experimental manipulations. One problem is that responses, as has already been demonstrated for stimuli, are global in nature. As an example, behaviors that an experimenter is scoring as outcome data may be less meaningful than other behaviors which preceded or accompanied the final performance. When interviewing in the Philippines, Sechrest had the experience of having respondents consult bystanding friends or family members before responding even to questions of personal opinion.

Another problem is that it is at times difficult to assess the meaning of responses from, or the impact of stimuli upon, even those who share the same cultural background as oneself. These problems are greatly exacerbated in cross-cultural research, for responses or stimuli which mean one thing to a researcher on the basis of his or her own ethnocentric experiences may mean something altogether different to people from another culture.

The problem of differential cultural meaning extends into both verbal and nonverbal areas. Perhaps the biggest issue which must be dealt with by the researcher who is trying to maintain equivalency in groups from different cultures is to achieve equivalent meaning of the stimuli rather than their formal equivalence. One would want, in a cross-cultural study of the effects of physical attractiveness on liking, to ensure that the two or more samples of stimulus people were equally attractive within their respective cultures, no matter how dissimilar that might make them from each other in actual physical appearance.

In the nonverbal realm, if the hypothesis being investigated concerns, for example, the relationship of physical closeness to types of communication, and the independent variable is the distance between experimenters and subjects, how physical distance is perceived in different cultures will have to be taken into account. As noted by Hall (1959), the same degree of physical closeness may prove facilitating to communication in some cultures, but threatening in others. Note that in resolving such problems a fundamental uncertainty arises: if two groups are equated for veridical distance, they may differ in psychological distance, and if equated for the latter, they will differ on the former.

Improving Construct Validity

The solutions to improving construct validity are numerous, but the choice of what specific steps to take depends upon a researcher's ability to foresee where threats may be introduced. Thus, the first step in the process is to try to identify all possible sources of confounding prior to the experimental manipulation, and then to correct for them methodologically.

The most obvious such correction is the inclusion of control groups to weaken some of the potential confounds. A common problem in therapeutic intervention studies, for example, is the possibility that results may be attributable to such nonspecific treatment effects as the placebo effect or demand characteristics (see Neale & Liebert, 1973). It is common in such studies to include one or more control groups receiving the same amount of attention as the experimental group or exposed to the same experimental setting and instructions, but not given what is regarded as the essential element in treatment. The use of carefully developed control groups can markedly enhance understanding of the exact nature of the treatment and lend confidence to the interpretation of the results in terms of a specific treatment effect.

Another possibility, one advocated and followed by Segall, Campbell, and Herskovits (1963) in their influential study of perceptual illusions, is to expose all subjects to special stimuli or treatment conditions which will help to reveal and define any confounds that exist. For example, one distinct possibility in explaining cultural differences in susceptibility to illusions is that members of some cultures may not understand the task as well as do those from other cultures and hence may show differences in response to illusion stimuli. Segall et al. helped to rule out such an explanation by including stimuli of a nonillusory nature; the subjects' responses would indicate whether the task was understood. Thus the critical "treatment" variable could with confidence be defined to exclude cultural bias in understanding task instructions.

Still another requirement for avoiding problems with construct validity is for careful description and documentation of the treatment administered. It is truly remarkable how infrequently journal articles indicate such important aspects of the treatment as whether the experimenter was male or female, young or old, attractive or ordinary, whether the experimenter's demeanor was relaxed and friendly or aloof and businesslike, what the subjects were told about the purposes of the experiment, and so on. Yet the write-ups will often specify the model number for a projector or the paper size for the response booklets. What does tend to get reported is the trivial but quantifiable fact; what tends not to get reported is the more important fact less precisely describable. Biases in reporting details of an experimental treatment may make it very difficult to know just what, in fact, the treatment was.

The maximization of construct validity in any research is achieved through multiple operations and methods (Cook & Campbell, 1975). Because of the many potential confounds in cross-cultural work, answering all questions in just one study will usually be impossible; the many operations and methods that would be needed would make the costs for the study prohibitive. As just one example, a huge sample size would be needed to have enough degrees of freedom to show a statistically significant effect in complex experimental designs. Therefore, the most appropriate means for settling questions about construct validity of causes is the successive use of experimental designs, each functioning to unsnarl a few of the possible confounds. Although such work might take more time, often it does appear to be the only economically feasible way to ensure construct validity of cause. Moreover, since establishing causal construct validity is one of the main goals of cross-cultural research, the investment of time and effort should be worthwhile. An additional benefit can be reaped from this approach if slight deviations in measures and analyses are introduced in each new study. Sometimes biases that experimenters are unaware of influence the choice of measures and statistical tests, but these biases may be eliminated by slightly changing the data-gathering methods and the means by which data are examined (Finifter, 1977; Campbell, 1957).

The situation is somewhat more easily handled in establishing the construct validity of effects. Multiple measures may yield enough information to satisfy the establishment of such validity (Cook & Campbell, 1975). These measures not only may encompass different methods of measurement, e.g., questionnaires, observations, etc., but also may include multiple items within questionnaires or multiple categories of behaviors in observations. The warning issued some years ago (Webb, Campbell, Schwartz, & Sechrest, 1966) about relying too heavily on any one method of measurement is still needed, as much in the field of cross-cultural psychology as anywhere. The use of measures not sharing common sources of error can help greatly to enhance the construct validity of outcome measures.

Comparison groups that are equivalent in pretreatment are necessary in any research, for preexisting differences present a powerful obstacle to firm conclusions and interpretations of findings. The problem of preexisting differences is inherent in cross-cultural research, for the cultural groups are, by definition, different to begin with. It is essential, however, that groups are as similar as possible with respect to all variables save that of cultural experience. Comparison of European college students with Eskimos would not produce data of an interpretable sort for most treatments. One might wonder if there is any way that Europeans and Eskimos could be compared at all, given the many irreducible differences that exist; certainly not easily and not with any assurance. However, some comparisons may be more meaningful than others. One could, for example, compare European and Eskimo political leaders on an experimental test of factors influencing decision making processes. The interpretation of findings would not be completely straightforward, but it would probably be enhanced if the groups were equated at least for age, size of community, and for in- or out-of-party status. The most important task would be to identify the dimensions of greatest potential competitive power with respect to the cultural difference and try as closely as possible to equate for those.

Another step toward enhancing the construct validity of individual experiments in cross-cultural research is to make them as nonreactive as possible. If there is cause to believe that groups have been differentially exposed prior to treatment to such measures as questionnaires, outcome data may be less confounded if measures other than questionnaires are used. Needless to say, there will be times when a manipulation or measure cannot be nonreactive, either because of ethical or practical considerations: obtaining observations without a subject's awareness that the data are being gathered will usually be unethical; at times certain measures which are likely to be reactive must be gathered, because there may be no other means of assessing the information needed. In such instances, cross-comparisons and manipulation checks may help to explain research results.

Statistical Conclusion Validity

In keeping with the premise that the primary goals of cross-cultural research are the testing of and addition to theory, statistical conclusion validity should be third in importance, following internal validity and construct validity (Cook & Campbell, 1975); it is necessary to have confidence in the statistical analyses used to assess experimental effects in order to extend a study's conclusions to a body of theory. Confounding from instability, a threat formerly listed with those that can detract from a study's internal validity (Campbell, 1969), was the source of the category of statistical conclusion validity. However, while instability was limited to such problems as unreliability of measures and changes in sampling individuals and/or components, statistical conclusion validity is a broader concept and encompasses any problems with the statistical analysis, whether they are introduced by instability or by some flaw in the application of a statistical test. At present, the maximization of internal and statistical validity presents diverse types of problems to researchers: internal validity is threatened by systematic sources of variance that are not themselves directly due to the experimental manipulation, and statistical conclusion validity is endangered by nonsystematic, or error, variance.

The analysis of experimental data by any statistical test is always beset by two potential types of error. If data from a given sample suggest there was an experimental effect, when in fact there was no effect, an ensuing decision to reject the null hypothesis would be a Type I error. Conversely, Type II errors are made when one fails to reject a null hypothesis on the basis of not detecting an experimental effect that actually does exist. The probabilities for the occurrence of these two types of error are inversely related in most cross-cultural work because researchers are unable to muster sufficient numbers of subjects to allow optimal settings of the error probabilities (see Cohen, 1969). However, the errors are not equally bothersome in cross-cultural research; the greater concern should be for Type II errors because it is difficult to replicate experimental findings in new settings and with new samples, and because there is more potential for error variance and other nontreatment related variance to creep into the necessarily less tightly controlled research conducted in the field. Therefore, it is usually more difficult to demonstrate a true experimental effect there than is the case for research done in a laboratory.

One of the goals of some cross-cultural work is to show no differences among groups. This goal causes the problem of Type II errors to take on added weight; when a researcher wants to demonstrate the universality of any given behavior or trait, the aim of the research is, in effect, to prove the null hypothesis. However, accepting the null hypothesis (concluding there are no differences among groups) is generally avoided in all research, because there is usually no assurance that all possible sources of random error have been eliminated, nor that treatments have been applied at an optimal strength, nor that all suppressor variables have been taken into account, nor that the most powerful statistical test has been used (Cook & Campbell, 1975). Still, the lure of the hypothesis of no difference is strong, and sometimes irresistible for theoretical reasons. A case in point is the theoretical hypothesis that there are no cultural differences in the fundamental forms of psychopathology, e.g., relative frequency of schizophrenia and manic-depressive psychosis. The empirical data to support such a hypothesis must, perforce, support or be compatible with the null hypothesis. Another example is provided by Berry's (1966) finding and conclusion that there is no difference in field independence-dependence between Eskimo males and females, a conclusion of considerable theoretical import since, if it is accepted, it disproves a cultural universal (Sechrest, 1977a).

Because the greater likelihood of the occurrence of Type II errors in field research gives the advantage to studies designed to show no effect, extreme caution must be exercised in all research testing hypotheses of universality. Conclusions favoring the acceptance of the null hypothesis can only be made if the experimental design is well enough planned and implemented to enhance the chances of showing an effect, and if all the theory-derived conditions that might strengthen the possibility of finding an effect have been included in the design (Cook & Campbell, 1975).

Controlling Threats to Statistical
Conclusion Validity

Awareness of the potential for Type II errors in field research is necessary to keep them from impeding the development of theory. The first preventive step should occur at the time that the sample size is selected, for the probability of making Type II errors is inversely related to the size of the sample. However, sight should not be lost of the fact that sample sizes can be increased to such a degree that statistical significance can be found for an effect that is in every other sense trivial. Therefore, if the goal for research is to produce outcomes that are both statistically and practically significant, as much care should be directed toward selecting the appropriate sample size as toward formulating the experimental design. The determination of an appropriate sample size must begin with a decision about the effect size, e.g., the difference between the means of two cultures that would be the smallest worth detecting. That is, the investigator must decide upon a point below which any difference would be considered trivial. Making such a decision is by no means simple, largely because most theories are insufficiently refined to permit much more than a statement concerning expected direction of differences. If the critical effect size can be established, it is a relatively straight-forward matter to determine the sample size needed to be able to detect the effect if it exists (see Cohen, 1977).

Another threat to statistical conclusion validity exists because much cross-cultural research is conducted on intact groups. With such samples, not only is randomized selection lost (with a concomitant forfeiture of claims for external validity), but the data from intact groups are independent for two reasons. First, it is unlikely that preexisting groups, be they villages or school classrooms, have been formed on a randomized basis. Second, the common history that groups share after being formed further increases the likelihood of dependencies among the members of them. However, most statistical tests are based on an assumption that it is equally as probable for one subject to be selected as another; furthermore, these probabilities are independent conditions that do not exist with the dependent nature of data from intact groups.

Moreover, outcome data collected from intact groups will be confounded with the variable of interest, i.e., culture, because there are different reasons for how and why clustering is achieved in different cultures. For example, the composition of villages may be reflective of matrilocal/patrilocal residential patterns, primogeniture, evidence that scarcity of resources results in the fittest leaving for better places to live, or any number of other factors.

The lack of independence in data from intact groups means that statistical analyses must be handled conservatively by treating the clusters as sampling units: e.g., testing should be for differences between cultures with the degrees of freedom equal to the number of classes tested rather than to the number of individual subjects within classes. The net result is that a smaller number of degrees of freedom will be used in testing for experimental effects, and it may be more difficult to demonstrate statistical significance. Therefore, the use of intact groups further increases the probability of making Type II errors in cross-cultural work.

Another equally troublesome problem is associated with taking intact groups for study: when fewer sampling units exist, as is the case when using intact groups, random assignment will be less likely to result in initially equivalent groups, thereby preventing the use of true experiments. However, various methods of experimental and statistical control do exist by which the researcher can compensate for the difficulty (Cook & Campbell, 1975).

An example of the application of experimental control to the problem of fewer sampling units might entail first forming groups of subjects that have been matched for variables that are considered theoretically relevant. These matched groups could then be randomly assigned to treatment conditions, thereby enhancing the chances of attaining initial group equivalency. Another possible experimental approach that can add to the statistical power is to increase the number of units being studied (although in many cross-cultural studies, the costs connected with this strategy might be prohibitive). It might also be possible to alter the design of the experiment to fit in with a quasi-experimental time-series design, or to use a design where the treatment is faded in and out.

If a decision is made to use statistical controls, one possible method is to analyze for differences between pretest and posttest measures with repeated measures tests. The advantages of this technique are greatest when it is expected that treatment scores may increase over time even without treatment; such an analysis can yield information about whether the interaction of treatment and time is increasing faster for experimentals than for controls. When analyzing data involving repeated measures, it is possible to do so either by ANOVA for repeated measures or by MANOVA. Which analysis is to be preferred depends upon characteristics of the data; the analyses are not equivalent (Boruch & Wortman, 1977).

Experimental approaches should be the first explored in endeavors to solve the problem of too few sampling units. While experimental controls do not preclude the use of statistical controls, good design may make complicated analyses unnecessary. Additional advantages to avoiding the use of statistical controls are: (1) not all data fit the assumptions inherent in the control techniques, and transforming them to fit may be beyond the statistical training of some researchers; and (2) nontransformed data may be easier for the nonsophisticated reader to understand and follow.

Another critical area for Type II errors arises from the alpha (α) level set as a point where experimental effects will be considered statistically significant. The interpretation of the usually reported .05 level is that, if a null hypothesis were true, and an experiment were repeated over and over, only five of every 100 repetitions would reach that level of statistical significance. Therefore, Type I errors (rejecting a null hypothesis that is true) would be made only about five percent of the time. However, there is an inverse relationship between Type I and Type II errors if sample sizes are held constant. In such cases, while setting a level of .05 helps to decrease the potential for making Type I errors, it also increases the possibility of making Type II errors. The important thing for the cross-cultural researcher to understand is that there is really no hard and fast rule for setting the alpha level, even though most times the .05 level is chosen. It may be that in the early stages of some cross-cultural work the .05 level is too stringent and that a different level, say .10, should be used. With such an approach, the greater problem for cross-cultural work—a higher probability of making Type II errors—may become less bothersome.

Although it is our position that at the present time Type I errors are not a great cause for concern in cross-cultural research, a change in research strategy may alter this situation. Much discussion has been given during the course of this chapter to the global nature of surrogate variables (both in the form of culture and sociodemographic characteristics of subjects). Should a search for the more meaningful variables that probably underlie surrogates be overzealously undertaken, the problem of increased Type I errors, resulting from too many statistical analyses being conducted on data sets, will need attention from researchers. This issue, known as the experiment-wise error rate, is the "probability that one or more erroneous conclusions will be drawn in a particular experiment" (Ryan, 1959). There are several ways in which the potential for Type I errors resulting from an escalated experiment-wise error rate can be controlled. First, if findings are supported by a body of theory, the researcher will be on safer ground in assuming that a true effect has been detected. Second, statistical analyses for individual effects should be preceded by an overall test; if an overall F-test shows that some underlying factors are indeed statistically significant, there is more certainty that effects revealed by subsequent multiple comparison tests (e.g., Newman-Keuls, Tukey, or Scheffé) are real. Another possible approach is for investigators to impose a more stringent level for significance on individual comparisons; if a level is set that is considered to be the outside of what one is willing to accept as a potential for error (say, .20), that level can be divided by the number of comparisons to be made, thereby yielding the probability level beyond which individual comparisons will not be considered as statistically significant (Cook & Campbell, 1975).

Other factors that may enter as threats to statistical conclusion validity are those widely recognized in all types of research: care must be taken to use reliable measures, to have reliability in the implementation of treatments, to reduce random irrelevancies in experimental settings, and to eliminate random heterogeneity of respondents (Cook & Campbell, 1975).

External Validity

Thus far, this chapter has dealt with the reasons for the priority ranking of three types of experimental validity. The one type that has yet to receive attention is external validity, a category that should be of the least concern to researchers testing theory. Because most theories are not specific to unique populations, occasions, or environmental settings, there is less need to worry about generalizability effects in theory-testing research (Cook & Campbell, 1975).

Moreover, designing a study with the goal of having good external validity may be detrimental to the theory-testing mission of cross-cultural research, primarily because random selection is a prerequisite to achieving external validity: a truly random selection introduces heterogeneity into the subject variable, and, as has been discussed earlier in this chapter, random heterogeneity of subjects can present a threat to statistical conclusion validity. Since the maximization of statistical conclusion validity is more important in the development of theory, attempts to maximize external validity may actually hinder theory-oriented research.

Generalizability theory suggests that the most appropriate model for measurement includes not only a component for persons and another for situations, but also a term for the interaction between those two variables (Cronbach et al., 1972). In most cross-cultural research it is almost certain that situations will be dissimilar, and there is the potential for differences among persons as a result of influences from the genetic pool. In such instances, differences among person and/or situation terms for particular cultures will most likely also produce a different interaction term. As disparity is introduced among all three terms of the equation for the generalizability model, it becomes apparent why external validity is an elusive dream for cross-cultural research. Moreover, the researcher who pursues the goal of enhancing external validity may find that the heterogeneity (both from situations and persons) introduced by random selection results in so much unexplained variance that the study's results are uninterpretable.

These arguments on face value appear to be at odds with the main thrust of this chapter. The reader may be ready to argue at this point that it is futile to advocate the use of cross-cultural research to test theory that is concerned with the universality of phenomena. After all, there seems to be no sense in testing universality by means of research that has no claims to generalizability.

However, we maintain that the very existence of generalizability problems in cross-cultural research adds to its potential for yielding valuable information about universality. If a finding endures despite the inherent rigors which result from the heterogeneous nature of cross-cultural work, conclusions of universality have a high probability of being correct. Therefore, cross-cultural research may be said to be an extremely conservative test of hypotheses of universality.

But what about theory-related research that does not have as its goal the testing of universality? Here again there are contributions to be made by cross-cultural studies. The answer to producing useable research is to aim for representativeness, in both situations and persons, and to forsake the goal of randomness when designing studies. The effect of achieving homogeneity for subject and situations in any experimental manipulation will be a higher probability for researchers to detect and eventually to correct for unwanted sources of variance. As has been suggested earlier in this chapter, this approach may require that work be repeated several times, with variations made in the design to correct for unwanted variance, but eventually the work should reach the level needed to have confidence in the results and to allow valid cross-cultural comparisons to be made.

Summary

The goal of this chapter has been to present cross-cultural research as a unique contributor to bodies of theory; cross-cultural research can fulfill a necessary and valuable role in the advancement of theoretical knowledge, particularly in those areas of study where answers cannot be found within an individual culture, or where there are too many natural sources of confounding in a culture to allow valid conclusions to be made.

However, just as cross-cultural work is a unique means for gathering information, it is also a difficult approach, necessitating exemplary methodological control. The best design that can be utilized to reduce the many sources of variance that are inherent in such research is the true experiment. Unhappily, true experiments are conspicuously absent in cross-cultural work, probably because they require more painstaking effort on the part of a researcher, and because of environmental, financial, or political reasons. These problems are commonplace to all field researchers, but the cross-cultural researcher seems to be particularly vulnerable in the absence of a true experimental design.

Cross-cultural research, even when properly done, is perhaps one of the most problematic areas in which to produce statistically significant findings that can be easily summarized to support the hypothesis of interest to the researcher. The reasons for the difficulties are numerous and have been expounded upon throughout this chapter: the global aspects of culture may obscure more important underlying dimensions; culture is by nature a quasi-experimental variable; differences in cultural personalities and situations make replications difficult to achieve; differential cultural reactions to experimental manipulations or stimuli can be expected; differential cultural responses may be hard to interpret; the sampling of intact groups, such as villages or classes, may provide too few degrees of freedom to permit demonstrations of statistical significance; hardships can be expected in the maintenance of stimulus equivalency across cultures; and the frequent goal of "proving the null hypothesis" of universality requires that no room be left in the experimental design for threats by confounding variables.

In order to sensitize researchers to some of the problems inherent in cross-cultural work, considerable attention has been given to threats of validity (see Cook & Campbell, 1975). We believe that knowledge of these possible sources of confounding and of some potential solutions for them is essential to the production of the best possible design to answer a research question. When statistical conclusion validity is assured and the possible confounds to construct validity are limited, a true experimental design can usually provide the type of information needed to add to theory.

The best alternative to the true experiment is unquestionably an appropriate quasi-experimental design, particularly one that can adequately handle all threats to internal validity (see Campbell & Stanley, 1963). However, it should be noted that even those studies whose quasi-experimental designs do seem to eliminate threats to internal validity may still be questioned by many who are unwilling to accept experimental conclusions. As a case in point, the reader should consider the large body of research that has time and again been reported on the frequency of mental disorders in various cultures. Despite the agreement of most of that area's research, individuals remain skeptical of the cultural differences in basic forms of mental disorders.

Therefore, while at first sight true experiments may appear to be more expensive because of additional time requirements and extra costs incurred by adding control groups and randomizing procedures, we contend that, viewed in a fuller perspective, true experiments may in fact be less expensive than quasi-experimental studies. Findings will be assimilated into bodies of theory more quickly if they have been demonstrated by well-conducted true experiments, thereby eliminating the need to continue trying to answer questions that could have already been laid to rest had a true experiment been the first approach.

References

BERRY, J. W. Temne and Eskimo perceptual skills. *International Journal of Psychology,* 1966, *1,* 207–29.

BORUCH, R. F., & GOMEZ, H. Sensitivity, bias and theory in impact evaluations. *Professional Psychology,* 1977, *8,* 411–34.

BORUCH, R. F., & WORTMAN, P. The effect of nutritional and educational intervention on the cognitive and physical development of malnourished Colombian preschoolers: a reanalysis of the Cali project. Unpublished manuscript, Northwestern University, 1977.

CAMPBELL, D. T. Factors relevant to the validity of experiments in social settings. *Psychological Bulletin,* 1957, *54,* 297–312.

———. Reforms as experiments. *American Psychologist,* 1969, *24,* 409–29.

CAMPBELL, D. T., & STANLEY, J. C. *Experimental and quasi-experimental designs for research.* Chicago: Rand McNally, 1966.

CARLSMITH, J. M., ELLSWORTH, P. C., & ARONSON, E. *Methods of research in social psychology.* Reading, Mass.: Addison-Wesley, 1976.

COHEN, J. *Statistical power analysis for the behavioral sciences.* New York: Academic Press, 1977.

COOK, T. D., & CAMPBELL, D. T. The design and conduct of quasi experiments and true experiments in field settings. In M. D. Dunnette (Ed.), *Handbook of industrial and organizational research.* Chicago: Rand McNally, 1975.

CRONBACH, L. J., GLESER, G. C., NANDA, H., & RAJARATNAM, N. *The dependability of behavioral measurements: theory of generalizability for scores and profiles.* New York: Wiley, 1972.

FINIFTER, B. M. The robustness of cross-cultural findings. In L. L. Adler (Ed.), *Issues in cross-cultural research.* New York: New York Academy of Sciences, Vol. 285, 1977.

FREEDMAN, R., & TAKESHITA, J. Y. Studies of fertility and family limitation in Taiwan. *Eugenics Quarterly,* 1965, *12,* 233–50.

HALL, E. T. *The silent language.* Greenwich, Conn.: Fawcett, 1959.

MALINOWSKI, B. *Sex and repression in a savage society.* New York: Harcourt, Brace, 1927.

McKAY, H., McKAY, A., & SINISTERRA, L. Stimulation of intellectual and social competence in Colombian preschool age children affected by the multiple deprivations of depressed urban environments. Second Progress Report, Human Ecology. Research Station, Cali, Colombia, 1973.

NEALE, J. M., & LIEBERT, R. M. *Science and behavior: an introduction to methods of research.* Englewood Cliffs, N.J.: Prentice-Hall, Inc., 1973.

ROHNER, R. P. Why cross-cultural research? In Issues in cross-cultural research, *Annals of the New York Academy of Sciences*, 1977, *285*, 3–12.

RYAN, T. A. Multiple comparisons in psychological research. *Psychological Bulletin*, 1959, *56*, 26–47.

SECHREST, L. Experiments in the field. In R. Naroll & R. Cohen (Eds.), *A handbook of method in cultural anthropology.* New York: Natural History Press, 1970.

———. On the need for experimentation in cross-cultural research. *Annals of the New York Academy of Sciences*, 1977a, *285*, 104–18.

———. On the dearth of theory in cross-cultural psychology: there is madness in our method. In Y. H. Poortinga (Ed.), *Basic problems in cross-cultural psychology.* Amsterdam: Swets and Zeitlinger, B. V., 1977b.

SECHREST, L., FAY, T. L., & ZAIDI, S. M. H. Problems of translation in cross-cultural research. *Journal of Cross-Cultural Psychology*, 1972, *3*, 41–56.

SECHREST, L., FAY, T. L., & FLORES, L. Motivational factors in blood donating. Midwestern Psychological Association, Cincinnati, Ohio, 1970.

SEGALL, M. H., CAMPBELL, D. T., & HERSKOVITS, M. J. Cultural differences in the perception of geometric illusions. *Science*, 1963, *139*, 769–71.

WEBB, E. J., CAMPBELL, D. T., SCHWARTZ, R. D., & SECHREST, L. *Unobtrusive measures: nonreactive research in the social sciences.* Chicago: Rand McNally, 1966.

WHITING, B. The problem of the packaged variable. In K. Riegel & J. Meacham (Eds.), *The developing individual in a changing world*, Vol. I. The Hague: Mouton, 1976.

9

Unobtrusive Methods in
Cross-Cultural Experimentation

~~~~~~~~~~~~~~~~~~~

Stephen Bochner

~~~~~~~~~~~~~~~~~~~

Contents

Abstract

The main *characteristics* of the unobtrusive method are: (a) subjects are unaware that they are participating in a psychological experiment; (b) most unobtrusive studies are conducted in the field rather than the laboratory; and (c) the dependent variable is usually an overt behavioral category. The main *advantages* of the unobtrusive approach are: (a) it reduces the effect of some of the artifacts that operate in laboratory research, such as the demand characteristics of the experimental situation, the enactment of subject roles, and the reactivity of the measurement process; (b) investigators generally manipulate and enumerate naturalistic behavior sequences due to the field orientation of the method; and (c) the procedure is particularly suited to a multimethod research strategy. The main *disadvantages* are: (a) there is some loss of experimental control; (b) there are problems in connection with inferring psychodynamic variables such as attitudes or motives from behavioral data; and (c) there is an ethical dilemma stemming from the methodological requirement that the subject's informed consent to participate cannot be obtained.

Because of its emphasis on behavioral dependent variables, the unobtrusive method is particularly indicated when the topic is socially desirable, taboo, embarrassing, or when the issue is subject to incompatible normative pressures.

This chapter is concerned primarily with cross-cultural experimental investigations, i.e., studies in which the experimenter has some control over the occurrence of the independent variable, and which include some cross-cultural or subcultural comparisons. Three types of experimental designs are distinguished: (1) where culturally homogeneous subjects are exposed to manipulations which systematically vary along some cultural dimension; (2) where subjects from different cultures are compared on some universal attribute; and (3) where both the culture of the subjects and the cultural connotation of the treatment are varied simultaneously in a factorial combination.

The first part of the chapter consists of a critical review of experiments representative of each of the three designs. Then, some cross-cultural replications are presented, followed by a discussion of the potential of the method for action research. The chapter continues with a summary of the general design principles of unobtrusive research; a treatment of some topics and procedures particularly suited for cross-cultural exploration; and it concludes with a summary of the ethical debate.

Introduction and Plan of Chapter

An anecdote provides an apt introduction to the topic of this chapter. The story concerns a young man who went into a bar for a drink. He looked around, and noticed a pretty girl at the other end of the room who was smiling at him. "That looks like a nice, friendly person," he thought to himself, walked over to her, and said, "Hello"; upon which, the girl in a loud and piercing voice answered: "What, go to your apartment with you? Certainly not!" The young man was taken aback by this turn of events, and returned to his corner of the bar in chagrin. But she was a very good-looking young lady, and after a while he could not resist casting another glance in her direction. To his surprise, she was smiling at him again. So he walked over to her once more, and this time asked her what she would like to drink, assuming that the lack of such an offer had been the cause of his earlier downfall. But no sooner had he spoken to her, when the woman exclaimed at the top of her voice: "What kind of a girl do you think I am? I certainly will not have sex with you." The young man, totally devastated by this second rejection, retired in confusion to his seat, and ordered a large whiskey soda with which to soothe his shattered nerves. When he was halfway through his drink, he was amazed to see the girl come over to his table. She sat down, and whispered in his ear that she was a psychology student doing research on how people react to embarrassing situations; upon which he turned to her, and in a voice that could be heard across the street, thundered: "Fifty dollars? That is much too much. I'll give you ten."

The story illustrates some of the major aspects of the unobtrusive approach in gathering psychological data. The most important feature in the example was the young man's total lack of awareness that he was participating in a psychological experiment. Indeed, an essential and defining characteristic of the unobtrusive method is that individuals who serve as subjects in these studies are completely ignorant of their status as helpers in a scientific investigation. Recurring in this chapter will be the consideration of the advantages and disadvantages of keeping experimental subjects in the dark regarding their role as sources of psychological data.

Another feature of the anecdote that is highly characteristic of unobtrusive studies is that the "experiment" took place in a real-life setting, with real people engaged in "natural" behavior. There was nothing contrived or unusual or esoteric about the setting, nor about the behavior in question—a man having a quiet drink in a neighborhood bar is an event that occurs a million times each day, in thousands of cities and towns all over the world. Again, the advantages and disadvantages of conducting research in natural settings will receive major attention in this chapter.

A further aspect of the unobtrusive approach, which the anecdote illustrates rather well, is related to the ethics of the method. Whenever we observe or stimulate or record someone without their knowledge and/or permission, we are breaking an ethical rule, and the immorality is compounded if the subject is embarrassed, or made to look foolish, or otherwise demeaned by the procedure. The anecdote is particularly revealing of a central issue in the debate on the ethics of experimentation, by suggesting that neither the loftiness of the purpose, nor an apology after the event, was capable of undoing the harm done. The young man, after being debriefed by the lady experimenter, did not say, "How clever, interesting, scientifically useful, and personally enriching this experience has been."

Rather, he showed by his own aggressive and retaliative response that he still felt angry and humiliated by the encounter.

The primary focus of this chapter will be to relate the unobtrusive method to research aims, areas, and topics that have a cross-cultural perspective. The purpose of the presentation will be to equip researchers with the basic concepts, precepts, and essential software necessary for designing and conducting an unobtrusive cross-cultural experiment. Consequently, both the advantages and the disadvantages of the approach will be discussed, in terms of the appropriateness of the method to the research purpose in hand. The choice of research strategies is always a compromise; there are no perfect methods, only more or less appropriate ones.

The scope of this chapter has been restricted to the analysis of designs that are *experimental* in the generally accepted definition of that term. The minimum requirements of an experiment are that the investigator has had some control over the occurrence of the independent variable. As will be seen, there is a great deal of latitude in the degree of control different experiments achieve. In general though, for a design to qualify for the honorific "experimental," the investigator must have had some say in making the independent variable event happen, in establishing its intensity, and in either regulating the constancy of the stimulus or deliberately varying it in some essential respect. Quasi experiments in which subject characteristics constitute the main variation will also be included in the discussion. However, studies that rely purely on the observation and recording of naturally occurring events will not be treated, even though such data are often unobtrusively gathered and yield a wealth of naturalistic information. This should in no way be construed as an indication that such methods lack respectability. Quite the contrary. The nonexperimental approach is an important specialty in its own right, and has been treated extensively elsewhere in this *Handbook*, particularly in the chapters by Longabaugh and Pareek.

Most of the experiments described in this chapter have a cross-cultural perspective in their design. Broadly, there are two ways in which an experiment can fall under the cross-cultural rubric: (1) by exposing culturally homogeneous subjects to manipulations that systematically vary in their cultural connotation, or (2) by comparing the responses of subjects from different cultures on some universal dimension. The sophisticated study will combine both of these aspects in a factorial design. An example of the first type might be a study in which members of one cultural group, such as white Australians, respond to the same request from experimenters who differ in their racial characteristics (e.g., Bochner, 1971a). The second type might involve recording the physical distance at which people from different cultures interact with each other (e.g., Baxter, 1970). An example of a sophisticated factorial experiment might be a study in which either black or white subjects are asked to help either a black or a white "victim" (e.g., Gaertner & Bickman, 1971). A variant of the factorial design is the cross-cultural replication, in which an investigator repeats an experiment that was done by someone else in a different cultural setting (e.g., Innes, 1974). The bulk of this chapter consists of research examples that illustrate each of these experimental designs.

A broad definition of the adjective "cross-cultural" will be adopted. Thus, studies that compare well-defined subcultures will be included. For instance, experiments that contrast black with white Americans (e.g., Wispé & Freshley, 1971), or "freaks" and "straights" (e.g., Darley & Cooper, 1972), qualify. However, studies will be preferred that encompass a sizeable cultural variation in their design. Generally speaking, it is desirable to maintain a fairly stringent cutoff point about what is and what is not a cross-cultural experiment. After all, every experiment by definition contains contrasting groups or manipulations, and the label would have no utility whatsoever if "cross-cultural" simply became a synonym for "contrasting."

It is not within the scope of this chapter to mention and review all unobtrusive studies, or even mention and review all cross-cultural unobtrusive studies. The primary aim of the literature that will be cited in this chapter is to describe, illustrate, and critically examine the unobtrusive method in the conduct of cross-cultural research. This aim is better achieved by discussing in relative detail a few prototypical and representative studies than by swamping the reader with a long list of titles and brief abstracts.

The first section of the chapter describes the essential characteristics of the unobtrusive method, its main strengths and weaknesses, and the research conditions under which the unobtrusive approach has particular utility. Subsequent sections will present research examples that illustrate the following designs: (1) experiments in which culturally diverse treatments are administered to culturally homogeneous subjects; (2) experiments in which culturally diverse groups of subjects are compared on measures which are culturally constant, with the culture in a sense providing the "experimental" treatment; (3) experiments in which both the cultural significance of the experimental treatment, as well as the cultural or subcultural affiliation of the subjects, is varied in a factorial or quasi-factorial design; and (4) experiments that are replications of studies carried out by other investigators in other cultures. This material will be followed by a section on unobtrusive measures in action research, a section drawing together and identifying the general principles of designing an unobtrusive experiment, and a section devoted to ethical considerations. The commentary accompanying the research examples will draw attention to several theoretical and methodological issues, problems, and solutions peculiar to unobtrusive cross-cultural research. Each section concludes with a summary listing the main issues that were treated in the preceding material. Finally, it should be noted that most of the research examples come from what might be called the sub-cross-cultural literature. This apparent bias in the material simply reflects the realities of the situation. The literature contains relatively few unobtrusive experiments which contain major cultural contrasts. Thus, in this area there still exist many opportunities for conducting basic pioneering research, unlike the situation in some of the more overworked areas of psychology.

Section Summary

The anecdote of the young man being publicly embarrassed so that a researcher could study his reactions introduced three main characteristics of the unobtrusive method: subjects are unaware of their participation in a psychological study; the research is conducted in natural settings; and failing to ask subjects' consent to serve in an experiment raises an ethical issue.

The stated aim of this chapter was to provide the necessary tools for conducting unobtrusive cross-cultural research. The scope was restricted to experimental studies that contained a sizeable cultural variation in their design. The plan of this chapter was presented, the organizing principle being the different types of experimental designs utilized in cross-cultural research. The main issues, problems, and solutions of unobtrusive cross-cultural research will now be raised in the context of specific research examples, and then systematically reiterated in the respective section summaries. A separate section will be devoted to the ethics of unobtrusive research.

Characteristics of the Unobtrusive Method

Behavioral scientists have been conducting unobtrusive research at least since the thirties (LaPiere, 1934). However, the systematic introduction of the method into the literature occurred relatively recently, with the monograph by Webb, Campbell, Schwartz, & Sechrest (1966). The defining attribute of the unobtrusive method is the lack of awareness by the subject that he is participating in a psychological experiment. The condition of the subject's being ignorant of his experimental status has two sets of methodologically advantageous consequences.

(1) Some of the problems that characterize studies in which subjects are openly recruited can be solved, minimized, avoided, or circumvented. The major problems of orthodox research, whether in the laboratory or in the field, are: (a) the biases produced by the experimental situation; (b) the biases associated with the measurement process; and (c) the biases intro-

duced by the presence of the experimenter in the subject's phenomenal field. The absence of these influences enhances the internal validity (Campbell, 1957) of an experiment. The structure of the unobtrusive framework eliminates or greatly minimizes the operation of these biases.

(2) In addition, the condition of subject unawareness also has some intrinsically positive consequences. In particular, experimenters employing unobtrusive methods are encouraged, inspired, or forced by necessity into devising procedures that will manipulate and capture naturalistic behavior sequences. Several desirable features tend to be positively correlated with a naturalistic orientation toward psychological research, among them: (a) the greater likelihood that the experiments will address phenomena that have a real-world impact; (b) the expectation that the experiments will confirm or disconfirm hypotheses previously demonstrated only in a laboratory setting; and (c) the likelihood that the experiments will be part of a multimethod approach. The presence of these attributes contributes to the external validity (Campbell, 1957) of an experiment. The biases that the unobtrusive method avoids, the positive effects of subject unawareness, and the concepts of internal and external validity, will be expanded on later in this section of the chapter.

Not all the consequences stemming from the condition of subject unawareness are positive. In particular, the failure to obtain the subject's informed consent to participate raises a fundamental ethical question. The other major problem is the psychological interpretation of behavioral data, specifically, the difficulties associated with making inferences about underlying psychodynamic variables from behavioral responses. Most unobtrusive studies reveal only *what* a subject did, not *why* he did it, or what he *felt* while he was making the response. This of course is not a problem if the research aim is restricted to the prediction of behavior in specific situations, but many investigators may not be content to limit their scope to a behavioral level of analysis. Finally, the social distance between investigator and subject sometimes makes it difficult to run an adequate check on the success of the experimental manipulation.

The ethical question, and the problem of the psychological interpretation of behavioral measures, will receive fuller attention in subsequent portions of this chapter. This section will concentrate on the two earlier mentioned consequences stemming from the subject not being aware of his status: (1) the methodological problems that can be avoided when that condition prevails, and (2) the positive effects of subject unawareness.

(1) *Problems that can be avoided if the subject is unaware of his experimental status.* In the discussion that follows, a distinction is being made between *being in an experiment*, the act of *measurement*, and the physical *presence of the investigator* in the experimental situation. All three conditions are present in orthodox experiments, but absent, as far as the subject is concerned, in studies employing an unobtrusive approach. There is empirical evidence

that under certain circumstances each of these conditions can produce artificial effects that reduce the internal validity of an experiment. Internal validity prevails when the dependent variable effects are unequivocally produced by the experimental treatment. But if these effects are the outcome of, or contaminated by, influences extraneous to the experimental manipulation, the internal validity of the experiment is compromised in proportion to the operation of these variables.

A brief list of those artifacts empirically identified as potential troublemakers will now be presented, using as an organizing framework the distinction among *being in an experiment, being measured,* and *having an encounter with an investigator.* It should be emphasized that not all of these artifacts are present in all experiments, or if they are, it is often possible to take successful precautions that minimize their deleterious effects. Nevertheless, the potential limitations of the conventional laboratory method should be taken into consideration when decisions about design strategies are being made. For example, there are certain substantive topics, to be identified later, which are particularly susceptible to distortion by artifacts. In these circumstances, rather than expending extra resources to increase the "realism" (Aronson & Carlsmith, 1968) of his laboratory situation, the investigator may instead decide to invest that energy in an unobtrusive field experiment. The material below has been included to provide empirically based guidelines for the choice of different research strategies.

(*a*) *Artifacts produced by the experimental situation.* The behavior of individuals is greatly influenced by the social role that they are enacting (Secord & Backman, 1964). The psychological experiment is a well-defined social situation, evoking its own idiosyncratic role performances. Five major subject roles have been empirically identified: the good, the faithful, the negativistic, the apprehensive (Weber & Cook, 1972), and the enlightened subject (Gergen, 1973).

The *good* subject is concerned about the utility of his performance. He wants to be helpful, and to make a contribution to research. From the best of motives, the good subject responds to the demand characteristics (Orne, 1962, 1970) of the experimental situation by striving to guess the hypothesis and emit responses that will confirm it, in the mistaken belief that he is thereby assisting the investigator.

The *faithful* subject (Fillenbaum, 1966) believes that a high degree of docility is required, that he must scrupulously follow experimental instructions, and that he must avoid acting on the basis of any suspicions that he might have about the true purpose of the study. Consequently he tends to behave in an artificially passive and submissive manner.

The *negativistic* subject exhibits what Masling (1966) called the "screw you effect" (p. 96). Such subjects will actively sabotage what they think is the purpose of the experiment by producing responses that are contrary to the hypothesis, or otherwise "useless" to the experimenter. For example, in a postexperimental interview, one resentful subject admitted that "I chose the tastes, because I knew you wanted me to pick the weights" (Goldberg, 1965, p. 897). Subjects such as these are covertly expressing their hostility toward the investigator, possibly because their suspicion has been aroused that they are being deceived about the true purpose of the study. Most subjects expect to be deceived even in studies where no deception is involved (Argyris, 1968; Kelman, 1967), but not all subjects necessarily agree with the practice.

Weber and Cook (1972) have extended Rosenberg's (1965, 1969) notion of evaluation apprehension to draw attention to the *apprehensive* subject role. Early in the history of attitude measurement, it was noticed that subjects tended to give responses which were socially desirable (Edwards, 1953, 1957). Thus, some subjects were reluctant to express opinions that they thought might be contrary to the prevailing social climate of the testing situation. This reluctance to make "unpopular" responses is often allied with the subject's wish to present himself in as favorable a light as possible, and to seek approval (Crowne & Marlowe, 1964) for his performance. Rosenberg has suggested that the setting of the psychological experiment is particularly evocative in arousing evaluation apprehension. Many of the subjects' routine tasks can be construed as tests of ability, or as measures of personal adjustment. Possible loss of self-esteem is further exacerbated because the experimenters are also psychologists and therefore acknowledged experts in evaluating intelligence and mental health. Consequently, the apprehensive subject will tend to suppress any responses that threaten his security, or that lead to an imagined negative evaluation of his capacity.

With the expansion in education, and the greater communication of psychological knowledge by the media, many of the central ideas in the social sciences have become common knowledge. This has led to a gradual shrinkage in the availability of naive subjects. Most people who now participate in psychological experiments are what Gergen (1973) has called *enlightened* subjects, i.e., individuals who are reasonably well informed about the concepts and findings of scientific psychology. The problem is that the person who is psychologically enlightened may deliberately contradict, conform with, or subvert the principle being tested in the experiment. In general, as society becomes more informed psychologically, theories that are known to the subjects will become increasingly difficult to test with traditional experimental methods.

Subjects in unobtrusive studies do not enact the various social roles of a psychological subject, because they are unaware of the demand characteristics of the experimental situation.

(b) *Artifacts produced by the act of measurement.* A basic problem in psychological research is that the mere act of observing behavior tends to alter and distort the very phenomenon the investigator set out to study. Psychological measures are reactive (Campbell, 1969a) if the subject knows he is being scrutinized. Measurement reactivity is the underlying determinant of all of the subject roles discussed in the preceding pages, in that the act of measurement tends to trigger whatever role is most salient for the subject at the time. Unobtrusive measures are nonreactive, because the subject is not aware that his behavior is being observed and measured.

(c) *Artifacts produced by the presence of the investigator in the experimental situation.* A basic problem in psychological research is that the characteristics of the investigator, whether actual or attributed, tend to influence the responses that subjects make. As was noted in relation to the apprehensive subject role, many individuals associate psychologists with evaluation, and consequently modify their behavior when they are in the presence of such a person. In general, the source of the experimental manipulation tends to interact with the content of the treatment. Thus the investigator's age, sex, race (Forrester & Klaus, 1964; Pedersen, Shinedling, & Johnson, 1968) all generate unintended variance, particularly in experiments with a cross-cultural component. For example, Kubany, Gallimore, and Buell (1970) found that the presence or absence of an experimenter changed the performance of Filipino Ss on a test of achievement motivation. Similarly, Lazarus, Tomita, Opton, and Kodama (1966), in a cross-cultural study of stress, found that Japanese subjects were much more sensitive to the disturbing aspects of the experimental situation as a whole than were Americans. The massive state of apprehension directed at the general situation by the Japanese Ss swamped the experimental induction of stress, so that, unlike their American counterparts, the Japanese gave distress responses that were independent of the stimulus features constituting the threat manipulation. Such unwanted variance can be eliminated from studies that use an unobtrusive approach, since the experimenter can, if he wishes, make himself invisible as far as the subject is concerned.

(2) *Positive consequences of a naturalistic orientation.* In the discussion that follows, some of the positive features associated with a naturalistic orientation towards psychological research will be briefly discussed. What unites these features is that they contribute to the external validity of an experiment. External validity refers to the generalizability of a particular set of results to other settings and populations, and the criterion applies equally to both laboratory and field studies. If a phenomenon is highly specific to a particular set of procedures, then that experiment lacks external validity.

External and internal validity may be independent of each other, i.e., results from experiments with high internal validity need not necessarily generalize beyond the specific situation that generated the data. Traditionally, internal validity has been associated with theory testing and building, for which external validity was not considered crucial. It was argued that as long as a predicted outcome could be produced, then the theory it implied was confirmed, even if the circumstances under which the phenomenon occurred were highly artificial or unusual. This viewpoint, together with considerations of convenience and expediency, was used to justify the large scale use of university undergraduates as experimental subjects, leading many critics to assert that the discipline was merely ". . . engaged in constructing the psychology of the college sophomore" (McGuire, 1969, p. 32).

In the last decade, more and more scientists in general and psychologists in particular have become persuaded that they ought to be making a greater professional contribution toward curing specific social problems (for an eloquent statement of this viewpoint, see Campbell, 1969b; for a case study that brought into the open some of the problems that arise when psychologists become professionally involved in social reform, see Zuniga, 1975). Not so long ago, the "pure" experiment testing some abstruse theoretical point enjoyed high status among the scientific fraternity, and the fact that such experiments had only the remotest applied payoffs did not seem to matter. A definite change in attitude has occurred in recent years (Elms, 1975). Although not rejecting the pursuit of knowledge for knowledge's sake, many writers have been expressing the wish that the behavioral sciences might also have something more immediate and relevant to offer (McGuire, 1969; Tarter, 1973; Wertheimer, 1970). Finally, questions are now being asked not only about the practical value of social science research, but increasingly about the benefits that actual subjects serving in a particular study are entitled to in return for their participation (Bochner, Brislin, & Lonner, 1975).

One consequence of the growing professional concern with social action has been to place greater emphasis on the external validity of research programs. However, achieving external validity can also be justified on traditional academic grounds. Thus a number of writers starting with Lewin (1948) have argued persuasively that the most powerful test of a theory occurs when it is confirmed within a real-world context. The problem with many otherwise admirable experiments is that they lack what Sells (1969) called ecological relevance. Conditions in the typical laboratory are too often unrepresentative of real-life encounters (Weick, 1967), and typically involve subjects who are also highly unrepresentative of the population at large. The solution increasingly advocated is to take some of the more desirable features of the laboratory out into the natural field (Campbell, 1969a; McGuire, 1969). Specifically this has meant conducting manipulated and controlled research in natural settings.

Practically all unobtrusive studies are conducted in natural settings. Therefore, such experiments are predisposed toward achieving ecological relevance and external validity, although it should be noted that neither feature is a necessary correlate of field studies. The core notion of the concept of external validity is the generalizability of the phenomenon beyond the particular experiment that identified it, and not merely whether a laboratory event "works out there." Thus in the case of a field experiment, the criterion for assessing its external validity must be the extent to which the outcome generalizes to other situations and other subject populations—exactly the same procedure by which the external validity of laboratory studies is judged. If field experimenters select unusual or exotic settings or populations in which to carry out their studies, or if their studies only "work" in unusual situations, then they will have fallen into exactly the same error that laboratory buffs commit when they contrive a situation in order to squeeze out some effect.

Finally, as Campbell (1969a) has reminded us, experiments cannot prove theories, only probe them. This is particularly true of the isolated, "one-shot" investigation. Such studies are incapable of confirming a theory, or even establishing the existence of some functional relationship, because most phenomena have many plausible rival explanations. The main function of science is to rule out rival hypotheses, and the strategy most likely to achieve this aim is a multimethod approach. Thus it is most desirable that a research question be tackled from many angles, with many different procedures (Campbell & Fiske, 1959), and by many different investigators. Webb et al. (1966), have likened this strategy to a process of triangulation, using the analogy of oil exploration and the sinking of test wells to determine the extent of the subterraneous deposits. From this point of view, unobtrusive field experiments can be thought of as fulfilling the important function of providing multiple corroboration (Lykken, 1968) for findings that were previously established only under laboratory conditions.

Topics and issues that are distortion-prone. This section concludes with a brief listing of some topics and issues that are particularly susceptible to distortion in the laboratory, thereby making them specially suited for study with nonreactive measures. Studies whose primary aim is to predict actual behavior in specific situations are a case in point. Although both common sense and theoretical expectations (Aronson, McGuire, Newcomb, Rosenberg, & Tannenbaum, 1968; Festinger, 1957; Heider, 1958; Osgood & Tannenbaum, 1955; Rosenberg & Abelson, 1960) assume agreement between what a person does and what he thinks, believes, and feels, some of the empirical evidence does not confirm this supposition. Thus under certain conditions, attitudes and actual conduct are unrelated, or even negatively associated (Wicker, 1969a).

The apparent discrepancy between attitudes and behavior is one of the major unresolved issues in social psychology, and has attracted a great deal of theoretical and empirical attention (Calder & Ross, 1973; Cohen, 1964; Fishbein, 1967; Kiesler & Munson, 1975; Liska, 1974; Mischel, 1968;

Rokeach, 1966, 1968; Wicker, 1969a, 1971). It would be outside the scope of this chapter to review this literature. However, the conclusion to be drawn is that because of the complex relationship between attitudes and behavior, some research questions in this domain are best served by an experimental design that directly measures behavior, thereby avoiding the necessity of making action-oriented inferences from a subject's verbal responses. Several writers (Bochner, Buker, & McLeod, 1976; Kelman, 1974; Weitz, 1972) have suggested that behavior-oriented research designs might be particularly appropriate in those areas where there exist strong societal and institutional norms, an example of which might be the prescription towards tolerance and cooperation in interrace relations. Whenever a topic is enveloped by a powerful cultural "ought," conventional attitude studies of behavioral intentions are particularly susceptible to the intrusion of social desirability, and hence more likely to reveal ideal rather than actual behavior patterns. Consequently, designs employing behavioral dependent variables will be most useful in those social areas where there is a large gap between actual and ideal practice, that is, if the research aim is to describe behavior. Naturally, if the research aim is to describe value systems without being particularly interested about the connection between values and action, then there is nothing inappropriate about using a battery of attitude questionnaires. The appropriateness of a particular method will depend entirely on what inferences an investigator wishes to make from his data.

Even when the primary target of a study is not action, and the investigator is really interested in some of the underlying dynamics, there are several areas in which it may nevertheless be advisable to use unobtrusive measures and then attempt to infer phenomenal variables from the behavioral responses. In general, unobtrusive methods are particularly apposite if the topic is sociopolitically sensitive, socially desirable, taboo, or embarrassing. An empirical example is research on "reverse discrimination." Thus several unobtrusive studies have shown that when middle class whites are manipulated into nonintimate interaction with members of discriminated-against groups, the minority member will receive preferential treatment over a comparable white person (Bochner & Cairns, 1976; Dutton, 1971, 1973). It is unlikely that this phenomenon would have appeared so clearly on a conventional questionnaire of behavioral intentions. The principle is neatly captured by Guthrie's (1977) comment that the results of a supplementary school feeding program are much more likely to show up on a set of bathroom scales than on psychological scales measuring the attitudes of mothers toward infant nutritional practices.

Finally, because of the compelling nature of unobtrusively gathered data, the method has a special place in action research (Lewin, 1948), where the primary aim is to change social attitudes and practices. The research examples that now follow expand on and illustrate the special uses, strengths, and limitations of the unobtrusive method in psychological research, with particular reference to gathering data with a cross-cultural perspective.

Section Summary

Unobtrusive methods contribute to the internal validity of an experiment by minimizing those biases that are a function of the subject's knowing that he is participating in a psychological study. In particular, unobtrusive experiments avoid the effects of measurement reactivity, do not evoke any of the various subject roles, and eliminate artifacts due to the presence of the investigator. Because most unobtrusive studies are conducted in natural settings, their ecological relevance and external validity tends to be higher than that of the typical laboratory study. The main limitations of the unobtrusive method are the ethical problem associated with not asking the subject's permission to participate, and the difficulties of inferring underlying psychodynamics from behaviorally couched raw data. As a genre, unobtrusive experiments tend to address themselves to real world issues, are part of a multimethod approach, and provide field corroboration for heretofore laboratory-bound phenomena. The method is particularly useful in behavior-oriented research, and in areas that are socially sensitive, including the special case of an investigator who is working in a culture other than his own.

Design 1 Studies: Cultural Connotation of Treatment Varied; Culture of Subjects Constant

It is fitting to begin the literature survey with a description of the classic study by LaPiere (1934). Notwithstanding the criticism that this study has attracted (Campbell, 1963; Dillehay, 1973; Triandis, 1971), the method used by LaPiere served as the prototype for a whole genre of nonreactive research, as well as opened up the substantive issue of attitude-behavior inconsistency. LaPiere made a genuine contribution to psychology, although, if he were to submit his paper for publication today, it would probably be rejected on the grounds of having a faulty research design. But that limitation would apply to many of the classic pioneering studies, and simply reflects the methodological advances that have accompanied the development of psychology as a scientific discipline.

LaPiere traveled around the United States in the early 1930s with a young Chinese couple. The group stopped at sixty-seven establishments to sleep and at 184 restaurants to eat, and they were refused service only once. After a lapse of six months, LaPiere sent a questionnaire to each of the 250 places which had catered to the travelers. The questionnaire contained the item: "Will you accept members of the Chinese race as guests in your establishment?" to which 92 percent of the respondents replied "No." The discrepancy between the two sources of data—the visits and the questionnaire—lit the fuse under the attitude-behavior controversy, an issue which to this day has not been satisfactorily resolved (Wicker, 1969a).

Undoubtedly, the LaPiere (1934) study contains some major flaws. For instance, because of the method employed, there was no way of ascertaining whether the person who responded to the questionnaire was also the same individual who had admitted the Chinese couple. This question is important because if two separate persons were involved, then strictly speaking no inferences can be made about the nature of the relationship between attitudes and behavior. Critics have also pointed out that LaPiere accompanied the Chinese couple to the various establishments, whereas in the questionnaire, no mention was made of the prospective Chinese guest being part of a three-person group, the third member of which was a white American. Thus the verbal index did not parallel the behavioral index of the attitude that both measures were supposed to reflect. The study also suffered subject loss (not all establishments returned the questionnaire), and lacked a control group. Nevertheless, there were many redeeming features that served as a model for subsequent investigators. For instance, the experimental treatment was quite powerful, in the sense that subjects could not help noticing that some of the visitors who had just arrived at the desk were Chinese. Likewise, the measurement of the dependent variable was utterly precise—the guests either were or were not accommodated. Thus despite some problems of internal validity (Campbell, 1957), LaPiere (1934) is an important landmark in the unobtrusive literature, primarily because of the liberating effect of the method on the imagination of future investigators.

The literature contains several studies that were directly patterned after LaPiere's (1934). An example is the Kutner, Wilkins, & Yarrow (1952) experiment, in which three female investigators—two white and one black—visited eleven quality restaurants. In every place the women were served. Two weeks later each restaurant was sent a letter requesting reservations for a group of the writer's friends, adding that ". . . since some of them were colored, I wondered whether you would object to their coming" (p. 650). After seventeen days, not a single reply to any of the letters had been received. Each restaurant was then telephoned, and the caller reminded the manager of the letter and then asked for reservations. No manager unconditionally accepted a telephone request that sought to make reservations for a racially mixed social affair. However, all managers routinely accepted reservations from the same person making a control call the next day, in which he simply requested space for a "party of friends." The feature to note about this study is that three degrees of interpersonal cross-racial contact were manipulated—impersonal contact (letter), partial personal contact (telephone), and direct contact (face-to-face confrontation). The results are consistent with LaPiere's findings that the hypothetical minority member is more readily discriminated against than such an individual in the flesh. Unfortunately, Kutner et al. (1952) also share LaPiere's (1934) design error of not controlling the identity of the respondents across the various indices of attitude.

A more recent study by McGrew (1967) illustrates the increasing sophistication and refinement of the LaPiere method. McGrew had experimenters posing as married couples who were viewing apartments for rent. The racial composition of the couples was systematically varied for four conditions: a white couple, a black couple, a white male–black female couple, and a black male–white female couple. Several weeks after the visit to view the apartment, the landlord was telephoned and asked if he would rent to a Negro couple. The results in the visit conditions showed that landlords were less willing to rent their apartments to black than white couples. But in response to the telephone inquiry, all of the landlords who had in fact refused to rent to a Negro couple, gave verbal responses that were inconsistent with their earlier action. Thus whereas LaPiere (1934) and Kutner et al. (1952) are both instances of a situation in which a negative verbal attitude was joined with positive action, the McGrew study illustrates one condition under which the verbal statements were positive, but the behavior was not.

A major aim of the LaPiere, Kutner et al., and McGrew studies, and many similar experiments, was to draw attention to the complex relationship between attitudes and behavior, particularly in the domain of race relations. The theoretical account of the often observed inconsistency between actions and verbal statements of intent is itself a complicated matter, and could be only briefly treated in this chapter. However, the practical lesson that may be derived from these experiments is relatively straightforward: if the investigator's primary research purpose is to predict interpersonal actions, then he would be well advised to measure the target behavior directly, rather than to rely on having to make inferences from verbal statements of intent. Furthermore, it is possible to identify four conditions where this recommendation makes special sense: (1) if the topic is a socially sensitive one; (2) if the topic is taboo; (3) if the topic-related behavior is socially desirable; and (4) if the topic is subject to strong normative pressures (Triandis, 1975). If one or all of these conditions prevails, then the likelihood that people will say one thing and do another is increased. Many of the research examples in this chapter illustrate the above proposition, and thus, rather than defend the argument formally here, the case will be assembled cumulatively in conjunction with the description of relevant empirical studies.

Bochner's studies of Australian intergroup relations (Bochner, 1971a, 1971b, 1972; Bochner & Cairns, 1976; Cairns & Bochner, 1974) illustrate some of the points made in the preceding paragraph. Bochner was primarily interested in how different groups would be *treated*, and thus did not include a measure of verbal attitude in the design of his studies. This is not to say that a verbal measure might not have been desirable, just that such data were not needed to achieve the aim of those particular investigations. For many research purposes it is not necessary to design overcomplicated experiments. Indeed, as some examples below indicate, an overly complex design may be self-defeating by rendering the data difficult to interpret. Another reason for keeping experiments simple is the need to match design requirements against the availability of resources. Many of the American studies that are described in this chapter would be out of the question in some parts of the world, purely on the grounds of cost. Probably one reason why the literature contains relatively few genuine cross-cultural replications is that most non-Western investigators do not have the resources to mount time, material, and personnel consuming studies. The three Australian studies that will now be reviewed are all examples of relatively simple experiments which cost practically nothing to run, were analyzed by hand, and were yet able to speak quite adequately to the research question they were addressing.

The specific aim of the research program was to investigate how Australian Aborigines living in predominantly white urban communities were being treated. Bochner (1972) studied the responses of landlords to potential Aborigine tenants. The purpose of the study was very similar to McGrew's (1967), although a different and a less elaborate method was employed. The manipulation consisted of the following two advertisements, which appeared on the same day in the "Wanted to Rent" classification of a Sydney newspaper:

> Young couple, no children, want to rent small unfurnished flat up to $25 per week. Saturday only. 759-6000.
>
> Young Aboriginal couple, no children, want to rent small unfurnished flat up to $25 per week. Saturday only. 759-6161. (Bochner, 1972, p. 335)

Different investigators manned the two telephones, and recorded the responses of the callers. Altogether twenty-two phone calls offering accommodation were received, fourteen for the "young couple," two for the "Aboriginal couple," and three landlords phoned both the numbers. An analysis of these data revealed a significant bias in favor of the ethnically nonspecific advertisement. The conclusion the author drew was that advertisements for accommodation are less likely to be answered if the prospective tenant identifies himself as being of Aboriginal descent. No conclusions were drawn, nor was there any intention of so doing, about the motives and attitudes that contributed to that effect.

The "Wanted to Rent" study employed a symbolic variation of the independent variable of ethnic identity. In the next two studies to be described, the cultural significance of the independent variable was directly manipulated, by using Aboriginal or white confederates to administer the experimental treatment. Both studies are reported in Bochner (1971a), and illustrate the research strategy of comparing naturally occurring social behavior toward members of different ethnic groups, under conditions controlled by the experimenter. The studies will be used here to introduce and illustrate some of the main problems that the unobtrusive method is rather prone to, and some of the solutions that are available. In particular, the discussion will refer to experimenter expectancy, inadequate sampling, the low spontaneous emission rate of the target behavior, and the predictive validity of behavioral data.

In Experiment 1, a white and a black (Aboriginal) girl walked a small dog in a public park, during the lunch hour. Both girls were in their early twenties and were similarly dressed. The park was divided into four comparable geographic areas, and each of the girls was randomly assigned to two of the sectors. The population density and demography in each of the four sectors were roughly equal, as determined by prior observation. Each sector was traversed by the experimenter dog walker for ten minutes.

As E (the experimenter) and the dog proceeded on their route, they were followed by two observers. These confederates gave the appearance of being on a stroll through the park, but in actuality were recording the responses of the people in the park toward the experimenter. Independently of each other, the two observers measured the frequency of smiles, verbal approaches, and nods that were directed at E. A record was also kept of the sex and age of the respondents. The strategy of using a dog was chosen in order to raise the base rate of the focal response to a level where sufficient data could be collected in a reasonable period of time. Prior observation had indicated that a person who is simply walking through a park will be mostly ignored by other passersby. However, a person walking a dog attracts a considerable amount of attention, a phenomenon that Bochner has called the Fifi effect (in preparation). In the study under discussion, the Fifi effect was exploited to overcome a problem that all field experiments face—how to evoke, provoke, or increase the emission rate of the target response. Thus the question at issue was whether Fifi would be equally effective in facilitating social contact regardless of the race of the person holding the leash. The results showed otherwise: the white girl attracted a combined total of 50 communication units, compared to the other E's 18, a highly significant difference. However, these results must be treated with caution, as a dissection of the study will now reveal.

One reason for describing the procedure in detail was to be able to discuss the problem of experimenter expectancy with a concrete example. Experimental psychologists have always realized that their own behavior is a crucial component of the research situation (Underwood, 1966). Consequently, much thought goes into standardizing the instructions to subjects, the conditions under which the treatment is administered, and the conditions under which the dependent variable measures are collected. Often, various mechanical stimulus-emitting and recording devices are used as a further means of lowering the inconsistency and unreliability that human beings exhibit when they function unaided as data gatherers. Unfortunately, the experimenter's inefficiency is only one part of the problem. An additional component, known in psychological research as the experimenter effect, is the experimenter's own motives and preconceptions. A sizable body of empirical evidence indicates that the investigator's expectations may influence, and sometimes even determine, the outcome of a study (Rosenthal, 1963; 1966; Rosenthal & Fode, 1963; Rosenthal & Jacobson, 1968). Although this literature has been challenged (Barber & Silver, 1968a, 1968b; Snow, 1969), there are at least two conditions under which experimenter expectancy has an increased probability of occurring. A high risk should be assumed in: (1) studies where investigators from one culture are collecting data in other-culture settings (Campbell & LeVine, 1970; Campbell & Naroll, 1972); and (2) studies where the dependent variable measure is imprecisely defined. Both conditions were present to some extent in the dog-walking study. Bochner worked with a confederate from a culture different from his own, and the nature of the dependent variable did not lend itself to a high degree of precision.

The behaviors constituting the raw data—smiles, verbal approaches, and nods—were not simple, unambiguous categories. Rather, the responses were complex signals of short duration, embedded in a rapidly changing ongoing situation. In trying to detect and accurately interpret what it was that passersby were emitting, the judges could have been influenced by their knowledge of the social standing of Aborigines in contemporary urban Australia. As it turned out, there was almost unanimous agreement between the two sets of independently-arrived-at observations. Still, even that result needs to be viewed cautiously. High interjudge reliability does not necessarily guarantee accuracy of measurement, particularly in situations like the dog-walking study. Both judges shared the same set of expectancies about Aboriginal-white relations, and could therefore have been distorting reality isomorphically. Probably the best way to reduce the operation of experimenter expectancy is to employ a dependent variable that can be objectively and unambiguously categorized. Later in this chapter, several examples of such measures will be presented and discussed.

The dog-walking study also illustrates the difficulties that are ever present in connection with the interpretation of unobtrusive data. Why did the passersby communicate less with the Aboriginal than with the white girl? A number of plausible alternate hypotheses can be entertained. Thus it is more than likely that prejudice accounted for the relative lack of warmth encountered by the Aboriginal girl. On the other hand, perhaps passersby ignored the Aboriginal, not because they disliked her, but because they felt that a personal approach might be misconstrued as patronizing. The solution to the problem of interpreting the results of this and similar studies is to conduct a number of interconnected experiments in which the situational context is systematically varied, and to supplement the unobtrusive observations with questionnaire and interview data. Webb et al. (1966) likened this strategy to a process of triangulation. The overall aim of such an integrated research program would be to eliminate all plausible rival hypotheses (Campbell, 1969a). Indeed, the principle of tackling a research question from many angles and with many different procedures (Campbell & Fiske, 1959) applies equally to the interpretation of all psychological data, not just results generated by an unobtrusive study. But the need for multiple corroboration (Lykken, 1968) becomes much more visible when the dependent variable is expressed exclusively in behavioral terms. Somehow, experimenters are less willing to believe their eyes than their ears, metaphorically speaking. Thus the question "What does it all mean?" is heard more frequently in respect to behavioral data than when verbal responses are being considered. This differential attitude toward the two data categories is not warranted, since the process of establishing the validity of both behavioral and verbal responses is based on an identical rationale. These brief comments on data interpretation will be supplemented later in this chapter with a further discussion and illustration of some of the issues involved in establishing the predictive validity of behavioral measures.

Some of the unanswered questions raised by the dog-walking study prompted the second experiment reported by Bochner (1971a). In this study, a white or a black girl walked into a butcher's shop, and asked for ten cents' worth of bones for her pet dog. Such a request is perfectly normal, and is made by customers from all walks of life. Prior observation had indicated that the amount and quality of bones that a customer receives in response to such a request will vary considerably. Indeed, this item is one of the few grocery lines still left in Australia that is neither prepackaged nor prepriced—a butcher just reaches into a bin and wraps up what he thinks is an appropriate amount. That is precisely the reason why the experiment was built around the request for bones, since the situation gives the butcher-subject leeway to behave more or less positively toward the experimenter posing as a customer.

Two dependent variables of social attitude were used: the weight of the bones, and their quality. Quality was established by an experienced dog lover, who rated the bones on a three-point scale, unaware of the circumstances under which the items had been acquired. The experiment was conducted in a busy middle class shopping district, which contained fourteen butcher's shops. The fourteen shops were randomly allocated to the two experimental conditions. Each girl visited seven butcher's shops, walked over to the nearest assistant, and said: "Can I have ten cents' worth of dog bones, please?" A confederate, posing as a customer, was also present in the store to lend social support and record any incidental information. The entire experiment was completed in about an hour. A comparison of the mean weight and quality of the bones in the two conditions revealed that the white E was given a larger measure than the Aboriginal E (20 lb. 2 oz., or a mean of 46.00 oz., per trial, versus 16 lb. 8 oz., or a mean of 37.71 oz.). However, this difference was not statistically significant. Likewise, the quality of the bones was marginally higher in the white than in the Aboriginal condition, but again not significantly so.

The somewhat inconclusive nature of these results can be attributed to two features which, in varying degrees, constitute a problem in many unobtrusive field studies: inadequate sampling, and a small N. Thus in the study just reviewed, an N of seven per E was probably insufficient to randomize the host of extraneous influences intruding into the experimental situation. And although the sample constituted the entire population of butcher's shops in the particular suburb where the study was conducted, the greater Sydney area contains several thousand such establishments. But before selling this and similar studies short, it should be acknowledged that most psychological research is conducted with samples that are not large or representative enough.

What does differentiate some unobtrusive field experiments from most laboratory studies is the *heterogeneity* of the subject population. This point can be illustrated by considering the makeup of the samples in the two Bochner (1971a) studies. In the dog-walking study, the subjects were drawn from the entire spectrum of socioeconomic and age variables in Australian urban society. These subjects therefore comprised an extremely heterogeneous group of people. In the dog-bone study, the subjects were united by a common occupation, but still differed in age, and probably in marital status, political leanings, and other sociological variables. Thus, there was more heterogeneity, and much greater variance than in the typical sophomore sample, where all or most of the subjects are young, middle class, well educated, and generally rather mundanely alike.

Since both subject homogeneity and subject heterogeneity have theoretical advantages and disadvantages, what kind of sample an experimenter selects will depend on the research aim of the study. For instance, if the purpose is to generalize the findings to the populace at large, then the investigator will probably choose a design that uses a heterogeneous subject population, and, if he is able to, a variety of different settings as well. On the other hand, if the investigator happens to be constrained by circumstances to a small N, he may decide to select a homogeneous subject population to reduce the variability produced by extraneous effects (or noise, as it is sometimes called). In general terms, unobtrusive studies that are conducted in institutional settings such as shops, hospitals, or office buildings, will contain a more homogeneous group of subjects than unobtrusive studies that have public settings such as streets, parks, or amusement centers.

Finally, the studies just reviewed illustrate a very desirable feature of psychological research. The studies were "coupled" (Webb, 1968), i.e., they were related to each other by a common theme, subject matter, and methodology. If each experiment is looked at in isolation, it makes a very limited impact. But when, for example, the LaPiere (1934), Kutner et al. (1952), and McGrew (1967) studies are taken together, a compelling picture begins to emerge of the complex nature of the attitude-behavior relationship in the area of race relations. Likewise, the programmatic nature of the Australian studies, taken together, underlines the likelihood that in a variety of contexts, Aborigines living in the cities are going to be treated less positively than their white counterparts.

An implication for the conduct of effective research is that the investigator must know the relevant empirical literature, so that he can couple his *original* experiment to current issues as well as past methods and findings. The *de novo* breakthrough experiment is a very rare event. Unfortunately, one-shot studies that are totally unrelated to anything that has been done previously are still alive, although not too well. One-shot research should be eschewed—it is difficult to interpret, and, because it cannot be easily integrated into an existing strand of thought, is very easily forgotten and ignored. The exception is a study that is clearly derived from some theoretical position and that has been explicitly designed to test some specific hypothesis. An example of such an experiment is Knox and Inkster's (1968) race track study, which tested a dissonance-theory derived hypothesis about postdecision cognitive processes. Immediately before or immediately after placing a bet, bettors were asked how confident they were that the horse they had selected would win the next race. Although no one had previously used such a technique in such a setting, the Knox and Inkster study nevertheless made a contribution because it was easily integrated into the dissonance literature, because it extended knowledge in an established substantive area (decision making), and because it confirmed an effect in the natural field that had previously been observed only under laboratory conditions.

Thus the most useful unobtrusive experiment is a study that has been coupled to and extends previous methods, addresses an established substantive issue, and has some explicit connection with a systematic theoretical position. The reason for devoting space to pointing out what may be obvious is that there is a tendency in unobtrusive research to get carried away by the ingenuity, novelty, or general brilliance of a particular procedure, sometimes to the point of forgetting that method is but the handmaiden to collecting scientific data. Probably the only sure way to overcome this occupational hazard is to begin with a research problem and then fit a method to it. Too often, however, an exciting method dictates the sort of problem that will be investigated. That sort of coupling is undesirable because it has the effect of stultifying rather than advancing a research area.

The presentation of research examples with what are here being called Type 1 designs continues with a review of the Bryan and Test (1967) studies. These studies are noteworthy because of the ingenious way in which modeling was used to deliver the independent variable manipulation. The modeling device has subsequently been employed in a number of more sophisticated studies (e.g., Huang & Harris, 1973, to be reviewed later), and the procedure seems to have wide applicability to a variety of issues and settings.

Bryan and Test (1967) built their experiments around a fund raising situation. Thus in one study, two Salvation Army kettles were manned, one by a black and one by a white female solicitor; both were dressed in the Salvation Army uniform. The dependent variables were: (a) the average number of donors in a set period of time in each condition; and (b) the amount of money collected by each solicitor. The data showed that more passersby donated to the white than to the black solicitor, although there were no differences in the amount of money collected by the two solicitors. In a later study, Bryan and Test introduced a model manipulation. In the model condition, a male confederate approached the kettle and contributed five cents. The subsequent twenty-second period constituted the duration of the treatment condition, and alternated with twenty-second no-model periods. An analysis of the data revealed no effect for the race of the solicitor, but significantly more passersby contributed in the model than in the no-model condition.

The actual results of the Bryan and Test studies are less interesting than the method that was employed. In addition to the modeling manipulation already commented on, Bryan and Test also showed resourcefulness in their indexing of the dependent variable. Earlier, in connection with the Bochner (1971a) dog-walking study, some of the difficulties of recording ongoing social interactions in natural settings were noted, together with the observation that the problem is less acute when the dependent variable event can be unambiguously categorized. Bryan and Test provide a good illustration: it is much easier to add up the cash in a collection box, or make a head count of donors, than it is to record the smiles and nods of people streaming by. Thus the relatively more objective nature of the behavioral events measured by Bryan and Test made their data less prone to experimenter-induced distortion than the rather ephemeral responses studied by Bochner (1971a).

As a general rule, the more complex and ambiguous the phenomena constituting the dependent variable, the greater the likelihood that experimenter-expectancy may intrude and bias the results in favor of the hypothesis. It follows that investigators should give much thought to devising dependent variable measures that are defined as objectively as possible.

Section Summary

In this section, some studies with a Type 1 design were reviewed. Such studies have a simple structure, and consist of varying the cultural connotation of the experimental treatment. Usually, a two-group design is employed. The relatively unsophisticated nature of these studies makes them suitable models for investigations in which time, personnel, materials, and technological resources are limited. A common theme running through the studies was their concern with the social treatment of minority members (Chinese, blacks, Aborigines) by the dominant majority. Several methodological issues were raised in connection with the presentation of the research examples, among them: (1) the conditions under which it is advantageous to measure behavior directly; (2) dependent variable categories, measurement, and experimenter expectancy; (3) sampling; (4) increasing the spontaneous rate of the target behavior; (5) the psychological interpretation of behavioral data; and (6) "coupling."

Design 2 Studies: Cultural Connotation of Treatment Constant; Culture of Subjects Varied

The cross-cultural literature is replete with studies that compare subjects from different cultural backgrounds, on some *etic* (Berry, 1969; see also Berry, Chapter 1 in this volume; Brislin, Chapter 10 in this volume for elaboration) or universal variable. In the language of experimental psychology, the culture of the various subject groups constitutes the treatment or independent variable, and the score or position on the dimension on which the Ss (Subjects) are being compared constitutes the dependent variable. Studies with such a design are very often (although not necessarily) atheoretical in their derivation and/or exploratory in their aim, in which case, the primary interest is to describe, compare, and contrast subjects on some variable, rather than to test a hypothesis or confirm a prediction. Studies of this type are useful in the initial stages of the accumulating knowledge in a hitherto unexplored field. However, once the basic observations have been made, further advances in *understanding* a phenomenon will come from studies that are explicitly linked to some theoretical framework. The link need not be forged in chains of steel, but it is desirable prior to embarking on a study to have a minimal idea on the order of "If X were the case, then the data should come out this way, but if Y were true, then such and such can be expected to happen." The unobtrusive research example that will now be described was chosen because it is an appropriate model for studies that employ the culture of the subjects as the experimental treatment, but at the same time are guided by a set of theoretical considerations.

Campbell, Kruskal, and Wallace (1966) compared the class seating pattern of black and white students in two colleges. The colleges were similar in most relevant respects, but differed greatly in the attitude of the white students toward racial integration. In the first college, the white student population was predominantly liberal, whereas the whites in the second college held traditional, nonintegrationist attitudes. Campbell et al. reasoned that these two college "cultures" (Bochner's term) would be reflected in the seating aggregation of black and white students. The data on seating patterns was unobtrusively collected by an observer posing as a student, and confirmed that significantly more blacks and whites sat adjacent to each other in class in the "liberal" than in the "traditional" college. These results may not appear very startling. However, it would be a mistake to disparage this study merely because the outcome was obvious. By demonstrating the discriminatory power of the seating aggregation measure in a reasonably known situation, the study opened up the possibility of using similar indices in situations where the outcome might be less predictable. Thus, as Campbell et al. point out, a version of the aggregation index might be used as a before-and-after measure of the effect of persuasive communications on reducing intergroup hostility, or, if the method was extended to more public settings such as shops, buses, and streets, aggregation might be used as an index of racial tension.

More generally, many of the more sophisticated unobtrusive studies explicitly build into their design some way of gauging the predictive validity of the measure or behavior serving as the dependent variable. In the Campbell et al. study this was done by predicting an almost (but not quite) known event, because the primary interest of the investigators was to validate the method. In experiments with a greater emphasis on substantive outcomes, the prediction may be to other actions considered on logical grounds to be related to the target behavior (Feldman, 1968, to be discussed below). Another (and probably the least preferred) method of establishing predictive validity is to seek verbal or attitudinal verification of the focal behavior. Limiting the latter strategy is the problem of potential attitude-behavior inconsistency and the consequent difficulty of interpreting such data, unless high face validity can be assumed for the mutuality of the attitudinal and behavioral measures. A good cross-cultural example incorporating both attitudinal and unobtrusive behavioral dependent variables, in which the two indices could be expected to agree, is Brislin (1971). This study's relevance to the present discussion is further enhanced because Brislin used seating aggregation as his behavioral measure, employing a Type 2 design.

Brislin studied the friendship choices and degree of interaction among students from nine ethnic groups attending the University of Guam. A conventional questionnaire was used to measure friendship. In addition, Brislin unobtrusively recorded seating patterns in the University cafeteria; his index was the frequency between, versus within, ethnic group interactions. For both sets of measures the investigator predicted intergroup interaction to be a positive function of objective similarity in the backgrounds of the participants. This hypothesis can be derived from reinforcement as well as cognitive theories of interpersonal behavior (e.g., Byrne, 1969; Heider, 1958; Newcomb, 1956), and has over the years achieved substantial empirical verification. Brislin found that both the behavior and the questionnaire data were consistent with the hypothesis and with each other, and thus also provided confirmation for the predictive validity of seating interaction as an index of friendship choice.

The importance of establishing the predictive validity of unobtrusive measures cannot be overemphasized. In essence, there is little point in carefully and systematically measuring some behavioral sequence, if the meaning of the behavior is obscure or ambiguous. What is urgently needed is a series of interrelated studies whose primary aim is to establish the predictive validity of some of the more frequently used behavioral dependent variables. A good place to start would be on the connection between physical proximity and liking, because the evidence does point to a positive relationship between these two variables (see Brislin's 1974 review of the literature). However, even in this relatively well researched area, because of the heterogeneous methods and procedures employed, it cannot be uncritically assumed that physical closeness provides a reliable index of interpersonal attraction. Thus there would be much utility (and probability of success) in running a series of coordinated studies that systematically measured a variety of different proxemic behaviors (nonverbal social behaviors, such as looking, touching, and kissing) of known friends, strangers, and enemies, in a large variety of public, institutional, and private places. If such a program of research revealed a high degree of overlap between the variables of friendship and physical closeness, and if this relationship held across most situations, then proximity could be used in less obvious contexts as an unobtrusive measure of liking.

Other behavior–attitude relationships that could be subjected to a predictive validity analysis might be the connection between overt obedience (to stop lights, to institutional rules) and psychological conformity; between sex role behavior (women taking care of babies and men fighting) and attitudes toward sex role typing; and between eye contact and linguistic forms (using "sir," pauses), and dominance and submission. To date, such basic research has not been done for the purpose of establishing the predictive validity of behavioral marker variables that subsequently can be used as dependent variables in unobtrusive studies. Some of the work in relating body movement, facial expressions, and other nonverbal behaviors to emotions and feelings (Duncan, 1969; Ekman & Friesen, 1972, 1974; Ekman, Friesen, & Ellsworth, 1972; Hall, 1959, 1966; Knapp, 1972; Mehrabian, 1972; Sommer, 1969) is highly relevant to the establishment of such a bank of marker variables, but the voluminous research in that area does not seem to have attracted the notice of the unobtrusive practitioner. Thus it is likely that the next major development in unobtrusive methodology will occur when the link between proxemics research and the predictive validity issue is fully recognized and exploited. It would be highly desirable if this development extended into conducting further basic research into *cross-cultural* differences in proxemic behavior. As Jones (1971) and others have noted, Hall's (1959, 1966) hypotheses that cultures (and subcultures) differ systematically in the way that people relate spatially has not received adequate empirical inquiry. To fill this gap, several recent unobtrusive investigations have explored the proxemic behavior of different subcultural groups (Aiello & Jones 1971; Scherer, 1974); the following study is an instance of the kind of well-conducted basic research which can make an important contribution to this field.

Baxter (1970) recorded the distances at which people interacted with each other. Four locations at the Houston Zoo provided the setting, and the subjects were members of three different subcultural groups—Anglos, blacks, and Mexican-Americans. The procedure will be described in some detail, because it illustrates a problem that many unobtrusive field studies face—how to secure an unbiased sample of subjects. The principle underlying the solution to the sampling problem is to set up *a priori* selection categories. Thus in the Baxter study, passersby were inducted into the experiment if: (a) they arrived at the observation post in a two-person combination; (b) if the people could be clearly identified as either Anglos, blacks, or Mexicans; and (c) if the pairs were homogeneous with respect to age and ethnic grouping. Passersby were excluded from the study if they were members of a larger group, of a mixed group, if they were carrying parcels or pushing strollers, or if they could not readily be classified by age and ethnicity.

The dependent variable was how close to each other the subjects stood. Ten seconds after a selected pair of subjects passed a previously designated point, an observer judged the distance between the two persons to the nearest one-quarter foot, from nose to nose. The main reason for the ten-second interval was to take the decision of when to judge interpersonal distance out of the rater's hands, thereby reducing a major potential source of bias. Other precautions were to use a primary judge who was not acquainted with the expectations of the investigator, and to have additional raters do reliability spot checks as the experiment progressed. The data showed that Mexican pairs stood closest to each other, blacks stood most distant, and the Anglo pairs were intermediate relative to the other two groups.

The Baxter study was described primarily for its procedure. Field studies that employ passersby as subjects fall into two broad categories: (1) where every passerby is a potential subject (e.g., Bochner's 1971a dog-walking study, or Bryan & Test, 1967); and (2) where specific subjects are selected for inclusion, as in the Baxter (1970) experiment. In designing experiments of the latter kind, two general guidelines should be kept in mind: (a) the selection and exclusion categories must be centrally relevant to the research hypothesis; and (b) individuals who do meet the criteria for inclusion should not be excluded because they might contradict the hypothesis, nor should subjects likely to confirm the hypothesis be overrepresented. The latter principle is preferred to the more conventional interpretation of random sampling as a technique which gives everyone who ought to be included on theoretical grounds an equal opportunity to participate. It is often not practicable to follow textbook prescriptions for sample drawing. Thus it is more realistic to guard against specific biases, than to settle for nothing less than a perfectly random sample.

The next research example illustrates the method of inferring psychodynamic variables from the traces that they leave in the environment. The assumption of trace analysis is that those tendencies which are strong in an ecosystem may be expected to leave some mark, either in the form of erosion or accretions. For example, it is usually possible to infer the prevailing wind from the slant of the trees and the bare patches in the landscape, and inscriptions on tombstones may be used to estimate the average life span of an era. The same principle applies to more culturally determined manifestations. For instance, one might be able to infer some quite telling data on the social and recreational habits of a people from a cross-sectional and cross-temporal analysis of the bars, houses of ill repute, and houses of worship in a given society at a given time. The attempt by newspaper reporters to trace-analyze the garbage produced by the household of the American Secretary of State was based on a similar rationale—that the data would reveal some heretofore obscure aspects of Dr. Kissinger's life style.

Sechrest and Flores (1969) used a trace-analysis procedure to test the hypothesis that there was more psychological conflict about homosexuality in the United States than in the Philippines. Recurring in this chapter is the theme that unobtrusive methods are particularly suited to the conduct of research in socially sensitive areas. Elsewhere this point was made in connection with issues that have a high degree of social desirability (such as appearing helpful), and where there are strong and ubiquitous normative pressures that prescribe how one is to behave (e.g., racial equality). A further case is where people may be reluctant to speak their mind because the subject matter is embarrassing or taboo (see also a later discussion of this problem in connection with the review of Spector, Torres, Lichtenstein, Preston, Clark, & Silverman, 1971). The Sechrest and Flores (1969) study addressed such a topic—homosexuality—and the sensitive nature of that issue made it advisable to use a measure of the dependent variable which did not rely exclusively on the cooperation and candor of the respondents. Their solution was to use the writing on the walls of public toilets in Manila and Chicago as the source of raw data. Sechrest and Flores reasoned that the two cultures' relative degree of conflict about homosexuality would be reflected in the graffiti each group produced. An analysis of the graffiti recorded in each city confirmed the author's expectations that there is less concern about homosexuality in the Philippines than in the United States. Thus, although the proportion of heterosexual inscriptions was about equal in the two samples, 42 percent of all of the American graffiti involved homosexuality in some way, whereas only 2 percent of the Filipino expressions were on that topic.

Sechrest and Flores (1969) is one of the very few unobtrusive research examples in this chapter (and indeed in the literature) in which a major cultural comparison was involved. This aspect of the study provides a point of departure for commenting on the special problems of designing cross-cultural experiments with a capital C. Sechrest and Flores provide a positive model for most aspects of the process. Thus the experiment was jointly planned and conducted by individuals indigenous to each of the two cultures being compared. This ensured that any conceptual, logistic, or sociopolitical difficulties that might have marred the study were ironed out at the design stage. The study has been criticized on the grounds that different norms could exist in the two societies regarding the use of graffiti as a communication channel. Presumably, this kind of issue was resolved by drawing on the cultural experiences of the respective investigators. Joint authorship also ensured that the topic was of interest to both cultures and not just an American or Filipino preoccupation. At the same time, the results had some nontrivial implications for a general theory of sexuality. Translation of the items was not required, because the data for each country—the relative frequency of homosexual references—were analyzed from an emic (Berry, 1969) perspective. Yet the comparisons were made within the etic framework provided by the operational definition of homosexuality in behavioral terms.

This section concludes with a research example that illustrates a problem potentially present in experiments that are not clearly embedded in a precise theoretical framework. Berkowitz (1971) observed pedestrians walking at three standardized locations (shopping area, public park, and downtown entertainment area), in twenty-four cities in eight different countries (Italy, West Germany, Sweden, England, United States, Afghanistan, Iran, and Turkey). The dependent variables were whether the pedestrians were alone or in a group, and whether those people observed in groups were interacting and were touching each other. Altogether, the responses of 21,316 pedestrians were recorded, and generated a superabundance of data. However, despite the huge effort that went into this investigation, there is very little that can be said in its favor. The basic problem is that Berkowitz had practically no theoretical notion of why he was collecting the data, or indeed what he was looking for. Consequently, the data analysis consisted of an aimless hunt for similarities and differences across a variety of behavioral and demographic variables. This search was accompanied by a post hoc running commentary. The study's main contribution to the literature is to provide an outstanding example of how not to do cross-cultural unobtrusive research.

Section Summary

In this section, some studies with a Type 2 design were reviewed. These are studies in which different cultural groups are compared on an etic or pancultural dimension. In the strict sense, studies with such a design are nonexperimental, since the independent variable is not being manipulated by the investigator. Rather, variation is achieved by selecting different groups of subjects to serve as the "experimental" treatment. Designs of this kind are most frequently used in investigations whose primary aim is to reveal similarities and differences between cultural groups. The value and interpretability of such data tends to be enhanced if their collection and analysis is guided by theoretical considerations.

A common theme running through all but one of the studies was their concern with proxemic behavior. Several methodological issues were raised in connection with the presentation of the research examples, among them: (1) the advantage of theory-guided research; (2) a further treatment of the psychological interpretation of behavioral data, extending into a discussion of predictive validity; (3) procedures for selecting and excluding specific subjects; (4) a further treatment of the conditions under which it is advantageous to measure behavior directly; (5) trace analysis; and (6) the cross-cultural genesis of cross-cultural studies.

Design 3 Studies: Cultural Connotation
of Treatment and Culture of Subjects
Varied Simultaneously

This section is devoted to studies that simultaneously vary the cultural connotation of the experimental treatment, together with variations in the cultural membership of the subjects. In a sense, such designs can be thought of as Design 1 studies with a replication to another culture. This point can be illustrated with reference to LaPiere (1934). Say that LaPiere had also crossed China in the company of one European and one Chinese, and recorded the verbal and behavioral responses of local innkeepers toward his group. Then he might have been able to answer questions such as whether his data reflected a uniquely American phenomenon, or whether a more general problem was being identified. LaPiere's hypothetically extended study would have been even more illuminating had each cultural replication contained a control condition, i.e., a group of three Americans and three Chinese seeking hospitality in the United States and China respectively. The research example which now follows was chosen partly because its design has such a factorial structure, and also because the substantive area—the treatment of strangers—is related to the topic of that earlier experiment.

Feldman (1968) studied the responses of people in the street to a stranger requesting assistance. Five types of request for help were carefully staged: (1) passersby were asked for directions; (2) passersby were asked to mail a letter; (3) passersby were shown some money and asked if they had just dropped the bill; (4) shopkeepers were deliberately overpaid; and (5) taxicabs were engaged to see whether the driver would take the shortest route. The experiment was done in three cities, Paris, Athens, and Boston, and in each city the procedures were carried out either by a foreigner or a compatriot. The design therefore consisted of two levels of the culture of the treatment (foreigner or compatriot seeking assistance); three levels of the culture of the subjects (Parisians, Athenians, or Bostonians); and five separate and independently arrived at indices of helping behavior. Thus the Feldman study can be thought of as having replicated the basic experiment (stranger versus compatriot asking for help) in three cultures, with five conceptual replications of the focal behavior (responding to a request for help). The comparisons across the several domains of helping behavior were used to evaluate the predictive validity of the dependent variable measures, although that is not the term that Feldman used. The rather complex results will not be summarized here, other than to report the main findings: compatriots were treated better in Paris and Boston, and foreigners were treated better in Athens.

The Feldman study illustrates both the advantages and disadvantages of employing a sophisticated factorial design. Inevitably, such studies tend to yield a large and complex body of data. Despite assurances to the contrary, Feldman had very few compelling reasons for predicting a specific set of outcomes, either as main or interaction effects. Thus, in those areas where the data did not form a coherent pattern, the author had to resort to post hoc speculation to explain his findings. However, it should be noted that this experiment provided some useful behavioral data supporting the cultural differences in the cognitive definition of ingroup-outgroup relations, as measured by the role differential (Triandis, Vassiliou, & Nassiakou, 1967).

The lesson to be learned is that investigators planning a complex unobtrusive study should be particularly sensitive to the problem of data interpretation. "It would be interesting to see what would happen if" variations have no place in a complex factorial design, because unless the experimenter is lucky, the interaction oᶠ these effects with the theory-derived variables may render the total set of data difficult or impossible to interpret. As a general rule, the investigator should have a sharply defined and theoretically derived *reason* for each of the manipulations or factors that constitute the various treatments. The next research example is a complex factorial study that was shaped rather more than Feldman's (1968) by specific theoretical considerations. This study is a particularly good illustration of the benefits of knowing beforehand the meaning of all of the possible outcomes of an experiment.

From a set of theoretical principles, Huang and Harris (1973) reasoned that the Chinese are less individualistic and more conforming than Americans. They designed an ingenious unobtrusive field experiment to test this hypothesis. The method was similar to Feldman's (1968), in that subjects were passersby who were accosted in the street. The experiment was conducted in two locations—Taipei (Taiwan), and Albuquerque (New Mexico). In each city, two experimenters were used, one E serving as a model (M), and the other E pretending to be conducting a survey. A two-step strategy was employed. First, M would select a subject (S), and go and stand next to him. Then, E would approach S and M, and ask the two people if they would be willing to participate in a brief survey. M would immediately agree on behalf of S and himself. E would then show both people sets of pictures of plants and flowers, and test the respondents' general knowledge about these items by asking questions such as: "Which plant would make the best slope covering?" or "Which flower would multiply the fastest?" Prior investigation had established that there were no objectively correct answers to these questions. M always answered before S, and whether S gave the same response as M constituted the dependent variable. These data were interpreted to reflect conformity.

In addition to the culture of the Ss, two further independent variables were manipulated: the status of the model, and his competence. In the low status condition, M wore shabby clothes, and in response to a question by E revealed his profession as a garbageman. In the high status condition, M was well dressed and described himself as a college professor. In the low-competence condition, M asserted that he knew nothing about plants, whereas in the high-competence condition, he asserted that plants were his hobbies and that he spent hours each day in his garden. Thus the design of the experiment consisted of two levels of culture (Chinese and American), two levels of status (high and low), and two levels of competence (high and low). An analysis of variance revealed the predicted main effect for culture, i.e., Chinese Ss imitated the model more than the Americans. There was also a main effect for status, with the high status M being imitated more than the low status M. Finally, a significant interaction between status and competence indicated that a low status model was imitated only if he was high in competence. None of the other comparisons were significant.

Data such as these present no problems of interpretation. The study unequivocally revealed both differences and similarities between Chinese and Americans. Thus the Chinese conformed more than the Americans, but both groups were equally susceptible to the status manipulation. The Huang and Harris (1973) study rates high on the ingenuity of its procedures, and on the clear thinking that went into its design.

The research example to be presented next (Bochner & Cairns, 1976), provides a further instance of a theory-oriented factorial design. However, the main reason for reviewing this particular study is to draw attention to a distinctive unobtrusive technique. Generally, the technique might be described as the *lost-object* method. Historically, the first objects to be "lost" under systematic conditions were letters. The *lost-letter* technique, as it became known, was originally introduced to the literature by Merritt and Fowler (1948), and was subsequently developed and extended by Milgram (Milgram, 1969a; Milgram, Mann, & Harter, 1965).

The method consists of distributing a large number of stamped and addressed envelopes in public places. When a person comes across one of these envelopes, the letter appears to have been lost, and the finder has a choice: he can either mail, disregard, destroy, or in some other manner treat the article that he has "found." The finder's behavior is presumed to be an indication of how the subject relates to the person to whom the letter was addressed. Thus if the subject mails the letter, this is interpreted as helping behavior and/or holding a positive attitude toward the addressee. But if the subject disregards or destroys the article, a negative attitude on the part of the subject toward the addressee is inferred. The experimental manipulation consists of systematically varying the name and address on the front of the "lost" envelope, thereby presenting finders with the symbols of people or organizations that differ in their social, political, or racial affiliation.

The names and addresses on the "lost" letter are either fictional or various pseudonyms that the experimenter has acquired for the purpose of the study, or names of genuine people and organizations willing to cooperate with the investigator. Consequently, all the letters that subjects find and mail make their way back to the investigator, and the dependent variable is the return rate of a particular name relative to some other name or organization that has been chosen to function as a control. If it can be assumed that no sampling or other research errors were operating, and if significantly more (or fewer) experimental than control letters duly appear within a specified length of time, the hypothesis is deemed to be confirmed, and certain inferences are drawn about the perceived psychological characteristics of the target name or organization.

The lost-letter technique has been used successfully in Australia, the United States, and Hong Kong (Berkowitz, 1970; Bickman, Teger, Gabriele, McLaughlin, Berger, & Sunaday, 1973; Cairns & Bochner, 1974; Forbes & Gromoll, 1971; Hornstein, Masor, Sole, & Heilman, 1971; Milgram, 1969a, 1969b; Milgram et al., 1965; Shotland, Berger, & Forsythe, 1970; Simon & Gillen, 1971) with relatively few dissenting opinions regarding the utility of the procedure (Baskett, Peet, Bradford, & Mulaik, 1973; Jacoby & Aranoff, 1971; Wicker, 1969b). The obvious potential of the method led to its extension beyond the use of letters as the stimulus. For example, Deaux (1974) and Korte and Kerr (1975) distributed post cards, thereby manipulating the content of the message in addition to the characteristics of the recipient and the sender. Gross (1975) dropped letters showing clearly visible "valuable" coupons, and in one series of studies, wallets containing various personal items (as well as money!) were "lost" in a number of public locations (Hornstein, 1970; Hornstein, Fisch, & Holmes, 1968). In another study, a woman shopper would drop a small bag in the street, ostensibly without realizing that she had lost it (Moss & Page, 1972).

There are several problems with the method of distributing letters or other apparently lost items in a public place. Thus the *diffusion of responsibility* phenomenon (Darley & Latané, 1968) may introduce some unwanted variance. This is the tendency to expect someone else in public settings to take care of an emergency, leading to a delay in anyone making the appropriate response. Two further problems are the difficulty of selecting specific subjects for inclusion (unless the letter is actually dropped in front of a target S), and the near impossibility of following up or debriefing subjects. Once a letter or a wallet has been distributed, it is usually anyone's guess who will appear on the scene and respond to the "lost" item. Even if the pickup point is under surveillance, the experimenter still has no control over who will come by, although at least he can record the demographic characteristics of both "pickers up" and "leavers alone." However, once a subject has left the locale of the experiment, he usually cannot be interviewed or otherwise followed up. The lost-object technique that will now be described was specifically evolved to achieve greater control over the selection of subjects, and to enable the investigator to identify the subjects who generated the data.

Bochner and Cairns (1976) devised a company identification card which contained the photograph of either a white or an Aboriginal woman employee, her name, and the address of the firm where she worked. The name of the employee and the company were fictional, but the address was real. The procedure consisted of placing the identification cards in the mail boxes of selected households. To make the householders think that a passerby had lost the identification card in the street outside his residence and that another passerby had found the card and dropped it in the letter box, the phrase "I found this near your letter box" had been written in pencil across the face of the instrument.

A 2 x 2 factorial design was employed. Fifty black or fifty white identification cards were deposited in either an upper-middle class or a working class residential district. Using large scale maps, 100 blocks of comparable size were identified in each area. From each of these blocks, one dwelling was randomly selected to serve as the target household. The actual address was confirmed and recorded when the drop was made. All cards were number coded, and their numbers recorded against the address of their destination. Thus the procedure achieved precise control over which subject-household was to serve in the study; households could be followed up later if so desired, and the "lost" object had been taken out of the public domain.

The dependent variable was the relative frequency of returned identification cards in each of the four experimental conditions. The return rate was considered to be an index of helping behavior, because the act of returning the cards required some effort on the part of the finder. He had to place the card in an envelope, transcribe the address, provide a stamp, and mail the article. A higher overall return rate was predicted for the upper-middle than for the working class suburbs, together with a lower proportion of Aboriginal cards returned in the working class than in the upper-middle class condition. Altogether eighty-three out of the 200 "lost" cards were returned, and the pattern of the data confirmed both predictions. Additionally, it was possible to infer some of the underlying dynamics from the many spontaneous comments which accompanied the cards.

The study illustrates how a relatively high degree of control can be achieved with a variant of the "lost object" method. The next development in this particular technique will occur when the tendency of respondents to include personal notes is exploited to gain a fuller understanding of the reasons why the object was returned. In the Bochner and Cairns study approximately one third of the respondents spontaneously revealed some of their thoughts and feelings about the incident. What is required is some device that maneuvers all of the subjects into providing such information, preferably in some systematic form. The method discussed below may have this potential.

The next two research examples illustrate the "wrong number" technique, which, as far as can be ascertained, was introduced to the literature by Gaertner (Gaertner, 1973; Gaertner & Bickman, 1971). As in the case of the previous study, the substantive topic was cross-race helping behavior. Other similarities include the systematic exploitation of geographic differences to obtain two different groups of homogeneous subjects, and the ability to select and follow up participants.

The procedure is built around a phone call, purportedly originating from a public telephone, to "Ralph's Garage." A motorist explains that his car has broken down on the parkway. When the subject indicates that this must be a wrong number since he is not "Ralph's Garage," the caller exclaims that he has no more change with which to make a further phone call. E then waits for the S to volunteer to call the garage on E's behalf. If S does not make a spontaneous offer to do so, E directly requests S to call for help. The dependent variable is the frequency of calls received at the "garage," and subjects in different conditions are given idiosyncratic telephone numbers to ring, so that the source of the call can be identified.

In the Gaertner and Bickman (1971) study, the independent variables were the apparent race of the victim (black or white), and the race of the subject (black or white). The apparent race of the victim was manipulated by varying his speech characteristics. In the black victim condition, the caller spoke with a "southern Negro" dialect, whereas in the white condition, he used a recognizably white speech pattern. The race of the subjects was manipulated by drawing the two groups from residential areas that were either inhabited almost totally by blacks, or almost totally by whites. The results showed that males helped more than females, that blacks helped blacks and whites equally, and that whites tended to help blacks less than they did members of their own race.

In the Gaertner (1973) study, the independent variables were the sex of the victim, the victim's race (black or white), and the registered political party membership of the subjects (Liberal or Conservative). All Ss were white. Both groups of subjects offered less help to blacks than to whites, with the Conservatives exhibiting more antiblack discrimination than the Liberals. Females were helped at the same rate as males. Finally, male subjects offered help more frequently than females, which is incidentally one of the most robust findings in the literature (see further instances of this effect in subsequent research examples).

Gaertner (1973) gave his study an interesting twist by interviewing a separate sample of Liberal and Conservative party members. These individuals were phoned and asked what they would do if they received a wrong-number call from a stranded motorist. The identity of this hypothetical victim was varied to parallel the experimental conditions of the main study. Data from this segment of the investigation did not correspond with the behavioral responses gathered earlier. Thus, on the basis of what subjects claimed that they would do, black victims would have been helped as frequently as white ones; the absolute level of expected helping would have been substantially higher than the actual help extended, and there would have been no differences between the Liberals and Conservatives regarding their expected degree of helpfulness. This study provides further empirical support for the contention made elsewhere in this chapter that the unobtrusive method is particularly suited for investigating topics that are socially sensitive. The point is important enough to warrant restating here in the context of the Gaertner studies.

Most people genuinely believe, and/or want other people to believe, that they are socially responsible individuals who are willing to give aid to anyone who needs it, regardless of race or creed. Consequently, asking subjects what help they would or might offer in a given emergency is unlikely to be the most accurate predictor of the actual behavior in that specific situation. Generally, the accuracy of any prediction increases as a direct function of the similarity between the procedure or test and its criterion. The implication of this theorem for the present discussion is quite straightforward: if the research (and social) problem is the reluctance of people to help each other when their cars stop (Graf & Riddell, 1972), or their shopping bags burst (Wispé & Freshley, 1971), or they stumble and fall (Piliavin & Piliavin, 1972), then the nontrivial procedure is to determine the actual rather than imagined antecedents and consequents of these phenomena. The point is not how people feel about these events, or how they would like them to turn out, but what it is that people actually do in the circumstances. Properly used, the unobtrusive approach is a very powerful technique for attaining such knowledge.

The next research example is another instance of an experiment in which race and neighborhood were systematically varied, this time in Tallahassee, Florida. West, Whitney, and Schnedler (1975) also built their study around the incident of a motorist in distress. The basic procedure, borrowed from Bryan and Test (1967), consisted of a car with its hood up. The "victim" stood next to the disabled car, facing the approaching traffic. The dependent variable was the time elapsed from when the hood of the car was raised, to when a motorist stopped and offered assistance. The race and sex of the helper were also recorded, as were the race and sex of the motorists who passed by the disabled car without stopping.

The independent variables were the sex of the victim, the race of the victim (black or white), and the racial composition of the neighborhood (black or white) in which the incident was staged. The analysis of the results revealed that: female victims were offered help faster than male victims; black victims were helped sooner in black neighborhoods and white victims were helped sooner in white neighborhoods; males offered more help than females; and victims were helped primarily by others of the same race. In a second experiment, West et al. (1975) added a further independent variable—the proximity of the incident to a college campus, illustrating the flexibility of the procedure to test a variety of different hypotheses. The special contribution of these studies is to show how an everyday occurrence—a broken down car—can be made to serve as the cornerstone for a complex, theory-derived psychological experiment.

The factorial design is increasingly employed in unobtrusive field research, and the treatment of this burgeoning literature must of necessity be selective. The present review of factorial experiments concludes with a brief look at several studies whose procedure elevates them from the run-of-the-mill investigation.

Thayer's (1973) study of helping behavior simultaneously varied the race and sex of both the person in need and the potential helper. A black male, a black female, a white male, or a white female, each conspicuously wearing a hearing aid, approached ten black and ten white males, and ten black and ten white females, in New York's Grand Central Station. The confederate held out a dime to the subject, and a notebook opened at a page which displayed the message: "I am deaf. Could you please help me? Dial (phone number) and just ask if Harold will pick me up at school. Thank you." The phone was manned by an assistant, and the frequency of calls in each of the sixteen experimental cells constituted the dependent variable measure.

Fun-and-Games or Creative Ingenuity?

Some investigators will go to extraordinary lengths to create a vivid and naturalistic situation for their studies. However, there is a division of opinion about the desirability of creating elaborate scenarios in public places, paralleling the debate regarding the alleged "fun-and-games" mentality (McGuire, 1967; Ring, 1967) in laboratory research. In the final analysis, it is a personal decision whether experiments loading high on the dramaturgical factor will be labelled as "cute" and "frivolous," or "creative" and "ingenious." The next two research examples are being presented primarily because they epitomize the dramaturgical approach to designing field experiments. At the same time, both studies are also linked substantively to the previous discussion in that they too address the problem of cross-race versus within-race helping behavior.

Wispé and Freshley (1971) built their experiment around a staged mishap at the exit to a supermarket. A young woman experimenter leaves the store, carrying a large bag full of groceries. When a passerby appears who meets the design criteria for subject selection, the shopping bag suddenly disintegrates. Groceries are strewn all over the pavement, with E making the appropriate gestures and noises of dismay, and the dependent variable is the degree of help offered.

Specifically, Wispé and Freshley classified the Ss' behavior into four categories: (a) ignore; (b) react without help; (c) help perfunctorily; and (d) help positively. The independent variables were the race of the young woman who dropped the bag (black or white); the sex of the subjects; and the race of the subjects (black or white). The latter variation was achieved by running the relevant trials in different neighborhoods. No clear cut results emerged from this study, other than an overall finding that men helped more than women. The somewhat cloudy outcome is compensated by the ingenuity of the independent variable treatment and by the manner in which the dependent variable was classified into four easily discriminable categories. The device of a disintegrating bag has inspired subsequent emulations, of which the most recent are the "accidental" dropping of a deck of 500 computer cards (Wegner & Crano, 1975) and the scattering of an armful of books across the sidewalk (Mathews & Canon, 1975).

The second dramaturgical example is the series of experiments conducted by Piliavin and his associates. These studies also employ a "dropping" device as their experimental treatment, except that it is the much more dramatic incident of a person staggering, collapsing, and then remaining supine on the floor of a moving subway car (Piliavin, Rodin, & Piliavin, 1969). As if that were not enough, in subsequent studies, collapsing victims have been made to apparently bleed from the mouth (Piliavin & Piliavin, 1972), or to appear disfigured by means of a large facial birth mark (Piliavin, Piliavin, & Rodin, 1975).

Experiments such as these have much in common with street theater, except that they are not cheap to run. Thus, in addition to the main character playing the victim, a large supporting cast of observers, confederate bystanders, and data recorders is required, all in appropriate costume. In addition, it is necessary to have access to props, make-up, and in the case of the Piliavin studies, a large quantity of subway tokens. Investigators contemplating unobtrusive experiments on this scale should first take careful stock of their human and material resources. More generally, there is a basic methodological issue in connection with studies of this nature: the internal validity of elaborately staged experiments, whether in the laboratory or in the field, is greatly dependent on the successful acting ability of the confederates. There are many ways in which a confederate could behave differently from a genuine person whose role he is playing. This is an unknown quantity limiting the conclusions which may be drawn from any experiment employing the confederate strategy. One way of reducing this effect is to design studies that make fewer demands on the acting skills of the confederates.

Just the Piliavin et al. (1969) study will be reviewed, since it is the only one of the series with a cross-cultural component. The setting was a subway car traversing a seven and one-half minute nonstop route between two New York stations. The riders became the captive audience of a staged incident, turning them into bystanders to an emergency situation. Seventy seconds after the train left the initial subway station, the "victim" staggered forward and collapsed, lying on the floor and looking at the ceiling until someone came to his aid. If no one came to the victim's assistance by the time the train slowed to a stop at the next station, an experimenter would help him to his feet. Other confederates in the car unobtrusively recorded data. The dependent variables were the frequency of help (whether a victim did or did not receive help), and the latency of help arriving. The race and sex of the helpers was also recorded. The independent variable was the race of the victim (black or white). In some of the conditions the victim smelled of liquor and carried a bottle in a brown bag, whereas in the remaining conditions he appeared sober and carried a black cane.

There was an uneven distribution of trials across conditions, so that this experiment cannot be considered as a pure instance of a factorial design. As a rule, an inelegant design is not just a matter of aesthetics, but also leads to difficulties when the time comes to analyze the data. The Piliavin et al. (1969) study is no exception to this rule. Nevertheless, some conclusions could be drawn, in particular: the victim with the cane received more frequent and earlier spontaneous help than the apparently drunk person; men helped more than women; and there was a slight tendency toward same-race helping, especially in the drunk condition.

The methodological lesson to be learned is that when planning a complex field study every effort should be made to fit the procedures into a balanced, genuinely factorial design. Only the inexperienced investigator relies on luck to produce an adequate and roughly equal N in each cell. The professional, on the other hand, makes explicit plans for allocating precisely the number of subjects to each condition as are required to fulfill the research purpose of the experiment. Luck, both good and bad, is certainly a factor in research, as it is in all human endeavor, but the negative contribution of chance can be minimized by competent planning and foresight.

Two ever-present problems in unobtrusive field research are to recruit subjects economically (in terms of time and effort), and then, after they have served their purpose, to get them out of the field so that they will not contaminate the behavior of their successors. The subway car used in the Piliavin studies provided an elegant solution to both these problems: every five minutes a new batch of subjects was delivered to the experiment, and encapsulated in a sealed environment while the treatment was being administered. At the termination of each trial, the subjects were dispersed miles away from the original pick-up point. In the meantime, a new batch of subjects had already arrived and was even then being processed. Thus the procedure automatically ensured that subjects in the different conditions would not contaminate each other, and that no individual served as a subject more than once. The logical principles behind the Piliavin procedure can be extended to settings other than subway cars, and can thus provide a valuable set of general guidelines for recruiting subjects for field studies.

Section Summary

In this section, some studies with a Type 3 design were reviewed. These were studies with a factorial design, in which the cultural significance of the treatment is varied simultaneously with the cultural affiliation of the subjects. Thus such studies can be thought of as Design 1 studies with a replication to another culture.

A common theme running through the studies was their concern with cross-race versus within-race helping behavior. Two specific methods—the *lost-object* and the *wrong-number* techniques, were described in detail. Several theoretical and methodological issues were raised in connection with the presentation of the research examples, among them: (1) a further treatment of the advantages of theory-guided research; (2) a further treatment of procedures for selecting and excluding specific subjects; (3) a further treatment of the conditions under which it is advantageous to measure behavior directly; (4) the "fun-and-games" versus "serious" research debate; (5) the advantages of a balanced factorial design; and (6) the principles of recruiting subjects for field studies.

Cross-Cultural Replications

The previous section was devoted to research examples of studies with a factorial design, i.e., studies in which the cultural significance of the treatment and the cultural membership of the subjects were varied simultaneously. Such designs, it was noted, could be thought of as replicating the focal manipulation across different cultural domains within a single investigation, thereby permitting direct comparisons to be made across all of the various experimental conditions. Thus the figures appearing in a typical summary table of results generated by a factorial study can be compared horizontally, vertically, and diagonally—a very powerful paradigm indeed. However, it is rare to find more than two or three cultural subject conditions in the typical factorial experiment, particularly in the unobtrusive literature. The reason for the relatively narrow scope of most studies is that there are limits to what can be included in any single investigation in terms of time, energy, and resources.

One alternative to the strategy of extending a single experiment to a multitude of cultures is for different investigators to replicate each other's studies in a variety of cultural settings. However, there are several obstacles to doing such desirable research. One problem, referred to earlier, is the cultural differential in research resources that mitigates against the replication of high-budget studies in countries where research funds are scarce or absent. The other major obstacle is that many journals will not publish replications, no matter how competently these may have been executed. This journal policy reinforces the attitude that replication research is an uncreative pursuit, rather like the activity of the artist who sits in a museum and makes copies of original masterpieces. What is overlooked is that the application of the same procedures to people in a different culture constitutes a *new* finding, in every sense of that term.

Until and unless replications achieve a higher status, and are rewarded more than at present, this area of research will remain underdeveloped. An extensive survey of the literature uncovered only one straight (i.e., unaltered) cross-cultural replication of an unobtrusive study—Innes's (1974) Scottish replication of Langer and Abelson's (1972) American "asking for a favor" experiment. Student members of Bochner's research team have replicated (or failed to replicate) some of the better known American unobtrusive studies (Bryan & Test, 1967; Ellsworth, Carlsmith, & Henson, 1972; Isen & Levin, 1972; Knox & Inkster, 1968; Sommer & Becker, 1969), but none of these reports has appeared in journals.

The preceding observations may help to explain why the replications literature is so sparse. The most visible research examples are some experiments using the *lost-letter* technique reviewed earlier; the replications and *extensions* in several cultures of Doob and Gross (1968); and the Innes (1974) replication of Langer and Abelson (1972). A brief review of the Doob and Gross paradigm will conclude this section. The substance of the studies is less important than the general model they convey of different investigators conducting the same basic experiment, with the same basic procedures, in a variety of different places.

Doob and Gross (1968) cleverly exploited an incident that most motorists may be embarrassingly familiar with—their automobile stalling at an intersection. This situation was staged under two experimental conditions. Either a new car with a well-dressed driver or an old car with a shabbily dressed driver drew up at a controlled intersection. After the lights turned green, the experimental vehicle remained stationary for fifteen seconds, thus blocking the cars behind. Doob and Gross reasoned that this manipulation would produce frustration in the driver of the blocked car, and the frustrated driver could vent his aggression by sounding the car's horn. Thus the dependent variable of the study was expressed aggression, indexed by the number of times a driver honked, and how soon after the lights had turned green, horn sounding commenced. An analysis of the results found less horn sounding, and a higher average latency for the first honk, in the new car condition. These differences were attributed to the inhibitory effect of the new, high status car on the expression of overt aggression.

What is noteworthy about this study is its ingenious method for unobtrusively measuring and quantifying aggression. Perhaps that is the reason why the basic paradigm has been replicated and extended several times. In the United States, the country where the original Doob and Gross study was carried out, there have been at least two replications (Deaux, 1971; Turner, Layton, & Simons, 1975), and the experiment has also been conducted in Canada (Ross, Baran, Beatty, Huebert, Humphrey, Kerr, & Stanley, in preparation) and Australia (Bochner, 1971b). A perusal of the data from these studies revealed one intriguing cross-national difference that illustrates the potential contribution of systematic cross-cultural replications. Thus in the American study conducted by Deaux (1971), subjects directed more aggression toward female than male drivers. But in the Australian and Canadian studies, females elicited significantly less horn sounding than males. Do these differences reflect different cultural attitudes toward the status of women? The data have some face validity, in that women in American society seem to have achieved a more egalitarian status than Australian women. From these assumed differences in status it is possible to derive the prediction that a "dumb" female American driver would be yelled at in the same way as a male doing something stupid, whereas allowances would be made for an Australian female's "dumb" behavior, on the grounds of her inferiority. Similarly, the Innes (1974) replication of Langer and Abelson (1972) revealed a much higher level of helping behavior in the Scottish than in the American sample, perhaps a reflection of genuine cultural differences, perhaps not. The question is an empirical one, and systematic research of the type reviewed in this section is eminently suited to the further exploration of such general propositions.

Section Summary

The paucity of cross-cultural replications was attributed to the cultural differential in research resources, and to the low status of replications. The advantages of cross-cultural replications were illustrated by offering a cultural interpretation of the cross-national differences in female-directed aggression found in the horn-honking studies.

Unobtrusive Measures in Action
Research

The following examples of action research have been carried out by non-indigenous investigators. This is a rather frequent phenomenon and important enough to warrant being singled out for treatment in this chapter. Action research (Lewin, 1948; Lippitt, 1949) is the term used in referring to studies which have a specific applied aim, such as changing social attitudes or practices. Two instances of action research will be briefly described, an older study which had the aim of advancing the civil rights of American blacks, and a more recent experiment whose aim was the diffusion of innovations in a developing country.

In 1950 a group of citizens organized a campaign to reduce discrimination against blacks in the restaurants of New York (Selltiz, 1955). The group explicitly adopted the strategy of achieving the desired results by means of a research project. The design of the investigation was patterned after the LaPiere (1934) and Kutner et al. (1952) studies. A black and a white team were dispatched to a sample of sixty-two restaurants, and a comparison was drawn between the treatment that the two groups of diners received. The results indicated that the black patrons were accorded inferior treatment. Although no restaurant refused service to the black party, they were usually assigned tables in less desirable parts of the dining room than the white control team. Quality of service was the other main dependent variable. Here again, the blacks fared much worse than their white controls, being treated more rudely, receiving unduly slow service, or being harried by the waiters to the point of inconvenience.

Armed with these data, the Citizens' Committee that had commissioned the study mounted a campaign to initiate social change. The results were discussed with the Restaurant Owners' Association and with representatives of the restaurant employees' unions. Many members of the food industry responded by pledging support for the campaign. Finally, details of the study and the subsequent action program were released to the press. Two years later, the experiment was repeated. The retest indicated that although some discrimination against blacks persisted, there was a marked drop from the levels experienced in the earlier study.

The Selltiz (1955) study is noteworthy for two reasons. First, it provides a clear illustration of the action research process—how objective fact finding, followed by educational and persuasive action, can be used to implement social change. Second, the study demonstrates the compelling nature of behavioral data, particularly when these are collected unobtrusively.

The second illustration of action research was a study carried out in rural Ecuador (Spector et al., 1971). The program had four purposes: to promote the construction of latrines, smokeless stoves, the making of marmalade, and smallpox immunization. The study was also designed to evaluate the relative effectiveness of three modes of presenting the persuasive communication: (1) radio broadcasts; (2) radio and audio-visual media such as films, slides, lectures, etc.; and (3) audio-visual media without radio. The design involved randomly assigning different towns to each of the three experimental treatments (the three different communication modes). Three additional towns served as controls. At the termination of a nine week campaign, all of the households in the three experimental towns and a random sample of households in the control towns were surveyed. Of interest to the present discussion is that a major set of dependent variables was the objective (and unobtrusive) count of latrines, stoves, marmalade, and vaccinations. The results showed that significantly more of the behaviors being encouraged occurred under the treatment conditions than in the control towns. However, contrary to expectation, there were no differences in the effectiveness of the three modes of presenting the persuasive communication.

The Spector et al. (1971) study provides an excellent model for research that combines theory testing with problem solving. Thus the study suggested a solution to a real life problem; it made a contribution to the health of the people who served as subjects; and it achieved a nontrivial addition to the theoretical literature on attitude change. Furthermore, the study probably would have run into serious methodological and practical difficulties had the authors not employed an unobtrusive and behavioral dependent variable. In particular, the strategy avoided the problems of translation described elsewhere in this *Handbook* and the demand characteristics and suspicion that would have been aroused by an outside expert asking all sorts of intimate questions.

Generally, the Spector et al. (1971) research program illustrates how topics that are considered taboo may be studied, particularly when the investigator is working in a culture or subculture other than his own. Thus, whereas people may be embarrassed or repulsed by talking about their bodily functions, the problem is circumvented when the observation consists of counting newly built latrines, or monitoring the sale of contraceptives. The Spector et al. experiment is a good prototype for studies that evaluate the effectiveness of diffusion of innovation programs, not just in developing countries, but wherever there is a serious and concentrated effort to promote social change.

Section Summary

The primary aim of action research is to change attitudes and/or practices. The unobtrusive method is especially suited to the conduct of cross-cultural action research, because: (1) actions speak louder than verbal intentions, and should therefore be more effective in producing social change; (2) taboo topics can be broached; and (3) once the criterion behavior has been identified, no further translation problems are likely to arise.

General Principles of Unobtrusive Research and Some Further Special Techniques

At different stages in the preceding discussion various design principles of unobtrusive research were identified. These principles will now be brought together in the form of a set of guidelines that investigators may find helpful at the planning stages of an unobtrusive field study. The section ends with a brief description of several techniques so far primarily used only in monocultural settings, but which seem to have a special potential for cross-cultural research. The main purpose of this section is to provide practical guidance and inspiration.

The core of an unobtrusive field study is the dependent variable behavior that constitutes the raw data. The selection of the dependent variable behavior and its contextual setting should take into account the following criteria: (a) the behavior must be centrally relevant to the investigator's research purpose, and have construct validity in terms of the conceptual framework of the study; (b) the experimenter should have as much control as possible over the occurrence and shaping of the event— ideally, the antecedents of the behavior should be experimentally manipulated; (c) the behavior should be naturalistic and representative, i.e., not exotic or esoteric; (d) the behavior should have a relatively high spontaneous probability of occurrence, or be capable of having its emission rate increased experimentally, so that instances of the event will occur with sufficient frequency within a reasonable period of time; (e) the flow sequence of participants should follow a pattern in which subjects enter and remain in the experiment just long enough to be exposed to the treatment and to emit the predicted response, and then leave the setting for good. Such a sequence ensures that subjects do not contaminate each other, that each subject serves only once, that subjects can be randomly assigned to different treatments, and that sufficient trials can be run in a reasonable period; (f) the behavior must have the property of being reliably observed, quantified, and recorded; (g) the experimenter must be able to observe and record the behavior without drawing the attention of the subject, passersby, the media, or the authorities; (h) the activities of the experimental team should not contravene the law or endanger the public in any way; and (i) the procedure should not violate the professional code of ethics (see the discussion on ethics in the next section).

The other major decision an investigator faces is how the subjects will be recruited. Two broad methods can be distinguished in the unobtrusive literature, the method of "accosting" specific subjects, and the method of providing a stimulus to which any person present in the experimental field may respond. Both of these recruiting procedures can be applied in either public or semipublic (e.g., institutional) settings.

(a) The "accosting" strategy. Research examples where subjects were "accosted" in an institutional setting were the LaPiere (1934) study, and Bochner's (1971a) butcher shop study. In these experiments, the treatment was administered to employees of preselected hostelries and stores. Examples of the same tactic in a public setting were the Feldman (1968) study of compatriots or foreigners seeking assistance, the Huang and Harris (1973) study of Chinese and American conformity behavior, and the Gaertner (1973) "wrong-number" studies. Here, individual subjects rather than institutions are preselected in terms of criteria related to the research purpose of the study. The assumption that must be satisfied is that once a subject has been identified, his subsequent disposition to the experimental condition must occur randomly. Likewise, the criteria for inclusion or exclusion must be rigidly adhered to.

In experiments where the subjects are recruited via the "accosting" method, the dependent variable is the selected subject's response to the experimental intervention. Usually, this response is quantified into a simple "Yes-No" dichotomy, although sometimes magnitudes of reaction can also be measured. In the case of a "Yes-No" design, the analysis consists of comparing the proportion of "Yes-No's" in the various experimental conditions. If the different cells have an equal N (of observations or subjects), the data are usually analyzed with a Chi Square, Fisher's exact, or a similar test. Nonparametric analyses of variance for frequency data are also available, although not often used, perhaps because researchers are unfamiliar with the method. In this regard, some useful sources are D'Agostino (1971), Lunney (1970), Sutcliffe (1957), and Wilson (1956).

(b) The "street theater" strategy. Examples in which the experimenter stages an incident open to all passersby were the Bochner (1971a) dog-walking study, and the Bryan and Test (1967) Salvation Army donation experiment. In these studies, the dependent variable is the number of subjects in each condition who emit the focal response. However, for these comparisons to have any meaning, three important assumptions must be satisfied: (1) the population N of potential subjects in each condition must be identical (or known, so that appropriate ratios of responders to nonresponders can be calculated); (2) the demographic make up of the population must remain constant over the term of the experiment; and (3) the duration of each data-collecting sequence must be controlled. For example, in the Bochner (1971a) dog-walking study the population density in the four sectors of the park was approximately equal, the same sorts of people frequented each of the four different sectors, and each excursion lasted exactly ten minutes. Similarly, although the people streaming past the Bryan and Test (1967) Salvation Army kettles were an extremely heterogeneous lot, the authors assumed that the number of passersby, and the range and frequency of person characteristics in each experimental condition, would be comparable.

In general, the strategy of "accosting" specific subjects, i.e., preselecting a passerby, motorist, shop, or household; randomly allocating this subject to an experimental condition; and then measuring *his* response, gives the investigator more control than the method of staging a "public" incident, and then counting the nature and frequency of the responses made by those witnessing the event. But, as was noted in connection with the Piliavin subway studies (Piliavin et al., 1969), investigator ingenuity can overcome the problem of experimental control even under conditions when subjects are not preselected.

Identifying the principles of unobtrusive design is one thing; putting them into practice is another. The method that takes up six lines in a research report may be the product of weeks of brainstorming, pilot testing, and tinkering "to make it work." To aid the process of selecting, adapting, or inventing an unobtrusive procedure to serve a particular research purpose, several further techniques not yet referred to will now be described. This review will emphasize specific methods and topics, rather than individual studies or types of research designs. The majority of the experiments from which these examples were derived have only a tenuous cross-cultural component, or are strictly monocultural in their coverage. Nevertheless, their procedures hold the promise of being applicable to more than one cultural setting, i.e., of being potentially capable of making comparisons along etic dimensions.

Petition Signing and Related Techniques

A number of studies have been built around the soliciting of signatures for a petition (Bryant, 1975; Suedfeld, Bochner, & Matas, 1971). This context permits the manipulation of independent variables such as the appearance, cultural affiliation, and reference group of the petitioner; and the content and orientation of the petition—whether it is pro, anti, or neutral toward literally an infinite number of social concerns. The dependent variables can be the frequency of signatures obtained in each experimental condition, the nature of the refusals (polite, reasoned, or evasive) or any other aspect of the encounter deemed relevant.

Techniques conceptually related to the petition signing procedure are handing out leaflets (Darley & Cooper, 1972), and begging for money or favors (Emswiller, Deaux, & Willits, 1971). Variations possible are the source of the leaflet and its contents, and the source of the request, the nature of the favor, and its "size." There are no obvious difficulties regarding the face validity of the various dependent variables, and all of the measures can be objectively quantified. Finally, all of the methods can be widely generalized to different topics, subject populations, theoretical considerations, and cultural or subcultural settings.

Another related method moves the experimental situation into people's homes. In one study, door-to-door salesmen-experimenters delivered the experimental treatment within the natural context of the family setting (e.g., Leventhal, Younts, & Lund, 1972). Katz, Cohen, and Glass (1975) used the telephone to manipulate assertiveness and race, and measured racial attitudes, under the guise of conducting consumer surveys and opinion polls. Cann, Sherman, and Elkes (1975) explored the "foot-in-the-door" technique (Freedman & Fraser, 1966) by telephoning subjects on the pretext of promoting traffic safety. In another study, the dependent variable measure was the response to a petition administered on the doorstep of a residence. The petition was related to the subject matter of a persuasive communication that had earlier been delivered under the guise of canvassing either for or against American involvement in Indochina (Nesbitt, 1972).

Eye Contact

Several studies have used the stare—a steady direct gaze—to manipulate, threat, or create interpersonal tension. For example, Ellsworth et al. (1972) stared at pedestrians waiting at an intersection, and found that stared-at subjects crossed the street at a faster pace than nonstared-at controls. This study may be the first recorded instance of the jelly bean method of randomly assigning subjects to experimental conditions. Each experimenter had a supply of sixteen jelly beans, corresponding to the number of subjects he was to run. Eight jelly beans were of one particular color, signifying the stare condition, whereas the other eight beans were of a different color, and signified the no-stare condition. When a potential subject arrived at the crosswalk, E would pull out a jelly bean, note its color, eat it, and then administer the appropriate experimental treatment.

Ellsworth et al. also stared at motorists pulled up at a red light. The stare was variously delivered by a motorcyclist adjacent to the subject's car, or by a pedestrian standing at the curb. Both manipulations had the predicted effect: subjects who were stared at drove across the intersection faster than subjects in the no-stare condition. However, the stare does not always serve as a stimulus to flight. Snyder, Grether, and Keller (1974) conducted a field experiment in which hitchhikers soliciting a ride either did or did not stare at oncoming cars. More rides were offered in the stare than in the no-stare condition, suggesting that the general context in which a stare is embedded determines whether it will elicit avoidance or approach behavior. This hypothesis has been supported by recent research. Thus, an unobtrusive study by Ellsworth and Langer (1976) found that flight is not elicited when the context suggests a clear explanation for the stare.

The stare manipulation may open the door for an unobtrusive study of one aspect of the "psychic unity of mankind" (Boas, 1911; Kluckhohn, 1949, p. 50), or the universalists' search for species-wide generalizations about human behavior. Universalistic assumptions about the nature of man are very difficult to test empirically; thus any new method should be welcomed by workers espousing such an approach. A cross-cultural unobtrusive study of the stare-flight relationship would be able to test for panhuman regularities in this domain, and has the further advantage that the interpretation could include a cross-species extension, since the gaze-threat relationship has also been studied in primates (Altmann, 1967; Schaller, 1963; Van Hooff, 1967; Van Lawick-Goodall, 1968).

Personal Space

A related phenomenon is the flight behavior of individuals whose personal space has been violated (Sommer, 1969). Felipe and Sommer (1966) have provided an excellent paradigm for studying this phenomenon unobtrusively. Confederates systematically sit or stand "too close" to various victims under a variety of experimental conditions. The dependent variable is the latency of the subject's withdrawal from the field. There would seem to be unlimited opportunities to extend this paradigm to any number of cultural variations and settings, with the certainty of making a valuable contribution not only to the theory of personal space, but also to those professions where phenomenal space is an important design consideration.

The Experience of Living in Cities

The growing concern about cities has generated a number of unobtrusive studies specifically aimed at exploring and quantifying the quality of urban life (Forbes & Gromoll, 1971; Korte & Kerr, 1975; Lesk & Zippel, 1975; Merrens, 1973; Milgram, 1970; Zimbardo, 1969). For instance, the urban incivility hypothesis has been tested by comparing city and country responses to contrived situations such as being asked for assistance by a wrong-number phone caller, store clerks being overpaid, a stranger at the door wishing to use the telephone, finding a "lost" post card, requesting signatures, being asked for a dime, changing a quarter, seeking directions, and finding an "abandoned" car. Recently, Milgram's (1970) "input over-load" explanation of urban inconsiderateness was the topic of an unob-trusive field experiment conducted in Holland (Korte, Ypma, & Toppen, 1975), in which the situations were a request for an interview, a person dropping a key "without realizing it," and an apparently lost person scru-tinizing a map, under either high or low environmental input conditions.

Cities throughout the world share many similarities, but intuitively there appear to be vast cross-cultural differences in the way that human beings respond to the urban environment. The unobtrusive method seems particularly suited for conducting pure, applied, comparative, and action research in this area of vital social concern.

The Social Power of a Uniform

Another unobtrusive method with apparent high cross-cultural compara-bility is the Bickman (1974) paradigm of a uniformed individual stopping people in the street. In the Bickman (1974) study, experimenters were dressed either as a guard, milkman, or in civilian clothes. Subjects were asked to pick up a paper bag lying in the street, give a dime to a stranger for an expired parking meter, or to move away from a bus stop because the sign read "No Standing." The dependent variable was the degree of compliance to these requests, and in accordance with expectation, the guard was more effective than either the milkman or the civilian. Since practically all cultures use the uniform as a device to signify and signal power, this method may provide a general pancultural framework for the study of conformity and compliance.

To date, probably the method with the largest claim to panculturality in conceptualization and application is the semantic differential (Osgood, 1971). The semantic differential has now been administered in some thirty different countries, using indigenously developed adjectives. Three domi-nant, orthogonal factors consistently appear across all the language and culture groups—evaluation, potency, and activity. The apparent cross-cul-tural invariance of these three factors means that they can serve as refer-ence points for comparing otherwise culture bound concepts. For example, the procedure for comparing the Malay and Danish conceptualizations of "self" is to plot the position of the two emic concepts on a three-dimensional semantic atlas. Although the notions of "self" may be quite different in the two cultures, they are made comparable by each being necessarily and sufficiently defined in terms of the universal dimensions of evaluation, potency, and activity.

The Osgood paradigm is not restricted to rating scales. It could serve as a model for the systematic cross-cultural exploration of behavioral stimuli. In the present section we have reviewed several phenomena, all of which are naturally present in many different cultures. Thus, for example, practically all people everywhere use the gaze in interpersonal communication, just as people everywhere apparently interpret the world in evaluative, potency, and activity terms. But just as different cultures may assign different values for each factor to phenomena defined as identical on other grounds, the antecedents and consequents of the stare may also differ across cultures. More generally, as Price-Williams (1974) has noted, just as an assertion has meaning only in a certain kind of context, a behavioral act (such as a gesture) also derives meaning from its context, made up largely of culture-specific rules. Nevertheless, universal behaviors like the stare could serve as a pivot for the integration of a further class of otherwise unconnected observations, provided the investigator also has a good theory for selecting those situations most likely to make a contribution.

Most of the search for behavior universals has, paradoxically, been in the cognitive domain. In addition to the work of Osgood, already referred to, probably the best known and most systematic contribution is that of Triandis and his colleagues (Triandis, 1977) in their exploration of subjective culture. Behavior, particularly when it occurs naturally, has been largely neglected by psychologists, probably because the methodology was lacking, although this never deterred the anthropologists. Recent developments in the unobtrusive method may overcome the logistical problem and perhaps stimulate some much needed *behavioral* research. A major breakthrough is likely to come when naturally occurring behavior universals (or part-universals) such as the stare are deliberately and systematically exploited for research and theory building.

Section Summary

Investigators were presented with a set of guidelines for selecting, adapting, or inventing unobtrusive procedures to serve their research needs. Then, some further techniques were described, chosen for their pancultural applicability. Finally, a paradigm was suggested for unobtrusive research on behavior universals.

Unobtrusive Research and Ethics:
Issues and Guidelines

The last decade has seen a self-conscious effort by the profession to develop, codify, and enforce ethical guidelines for the conduct of psychological research with human subjects (American Psychological Association, 1963, 1973; Kelman, 1967). The increasing recognition of the human rights of experimental subjects has not been confined to the United States, but is a worldwide phenomenon, or to be more accurate, is apparent in those parts of the world inhabited by a critical mass of experimental psychologists. For example, the Australian, Canadian, and British Psychological Societies (Australian Psychological Society, 1970; Sasson & Nelson, 1969; Summerfield, 1972) have all been engaged in drawing up ethical principles for their members, as has the International Committee of the American Psychological Association (Tapp, Kelman, Triandis, Wrightsman, & Coelho, 1974), and the International Association for Cross-Cultural Psychology (Tapp, 1972).

The kernel principle of ethical research with human subjects is that the experimenter should do nothing that will in any way lower the self-esteem of the subject. In the domain of cross-cultural research, one further ethical rule has been proposed: that the cultures or subcultures generating the data should benefit in some material, practical, or theoretical way (Tapp et al., 1974; Bochner et al., 1975). Thus subjects should emerge from a research experience not only unharmed but also enriched. The most general statement of the current position on ethics is an absolute prescription against exploiting human subjects. This means that experimenters can no longer appeal to some lofty scientific or humanitarian purpose to justify their actions. In practice, most of the research being conducted today does not conform to the ideals set out in official Codes of Conduct. However, the frequency of really "outrageous" experiments seems to be declining. Furthermore, the concept of "outrageous" appears to be shifting, so that experiments that once would have rated hardly a lifted eyebrow now generate a serious debate. The research example to be presented shortly illustrates this change in ethical perspective.

Respect for the subject and his culture is not incompatible with experimental rigor and control. The two requirements can be reconciled by exercising care and ingenuity in devising procedures that meet both ethical and methodological criteria. However, in the special case of the unobtrusive experiment, there is a particular ethical problem which appears insoluble, because it stems from an integral aspect of the method. Subjects in unobtrusive studies have by definition not given their informed consent to be included in a research project.

The problem has to be faced squarely and without equivocation. Unobtrusive research intrudes into a person's private life, without his consent or knowledge. The experiments interfere with the subject's everyday activities; record, dissect, and analyze his behavior and motives; and then disseminate this information to the world. Frequently, aspects of the published data directly or implicitly defame and derogate some actual group of human beings, too often readily identifiable. Finally, to add insult to injury, in almost all unobtrusive experiments subjects are neither thanked for their participation nor debriefed.

To date, no one has suggested a satisfactory solution to the ethical dilemma of nonreactive measurement. Getting a subject's permission to participate in a psychological experiment—the ethical imperative—is just not compatible with the requirements of unobtrusive research. In the circumstances, the best that an investigator can do is to tone down the noxious effects of his manipulations and procedures and trade off the human cost against the experiment's potential contribution to knowledge. It should be noted that many research workers are not comfortable with such a justification, and have for that reason eschewed using unobtrusive methods. On the other hand, it has been argued that the amount of intrusion and interference the typical unobtrusive study causes is so minimal and so infrequent that it is hardly worth making a fuss about. After all, in their daily lives people are constantly being bombarded by "intrusive" stimuli.

There is no consensus in the profession about the ethical status of unobtrusive research. However, judging by the relatively large number of unobtrusive studies being published, there must be a sizeable group of experimental psychologists who have no moral qualms about the nonreactive paradigm. The debate continues and is fuelled by the occasional appearance of studies like the research example that will now be presented. The study by West, Gunn, and Chernicky (1975) does not have a cross-cultural perspective. It is included here because the experiment had the singular distinction of being defined empirically as "outrageous" in the sense that a rejoinder on ethical grounds was published cheek by jowl with it (Cook, 1975). Only those aspects of the procedure that are relevant to the ethics issue will be summarized.

The study simulated the Watergate incident. Subjects were invited by the experimenter to E's house or to a restaurant to discuss "a project you might be interested in." The experimenter was known to the subjects as a local private investigator. At the meeting the experimenter was accompanied by a confederate. A briefcase was produced containing elaborate plans for the burglary of a local advertising firm. Ss were told that a four-person team would be necessary to carry out the plan. This team would consist of: (a) the experimenter who would monitor police calls from an office in the building; (b) the confederate, who would serve as an outside lookout; (c) a lock-and-safe expert (not present in the experimental situation); and (d) the subject who was to be the inside lookout and make microfilms of the advertising agency records. The crime was presented to the subjects in elaborate detail, including aerial photographs of the building and the surrounding area, lists of police cars and their routes and times, and blueprints of the advertising office. The total effect was to convince subjects that this was a well-planned, professional job with only a minimal chance of being caught.

Subjects were randomly assigned to one of four experimental conditions. In the first two conditions, the subjects were told that the burglary was to be committed for a government agency to microfilm an illegal set of accounting records maintained by the advertising firm to defraud the U.S. Government out of millions of tax dollars. In the first condition, Ss were promised immunity from prosecution if caught. In the second condition, Ss were warned that there would be no immunity from prosecution if they were apprehended. In the third condition, Ss were told that the burglary was being committed on behalf of a competing local advertising firm, and that they would be paid $2,000 for their participation in the crime. In the fourth condition, Ss were told that the crime was being committed merely to determine whether the burglary plans would work, and that actually nothing would be stolen from the office. The dependent variable was the subject's agreement or refusal to participate in the burglary. The highest degree of compliance occurred in the government sponsorship-immunity condition, a result that parallels the alleged inducements offered to the real Watergate burglars.

The West et al. (1975) procedure was described in detail because it is a particularly good illustration of the increasingly frowned-on practice of manipulating a subject into violating his or the community's moral code. The temptation paradigm has fallen into disrepute because it appears that even after extensive postexperimental debriefing, subjects may nevertheless retain feelings of guilt, shame, and anxiety about the ease with which they were seduced into committing evil acts (Ross, Lepper, & Hubbard, 1975; Walster, Berscheid, Abrahams, & Aronson, 1967). Such self-blame effects are more probable in unobtrusive field studies than in laboratory experiments. In a laboratory setting, subjects more or less consciously cede control over events to the experimenter, and can therefore also more readily shift the blame for their "reprehensible" behavior to the investigator. However, this avenue of dissonance reduction is not available to the subject who, at the time when he succumbed to the blandishments of his tempter, was under the impression that he was participating in a real-life encounter.

Finally, experiments such as the West et al. (1975) study tend to attract wide publicity. This is undesirable for several reasons. The public, largely uninformed about the nature and complexity of psychological research, will tend to ignore whatever positive contributions such studies do make and concentrate on their odious aspects. There is a real danger that the opprobrium generated by a few dubious unobtrusive field studies may cumulatively generalize to the parent discipline and lower both the standing and the effectiveness of the profession. As Kelman (1967) noted, in the universities psychologists have the reputation of being liars, at least in their professional capacity, because of the prevalence of the deception paradigm in research with human beings. There is a danger that, with the increasing use of deception in natural settings, the world beyond the cloisters will start taking a dim view of psychological research. The muted tones of polite criticism emanating from colleagues and students may soon be joined by the strident voice of the popular press.

If unobtrusive experiments are overdone, both in terms of their frequency and their notoriety, it may become increasingly more difficult to recruit subjects who are genuinely naive as to their experimental role. Based on present trends, it is not too fanciful to foresee the day when the first thought entering the mind of a person encountering something unusual in a natural setting will be the question, "Is it an experiment?" Thus ethically marginal field research is similar to pollution. It is not just morally wrong; it is self-defeating. If the literature should become fouled with doubtful experiments, it will certainly become more difficult to mount successful nonreactive studies in the future.

Because of the methodological focus of this chapter, the preceding discussion on ethics has been primarily concerned with the relationship between ethically dubious research and the technical problem of collecting genuinely nonreactive data. However, there are other issues of concern. As Warwick (1975) has noted, in the case of research with human subjects, at least four parties are involved: the subject, the researcher, the larger society, and the researcher's profession. This section concludes with a summary of the ethical implications of the unobtrusive method for each of these four groups.

From the particular perspective of the unobtrusive method, *subjects* categorically do not have the opportunity to give their informed consent, nor do they have the freedom to decline participation. Other subject problems generally, although not inherently, associated with the method are a concomitant and frequent failure to debrief subjects. Thus subjects in unobtrusive experiments are seldom given the reason for the deception or told about the findings and implications of the research. Occasionally, as in Humphreys' (1975) unobtrusive study of male homosexual activity in public restrooms, the confidentiality of the subjects may be violated. It is the responsibility of the investigator to employ a design that is consistent with his research purpose and also respects the rights of the subjects serving in the study.

The effect on the *researcher* is to place him in the potential role of a sociological voyeur (Wiesenthal, 1974). Whether this label connotes opprobrium must be left up to the individual investigator. The effect on the *larger society* may be to incense the public about having its privacy insidiously invaded by behavioral science researchers. Not just individuals, but institutions, like the Salvation Army or the Butcher's Guild, may object to serving as involuntary participants in research. Some specific undesirable consequences have also been predicted to follow from the greater incidence of unobtrusive field studies (e.g., Wiesenthal, 1974). For example, if the public at large were to become as familiar with the literature as is the reader of this chapter, how would they respond to a genuine wrong-number call, broken down car, or a person collapsed on the floor with blood oozing from his mouth? Is the genuine victim more likely to be ignored because the passerby assumes the incident to be "just another experiment"? Probably not, but the possibility cannot be discounted.

Finally, it is sometimes said that the effect of the unobtrusive method on the *profession* has been to contaminate the environment for other branches of behavioral science, thus making it more difficult to carry out any kind of social research (Warwick, 1975). To that charge, a plea of "not guilty" can be entered. The general suspicion against psychology is due to the sheer overexposure of the public to all types of research, including surveys, consumer and market probes, opinion polls, and government and institutional information gathering. The backlash has been exacerbated by the deception paradigm of laboratory research, the arrogance and condescension of some anthropologists toward their subjects, and the illegal intrusion by intelligence-gathering and similar bodies into the private lives of law-abiding citizens. The unobtrusive method has played a minute part in this plethora of noxious influences.

The real danger is that the criticisms of unobtrusive research on doctrinaire grounds will deter investigators from using the method even in situations where it is particularly indicated, and where the ethical costs are minimal. In this regard, the following observation by Elms (1975) may be helpful in coming to a sensible decision:

> Social psychologists are obligated to be attentive to ethical issues, especially because their research is largely directed toward other humans. But their attentiveness should be of the kind that allows them to work through an ethical issue, to arrive at a satisfactory resolution in their own eyes and as much as possible in the eyes of other informed observers, and then to go ahead with ethically sound *and* meaningful research. (p. 974)

Section Summary

The unobtrusive method presents a peculiar ethical dilemma: subjects should have the right to give or withhold their informed consent to serve in a psychological experiment. However, this ethical imperative is incompatible with the very essence of the unobtrusive method.

Two general ethical principles of cross-cultural research with human participants are (a) that subjects' self-esteem should not be lowered, and (b) that participation in the experiment should enrich the subjects in some way. An unobtrusive study violating both these principles was described. The experiment used the temptation paradigm, where subjects are manipulated into violating their moral code. Subjects who succumb to such a manipulation are almost certain to experience guilt and lowered self-esteem, extensive debriefing notwithstanding.

Maintaining a high standard of propriety in unobtrusive research can be justified on both intrinsic and pragmatic grounds. Thus, ethically impeccable procedures are usually also likely to be methodologically sound, to contribute to the experimenter's self-esteem, to enhance the image of the profession, and to reduce the risk of fouling the nest through public exposure.

The section closed with a recapitulation of the ethical implications of the unobtrusive method on the subject, the researcher, society, and the behavioral sciences.

Conclusion

The characteristics, uses, special features, strengths, and limitations of the unobtrusive method were described, and illustrated with representative sets of research examples. Can any conclusions be drawn about the special contribution of unobtrusive methods in cross-cultural research? The answer to this question must be speculative, since there is relatively little substantive precedent to go on. However, extrapolating from the trends that were identified in the preceding discussion, probably the major contribution of the unobtrusive method will be to foster the development of a cross-cultural psychology of social behavior. Currently, the predominant orientation in cross-cultural research is in the area of cognition and perception, with some spillover into attitudes (Cole, 1975; Cole, Gay, Glick, & Sharp, 1971; Dasen, 1972; Osgood, 1971; Triandis, 1977; Witkin & Berry, 1975).

The theoretical framework of the cognition-perception-attitude areas is essentially personalistic, or at best interpersonalistic. With a few exceptions (Cole, 1975), most workers in these fields adopt what Mann (1969) called a "within-skin" model of man, with some concessions made to "between-skin" phenomena. But implied in a cross-cultural psychology of social behavior is a much greater emphasis on situational determinants of conduct. Thus a further contribution of the unobtrusive method will be to speed up the development of a cross-cultural psychology of behavior settings, paralleling the work of Barker and his colleagues (Barker, 1968) in the United States.

An orientation towards a situational-behavior setting draws attention to environmental determinants of behavior, in particular the role of the *built* environment in shaping and giving meaning to interpersonal encounters. The unobtrusive method will be able to make a major contribution toward the development of cross-cultural environmental psychology. Probably the greatest impact will occur in the general area of architecture and planning, already a growing specialization (Proshansky, Ittelson, & Rivlin, 1970).

As Gadlin and Ingle (1975) and others have noted, the current emphasis in psychology is to select for research those phenomena suited to existing methods. The unobtrusive approach reverses this trend by shaping and developing experimental procedures to fit phenomena. That is why the unobtrusive method will continue to be used in studies that address real-life problems. In particular, the method will gain wider currency in cross-cultural action research and evaluation, both in regard to implementing change, and in assessing the effectiveness of the interventions.

The unobtrusive method will be increasingly used as part of a multimethod, multicultural approach to corroborating both cross- and monocultural laboratory and attitude-survey findings. It is also likely that there will occur a reassessment of the value of replications, in which case research workers in different societies will increasingly replicate and extend each other's studies. The relative ease with which an unobtrusive study can be replicated in other cultural settings should produce a substantial literature of cross-cultural replications.

Finally, the increasing use of the unobtrusive method in cross-cultural research will have an impact on some of the major theoretical issues in the area. In particular, the problems of cross-cultural equivalence, comparability, and the translation of items and procedures will be affected. Just because unobtrusive procedures and measurements are couched in behavioral terms does not mean that the equivalence or translation problem is not operative. As investigators begin to grapple with these theoretical issues in the context of behavioral rather than verbal "items," the whole area should benefit from being viewed through such a new perspective.

The major unresolved issue is the ethical dilemma posed by the unobtrusive paradigm. In their own self-interest, workers using nonreactive procedures should be extremely careful not to overstep the bounds of propriety, but should explore only topics and issues that are nontrivial and that can provide experimental results that will make some positive contribution to society.

Note

1. This chapter was written while the author was a Visiting Researcher at the Culture Learning Institute of the East-West Center. The Center's support is gratefully acknowledged. I would also like to express my gratitude to Ms. Joy Y. Ichiyama for the secretarial assistance she rendered to this project.

References

ABELSON, R. P., ARONSON, E., McGUIRE, W. J., NEWCOMB, T. M., ROSENBERG, M. J., & TANNENBAUM, P. H. *Theories of cognitive consistency: a sourcebook.* Chicago: Rand McNally, 1968.

AIELLO, J. R., & JONES, S. E. Field study of the proxemic behavior of young school children in three subcultural groups. *Journal of Personality and Social Psychology,* 1971, *19,* 351–56.

ALTMANN, S. A. The structure of primate communication. In S. A. Altmann (Ed.), *Social communication among primates.* Chicago: University of Chicago Press, 1967.

AMERICAN PSYCHOLOGICAL ASSOCIATION. *Ethical standards for psychologists.* Washington, D. C.: American Psychological Association, 1963.

————. *Ethical principles in the conduct of research with human participants.* Washington, D. C.: American Psychological Association, 1973.

ARGYRIS, C. Some unintended consequences of rigorous research. *Psychological Bulletin,* 1968, *70,* 185–97.

ARONSON, E., & CARLSMITH, J. M. Experimentation in social psychology. In G. Lindzey & E. Aronson (Eds.), *The handbook of social psychology,* Vol. 2. Reading, Mass.: Addison-Wesley, 1968.

AUSTRALIAN PSYCHOLOGICAL SOCIETY. Code of professional conduct and advice to members, 1970. *Australian Psychologist,* 1970, *5,* 75–95.

BARBER, T. X., & SILVER, M. J. Fact, fiction, and the experimenter bias effect. *Psychological Bulletin Monograph Supplement,* 1968a, *70,* 1–29.

————. Pitfalls in data analysis and interpretation: a reply to Rosenthal. *Psychological Bulletin Monograph Supplement,* 1968b, *70,* 48–62.

BARKER, R. C. *Ecological psychology: concepts and methods for studying the environment of human behavior.* Stanford, Calif.: Stanford University Press, 1968.

BASKETT, G. D., PEET, J. G., BRADFORD, D., & MULAIK, S. A. An examination of the lost-letter technique. *Journal of Applied Social Psychology,* 1973, *3,* 165–73.

BAXTER, J. C. Interpersonal spacing in natural settings. *Sociometry,* 1970, *33,* 444–56.

BERKOWITZ, W. R. Spectator responses at public war demonstrations. *Journal of Personality and Social Psychology,* 1970, *14,* 305–11.

————. A cross-national comparison of some social patterns of urban pedestrians. *Journal of Cross-Cultural Psychology,* 1971, *2,* 129–44.

BERRY, J. On cross-cultural comparability. *International Journal of Psychology*, 1969, 4, 119–28.

BICKMAN, L. The social power of a uniform. *Journal of Applied Social Psychology*, 1974, 4, 47–61.

BICKMAN, L., TEGER, A., GABRIELE, T., McLAUGHLIN, C., BERGER, M., & SUNADAY, E. Dormitory density and helping behavior. *Environment and Behavior*, 1973, 5, 465–90.

BOAS, F. *The mind of primitive man*. 1911. (Reprinted, New York: Free Press, 1965.)

BOCHNER, S. The use of unobtrusive measures in cross-cultural attitudes research. In R. M. Berndt (Ed.), *A question of choice: an Australian Aboriginal dilemma*. Nedlands, W. A.: University of Western Australia Press, 1971a.

———. Inhibition of horn-sounding as a function of frustrator's status and sex: an Australian replication and extension of Doob and Gross (1968). *Australian Psychologist*, 1971b, 6, 194–99.

———. An unobtrusive approach to the study of housing discrimination against Aborigines. *Australian Journal of Psychology*, 1972, 24, 335–37.

———. The Fifi effect. In preparation.

BOCHNER, S., BRISLIN, R. W., & LONNER, W. J. Introduction. In R. W. Brislin, S. Bochner, & W. J. Lonner (Eds.), *Cross-cultural perspectives on learning*. New York: Wiley/Halsted, 1975.

BOCHNER, S., BUKER, E. A., & McLEOD, B. M. Communication patterns in an international student dormitory: a modification of the "small world" method. *Journal of Applied Social Psychology*, 1976, 6, 275–90.

BOCHNER, S., & CAIRNS, L. G. An unobtrusive measure of helping behaviour toward Aborigines. In G. E. Kearney & D. W. McElwain (Eds.), *Aboriginal cognition: retrospect and prospect*. Canberra: Australian Institute of Aboriginal Studies, 1976.

BRISLIN, R. W. Interaction among members of nine ethnic groups and belief-similarity hypothesis. *Journal of Social Psychology*, 1971, 85, 171–79.

———. Seating as a measure of behavior: you are where you sit. In R. W. Brislin (Ed.), *Topics in culture learning*. Honolulu, Hawaii: East-West Center, 1974, 2, 103–18.

BRYAN, J. H., & TEST, M. A. Models and helping: naturalistic studies in aiding behavior. *Journal of Personality and Social Psychology*, 1967, 6, 400–07.

BRYANT, N. J. Petitioning: dress congruence versus belief congruence. *Journal of Applied Social Psychology*, 1975, 5, 144–49.

BYRNE, D. Attitudes and attraction. In L. Berkowitz (Ed.), *Advances in experimental social psychology*, Vol. 4. New York: Academic Press, 1969.

CAIRNS, L. G., & BOCHNER, S. Measuring sympathy toward handicapped children with the "lost-letter" technique. *Australian Journal of Psychology*, 1974, 26, 89–91.

CALDER, B. J., & ROSS, M. *Attitudes and behavior*. Morristown, N.J.: General Learning Press, 1973.

CAMPBELL, D. T. Factors relevant to the validity of experiments in social settings. *Psychological Bulletin*, 1957, 54, 297–312.

———. Social attitudes and other acquired behavioral dispositions. In S. Koch (Ed.), *Psychology: a study of a science*, Vol. 6. New York: McGraw-Hill, 1963.

————. Prospective: artifact and control. In R. Rosenthal & R. L. Rosnow (Eds.), *Artifact in behavioral research.* New York: Academic Press, 1969a.

————. Reforms as experiments. *American Psychologist,* 1969b, *24,* 409–28.

CAMPBELL, D. T., & FISKE, D. W. Convergent and discriminant validation by the multitrait-multimethod matrix. *Psychological Bulletin,* 1959, *56,* 81–105.

CAMPBELL, D. T., KRUSKAL, W. H., & WALLACE, W. P. Seating aggregation as an index of attitude. *Sociometry,* 1966, *29,* 1–15.

CAMPBELL, D. T., & LEVINE, R. A. Field manual anthropology. In R. Naroll & R. Cohen (Eds.), *A handbook of method in cultural anthropology.* New York: Natural History Press, 1970.

CAMPBELL, D. T., & NAROLL, R. The mutual methodological relevance of anthropology and psychology. In F. L. K. Hsu (Ed.), *Psychological anthropology.* Cambridge, Mass.: Schenkman, 1972.

CANN, A., SHERMAN, S. J., & ELKES, R. Effects of initial request size and timing of a second request on compliance: the foot in the door and the door in the face. *Journal of Personality and Social Psychology,* 1975, *32,* 774–82.

COHEN, A. R. *Attitude change and social influence.* New York: Basic Books, 1964.

COLE, M. An ethnographic psychology of cognition. In R. W. Brislin, S. Bochner, & W. J. Lonner (Eds.), *Cross-cultural perspectives on learning.* New York: Wiley/Halsted, 1975.

COLE, M., GAY, J., GLICK, J., & SHARP, D. *The cultural context of learning and thinking.* New York: Basic Books, 1971.

COOK, S. W. A comment on the ethical issues involved in West, Gunn, and Chernicky's "Ubiquitous Watergate: an attributional analysis." *Journal of Personality and Social Psychology,* 1975, *32,* 66–68.

CROWNE, D. P., & MARLOWE, D. *The approval motive.* New York: Wiley, 1964.

D'AGOSTINO, R. B. A second look at analysis of variance on dichotomous data. *Journal of Educational Measurement,* 1971, *8,* 327–33.

DARLEY, J. M., & COOPER, J. The "clean for Gene" phenomenon: the effect of students' appearance on political campaigning. *Journal of Applied Social Psychology,* 1972, *2,* 24–33.

DARLEY, J. M., & LATANE, B. Bystander intervention in emergencies: diffusion of responsibility. *Journal of Personality and Social Psychology,* 1968, *8,* 377–83.

DASEN, P. R. Cross-cultural Piagetian research: a summary. *Journal of Cross-Cultural Psychology,* 1972, *3,* 23–39.

DEAUX, K. Honking at the intersection: a replication and extension. *Journal of Social Psychology,* 1971, *84,* 159–60.

————. Anonymous altruism: extending the lost letter technique. *Journal of Social Psychology,* 1974, *92,* 61–66.

DILLEHAY, R. C. On the irrelevance of the classical negative evidence concerning the effect of attitudes on behavior. *American Psychologist,* 1973, *28,* 887–91.

DOOB, A. N., & GROSS, A. E. Status of frustrator as an inhibitor of horn-honking responses. *Journal of Social Psychology,* 1968, *76,* 213–18.

DUNCAN, S. Nonverbal communication. *Psychological Bulletin,* 1969, *72,* 118–37.

DUTTON, D. G. Reactions of restaurateurs to blacks and whites violating restaurant dress requirements. *Canadian Journal of Behavioural Science,* 1971, *3,* 298–302.

————. Reverse discrimination: the relationship of amount of perceived discrimination toward a minority group on the behaviour of majority group members. *Canadian Journal of Behavioural Science*, 1973, 5, 34–45.

EDWARDS, A. L. The relationship between the judged desirability of a trait and the probability that the trait will be endorsed. *Journal of Applied Psychology*, 1953, 37, 90–93.

————. *The social desirability variable in personality assessment and research.* New York: Dryden Press, 1957.

EKMAN, P., & FRIESEN, W. V. Hand movements. *The Journal of Communication*, 1972, 22, 353–74.

————. Detecting deception from the body or face. *Journal of Personality and Social Psychology*, 1974, 29, 288–98.

EKMAN, P., FRIESEN, W. V., & ELLSWORTH, P. *Emotion in the human face: guidelines for research and an integration of findings.* New York: Pergamon Press, 1972.

ELLSWORTH, P. C., CARLSMITH, J. M., & HENSON, A. The stare as a stimulus to flight in human subjects: a series of field experiments. *Journal of Personality and Social Psychology*, 1972, 21, 302–11.

ELLSWORTH, P. C., & LANGER, E. J. Staring and approach: an interpretation of the stare as a nonspecific activator. *Journal of Personality and Social Psychology*, 1976, 33, 117–22.

ELMS, A. C. The crisis of confidence in social psychology. *American Psychologist*, 1975, 30, 967–76.

EMSWILLER, T., DEAUX, K., & WILLITS, J. E. Similarity, sex, and requests for small favors. *Journal of Applied Social Psychology*, 1971, 1, 284–91.

FELDMAN, R. E. Response to compatriot and foreigner who seek assistance. *Journal of Personality and Social Psychology*, 1968, 10, 202–14.

FELIPE, N. J., & SOMMER, R. Invasions of personal space. *Social Problems*, 1966, 14, 206–14.

FESTINGER, L. *A theory of cognitive dissonance.* Evanston, Ill.: Row, Peterson, 1957.

FILLENBAUM, S. Prior deception and subsequent experimental performance: the "faithful" subject. *Journal of Personality and Social Psychology*, 1966, 4, 532–37.

FISHBEIN, M. Attitude and prediction of behavior. In M. Fishbein (Ed.), *Readings in attitude theory and measurement.* New York: Wiley, 1967.

FORBES, G. B., & GROMOLL, H. F. The lost letter technique as a measure of social variables: some exploratory findings. *Social Forces*, 1971, 50, 113–15.

FORRESTER, B. J., & KLAUS, R. A. The effect of race of the examiner on intelligence test scores of negro kindergarten children. *Peabody Papers in Human Development*, 1964, 2, 1–7.

FREEDMAN, J. L., & FRASER, S. Compliance without pressure: the foot-in-the-door technique. *Journal of Personality and Social Psychology*, 1966, 4, 195–202.

GADLIN, H., & INGLE, G. Through the one-way mirror: the limits of experimental self-reflection. *American Psychologist*, 1975, 30, 1003–09.

GAERTNER, S. L. Helping behavior and racial discrimination among liberals and conservatives. *Journal of Personality and Social Psychology*, 1973, 25, 335–41.

GAERTNER, S., & BICKMAN, L. Effects of race on the elicitation of helping behavior: the wrong number technique. *Journal of Personality and Social Psychology*, 1971, 20, 218–22.

GERGEN, K. J. Social psychology as history. *Journal of Personality and Social Psychology*, 1973, *26*, 309–20.

GOLDBERG, P. A. Expectancy, choice, and the other person. *Journal of Personality and Social Psychology*, 1965, *2*, 895–97.

GRAF, R. G., & RIDDELL, J. C. Helping behavior as a function of interpersonal perception. *Journal of Social Psychology*, 1972, *86*, 227–31.

GROSS, A. E. Generosity and legitimacy of a model as determinants of helpful behavior. *Representative Research in Social Psychology*, 1975, *6*, 45–50.

GUTHRIE, G. M. Problems of measurement in cross-cultural research. *Annals of the New York Academy of Sciences*, 1977, *285*, 131–140.

HALL, E. T. *The silent language.* Garden City, N.Y.: Doubleday, 1959.

————. *The hidden dimension.* Garden City, N.Y.: Doubleday, 1966.

HEIDER, F. *The psychology of interpersonal relations.* New York: Wiley, 1958.

HORNSTEIN, H. A. The influence of social models on helping. In J. Macaulay & L. Berkowitz (Eds.), *Altrusim and helping behavior.* New York: Academic Press, 1970.

HORNSTEIN, H. A., FISCH, E., & HOLMES, M. Influence of a model's feeling about his behavior and his relevance as a comparison other on observers' helping behavior. *Journal of Personality and Social Psychology*, 1968, *10*, 222–26.

HORNSTEIN, H. A., MASOR, H. N., SOLE, K., & HEILMAN, M. Effects of sentiment and completion of a helping act on observer helping: a case for socially mediated Zeigarnik effects. *Journal of Personality and Social Psychology*, 1971, *17*, 107–12.

HUANG, L. C., & HARRIS, M. B. Conformity in Chinese and Americans: a field experiment. *Journal of Cross-Cultural Psychology*, 1973, *4*, 427–34.

HUMPHREYS, L. *Tearoom trade: impersonal sex in public places. Enlarged edition with a retrospect on ethical issues.* Chicago: Aldine, 1975.

INNES, J. M. The semantics of asking a favour: an attempt to replicate cross-culturally. *International Journal of Psychology*, 1974, *9*, 57–61.

ISEN, A. M., & LEVIN, P. F. Effect of feeling good on helping: cookies and kindness. *Journal of Personality and Social Psychology*, 1972, *21*, 384–88.

JACOBY, J., & ARANOFF, D. Political polling and the lost-letter technique. *Journal of Social Psychology*, 1971, *83*, 209–12.

JONES, S. E. A comparative proxemics analysis of dyadic interaction in selected subcultures of New York City. *Journal of Social Psychology*, 1971, *84*, 35–44.

KATZ, I., COHEN, S., & GLASS, D. Some determinants of cross-racial helping behavior. *Journal of Personality and Social Psychology*, 1975, *32*, 964–70.

KELMAN, H. C. Human use of human subjects: the problem of deception in social psychological experiments. *Psychological Bulletin*, 1967, *67*, 1–11.

————. Attitudes are alive and well and gainfully employed in the sphere of action. *American Psychologist*, 1974, *29*, 310–24.

KIESLER, C. A., & MUNSON, P. A. Attitudes and opinions. In M. R. Rosenzweig & L. W. Porter (Eds.), *Annual Review of Psychology*, 1975, *26*, 415–56.

KLUCKHOHN, C. *Mirror for man.* New York: McGraw-Hill, 1949.

KNAPP, M. L. *Nonverbal communication in human interaction.* New York: Holt, Rinehart and Winston, 1972.

KNOX, R. E., & INKSTER, J. A. Postdecision dissonance at post time. *Journal of Personality and Social Psychology*, 1968, 8, 319–23.

KORTE, C., & KERR, N. Response to altruistic opportunities in urban and nonurban settings. *Journal of Social Psychology*, 1975, 95, 183–84.

KORTE, C., YPMA, I., & TOPPEN, A. Helpfulness in Dutch society as a function of urbanization and environmental input level. *Journal of Personality and Social Psychology*, 1975, 32, 996–1003.

KUBANY, E. S., GALLIMORE, R., & BUELL, J. The effects of extrinsic factors on achievement-oriented behavior: a non-Western case. *Journal of Cross-Cultural Psychology*, 1970, 1, 77–84.

KUTNER, B. WILKINS, C., & YARROW, P. R. Verbal attitudes and overt behavior involving racial prejudice. *Journal of Abnormal and Social Psychology*, 1952, 47, 649–52.

LANGER, E. J., & ABELSON, R. P. The semantics of asking a favor: how to succeed in getting help without really dying. *Journal of Personality and Social Psychology*, 1972, 24, 26–32.

LAPIERE, R. T. Attitudes versus actions. *Social Forces*, 1934, 13, 230–37.

LAZARUS, R. S., TOMITA, M., OPTON, E., JR., & KODAMA, M. A cross-cultural study of stress-reaction patterns in Japan. *Journal of Personality and Social Psychology*, 1966, 4, 622–33.

LESK, S., & ZIPPEL, B. Dependency, threat, and helping in a large city. *Journal of Social Psychology*, 1975, 95, 185–86.

LEVENTHAL, G. S., YOUNTS, C. M., & LUND, A. K. Tolerance for inequity in buyer-seller relationships. *Journal of Applied Social Psychology*, 1972, 2, 308–18.

LEWIN, K. *Resolving social conflicts.* New York: Harper, 1948.

LIPPITT, R. *Training in community relations.* New York: Harper, 1949.

LISKA, A. E. Emergent issues in the attitude-behavior consistency controversy. *American Sociological Review*, 1974, 39, 261–72.

LUNNEY, G. H. Using analysis of variance with a dichotomous dependent variable: an empirical study. *Journal of Educational Measurement*, 1970, 7, 263–69.

LYKKEN, D. T. Statistical significance in psychological research. *Psychological Bulletin*, 1968, 70, 151–59.

MANN, L. *Social psychology.* New York: Wiley, 1969.

MASLING, J. Role-related behavior of the subject and psychologist and its effects upon psychological data. In D. Levine (Ed.), *Nebraska symposium on motivation*, 1966, 14, 67–103.

MATHEWS, K. E., JR., & CANON, L. K. Environmental noise level as a determinant of helping behavior. *Journal of Personality and Social Psychology*, 1975, 32, 571–77.

McGREW, J. M. How "open" are multiple-dwelling units? *Journal of Social Psychology*, 1967, 72, 223–26.

McGUIRE, W. J. Some impending reorientations in social psychology: some thoughts provoked by Kenneth Ring. *Journal of Experimental Social Psychology*, 1967, 3, 124–39.

————. Theory-oriented research in natural settings: the best of both worlds for social psychology. In M. Sherif & C. W. Sherif (Eds.), *Interdisciplinary relationships in the social sciences.* Chicago: Aldine, 1969.

MEHRABIAN, A. D. *Nonverbal communication.* Chicago: Aldine, 1972.

MERRENS, M. R. Nonemergency helping behavior in various sized communities. *Journal of Social Psychology,* 1973, *90,* 327–28.

MERRITT, C. S., & FOWLER, R. G. The pecuniary honesty of the public at large. *Journal of Abnormal and Social Psychology,* 1948, *43,* 90–93.

MILGRAM, S. The lost-letter technique. *Psychology Today,* 1969a, *3,* 30–33, 66–68.

———. Comment on "A failure to validate the lost-letter technique." *Public Opinion Quarterly,* 1969b, *33,* 263–64.

———. The experience of living in cities. *Science,* 1970, *167,* 1461–68.

MILGRAM, S., MANN, L., & HARTER, S. The lost-letter technique: a tool of social research. *Public Opinion Quarterly,* 1965, *29,* 437–38.

MISCHEL, W. *Personality and assessment.* New York: Wiley, 1968.

MOSS, M. K., & PAGE, R. A. Reinforcement and helping behavior. *Journal of Applied Social Psychology,* 1972, *2,* 360–71.

NESBITT, P. D. The effectiveness of student canvassers. *Journal of Applied Social Psychology,* 1972, *2,* 252–58, 343–49.

NEWCOMB, T. M. The prediction of interpersonal attraction. *American Psychologist,* 1956, *11,* 575–86.

ORNE, M. T. On the social psychology of the psychological experiment: with particular reference to demand characteristics and their implications. *American Psychologist,* 1962, *17,* 776–83.

———. Hypnosis, motivation, and the ecological validity of the psychological experiment. In W. J. Arnold & M. M. Page (Eds.), *Nebraska symposium on motivation,* 1970, *18,* 187–285.

OSGOOD, C. E. Explorations in semantic space: a personal diary. *Journal of Social Issues,* 1971, *27,* 5–64.

OSGOOD, C. E., & TANNENBAUM, P. H. The principle of congruity in the prediction of attitude change. *Psychological Reivew,* 1955, *62,* 42–55.

PEDERSEN, D. M., SHINEDLING, M. M., & JOHNSON, D. L. Effects of sex of examiner and subject on children's quantitative test performance. *Journal of Personality and Social Psychology,* 1968, *10,* 251–54.

PILIAVIN, I. M., PILIAVIN, J. A., & RODIN, J. Costs, diffusion, and the stigmatized victim. *Journal of Personality and Social Psychology,* 1975, *32,* 429–38.

PILIAVIN, I. M., RODIN, J., & PILIAVIN, J. A. Good Samaritanism: an underground phenomenon? *Journal of Personality and Social Psychology,* 1969, *13,* 289–99.

PILIAVIN, J. A., & PILIAVIN, I. M. Effect of blood on reactions to a victim. *Journal of Personality and Social Psychology,* 1972, *23,* 353–61.

PRICE-WILLIAMS, D. Psychological experiment and anthropology: the problem of categories. *Ethos,* 1974, *2,* 95–114.

PROSHANSKY, H. M., ITTELSON, W. H., & RIVLIN, L. G. (Eds.), *Environmental psychology: man and his physical setting.* New York: Holt, Rinehart and Winston, 1970.

RING, K. Experimental social psychology: some sober questions about some frivolous values. *Journal of Experimental Social Psychology,* 1967, *3,* 113–23.

ROKEACH, M. Attitude change and behavioral change. *Public Opinion Quarterly,* 1966, *30,* 529–50.

————. The nature of attitudes. In D. L. Sills (Ed.), *International encyclopedia of the social sciences*, Vol. 1. New York: Macmillan, 1968.

ROSENBERG, M. J. When dissonance fails: on eliminating evaluation apprehension from attitude measurement. *Journal of Personality and Social Psychology*, 1965, *1*, 28–42.

————. The conditions and consequences of evaluation apprehension. In R. Rosenthal & R. L. Rosnow (Eds.), *Artifact in behavioral research*. New York: Academic Press, 1969.

ROSENBERG, M. J., & ABELSON, R. P. An analysis of cognitive balancing. In M. J. Rosenberg, C. I. Hovland, W. J. McGuire, R. P. Abelson, & J. W. Brehm (Eds.), *Attitude organization and change*. New Haven: Yale University Press, 1960.

ROSENTHAL, R. On the social psychology of the psychological experiment: the experimenter's hypothesis as an unintended determinant of experimental results. *American Scientist*, 1963, *51*, 268–83.

————. *Experimenter effects in behavioral research*. New York: Appleton-Century-Crofts, 1966.

ROSENTHAL, R., & FODE, K. L. The effect of experimenter bias on the performance of the albino rat. *Behavioral Science*, 1963, *8*, 183–89.

ROSENTHAL, R., & JACOBSON, L. *Pygmalion in the classroom: teacher expectation and pupils' intellectual development*. New York: Holt, Rinehart and Winston, 1968.

ROSS, A. S., BARAN, C., BEATTY, J. G., HUEBERT, J., HUMPHREY, E., KERR, M., & STANLEY, L. Status of frustrator as an inhibitor of horn honking response: an attempted replication. In preparation.

ROSS, L., LEPPER, M. R., & HUBBARD, M. Perseverance in self-perception and social perception: biased attributional processes in the debriefing paradigm. *Journal of Personality and Social Psychology*, 1975, *32*, 880–92.

SASSON, R., & NELSON, T. M. The human experimental subject in context. *Canadian Psychologist*, 1969, *10*, 409–37.

SCHALLER, G. B. *The mountain gorilla: ecology and behavior*. Chicago: University of Chicago Press, 1963.

SCHERER, S. E. Proxemic behavior of primary school children as a function of their socioeconomic class and subculture. *Journal of Personality and Social Psychology*, 1974, *29*, 800–05.

SECHREST, L., & FLORES, L. Homosexuality in the Philippines and the United States: the handwriting on the wall. *Journal of Social Psychology*, 1969, *79*, 3–12.

SECORD, P. F., & BACKMAN, C. W. *Social psychology*. New York: McGraw-Hill, 1964.

SELLS, S. B. Ecology and the science of psychology. In E. P. Willems & H. L. Raush (Eds.), *Naturalistic viewpoints in psychological research*. New York: Holt, Rinehart and Winston, 1969.

SELLTIZ, C. The use of survey methods in a citizens campaign against discrimination. *Human Organization*, 1955, *13*, 19–25.

SHOTLAND, R. L., BERGER, W. G., & FORSYTHE, R. A validation of the lost-letter technique. *Public Opinion Quarterly*, 1970, *34*, 278–81.

SIMON, W. E., & GILLEN, M. J. Return rates of "lost" letters as a function of whether the letter is stamped and amount of money apparently in the letter. *Psychological Reports*, 1971, *29*, 141–42.

SNOW, R. E. Review of R. Rosenthal & L. Jacobson, Pygmalion in the classroom. *Contemporary Psychology*, 1969, *14*, 197–99.

SNYDER, M., GRETHER, J., & KELLER, K. Staring and compliance: field experiment on hitchhiking. *Journal of Applied Social Psychology*, 1974, *4*, 165–70.

SOMMER, R. *Personal space: the behavioral basis of design.* Englewood Cliffs, N.J.: Prentice-Hall, 1969.

SOMMER, R., & BECKER, F. D. Territorial defense and the good neighbor. *Journal of Personality and Social Psychology*, 1969, *11*, 85–92.

SPECTOR, P., TORRES, A., LICHTENSTEIN, S., PRESTON, H. O., CLARK, J. B., & SILVERMAN, S. B. Communication media and motivation in the adoption of new practices: an experiment in rural Ecuador. *Human Organization*, 1971, *30*, 39–46.

SUEDFELD, P., BOCHNER, S., & MATAS, C. Petitioner's attire and petition signing by peace demonstrators: a field experiment. *Journal of Applied Social Psychology*, 1971, *1*, 278–83.

SUMMERFIELD, A. Ethical problems in research with individuals. *Bulletin of the British Psychological Society*, 1972, *25*, 127.

SUTCLIFFE, J. P. A general method of analysis of frequency data for multiple classification designs. *Psychological Bulletin*, 1957, *54*, 134–37.

TAPP, J. L. Symposium on ethical considerations in the conduct of cross-cultural research. In J. Dawson (Ed.), *First IACCP international conference abstracts.* Hong Kong: University of Hong Kong, 1972.

TAPP, J. L., KELMAN, H. C., TRIANDIS, H. C., WRIGHTSMAN, L. S., & COELHO, G. V. Continuing concerns in cross-cultural ethics: a report. *International Journal of Psychology*, 1974, *9*, 231–49.

TARTER, D. E. Heeding Skinner's call: toward the development of a social technology. *American Sociologist*, 1973, *8*, 153–58.

THAYER, S. Lend me your ears: racial and sexual factors in helping the deaf. *Journal of Personality and Social Psychology*, 1973, *28*, 8–11.

TRIANDIS, H. C. *Attitudes and attitude change.* New York: Wiley, 1971.

———. Culture training, cognitive complexity and interpersonal attitudes. In R. W. Brislin, S. Bochner, & W. J. Lonner (Eds.), *Cross-cultural perspectives on learning.* New York: Wiley/Halsted, 1975.

———. Subjective culture and interpersonal relations across cultures. *Annals of the New York Academy of Sciences*, 1977, *285*, 418–34.

TRIANDIS, H. C., VASSILIOU, V., & NASSIAKOU, M. Some cross-cultural studies of subjective culture. Technical Report No. 45, 1967, Group Effectiveness Research Laboratory, University of Illinois.

TURNER, C. W., LAYTON, J. F., & SIMONS, L. S. Naturalistic studies of aggressive behavior: aggressive stimuli, victim visibility, and horn honking. *Journal of Personality and Social Psychology*, 1975, *31*, 1098–1107.

UNDERWOOD, B. J. *Experimental psychology,* 2nd ed. New York: Appleton-Century-Crofts, 1966.

VAN HOOFF, J. A. R. A. M. The facial displays of the Catarrhine monkey and apes. In D. Morris (Ed.), *Primate ethology.* Chicago: Aldine, 1967.

VAN LAWICK-GOODALL, J. A preliminary report on expressive movements and communication in the Gombe Stream chimpanzees. In P. C. Jay (Ed.), *Primates: studies in adaptation and variability.* New York: Holt, Rinehart and Winston, 1968.

WALSTER, E., BERSCHEID, E., ABRAHAMS, D., & ARONSON, V. Effectiveness of debriefing following deception experiments. *Journal of Personality and Social Psychology*, 1967, *6*, 371–80.

WARWICK, D. P. Tearoom trade: means and ends in social research. In L. Humphreys (Ed.), *Tearoom trade: impersonal sex in public places. Enlarged edition with a retrospect on ethical issues.* Chicago: Aldine, 1975.

WEBB, E. J., CAMPBELL, D. T., SCHWARTZ, R. D., & SECHREST, L. *Unobtrusive measures: nonreactive research in the social sciences.* Chicago: Rand McNally, 1966.

WEBB, W. B. A "couple" of experiments. *American Psychologist*, 1968, *23*, 428–33.

WEBER, S. J., & COOK, T. D. Subject effects in laboratory research: an examination of subject roles, demand characteristics, and valid inference. *Psychological Bulletin*, 1972, *77*, 273–95.

WEGNER, D. M., & CRANO, W. D. Racial factors in helping behavior: an unobtrusive field experiment. *Journal of Personality and Social Psychology*, 1975, *32*, 901–05.

WEICK, K. E. Promise and limitations of laboratory experiments in the development of attitude change theory. In C. W. Sherif & M. Sherif (Eds.), *Attitude, ego-involvement, and change.* New York: Wiley, 1967.

WEITZ, S. Attitude, voice, and behavior: a repressed affect model of interracial interaction. *Journal of Personality and Social Psychology*, 1972, *24*, 14–21.

WERTHEIMER, M. Introduction. In M. Wertheimer (Ed.), *Confrontation.* Glenview, Ill.: Scott, Foresman, 1970.

WEST, S. G., GUNN, S. P., & CHERNICKY, P. Ubiquitous Watergate: an attributional analysis. *Journal of Personality and Social Psychology*, 1975, *32*, 55–65.

WEST, S. G., WHITNEY, G., & SCHNEDLER, R. Helping a motorist in distress: the effects of sex, race, and neighborhood. *Journal of Personality and Social Psychology*, 1975, *31*, 691–98.

WICKER, A. W. Attitudes versus actions: the relationship of verbal and behavioral responses to attitude objects. *Journal of Social Issues*, 1969a, *25* (4), 41–78.

———. A failure to validate the lost-letter technique. *Public Opinion Quarterly*, 1969b, *33*, 260–62.

———. An examination of the "other variables" explanation of attitude-behavior inconsistency. *Journal of Personality and Social Psychology*, 1971, *19*, 18–30.

WIESENTHAL, D. L. Reweaving deception's tangled web. *Canadian Psychologist*, 1974, *15*, 326–36.

WILSON, K. V. A distribution-free test of analysis of variance. *Psychological Bulletin*, 1956, *53*, 96–101.

WISPE, L. G., & FRESHLEY, H. B. Race, sex, and sympathetic helping behavior: the broken bag caper. *Journal of Personality and Social Psychology*, 1971, *17*, 59–65.

WITKIN, H. A., & BERRY, J. W. Psychological differentiation in cross-cultural perspective. *Journal of Cross-Cultural Psychology*, 1975, *6*, 4–87.

ZIMBARDO, P. G. The human choice: individuation, reason, and order versus deindividuation, impulse, and chaos. In W. J. Arnold & D. Levine (Eds.), *Nebraska Symposium on Motivation*, 1969, *17*, 237–307.

ZUNIGA, R. B. The experimenting society and radical social reform: the role of the social scientist in Chile's unidad popular experience. *American Psychologist*, 1975, *30*, 99–115.

10

Translation and Content Analysis
of Oral and Written Materials

Richard W. Brislin

Contents

Abstract

The use of content analysis and the analysis of folktales is explored, taking into account the emic and etic elements of written messages, stories, folktales, and myths. The chapter examines the problems of sampling, the coding, reliability, and validity of the procedures, and gives examples of the use of these methods in cross-cultural research. The utility of these procedures is critically evaluated. Other approaches such as ethnoscience methods are also reviewed. The last section of the chapter focuses on the problems of translation between languages, considers the importance of context and redundancy, and offers some procedures that can be used to avoid translation and yet obtain comparable data from more than one culture.

Introduction

Since the range of topics that could be included in a treatment of oral and written materials for cross-cultural research is vast, there had to be a careful selection of the subject matter to be reviewed in this chapter. An attempt has been made to review the *uses* of oral and written materials, with special attention to how researchers may benefit from the analysis of these. In addition, methodological issues that arise in the use of these materials are covered, especially translation between languages. It is argued that every cross-cultural researcher, at one time or another, will deal with oral and written materials in the form of instructions to subjects, response protocols obtained from subjects, content analysis of existing materials, ordering the seeming chaos of input from informants, and so forth. Hence some knowledge concerning the processing of such materials is mandatory. In addition (and similar to the treatment by Lonner in his chapter, in Volume 1 of this *Handbook*), it is assumed that every researcher will have to deal with translation problems many times while carrying out cross-cultural studies. Finally, there is a general approach to cross-cultural methodology, the emic-etic distinction that has demonstrated its usefulness in integrating the seemingly diverse approaches designed to solve specific problems. This distinction has also been used in other chapters for this *Handbook* (e.g., Davidson and Hilton in Volume 5; Lonner in Volume 1). Since it will be referred to many times throughout this chapter, it will be introduced at the very beginning. This treatment will be followed by a presentation of methods in content analysis, including two topic areas in cross-cultural studies where researchers can use the general approach of content analysis: folklore and ethnoscience studies. The final section will be a treatment of translation between languages, as well as a discussion of alternative techniques designed to minimize the need for translation.

The Emic-Etic Distinction in
Cross-Cultural Research

The emic-etic distinction is one of the central concepts in current thinking about cross-cultural research; it has received a good deal of attention recently (Berry, 1969; Triandis, 1972; Brislin, Lonner, & Thorndike, 1973; Price-Williams, 1974; Irwin, Klein, Engle, Yarbrough, & Nerlove, 1977). Berry also covers the distinction and its implications in the Introduction to this volume. Specific examples will be covered in this chapter. Briefly, the distinction relates to two goals of cross-cultural research. The first goal is to document valid principles that describe behavior in any one culture by using constructs that the people themselves conceive as meaningful and important; this is an emic analysis. The second goal of cross-cultural research is to make generalizations across cultures that take into account all human behavior. The goal, then, is theory building; that would be an etic analysis. The distinction may become clear after a few examples from cross-cultural investigations are discussed.

Some Research Examples of Emics and Etics

Comparing interpersonal relations among people in Greece and the United States, Triandis, Vassiliou, and Nassiakou (1968) discovered that the concepts *ingroup* and *outgroup* had different definitions. In the United States it is well known that an ingroup consists of family, close friends, and fellow countrymen (if a choice is demanded between other Americans and visitors to the United States). In Greece, however, the "ingroup" consists of family, close friends, and visitors, but excludes other Greeks; the latter are part of an individual's outgroup. The concepts of ingroup and outgroup are theoretically useful for explaining people's reactions to others, since perception of ingroup-outgroup membership affects much social behavior, such as the degree of social distance which a person allows others. These concepts have been very useful in another large scale investigation into ethnocentrism (Brewer, 1968, 1977; LeVine & Campbell, 1972). This general aspect of an ingroup-outgroup distinction affecting interpersonal relations has implications for theoretical generalizations across cultures, and can be termed *etic*. The exact content of the ingroup and outgroup, however, differs in the United States as compared to Greece, and centers on differing reactions to visitors and fellow countrymen. This is the *emic* aspect of the ingroup and outgroup concepts in the two countries. By documenting the emic-etic aspects of ingroup-outgroup relations, Triandis and his colleagues have both identified theoretically important concepts for cross-cultural generalizations and indicated how people in the United States and Greece define ingroup in their own terms and from their own point of view. Triandis's group has also shown that the range of the independent variable, ingroup versus outgroup membership, is expanded when comparisons are made between Greece and the United States. This is one of the possible contributions of cross-cultural studies.

In fact, an experimental assessment of the effects of ingroup versus outgroup membership has been done in an important, independent verification of the Triandis work. Feldman (1968) staged parallel, natural investigations of helping behavior in Paris, Athens, and Boston. Experimental accomplices (based on random assignment for different subjects) presented themselves as either a foreign visitor to the country or as a fellow countryman. The entire project is well worth careful study but only the Athens-Boston comparisons will be reviewed here. In Boston, helping behavior followed the American definition of ingroup versus outgroup, with fellow countrymen receiving more help than visitors. In Athens, helping behavior followed the Greek definition of ingroup versus outgroup, with visitors receiving far more help than fellow countrymen. Some of the results were striking. For instance, 93 percent of the Greeks did not respond to a simple request to help a fellow countryman mail a letter, compared to 32 percent (refusal to help a countryman) of the Bostonians.

As another example, a number of researchers have investigated the nature of the need for achievement (nAch) among Pacific Islanders, with special attention to Hawaiian-Americans (Gallimore, Weiss, & Finney, 1974; Howard, 1974). The major method was content analysis, which will be reviewed later in this chapter. Their results can be interpreted in terms of emics and etics, although the researchers themselves did not use this language. They found that the concept of need for achievement (as identified by McClelland, 1963) with its operational definition of realistic goal setting, work for the attainment of objectives, and so forth, was useful as an etic concept. Using the concept allowed for linkage and integration of their studies with those of other researchers in other parts of the world. Yet the exact interrelation of nAch with other cultural patterns and practices was different from that found in the United States (where most of the nAch research was done and hence the concept was established). Specifically, nAch interacted with the need for affiliation (nAff) such that the Hawaiian-Americans would exhibit nAch behaviors only if people whom they liked asked for it, or only if the nAch behaviors would lead to an end (e.g., money) which they could use to help satisfy their affiliative needs (e.g., giving the money away or throwing a big party). This relation between nAch and nAff is different from that found in the United States where the needs are posited to be independent, i.e., people engage in high nAch behavior whether they like their coworkers or not.

Thus the concept of nAch is a useful and important etic, but to understand fully its workings in various cultures the emics of it must be taken into account. As another example, Sinha (1968) demonstrated in a laboratory experiment carried out in India that given limited resources with which to work people accomplished the most (engaged in nAch behaviors) when they had a mental set to cooperate rather than to compete with others. This finding is of obvious relevance to people who might wish to apply the nAch concept in countries that do not have the natural resources or the opportunities for advancement into higher social classes as exist in the United States (the place where the concept was first researched).

Methods for the Emic-Etic Distinction

Research methods meant to yield both emic and etic findings will not be reviewed. One approach is that suggested by Przeworski and Teune (1966, 1970), who gave special attention to questionnaire research, which is an etic since people in all cultures are not equally familiar with questionnaires. To date, some psychologists have used the thinking behind the procedure as a guide in their work but have never followed the procedure step-by-step. Again, although the developers of the method did not use the terms *emic* and *etic*, their thinking fits well into this conceptualization and so their work will be presented here using the concepts (as was done by Brislin et al., 1973, pp. 27–28). Przeworski and Teune suggest that a core of items be written that are meaningful and hence answerable by members of each culture under study. Using the two examples already reviewed, a set of *core items* would be written that are expected to tap etic aspects of ingroup-outgroup relations, or etic aspects of the need for achievement. These items would be relevant to all cultures. In addition, *culture-specific items* would be written that are different for each culture. These items would be designed so as to tap the emic aspects of ingroup-outgroup relations or emic aspects of the need for achievement.

Interpretable statistical interrelations (such as statistically significant correlations), computed separately for individual responses in each culture, would be expected between culture-general and culture-specific items. No relationships would be expected between the emic items for the different cultures since they were designed specifically for each culture; therefore, they would be irrelevant to people who are not members of that culture. Figure 10-1 gives an overview of the procedure.

From the results of this procedure the investigator can formulate general theoretical statements (etics) that summarize the data. These statements can then be refined by the results of the culture-specific questions (emics). An additional benefit of the procedure is that practical information which is useful to members of each culture can be obtained since a set of questions would be compiled to measure the specific concerns of each culture. Answers to such questions should be of more use than answers to questions based on imposed or even derived etics.

A central question remains: how can researchers discover a set of culture-specific items so that the procedure can be profitably used? A number of general guidelines can be suggested. Ideally, a researcher will use many of these approaches since the strengths of one will often offset the weaknesses of another. This is the key to the multiple method approach recommended by Campbell (Campbell & Fiske, 1959; Campbell & Stanley, 1966). (1) Collaborative research with colleagues from other countries who have first-hand knowledge about various cultures is desirable. Extensive discussions between investigators from different countries should

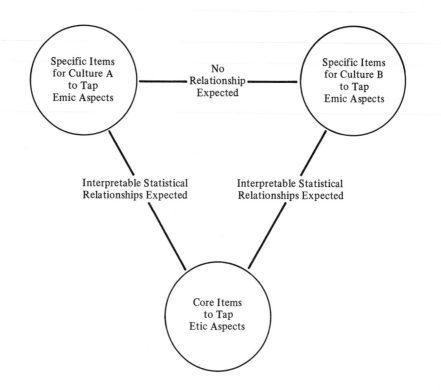

Figure 10-1. Overview of Method Involving Core Items (Etic) and Culture-Specific Items (Emics).

result in sets of core items and culture-specific items for many issues. (2) Wesley and Karr (1966) have suggested that researchers might seek out people who have lived in more than one of the cultures under investigation. After careful questioning, researchers should be able to obtain items from these "informants" that seem to be meaningful and appropriate for more than one of the cultures, as well as culture-specific items. (3) Sentence completion, free association, and similar techniques may be used to *elicit* appropriate items. People in various cultures could respond according to these techniques and the researcher would then look for common responses across cultures and specific responses that appear in the protocols of only one culture. (4) Another way, which is now a sine qua non in cross-cultural psychological research, is to study the anthropological literature on the cultures to be investigated, searching for relevant similarities and differences in people's behavior relevant to the issue under investigation. Help in finding information on a given topic might be provided by the developers of the Human Relations Area Files (HRAF;

explained by Whiting, 1968; Barry, this volume of the *Handbook*). The HRAF organization has created a massive, efficient reference/cross-reference system to guide readers through the many anthropological ethnographies on different cultures all over the world. (5) Finally, there is no substitute for first-hand contact with a culture other than the one in which the researcher grew up. Irvine (1968, p. 3) discussed the possibility as it relates to psychologists:

> To collect valid data the psychologist needs adequate and sympathetic training in understanding a society system that is alien, complex, and conceptually different. Participant observer research will acquire greater scientific status, it seems, as a result.

These comments about the low status of participant observation refer to its place in psychology, not in other fields such as sociology or anthropology. It is hoped that participant observation in cross-cultural psychology will develop as a method so that it can take a prominent place along with experiments, correlational analyses, psychometrics, and so forth.

With this discussion of the emic-etic distinction as background, the methods of content analysis for cross-cultural research will be reviewed. The most effective uses of content analysis will incorporate the emic-etic distinction.

Content Analysis for
Cross-Cultural Studies

The term *content analysis* will be used in its broadest sense, referring to the systematic scrutiny of any set of material (e.g., oral, written, pictorial representations, communications through bodily movements, etc.) that might yield important generalizations about human behavior. Two more formal definitions have been suggested by Holsti (1968) and Janis (1949). The definition by Holsti (1968, p. 601) was designed to be a concise but general description: "Content analysis is any technique for making inferences by systematically and objectively identifying specified characteristics of messages." This definition was suggested by Holsti after he completed an excellent, wide-ranging review of content analysis in the behavioral and social sciences. The definition by Janis is longer and begins to explain content analysis in operational terms, or in terms of "what happens."

> "Content analysis" may be defined as referring to any technique (a) for the *classification* of the sign-vehicles, (b) which relies solely upon the *judgments* (which theoretically, may range from perceptual discriminations to sheer guesses) of an analyst or group of analysts as to which sign-vehicles fall into

which categories, (c) on the basis of *explicitly formulated rules*, (d) provided that the analyst's judgments are regarded as the reports of a *scientific observer* (Janis, 1949, p. 55, emphases in the original).

If a general use of the term is accepted, content analysis has been used frequently in cross-cultural research, perhaps more frequently than would be estimated on first guess. For instance, Cole, Gay, Glick, and Sharp (1971) analyzed the classification of everyday objects and concepts by the Kpelle of Liberia, subsequently using the Kpelle's own classification system as the basis of experiments designed to measure learning and memory. Colby (1966) analyzed folktales from various cultures to obtain meaningful similarities and differences in word groups found in the tales. Themes emerged from the word groups, and these were related to known differences among the cultures. Folktales from various cultures were also analyzed by McClelland and Friedman (1952), who designed a coding scheme to measure achievement imagery (e.g., characters in the tales setting goals and working to attain them). They related these results to ratings on child-training practices developed from data in the Human Relation Area Files (see the chapter by Barry, in this volume of the *Handbook*). By studying pictures and films, Mann (1974) analyzed different forms of crowd behavior in various countries and concluded that there may be cross-national differences in the forms and meanings of riots. Ekman and Friesen (1971) analyzed facial movements of people in the United States and developed pictures used in a cross-cultural study meant to test the universality of a hypothesis that related particular facial muscular patterns to various emotions. These and other cross-cultural studies will be reviewed in more detail later. They are presented here only to show the range of applications of content analysis.

For a variety of reasons, the methods of content analysis are likely to be used more frequently in future cross-cultural research. A major objection to much recent cross-cultural research is that the materials researchers used were artificial, alien, and simply not meaningful to the members of the culture in which a given study was done (Guthrie, 1977). The most notorious example is the use of intelligence tests, which were developed in one part of the world (the United States), and used in other parts of the world where the concepts found in the tests are alien (see Brislin et al., 1973, Chapter 8, for a longer discussion). Most intelligence tests are based on content analyses of materials and concepts familiar to children at different age levels in the United States, and the results of the analyses suggest that certain types of test items will achieve the goals of the test. But the results of such content analyses are not valid in other cultures where people have had different experiences, value different ideals, and use different materials in their everyday behavior. When tests from one culture are used in another, this represents a blatant misuse of psychological research methods and yields studies which present incorrect conclusions that can be harmful to people in the cultures. Yet more subtle examples of imposing a set of materials (an example of the emic-etic distinction discussed previously) occur frequently. For example, consider Piagetian studies in which children in various cultures are asked to make judgments about the quantity of different substances. The children make their judgments after seeing materials developed by Piaget and his colleagues in Geneva. The criticism of this procedure is that if the materials are *less* familiar to children in the cultures investigated than to the comparison group of children in Geneva, this can lessen performance on the conservation task. The diminished performance can then lead to the mistaken conclusion that children in certain cultures reach certain levels of development later than do children in Geneva. Sensitive to this problem, Price-Williams (1961) used nuts rather than beads in a task meant to tap the conservation of discontinuous qualities among the Tiv of Central Africa. He substituted nuts after discovering that it was difficult to explain the task when beads (used in the comparison studies in Geneva) were the materials the children were to see. Price-Williams used the basic techniques of content analysis to find materials in the culture that were familiar to the children and this procedure allowed a good experiment to be designed. Is it only chance that the study reported by Price-Williams represents one of the very few cases in which children from a nontechnical (sometimes called non-Western) culture performed at comparable levels to the Geneva comparison group? Probably not. A more formal investigation into the use of content analysis of familiar objects and concepts was performed by Cole et al. (1971), as noted above, in preparing for experiments on learning and memory.

Another reason that will encourage the more frequent application of content analysis is that other methods, long used by psychologists, are likely to decrease in frequency of use. Specifically, complex experiments involving trained accomplices and deception will be a method which cross-cultural researchers will have to forego. Such experiments run too great a risk of alienating members of cultures in which psychologists work. All experimentation is not ruled out (see the chapters by Bochner and Ciborowski in this volume), but the type that includes complex manipulation and deception should be avoided. The kind of experiment to be avoided is what Daniel Katz (1970) called the "frustrated playwright" type. For example, the experimenter may train assistants who act in a hostile manner toward subjects, or the experimenter might tell subjects that the test they are about to take measures IQ, in order to raise the subjects' anxiety level. Such studies are to be eschewed for two reasons. One is the probable negative response of people in the culture to visiting researchers who do such experiments in the name of "careful scientific inquiry." Such inquiry is a hard concept to communicate in many cultures that place a higher value on truth in interpersonal relations than (for instance) the United States does. The chapter by Warwick, in Volume 1 of this *Handbook*, covers such ethical issues in research. The second reason is that there are so many variables manipulated in the complex scenarios of such experiments that it is impossible to pinpoint the exact factors which influenced the results. It is safe to presume that people in various cultures will react differently from college students in highly technical societies— the group most frequently studied in complex manipulation/deception experiments. These differing reactions will only add more possible reasons, in addition to the researchers' preferred hypothesis, for the obtained results.

Finally, the use of content analysis in cross-cultural research will increase as more established scholars and neophyte students become attracted to the field. Because of time and expense, field trips to various cultures are a rare event for senior researchers. Further, access to cultures is likely to *decrease* if poorly trained students impose themselves on other cultures, particularly during these times when leaders of cultures are saying "no" to requests to do research (Bochner, Brislin, & Lonner, 1975, pp. 7–13). But if established researchers can keep in touch with cross-cultural research problems through content analyses, such as Mann's (1974) analysis of films to make generalizations about crowd behavior, then the rare field research opportunity (during which original data can be gathered) is likely to yield important results. Similarly, if students can learn about basic cross-cultural methods (e.g., emic-etic distinction; formulating important hypotheses; generating research of use to the cultures under study) by performing content analyses, then during their field study they will be likely to do good research which might even yield an invitation to return to the culture.

Basics of Content Analysis

Although disagreements can be found in the literature concerning the exact scope of content analysis, there are three characteristics on which there is wide agreement (Holsti, 1968). The first is objectivity, meaning that content analysis must proceed according to explicit rules, so that a wide range of content will be examined, not simply that content which is likely to support the researcher's hypothesis. Second, categories into which the analysts place different parts of the content should be formulated according to rules so that there is no bias in favor of a given hypothesis during this category-formation stage. The third characteristic is generality, meaning that findings must have theoretical relevance. There are pure descriptive analyses available in the published literature, such as analyses of the stereotypes assigned to Afro-Americans in magazines (Cox, 1969), but these are of little value if there is no clear link made between the results of a given content analysis and other research and/or theoretical formulations. In other words, the summary report of a good content analysis will be read not only by people interested in the specific content (in Cox's case, stereotypes of Afro-Americans), but also by people interested in a wide range of theoretical issues (e.g., social change, minority group influence, learning of stereotypes). The person who does a good content analysis according to this third characteristic will create a wide audience for the research report since the theoretical issues addressed will interest many readers.

The first two points can be summarized succinctly by saying that good content analysis allows for replicability. The old criterion of a well-designed study—if someone else can read the write-up and repeat the exact procedure—is still a good one. The third characteristic has to do with theory building, and it is on this basis that the whole field of cross-cultural research will either rise or fall.

Content analysis is especially useful when the application of less precise methods: (a) might not allow the researcher to discover subtle indicators, or (b) might not allow the discovery of findings that take the form of an interaction between two variables. As an example of the first point, Holsti (1968) reviewed White's (1947) analysis of an autobiography, Richard Wright's *Black Boy*. Although White was a trained psychologist, his first analysis did not yield certain important indicators which were later found by a systematic content analysis. The themes found by the content analysis included an "emphasis on personal safety (18 percent of all value judgments), failure to identify with other Negroes, and lack of interest in social goals" (Holsti, 1968, p. 602). As an example of the second point, Mann (1974) tabulated different criteria of riot behavior in various countries. He showed that the convergence mechanism (i.e., the idea that the prime riot mechanism is the coming together of similar people, in contrast to contagion, in which rational individuals are caught up in the hysteria of the moment) was prominent in Japan but not in France or India.

> The fact that the Japanese rioter is always prepared, and demonstrates group affiliation through his uniform and slogan-printed helmet, provides evidence that the coming together of coordinated, highly disciplined activists is a major mechanism underlying Japanese riot behavior. (Mann, 1974, p. 332)

This interaction between country and riot mechanism (that a mechanism is prominent in one country but not another) could not have been discovered without the careful tabulation of category frequencies, which is part of content analysis.

For the vast majority of cross-cultural studies, a sine qua non of basic methodology is relating the results from the content analysis to external, independent criteria. Any result from a content analysis will rarely be of significance by itself; a result must be related to other theoretically significant indices of behavior. The most massive effort along these lines and the most frequently cited cross-cultural use of content analysis is McClelland's work with the need for achievement (nAch) variable. In the McClelland and Friedman (1952) study, nAch themes from a content analysis of folktales were related to independent ratings of child-rearing practices gathered from ethnographies of various cultures. In other work (summarized in McClelland, 1963) content analysis of nAch themes from children's school primers in various countries were related to indices of economic attainment of the same countries, such as the gross national product. By relating these separate sets of evidence McClelland was able to formulate a theory relating nAch to parent-child relations and to relate nAch in children to the economic growth of countries. The hypothesis relating the elements in the latter point is that nAch is instilled in the children when they read the primers with the nAch themes; the children then engage in nAch behaviors when they become older and have a chance to participate in adult society. McClelland's work deserves more space, but it will be covered in other chapters of this *Handbook* (see chapters by Berry in Volume 5, Jahoda in Volume 1, and Zavalloni in Volume 5). More recent studies in this genre (e.g., Suleiman, 1977) have not linked themes from content analysis to independent criteria, and are weaker because of this lacuna.

The general point about cross-cultural methods exemplified by the work of McClelland is that research based on multiple methods will be stronger than research which is dependent on one method. When the results of a content analysis are compared to independent criteria, two methods are being used. Campbell's (1968; Campbell & Fiske, 1959) analysis of cross-cultural methods is important in pointing out that each method researchers might use has biases associated with it (e.g., content analysis is dependent upon what content is available; experiments are often artificial). But if several methods are used, each with its own different, nonoverlapping biases, then a theory must be strong if research based on different methods leads to the same conclusions. The use of multiple methods in research is always more desirable than the use of only one. Teitelbaum (1967, p. 12) quotes von Bekesy, Nobel Prize winner in Physiology and Medicine, as saying, "I never publish a finding until I have measured the phenomenon by at least five different methods. . . . I expect a fact determined this way to stand unchanged for about fifty years." Webb, Campbell, Schwartz, and Sechrest (1966) have presented an eloquent defense of multiple methods in the social and behavioral sciences, and have paid special attention to unobtrusive measures (see the chapter by Bochner in this volume of the *Handbook*) as one method which should be complemented by others.

Sampling, Coding, Reliability, and Validity

Four aspects of content analysis: (a) the sampling of materials to be analyzed, (b) the development of categories and subsequent coding of material into them, (c) the establishment of reliability of the coding procedure, and (d) the establishment of validity for the results, are closely interrelated. A problem with one aspect can cause difficulties with the others, and (to use a cliché) content analysis is only as strong as its weakest aspect. For instance, poor sampling can cause an unrepresentative selection of material to be analyzed, and errors here will eventually lower validity. That is, validity is dependent upon actual measurement of what was intended to be measured, and this cannot be done by analyzing unrepresentative materials. A poor coding scheme will not allow different analysts to agree as to what content goes into what categories, and reliability is thus affected. As with all psychometric measurement, there cannot be high validity without adequate reliability. Thus each aspect has to receive a great deal of attention from the researcher.

Sampling.   The sample of materials that is to be analyzed will determine the extent to which the researcher can make conclusions about the results of the analysis. For instance, if only prestige newspapers in a country are sampled, conclusions cannot be drawn about coverage of a certain topic in all types of newspapers (e.g., local weeklies, high-readership newspapers). Another type of sampling problem is the ratio of available material to relevant material. Often, desired material which is relevant is not available for many reasons (e.g., location, political considerations, legal stipulations). The researcher should have a good estimate of the available/relevant ratio so as not to overdraw conclusions. In addition to this central methodological issue of representativeness, there is a practical reason for attention to sampling. The tremendously time-consuming procedures of category development, coding, assessment of reliability, and so forth, are simply not worth the effort if an inadequate sample of material is to be analyzed.

How should sampling be done? The thoroughly desirable methodological goal of random sampling seems out of the question for every piece of research because of the impossibility of defining the universe from which to draw randomly. The extent of the available material is simply not known in many cases. Substitutes for random sampling have to be found that retain as many of its benefits as possible.

The general rule that the sampling procedure should follow from the problem to be investigated seems obvious, and yet it is a helpful point. Many content analyses in cross-cultural psychology will have as their goal the demonstration that a certain set of material has a certain set of effects upon people. Given this general goal, Holsti (1968) has suggested three sampling guidelines. The first is a criterion of popularity—what content has been seen or heard by a large number of people? A cross-cultural example is that of McGranahan and Wayne (1948), who compared themes in highly popular German and American dramas. As their criterion for selection of plays, they used such popularity indices as length of a play's run, a figure easily available from newspaper (and other) records. The second guideline is to select those materials that have the explicit function of instilling social norms. This was the reasoning behind McClelland's (1963) selection of school primers to analyze need for achievement themes. It was also the basis for Colby's (1966) work with folktales and Lewin's (1947) comparison of youth manuals in Germany and the United States (materials from Hitler Youth as compared to material from the Boy Scouts). The third guideline is to compare several sets of data to determine if the same conclusions can be drawn. For instance, in the McGranahan and Wayne study, the results of the content analysis of dramas was compared to an analysis of German reactions to movies that had been successful or unsuccessful in the United States. The rationale behind this guideline, of course, is the same as the rationale behind the use of multiple methods in cross-cultural research, as discussed previously.

In an analysis of the sampling of individuals in cross-cultural research, Brislin and Baumgardner (1971) pointed to the desirability but near impossibility of random selection, but they concluded that certain nonrandom sampling techniques could lead to good research. Generalized to the selection of content for analysis, these guidelines suggest that the sample should be described in considerable detail. This would serve a number of purposes. (1) Subsequent researchers could then choose their samples with a greater certainty of obtaining important results. One study may determine that a certain set of content is very fruitful for analysis, and so the same or similar content may be useful to another researcher. For instance, Lewin (1947) analyzed youth manuals in Germany and the United States; this was followed by Sebald's (1962) analysis of songbooks in the same countries. Both studies obtained results leading to the same conclusions. (2) Researchers can incorporate the findings from any given study into their own work. If samples are not described, subsequent researchers will be unable to determine whether or not the results of a study can be integrated into their own work. For instance, if a researcher in 1980 wanted to study current newspapers to determine coverage of a certain topic and wanted to integrate similar research that examined coverage of the same topic, he or she would find this impossible if the other relevant studies did not indicate the published dates of the newspapers they analyzed, criteria for including and excluding specific newspapers, and so forth. (3) Careful description also allows researchers and their readers to evaluate any plausible rival hypotheses (to be described in more detail later) that might be attributable to sampling. A major problem with content analysis is that the method is dependent upon what content is available. For instance, analysis of folktales can be done only on those folktales which have been collected. If there are selection biases that determine what tales (out of many in a culture) are available (e.g., an anthropologist in a given culture collected only those tales dealing with stress between people, since that was his interest), then these biases must be pointed out as clearly as possible when the sample is described. If this is done, the researcher and reader can then analyze the plausible rival hypothesis that the type of sample available for analysis affected the results. Of course, this practice will also make clear what types of material must be collected in the future.

If the sample can be described in sufficient detail to allow a reasonable case that the above three points can be handled, then an additional benefit can be obtained. If, after such description, there is more material than can be processed given the limitations of the research project (e.g., budget, staff), it would be desirable to sample randomly from those materials available. This would alleviate the possible bias that the researcher might choose only that final set of material likely to support the study's hypothesis.

Coding.   The link between a researcher's hypothesis and the raw data to be content analyzed is the coding process. In coding, the usually massive set of original material is transformed, according to a careful set of rules, into a limited number of well-defined categories. Ideally, this results in an economical reduction of the data to manageable proportions, and it allows the researcher to draw conclusions about the study's hypotheses. Without good categories and good coding rules, it is impossible to make any sense out of the original content and it is impossible to link the original data and the researcher's hypothesis. A helpful, operational way of viewing category formulation and coding is to remember that a number of different analysts must be able to place the same parts of the content into the same categories. The rules for doing so must be made explicit if more than one person is to do the analysis, and there *has to be* more than one analyst if the reliability of the procedure is to be determined. The material on emics and derived etics in the Introduction to this volume by Berry may be helpful in guiding the development of categories and codes. In cross-cultural studies most categories will resemble either emics or derived etics. There is also useful material on coding by Pareek and Rao and by Longabaugh in this volume, in their chapters on interviewing and systematic observation. The nature of coding in these two methodological domains is very similar to coding in content analysis.

Some content analyses have as their base very clear categories and rules for coding material into those categories (e.g., Truex, 1977). When this level of clarity can be achieved, it is sometimes possible to use computers to do the coding, as with the General Inquirer System (Stone, Dunphy, Smith, & Ogilvie, 1966). The entire body of material can be put on computer cards or tape, and the coding rules can be arranged in the form of a program. The computer output will consist of tables showing the frequency of material in different categories, as well as indications of what exact content went into what categories. For instance, Colby, Collier, and Postal (1963, p. 319) described their computer program for the analysis of folktales:

> The instructions tell the computer how to compare each word of the folktale text with the list of themes contained in the dictionary. Every time a word in one of the theme categories is found it is "tagged" and a score is recorded for that particular theme. Thus the initial output from the computer run is a "tag tally" giving the total number of times each theme has appeared in each sample of texts. . . . It should be emphasized that the program is essentially a clerical aid. The definition of themes was made prior to the computer analysis so that all computations by the machine are simply applications of the original plans and ideas of the investigators.

Colby had developed 180 themes at this stage of his research (1966a,b). As an example, here are the entries that are tagged for the theme called "Rational":

> *Rational:* Belief, consider, contemplate, explanation, deem, define, guess, idea, inform, information, instruct, judge, knowledge, learn, logic, memory, mind, opinion, remember, realize, reason, reflect, remind, riddle, think, thought, understand, teach. (Colby et al., 1963, p. 320)

A computer, of course, cannot "think" or even "fill in" for the minor errors the researcher makes with the rules for coding into categories. In many cases, even though humans are to do the coding, it would probably be a good idea to develop the rules *as if* a computer were to do the coding. Such clarity can yield only positive benefits.

Other content analyses have as their base a set of categories dependent upon more subtle rules that demand a great deal of judgment on the part of analysts. In such cases, the analysts have to be highly trained, and they have to be highly motivated to keep the same keen level of attention throughout their examination of the entire content. As an example of this more difficult analysis, McClelland and Friedman (1952) analyzed folktales from American Indian cultures. They trained analysts to find themes of achievement motivation, or "characters in the story competing with standards of excellence, or in more simple terms, trying to do well in relation to some achievement goal" (p. 325). As an example, they presented the following section of a Comanche tale to analysts. The portions of the tale that are italicized constitute McClelland and Friedman's own indications of achievement-related phrases, according to the scoring system.

> Coyote was always knocking about hunting for something. He came to a creek, where there was nothing but green willows. Two little yellow-birds were playing there. He came up to them. Laughing, they pulled out their eyes and threw them on the trees, while they stood below. "Eyes, fall!" they said. Then their eyes fell back into their sockets. Coyote went to them. *He greatly admired their trick. "Oh, brothers! I wish to play that way, too."* "Oh, *we won't show you*, you are too mean. You would throw your eyes into any kind of a tree and lose them."—"Oh, no! I would do just like you." At last *the birds agreed to show him*. They pulled out his eyes, threw them up, and said, "Eyes, fall!" They returned to their places. "Let us all go along this creek!" said the birds. *"Other people will see us and take a fancy to us."* They went along playing. Coyote said, "I am going over there. I know the trick well now." He left them. He got to another creek. A common willow tree was standing there. *"There is no need to be afraid of this tree. I'll try it first."* He pulled out his eyes, and threw them at the tree. "Eyes, fall!" he shouted. His eyes did not fall. He thus became blind. He tied something around his eyes, and left (McClelland & Friedman, 1952, p. 246).

I do not doubt that the italicized portions indicate need for achievement according to the scoring scheme—there is a certain "sense" of achievement conveyed—but I would guess that only highly trained analysts could indicate the exact phrases that should be scored as achievement related.

Another way to perform a content analysis is to develop a set of scales on which analysts rate a section of material, of defined length. Thus a large amount of original material might be divided into 100 word segments, all segments read by the analysts, each reread individually, and each segment then rated on such scales as the following one, developed according to the purpose of the study.

This segment shows achievement motivation to this degree:

_____	_____	_____	_____	_____
a very large amount	a large amount	average, for all segments read	a small amount	none at all

This is a tempting alternative, especially given advances in psychometrics that could be used to develop sophisticated scales. Disadvantages are: (1) that there is no record of exactly which aspects of each segment led each analyst to his or her final rating. There is no "tag" on individual words or phrases. In addition, (2) it is apparently very hard to obtain reliable ratings of this type that involve an intensity dimension (very large versus large amount of a certain theme [Holsti, 1968]). Finally, (3) there is a decreased opportunity for discovering serendipitous findings, those totally unexpected by the researchers, if the analysts read, but do not mark, the original material, and rate on preestablished scales after reading.

It would be desirable if there were an extensive literature on training and working with analysts, but unfortunately there is not. There is a certain "folklore" that has developed about analysts, however, heard during coffee breaks at research institutes and during professional meetings. Analysts, more frequently called "coders," are often undergraduate students who hire on to a research project to pay part of their way through school. In addition to money, another goal of the analyst-student is to obtain academic credit under the "directed research" course option available at some universities. This analysis-for-credit becomes ethically questionable when the student is no more than a clerk for a senior researcher and learns little about the range of issues involved in content analysis. There is a difficult-to-reconcile contradiction in the requirements for good analysts: they should be bright enough to make difficult judgments and even, perhaps, after working through a good deal of the content, be creative enough to suggest a new category or a new idea for research. However, such bright analysts often become bored with the drudgery of processing and coding a large amount of material, which after all is an integral part of content analysis. A person involved with one major project told me recently that the project's coding rules were too complex for a computer and so human analysts had to be hired. Over time, however, the project director found that bright analysts either quit because of boredom or coded differently than others because they "thought too much" about the content and the categories. They went too far beyond the manifest content and the coding rules; this led to esoteric judgments different from those of the other raters. After several such experiences, the project director made it a point to hire people of average or just below average intelligence.

I have also spoken to analysts on various projects, and they provided this input. One was able to verbalize the contrast effect (Helson, 1964): namely, that after reading a segment with a large number of the themes for which one is looking, the *next* segment seems to have fewer than it really does. Or, after reading a segment with no themes, the next one seems to have more than it really does. Explicit coverage of this potential problem during training sessions will probably help to alleviate it. Another coder indicated an emic-etic problem when she said, after working on a cross-cultural study, that it was difficult to code the content from cultures other than the United States into the categories designed by the researcher (who was from the United States). This comment may indicate that an etic set of categories had been developed where a combined etic-emic set would have worked better. The emic categories would have been developed *from* the content of the other cultures, not imposed on the basis of content from another culture of which the researcher is a member. Finally, a coder (of above average intelligence) told me that boredom wasn't a factor but motivation was. One of the categories dealt with the length of the phrase devoted to a theme, supposedly a measure of importance. She argued, however, that importance could also be indicated by a short, concise phrase of a few well-chosen words. But she was "locked in" to the coding scheme and was not allowed to have any input, causing frustrations that may have affected her judgment on other, more subjective categories. The solution here seems to be that the researcher should give the *reasons* behind each category and coding rule during training sessions, and that provisions should be made to allow input from the coders. In many cases, these people will have studied more of the original content than the research project directors themselves, and so their opinions should be cherished. Systematic research on factors to alleviate boredom and to increase interest among coders would be a valuable area for further investigation.

Finally, a conclusion from one actual methodological study by Stempel (1955) is that there will be more agreement among untrained coders working with clear categories than among well-trained coders working with ambiguous categories. Realizing this fact, Brislin and Holwill (1977) specified, in descriptions of their categories, what the difficult choices were likely to be. That is, they specified reasons why two or even three categories *might* be assigned the same content, but *why* only one would be appropriate.

Any coverage of category formulation and coding should include the common-sense, but often ignored, reminder that generalizations from the data are limited by the categories and the coding rules. For instance, Ekman and Friesen (1971) attempted to demonstrate that "the association between particular facial muscular patterns and discrete emotions is universal" (p. 124). Their method consisted of telling stories involving a particular emotion, and then asking subjects to choose, among three pictures of posed faces, the one that showed the emotion described in the story. Subjects were the Dani of New Guinea who, it was argued, had engaged in minimal contact with "Western facial behavior" (p. 125). Previous content analysis of the pictures had shown that there were distinct aspects (e.g., position of eyebrows, shape of mouth, amount of white in the eyes) that differentiated one theorized primary emotion from another. Pretest judges rated the stories told in order to insure that only one emotion was contained in each story, again a content-analysis-like procedure. The researchers concluded that: "The results for both adults and children clearly support our hypothesis that particular facial behaviors are universally associated with particular emotions" (p. 128). The researchers presented some limitations to their data, as with the use of the words "discrete emotions" in the first direct quote from them, above, but they should have tempered their overstated conclusion to a much greater degree. The nature of their categories should have determined the limitations on their generalizations. All emotions were not studied, only happiness, sadness, anger, surprise, disgust, and fear. Another, "interest," was mentioned as a seventh in the Introduction to the article (p. 124), but was eliminated from the study for unexplained reasons. No "blends" of emotions were studied, such as happiness and surprise expressed on the face at the same moment. The authors found that fear could not be distinguished from surprise by the Dani, either in the development of the stories or in the subjects' selection of the pictures; this point was made several times in the report. In addition and most importantly, the pictures used were the most intense forms of the emotions, reminiscent of American silent movies of the 1920s in which actors had to overact to compensate for the lack of opportunity to express emotion through their voices. The types of pictures used by the Ekman research group have been reprinted, including three used in the New Guinea study (Ekman, Friesen, & Ellsworth, 1972, especially p. 160; see also Ekman, 1975). Such intense forms of the emotions would not be seen by people in their everyday lives. Thus, the conclusion about the cross-cultural, universal nature of emotion and facial behavior is severely limited by the small number of emotions studied (the categories, in the language of this chapter), the lack of attention to combined elements or blends, and the atypical intense forms of the emotions displayed in the pictures.

Reliability.   In a somewhat unguarded moment the author of this chapter once made an analogy, during a talk with some students, between pornographic movies and research in the behavioral sciences. Citing the fortunes that have been made in pornography, he said that no one ever lost money by underestimating the tastes of the American movie-going public. Similarly, no one ever made money by overestimating people's concern with reliability and validity. Even though concepts of reliability and validity have been at the core of research methods for decades, the reasons behind much poor research are based on a lack of attention to these two concepts. Judging from Lonner's (1975; 1977) analysis of reasons for referees' recommendation of "accept" or "reject" with regard to articles submitted to the *Journal of Cross-Cultural Psychology,* lack of attention to reliability and validity eventually takes its toll.

In considering reliability, it is important to remember exactly what each type of reliability estimate means, and to remember what the operations are that yield the reliability estimate. One form of reliability is not the same as another. When reliability in content analysis is described, it usually refers to interrater reliability, where the judgments of two or more analysts are compared. This means that a number of different people can look at the same content and code it into the same categories. It is likely that the more dissimilar the coders are, the more robust the results of the content analysis will be to the critical scrutiny of others. If the senior professor and his/her top graduate student, who have been working together for four years, are the analysts whose judgments show high reliability, this *may* mean that only these two people, who may think completely alike, can yield a certain set of results. Another, uninitiated person might be able to make a reasonable set of judgments about the content but not the same judgments as the similar duo because this third person is not "tuned in" to the way the duo has been thinking over the last four years. The best procedure, then, is to have quite dissimilar people trained according to a carefully prepared set of categories and coding rules. But the training should not be for such a long period that critical readers might conclude that "All the training is doing is showing that the coders have to think exactly like professor X to keep their jobs (and no one in his or her right mind thinks like X)."

In cross-cultural research an additional problem occurs for those researchers working along the lines suggested by the emic-etic distinction. Analysts from the various cultures under study should be able to reach agreement on coding into etic categories (as these are proposed to be valid for all cultures under study), and two or more analysts from within each culture should be able to reach agreement on coding into the emic categories. Asking people from different cultures to code the material (from all the cultures) into the etic categories will yield two benefits. It will satisfy the recommendation to obtain dissimilar raters, as discussed above, and it will add evidence that the etic categories are indeed etic. That is, if the raters can code the material into the proposed etic categories without difficulty and if they can agree on their judgments, the categories are likely to be truly etic.

However, this recommendation is not likely to become standard practice. If for no other reason, it will be difficult to hire analysts from the various cultures under study to agree to code the entire set of material. But there is the possibility of analysts from the different cultures coding a random sample of the content. The sample would be small enough to be coded according to the demands of convenience necessitated by complex field research, but large enough to provide evidence (in addition to other indices) in the researcher's arsenal that the proposed etic categories are indeed etic and that diverse coders can agree on their judgments.

Another type of reliability is split-half, where evidence is presented that there is consistency across random halves of the sample of material. If this type of reliability figure is presented it does *not* mean that there is consistency across raters. Rather, it means that there is consistency across the sample of materials according to one rater. It would not be difficult to obtain both interrater and split-half reliabilities if the coding were done according to this two-by-two design:

	First Random Half of Sample	Second Random Half of Sample
Analyst 1	A	B
Analyst 2	C	D

The average correlation between cells A-C and between B-D would be the interrater reliability. The average correlation between A-B and between C-D would be the split-half reliability. Both figures should be high.

Confusion between interrater and split-half reliabilities has caused errors to be made. For instance, in discussing the use of computers in content analysis, Holsti (1968, p. 673) wrote that "When computers are used the problem of scoring reliability is completely resolved." This is true only to a very limited degree. The interrater problem is partially resolved since, after one run on a computer, another run will give the same results, as will a run through another computer. However, the use of computers does not solve the problem that the results may be due to an esoteric scheme which is irreproducable by another researcher. One researcher's program for a content analysis which is fed into the computer may give clear results to that one researcher, but perhaps not to someone else. The advantage resulting from using dissimilar human coders, as already discussed, would be lost. In addition, the results of a computer run say nothing about split-half reliability. There may be a stable score which is repeated after a run on another computer, but there is no evidence that there is consistency across the sample of material, and there should be such evidence. If a different number of phrases indicating a certain theme are found in one random half of the sample as compared to the other random half, then this result should cause close examination to determine the reasons why. Of course, it would be easy to program a computer to split the content into random halves and subsequently to carry out an independent scoring for each.

Validity. Certain aspects of validity have already been covered in the discussion of such central aspects in content analysis as "comparing with independent criteria" and "the use of multiple methods," as well as in the earlier discussion of the emic-etic distinction. These tremendously important aspects of content analysis are part of what has become known as "construct validity" (Cronbach & Meehl, 1955; Cronbach, 1975). In its simplest terms construct validity means that a concept (or construct) is surrounded by pieces of evidence to show its importance, what it is similar to and different from, how it is logically related to other concepts, and so forth. Another form of validity is "predictive." It occurs when the results of a content analysis lead to specific predictions, and when these predictions are proven accurate according to independent indices. Holsti (1968) points out that predictive validity is one of the least-attended-to aspects of content analysis; he had to search widely for examples. He pointed out one example in his commentary on a study of Knut Hamsun's novels: "The inference that Hamsun was a latent fascist was later validated by his collaboration with the Nazis (Lowenthal, 1949)."

A more familiar example is McClelland's (1961; 1963) analysis of school primers, already reviewed. Predictions relating themes found in the primers to independent criteria of a country's economic growth were supported. Another, more recent, example is his (McClelland, 1975) prediction of wars in various countries based on a content analysis of the theme of power and its relation to the theme of affiliation between people. Again, results based on predictions compared to actual records of warfare were impressive.

Content Analysis in Cross-Cultural Research:
Some Conclusions

There are very few pieces of research based on content analysis that have become part of the widely cited, influential "core" studies of cross-cultural psychology. The reasons are probably twofold: one is that few researchers have given attention to the validity of their results according to the guidelines already suggested. Related to this problem, when good content analyses have been done, there has not been sufficient integration of the findings into a theoretical framework. It is as if the researcher is saying, "I did all this work on the content analysis. Now make what you will of the results." It is the job of the researcher, not readers, to place the results of a given study into a framework, and to make a link between one study and other published research.

The second reason is that there have been few good ideas or central theoretical conceptualizations studied through content analysis. Too often, content analysis is nothing but busywork, an activity more like a smokescreen than inspired research. Some psychologists have spent two years or more examining a certain topic in another culture, failed in the use of other methods such as experiments, and then at the last minute gathered some "content" that they planned to analyze after returning to their home base. At the time of data collection, however, they had no idea about how the content analysis would proceed, and so after returning home they engaged in a flurry of activity: hiring students to do the coding, running data through the computer, and so forth. They seemed determined to "get something" out of their two years spent in the other culture, but the resultant activity was just busywork to persuade others that something was going on. Researchers have also admitted that if they were carrying on two projects at the same time, the one involving content analysis was a respite, or a chance to relax. Again, use of content analysis in this way will not lead to important results.

The proper place of content analysis cannot be summarized better than it was by Berelson (1952, p. 198) twenty-five years ago:

> Unless there is a sensible, or clever, or sound, or revealing, or unusual, or important notion underlying the analysis, it is not worth going through the rigor of the procedure, especially when it is so arduous and so costly of effort.

Possible Content for Cross-Cultural Analysis

With a general treatment of methods of content analysis as background, it may now be useful to review possible content areas that may yield fruitful findings in cross-cultural studies. Much attention has been given to folktales, a general term encompassing

> any traditional dramatic, oral narrative. This includes serious myths dealing with the supernatural, as well as tales told primarily for entertainment; purportedly factual accounts of historical events; moralistic fables; and other varieties of narrative which may be distinguished in varying grounds of classification. (Fisher, 1963, p. 236)

Anthropologists have given more attention to the analysis of folktales than psychologists have, with the rare psychologist's effort standing out, such as the work of McClelland already reviewed. The long article entitled "The socio-psychological analysis of folklore" by Fisher (1963), followed by a helpful set of comments by various scholars (in the *Contemporary Anthropology* format), is the most detailed treatment of issues that interest most psychologists. More recent reviews of folklore and narrative by Colby and Peacock (1973) and Dorson (1972, 1973) are useful in pointing out the availability of recent anthologies of material for possible analysis and in indicating the general directions which anthropologists and folklorists have taken. Recently, a symposium at the annual meeting of the American Psychological Association (1975) entitled "Psychology and Folklore: Social, Developmental, and Aesthetic Considerations" may indicate renewed interest in this area by psychologists.

Much of the sociopsychological analysis of folktales has dealt with their functions in society. The theory of "cultural models" (Roberts & Sutton-Smith, 1962; Roberts, Sutton-Smith, & Kendon, 1963) has attracted a good deal of attention. Their theory "deals with what is probably the most important, predominant, and important function (of folktales): the modelling of strategies and behavioral modes in ways that are culturally important in socialization (Colby, 1966, p. 385)." An example of this function in socialization, of course, is McClelland's analysis of the inculcation of the need for achievement in children. An extension of the "folktales as cultural models" point of view would be that the analysis of folktales, properly validated, could reveal the central values of various cultures which must be communicated from generation to generation so that the society will survive. Further, in times of pressure from other societies (or in times of pressure to change or "modernize"), it should prove fruitful to analyze the changes in traditional folktales, or the adoption of new folktales that have the function of socializing values congruent with the new demands placed on the society.

If psychologists begin to analyze folktales more than they do currently (which is probable, given the reasons for predicting increased use of content analysis that were reviewed earlier), they will be able to apply the methods of psychology to increase the sophistication of folklore studies. Psychologists will undoubtedly be no more brilliant than anthropologists and folklorists, but they *will* be able to make a unique contribution. The psychologist should be able to show how hypotheses, and ultimately theories, can be formulated and then tested by reliable, valid methods. Clear links would be made between the content of the folktales and the hypotheses with enough specificity so that the ideas behind the hypotheses can be supported or discarded. The procedures of the analysis would be given in sufficient detail so that it could be replicated by another investigator, and/or so that it could be integrated into another investigator's analysis of a different set of folktales. At present, and as is pointed out by such anthropologists as Fisher (1963) and folklorists as Dorson (1963), folklore analysis is not done in a sufficiently clear manner so that the basis of a given investigator's decisions can be seen. Rather, evidence in support of an idea is often vague; certain folktales are brought forth to bolster the idea while nonsupporting folktales are ignored. Of course, not all psychological studies in various fields of investigation follow the desirable points in the above scenario, but the standards of the discipline are clear enough so that studies which do not contain these elements can be labelled "bad psychology." Good methodology demands examination of all cases, both those potentially supportive and those potentially damaging to an idea. Such improvements in methodology should benefit folklore studies. The anthropologist Colby (1963, p. 275), for instance, has pointed to the potential contribution of psychologists: "The new canons that are emerging (for folklore studies) in anthropology require control for both descriptive and predictive validity."

It would be unfair to anthropologists if their major criticism of cross-cultural psychology went unmentioned: that psychologists' methods are artificial and are used to examine trivial hypotheses. The only defense to the criticism (often fair) is to give much more attention to investigating important hypotheses (McGuire, 1973), perhaps by asking colleagues to criticize the ideas behind a study as well as the methods. At present, psychologists ask their colleagues for methodological guidance but rarely for guidance regarding the perceived importance and centrality of the idea to be investigated. Bochner (in his chapter of this volume of the *Handbook*) discusses the issue of artificiality in psychological studies, pointing out that artificiality is not a necessary aspect of psychologists' methods.

Other possible contributions of psychologists include methodological treatments of (1) sampling; (2) reliability; (3) emics-etics; and (4) the relation between a folktale and its place in a social context. The latter is an issue similar to current thinking about an individual's personality being interpretable only in relation to a social situation (Mischel, 1972; Cronbach, 1975; Endler & Magnusson, 1976). With regard to (1) sampling, Fisher (1973, p. 272) has indicated several criteria for choosing folktales to be analyzed, and these are similar to those already discussed above for any content analysis. They include choice for analysis based on social function (such as tales designed to explain origins of a society's people); popularity; social roles central to the stories (father-son, chief-subject); or similarity of conflict objects across tales (food, property). In discussing (2) reliability, Fisher is also sensitive to the problem that themes emanating from one tale or from one informant may be biased and that more reliable indicators will be generated from the analysis of multiple tales (or multiple versions of one tale) gathered from many informants. Dorson (1963) pointed out (3) an emic-etic problem while discussing the issues involved when investigators in one study imposed characters drawn from modern Europe and classical Greek literature on tales from the Clackamas culture. In doing so they made many errors about the Clackamas.

Finally, several reviews of the writings of anthropologists show the concern with (4) the relation between a folktale and its social context. Fischer (1963, p. 247) wrote:

> La Barre (1948) presents a cogent plea for interpreting myths only with the help of additional information about their broader context. For each act we would like to know what the cultural norm is, what the purpose is, who is supposed to do it, what artifacts are normally employed and how, etc. For each role mentioned we would like to know the specific standards, privileges, and disabilities.

In addition, Dorson (1963, p. 103) pointed out that:

> Both Jacobs and Herskovits recognize the need for furnishing considerable additional information about the "givens" of the culture, whose cosmogony, social arrangements, economic habits, linguistic structure, and value system, so alien to the reader, form constant reference points within the tales.

This issue of surrounding a given piece of folklore with information concerning its social context is similar to the concept of construct validity (Cronbach & Meehl, 1955; Cronbach, 1975) in psychology. The issue is also important in analyzing translation of material across languages, and it will be raised again in the section on translation in this chapter. In general, the issue demands that psychologists become familiar with all aspects of a culture that might have relevance to a given folktale, and the extent of this familiarity will be necessarily greater than that found in most current cross-cultural studies in psychology. An "image" that has been helpful in conceptualizing the type of product necessary for a complete analysis of folklore is that of a compendium like the Oxford English Dictionary. In such a dictionary words and concepts would be given not only with an accompanying definition, but also with examples of how they are used in a wide ranging series of sentences or paragraphs. A very similar "image" is that of a Folger edition of Shakespeare's plays in which there are many footnotes explaining how a given word was used that may connote a different meaning from that of present-day common usage, or explaining the social context in Elizabethan times against which a given word or phrase should be interpreted.

What Can the Analysis of Folktales Yield?

Since psychologists have not often worked with folktales, it is by no means clear what the analysis of folktales can yield. There is a difference of light years' magnitude between the amount of research done with performance on (for example) standardized tests and the amount of research done with folktales. Psychologists know what the former basis for comparison is (an individual's performance at one point in time as compared to norms gathered from a large sample in a population), but do not have such knowledge about the latter. In any research which psychologists might undertake, they will necessarily be making a contribution to folklore methodology (as well as a contribution to the topic area under study) since there are, at present, so few models to give methodological guidance. In every study there will have to be links made between the content of the folktales and independent, external criteria for the purpose of pinning down exactly what folktales mean in different social situations. Anthropologists have also expressed this opinion: "There is much to be learned about texts themselves before we can successfully attack this larger question of how a text relates to its cultural environment" (Colby, 1966, p. 386). There is disagreement regarding whether or not the analysis of folktales can tell us anything. Comparing possible cultural differences in the use of such materials Dorson (1963, p. 101) wrote that ". . . American historians are singularly distrustful of folk materials. Unlike their

European colleagues, they regard oral tradition as insubstantial and untrustworthy, failing to recognize its value as a record of social thought." Examples concerning the use of folklore are then suggested by Dorson for such important topics in United States history as immigration, the westward movement, Negro slavery, and industrialization.

Assuming that the possible value of folktale analysis is at least tentatively accepted, it may be useful to list some areas in which folktale studies can make a contribution. Unless otherwise noted, these suggestions about "what do the tales mean?" and "what can they tell us?" are taken from the review by Fisher (1963). It should be remembered that these are only *suggestions* as to what folktale analyses can yield. Psychologists, in their empirical studies, will have to determine and document that folktales *do indeed* have a certain meaning or serve a certain function.

(1) The folktale can serve to justify the demands placed on individuals by a society, such as the relinquishing of certain individual freedoms for the "good" of society. It can also serve to justify the status quo of the existing social structure, and the relative position of the privileged and not-so-privileged. This function is relevant to Brislin's memories of his own socialization when a story was used to justify why his older brother should not accept a full scholarship to a certain college. There were four children in the family, raised in a strict Irish-Catholic household, but the scholarship (to play basketball) was to a Protestant college. With the other three children planning on attending college, the scholarship money would have been welcome. In deciding whether to accept the scholarship or not, this story was told about a character named Marty who worked for Carrigan's, a small neighborhood grocery store in his home town. Marty asked Mr. Carrigan whether he could leave fifteen minutes early one evening so that he could shop at A & P, part of an extensive chain of large stores. Mr. Carrigan asked, "Why do you want to shop at A & P? You can buy your groceries here." Marty replied, "Well, the prices at A & P are a little less." Mr. Carrigan then opined, "Maybe you should go work for the A & P." In case it is not obvious, the moral of the story is that a person should be faithful to one person or group and should not gather some benefits from one group, some from another, and so forth.

(2) Dorson (1963, p. 102) analyzed the functions of various narrative forms in his review of folklore theories.

> Expanding the viewpoint of Malinowski (1926) in *Myth in Primitive Psychology*, Bascom (1954) calls attention to the functional roles of folklore. Proverbs help settle legal decisions, riddles sharpen wits, myths validate conduct, satirical songs release pent up hostilities. So the anthropologist searches for context as well as text . . . (Folklore also serves) the reinforcement of custom and taboo, release of aggression through fantasy, pedagogical explanations of the natural world, and applications of pressure for conventional behavior.

(3) Ruth Benedict (1935) was one of the first to suggest the influential concept that tensions common to individuals in a given society are released and can be handled openly in oral literature. Fisher (1963, p. 257) goes further in suggesting that:

> The view of folktales as exciting the individual's emotions for socially desirable ends is complementary to the view of folktales as draining off surplus antisocial emotion. In fact, if one combines the two views, folktales and expressive culture generally can be regarded as converting antisocial emotion into socially desirable emotion by linking them together.

The general issue of how socially undesirable tensions, or socially censured tensions, can be expressed is an important topic for cross-cultural study. It is reported, for instance, that the bureaucracy and red tape of the government of the USSR can be criticized only by clowns in the circus, as part of their skits. Such skits are extremely well received by audiences.

(4) It has also been suggested that folktales serve an important function in the individual's search for identity, that is, to find out exactly who he or she is. Jerome Bruner (1959, p. 353), for instance, described "the corpus of myth as providing a set of possible programmatic identities for the individual personality."

(5) More closely related to issues in clinical psychology, Jacobs (1959) has suggested that repetition of a certain theme or point is a type of defense mechanism by which people desensitize themselves to a painful stimulus or to a threatening idea. Topics such as these enter an area already studied by anthropologists and psychologists who have followed Freudian theory in their analyses. Dorson (1963, p. 105) cautions that "the most speculative body of current folklore theory belongs to the psychoanalytic school that memorializes Sigmund Freud. This is also the school of interpretation most abhorrent to orthodox folklorists." In the same article Dorson uses words like "fantastic" and "absurd" to describe certain Freudian analyses. He points out (as have many others, many times) the complete lack of emphasis on proving the validity of their claims made about a set of folktales.

(6) Even the ambiguity of some folktales has received attention as a possible indicator of important cultural themes. Those aspects of a culture about which people are most confused or uncertain may become manifest through symbols in folktales, and hence the tales themselves may seem ambiguous upon first glance. This might be called the "Hamlet" function of tales. Since social reality is not completely understandable and predictable, there is no reason to expect folktales to be so.

(7) The eventual, perhaps long-in-the-future goal of folklore analysts has been expressed by Fisher (1963, p. 285):

> Ultimately I would like to be able to take a collection of folktales without knowing the associated social structure and say, in view of this group of tales, the society from which these come has the following features, and the people of the society have the following basic personality or human image . . .

Psychologists may be taking a risk if they choose to study folktales because there is no promise that "they will live up to their billing." But consider some definite advantages: most folktales have been part of society for a long period of time and this fact has allowed the subjective processes of sharpening and levelling to take their effect, yielding a product meaningful to many members of society. If the stories did not have some meaning to people in various societies, they would have disappeared. In addition, folktales are in a form more readily analyzable than other manifestations of culture such as children's play or dance rituals. The latter are more ambiguous and open to a number of different interpretations dependent upon the structure suggested by the investigator. Methods exist to allow structures to emerge from folktales so that dependence on an imposed framework is no longer necessary. One such method will now be reviewed.

A Specific Method for Folktale Analysis

A method for folktale analysis which has been presented in great detail is that of Colby (Colby, Collier, & Postal, 1963; Colby, 1966a, 1966b). His work is based on the premise that natural languages have three attributes: (1) similar kernel structures, (2) parallelism between formal classes and basic function classes in transforms, and (3) a large number of similar semantic fields. The first two attributes are based on the influential work of Chomsky (see his 1972 collection of essays for a readable introduction) and developments in the field of transformational grammar. Colby's approach is to "take the semantic field as the basic unit and work toward the description of the field's structure and the sense typically held by its representative word-forms through interviewing techniques or distributional studies" (Colby, 1966, p. 374). The distributional-studies approach has received the greater share of attention. The primary method is to obtain word counts of folk narratives with the help of computers. Words are "tagged" to indicate different conceptual domains, such as affection, competition, perception, and so forth. The words that are tagged for the theme "rational" have been presented earlier in this chapter. After word counts are obtained from a number of cultures, each represented by a large number of folktales, comparisons can take the form of the frequency with which different conceptual domains are used. Colby is clear in detailing the problems of the method which might influence the acceptance or rejection of the approach by other researchers. For instance, words are counted by the computer without regard to the surrounding context of the words, and of course context plays an important part in determining the meaning of words. The "defense" to many possible criticisms is that meaningful cross-cultural findings and meaningful relationships between variables are being found.

As an example, a number of anthropologists, in their ethnographic work (e.g., Kluckhohn, 1949), have found a theme of travel and movement among the Navajo. The folktales of the Navajo and Zuni Indian cultures were compared, and the frequency of the TRAVEL word group (e.g., bridge, departure, embark) was higher for the Navajo. A breakdown of the TRAVEL category

> showed that the Navajo used word forms in the TRAVEL group to indicate the idea of travel, the Zuni used word forms in the TRAVEL group for orientation and setting, suggesting the existence of two different conceptual areas that are culturally distinctive. Similarly the PLACE word group was broken down into areas and orientation on the one hand and places associated with means of travel on the other. As would be expected, the Navajo were high in the travel subdivision and the Zuni high in the areas and orientation subdivision. Thus distinction is noted within several word-groups, the distinction gains in validity as a cultural distinction. In such a case the original word-groups can be recomposed in culture-specific studies. (Colby, 1966a, p. 379)

This concern with validity and the search for similar findings across different analyses shows Colby's awareness of advances in modern cross-cultural research methodology such as triangulation, multiple methods, methods with nonoverlapping biases, and so forth, as presented earlier in this chapter.

After presenting his method, Colby (1966a) criticizes the work of other anthropologists such as Propp and Levi-Strauss for nonclarity of procedures and for imposing a framework (in the language introduced earlier in this chapter, imposing an etic) on folktales before the analysis even takes place. Colby thinks his method allows a framework to be objectively determined since it is a product of the computer analysis and ultimately of the words themselves in the folktales (i.e., the procedure allows emic categories to be generated). Problems with the method are the same as for those of content analysis in general. Just two are (1) the incredible amount of time that must be spent in developing the conceptual categories, word entries for each, preparing the text for computer analysis, processing the output from the computer, and so forth. A major, legitimate question will always be whether or not the time involved is commensurate with the benefits. The other problem is that (2) the method is dependent upon which folktales are available for analysis, and it is likely that many sets of folktales were gathered in a biased manner unknown to the analyst who uses them at a later date.

Needed Methods for Folktale Analysis

Certain methods have been presented, both in the general section on content analysis and in this section, which may be useful in folktale studies. Other methods will have to be developed, however, or present methods will have to be improved, to answer certain questions of interest to workers in this area. For instance, Fisher (1963, p. 261) asks this important question:

> Is there a determinate relationship between folktales and social reality? If so, what aspects of social reality are related to folktale content, and how are they related—by exaggeration? by inversion? by direct relation? How reliable are these relationships?

There are no good methods available to help answer those questions. A predictable set of answers has been put forth by researchers of a psychoanalytic persuasion, but the bases of their conclusions are unclear and the researchers can be accused of arbitrariness. More specifically, on the issue of manifest and latent functions of folklore, Spiro (1963, pp. 282–83) argues:

> Unless explicit distinctions are made between manifest and latent functions, functional theory will remain in its present fuzzy state. And until more adequate methods are devised to measure both types of functions, we shall only perpetuate the weary game of proving functions by assertion or attribution.

The solution to this and other problems related to the meaning of folktales may be to make much greater use (while gathering the tales) of questioning people after they relate a folktale (Berndt, 1963; Chowning, 1963). Questions such as, "When you hear that story, what else do you think of?" or "Are there certain times when people like to hear this story?" should yield important results. However, story tellers (1) may not know or (2) may not be willing to reveal such information. On the second point, it is doubtful that the intimacy and sensitivity of the secrets will be any greater than those regularly reported by ethnographers (who maintain proper safeguards as to the dissemination of the secrets) after good fieldwork. On the first point, the investigator may want to explain the nature of free association and then gather such associations from story tellers at different times during their narration of tales. A more formal technique that might be applied is the antecedent-consequent method (Triandis, 1972), which is designed to obtain information on what is likely to precede a certain concept, and what is likely to follow it. Questions would take this form:

Antecedent

If you have ————, then you want to tell this tale; or

If you have————, then it reminds you of such-and-such a character in this tale.

Consequent

If you tell this tale, people will probably————; or

When you tell about such-and-such a character in this tale, people often think about————.

Of course, these are just examples of hundreds of questions that could be written in this or similar formats (see Triandis, 1977).

Another possible solution is to use the formal methods of content analysis (already described in the section on sampling, coding, reliability, and validity). To date, folklore analysts have rarely used these objective methods (Colby's work is an exception) and have relied instead on subjective impressions after reading and studying a large number of tales. Fisher (1963) points to the advantages of these methods, and he feels that such methods allow researchers to come closer to the desirable goals of controlled experimentation. He emphasizes that these methods force examination of possible negative examples, not just examination of those tales likely to support a hypothesis.

There is a great deal of unmined raw ore in oral narratives that may possibly yield large fortunes. Psychologists may want to apply their pick-and-shovel methods to determine if they can share in, and contribute to, the analysis of folktales. This recommendation holds for all folklore, including its components and related areas such as dreams and rituals, humor, jokes, superstitions, puppet shows, court cases, movie stories, and so forth. All of these areas can be analyzed according to the methods of content analysis.

Ethnoscience

Ethnoscience is the most widely used term to denote the search for classifications of various domains in a culture, as seen by members of that culture (see Sturtevant, 1964; and Berry's Introduction to this volume). The goal of ethnoscience is to determine emic systems for classifications, with etic impositions eschewed. It is a content analysis based on categories and codes of the people in the culture. A premise of ethnoscience studies is that since there are so many stimuli which people encounter, they must group some of them together and respond to different stimuli in the grouping as if they were the same. Such groupings of stimuli allow people to make sense out of their world. More formally, Goodenough (1957, pp. 167–68) has stated that:

> A society's culture consists of . . . the forms of things that people have in mind their models for perceiving, relating, and otherwise interpreting them . . . description, then, requires methods of processing observed phenomena such that we can inductively construct a theory of how our informants have organized the same phenomena. It is the theory, not the phenomena alone, which ethnographic description aims to present.

Learning about another culture, then, consists in large part of learning how people in the other culture classify things and how classes relate to one another. One of the goals of formal cross-cultural training devices (Brislin & Pedersen, 1976) such as the culture assimilator (Fiedler, Mitchell, & Triandis, 1971), is to communicate such knowledge. For instance, in the United States the acts of "being a friend" and "being a critic" are separate: a person can criticize a friend. But in many Asian countries this is not possible: the categories are not separated. If an Asian perceives a certain American as a friend, and if the American criticizes the Asian, a tremendous tension results. The problem could be avoided or at least alleviated if both parties know the other's classification system. Another example of ethnoscience studies is covered in the chapter by Lonner (Volume 1 of this *Handbook*) in his review of the color categorization work of Berlin and Kay (1969) and the related work of Rosch (1975).

Many researchers using ethnoscience techniques have not been interested in the theoretical ramifications of their work. Rather, their product is much like a content analysis done for its own sake. For instance, Krauss (1974) started her monograph on the classification of plants as seen by the ancient Hawaiian people by using the term "ethnobotany" as a combination of botany and ethnology. But this was the extent of her general comments, since she then immediately began her coverage of Hawaiian plants (with excellent pictures, lists of uses to people, etc.). This is not in and of itself bad: her work should be read by anyone interested in the flora and fauna of the Pacific. But if there is to be a theoretical integration of this work with that of other ethnoscientific studies, someone else will have to do it. This example is not unique. There are many ethnoscientific studies of various domains which have not been related to the work of other researchers, and so there has been no integration of knowledge and no theoretical advance. If a person is interested in the specific domain (such as Hawaiian botany), then the studies are invaluable. But the audience is limited to like-minded specialists if there is no theoretical background for the work. This conclusion is similar to the one reached by

Davidson and Thomson (Volume 5 of this *Handbook*) after their review of attitude studies. As a possible antidote, the theoretical work of Rosch (1977) can be recommended. She shows how classification of objects can be viewed as part of a much more general theory of psychological functioning, with implications for physiology, linguistics, perception, cognition, and human development from birth to maturity. Rosch's argument is that categories are formed on the basis of prototypes, and other members as judged on the basis of perceived distance from that prototype. Crosscultural work could include identification of prototypes and the dimensions used in determining distance between possible category members and the prototype. Research to date (Rosch, 1977) indicates that some prototypes (e.g., color, two-dimensional geometric forms) are probably universal.

There have been some aspects of culture that have received more attention from ethnoscientists than other aspects. Certainly there are advantages to the approach that are similar to those of content analysis generally: precision, control, opportunities for validation, and so forth. But Colby (1966b, p. 793) writes that:

> The emphasis on control has, unfortunately, imposed a bias in the selection of ethnographic subject matter toward the more explicit aspects of culture, where there is high consensus among culture members, as in semantics. The more abstract aspects—art, religion, and folk literature—have usually been neglected.

Colby then describes his own techniques as an approach to generating the basis of a classification system in a complex area such as oral narrative.

Componential Analysis and Facet Analysis

Some ethnoscience studies attempt to discover a number of components which, when combined according to a set of rules, describe the entire content of a certain general class. This approach is called componential analysis (Goodenough, 1956). The basics of the procedure are to isolate the components and then to determine the rules for combining the components to form each and every member of the class. The greatest amount of work has been undertaken on kinship systems in different cultures, probably for the reasons Colby suggested (above), and indeed the clearest examples are in that domain. For instance, Goodenough (1965) has done a componential analysis on Yankee kinship terminology, a content area which at least in part will be familiar to all speakers of English. That 1965 article may be the best first step for researchers interested in how a familiar content area can be precisely described. The entire volume (Hammel, 1965) in which the article appeared is a useful source. Goodenough isolated such components as these:

1. Degree of collateral distance between ego (person whose kinship ties are being analyzed) and alter (person analyzed in relation to ego);
2. Degree of genealogical distance between ego and alter;
3. Generational seniority;
   and others.

Tables are then presented showing combinations of the components (with respect to the indicators subsumed under each component, not presented here due to space limitations). For other, more complex relationships, certain derivational rules are presented. For instance, rule 7 describes a complex relationship over which English speakers become tongue-tied during introductions at social gatherings: "Affinal kin types that are more than one degree of collateral distance from ego are not denoted by any kinship lexemes but by two or more lexemes in descriptive constructions (e.g., my cousin's wife; my husband's cousin)" (Goodenough, 1965, p. 278).

Goodenough (1965, p. 286) summarizes some of the benefits of the method:

> Componential analysis enables us to summarize in a succinct way what we think we know about the categorical organization of phenomenal domains as revealed by the use of linguistic labels for the categories within them. It forces us to be precise and rigorous in stating what we think we know, thereby helping us to clarify to ourselves our knowledge and its limitations. The results of analysis, as illustrated in tables portray in an objective manner complicated relationships for which otherwise we have only a subjective feel. These relationships and the structures they form thus are made much more amenable to systematic comparison for scientific purposes.

There are at least two types of componential analysis (Sturtevant, 1964). One aims for "psychological reality," since the components should be "cognitively salient" to the members of the culture under study (Wallace & Atkins, 1960, p. 64). This type then, is in line with the explanation of ethnoscience studies in general, presented earlier. But finding such components is not easy because informants may not be able to communicate the components readily even though they have a "sense" of them. Most readers, for instance, have a "sense" of the Yankee kinship terminology but there are those who would have to struggle with it if they were chosen as informants by the proverbial anthropologist from Mars. The other type of componential analysis aims at structural reality with the "reflection of the cognitive world of a culture's members" requirement being dropped. The goal here is an economical componential analysis which will describe the largest number of concepts based on the fewest number of components and the fewest number of rules. "Occam's razor" becomes the prime guide.

Another approach to determining basic components of a complex content area is facet analysis (Foa, 1965; Jordan, 1974). Psychologists have used this approach much more often than componential analysis. A content area would be broken down into what Guttman called "facets," and the area would be rebuilt based on combinations of the facets. For instance, Guttman (1959)

> defined attitude as a "delimited totality of behavior with respect to something" and later proposed that such a delimited totality of behavior be viewed as an attitude universe which could be sub-structured into subuniverses which are systematically related according to the number of identical conceptual elements they hold in common. (Jordan, 1974, p. 40)

Jordan then used five facets to begin to define the attitude universe for a number of studies which he and his colleagues have carried out.

- Facet A—Referent (other$_{a1}$ vs. self-I$_{a2}$)
- Facet B—Referent behaviour
             (belief$_{b1}$ vs. overt behaviour$_{b2}$)
- Facet C—Actor (other$_{c1}$ vs. self-mine/my$_{c2}$)
- Facet D—Actor's intergroup behaviour
             (comparison$_{d1}$ vs. interaction$_{d2}$)
- Facet E—Domain of actor's behaviour
             (hypothetical$_{e1}$ vs. operational$_{e2}$)

There are mathematically $2^5 = 32$ combinations (called "profiles"), but only twelve make any sense (Maierle, 1969). Six profiles were chosen by Jordan based upon capability of instrumentation, face validity, and their forming a simplex order. This latter criterion means that an intercorrelation matrix of the profiles will show high correlations near the main diagonal but lower correlations away from the main diagonal. Such statistical demonstrations determine whether or not there was a good basis for choosing a certain set of facets in the first place, an issue very similar to the choice of etics in the Triandis research procedures to be reviewed later. The six profiles were:

1—Societal Stereotype (a_1 b_1 c_1 d_2 e_1), or, Others believe others' comparisons hypothetically
2—Societal Norm (a_1 b_1 c_1 d_2 e_1), or, Others believe others' interactions hypothetically
3—Personal Moral Evaluation (a_2 b_1 c_1 d_2 e_1), or I believe others' interactions hypothetically
4—Personal Hypothetical Action (a_2 b_1 c_2 d_2 e_1), or, I believe my interactions hypothetically

5—Personal Feeling (a_2 b_2 c_2 d_2 e_1), or, I experience my interactions hypothetically

6—Personal Action (a_2 b_2 c_2 d_2 e_2), or, I experience my interactions operationally

Note that only one level of one facet changes in moves from one profile to another. Five other facets were used to define the content of items for the resulting attitude scales (which would be very different for each research study), and two final facets were used to indicate the degree of favorableness and intensity. Jordan (1974) covers the development of the attitude scales in more detail, indicating relationships between this method and others covered elsewhere in this Handbook (chapter in Volume 5 by Davidson & Hilton).

Some powerful techniques such as ethnoscience methods, componential analysis, and facet analysis now exist so that researchers can organize and bring precision to the investigation of various content areas as studied cross-culturally. Dangers in using them include: (1) the choice of a topic area for investigation becomes based on the availability of one of these methods, not on the importance of the topic itself. The latter is the important "facet" or "component" central to the future of cross-cultural research; (2) the overutilization of these techniques can cause the imposition of etics where they do not belong; and (3) the idea behind the study, or the important generalization which the researcher is trying to establish, will become lost as the data gathered through the application of these techniques (and the resulting data will be vast!) has to be processed. A person can be so in love with the data, running post hoc subanalyses and cross-category analyses on the computer, that the idea behind the study is lost during trips to and back from the computer center.

Translation of Material between Languages

It is easy to overestimate the importance of one's own chapter in a cooperative venture such as the development of this Handbook, but the problems of translation have stimulated such impassioned pleas for solutions that a person wants to put forth any possible contribution in a forthright manner. Lonner (Volume 1 of this Handbook) discussed the ubiquity and difficulty of the translation problem, and Richards (1953, p. 25) has probably echoed the feelings of many researchers in asserting that translation is "probably the most complex type of event yet produced in the evolution of the cosmos." The many, many ways that meaning (in its most general

sense) can be conveyed through language, and the fact that we often mis-
understand people we know very well and who speak the same language
as ourselves, is enough of a problem to occupy the careers of many researchers. And when such meaning and potential for misunderstanding
must be taken into account while transferring material from one language
to another, the number of seemingly unsolvable problems surely causes
frustration on the part of researchers who are faced with these problems.

Recently, a number of scholars from different disciplines have contributed chapters to a book on translation theory, addressing its application,
research possibilities, and research needs (Brislin, 1976a). Much attention
was given to the issue of how the translator can be helped on his/her job
(see also the collection edited by Gerver and Sinaiko, 1978); highly philosophical discussion, on such topics as the determinacy and indeterminacy
of translation, was omitted in these collections. Much of the material
below follows the presentation by Brislin (1976b) which introduced the
chapters.

A useful start to any discussion of translation is a consideration of different categories, or different purposes of translation. A useful set of categories is that of Casagrande (1954), who wrote of the four "ends" of
translation. The expansions on each of the four types draws from analyses
done since 1954. Type one is *pragmatic translation* and it refers to the translation of a message with an interest in the accuracy of the information that
was meant to be conveyed in the source language form. Pragmatic translation is *not* concerned with other aspects of the original language version
(e.g., aesthetic form) that would be considered as part of the other three
ends of translation (below). The clearest example of pragmatic translation
is in the treatment of technical documents in which information, e.g.,
about repairing a machine, is translated into another language (Sinaiko &
Brislin, 1973). Mechanics should be able to repair the machine using the
translated materials. Translators would have no concern other than getting
the information across in the second language. This approach contrasts
sharply with type two, *aesthetic-poetic translation*, in which the translator
takes into account the affect, emotion, and feelings of an original language
version; the aesthetic form (e.g., sonnet, heroic couplet, dramatic dialogue)
used by the original author; as well as any information in the message.
The clearest examples are in the translation of literature.

The third type is *ethnographic translation*, and its purpose is to explicate
the cultural context of the source and second language versions. With this
as their goal, translators have to be sensitive to the way words are used
(e.g., "yes," versus "yea" in American English), and must know how the
words fit into the cultures which use the sources and the target languages.
This type is similar to that discussed by Nida (1976) under the heading,
"Sociolinguistics and Translation," and his most compelling example was
a description of a translation from the Bible used by students who were

protesting social injustice in a Latin American country. Their translation was phrased in common, everyday language, and it was mimeographed on the inexpensive type of paper often used in the past for their activist communications. The translation and the form in which it appeared thus fit the cultural context. At a recent meeting in Australia, anthropologists were discussing how people from specific cultural groups (e.g., Aboriginal Australians) used certain words very roughly translated into English as "myth," "folklore," "narrative," "tale," "story," "fable," and so forth. The conference participants were interested in how the people themselves (*not* the anthropologists studying them) use the terms and the participants were concerned also with the context in which the terms would be used. They called for an "Oxford English Language Dictionary" type of analysis in which the terms would be given (in long passages with as much context as possible) as they are actually used. This is another example of ethnographic translation, since the concern is with use in a social situation. It also introduces the importance of context in translation, which will be covered below.

The fourth type is called *linguistic translation* and is concerned with "equivalent meanings of the constituent morphemes of the second language" (Casagrande, 1954, p. 337) and with grammatical form. In a description of an operational machine translation system, Peter Toma (1976) points out the necessity for linguistic analysis of both the source and target languages. The corresponding structures specified in the analysis become a central part of the computer program that constitutes the step between the source language input and the machine's target language output. Lack of such analysis has been a major reason for past failures in attempts at machine translation. Nida (1976) discusses linguistic translation in more detail.

Of course, any one translation can rarely be categorized into only one of Casagrande's four types. Certain information that would be a concern of pragmatic translation, for instance, is conveyed by the way certain words are used in a cultural context. Likewise, certain aesthetic-poetic forms, such as heroic couplets used in narratives designed to tell a long story, do not fit today's social context in such places as the United States where readers are accustomed to long narratives in the form of novels. Awareness of Casagrande's four types should help the translator to decide upon specific goals in a given translation since there have to be compromises made between elements subsumed under the four types. Questions concerning quality of translation, then, depend on which of several purposes the translator chooses to emphasize. However, several areas of research findings and analyses will help in the quest for quality no matter what the goals of a translator are, and these will now be reviewed.

The Importance of Context and Redundancy

Researchers who have investigated translation have indicated that context and redundancy in the original language version have major effects on the quality of the translated version. Experienced practitioners have come to the same conclusion (Seleskovitch, 1976). Redundancy helps in the construction of material likely to be translatable; two phrases in a passage that refer to the same concept allow the translator to be sure of the passage's meaning. It also allows any translation-checker to note errors when one of the phrases in the translation differs in meaning when compared to the other. As an example of applying knowledge about redundancy, Campbell (1968) made suggestions about research in which questionnaires are to be used, with the goal of using the questionnaire to interview large numbers of people who speak different languages. He has suggested that every concept under investigation be represented by at least two differently worded questions if at all possible. If the two or more questions show similar results, a researcher may have more faith in his measuring instruments, and can also add more credence to his claim that the obtained results are not due to translation errors.

Descriptions of the advantages of redundancy are also found in the writings of information theorists. A quotation from one of the most prominent proponents of information theory in psychology, George Miller (1953, p. 8), points out the advantages of redundancy for all communication.

> It is reasonable to ask why we are so redundant. The answer lies in the fact that redundancy is an insurance against mistakes. The only way to catch an error is to repeat. Redundant information is an automatic mistake catcher built into all natural languages.

The principle of providing ample context for difficult terms has been suggested by various analysts. Werner and Campbell (1969) pointed out that a word is translated least adequately when it is translated as a single item. Translation improves when a word is a part of a sentence, and is even better when the sentence is part of a paragraph. Longacre (1958) writes that in translating Biblical passages, the long passages are easier to translate than short ones since long passages provide more context for any one concept. Phillips (1960) noted that the translation procedure of the well known anthropologist Bronislaw Malinowski included a careful addition of clarifying terms to provide more context.

Chapanis (1965, p. 73), a psychologist interested in human factors engineering, described context cues for improving understanding of human speech. "A word is much harder to understand if it is heard in isolation than if it is heard in a sentence." And in discussing the NATO alphabet,

Chapanis (p. 75) said that it "is a specially selected one, full of context and redundancy for getting the maximum amount of information across."

This emphasis on the writings of Chapanis provides a background for a set of rules he designed for a "language to be used under adverse conditions" (p. 75). Citing Richards (1953) again, the translation process can be considered as an example of an adverse, difficult state of affairs. Chapanis's rules should have value in writing the original language form which a researcher wants bilinguals to translate. Three of his five rules apply (pp. 75–76):

2. Use as small a vocabulary as possible and make sure that vocabulary is known to all the communicators.
3. Use familiar rather rather than unfamiliar words. (Chapanis suggests the Thorndike-Lorge (1944) word count as a source.)
4. Supply as much context for your words as possible. Put the difficult ones in a sentence if you can.

Chapanis's principles of maximum communication with human speech seem to echo researchers' and practitioners' suggestions for maximum translatability.

Translation as a research tool.   The most careful and formal checks on translation quality have been designed (and used) for empirical research in the social and behavioral sciences. A survey researcher may want to ask the same set of questions in two or more cultures, and members of the cultures may speak different languages. Questions about people's responsibility during election time serve as an example of the survey's content. If the people in the research study speak different languages, and the researcher wants to ask the same set of questions (an important decision step since the procedure Triandis outlines, as reviewed below, does not demand that the same questions be asked), then a translation between languages is necessary. Obviously, if the researcher obtains different results he wants to be sure that they are based upon respondents' feelings about responsibility during elections, not upon differences in the original language form of the questionnaire and its translation. In cross-cultural work (or the comparison of behavior across cultures), there have long been pleas from psychologists, sociologists, and anthropologists alike (e.g., Goodenough, 1926; Bartlett, 1937) that the most careful precautions be taken during the stage of research when instruments are developed. Instruments include questionnaires or tests—these often demand translation—hence the concern with assuring equivalent versions in the languages of the cultures under study.

Procedures for quality checks when instruments are translated have been developed by a number of behavioral scientists (Werner & Campbell, 1970; Prince & Mombour, 1967; Brislin et al., 1973). Procedures when translation is *not* to be a major method have been developed by Triandis (1976) and these are described later in this chapter. Triandis rightly points out that by defining exactly where translation is and is not needed, and what it can and cannot do, the analysis of the research process is sharpened. In addition to the Triandis approach, empirical methods will be discussed for use by researchers who decide that translation is necessary for a given study. Triandis (1976) recognizes the necessity of some translation for research purposes, as in the instructions to respondents for answering questions, or as in helping put people who speak different languages in the same frame of mind (e.g., frank, open, free to admit that they don't know certain answers) before answering any questions. The procedures will be detailed without elaboration on how they were developed, but references will be given to places where such information can be found.

   Translation methods.   There are four basic translation methods that can be combined for the special needs of any one research project.

1. *Back translation,* in which a researcher prepares material in one language and asks a bilingual to translate into another (target) language. A second bilingual independently translates the material back into the original language. The researcher then has two original language forms to examine and, even if he/she does not know the target language, can make a sound judgment about the quality of the translation. There are reasons, however, why the back translation technique can give a false sense of security, so other devices to assess the the quality of the translated version have been developed (Brislin, 1970). These devices can be used by people who do not know the target language, a common problem in cross-cultural research, especially difficult to avoid in studies comparing three or more cultures.

2. The *bilingual technique,* in which bilinguals take the same test, or different groups take different halves of a test, in the two languages that they know. Items yielding discrepant responses, or differing frequency of responses, can be easily identified. The advantage of the technique is its preciseness and the potential for using sophisticated statistics and test concepts such as split-half reliability assessment. The disadvantage is that the research instrument is being developed on the basis of responses from an atypical group, bilinguals (see Segalowitz's chapter, Volume 4 of this *Handbook,* for more information on this point).

3. The *committee* approach, in which a group of bilinguals translates from the source to the target language. The mistakes of one member can be caught by others on the committee. The weakness of the method is that committee members may not criticize one another, and may even unify against the researcher (see earlier discussion on interpersonal criticism among Asians).

4. *Pretest* procedures. After a translation is completed, it should be field tested to insure that people will comprehend all material to which they will be expected to respond. There is no weakness per se with this

method. Indeed, all translated material should be field tested. But, of course, the technique will only be as good as the interviewers doing the pretesting (see Frey, 1970; Brislin et al., 1973; Pareek & Rao, Volume 2 of the *Handbook*).

Any of these methods can be used if the strengths and weaknesses of each are recognized and if steps are taken to accentuate the former and eliminate the latter. No matter which technique is chosen, there has to be a starting point, and this is usually some material in one of the languages to be used in the cross-cultural study. The material can be questionnaires, instructions to respondents, test items, and so forth. English will be used as an example only because more analysis for cross-cultural research has been done on English than on any other language. Guidelines have been formulated for writing translatable English, that is, English that is easier to translate than corresponding material in which these suggestions are not followed. These rules were developed by giving a wide variety of English language materials to bilinguals competent in English and in a variety of other languages, and then determining successes and failures in their translation efforts (described more fully in Brislin et al., 1973).

The suggested rules are as follows:

1. Use short, simple sentences of less than sixteen words.
2. Employ the active rather than the passive words.
3. Repeat nouns instead of using pronouns.
4. Avoid metaphor and colloquialisms. Such phrases are least likely to have equivalents in the target language.
5. Avoid the subjunctive mood, e.g., verb forms with "could", "would".
6. Add sentences which provide context for key ideas. Reword key phrases to provide redundancy. This rule suggests that longer items and questions be used in single-country research.
7. Avoid adverbs and prepositions telling "where" or "when" (e.g., frequent, beyond, upper).
8. Avoid possessive forms where possible.
9. Use specific rather than general terms (e.g., the specific animal such as cows, chickens, pigs, rather than the general term, "livestock").
10. Avoid words indicating vagueness regarding some event or thing (e.g., probably, frequently).
11. Use wording familiar to the translators where possible.
12. Avoid sentences with two different verbs if the verbs suggest two different actions.

If these suggestions are followed the next step would be to translate the material into another language. Assume that a questionnaire is to be translated; if the back translation technique is used it has the additional advantage of "decentering" the questionnaire away from the original language form. Decentering is a translation concept, first outlined by Werner and Campbell (1970), that refers to a process by which one set of materials is *not* translated with as little change as possible into another language. Rather, material in one language is changed so that there will be a smooth, natural-sounding version in the second language. The result of decentering contrasts with the awkward, stilted versions common when material in one language is taken as the final content that must be translated with minimal change into another language. Decentering means that the research project is not centered around any one culture or language. Instead, the idiosyncrasies of each language under study contribute to the final version of the questionnaire.

Here is how the decentering procedure works in actual practice (Brislin et al., 1973, pp. 38–39). An original language version of a question or test item such as the following is given to a translator. This item is from the Marlowe-Crowne Social Desirability scale (Crowne & Marlowe, 1964); respondents would answer "true" or "false" as the item applies to them.

I don't find it particularly difficult to get along with loud-mouthed, obnoxious people.

Brislin (1970) had this translated into Chamorro, the native language of Guam and the Marianas Islands, and then back translated into English. The terms "particularly" and "obnoxious" were not in the back translation, and the bilinguals explained that there were no good Chamorro equivalents. The first back translated version was given to another bilingual (not the original version, as above). The decentering process had started, as the nature of the Chamorro language determined the decisions made about the English language version. In the second back translation, "get along with" was replaced by "talk with," the bilinguals pointing out that the Chamorro term for the latter would be more understandable to the projected population of respondents. Another translation and back translation showed word-for-word equivalence (this is probably not a necessary criterion in all cases), and the final version was:

It is not hard for me to talk with people who have a big mouth.

This is the version subsequently used for the cross-cultural study comparing English-speaking and Chamorro-speaking people. This version led to a good Chamorro translation, the original version did not, and hence the revised version was used. The decentering process determines the changes that must be made. A combination of examining the back translated versions and discussions with translators will lead the researcher to the best choice for an original language wording that will be best for obtaining reliable and valid research results. Procedures exist to relate data gathered using the revised version to data gathered using the original version (Brislin, 1970, pp. 200–01). This would be useful if the researcher desired to compare some newly gathered cross-cultural data with the results of other, already published, studies.

In many cases, of course, use of the rules for writing translatable English and application of the decentering procedure will help formulate a revised version that is more easily understandable to speakers of English than if these aids were not used. Designers of questionnaires and tests are constantly looking for ways to write questions or statements that are easily understandable. The decentering procedure may help.

Other original and revised items were as follows:

original: I like to gossip at times.
revised: I sometimes like to talk about other people's business.
original: I sometimes think when people have a misfortune they only got what they deserved.
revised: Sometimes I have thought that if people have hardships it's their own fault.

Another by-product of back translation and decentering is that research ideas may be generated by the results of the translation efforts. For instance, in the item above, "gossip" did not translate well because Chamorro has terms for "male gossip" and "female gossip," but the sex is not specified in the item. Phillips (1960, p. 302) could not have the sentence stem, "Sometimes a good quarrel is necessary because . . ." translated into the Thai language. "After much discussion the translators decided that, although it was conceivable that an American might enjoy a quarrel for its cathartic effect, the notion would be incomprehensible to a Thai." Such results can suggest fruitful lines for further study.

The products of the decentering procedure can be related to emics and etics. Using the decentering approach, etic concepts would be those that "survive" the translation-back-translation procedure since terms would have to be readily available in both languages if the concepts are to survive. Emic concepts would be those that are "lost" (such as "gossip" and "daydreaming"), since, after a concept is described in one language, losing it means that no equivalent could readily be found in the other language(s) that are part of the research study. Etic and emic concepts would then be interrelated through statistical techniques, as described early in this chapter.

Procedures Suggested by Triandis

The basic procedure in the back translation, decentering approach, then, is to prepare materials in one language following rules that have been shown to help during this stage of the research. Material that is retained or eliminated in the decentering process yields the etic and emic dimensions. In the Triandis procedure, on the other hand, all instrument development is carried out within each culture in the study. There is no translation of material from one language to another, with the exception of instructions to subjects and descriptions of other procedural matters. The details of their procedure are very complex, with multivariate statistics frequently being used; more complete discussions are available in several places (Triandis, 1972, 1976; Davidson, Jaccard, Triandis, Morales, & Diaz-Guerrero, 1976). The highlights will be presented here. An important issue is that the method has not been used outside of the University of Illinois group whose central person is Triandis. One reason may be that no one outside the University of Illinois has written about the method using different explanatory devices than those to which the Illinois people have become accustomed.

Using the Triandis approach, the researcher starts with a set of proposed etics and then writes (or works with colleagues who write) emic items in each culture for the etic concept. The emic items are written by people intimately familiar with the culture. For instance, in research in Japan and Germany (Triandis, Davis, & Takezawa, 1965), the investigators were interested in interpersonal social distance as a function of the race, religion, occupation, and nationality of different target people. The researchers then did pretest questioning to discover the recognized races, religions, occupations, and nationalities with whom people in each culture would commonly come into contact. This pretesting, for instance, would yield members of the Buddhist religion in Japan, but not in Germany. Note the similarity to content analysis procedures. Then approximately one hundred statements implying differing degrees of social distance were generated, in the language of each culture, by other pretest subjects or by colleagues who were members of the culture. Thurstone scaling of the items was then carried out, again within each culture, so that ambiguous items (those on which subjects did not agree on the scales) could be discarded. Most of the items on the scales for one culture were quite different from the items for the other culture. In those cases where an item was similar, the scale value could be different in the two cultures. But because the emic items were written to measure etic constructs, cross-cultural comparisons could still be made; for instance, regarding the relative importance of the etic concepts in each culture. Triandis (1976) points out that in this procedure the etic concepts such as race, nationality, religion, or occupation are at a much higher level of generality than the emic manifestations of them within each culture.

How can the reality of the etic dimensions be established so that the emic development of instruments can follow? After all, scholars are not going to accept researchers' assurances that their dimensions are etic unless there is supporting data. One way is to propose a set of etics, as

Triandis did in the above example, to carry out the emic development of instruments, and then to factor analyze the data that is gathered using the instruments. The major factors derived from the data should be the proposed set of etics, as they were in the Triandis study. Of course, the factor analysis can also show that there could be a better set of etics than that originally proposed, and this would start another round of research using the same procedures as outlined above.

Another way to derive etics is to relate new areas of investigation to older, established areas. Osgood (1965, 1971, 1977) has convincing data to show that the basic dimensions of connotative meaning are cross-culturally invariant. These basic dimensions are evaluation (which accounts for the highest proportion of the variance), potency, and activity. Incidentally, Osgood used the emic procedure of eliciting descriptors of words within each culture in his massive study, obtained ratings from subjects, and factor analyzed the results to determine the etic factors in each culture. In all cases (over thirty languages studied to date), the same set of three dimensions appeared. Triandis (1976) has expressed his debt to the Osgood work.

In developing a new area of investigation, role behavior, Triandis et al. (1968) generated a large number of statements expressing how people behave toward one another. The emic procedure of instrument development was followed. After subjects completed a set of ratings on the probability of behavior between two people occupying different roles, the data were factor analyzed. The results showed four factors: association versus disassociation; superordination versus subordination; active hostility versus no hostility; and intimacy versus formality. The first two factors, which accounted for most of the common variance, shared a strong similarity to Osgood's evaluation and potency factors. Such replication and linkage of one set of results to another allow for reasonable assurance that etic dimensions have been established (Triandis, 1977).

The Triandis procedure is a carefully-thought-out set of methods specifically aimed at obtaining valid cross-cultural data. One possible problem, however, is that in the emic development of instruments within each culture, the etic may be lost. For instance, in the Davidson et al. (1976) study, a number of predictor variables were related to the behavioral intention of having children; the research was carried out in the United States and Mexico. In the United States the variable *Aact*—affect toward the act of having a child during the next two years—was the best predictor of behavioral intentions. In the Mexican lower socioeconomic status samples, however, the variable *PNB*—personal moral belief concerning a moral obligation to have a child during the next two years—was the best predictor. This cross-cultural difference, if valid, would have obvious application to population control campaigns, and the conclusion would be that different sorts of persuasive communications would have to be written for the different audiences. However, because all items for Aact and PNB were emic, it is not clear whether or not there is still an etic. In other words, are the etics of Aact and PNB still present after the emic type of instrument development which led to different items? Would the emic items be better labeled something besides Aact and PNB for either the United States or Mexican samples? No obvious link was made between the emic items, and an established etic, such as a set of identical, core items as in the Przeworski-Teune procedure.

The other possible problem with the Triandis procedure is the potential misuse of factor analysis. If they were to adopt the Triandis procedure, cross-cultural researchers would be placing their bets on a data analysis method that methodological specialists do not agree about. There is no agreed-upon best method for rotation, estimates of communality, determining the number of factors, choice of a factor model, and so forth (Brislin et al., 1973, Chapter 9). Just one quote from specialists should communicate the hard road to travel, should factor analysis be chosen as the method for data analysis:

> It has become practice for researchers to report in professional journals the results of factor and component analyses of various correlation matrices. Undoubtedly this is, at least in part, due to the accessibility of computer programs that perform these tasks. . . . Seldom, however, is evidence provided that the sample correlation matrices at hand are appropriate for factor-analytic methods. (Dziuban & Shirkey, 1974, p. 358)

Any method, of course, has problems associated with it. The procedures involved in the back translation/decentering approach and in the Triandis approach provide a smorgasbord for researchers. According to the special needs of their project, researchers can consider the advantages and disadvantages of the various techniques and proceed accordingly.

A More General Approach to Cross-Cultural Methodological Problems

A number of specific procedures with the emic-etic distinction as their starting point have been covered in some detail. In doing so, certain methodological problems have been raised and some solutions suggested. Every specific problem that might be faced in a given study, however, cannot be covered. A more general approach to solving cross-cultural methodological problems is the plausible rival hypothesis analysis, suggested by Campbell (1968, 1969).

In performing such an analysis, researchers consider their preferred interpretation of the data along with all other plausible explanations. The preferred interpretation is usually a theory-based concept meant to explain cross-cultural differences, while the plausible alternatives are most often methodological difficulties such as sampling of subjects (Brislin & Baumgardner, 1971), instrumentation, rapport with subjects, representativeness of experimental tasks in relation to everyday tasks that the subjects are familiar with (given special attention by Cole et al. 1971), and so forth. Each alternative explanation of the data is listed and considered individually. Were college students the sample? Then what factors associated with this sample might have caused the results or would limit the generalizability of the results (e.g., literacy, practice in working with abstractions)? Did subjects in cultures other than the United States perform poorly on the experimenter's task? Then perhaps it is the experimenter's fault for not communicating what was to be done, or for not communicating why the subjects should bother spending time and effort on the task (Cole, 1975; Guthrie, 1977). An operational way of viewing the analysis is that researchers should presuppose every criticism that journal reviewers could possibly suggest as a reason for rejecting their article. Data or arguments should be presented to convince the journal reviewers that the author's preferred interpretation is the most reasonable and that all alternative explanations have been taken into account. Aid in presupposing reviewers' comments can be derived from Lonner's (1975; 1977) content analysis of reasons reviewers gave for recommending acceptance and rejection of articles submitted to the *Journal of Cross-Cultural Psychology*.

A Final Comment

The purpose of this chapter was to review some methods for cross-cultural research, which hopefully does not overshadow the more important aspect of research, that is, the decision on a topic area for investigation. The future of cross-cultural research will depend on its contribution to theory in general psychology, and methods will be only a means to the major goal of discovering important, central facts about human behavior. Further, the future will hopefully see the elimination of the modifier "cross-cultural" as psychologists continue to deal with all aspects of human behavior in all parts of the world.

References

AMERICAN PSYCHOLOGICAL ASSOCIATION. Psychology and folklore: social, developmental, and aesthetic consideration. *Proceedings*, 1975 (P. Machotka, Chairman).

BARTLETT, F. Psychological methods and anthropological problems. *Africa*, 1937, *10*, 401–19.

BASCOM, W. Four functions of folklore. *Journal of American Folklore*, 1954, *67*, 333–49.

BENEDICT, R. *Zuni mythology*. New York: Columbia University, 1935.

BERELSON, B. *Content analysis in communication research.* Glencoe, Ill.: Free Press, 1952.

BERLIN, B., & KAY, P. *Basic color terms: their universality and evolution.* Berkeley: University of California Press, 1969.

BERNDT, C. Comments. *Contemporary Anthropology*, 1963, *4*, 273–74.

BERRY, J. On cross-cultural comparability. *International Journal of Psychology*, 1969, *4*, 119–28.

BOCHNER, S., BRISLIN, R., & LONNER, W. Introduction. In R. Brislin, S. Bochner, & W. Lonner (Eds.), *Cross-cultural perspectives on learning.* New York: Wiley/ Halsted, 1975, pp. 3–36.

BREWER, M. Determinants of social distance among East African tribal groups. *Journal of Personality and Social Psychology*, 1968, *10*, 279–89.

————. Perceptual processes in cross-cultural interaction. In D. Hoopes, P. Pedersen, & G. Renwick (Eds.), *Overview of intercultural education, training, and research: Volume 1, theory.* Washington, D. C.: Georgetown University, Society for Intercultural Education, Training, and Research, 1977, pp. 22–31.

BRISLIN, R. Back-translation for cross-cultural research. *Journal of Cross-Cultural Psychology*, 1970, *1*, 185–216.

————. Translation research and its applications: an introduction. In R. Brislin (Ed.), *Translation: applications and research.* New York: Wiley/Halsted, 1976a.

———— (Ed.), *Translation: applications and research.* New York: Wiley/Halsted, 1976b.

————. Methodology of cognitive studies. In G. Kearney & D. McElwain (Eds.), *Aboriginal cognition.* Canberra, Australia: Australian Institute for Aboriginal Studies, 1977, pp. 29–53.

BRISLIN, R., & BAUMGARDNER, S. Nonrandom sampling of individuals in cross-cultural research. *Journal of Cross-Cultural Psychology*, 1971, *2*, 397–400.

BRISLIN, R., & HOLWILL, F. Reactions of indigenous people to the writings of behavioral and social scientists. *International Journal of Intercultural Relations*, 1977, *1*(2), 15–34.

BRISLIN, R., & PEDERSEN, P. *Cross-cultural orientation programs.* New York: Gardner Press and Wiley/Halsted, 1976.

BRISLIN, R., LONNER, W., & THORNDIKE, R. *Cross-cultural research methods.* New York: Wiley, 1973.

BRUNER, J. Myth and identity. *Daedalus, Proceedings of the American Academy of Arts and Sciences*, 1959, *88*, 349–58.

CAMPBELL, D. A cooperative multinational opinion sample exchange. *Journal of Social Issues*, 1968, *24*, 245–58.

————. Perspective: artifact and control. In R. Rosenthal & R. Rosnow (Eds.), *Artifact in behavioral research.* New York: Academic Press, 1969, pp. 351–82.

CAMPBELL, D., & FISKE, D. Convergent and discriminant validity by the multitrait-multimethod matrix. *Psychological Bulletin*, 1959, *56*, 81–105.

CAMPBELL, D., & STANLEY, J. *Experimental and quasi-experimental design for research.* Chicago: Rand McNally, 1966.

CAMPBELL, D., & ERLEBACHER, A. How regression artifacts in quasi-experimental designs can mistakenly make compensatory education look harmful. In J. Hellmuth (Ed.), *Compensatory education: a national debate*. New York: Brunner/Mazel, 1970.

CASAGRANDE, J. The ends of translation. *International Journal of American Linguistics*, 1954, *20*, 335–40.

CHAPANIS, A. *Man-machine engineering*. Belmont, Calif.: Wadsworth, 1965.

CHOMSKY, N. *Language and mind*, enlarged ed. New York: Harcourt, Brace, Jovanovitch, 1972.

CHOWNING, A. Comments. *Contemporary Anthropology*, 1963, *4*, 274–75.

COLBY, B. The analysis of culture content and the patterning of narrative concern in texts. *American Anthropologist*, 1966a, *68*, 374–388

———. Cultural patterns in narrative. *Science*, 1966b, 151, 793–798.

COLBY, B., COLLIER, G., & POSTAL, S. Comparison of themes in folktales by the general inquirer system. *Journal of American Folklore*, 1963, *76*, 318–23.

COLBY, B., & PEACOCK, J. Narrative. In J. Honigmann (Ed.), *Handbook of social and cultural anthropology*. Chicago: Rand McNally, 1973, pp. 613–35.

COLE, M. An ethnographic psychology of cognition. In R. Brislin, S. Bochner, & W. Lonner (Eds.), *Cross-cultural perspectives on learning*. New York: Wiley/Halsted, 1975, pp. 157–75.

COLE, M., GAY, J., GLICK, J., & SHARP, D. *The cultural context of learning and thinking*. New York: Basic Books, 1971.

COX, K. Changes in stereotyping of negroes and whites in magazine advertisements. *Public Opinion Quarterly*, 1969, *33*, 603–06.

CRONBACH, L. Beyond the two disciplines of scientific psychology. *American Psychologist*, 1975, *30*, 116–27.

CRONBACH, L., & MEEHL, P. Construct validation in psychological tests. *Psychological Bulletin*, 1955, *52*, 281–302.

CROWNE, D., & MARLOWE, D. *The approval motive*. New York: Wiley, 1964.

DAVIDSON, A., JACCARD, J., TRIANDIS, H., MORALES, M., & DIAZ-GUERRERO, R. Cross-cultural model testing: toward a solution of the emic-etic dilemma. *International Journal of Psychology*, 1976, *11*, 1–13.

DORSON, R. (Ed.), *Folklore and folklife, an introduction*. Chicago: University of Chicago Press, 1972.

———. Mythology and folklore. *Annual Review of Anthropology*, 1973, *2*, 107–26.

DZIUBAN, C., & SHIRKEY, E. When is a correlation matrix appropriate for factor analysis? Some decision rules. *Psychological Bulletin*, 1974, *81*, 358–61.

EKMAN, P. The universal smile: face muscles talk every language. *Psychology Today*, 1975, *9* (4), 35–39.

EKMAN, P., & FRIESEN, W. Constants across cultures in the face and emotion. *Journal of Personality and Social Psychology*, 1971, *17*, 124–29.

EKMAN, P., FRIESEN, W., & ELLSWORTH, P. *Emotions in the human face: guidelines for research and an integration of findings*. New York: Pergamon, 1972.

ENDLER, N., & MAGNUSSON, D. (Eds.), *Interactional psychology and personality*. Washington, D.C.: Hemisphere, 1976.

FELDMAN, R. Response to compatriot and foreigner who seek assistance. *Journal of Personality and Social Psychology*, 1968, *10*, 202–14.

FIEDLER, F., MITCHELL, T., & TRIANDIS, H. The culture assimilator: an approach to cross-cultural training. *Journal of Applied Psychology*, 1971, *55*, 95–102.

FISHER, J. The sociopsychological analysis of folktales. *Current Anthropology*, 1963, *4*, 235–95.

FOA, U. New developments in facet design and analysis. *Psychological Review*, 1965, *72*, 262–74.

FREY, F. Cross-cultural survey research in political science. In R. Holt & J. Turner (Eds.), *The methodology of comparative research*. New York: Free Press, 1970, pp. 173–264.

GALLIMORE, R., WEISS, L., & FINNEY, R. Cultural differences in delay of gratification: a problem of behavior classification. *Journal of Personality and Social Psychology*, 1974, *30*, 72–80.

GERVER, D., & SINAIKO, H. (Eds.), *Language interpretation and communication*. London: Plenum, 1978.

GOODENOUGH, F. Racial differences in the intelligence of school children. *Journal of Experimental Psychology*, 1926, *9*, 388–97.

GOODENOUGH, W. Componential analysis and the study of meaning. *Language*, 1956, *32*, 195–216.

————. Cultural anthropology and linguistics. In P. Garvin (Ed.), *Reports of the 7th annual round table meeting on linguistics and language study*. Washington, D.C.: Institute of Languages and Linguistics, Georgetown University, 1957, pp. 167–73.

————. Yankee kinship terminology: a problem in componential analysis. *American Anthropologist*, special publication on "Formal Semantic Analysis," E. Hammel (Ed.), 1965, *67*, 5(part 2), 259–87.

GUTHRIE, G. Problems of measurement in cross-cultural research. In L. Loeb Adler (Ed.), Issues in Cross-Cultural Research. *Annals of the New York Academy of Sciences*, 1977, *285*, 131–40.

GUTTMAN, L. A structural theory for intergroup beliefs and action. *American Sociological Review*, 1959, *24*, 318–28.

HELSON, H. *Adaptation-level theory*. New York: Harper, 1964.

HAMMEL, E. (Ed.), Formal semantic analysis. *American Anthropologist*, 1965, *67*, 5(part 2), entire issue.

HOLSTI, O. Content analysis. In G. Lindzey & E. Aronson (Eds.), *Handbook of social psychology*, 2nd ed., Vol. 2. Reading, Mass.: Addison-Wesley, 1968, pp. 596–692.

HOWARD, A. *Ain't no big thing*. Honolulu, Hawaii: University Press of Hawaii, 1974.

IRWIN, M., KLEIN, R., ENGLE, P., YARBROUGH, C., & NERLOVE, S. The problem of establishing validity in cross-cultural measurements. In L. Loeb Adler (Ed.), Issues in Cross-Cultural Research. *Annals of the New York Academy of Sciences*, 1977, *285*, 308–25.

IRVINE, S. Human behavior in Africa: some research problems noted while compiling source materials. Paper presented to the East Africa Institute of Social Research Workshop in Social Psychology in Africa, New York City, 1968.

JACOBS, M. *The content and style of an oral literature*. Viking Fund Publication in Anthropology, 1959, *26*, entire issue.

JANIS, I. The problem of validating content analysis. In H. Lasswell & N. Leites

(Eds.), *The language of politics: studies in quantitative semantics.* New York: George Stewart, 1949, pp. 55–82.

JORDAN, J. Facet theory and cross-cultural research methodology. In J. Dawson & W. Lonner (Eds.), *Readings in cross-cultural psychology.* Hong Kong: University of Hong Kong Press, 1974, pp. 39–50.

KATZ, D. Review, *Handbook of social psychology. Contemporary Psychology,* 1971, *16,* 273–82.

KLUCKHOHN, C. The philosophy of the Navajo Indians. In F. Northrop (Ed.), *Ideological differences and world order.* New Haven: Yale University Press, 1949.

KRAUSS, B. *Ethnobotany of the Hawaiians.* Honolulu, Hawaii: Harold L. Lyon Arboretum, 1974.

LABARRE, W. Folklore and psychology. *Journal of American Folklore,* 1948, *61,* 382–390.

LEVINE, R., & CAMPBELL, C. *Ethnocentrism.* New York: Wiley, 1972.

LEWIN, H. Hitler youth and the boy scouts of America: a comparison of aims. *Human Relations,* 1947, *1,* 206–27.

LONGACRE, R. Items in context—their bearing on translation theory. *Language,* 1958, *34,* 482–91.

LONNER, W. An analysis of the prepublication evaluation of cross-cultural manuscripts: implications for future research. In R. Brislin, S. Bochner, & W. Lonner (Eds.), *Cross-cultural perspectives on learning.* New York: Wiley/Halsted, 1975, pp. 305–20.

LONNER, W. Issues relating to the publication and dissemination of cross-cultural research data. In L. Loeb Adler (Ed.), *Issues in Cross-Cultural Research, Annals of the New York Academy of Sciences,* 1977, *285,* 203–14.

LOWENTHAL, L. The sociology of literature. In W. Schramm (Ed.), *Communications in modern society.* Urbana: University of Illinois Press, 1949, pp. 82–100.

MAIERLE, J. An application of Guttman facet analysis to attitude scale construction: a methodological study. Unpublished doctoral dissertation, Michigan State University, 1969.

MALINOWSKI, B. *Myth in primitive psychology.* New York: Norton, 1926.

MANN, L. Cross-national aspects of riot behavior. In J. Dawson & W. Lonner (Eds.), *Readings in cross-cultural psychology.* Hong Kong: University of Hong Kong Press, 1974, pp. 327–37.

McCLELLAND, D. *The achieving society.* Princeton, N.J.: Van Nostrand, 1961.

———. The achievement motive in economic growth. In B. Hoselitz & W. Moore (Eds.), *Industrialization and society.* The Hague: Mouton, 1963. Reprinted in W. Lambert & R. Weisbrod (Eds.), *Comparative perspectives on social psychology.* Boston: Little, Brown, 1971, pp. 274–95.

———. *Power: the inner experience.* New York: Wiley/Halsted, 1975.

McCLELLAND, D., & FRIEDMAN, G. A cross-cultural study of the relationship between child-training practices and achievement motivation appearing in folktales. In G. Swanson, T. M. Newcomb, & E. L. Hartley (Eds.), *Readings in social psychology.* New York: Holt, Rinehart and Winston, 1952.

McGRANAHAN, D., & WAYNE, I. German and American traits reflected in popular drama. *Human Relations,* 1948, *1,* 429–55.

McGuire, W. The yin and yang of progress in social psychology: seven koan. *Journal of Personality and Social Psychology*, 1973, *26*, 446–56.

Miller, G. What is information measurement? *American Psychologist*, 1953, *9*, 3–11.

Mischel, W. Toward a cognitive social learning reconceptualization of personality. *Psychological Review*, 1973, *80*, 252–83.

Morrison, D., & Henkel, R. *The significance test controversy.* Chicago: Aldine, 1970.

Nida, E. A framework for the analysis and evaluation of theories of translation. In R. Brislin (Ed.), *Translation: applications and research.* New York: Wiley/Halsted, 1976, pp. 47–91.

Osgood, C., Cross-cultural comparability in attitude measurement via multilingual semantic differentials. In I. Steiner & M. Fishbein (Eds.), *Current studies in social psychology*, New York: Holt, Rinehart and Winston, 1965, pp. 95–106.

———. Exploration in semantic space: a personal diary. *Journal of Social Issues*, 1971, *27*(4), 5–64.

———. Objective indicators in subjective culture. In L. Loeb Adler (Ed.), *Issues in Cross-Cultural Research. Annals of the New York Academy of Sciences*, 1977, *285*, 435–50.

Phillips, H. Problems of translation and meaning in field work. *Human Organization*, 1960, *18*(4), 184–92.

Price-Williams, D. A study concerning concepts of conservation of quantities among primitive children. *Acta Psychologica*, 1961, *18*, 297–305.

———. Psychological experiment and anthropology: the problem of categories. *Ethos*, 1974, *2*, 95–114.

Prince, R., & Mombour, W. A technique for improving linguistic equivalence in cross-cultural surveys. *International Journal of Social Psychiatry*, 1967, *13*, 229–37.

Przeworski, A., & Teune, H. Equivalence in cross-national research. *Public Opinion Quarterly*, 1966, *30*, 33–43.

———. *The logic of comparative social inquiry.* New York: Wiley, 1970.

Richards, I. Toward a theory of translation. *Studies in Chinese thought.* American Anthropological Association, 1953, Volume 55, Memoir 75. Chicago: University of Chicago Press.

Roberts, J., & Sutton-Smith, B. Child training and game involvement. *Ethnology*, 1962, *1*, 166–85.

Roberts, J., Sutton-Smith, B., & Kendon, A. Strategy in games and folktales. *Journal of Social Psychology*, 1963, *61*, 185–99.

Rosch, E. Universals and cultural specifics in human categorization. In R. Brislin, S. Bochner, & W. Lonner (Eds.), *Cross-cultural perspectives on learning.* New York: Wiley/Halsted, 1975, pp. 177–206.

———. Human categorization. In N. Warren (Ed.), *Studies in cross-cultural psychology*, Vol. 1. London: Academic Press, 1977, pp. 1–49.

Sebald, H. Studying national character through comparative content analysis. *Social Forces*, 1962, *40*, 318–22.

Seleskovitch, D. Interpretation, a psychological approach to translation. In R. Brislin (Ed.), *Translation: applications and research.* New York: Wiley/Halsted, 1976, pp. 92–116.

SINAIKO, H., & BRISLIN, R. Evaluating language translations: experiments on three assessment methods. *Journal of Applied Psychology*, 1973, *57*, 328–334.

SINHA, J. The n-Ach/n-Cooperation under limited /unlimited resource conditions. *Journal of Experimental Social Psychology*, 1968, *4*, 223–46.

SPIRO, M. Comments. *Current Anthropology*, 1963, *4*, 282–83.

STEMPEL, G. Increasing reliability in content analysis. *Journalism Quarterly*, 1955, *32*, 449–55.

STONE, P., DUNPHY, D., SMITH, M., & OGLVIE, D. *The general inquirer: a computer approach to content analysis in the behavioral sciences.* Cambridge, Mass.: MIT Press, 1966.

STURTEVANT, W. Studies in ethnoscience. In A. Romney & R. D'Andrade (Eds.), *Transcultural studies in cognition. American Anthropologist*, 1964, *66* (3), part 2.

SULEIMAN, M. Values expressed in Egyptian children's readers. *Journal of Cross-Cultural Psychology*, 1977, *8*, 347–55.

TEITELBAUM, P. *Physiological psychology.* Englewood Cliffs, N.J.: Prentice-Hall, 1967.

THORNDIKE, E., & LORGE, I. *The teacher's word book of 30,000 words.* New York: Bureau of Publications, Teachers College, Columbia University, 1944.

TOMA, P. An operational machine translation system. In R. Brislin (Ed.), *Translation: applications and research.* New York: Wiley/Halsted, 1976, pp. 247–60.

TRIANDIS, H. *The analysis of subjective culture.* New York: Wiley, 1972.

———. Approaches toward minimizing translation. In R. Brislin (Ed.), *Translation: applications and research.* New York: Wiley/Halsted, 1976, pp. 229–43.

———. Subjective culture and interpersonal relations across cultures. In L. Loeb Adler (Ed.), *Issues in Cross-Cultural Research. Annals of the New York Academy of Sciences*, 1977, *285*, pp. 418–34.

TRIANDIS, H., DAVIS, E., & TAKEZAWA, S. Some determinants of social distance among American, German, and Japanese students. *Journal of Personality and Social Psychology*, 1965, *2*, 540–51.

TRIANDIS, H., VASSILIOU, V., & NASSIAKOU, M. Three cross-cultural studies of subjective culture. *Journal of Personality and Social Psychology Monograph Supplement*, 1968, *8*, No. 4, 1–42.

TRUEX, G. Measurement of intersubject variations in categorizations. *Journal of Cross-Cultural Psychology*, 1977, *8*, 71–82.

WALLACE, A., & ATKINS, J. The meaning of kinship terms. *American Anthropologist*, 1960, *62*, 58–80.

WEBB, E., CAMPBELL, D., SCHWARTZ, R., & SECHREST, L. *Unobtrusive measures: nonreactive research in the social sciences.* Chicago: Rand McNally, 1966.

WERNER, O., & CAMPBELL, D. Translating, working through interpreters, and the problem of decentering. In R. Naroll & R. Cohen (Eds.), *A handbook of method in cultural anthropology.* New York: Natural History Press, 1970, pp. 398–420.

WESLEY, F., & KARR, C. Problems in establishing norms for cross-cultural comparisons. *International Journal of Psychology*, 1966, *1*, 257–62.

WHITE, R. "Black boy": a value-analysis. *Journal of Abnormal and Social Psychology*, 1947, *42*, 440–61.

WHITING, J. Methods and problems in cross-cultural research. In G. Lindzey & E. Aronson (Eds.), *Handbook of social psychology*, 2nd ed., Vol. 2. Reading, Mass.: Addison-Wesley, 1968, pp. 693–728.

11

Description and Uses of the Human Relations Area Files

Herbert Barry III

Contents

Abstract

The Human Relations Area Files contain ethnographic source materials on more than 300 cultural units throughout the world. The Files include a comprehensive set of topical categories, each containing a copy of the pages of the source materials with information on that topic for the cultural unit. A set of paper files is available at more than twenty locations, and a set of microfiche files is available at more than 200 locations. The Files have many applications to cross-cultural research and have stimulated studies on a wide variety of topics, especially using large samples of nonliterate societies. Associated resources include a recommended "probability sample" of sixty cultural units and sets of coded data and programs for research use with computers.

Overview

Scientific use of the enormous richness and diversity of ethnographic information is hampered by the difficulty of bringing together in a uniform format the various sources. The problem is magnified by the fact that most ethnographic accounts emphasize the uniqueness of the society described without attempting to establish a standard list of the topics for comparison with other ethnographic accounts.

The Human Relations Area Files provide a unique resource for standardizing the information and thus for enabling effective comparison among different accounts. Diverse information from various sources on the same society is brought together in the same topical category. These topical categories have been carefully constructed to cover the full range of cultural attributes. The information on different societies can be compared using a standardized classification system. This compilation has been applied by HRAF, Inc. to a large and gradually increasing number of cultural units, representing all areas of the world and the full range of cultural development, from small aboriginal tribes to modern nations. The full set of materials is available at more than twenty institutions, in widely separated locations, including one in Europe and three in Asia. A steadily increasing portion of the material is available at a much larger number of institutions in the form of microfilm.

The Files have attained a large and important role in cross-cultural research in the few decades since the initial formulation of the idea in 1936. The usefulness of this resource is demonstrated by a large number of publications reporting research in which the Files were used. Each new study with this sample of societies and set of topical categories enhances the value of the material for other researchers and encourages further growth of this type of research.

Since psychology is a comprehensive field, the wide scope of materials in the ethnographic literature should be especially attractive to many psychologists. Each specialty topic in psychology can find much pertinent and useful information in ethnographic accounts, which are made easily accessible and efficiently usable by the Human Relations Area Files.

This chapter begins with a summary of general characteristics of the Files, describing the availability of the two forms of the Files (paper and microfiche). The most distinctive and frequently used feature is the organization of ethnographic information in terms of topical categories. This section also summarizes the identification and evaluation of ethnographic sources and the sample of societies included.

The next major section of this chapter summarizes the origin, development, and uses of the Files. This information is intended to demonstrate the thoroughness and care with which the topical categories were formulated, and to identify some of the published studies based on the Files.

The last major section of this chapter points out various uses of the Files and discusses some considerations in selecting a sample of cultural units, using the topical categories, and collecting, summarizing, statistically evaluating, and publishing the data.

General Characteristics

The Human Relations Area Files (HRAF) consist of reproductions of various ethnographic accounts assembled on each cultural unit. The information from each source is reproduced in each topical category for which it is relevant. The user therefore can locate ethnographic material on a cultural unit and can select the material pertaining to a particular topic for that cultural unit.

These procedures have been applied to a large and progressively increasing world sample of societies, ranging from small, traditionally non-literate tribes to contemporary nations. Two types of Files are available (paper and microfiche) at many locations in the United States and at several sites in other countries.

An excellent manual for users of the Files, prepared by Lagacé (1974), is distributed by HRAF, Inc., Box 2054 Y.S., New Haven, CT 06520. In addition, a brief informational pamphlet entitled "A World of Research" is available without charge from HRAF. The present chapter summarizes this information and adds discussion of some general characteristics of the Files, especially the features that are most important for psychologists.

Paper Files and Microfiche

Two principal physical versions of the Files are available. One, the Paper Files, is more complete and convenient to use but available at fewer locations. The other, the HRAF-Microfiles, is more widely available and almost as complete, but requires the use of a microfiche reader.

The paper files consist of a large collection of thin slips of paper, twenty by thirteen centimeters (eight by five inches). One side of each slip reproduces in reduced size one page of each source included in the collection. The slips are stored in file drawers.

By July 1977 more than 500,000 pages of source material had been reproduced on slips. The duplications of source pages in different topical categories multiply the number of slips by about six, which totals about three million. More than forty cabinets, each containing seven rows of file drawers, are needed to house the collection.

The Paper Files are available at the HRAF headquarters, in New Haven, Connecticut, and at more than twenty other locations that are listed in the chapter by Naroll, Michik, and Naroll in this volume. Four of these locations are outside the United States (Kyoto, Osaka, Paris, and Seoul). Most of these sets of Files are in special collections at university libraries.

Most of the Paper Files have been reproduced on microfilm (in microfiche card format) as part of the HRAF-Microfiles program. The HRAF-Microfiles are currently available at over 200 member institutions around the world. Each microfiche, 105 by 148 millimeters (four by six inches), contains an average of 160 pages. The microfiche files include each of the sixty cultural units in the HRAF "Probability Sample" (Table 11-1). In an earlier version of the HRAF-Microfiles, the materials were reproduced on smaller microfilm cards in two different formats, jacketed microfilm cards and microfiche.

Table 11-1. The Sixty Cultural Units in the HRAF Probability Sample. The single letter after the identification code designates whether the form of marriage is monogamy (M), limited polygyny (L), or general polygyny (P), according to the code in the Ethnographic Atlas (Murdock, 1967).

Asia

AA1	M	Koreans
AD5	M	Taiwan Hokkien
A07	L	Central Thai
AR5	L	Garo
AR7	M	Khasi
AW42	L	Santal
AX4	M	Sinhalese
AZ2	M	Andamans

Europe

EF6	M	Serbs
EP4	M	Lapps
ES10	M	Highland Scots

Africa

FA16	L	Dogon
FE12	P	Twi (Ashanti)
FF57	P	Tiv
FK7	P	Ganda
FL12	P	Masai
F04	L	Pygmies (Mbuti)
F07	P	Azande
FQ5	P	Bemba
FQ9	P	Lozi

Middle East

MA11	L	Kurd
M04	P	Somali
MP5	M	Amhara
MS12	P	Hausa
MS14	P	Kanuri
MS30	P	Wolof
MT9	P	Libyan Bedouin
MW11	M	Shluh

North America

NA12	L	Tlingit
ND8	M	Copper Eskimo
NF6	P	Blackfoot
NG6	L	Ojibwa
NM9	M	Iroquois
NQ18	P	Pawnee
NR10	L	Klamath
NT9	M	Hopi
NU33	L	Tarahumara
NV9	L	Tzeltal

Oceania

OA19	M	Ifugao
OC6	M	Iban
OG11	M	Toradja
O18	P	Aranda
OJ29	P	Kapauku
OL6	L	Trobrianders
OQ6	P	Lau (Fijians)
OR19	M	Truk
OT11	P	Tikopia

Russia

| RV2 | P | Yakut |
| RY2 | P | Chukchee |

South America

SB5	L	Cuna
SC7	L	Cagaba
SF5	M	Aymara
SH4	L	Ona
S17	L	Mataco
SM4	M	Guarani (Cayua)
SO11	M	Bahia Brazilians
SP8	L	Bororo
SQ18	P	Yanoama
SQ19	P	Tucano
SR8	P	Bush Negroes

Topical Categories

The universe of cultural attributes is divided into categories that bring together the information on each specified topic in a convenient group, excluding irrelevant material. Two hierarchical levels are distinguished,
sections and categories. Table 11-2 names seventy-nine sections, identified by two-digit numbers ranging from ten to eighty-eight. Each section is
divided into several categories ranging from five to nine in number. These
categories are identified by three-digit numbers, the first two digits consisting of the number of the section in which they belong. Table 11-3
names the categories for a sample of four of the seventy-nine sections.

The two- or three-digit codes are marked for each paragraph of the
source material, and a copy of the page is included in the collection for
each category marked. Figure 11-1 shows a sample page with the three-
digit codes.

Table 11-2 divides the seventy-nine sections into eight groups. These
general groups are intended to help the readers to locate the categories
that are available and useful for them.

The first group consists of Sections 10-21, which summarize several
characteristics of the cultural unit, including language and historical material. In Section 11 (Bibliography), Category 111 identifies the ethnographic
and other written sources of information. In the same section, Category
116 reproduces each consecutive page of each source (except for copyright
restricted material), so that users can locate all the material on a particular
source or find adjacent pages if the page reproduced in a topical category
does not provide all the needed information. Table 11-3 lists the eight
categories in Section 12 (Methodology). This material is of special interest
for users who wish to assess the quality of the ethnographic information.

The second group, Sections 22-30, includes the topics of food and
clothing. Table 11-3 lists the categories for Section 27 (Drink, Drugs, and
Indulgence). Psychological information on people's feeling of thirst is
found in Category 271; behavior related to alcohol intoxication is described in Category 273; use and abuse of other drugs is covered in Category 276.

The third group, Sections 31-41, is on housing and technology. Many
of the categories within these sections pertain to heavy industry, which
has been developed only in modern nations, so they have no material on
nonliterate societies.

The fourth group, Sections 42-50, covers the general topics of economy and transport. This material is usually more extensive in industrialized nations than in nonliterate societies.

The fifth group, Sections 51-61, includes the diverse individual and
family activities that are involved in social behavior and family structure.
Among these are games, esthetics, and other leisure or expressive activi-

Table 11-2. The Seventy-nine Topical Sections (10-88) Are from the Outline of Cultural Materials (Murdock et al., 1971). The eight groups (I-VIII) are specified by Barry.

I General Characteristics
  10 Orientation
  11 Bibliography
  12 Methodology
  13 Geography
  14 Human Biology
  15 Behavior Processes and Personality
  16 Demography
  17 History and Culture Change
  18 Total Culture
  19 Language
  20 Communication
  21 Records
II Food and Clothing
  22 Food Quest
  23 Animal Husbandry
  24 Agriculture
  25 Food Processing
  26 Food Consumption
  27 Drink, Drugs, and Indulgence
  28 Leather, Textiles, and Fabrics
  29 Clothing
  30 Adornment
III Housing and Technology
  31 Exploitative Activities
  32 Processing of Basic Materials
  33 Building and Construction
  34 Structures
  35 Equipment and Maintenance of Buildings
  36 Settlements
  37 Energy and Power
  38 Chemical Industries
  39 Capital Goods Industries
  40 Machines
  41 Tools and Appliances
IV Economy and Transport
  42 Property
  43 Exchange
  44 Marketing
  45 Finance
  46 Labor
  47 Business and Industrial Organization
  48 Travel and Transportation
  49 Land Transport
  50 Water and Air Transport

V Individual and Family Activities
  51 Living Standards and Routines
  52 Recreation
  53 Fine Arts
  54 Entertainment
  55 Individuation and Mobility
  56 Social Stratification
  57 Interpersonal Relations
  58 Marriage
  59 Family
  60 Kinship
  61 Kin Groups
VI Community and Government
  62 Community
  63 Territorial Organization
  64 State
  65 Government Activities
  66 Political Behavior
  67 Law
  68 Offenses and Sanctions
  69 Justice
  70 Armed Forces
  71 Military Technology
  72 War
VII Welfare, Religion, and Science
  73 Social Problems
  74 Health and Welfare
  75 Sickness
  76 Death
  77 Religious Beliefs
  78 Religious Practices
  79 Ecclesiastical Organization
  80 Numbers and Measures
  81 Exact Knowledge
  82 Ideas About Nature and Man
VIII Sex and the Life Cycle
  83 Sex
  84 Reproduction
  85 Infancy and Childhood
  86 Socialization
  87 Education
  88 Adolescence, Adulthood, and Old Age

that a girl arrived at puberty, she was called *Mulongo*, a term used **857**
of a cow when it was old enough to have calves.

When a twin had grown up, and went to war for the first time, **727**
then if he killed a man, he had on his return to go to his father's
house and spend the night there. His father jumped over his mother **845**
that night, and the next morning he gave a barkcloth and a fowl to **852**
his son, who then went away to his own residence.

In more ancient times, before princes were killed when their **643**
brother began to reign, none of the King's brothers who married
were allowed to have sons; any male child born to a prince was put **847**
to death by the midwife, and only princesses were allowed to live.
The sons of the reigning king, however, might marry and have
children, and their sons were not killed, because they were not
regarded as dangerous to the sovereign.

Women who did not wish their daughters to be taken to be wives **304**
of the King, or of a chief in the yearly tribute of girls, sometimes **582**
scarified them on the forehead or some other visible place; this **651**
disqualified a girl from being taken to wife by the King.

Owing to the clan system, no occasion arose for the adoption of Adoption
orphans; children belonged to the clan, and when their father or was not
mother died, they were still under the care of some relative who followed.
took the place of the father. Women taken captive in war might **549**
become the wives of men in high positions, and the children which **614**
they had by such men would become full members of the clan, **727**
while they themselves were only slaves. On the death of the hus- **614**
band such a woman became the property of his heir; she might be
appointed to look after her husband's grave, and in some cases she
was respected by the clan. If she had borne children, she would
not be so likely to be sold by the heir as would a slave who had
never been taken to wife.

At puberty some of the women of the Kyagwe district scarified **881**
themselves on the stomach, the shape of the figure being usually a **304**
large W, the tips of which started below the breasts, while the mid- **184**
dle point was between the breasts; but among other women such
markings were discouraged.

G

**Figure 11-1. A Sample Page from the Files, Showing the Identifying Informa-
tion on the Source and Cultural Unit at the Top and the Three-Digit Categories
for Each Paragraph at the Right-Hand Margin.**

Table 11-3.   The Three-Digit Topical Categories for a Sample of Two-Digit Topical Sections from the Outline of Cultural Materials (Murdock et al., 1971).

12 *Methodology* (employed by the observers of the society)
    121 Theoretical Orientation
    122 Practical Preparations
    123 Observational Role
    124 Interviewing
    125 Tests and Schedules
    126 Recording and Collecting
    127 Historical Research
    128 Organization and Analysis

27 *Drink, Drugs, and Indulgence*
    271 Water and Thirst
    272 Nonalcoholic Beverages
    273 Alcoholic Beverages
    274 Beverage Industries
    275 Drinking Establishments
    276 Narcotics and Stimulants
    277 Tobacco Industry
    278 Pharmaceuticals

57 *Interpersonal Relations*
    571 Social Relationships and Groups
    572 Friendships
    573 Cliques
    574 Visiting and Hospitality
    575 Sodalities
    576 Etiquette
    577 Ethics
    578 Ingroup Antagonisms
    579 Brawls, Riots, and Banditry

86 *Socialization*
    861 Techniques of Inculcation
    862 Weaning and Food Training
    863 Cleanliness Training
    864 Sex Training
    865 Aggression Training
    866 Independence Training
    867 Transmission of Cultural Norms
    868 Transmission of Skills
    869 Transmission of Beliefs

ties. Table 11-3 shows that Section 57 (Interpersonal Relations) is divided into a number of categories describing particular types of organized or spontaneous activities among friends and companions.

The sixth group, Sections 62-72, is on the organization of the community and government. Detailed aspects of political, legal and military topics are covered in some of the categories.

The seventh group, Sections 73-82, encompasses diverse topics of welfare, religion, and science. These concepts concern the general customs and ideology of the society as a whole. Individual behavior is also described in the information on sickness and health, religious customs, and applications of scientific knowledge.

The eighth group, Sections 83–88, covers information on the wide range of behavior involved in sex and the life cycle. Important emotional aspects of the life of the individual are represented. Table 11–3 shows the nine categories that comprise Section 86 (Socialization). Categories 862–866 organize the information on training and behavior of the child according to five motivational systems (oral, anal, sex, aggression, dependence) that were presented by Whiting and Child (1953).

Sources

An important aspect of the Files is the use of a number of different ethnographic sources on each society. The sample page (Fig. 11–1) shows at the top several standard items of information, repeated on each page for the same source.

The first number "2" indicates that this is the second source in the File's serial numbering for this cultural unit. The first source is generally the most definitive ethnographic account. Brief articles describing technological specialties, such as methods of manufacturing beer, are usually at the end of the sequence of sources.

The name (Roscoe) identifies the last name of the author. The letter "M" is one of twenty-six codes for the type of source, in this case Missionary. The number "5" is a code designating the highest quality of source (excellent primary data), based on a scale of 1 to 5. The following dates show the dates of the fieldwork (ca. 1900) and publication (1911).

More detailed information about the sources is given in some of the categories in Section 11 (Bibliography). The categories in Section 12, shown in Table 11–3, provide further information about the techniques of observation or data collection.

Cultural Units

The sample page from the Files (Fig. 11–1) includes identifying information reproduced at the top of every page for the same File unit. The region is Africa (F), the subregion is Uganda (K), the serial number is "7" within the subregion, and the name is Ganda. Table 11–1 names the eight regions of the world and shows for each of sixty cultural units the identifying letters and number and the name. The classification is described by Murdock (1975).

In July, 1977, the Files contained material on more than 300 cultural units. A few of these File units are large regions (Southeast Asia, Europe,

Africa, Middle East, Baltic Countries), but most of them are names of specific societies or countries. A list available from HRAF, Inc. shows for each File unit the number of different sources included and the total number of text pages of this material. Each consecutive page of each consecutive source is usually reproduced in Category 116 and also in an average of five additional three-digit categories.

The average amount of source material for a File unit is almost 2,000 text pages, divided among ten sources. A few File units contain more than 10,000 text pages; more than half of the File units have fewer than 1,500 text pages. The largest amount of material is for Indochina (AM1), 19,633 text pages from 153 sources. Other File units with 3,000 or more text pages are Korea (AA1), China (AF1), Tibet (AJ1), Malaya (AN1), Thailand (AO1), Burma (AP1), Afghanistan (AU1), India (AW1), Poland (EA1), Czechoslovakia (EB1), Serbs (EF6), Lapps (EP4), Georgian Britain (ES3), Tudor Britain (ES14), Iran (MA1), Jordan (MG1), Saudi Arabia (MJ1), Philippines (OA1), Indonesia (OB1), and the Soviet Union (R1). The smallest amount of material is for the Maritime Arabs (MK2), 103 text pages (four sources). For a few of the File units, the material is designated as a subfile, which consists of a portion of a larger File unit.

Most of the File units are included also in the sample of more than 1000 societies called the Ethnographic Atlas (Murdock, 1967). These societies are coded for a number of cultural attributes, and the large amount of compact information on a large sample is useful for selecting or grouping societies and for correlating these attributes with each other or with other measures. Unfortunately, the Ethnographic Atlas divides the world into six instead of eight regions and identifies the societies by a different code of letters and numbers. This obstacle to comparisons between the two samples can be removed by using a concordance (O'Leary, 1969b), which lists the cultural units in four sequences: alphabetical order of names, Outline of World Cultures code, Ethographic Atlas code, and Ethnographic Atlas serial number.

The "probability sample" of sixty societies, listed in Table 11–1, has been selected on the basis of several criteria (Naroll, 1967; HRAF, 1967; Lagacé, 1970, 1976). This sample is recommended for use as a standard list of independent, well-described societies. The value of this sample will be enhanced by the accumulation of codings of various attributes by researchers who use this sample. The cultural unit in Table 11–1 with the largest amount of source material is Korea (AA1), 6,148 text pages from fifty-eight sources. The next largest amount of material is on the Ojibwa (NG6), 4,354 text pages from twenty-six sources. The society with the least material is the Guarani (SM4), 484 text pages from six sources.

Table 11–1 contains a few national or regional units: Korea (AA1), Serbs (EF6), and Highland Scots (ES10). The remaining fifty-seven cultural units in this sample are smaller, nonliterate societies. Most of them have undergone major changes since contact with Western European civilization. Many of the sources consist of accounts by ethnographers who attempted to describe the aboriginal customs at an early stage of this culture contact.

Origin, Development, and Uses

The historical background of the Files is of interest to anybody who uses this important resource. It is impressive that such a large, thoroughly organized, widely available body of material could have grown in the few decades since its development was begun in 1936 by G. P. Murdock with the help of a small interdisciplinary group of social scientists (C. S. Ford, A. E. Hudson, R. Kennedy, J. W. M. Whiting) at the Institute of Human Relations, Yale University. A special value of knowing the history of the Files is that it indicates some special attributes of this material. The successive stages in the development of the Files can guide the knowledgeable user to take into account certain characteristics in the formulation of the categories, the selection of the sample of societies, the forms of the material, and the locations of the collections.

The present account summarizes historical information given in Murdock (1975), Murdock, Ford, Hudson (and others) (1971), and Ford (1971). In addition, Table 11-4 gives a selected list of published studies on many of the topical categories (Table 11-2) applied to a world sample of societies. Most of these studies are included in one of the successive bibliographies of cross-cultural studies compiled by O'Leary (1969a, 1971, 1973).

Table 11-4. Studies of the Designated Variables, Identified by Eight Groups of Two-Digit Sections (Table 11-2), Using the Ethnographic Information in the Files. Each reference is followed by the specific topic studied, then the principal other variable if any related to it, and last the number of cultural units in the sample.

I Environment, Biology, History (Sections 13–21)

Whiting (1964; 1969)	Climate; Infancy	177
Whiting (1965)	Physical growth; Infant treatment	24
Gunders & Whiting (1968)	Physical growth; Infant treatment	69

II, III, IV Technology, Economy (Sections 22–50)

Horton (1943)	Alcohol use; Economy	57
Klausner (1964)	Alcohol use	48
Bacon et al. (1965)	Alcohol use; Child training	139
Goodenough (1969)	Subsistence economy	40
Murdock & Morrow (1970)	Subsistence economy	186
Whiting & Ayres (1968)	Shape of houses	52
Gouldner & Peterson (1962)	Technology; Morality	71
Hickman (1962)	Technology	70
Carneiro (1968)	Technological complexity	100
Murdock & Provost (1973b)	Technological complexity	186
Udy (1959; 1970)	Work organizations	150

V–A Individual Activities (Sections 51–57)

Roberts et al. (1959)	Games; Child training	51
Roberts & Sutton-Smith (1962)	Games; Child training	56
Roberts et al. (1963)	Games; Folk tales	141
Roberts & Forman (1971)	Riddles	146
Barry (1957)	Art; Child training	30
Fischer (1961)	Art; Social structure	29
Wolfe (1969)	Art	53
Hays et al. (1972)	Color perception	123
Bornstein (1973)	Color perception	127
Lomax (1968)	Folk songs	233
Lomax & Berkowitz (1972)	Folk songs	10
Ayres (1968)	Music; Infancy experiences	25
McClelland (1972)	Folk tales; Alcoholism	44
Barry et al. (1957; 1967)	Sex differences in childhood	110
Schlegel (1972)	Sex role; Authority in family	66
Whyte (1978)	Sex role	93
Murdock & Provost (1973a)	Sexual division of labor	186
Rohner (1977)	Sex differences in aggression	31
Roberts & Gregor (1971)	Privacy	42
Moore (1942)	Social stratification	36
Goggin & Sturtevant (1964)	Social stratification	42
Cohen (1964)	Sharing food	65
Cohen (1964)	Friendship	65

V–B Family and Kinship (Sections 58–61)

Rosenblatt (1966)	Romantic love; Child training	19
Rosenblatt (1967)	Romantic love; Residence	75
Rosenblatt & Cozby (1972)	Courtship	59
Ember (1967)	Marital residence	29
Ember & Ember (1971)	Marital residence	17
Ember (1973)	Marital residence	15
Murdock (1950)	Divorce	40
Ackerman (1968)	Divorce	62
Minturn & Lambert (1964)	Household; Child training	76
Murdock (1949)	Family and kinship	250
Brant (1948; 1972)	Kinship relations	220
Sweetser (1966)	Kinship role	102
Nerlove & Romney (1967)	Kinship terms	245
Driver & Sanday (1971)	Kin avoidances	277

VI Community and Government (Sections 62–72)

March (1955)	Group control	15
Broussard (1957)	Social power	100
Murdock & Wilson (1972)	Community organization	186
Ember (1963)	Political system; Economy	24
Otterbein (1971)	Political complexity	50
Tuden & Marshall (1972)	Political system	186
Wirsing (1973)	Political power	25
Roberts (1965)	Ordeals in legal trials	164
Otterbein & Otterbein (1965)	Feuding	50

Hoebel (1972)	Feuding and law	50
Otterbein (1968)	Warfare	50
Otterbein (1970)	Warfare	50
Divale (1976)	Warfare; Population control	112
Sipes (1973)	Warfare	20
Ember (1974)	Warfare; Polygyny	48

VII Welfare, Religion, and Science (Sections 73–82)

Allen (1967)	Social pathology; Child training	58
Bacon et al. (1963)	Crime; Child training	48
Palmer (1965)	Murder and suicide	40
Palmer (1970)	Aggression	58
Lester (1967a)	Aggression and suicide; Child training	33
Lester (1967b)	Aggression; Child training	67
Lester (1971)	Suicide and mutilation	34
Allen (1972)	Aggression and crime	58
Devereux (1955)	Abortion	365
Rosenblatt et al. (1976)	Mourning	78
Roberts (1976)	Evil eye	186
Lambert et al. (1959)	Religion; Child training	43
Swanson (1960)	Religion	50
Zern (1967)	Time; Technological complexity	29

VIII–A Sex (Section 83)

Ford (1939)	Sexual behavior	25
Ford (1945)	Reproduction	48
Ford (1952)	Control of conception	200
Brown (1952)	Deviations from sexual norms	110
Minturn et al. (1969)	Sexual behavior	135
Zern (1969)	Premarital sex; Family cohesiveness	37
Lester (1970)	Premarital sex; Adolescent suicide	40
Eckhardt (1971)	Sexual permissiveness	153
Stephens (1972)	Modesty; Child training	92
Braude & Greene (1976)	Sexual behavior	186

VIII–B Life Cycle (Sections 85–88)

Raphael (1969)	Infancy	168
Barry & Paxson (1971)	Infancy	186
Whiting & Child (1953)	Child training; Illness	75
Whiting (1959)	Child training; Social control	45
Barry et al. (1959; 1967)	Child training; Economy	110
Rohner (1975)	Child training	101
Barry et al. (1976)	Child training	186
Barry et al. (1977)	Child training	186
Herzog (1962)	Education; Household	111
Whiting et al. (1958)	Adolescent initiation	55
Norbeck et al. (1962)	Adolescent initiation	56
Brown (1963)	Adolescent initiation	75
Cohen (1964)	Adolescent initiation	65
Young (1965)	Adolescent initiation	54
Simmons (1945)	Role of the aged	71

Two Documents

The Files originated from two principal documents. The first is the inventory of the world's cultural units entitled *Outline of World Cultures* (Murdock, 1975), first published in 1954. The second document applies to each cultural unit a system of topical categories so that a particular category brings together all the pertinent ethnographic information from the various sources. The same information may be duplicated in a number of different categories. This topical classification is formulated in the *Outline of Cultural Materials* (Murdock et al., 1971), the first edition of which was published in 1937.

Both of these documents were difficult to prepare because cultural units and topics pertaining to culture are very numerous and diverse. Ford (1971) has given a good account of the problems he and his colleagues encountered in the initial development of the topical categories.

Murdock et al. (1971) have enumerated seven alternative criteria by which information can be classified. The following examples show applications of these criteria to the topic of child training: (1) Patterned activity (Household tasks or Games that are played), (2) Circumstances (Home or Playground), (3) Subject (Mother teaching child or child playing with toys), (4) Object (Firewood carried by children or Toys used by children), (5) Means (Techniques of punishment or Books for instruction), (6) Purpose (Teach adult skills or Maintain authority over child), and (7) Result (Traits inculcated or Emotional health).

The topical categories in the Files include various applications of each of the seven criteria. The principal guide was the material as it is organized in most ethnographic accounts rather than a theoretically oriented or systematic classification. Accordingly, the majority of topical categories are based on the first, third, and fourth of these seven criteria (Patterned activity, Subject, Object). A comprehensive classification would place each item of information into a different category for each of the seven criteria, so that the user could select the desired basis of classification. Instead, the Files minimize redundancy by a classification system that selects among the seven criteria, depending on the particular topic.

Revisions and Extensions

The Files have changed and grown greatly, as is indicated by the major revisions in each successive edition of the *Outline of World Cultures* (Murdock, 1975) subsequent to the initial edition in 1954 and in each successive edition of the *Outline of Cultural Materials* (Murdock et al., 1971) subsequent to the initial edition in 1937.

The second edition of the *Outline of Cultural Materials* was published in 1942 and reprinted in 1945 as Volume 2 of *Yale Anthropological Studies*. This classification system was applied to a total of about 150 societies during the development of the Cross-Cultural Survey, the predecessor to the HRAF Files. Most of the sample consisted of small, nonliterate societies. The passages pertinent to a topical category were typed on the slips of paper, without reproduction of entire pages. The only set of the Cross-Cultural Survey was located at the Institute of Human Relations at Yale University.

In 1950 the third edition of the *Outline of Cultural Materials* was printed, with major changes in the classification system. The number of topical categories was almost doubled, largely as a result of adding many categories of technological and specialized activities pertaining to industrial nations.

This third edition appeared soon after the founding of HRAF in 1949, which established more than twenty sets of the Files at different locations. The technique of making photo offset reproductions of each page was introduced in 1953, with the topical categories designated for each paragraph in place of retyping the relevant material. For many years the Cross-Cultural Survey remained available concurrently at the Institute of Human Relations and was used by a number of researchers because only a portion of the societies were duplicated by the new HRAF. In 1960 the Cross-Cultural Survey materials were moved to the Yale University Library, and subsequently to HRAF headquarters. The Cross-Cultural Survey seldom has been used since then, due to the single location and the gradual coverage of most of the societies in the HRAF Files.

The fourth edition of the *Outline of Cultural Materials* was issued in 1961, with a fifth printing in 1971 (Murdock, 1971). Changes of topical categories have been limited to a few minor items. Numerous cross-references to other topical categories have been added. The index of topics at the end of the volume has been greatly expanded.

The *Outline of World Cultures* (Murdock, 1975) has changed in a smaller degree since the initial edition in 1954. The classification of world regions has remained constant, and the list of known societies has expanded only moderately since then.

There has been a steady increase in the number of cultural units included in the Files. Special projects supported by outside sources of funds have resulted in thorough coverage of some regions. In 1943–44, a U. S. Navy project on Japanese-held islands in the Pacific led to the addition of many Polynesian, Micronesian, and Melanesian societies to the Cross-Cultural Survey. In 1946–47, the University of Nebraska supported a project on Plains Indian tribes that was also entered in the Cross-Cultural Survey.

Another project, during 1942–43, was on contemporary South and Central American nations, supported by the U. S. Agency of Inter-American Affairs. These materials were included in the Cross-Cultural Survey, and the experience of applying the *Outline of Cultural Materials* to contemporary nations contributed to the major expansion of the topical categories included in the third edition in 1950 (Murdock et al., 1971).

Starting in 1955, the U. S. Department of the Army sponsored a project on the Soviet Union, China, and a number of countries on or near the borders of these two large nations. These materials were included in the HRAF Files and resulted in extensive representation of these selected countries.

In 1958, HRAF initiated the microfilm edition called the HRAF-Microfiles. This greatly expanded the availability of the materials. The reduction in storage space helps the user to locate the desired material and thereby compensates for the inconvenience of using a microfilm viewer.

The expansion of the HRAF operation has resulted in an increase in services available. Magnetic tapes or punched cards are for sale, containing coded data on various samples of societies, notably the Ethnographic Atlas (Murdock, 1967) and a sample of 186 societies (Murdock & White, 1969; Barry & Paxson, 1971; Barry, Josephson, Lauer, & Marshall, 1976). Computer programs for various statistical analyses of the data are also available (Naroll & Michik, 1975). Their application to the HRAF Probability Sample of sixty cultural units is illustrated by Naroll, Michik, & Naroll (1976). A computerized bibliographic system called HABS (HRAF Automated Bibliographic System) has been developed and is in regular operation at HRAF. A modification of HABS is the Theoretical Information Control System (THINGS), that has resulted in a five-volume propositional inventory (Levinson, 1977).

Another development is a membership File Program in microfiche format, called the Human Relations Resource Files (HRRF). This Program consists of the sixty HRAF Probability Sample Files, and is intended primarily to support culture, area, and general social science studies at two-year colleges and senior high schools.

Studies Based on the Files

The Files have been developed as a tool for researchers. An indication of the effectiveness of the Files is the record of published studies that have used these materials. The topics of these studies identify measures that have already been used successfully, providing a good basis for new studies that apply the same measures to new societies or develop new related measures. Absence of published studies on other topics may indicate opportunities for research on novel variables.

Table 11–4 shows a sample of published studies, most of which used the Files. Most of those published before 1974 were included in lists published by O'Leary (1969a, 1971, 1973). The specified topical classifications are based on groups of Sections identified in Table 11–1.

The earliest studies using the Cross-Cultural Survey have had great influence on the subsequent research. The topics studied were diverse, including alcohol use (Horton, 1943), sexual behavior (Ford, 1945), the aged (Simmons, 1945), kinship (Murdock, 1949), divorce (Murdock, 1950), and child training (Whiting & Child, 1953). An early study on subsistence economy by Goodenough influenced the work of investigators at that time although it was not published until many years later (Goodenough, 1969).

Replicability of the specific features of these early studies is limited by the fact that the topical categories, sample of societies, and ethnographic materials in the HRAF are somewhat different from those in the Cross-Cultural Survey. Most of the studies in Table 11–4 have used the HRAF and therefore are based on the materials that are available currently.

Table 11–4 indicates only a few studies in Sections I–IV but so many in Sections V and VIII that both of these sections are divided into two subsections. There have been numerous studies on the topics of warfare, sexual behavior, and child training. A topic not included is acculturation or culture history, although Moore (1971) has commented that most societies have a large amount of material in Section 17 that covers this topic. It might have been preferable to divide this material into several sections, each more compact and unified. Some broad topics, on which there is usually much ethnographic information but very few studies using the Files, are social stratification, the environment, human biology, food, and clothing. Technological activities, such as manufacturing, are important in the industrialized societies but are the topics of very few of the studies listed in Table 11–4.

Research Techniques

The Files were developed as a technique to facilitate comparative studies of selected topics in a world sample of societies. This remains the principal use of the Files, but they are a versatile research resource. Other uses include selecting an individual cultural unit, content analysis of the ethnographic sources, formulating or testing hypotheses, and assessing reliability of the information from different sources.

Effective use of the Files requires careful selection among the many diverse cultural units available. The size and characteristics of the sample should be determined by multiple considerations, including the purposes of the research, the time or money available, the societies included in the Files, and prior studies on the same topic.

The most distinctive feature of the Files is the classification by topical categories that brings together the related information from various sources. Special techniques are needed for selecting the categories, searching for all the relevant material, and recording the needed information.

Some general functions, necessary for any good research, include formulation of the hypothesis; definition of the measures to be counted, coded, or quantitatively rated; and statistical analysis of the data. The Files can facilitate but cannot substitute for these components of the research project.

Uses of the Files

The topical categories (Table 11-2) have guided many of the studies cited in Table 11-4. The categories are especially useful when applying a single topic to a large world sample. An example is a study by Murdock (1950) on divorce that is one of the topical categories in Section 58 (Marriage). The article includes an account of the modest number of hours required to collect the information on forty societies in the Cross-Cultural Survey. The principal value of the Files, however, is not to enable the same work to be done more quickly but to allow more extensive and thorough studies in the time available.

Another use of the Files is to help the researcher to select an individual cultural unit for a comparative study or for field work (Berry, 1976). The cultural units with the desired attributes can be determined rapidly with the help of the topical categories.

Reading the source material in selected topical categories can help the researcher to formulate and test hypotheses about relationships between specified variables. For example, information about pharmacological or physical attributes of medicines or love potions can be tested by looking for the presence of both relevant categories in the same paragraph. The source material in a particular topical category for a cultural unit may show an association between two different variables, and this association can be tested by reading the source material in the same category for other cultural units.

The source material in a selected category can be used for content analysis, counting the number of repetitions of particular words or phrases. One study counted the number of references to suicide in ethnographic reports (Naroll & Cohen, 1970); another study counted the number of words expressing themes of power, inhibition, and anxiety in folktales (McClelland, Davis, Kalin, & Wanner, 1972). This method may be more efficient and powerful when limited to the source material in a relevant topical category.

Another specialized use of the Files is to assess the reliability of the sources by measuring the degree of agreement between different sources, which may be facilitated by the fact that the Files bring together the material from different sources on each topic. Lagacé (1970) suggests specific criteria for assessing the quality of the source material.

The Files are a valuable resource even without the use of the topical categories. Some researchers use the consecutive pages on each source (Category 116). This is appropriate if the material from each separate source is coded separately, or if the source material to be used is on a broad range of topics and the full context is needed. The Files provide a compilation in one location, in a standardized format, of the different sources on each of a large number of cultural units. Sources in foreign languages are translated into English. Even when the consecutive pages in Category 116 are used, the other category numbers in the margin (Fig. 11-1) can provide a useful guide to the presence of desired topics, in addition to the information in the table of contents and index.

Selection of Sample

The researcher usually wishes to generalize the findings to the hypothetical, infinite population of cultural units with the specified characteristics. This requires the use of a sample of numerous cultural units, which are independent of each other. Accordingly, most of the studies cited in Table 11-4 have been done with a sample of small, nonliterate societies, because there are many of them, mostly isolated from each other. Most of the cultural units in the Files consist of this type of society. The results can be generalized safely only to this type of society, but the wide range of variation among these societies in many cultural attributes provides at least suggestive evidence concerning the corresponding measures in technologically developed civilizations.

It is preferable to include technologically advanced civilizations in the sample if the results are to be generalized to all known types of human cultures. This advantage compensates for the diminished independence of the cultural units in the sample due to the worldwide commerce and communication that accompany technological development. The Files began with a sample of exclusively small, nonliterate societies but subsequently included many cultural units that represent technologically advanced civilizations. Several other samples constitute attempts to include all the major known cultural types.

The largest carefully selected sample is the Ethnographic Atlas (Murdock, 1967) containing 863 societies. Summaries of the coded characteristics are provided by Barry (1968) and by Bourguignon and Greenbaum (1973). A smaller sample (Murdock & White, 1969) specifies one representative in each of 186 world areas, with special effort to include the unusual cultural types. For example, ancient civilizations more than 1000 years ago characterize only three (0.3%) of the 863 societies in the Ethnographic Atlas and three (1.6%) of the sample of societies. Also, polyandry is the form of marriage in only four (0.5%) of the 863 Ethnographic Atlas societies and in two (1.1%) of the smaller sample. The smaller sample more effectively selects only one among societies that are closely related to each other, and another important advantage is that the ethnographic information has been summarized by many coded measures, covering a wide range of topics. These are indicated by the studies in Table 11–4 with 186 as the sample size. The coded or quantitatively rated measures are available to be related to each other and to new measures.

Naroll and Sipes (1973) have specified a sample of 273 well described, nonliterate cultural units. A higher degree of independence among the societies is represented by the "probability sample," listed in Table 11–1, which consists of one randomly chosen representative from each of sixty sampling groups (Naroll, 1967; Lagacé, 1977). Several of these are representatives of technologically advanced civilizations. The use of this sample in future research will undoubtedly be stimulated by the availability of adequate ethnographic information on each of the sixty cultural units in both the Paper and Microfiche editions of the Files. The coded information accumulated by these studies will constitute an incentive for use of this sample in further research.

A sample should include all regions if cultural variations throughout the world are to be represented adequately. For example, Table 11–1 lists and Figure 11–2 portrays the frequency of three forms of marriage (Murdock, 1967) among the sixty cultural units of the "Probability Sample," separately for the eight regions. Barry coded the information from the Files for the six cultural units not included in the Ethnographic Atlas (AD5, Taiwan Hokkien; AO7, Central Thai; ES10, Highland Scots; MT9, Libyan Bedouin; SO11, Bahia Brazilians; SR8, Bush Negroes). The form of marriage constitutes an important variable, related to many other cultural attributes summarized by Textor (1967). Figure 11–2 shows large variations among regions, with general polygyny predominant in Africa (F) and Russia (R) and monogamy predominant in Europe (E) and Asia (A). Region is not the only influence on form of marriage, however, because variation is seen among the societies within six of the eight regions.

Some research topics drastically limit the number of societies available having relevant information. An extreme example would be a study of ancient civilizations or of polyandry. Studies of these topics should include every available society. Many researchers might wish to study only societies with monogamous marriage in order to avoid differences in this respect from Western European civilization. Such a study should not use the Probability Sample because of an insufficient number of cultural units with this form of marriage.

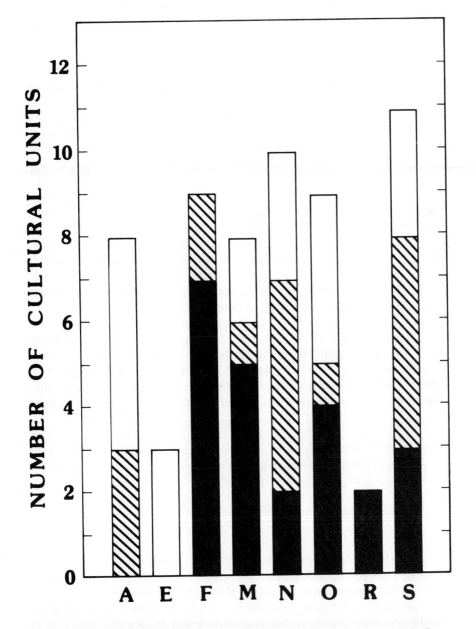

Figure 11–2.   Number of Cultural Units in Which the Form of Marriage Is General Polygyny (Filled), Limited Polygyny (Diagonal Lines), and Monogamy (Open), for the Sixty Cultural Units in the "Probability Sample." Separate bars show the eight regions: Asia (A), Europe (E), Africa (F), Middle East (M), North America (N), Oceania (O), Russia (R), and South America (S).

An alternative to a large sample of independent societies is the comparison between two cultural units that are similar in most attributes but differ in certain specified characteristics. This technique focuses effectively on the few characteristics that differ, equating the cultural units in most other attributes. Barry (1969) reported on relationships between child training and subsistence in a sample of twelve pairs of nonliterate societies. The two members of each pair were in the same cultural cluster (Murdock, 1967) and thus similar to each other in most respects. The member of the pair with the higher proportion of food production (agriculture or animal husbandry) usually trained children more strongly in compliance (obedience and responsibility). The Files contain many closely related pairs of cultural units which are suitable for such comparisons.

This technique might be especially suitable for studying different portions of the same nation. Comparisons can be made between two localities, two occupational groups, or two time periods in the same nation. Many suitable examples of such closely related pairs undoubtedly are available in the voluminous source materials of the Files on some contemporary nations.

The problem of defining and standardizing the cultural unit has been discussed by Lagacé (1967), and by Naroll, Michik, & Naroll (Chapter 12 in this volume of the *Handbook*). The researcher should specify the particular cultural unit, such as a local community, and a narrow range of dates to which the ethnographic material applies. This was done by Murdock and White (1969) for a world sample of 186 societies. A perplexing problem occurs when an ethnographic source pertains to a slightly different locality or time. Its inclusion may be a source of inconsistency in the information, but ignoring it may mean the loss of corroborative or additional information on a closely similar locality or time. An effective use of the information may be to study several such pairs of localities or times, focusing on the differences among the members of each pair.

Measures and Topics

The topical categories in the Files were formulated carefully and defined in detail with the benefit of many years of application to ethnographic sources. The ethnographic sources in the Files have been classified on the basis of these definitions. Therefore, a study of cultural characteristics should generally use measures that correspond closely to these topical categories. If a single measure refers to information that is in a single topical category, the material can be read more quickly, thereby allowing a larger number of measures or a larger sample of societies to be studied in the same amount of time. Examples of measures corresponding to a particular topical category in the Files are divorce (Murdock, 1950) and use of alcoholic beverages (Bacon, Barry, Buchwald, Child, & Snyder, 1965).

Even when a measure corresponds directly to a single topical category, it is wise to search the material in other categories of the same section as well as in other sections. A paragraph in the source materials may contain information on many categories, but to minimize redundancy it is usually assigned to a small number of categories, as can be seen in the sample page (Figure 11-1). Important information on a topic may not be filed in that category because it is overlooked or because it is only a minor part of the paragraph. Usually it can be found in related categories and sections. Information on divorce should be searched not only in the categories of Section 58 (Marriage) but also in Sections 57 (Interpersonal Relations), 59 (Family), and 73 (Social Problems). Information on alcohol consumption should be searched not only in Section 27 (Drink, Durgs, and Indulgence) but also in Sections 52 (Recreation), 57 (Interpersonal Relations), and 73 (Social Problems).

The measure should be defined precisely, with examples of the typical ethnographic statements that correspond to each code or numerical rating. Criteria for dealing with ambiguous or uncertain information should be specified in advance and applied in a uniform manner to each cultural unit.

If a cultural attribute is coded as absent, it is desirable to include a measure of the adequacy of the ethnographic information in order to assess the likelihood that the attribute is actually present but not reported. A search for information in additional topical categories and sections is especially important in this case.

Objective, quantifiable measures should be sought. For example, the distinction between general polygyny and limited polygyny (Murdock, 1967) is often based on ethnographic information on the number of monogamous and polygynous marriages in the community. Measures of the mode of carrying an infant (Barry & Paxson, 1971) are often based on photographs. It would be possible to include a measure of the proportion of pictures showing different carrying methods or positions. A study on the Evil Eye (Roberts, 1976) included a quantitative scale on the degree of certainty with which absence or presence of this belief was coded. The Ethnographic Atlas (Murdock, 1967) showed the relative dependence of the society on each of five types of subsistence activities by assigning to each subsistence activity a number between zero and ten, with ten as the total for the five activities.

Some studies use a wide range of variables, encompassing a large number of topical categories. For example, a major study by Murdock (1949) on family and kinship relations includes much of the material in Sections 58–61 as well as in many other sections, including 14 (Human Biology), 42 (Property), 51 (Living Standards and Routines), 57 (Interpersonal Relations), 73 (Social Problems), and 88 (Adolescence and Old Age). Nevertheless, the author, in the preface to the book, commented on the much greater speed and thoroughness with which the information was obtained on the portion of the sample that was included in the Cross-Cultural Survey.

It is desirable to formulate a group of related measures, some more objective and specific, others more general and taking into account the context of the information and the conclusions and evaluations by the ethnographers. The most general measure is often the most useful. Barry (1957) found that a number of specific measures of art style, such as crowdedness of space and degree of variety of figures, were usually correlated more highly with a measure of over-all complexity of design than with any of the other measures, and complexity of design was the measure most closely related to several independent measures of child training. Similar advantages have been found for a measure of general infancy indulgence compared to several specific measures such as constancy of presence of the nurturant agent and absence of pain (Barry, Bacon, & Child, 1967) and for measures of amount of alcohol consumption and frequency of drunkenness compared to specific measures of drinking context and types of drunken behavior (Bacon et al., 1965).

A quantitative, numerical scale is usually most suitable for a general measure. A large number of scale divisions allows more precise differentiations. Some cases inevitably will be at the border between two scale points and arbitrarily assigned to one of them. A large number of scale points minimizes the relative magnitude of this error. Most of the ratings on child training practices reported by Barry et al. (1967) constituted the sum for two raters, both on a 1–7 scale, thereby providing fourteen scale points. Later studies (Barry & Paxson, 1971; Barry et al., 1976; Barry, Josephson, Lauer, & Marshall, 1977) included ratings on a 1–5 scale, with each scale point being divided into a high, middle, and low portion, thereby allowing fifteen scale points.

Most studies have been limited to the average or typical custom. Measures of variability should be given more emphasis. Cultural units can be compared with respect to the degree of variation among individuals, ages, occupations, localities, and times of year. Sex differences also deserve greater emphasis. Separate ratings for males and females were routinely made in studies of child training (Barry et al., 1967, 1976, 1977) and alcohol use (Bacon et al., 1965), but in many cases a sex difference was not large enough to justify differential scale scores. Explicit measures of the occurrence and size of sex differences would be more sensitive.

Another desirable measure is an assessment of the quantity and quality of the ethnographic information. In addition to a rating or the cultural unit, a separate rating can be made for each source. Cultural units with low scores on this measure might be omitted from the final sample.

Methodological Considerations

The use of the Files constitutes only a portion of the research project. Other phases of the project must also be conducted carefully and thoroughly in order to take full advantage of the opportunities provided by availability of the Files. An article by Rohner, Naroll, Barry, Divale, Erickson, Schaefer, and Sipes (1978) gives general advice on cross-cultural research methods. LeBar (1970) and Moore (1969) discuss the important problems and procedures of coding.

The initial step is to formulate hypotheses that should be as explicit as possible. Otterbein (1969) has emphasized the planning and other preliminary stages of research. This procedure is compatible with receptiveness to new and unexpected findings at any subsequent stage of the research.

The measures should include several specific, objective items and at least one general, over-all rating. Since the time spent reading the material on a particular topic is great and fairly constant, it is most efficient to include a substantial number of measures for a particular topic. The decision on how many different topics to include depends on the time and other resources available, because each additional topic substantially increases the amount of time required to search the ethnographic sources.

At least two raters or coders are desirable, and their independent ratings allow an accurate measure of reliability of the measures. If it is not feasible to assign two raters to each cultural unit, they can perform the reliability check on a portion of the sample. A useful device is for the two raters to preserve the record of their original, independent ratings but to agree on a new set of ratings (Barry & Paxson, 1971; Barry et al., 1976, 1977). This method combines the advantages of independent measures with a consensus after discussion of disagreements.

The procedures should be consistent throughout the study. The definitions of the measures and the topical categories searched should be uniform for all the societies in the sample. It may be tempting to add an elaboration or improvement during the course of the study. If this is done, it should be applied systematically to all the societies previously coded. A useful device for maximizing uniformity of procedures is to apply the coding methods to an initial practice sample prior to starting with the sample selected for the study. A uniform procedure should be used also for searching the topical categories. For example, in testing the hypothesis that witchcraft tends to occur in societies with competitive games of strategy, an erroneous conclusion may be caused by the tendency to search more thoroughly for reports of witchcraft in societies that have competitive games of strategy.

A practical device for maximizing both uniformity of procedures and comprehensiveness of the information used is to make extensive notes on the ethnographic material, identifying the topical category, source, and page number for each item of information. The coding should be done by a uniform procedure, after all the notes have been assembled and inspected. It is useful to keep a list of the pertinent topical categories, and to search all of them in sequence of their importance.

When a large sample is studied, the sequence of societies coded should not follow any logical pattern, such as geographical region. Alphabetical sequence is acceptable, but a randomized sequence is preferable.

The user should be alert to the possibility of loss of material from the Files, because of misfiling or theft. This will usually pertain to entire topical categories or sections. If any material seems suspiciously meager, its absence can be detected by the presence of pages identifying the categories or sections in the consecutive source pages in Category 116. Loss of material from Category 116 can be detected by checking the list of sources in the same section. A multivolume subject index to the Files is available at most member institutions. This index lists for each File the source and page numbers for material in each topical category.

After the measures have been applied to the entire sample, the data should be summarized and related to other independent measures. An important and progressively growing resource for researchers is the collection of measures obtained by others on the same cultural units. In addition to the Ethnographic Atlas codes on a sample of 863 societies (Murdock, 1967), many of the studies cited in Table 11–4 report the codes or quantitative ratings on each cultural unit studied. A wide variety of topics is included.

Reviews by Naroll (1970) and by Harrington and Whiting (1972) are important reference materials for researchers. Searches for later articles can be helped by the Science Citation Index (Garfield, 1964) and its subsequently developed affiliate, the Social Science Citation Index. A selected key reference, such as one of those in Table 11–4, is used to identify the subsequent articles that have cited it.

Computer facilities are necessary for thorough analysis of the data. A widely available statistical package (Nie, Hull, Jenkins, Steinbrenner, & Bent, 1975), called the SPSS, contains many programs useful for cross-cultural data. The HRAFLIB (Naroll & Michik, 1975; Naroll et al., 1975–77) is a statistical package specifically designed for cross-cultural research. Methods of statistical analysis are discussed by Naroll, Michik, and Naroll in their chapter in this volume of the *Handbook*.

Cross-tabulations among many pairs of variables with tests of statistical significance have been compiled by Textor (1967) for 400 nonliterate societies and by Banks and Textor (1963) for 115 polities. These constitute only the first stage in effective analysis and communication of data. A publication should generally select the measures that are most important and closely related to each other. These should be analyzed thoroughly with the aid of multivariate tests, such as factor analysis.

The purpose of the complex statistical procedures is to condense an enormous amount of data into a simple, meaningful pattern. Bacon et al. (1965) used a factor analysis to identify cultural variations with respect to four principal drinking patterns from quantitative scores on many measures of alcohol use. Factor analyses have been used to condense diverse attributes into a few cultural types with emphasis on regional variations in an article by Erickson (1977), and in several prior articles cited by Erickson (1977).

Publications that report on new measures should include a list of the codes or quantitatively scaled scores for each cultural unit. This list provides a permanent addition to the materials available for use by subsequent researchers on the same sample of societies.

Conclusions

The development of a scientific specialty can be described in terms of the introduction and exploitation of technological resources, such as the microscope in biology and the digital computer in statistics. The Human Relations Area Files provide an important resource of this type for cross-cultural research. The extensive compilations of cultural information are powerful and widely available tools with applications to a wide variety of cross-cultural studies. Each cross-cultural researcher should be familiar with the Files and able to use them effectively. Part of the value of the Files is to encourage the use of their topical categories and sample of societies. Each new user can provide new codes on the same sample of societies, thereby increasing the materials available to future researchers.

The sample of cultural units in the Files has guided many cross-cultural studies. Earlier studies have been done predominantly on small, nonliterate societies, and the measures have most often been attributes of family or individual behavior that might be expected to be comparable in cultural units with a wide range of variation in degree of technological development. Many future studies are likely to use a standard sample of 186 cultural units (Murdock & White, 1969) or the "probability sample" of sixty cultural units (Lagacé, 1977). Both of these samples include some representatives of technologically developed civilizations. Other future developments may include more emphasis on multivariate analyses and comparisons between pairs of closely related cultural units. Information in the Files on different localities, occupations, and times in the same society or nation may provide useful source material for such comparative studies.

References

ACKERMAN, C. Conjunctive affiliation and divorce. In N. W. Bell & E. F. Vogel (Eds.), *A modern introduction to the family*, rev. ed. New York: Free Press, 1968, pp. 469–78.

ALLEN, M. G. Childhood experience and personality—a cross-cultural study using the concept of ego strength. *Journal of Social Psychology*, 1967, *71*, 53–68.

———. A cross-cultural study of aggression and crime. *Journal of Cross-Cultural Psychology*, 1972, *3*, 259–71.

AYRES, B. C. Effects of infantile stimulation on musical behavior. In A. Lomax, *Folk song style and culture*. Washington, D. C.: American Association for the Advancement of Science, Publication 88, 1968, pp. 211–21.

BACON, M. K., BARRY, H., III, BUCHWALD, C., CHILD, I. L., & SNYDER, C. R. A cross-cultural study of drinking. *Quarterly Journal of Studies on Alcohol*, Supplement 3, 1965.

BACON, M. K., CHILD, I. L., & BARRY, H., III. A cross-cultural study of correlates of crime. *Journal of Abnormal and Social Psychology*, 1963, *66*, 291–300.

BANKS, A. S., & TEXTOR, R. B. *A cross-polity survey.* Cambridge, Mass.: MIT Press, 1963.

BARRY, H., III. Relationships between child training and the pictorial arts. *Journal of Abnormal and Social Psychology*, 1957, *54*, 380–83.

———. Regional and worldwide variations in culture. *Ethnology*, 1968, *7*, 207–17.

———. Cross-cultural research with matched pairs of societies. *Journal of Social Psychology*, 1969, *79*, 25–33.

BARRY, H., III, BACON, M. K., & CHILD, I. L. A cross-cultural survey of some sex differences in socialization. *Journal of Abnormal and Social Psychology*, 1957, *55*, 327–32.

———. Definitions, ratings, and bibliographic sources for child training practices of 110 cultures. In C. S. Ford (Ed.), *Cross-cultural approaches*. New Haven: HRAF Press, 1967, pp. 293–331.

BARRY, H., III, CHILD, I. L., & BACON, M. K. Relation of child training to subsistence economy. *American Anthropologist*, 1959, *61*, 51–63. (Reprinted in C. S. Ford (Ed.), *Cross-cultural approaches*. New Haven: HRAF Press, 1967, pp. 246–58.)

BARRY, H., III, JOSEPHSON, L., LAUER, E. M., & MARSHALL, C. Traits inculcated in childhood: cross-cultural codes 5. *Ethnology*, 1976, *15*, 83–114.

———. Agents and techniques for child training: cross-cultural codes 6. *Ethnology*, 1977, *16*, 191–230.

BARRY, H., III, & PAXSON, L. M. Infancy and early childhood: cross-cultural codes 2. *Ethnology*, 1971, *10*, 466–508.

BERRY, J. W. *Human ecology and cognitive style: comparative studies in cultural and psychological adaptation.* Beverly Hills: Sage/Halsted, 1976.

BORNSTEIN, M. H. The psychophysiological component of cultural difference in color naming and illusion susceptibility. *Behavior Science Notes*, 1973, *8*, 41–101.

BOURGUIGNON, E., & GREENBAUM, L. S. *Diversity and homogeneity in world societies.* New Haven: HRAF Press, 1973.

BRANT, C. S. On joking relationships. *American Anthropologist*, 1948, *50*, 160–62.

————. A preliminary study of cross-sexual joking relationships in primitive society. *Behavior Science Notes*, 1972, *7*, 313–29.

BROUDE, G. J., & GREENE, S. J. Cross-cultural codes on twenty sexual attitudes and practices. *Ethnology*, 1976, *15*, 409–29.

BROUSSARD, J. A. A comparative study of the distribution of social power in one hundred pre-literate societies. *Dissertation Abstracts*, 1957, *17*, 310.

BROWN, J. K. A cross-cultural study of female initiation rites. *American Anthropologist*, 1963, *65*, 837–53.

BROWN, J. S. A comparative study of deviations from sexual mores. *American Sociological Review*, 1952, *17*, 135–46.

CARNEIRO, R. L. Ascertaining, testing, and interpreting sequences of cultural development. *Southwestern Journal of Anthropology*, 1968, *24*, 354–74.

COHEN, Y. A. *Social structure and personality: a casebook.* New York: Holt, Rinehart and Winston, 1961.

————. *The transition from childhood to adolescence.* Chicago: Aldine, 1964.

DEVEREUX, G. *A study of abortion in primitive societies.* New York: Julian Press, 1955.

DIVALE, W. T. Population, warfare, and the male supremacist complex. *American Anthropologist*, 1976, *78*, 521–38.

DRIVER, H. E., & SANDAY, P. R. Factors and clusters of kin avoidances and related variables. In P. Kay (Ed.), *Explorations in mathematical anthropology.* Cambridge, Mass.: MIT Press, 1971, pp. 269–79.

ECKHARDT, K. W. Exchange theory and sexual permissiveness. *Behavior Science Notes*, 1971, *6*, 1–18.

EMBER, M. The relationship between economic and political development in non-industrialized societies. *Ethnology*, 1963, *2*, 228–48.

————. The emergence of neolocal residence. *Transactions of the New York Academy of Sciences*, Series 2, 1967, *30*, 291–302.

————. An archeological indicator of matrilocal versus patrilocal residence. *American Antiquity*, 1973, *38*, 177–82.

————. Warfare, sex ratio, and polygyny. *Ethnology*, 1974, *13*, 197–206.

EMBER, M., & EMBER, C. R. The conditions favoring matrilocal versus patrilocal residence. *American Anthropologist*, 1971, *73*, 571–94.

ERICKSON, E. E. Factors and patterns: the nature of sociocultural variation. *Behavior Science Research*, 1977, *12*, 227–50.

FISHER, J. L. Art styles as cultural cognitive maps. *American Anthropologist*, 1961, *63*, 79–93.

FORD, C. S. Society, culture, and the human organism. *Journal of General Psychology*, 1939, *20*, 135–79. Reprinted in F. W. Moore (Ed.), *Readings in cross-cultural methodology.* New Haven: HRAF Press, 1966, pp. 130–65.

————. *A comparative study of human reproduction.* Yale University Publications in Anthropology, 32, 1945.

————. Control of conception in cross-cultural perspective. *Annals of the New York Academy of Sciences*, 1952, *54*, 763–68.

————. The development of the outline of cultural materials. *Behavior Science Notes*, 1971, *6*, 173–85.

GARFIELD, E. Science citation index—a new dimension in indexing. *Science,* 1964, *144,* 649-54.

GOGGIN, J. M., & STURTEVANT, W. C. The Calusa: a stratified, nonagricultural society (with notes on sibling marriage). In W. H. Goodenough (Ed.), *Explorations in cultural anthropology: essays in honor of George Peter Murdock.* New York: McGraw-Hill, 1964, pp. 179-219.

GOODENOUGH, W. H. Basic economy and community. *Behavior Science Notes,* 1969, *4,* 291-98.

GOULDNER, A. W., & PETERSON, R. A. *Notes on technology and moral order.* Indianapolis: Bobbs-Merrill, 1962.

GUNDERS, S. M., & WHITING, J. W. M. Mother-infant separation and physical growth. *Ethnology,* 1968, *7,* 196-206.

HARRINGTON, C., & WHITING, J. W. M. Socialization process and personality. In F. L. K. Hsu (Ed.), *Psychological anthropology,* rev. ed. Cambridge, Mass.: Schenkman, 1972, pp. 469-507.

HAYS, D. G., MARGOLIS, E., NAROLL, R., & PERKINS, D. R. Color term salience. *American Anthropologist,* 1972, *74,* 1107-21.

HERZOG, J. D. Deliberate instruction and household structure: a cross-cultural study. *Harvard Educational Review,* 1962, *32,* 301-42.

HICKMAN, J. M. Dimensions of a complex concept: a method exemplified. *Human Organization,* 1962, *21,* 214-18.

HOEBEL, E. A. Feud: concept, reality and method in the study of primitive law. In A. R. Desai (Ed.), *Essays on modernization of underdeveloped societies,* Vol. 1. Bombay: Thacker, 1972, pp. 1-15.

HORTON, D. The function of alcohol in primitive societies: a cross-cultural study. *Quarterly Journal of Studies on Alcohol,* 1943, *4,* 199-320.

HRAF. The HRAF quality control sample universe. *Behavior Science Notes,* 1967, *2,* 81-88.

KLAUSNER, S. Z. Sacred and profane meanings of blood and alcohol. *Journal of Social Psychology,* 1964, *64,* 27-43.

LAGACÉ, R. O. Principles and procedures of ethnographic unit identification; with particular reference to the HRAF files system. *Behavior Science Notes,* 1967, *2,* 89-103.

―――. The HRAF data quality control schedule. *Behavior Science Notes,* 1970, *5,* 125-32.

―――. *Nature and use of the HRAF Files; a research and teaching guide.* New Haven: HRAF, Inc., 1974.

LAGACÉ, R. O. (Ed.), *Sixty cultures: a guide to the HRAF probability sample files.* New Haven: HRAF, 1977.

LAMBERT, W. W., TRIANDIS, L. M., & WOLF, M. Some correlates of beliefs in the malevolence and benevolence of supernatural beings: a cross-cultural study. *Journal of Abnormal and Social Psychology,* 1959, *58,* 162-69.

LE BAR, F. M. Coding ethnographic materials. In R. Naroll & R. Cohen (Eds.), *A handbook of method in cultural anthropology.* New York: Natural History Press, 1970, pp. 707-20.

LESTER, D. Suicide, homicide, and the effects of socialization. *Journal of Personality and Social Psychology,* 1967a, *5,* 466-68.

―――. The relation between discipline experiences and the expression of aggression. *American Anthropologist,* 1967b, *69,* 734–37.

―――. Adolescent suicide and premarital sex behavior. *Journal of Social Psychology,* 1970, *82,* 131–32.

―――. Suicide and mutilation behaviors in non-literate societies. *Psychological Reports,* 1971, *28,* 801–02.

LEVINSON, D. (Ed.), *A guide to social theory: worldwide cross-cultural tests* (5 vols.). New Haven: HRAF, 1977.

LOMAX, A. (Ed.), *Folk song style and culture.* Washington, D. C.: American Association for the Advancement of Science, Publication 88, 1968.

LOMAX, A., & BERKOWITZ, N. The evolutionary taxonomy of culture. *Science,* 1972, *177,* 228–39.

MARCH, J. G. Group autonomy and internal group control. *Social Forces,* 1955, *33,* 322–26.

MCCLELLAND, D. C., DAVIS, W. N., KALIN, R., & WANNER, E. *The drinking man.* New York: Free Press, 1972.

MINTURN, L., & LAMBERT, W. W. *Mothers of six cultures: antecedents of child rearing.* New York: Wiley, 1964.

MINTURN, L., GROSSE, M., & HAIDER, S. Cultural patterning of sexual beliefs and behavior. *Ethnology,* 1969, *8,* 301–18.

MOORE, B., Jr. The relation between social stratification and social control. *Sociometry,* 1942, *5,* 230–50.

MOORE, F. W. Codes and coding. *Behavior Science Notes,* 1969, *4,* 247–63.

―――. The outline of cultural materials: contemporary problems. *Behavior Science Notes,* 1971, *6,* 187–89.

MURDOCK, G. P. *Social structure.* New York: Macmillan, 1949.

―――. Family stability in non-European cultures. *Annals of the American Academy of Political and Social Science,* 1950, *272,* 195–201. Reprinted in G. P. Murdock, *Culture and society.* Pittsburgh: University of Pittsburgh Press, 1965, pp. 312–23.

―――. *Outline of world cultures,* 5th ed., rev. New Haven: HRAF, Inc., 1975.

―――. *Ethnographic atlas.* Pittsburgh: University of Pittsburgh Press, 1967. Also in *Ethnology,* 1967, *6,* 109–236. Information on bibliographical sources is in vols. 1–6, 1962–67; subsequent additions and corrections are in vols. 6–10, 1967–71.

MURDOCK, G. P., & MORROW, D. O. Subsistence economy and supportive practices: cross-cultural codes I. *Ethnology,* 1970, *9,* 302–30.

MURDOCK, G. P. & PROVOST, C. Factors in the division of labor by sex: a cross-cultural analysis. *Ethnology,* 1973, *12,* 203–25.

―――. Measurement of cultural complexity. *Ethnology,* 1973, *12,* 379–92.

MURDOCK, G. P, & WHITE, D. R. Standard cross-cultural sample. *Ethnology,* 1969, *8,* 329–69.

MURDOCK, G. P., & WILSON, S. F. Settlement patterns and community organization: cross-cultural codes 3. *Ethnology,* 1972, *11,* 250–95.

MURDOCK, G. P., FORD, C. S., HUDSON, A. E. et al. *Outline of cultural materials,* 4th revised ed. New Haven: HRAF, Inc., 1971.

NAROLL, R. The proposed HRAF probability sample. *Behavior Science Notes*, 1967, *2*, 70–80.

———. What have we learned from cross-cultural surveys? *American Anthropologist*, 1970, *72*, 1227–88.

NAROLL, R., & COHEN, R. (Eds.), *A handbook of method in cultural anthropology.* New York: Natural History Press, 1970. Reprinted 1973. New York: Columbia University Press.

NAROLL, R., & MICHIK, G. L. HRAFLIB: a computer program for hologeistic research. *Behavior Science Research*, 1975, *10*, 283–96.

NAROLL, R., MICHIK, G. L., GRIFFITH, D. F., & NAROLL, F. *HRAFLIB: HRAF hologeistic program library.* New Haven: HRAF, 1975–77.

NAROLL, R., & SIPES, R. G. A standard ethnographic sample, 2nd ed. *Current Anthropology*, 1973, *14*, 111–40.

NAROLL, R., MICHIK, G. L., & NAROLL, F. *Worldwide theory testing.* New Haven: HRAF Press, 1976.

NERLOVE, S., & ROMNEY, A. K. Sibling terminology and cross-sex behavior. *American Anthropologist*, 1967, *69*, 179–87.

NIE, N. H., HULL, C. H., JENKINS, J. G., STEINBRENER, K., & BENT, D. H. *SPSS: statistical package for the social sciences*, 2nd ed. New York: McGraw-Hill, 1975.

NORBECK, E., WALKER, D. E., & COHEN, M. The interpretation of data: puberty rites. *American Anthropologist*, 1962, *64*, 463–85.

O'LEARY, T. J. A preliminary bibliography of cross-cultural studies. *Behavior Science Notes*, 1969a, *4*, 95–115.

———. Concordance of the ethnographic atlas with the outline of world cultures. *Behavior Science Notes*, 1969, *4*, 165–207.

———. Bibliography of cross-cultural studies: supplement I. *Behavior Science Notes*, 1971, *6*, 191–203.

———. Bibliography of cross-cultural studies: supplement II. *Behavior Science Notes*, 1973, *8*, 123–34.

OTTERBEIN, K. F. Internal war: a cross-cultural study. *American Anthropologist*, 1968, *70*, 277–89.

———. Basic steps in conducting a cross-cultural coding study. *Behavior Science Notes*, 1969, *4*, 221–36.

———. *The evolution of war: a cross-cultural study.* New Haven: HRAF Press, 1970.

———. Comment on "Correlates of political complexity." *American Sociological Review*, 1971, *36*, 113–14.

OTTERBEIN, K. F., & OTTERBEIN, C. S. An eye for an eye, a tooth for a tooth: a cross-cultural study of feuding. *American Anthropologist*, 1965, *67*, 1470–82.

PALMER, S. Murder and suicide in forty non-literate societies. *Journal of Criminal Law, Criminology and Police Science*, 1965, *56*, 320–24.

———. Aggression in fifty-eight non-literate societies: an exploratory analysis. *Annales Internationales de Criminologie*, 1970, *9*, 57–69.

RAPHAEL, D. L. The lactation-suckling process with a matrix of supportive behavior. *Dissertation Abstracts*, 1969, *30*, 1472–B.

ROBERTS, J. M. Oaths, autonomic ordeals, and power. *American Anthropologist*, 1965, *67*, 186–212. Reprinted in C. S. Ford (Ed.), *Cross-cultural approaches.* New Haven: HRAF Press, 1967, pp. 169–95.

————. Belief in the evil eye in world perspective. In C. Maloney (Ed.), *The evil eye.* New York: Columbia University Press, 1976, pp. 223–78.

ROBERTS, J. M., ARTH, M. J., & BUSH, R. R. Games in culture. *American Anthropologist,* 1959, *61,* 597–605.

ROBERTS, J. M., & FORMAN, M. L. Riddles: expressive models of interrogation. *Ethnology,* 1971, *10,* 509–33.

ROBERTS, J. M., & GREGOR, T. Privacy: a cultural view. In J. R. Pennock & J. W. Chapman (Eds.), *Privacy.* New York: Atherton, 1971, pp. 199–225.

ROBERTS, J. M., & SUTTON-SMITH, B. Child training and game involvement. *Ethnology,* 1962, *1,* 166–85.

ROBERTS, J. M., SUTTON-SMITH, B., & KENDON, A. Strategy in games and folk tales. *Journal of Social Psychology,* 1963, *61,* 185–99.

ROHNER, R. P. *They love me, they love me not: a study of the world-wide effects of parental acceptance and rejection.* New Haven: HRAF Press, 1975.

————. Sex differences in aggression: phylogenetic and enculturation perspectives. *Ethos,* 1976, *4,* 57–72.

ROHNER, R. P., NAROLL, R., BARRY, H., III, DIVALE, W. T., ERICKSON, E. E., SCHAEFER, J. M., & SIPES, R. G. Guidelines for holocultural research. *Current Anthropology,* 1978, *19,* 128–29.

ROSENBLATT, P. C. A cross-cultural study of child rearing and romantic love. *Journal of Personality and Social Psychology,* 1966, *4,* 336–38.

————. Marital residence and the functions of romantic love. *Ethnology,* 1967, *6,* 471–80.

ROSENBLATT, P. C., & COZBY, P. C. Courtship patterns associated with freedom of choice of spouse. *Journal of Marriage and the Family,* 1972, *34,* 689–95.

ROSENBLATT, P. C., WALSH, R. P., & JACKSON, D. A. *Grief and mourning in cross-cultural perspective.* New Haven: HRAF Press, 1976.

SCHLEGEL, A. *Male dominance and female autonomy; domestic authority in matrilineal societies.* New Haven: HRAF Press, 1972, p. 37.

SIMMONS, L. W. *The role of the aged in primitive society.* New Haven: Yale University Press, 1945. Reprinted in Hamden, Conn.: Archon Books, 1970.

SIPES, R. G. War, sports and aggression: an empirical test of two rival theories. *American Anthropologist,* 1973, *75,* 64–86.

STEPHENS, W. N. A cross-cultural study of modesty. *Behavior Science Notes,* 1972, *7,* 1–28.

SWANSON, G. E. *The birth of the gods: the origin of primitive beliefs.* Ann Arbor: University of Michigan Press, 1960.

SWEETSER, D. A. On the incompatibility of duty and affection: a note on the role of the mother's brother. *American Anthropologist,* 1966, *68,* 1009–13.

TEXTOR, R. B. *A cross-cultural summary.* New Haven: HRAF Press, 1967.

TUDEN, A., & MARSHALL, C. Political organization: cross-cultural codes 4. *Ethnology,* 1972, *11,* 436–64.

UDY, S. H., Jr. *Organization of work: a comparative analysis of production among nonindustrial peoples.* New Haven: HRAF Press, 1959.

————. *Work in traditional and modern society.* Englewood Cliffs, N.J.: Prentice-Hall, 1970.

WHITING, J. W. M. Sorcery, sin, and the superego: a cross-cultural study of some mechanisms of social control. In M. R. Jones (Ed.), *Nebraska symposium on motivation.* Lincoln: University of Nebraska Press, 1959, pp. 174–95. Reprinted in C. S. Ford (Ed.), *Cross-cultural approaches.* New Haven: HRAF Press, 1967, pp. 147–68.

————. The effects of climate on certain cultural practices. In W. H. Goodenough (Ed.), *Explorations in cultural anthropology: essays in honor of George Peter Murdock.* New York: McGraw-Hill, 1964, pp. 511–44.

————. Menarcheal age and infant stress in humans. In F. A. Beach (Ed.), *Conference on sex and behavior.* New York: Wiley, 1965, pp. 221–23.

————. Effects of climate on certain cultural practices. In A. P. Vayda (Ed.), *Environment and cultural behavior: ecological studies in cultural anthropology.* New York: Natural History Press, 1969, pp. 416–55.

WHITING, J. W. M., & AYRES, B. C. Inferences from the shape of dwellings. In Kwang-chih Chang (Ed.), *Settlement archaeology.* Palo Alto, Calif.: National Press Books, 1968, pp. 117–33.

WHITING, J. W. M., & CHILD, I. L. *Child training and personality.* New Haven: Yale University Press, 1953.

WHITING, J. W. M., KLUCKHOHN, R., & ANTHONY, A. S. The function of male initiation ceremonies at puberty. In E. E. Maccoby, T. M. Newcomb, & E. L. Hartley (Eds.), *Readings in social psychology,* 3rd ed. New York: Holt, Rinehart and Winston, 1958, pp. 359–70.

WHYTE, M. K. Cross-cultural codes dealing with the relative status of women. *Ethnology,* 1978, 17, 211–37.

WIRSING, R. Political power and information: a cross-cultural study. *American Anthropologist,* 1973, 75, 153–70.

WOLFE, A. P. Social structural bases of art. *Current Anthropology,* 1969, 10, 3–44.

YOUNG, F. W. *Initiation ceremonies: a cross-cultural study of status dramatization.* Indianapolis: Bobbs-Merrill, 1965.

ZERN, D. The influence of certain developmental factors in fostering the ability to differentiate the passage of time. *Journal of Social Psychology,* 1967, 72, 9–17.

————. The relevance of family cohesiveness as a determinant of premarital sexual behavior in a cross-cultural sample. *Journal of Social Psychology,* 1969, 78, 3–9.

12

Holocultural Research Methods[1]

Raoul Naroll, Gary L. Michik
and Frada Naroll

Contents

Abstract

Worldwide cross-cultural surveys, although neither as sensitive nor as accurate as other kinds of cross-cultural theory tests, must be used before a general theory of cultural variation can be scientifically established. Solutions to the technical problems of holocultural theory test method are reviewed here. Such tests face specific problems of statistical significance, both with respect to individual hypothesis tests and group tests. They face Galton's Problem—the confounding effect of cultural diffusion. They face special sampling problems. They face special problems of defining their unit of study—the society or culture; also problems of data accuracy and data paucity; of regional variation in correlations; of conceptualization, classification, and coding; of causal analysis of correlations; of deviant case analysis. The computer program and holocultural manual library of the Human Relations Area Files are specially intended to make the solution to many of these problems easier. With or without these programs and manuals, methods to solve each of these problems are offered—methods that are workable and, most of them, now well tested in practice.

Introduction: The Need for
Hologeistic Studies

A hologeistic (whole earth) study is a study that tests theories by correlational analyses using data from worldwide samples of entire societies or cultures; such samples are intended as representative samples of all known human cultures (or of a defined subset of that universe). There are three kinds of hologeistic studies: (1) a *holonational* study uses a sample selected from the population of nation states. (2) A *holocultural* study uses a sample drawn from the population of all known primitive cultures. (A primitive culture is defined as a culture without a surviving native-written historical tradition.) (3) A *holohistorical* study uses a sample selected from the universe of all historically known cultures. Hologeistic studies are distinguished from other types of cross-cultural research primarily because they use large worldwide samples of cultures.

The hologeistic method is a means for empirical testing of theories that attempt to explain some general characteristics of human culture. Theoretical variables are measured for a large, worldwide sample of cultures (measurement is usually based on archival data). Then the statistical associations among the variables are examined to see whether the intervariable relationships are as the theory predicted. Nearly all the necessary computations can be performed with the Human Relations Area Files hologeistic computer program package (Naroll & Michik, 1975). Within the last twenty-five years, the social sciences have produced a large body of hologeistic literature (see Moore, 1966; Ford, 1967; Gillespie & Nesvold, 1971; Naroll, 1973). While some of this literature is concerned with *developing* theories, the major contribution of the hologeistic method has been in *testing* theories. This chapter, therefore, deals primarily with the use of hologeistic methodology to test theories. Since detailed aspects of hologeistic methodology will be discussed concisely and technically, the reader will find a background in elementary statistics (e.g., Freund, 1967; or Dixon & Massy, 1969) helpful in following the discussion.

The need for cross-cultural comparisons, comparisons of many cases, has become widely realized by behavioral scientists in the last twenty-five years. This need is often not apparent to physical scientists or biologists. Only one set of laws governs physics and chemistry. All the plants and animals we know on earth follow a fundamental set of common rules, governed by a single genetic code. In the double helix there is only one genetic "language" with only four "phonemes."

In contrast there are some four thousand human languages spoken today. The speakers of each constitute a distinct culture with their own underlying laws of behavior and their own images of reality. (Nor do speakers of a common language necessarily, or even usually, share a homogeneous culture; there are often many local variants.) The degree of variation imposed by culture on human behavior—even on matters of physiology and perception—has been realized by psychologists only in the last quarter century. (See the reviews of this literature by Triandis, 1964; and Dawson, 1971.)

The limitation of individual case studies as tools for widely generalizing about society and culture has been set forth by Köbben (1970). The following inventory of conflicts is taken partly from his work. From his study of the Siriono of Bolivia, Holmberg (1950) concluded that hunting and gathering tribes tended to be underfed and obsessed with food. From his celebrated study of Western European nations during the 1880s and 1890s, Durkheim (1951) concluded that in general, social isolation tends to drive a person to suicide. Hauser's study (1959) of the Thai led him to believe that, in general, the more atomistic a society, the more it would resist modernization. Raulin (1959), studying the people of Gagnia and Daloa, concluded that, in general, uprooted peoples would be more interested in modernization than those still at home in the land of their ancestry.

But Needham (1954), studying the Punan of Borneo, concluded that hunting and gathering tribes were usually well fed and unobsessed with food. Asuni (1962), studying the people of western Nigeria, concluded that social isolation had nothing to do with suicide. Adair and Vogt (1949), studying the Zuni, concluded that the less atomistic a society, the more it would resist modernization. Malefijt (1963), studying the Javanese, concluded that uprooted peoples would be less interested in modernization than would stay-at-homes. Concomitant variation studies are similarly restricted in their scope by the cultural context of the region in which they are set (see Clignet, 1970).

Hologeistic theory testing is often crucial to testing theoretical models. This is true even though such tests are often less sensitive and less accurate than those using narrower, more rigorously generated data bases. (Such smaller scale studies are important as a means of generating models that can then be tested hologeistically to validate their worldwide applicability. Rohner's [1975] advocacy of multiple methods in establishing social science theory is supported here.) The reduction in sensitivity and accuracy is due mainly to the reliance on archival data to measure variables for hologeistic studies. Researchers often find that there is inadequate information to measure variables of interest for some cultures. In addition, archival data does not normally permit precise measurement of variables. These problems will be discussed further in the sections on data accuracy and data paucity. However, in spite of the cost of reduced sensitivity and accuracy, several benefits accrue.

First, the variation of social behavior is wider in hologeistic studies than in any other sort. The universe of all known human cultures constitutes a natural laboratory that has a greater variance with respect to many variables than can be found in any narrower data base.

Second, one can more confidently assume in a hologeistic test than in any other kind of theory test that the irrelevant variables vary randomly and so drop out of correlations. When looking at a single society, or at a few closely related societies, there is no real possibility of testing supposed functional linkages. There are so many common features, any of which may explain any one particular relationship. It is only when a large variety of societies that differ widely from each other in most respects are examined that the *irrelevant* attributes can be expected to vary. Thus when the Netsilik Eskimos of 1900 are compared with the English of that same date, almost nothing alike is found in their cultures. The Netsilik lived at the most primitive level of social complexity known; with incredible skill they used a highly specialized technology based on bone, stone, and sinew to forage a precarious living from winter sealing and summer hunting and fishing. The English in 1900 were a highly industrialized state, ruling a worldwide empire from a great city. In material culture, in religion, in moral attitudes, in modes of thought, these two cultures have almost nothing in common. And yet, as it happens, they do agree with respect to their basic kinship system, their family structure: the English of 1900 resemble the Netsilik Eskimos far more closely than they do the Ancient Romans or the Chinese or the Hindus—not to speak of the Crow, Omaha, or Iroquois Indians.

So if the English family system in 1900 is compared with that of the French or German of the same day (from the anthropological view), no difference of consequence will be found; but no conclusions can be drawn about associations of constituent elements in that family system from looking at all three peoples, because they share so many other traits in common. They have a common religion, a common moral system, a common economic system, to a considerable extent a common fund of literature, and so on. But when the English kinship system is compared with the Netsilik Eskimos', one finds that several crucial elements of their kinship system are shared, despite all the other differences in their societies and cultures. The so-called Eskimo kinship system that is also the English kinship system is, in fact, one of the six major types of kinship system, each of which has subtypes or variants. The hologeistic study surveys many examples of each of these types and subtypes, looking for correlation, for co-variation.

However, merely to compare the English and Eskimo kinship systems is not enough. The comparison of only two natural instances may prove a fruitful *source* of insight. (Most anthropological "case studies" of single primitive tribes are actually comparisons between the culture of the tribe studied and the culture of the ethnographer.) But such a comparison is an inadequate *test* of that same insight. Consider the comparison of the Oedipus complex in Freud's Vienna and Malinowski's Trobriands. As Donald T. Campbell said:

> Between Trobriand and Vienna there are many dimensions of differences which could constitute potential rival explanations and which we have no means of ruling out. For comparisons of this pair, the *ceteris paribus* requirement [that other things be equal] becomes untenable. (Campbell & Naroll, 1972, p. 449)

Hologeistic studies are studies of large worldwide samples. Culture presumably varies within the sample as much as usual. *So other things are presumed equal. Irrelevant factors are presumed to vary randomly.* This is the greatest strength of hologeistic studies. They are quasi experiments—not as good as controlled experiments, but the next best thing.

The third benefit of hologeistic studies is that the control of Galton's Problem—cultural diffusion—is easier in worldwide samples. This problem, overlooked or ignored by most social scientists, is a persistent confounding factor—a source of spurious correlations. (For more on this problem, see the discussion of solutions.)

The fourth benefit is that many important variables are discernible and measurable only as characteristics of entire societies. Level of cultural evolution is an important variable. Religion is another. Language is a third.

A fifth advantage of hologeistic studies is their relative objectivity. In most case studies, for example, investigators tend deliberately or unconsciously to select the data to fit their insights. Two case studies of the same society by two different investigators can lead to diametrically opposite conclusions about fundamental points. (For a discussion of such studies of Tepoztlan and of the Arapesh, see Naroll, 1970a, pp. 928–29.) Hologeistic studies are designed to seek out and count such inconsistent, discrediting evidence as fully as consistent, supporting evidence.

However, these benefits are not to be gained without costs, not only in terms of reduced accuracy and sensitivity but also in terms of the need for mastery of the special methodological problems that hologeistic research poses. Eight problems of method which require special treatment in holo-geistic studies will be discussed: (1) Group Significance; (2) Galton's Prob-lem; (3) Sample Selection; (4) Unit Definition; (5) Data Accuracy; (6) Regional Variation; (7) Special Problems in Conceptualization, Classifica-tion, and Coding; (8) Data Paucity. The problems of statistical signifi-cance, causal analysis, and deviant case analysis will also be considered. These issues will be discussed mostly from the standpoint of holocultural studies. For a more complete discussion of holonational research method-ology, see Przeworski and Teune (1970); Rokkan (1970); and Rummel (1970).

Hologeistic Method in General

For the usual routine of carrying out a hologeistic study, see Otterbein (1969). Naroll, Michik, and Naroll (1976) have provided a manual giving cookbook-type instructions on how to perform a holocultural study using the Human Relations Area Files Probability Sample of sixty cultures. This manual describes how to deal with the various methodological problems involved in holocultural studies, greatly simplifying the processes of data collection and analysis. It is recommended for investigators wishing to perform a holocultural study.

Hologeistic methodology has been widely criticised (Köbben, 1952, 1967; Schapera, 1953; Lewis, 1956; Barnes, 1971); the classic defense is Whiting (1954, 1968); Köbben's critiques are especially careful, responsi-ble, and measured. See also McEwen (1963); Cohen (1968); Pelto (1970); Holt and Turner (1970); Rokkan (1970); Przeworski and Teune (1970); Chaney (1971); Gillespie and Nesvold (1971); Campbell and Naroll (1972); Sipes (1972); Naroll (1973); Schweizer (1975); Wirsing (1975).

Statistical Significance

The widely used concept of *statistical significance* can best be understood in terms of its rarely used antonym—statistical insignificance. A relationship or measurement is statistically insignificant if it occurs merely by random sampling error—in other words, by chance. To say some quantity is sta-tistically insignificant is to say that it is no more than we would expect to get by chance through sampling error from a universe where the quantity in question did not exist, that is, was zero. The measurement of statistical significance is the subject matter of statistical inference; statistical infer-ence in turn is the main concern of the science of mathematical statistics. The elements of the mathematical reasoning underlying statisti-cal inferences are set forth in such introductory texts as Kenny and Keep-ing (1951) and Mood (1950). The general application of these techniques to the social sciences is outlined (without the underlying mathematical logic) in such texts as Freund (1967) and Blalock (1972).

There are two main types of statistical inference—inference about differences and inference about associations. Hologeistic studies deal chiefly with inference about associations. The present discussion assumes at least an elementary acquaintance with the statistics of inference about associations. Two aspects of statistical inference that bear with special force on hologeistic studies are: (1) the problem of applying inferential statistics to data that may not meet the necessary mathematical assumptions, and (2) the problem of arbitrarily dichotomizing probabilistic statements into those which support a hypothesis and those which do not. Hologeistic studies examine the relationships among variables in large, worldwide samples from the universe of all known cultures. They test theoretical predictions about the nature of those relationships. The relationships are described by measures of association (or correlation), and the probability of their existence in the sampling universe is assessed by tests of statistical significance (for discussions of these statistical operations see Freund, 1967, pp. 355–77; Blalock, 1972, pp. 361–464; Naroll, 1974a).

The significance tests measure the probability that the observed association would have occurred by chance in a sample representing a universe in which no associations actually existed, under the following assumptions: (1) that each of the units in the universe had an equal probability of inclusion in the sample; (2) that each of the units was defined in the same manner; and (3) that each of the units in the sample was independent of all other units in the sample.

Violation of these assumptions may produce errors in the determination of an association's probability of chance occurrence. However, a study of all the units in a universe—a 100 percent sample—may still be thought of as a study of a sample representing a hypothetically infinite macrouniverse with the characteristics of the universe studied. Here, too, significance tests can still be useful. The investigator often wants to know whether the relationship that is found in the actual universe is nothing more than might well have been expected by chance if the actual universe had in fact been a random sample from that hypothetical macrouniverse.

The data of most hologeistic studies do not meet the assumptions required for parametric measures. Consequently, although parametric statistics (e.g., Pearson's r) are more accurate than nonparametric statistics (e.g., gamma, phi, tau-b)—and should be used whenever possible because they are more sensitive (see Siegel, 1956; Dixon & Massey, 1969; Pierce, 1970; Blalock, 1972)—the discussion here will refer to nonparametric statistics unless otherwise stated. The logic of the manipulations involved is, of course, equally applicable to parametric statistics. Computer programs ORDMAT and RPHI (for nonparametric data), PROMO (for parametric data), and RPB (for combinations of parametric and nonparametric data) can compute the associations and significance levels for hologeistic studies (Naroll & Michik, 1975; Naroll, Griffiths, Michik, & Naroll, 1975, 1977).

Generally speaking, investigators choose an arbitrary probability value and decide that associations having a probability of chance occurrence less than or equal to that value are not attributable to chance, while those associations having a probability of chance occurrence greater than that value are attributable to chance. According to this decision rule, associations which are not attributable to chance are considered to be *statistically significant* at the probability level used to make the decision. (0.10, 0.05, 0.01, and .001 are common probability values used for this purpose.) Thus, when an investigator reports that the results are statistically significant at some probability level and asserts that the observed relationships actually exist in the universe being studied, the investigator may be wrong; some probability remains that the associations could have occurred by chance (see Winch & Campbell, 1969; Naroll, 1971b).

Rarely, if ever, are all the assumptions underlying the use of statistical significance tests met in hologeistic studies. Nevertheless, significance tests can still be useful in evaluating the probability that an observed association may be reasonably explained as a chance occurrence. Errors in determining the probability of chance occurrence produced by violating the assumptions underlying significance tests can be divided into two categories: random error and systematic error (or bias). It is important to note that these two kinds of error have different effects on the magnitude of the associations observed in the sample and on their probability of chance occurrence as determined by significance tests. Random errors, by definition, tend to cancel each other out. These errors always tend to lower associations and, thus, tend to increase the probability of chance occurrence indicated by significance tests. Paradoxically, despite circumstances suggesting considerable random error, one can have *even greater confidence* than the significance level suggests in an association that is found to be significant in the universe being studied. Accordingly, random errors need not be a matter of great concern.

Systematic errors, however, may well produce spurious inflation of observed associations, and thereby decrease the probability of chance occurrence indicated by significance tests. Therefore, if all systematic errors are measured and their influences on the magnitudes of the observed associations are statistically controlled, the results of the significance tests can be interpreted as the upper limit of the probability of chance occurrence (i.e., if a significance test indicates that $p=0.05$, then in fact $p \leq 0.05$). Although this application of significance tests does not produce accurate measurement of the probability of chance occurrence, the error is conservative; it favors acceptance of the hypothesis that the observed association does not exist in the universe studied. The general logic underlying the solutions to the various methodological problems discussed in this paper is to eliminate the plausibility of explaining an observed association on the basis of systematic error.

In order for a systematic error to have an effect on the magnitude of an association, it must be significantly associated with both of the theoretical variables. The question of whether the associations observed in a holo-geistic study have been influenced by systematic error can be answered empirically by: (1) measuring the hypothetical systematic error, and (2) testing the significance of its associations with the theoretical variables in each association (which, hypothetically, have been influenced by it). If some systematic error factor reveals an influence on an association be-tween two theoretical variables in this manner, then the magnitude that that association would have manifested—if it had not been influenced by the systematic error factor—may be estimated as the partial association between the two theoretical variables with respect to the systematic error factor. (See Blalock, 1972, pp. 433–42, for discussion and explanation of the concept of partial association.) Computer program PARTAU (Naroll, Griffiths, Michik, & Naroll, 1975) can compute the partial associations be-tween the theoretical variables with respect to each error factor.

To use partial association in this way, it must first be assumed that the error factor is measured accurately and that any other factors associated with it are also associated with the theoretical variables (Brewer, Camp-bell, & Crano, 1970). If these assumptions are not tenable, the partial asso-ciation may be spuriously inflated. However, if the influence of the biasing error factor is such that the resulting partial association between the theo-retical variables is no longer significant—when subjected to standard sig-nificance tests—the conclusion that the original association was determined to be significant because it had been spuriously inflated by systematic error is tenable. It is tenable regardless of the characteristics of the measure of systematic error. If the assumptions about the measure of systematic error are not tenable and the resulting partial association be-tween the theoretical variables is still significant, factor analysis is neces-sary to determine the nature of the influence of the biasing error factor on the theoretical association (Brewer et al., 1970).

It is well to remember that all measures of associations are valid de-scriptions of a relationship only when that relationship is monotonic—when the value of one variable is changed in a specific direction, the di-rection in which the other variable changes will remain constant (Blalock, 1972, pp. 415–16). An easy way to examine the relationship between two variables is first to plot each case on coordinate axes representing the two variables and then to determine, by inspection, whether the line approxi-mating the average value of the relationship changes direction with re-spect to either of the variable axes. If it does change, the relationship is nonmonotonic.

Group Significance

If a large number of associations are computed from the same data, a certain percentage of them can be expected to be "statistically significant" purely by chance. That chance significance is the concern of group significance tests. Leo Simmons (1945) presents no fewer than 1,145 coefficients of association. Most of these are not statistically significant. Are so few individually significant coefficients well within the number that might be expected by chance, even if the data were taken from a table of random numbers or other meaningless garbage? A hologeistic study designed to test a theory—or to select the most tenable of a number of theories—must determine whether the number of associations found to be significant is greater than the number of associations that would be expected to be found significant if none of the associations actually existed in the universe being studied. Murdock (1949) computed hundreds of coefficients of association to test his theory of kinship. It is the group of tests as a whole, not any one test, that constitutes his basic argument. Yet most of his tests were not statistically significant. If the number of significant correlations is too small, the results of the study as a whole may be plausibly explained as chance occurrences. When large numbers of associations are being computed in a hologeistic study, two comparisons are useful.

The first is the comparison between the number of observed significant associations and the number of significant associations that can be expected by chance. With parametric data the number of significant associations that might be expected by chance can be determined by multiplying the number of associations computed by the probability level used to determine significance. However, this procedure often will not work if the data are nonparametric because the distribution of the coefficients of association (and their probability levels) is not continuous. Thus Textor (1967, p. 56) computed 2,500 coefficients of association from four-fold contingency tables derived from random numbers—his so-called "Whiskers Variables." It is reasonable to expect 250 (10 percent) of these associations to be significant at the 10 percent level; in fact, only 126 were. Naroll (1969) ran a similar series of tests on his War, Stress, and Culture sample, with similar results. With nonparametric data the best way to estimate the number of significant associations expected by chance is the "Whiskers Variable" method of Banks and Textor (1963). (See also Textor, 1967, pp. 54–59; Tatje, Naroll, & Textor, 1970, pp. 649–52.) A Whiskers Variable is a nonsense variable coded from a table of random numbers or from the random numbers generator of a computer. A set of Whiskers Variables is generated for each substantive variable; the data for these variables are random with the restriction that each has the same frequency distribution as the substantive variable from which it was generated (see Naroll, Bullough, & Naroll 1974). Computer program MONTE (Naroll, Griffiths, Michik, & Naroll, 1975) can generate as many such Whiskers Variables for each substantive variable as are desired. The associations between each of these Whiskers Variables and the substantive variables are then computed to estimate the distribution of the coefficients of association (and their probability levels) expected by chance. In this manner the percentage of associations that could be expected to be "significant" can be estimated if none of them actually existed in the universe being studied.

A second comparison is useful when a researcher computes a number of associations, only some of which are relevant to testing the hypotheses. In such cases it is useful to compare the magnitudes of the predicted associations with those of the unpredicted associations as suggested by Guthrie (1971) using the methods of Campbell and Fiske (1959). This procedure can provide validation for theoretical discrimination of variables.

Galton's Problem

Most cultural characteristics tend to spread readily by borrowing or migration—by cultural diffusion. Galton's Problem is the problem of possible interdependence of the units of study in a hologeistic survey. If cultures are not independent of each other with respect to the characteristics being studied, statistical analyses of the relationships among those characteristics will be inaccurate. It has been demonstrated that this problem can lead investigators to conclude falsely that their study has provided support for some hypothesis (Erickson, 1974; Ross & Homer, 1976).

There are two aspects to Galton's Problem: (1) If some of the cultures are interdependent, the actual number of independent observations is less than the number of cultures the investigator examined. This inflation of N (number of cases) produces error in tests of the statistical significance of a relationship—error that favors rejection of the null hypothesis, since the standard errors of measures of association are all inverse functions of N. (2) Inclusion of interdependent cases can produce spurious inflation (or deflation) of coefficients of association (Loftin, 1972; Erickson, 1974; Strauss & Orans, 1975). For general reviews of Galton's Problem in hologeistic research, see Naroll (1970a); Schaefer (1974); and Naroll (1976a). The remainder of this section will discuss valid approaches to Galton's Problem.

The basic question is whether cultural diffusion is influencing the results of a hologeistic study. One fruitful approach to this question begins with the calculation of spatial autocorrelations as measures of a variable's tendency to diffuse among the cultures in the sample. The first step in obtaining such an autocorrelation is to arrange (align) the cultures in the sample so that geographical neighbors are grouped together. The second step is to generate an autocorrelation variable from the substantive variable on the basis of the geographical alignment. Suppose, for example, that the first culture in the alignment has a score of two (on the variable being autocorrelated), the second culture (neighboring the first) has a score of six, and the third culture has a score of nine. Then, autocorrelation variable scores would be six for the first culture, nine for the second culture, and so on. The spatial autocorrelation for the variable is the correlation between that variable and its autocorrelation variable. The spatial autocorrelation measures the degree to which geographical neighbors resemble each other. Thus, geographical propinquity is used to measure diffusion.

There is a weakness in the use of spatial autocorrelations as measures of diffusion. The spatial autocorrelations are based on linear alignments and therefore measure diffusion along a single dimension, whereas the cultures being studied are scattered about the earth in a two-dimensional manner. One approach to dealing with this weakness is to prepare more than one geographical alignment for the sample. For example, one alignment could group the cultures on the basis of propinquity along meridians and another could group them on the basis of propinquity along parallels (see Schaefer, 1969, for example). Murdock and White (1969) developed an alignment of culture clusters based on linguistic and other historical relationships as well as propinquity; Loftin and Hill (1974) developed a procedure (based on the Murdock-White culture cluster alignment) for preparing a single alignment for any holocultural sample. Such Loftin-Hill alignments have been shown to be more powerful than others using propinquity alone and are considered to be better for measuring diffusion in holocultural research (see Loftin, Hill, Naroll, & Margolis, 1976).

There are two stages involved in the autocorrelation approach to the question of whether an observed relationship was spuriously produced by cultural diffusion. The first stage is to analyse the autocorrelations of the two variables involved. *The proposition that the observed relationship has been influenced by diffusion is tenable only if both autocorrelations are positive.* If either of them is zero or negative, then Galton's Problem is not a problem for that relationship in that study.

If both of the autocorrelations are positive and significant, it is necessary to move on to the second stage of the autocorrelation approach. This involves two statistical procedures, one to control for diffusional effects on the strength of the relationship and the other to control for the inflated number of cases in the significance test. Using second-order partial correlation is a good way to control for diffusional effects on the strength of a relationship (i.e., partialing out the effects of both of the autocorrelation variables on the relationship between the substantive variables). For a discussion of the logic and mathematics of this partialing procedure, see Wirsing (1975), Loftin and Ward (n.d.), and Naroll (1976a).

The control for spurious inflation of the number of cases used in the significance test relies on the analogy between spatial and temporal autocorrelation pointed out by Simonton (1975). With spatial autocorrelation each culture is correlated with its geographical neighbor; with temporal autocorrelation each culture is correlated with itself at an earlier (or later) time. In both cases the problem is one of interdependence of observations. Orcutt and James (1948) derived a technique for estimating the effective number of independent observations on the basis of the autocorrelations. Thus it is possible to calculate the appropriate number of cases to use in the significance test computations for relationships that have been influenced by cultural diffusion. For further discussion of this procedure, see Naroll (1976a).

With these two control procedures it is possible to estimate what the strength and statistical significance of the observed relationship would have been, had it not been influenced by diffusion. In other words, these controls make it possible to test hologeistic hypotheses even when cultural diffusion has operated in the sample. It should be remembered, however, that the results produced by these procedures are conservative; they tend to favor acceptance of the null hypothesis because the two autocorrelation variables will never be equivalent unless the substantive variables are perfectly correlated. Thus it is possible to have a significant autocorrelation for variable A owing to diffusion in Africa and Asia, and a significant autocorrelation for variable B owing to diffusion in the Americas and Oceania. In such a case diffusion could not reasonably be considered to have influenced the observed relationship between the two variables. So it is possible that by using these autocorrelation control procedures, investigators may fail to reject the null hypothesis when it is false; but it is quite unlikely that the procedures will ever lead investigators to falsely reject the null hypothesis.

A second approach to Galton's Problem, applicable only when the variables being studied are measured at the dichotomous level, has been suggested by Strauss and Orans (1975). This method, called *Cluster Reduction*, appears to employ some sort of diffusion alignment similar to those used in the autocorrelation approach. This procedure involves reduction of cell frequencies in the two by two contingency table until the number of neighbor-pairs falling in the same cell does not exceed chance expectation. Analysis of the final contingency table yields results free of both kinds of diffusion effects (i.e., effects on strength of relationship and on number of cases used in calculation of statistical significance). For further discussion of the Cluster Reduction approach, see Naroll (1976a).

(A related approach to Galton's Problem, potentially more powerful than the autocorrelation or Cluster Reduction approach, is the use of worldwide historical matrices. In such matrices, the degree of historical relationship between every pair of cultures in the sample is estimated by using whatever factors the investigator considers relevant. For examples of this technique, see Wirsing [1974] and Pryor [1978]. At this writing, however, there is no worldwide matrix method that has been sufficiently developed for general holocultural research.)

The autocorrelation approach (for interval and ordinal scale data) and the Cluster Reduction approach (for dichotomous data) are practical ways of getting at Galton's Problem in holocultural studies. However, a different approach, the *Cluster Difference test*, is useful when either Cluster Reduction or autocorrelation indicates that diffusion has played a large part in the results of a study. The Cluster Difference test uses the process of diffusion to test hypotheses. The working assumption underlying this test is that if two variables are functionally related, they will diffuse together as a unit rather than independently. In other words, the "hits" (cases that support the theoretical hypothesis) should have a greater tendency to be geographically clustered than the "misses" (cases not supporting the hypothesis), if the hypothesis is valid. The Cluster Difference test uses diffusion alignments similar to those used in the autocorrelation approach. See Zucker (1976) for a description of how this test can be operationalized. The Cluster Difference test is distinguished by the fact that it constitutes a direct test of functional hypotheses that is independent of the usual correlational procedures.

In summary, either the autocorrelation or Cluster Reduction approaches (depending on the level of measurement of the variables) is advocated for evaluation of the relevance of Galton's Problem in a hologeistic study. If diffusion is found to be pervasive, then further analysis with the Cluster Difference test is necessary. The computations necessary for all three of these approaches to Galton's Problem can be done by computer, using HRAFLIB library programs (Naroll & Michik, 1975; Naroll, Griffiths, Michik, & Naroll, 1975, 1977).

Sample Selection

This section discusses how to obtain a sample of cultures having the same characteristics as the universe of interest. Has each unit of study in the sampling universe an equal probability of being included in the sample? This is the assumption underlying the use of significance tests to evaluate the probability that an association observed in the sample exists in the sampling universe. However, because most of the units in the universe of all known primitive cultures are not described well enough to be studied, it is not possible to use such strictly probabilistic methods in holocultural studies.

The salience of this departure from the assumptions underlying significance tests has been demonstrated by a number of studies of systematic sampling bias in holocultural studies. In a restudy using a different sample, Murdock (1957) has reported that the relationships examined in the earlier study (Murdock 1949) were influenced by systematic sampling error. Chaney (1966) has demonstrated that the sample used by Spiro (1965) was systematically biased; Spiro (1966) has conceded that his sample was biased, causing him to conclude falsely that one of his propositions was supported by the data in his earlier study. Further evidence of variation in relationships between variables as a function of the sample examined is provided by Köbben (1952, p. 140); Chaney and Ruiz Revilla (1969); Chaney (1970); Naroll (1970b); Rohner and Pelto (1970); Tatje et al. (1970, pp. 657–75).

The solution proposed here to this problem of systematic sampling bias is two-fold: (1) Limit sampling bias to a few well-defined restrictions and otherwise use probability sampling. (2) Measure the biases involved in these restrictions and control for their influence on the relationships being examined. Ideally, the sampling universe for holocultural studies should be all known "primitive" cultures. Murdock's *Outline of World Cultures* (1975) represents an attempt to list this universe; even here, because of the difficulty of the task rather than any departure from principle, the areas of Australia and New Guinea are incomplete. Murdock's list, combined with Capell's linguistic survey and Greenway's Australian bibliography (1963), yield a sampling universe that is not significantly different from the universe of all primitive cultures. The greatest bias inherent in the selection of samples from this universe is a bibliographic one. The variables under study must be described well enough to be examined in each unit. By accepting this bias, one can produce a bibliographically defined universe from which probability samples can be selected. It is well to remember that the more stringent the bibliographic restrictions, the smaller the bibliographic universe, and the greater the probability of its being systematically different from the universe of all known cultures.

The bibliographic restrictions may produce differences between the relationships observable in the sample and the actual relationships in the universe of all known cultures. Since some of the units in the sample can be expected to fulfill the bibliographic selection requirements to a greater degree than others, measurements of this variation can be considered estimates of bibliographic error. The hypothesis that bibliographic error influences the results of the study can be tested, and, if necessary, the influence can be controlled statistically.

The validity of this procedure for controlling bibliographic sampling error depends on the following assumption: the observed influences of bibliographic quality in the sample must reflect the actual influences of sampling selection bias on the association in question. In other words, bibliographic controls must estimate the degree to which the relationships in the universe of all known primitive cultures have been misrepresented in the sample because of systematic sampling errors produced by the bibliographic restrictions on sampling. The validity of this assumption is doubtful (1) if the relationships between selection bias and the variables are not monotonic, or (2) if examination of a different sample (drawn with the same bibliographic restrictions) yields results significantly different from those of the original sample. Demonstrating that the bibliographic restrictions on sample selection produce systematic errors in representation of some specified culture types or culture areas would also cast doubt on this assumption. If by one or more of the strategies described above, the investigators attempt to demonstrate that they are not able to rely on the control procedures for bibliographic error, and if they fail to do so, then there is an empirical basis for presuming that the bibliographic bias has been controlled. A conclusive test would require examination of a sample selected without bibliographic restrictions; with such a sample, the bibliographic restrictions would not have been imposed in the first place. For further discussion of bibliographic error and how it may be controlled, see Naroll (1970a, pp. 911ff.).

Additional restrictions on sample selection may be imposed to satisfy the requirement that all units in the sample are defined in the same manner. These additional restrictions may cause the investigator to deviate from probability sampling procedures in selecting the sample from the bibliographically defined universe. Such errors are, by definition, immeasurable and require qualification of the definition of the universe being studied—the universe of all known primitive cultures, for example. (For a more complete discussion of holocultural sampling methods, see Naroll, 1970a, pp. 889–926; and Otterbein, 1976.)

Unit Definition

A unit definition is a statement of the boundaries of the tribal or the societal unit of study in a hologeistic survey. What is the "skin" of a society or culture? Consider the people of the Gyem area of the Gabor district of Gabon. This area is in effect the boundary between the Fang people and the Ntumu people. Both Fang and Ntumu are names of languages. Fang and Ntumu lie along a single language chain (linguistic continuum). The Ntumu of Bitam call the Gyem people Fang. The Fang of Mitzik call them Ntumu. The Gyem people themselves say that they do not know whether they are Fang or Ntumu (Fernandez, 1963, p. 8). As already stated, Murdock's *Outline of World Cultures* (1975), together with Capell (1962) and Greenway (1963), constitute a satisfactory definition of the universe of all known primitive cultures. The problem with using these lists is that the definition of the cultures in them is neither consistent nor explicit.

How may the culture-bearing units that form the basis for holocultural surveys be defined? There has been no agreement among anthropologists. (See Naroll, 1964; Helm, 1967; Barth, 1969; Jorgensen, 1969; Murdock & White, 1969; Naroll, 1970a, pp. 721–65; Naroll, 1971a.) The definition of the culture-bearing units in a hologeistic study depends on the nature of the theoretical variables being studied. If differences in state organization are of interest, for example, it may be appropriate to use states as units of study; in such a case the universe of all known states rather than that of all known cultures is being studied. A state is here defined as a group of several territorially distinct subgroups, whose leaders assert and wield the exclusive right to declare and conduct warfare.

For such variables as child-rearing practices, kinship organization, and descent rules, it may be possible to forego exact delineation of cultural boundaries and use as the data point for that culture a particular local community falling within one of the "cultures" listed in Murdock (1975), Capell (1962), or Greenway (1963). One solution to such a unit definition problem relies on language to isolate the parameters of the culture-bearing unit (Naroll, 1971a). The most recent and perhaps the most useful summary of the difficulties in using language to define culture-bearing units is that by Hymes (1967). Hymes provides a clear discussion of the two major objections: (1) speech communities often have fuzzy, vague, indistinct boundaries, in practice sometimes impossible to delineate; and (2) speech communities are often culturally heterogeneous and do not have one homogeneous culture. The difficulty in delineating speech communities may be solved by separating each community from all other communities being studied by a double language boundary: instead of attempting to locate one vague boundary between two speech communities, require that each of the units has at least two such boundaries between it and all other units in the sample studied. If more than one language appears to be spoken in a community, a specific language or dialect should be named as the speech community being studied—ordinarily the one spoken by the fieldworker's principal informants. For further discussion of this approach to unit definition see Naroll (1971a).

The problem of cultural heterogeneity within speech communities is concerned with the extent to which the description of a single community represents the speech community to which it belongs. It is generally accepted that cultural characteristics usually change from local group to local group, indeed from subculture to subculture, and even from household to household (see Murdock, 1953, pp. 477–79; Whiting, 1954, p. 526). The major justification for the use of communities as units of study is that nearly all the ethnographic descriptions of cultures are primarily based on information gathered in such units. However, that justification provides no logical basis for presuming that such data are representative of the entire culture. Presumably, the selection bias introduced in this way is measured indirectly by the measures of bibliographic sampling error discussed in the preceding section of this paper.

The most elaborate and precisely tested attempt at a general theory of ethnic unit definition for hologeistic research is Naroll's *cultunit* concept. Naroll distinguishes four types of ethnic units: (1) a Hopi type—a stateless society defined solely by language and community contact; (2) a Flathead type—a linguistically homogeneous state; (3) an Aymara type—a linguistically defined subordinate, politically subject people in a linguistically heterogeneous state; and (4) an Inca type—a linguistically homogeneous group of imperial rulers in a linguistically heterogeneous state (Naroll, 1970a, pp. 731–65). This typology supplements the distinction between holocultural and holonational studies.

Culture varies temporally as well as spatially. Since the investigator often finds more than one bibliographic source for some of the units, and since these sources may be describing the same unit at different times, it is necessary to choose a specific temporal focus for each unit. Normally this selection will be based on the relative quality of the descriptions of the variables being studied. However, if the theory does not predict that the relationships among the variables can be observed if the cultures are examined at only one moment in time, then, in order to test the theory, it will be necessary to select at least two separate time foci for each unit to study.

The general approach to the problem of unit definition advocated here can be described as follows: ordinarily, the language is used as a sampling unit. For each sampling unit, a focal community is chosen (together with one or more time foci). The double language boundary method may then be used to ensure that no two focal communities in the sample speak mutually intelligible dialects—deciding all doubts and questions in favor of the hypothesis of mutual intelligibility. If the natural unit of study is wider than a community—for example, a state or a language group—that unit should be defined from the point of view of the focal community. If the wider unit is an entire language group, the double boundary method will have to be used to make sure that no two such groups in the sample overlap. This method permits the language groups to have fuzzy, vague, and indeterminate boundaries.

Data Accuracy

Data accuracy is concerned with errors that may be introduced into holocultural studies by informants, reporters, and comparativists. The data in hologeistic surveys may be defined as the results of the measures of the variables that are used to compute the associations. These measurements are based on reports of observations of the units being studied. There are, then, three general sources that may produce inaccuracies in hologeistic data: (1) Informant error—the people from whom the information was gained may not have known their own culture accurately. (2) Reporter error—the writers of the reports on the culture may be inaccurate in their interpretations of what the informants told them about the culture; they may not have gathered enough of the available information for an accurate report; and they may not report all the relevant information that they have gathered. Or, most important of all, their informants may have deliberately deceived them. (If the informants deliberately deceived them, they were making no mistake; their mistake was to believe the informants, to fail to check them and thus detect the error and the practice of deception.) (3) Comparativist error—holocultural investigators may be inaccurate in interpreting the observers' reports and may indicate that the reports show presence of the variables of interest when those variables are in fact absent.

The accuracy of holocultural data has been seriously questioned on the basis of errors arising from all three of these sources (Webb, Campbell, Schwartz, & Sechrest, 1966; Haekel, 1970; Naroll, 1970a, pp. 928–30). It has been demonstrated that the results of some holocultural studies can be at least partially explained as artifacts caused by inaccurate data; in some cases, data inaccuracy itself constitutes a sufficient and plausible explanation for some of the associations (Naroll, 1962, pp. 146–51; Rohner, Dewalt, & Ness, 1973; Rohner, 1975, pp. 101, 200–04).

To guard against the real possibility that inaccuracy of data is influencing the results of a holocultural study, the control factor method of data quality control can be used. This method assumes that there is variation in the degree of accuracy of holocultural data and that this variation is related to characteristics of the data generation process. A control factor can be any characteristic of the data generation process that is thought to be related to the accuracy of the data. Did the reporters participate in the activities they describe? Did the reporters obtain their information directly from people who observed the phenomena, or did they obtain it through intermediaries? Control factors should be measured for each of the variables in each of the units of study and should deal with possible errors from all three of the major categories of sources (discussed below) which may produce data inaccuracy. The hypothesis that the data on a variable are inaccurate may be examined by computing associations between that variable and the control factors suspected of being related to its accuracy. If the associations are not significantly different from zero, it can be presumed that the data on the variable are not systematically distorted by errors in data generation and that associations between this and other variables are not artifacts of data inaccuracy. Computer programs ORDMAT, PROMO, and RPB (Naroll & Michik, 1975; Naroll, Griffiths, Michik, & Naroll, 1975, 1977) can perform these computations. Computing associations will not measure random errors in data generation, but since random errors tend to lower associations, it need not be a matter of great concern.

The fact that control factors are associated with the data does not necessarily imply that those data are inaccurate. For example, an association between witchcraft attribution and length of time the fieldworker spent collecting data may indicate: (1) that fieldworkers who spend more time collecting data tend to be more accurate in learning about witchcraft; (2) that fieldworkers who spend more time collecting data tend to exaggerate the importance of witchcraft; or (3) that cultures with much witchcraft are more interesting and therefore encourage fieldworkers to study them longer. The association, like any other, needs to be explained. If investigators are able to rule out plausible alternative explanations of the associations between the control factors and the variables, if they can provide evidence that people in cultures high in witchcraft attribution are reluctant to talk about witchcraft with field workers they do not know well, and if they can assume that at least *some* of the data are really accurate, then they can treat those associations as measures of systematic error and, if necessary, control for influences on their results statistically. Causal analysis of associations between theoretical variables and control factors may also be helpful in explaining them.

Five control factors are now known to be especially useful and sensitive to systematic error. These five factors are given by the answers to the following questions: (1) How long did the ethnographers live among the people they describe? (2) How well do they claim to know the native language—the language the natives speak among themselves at home? (3) Do the ethnographers describe the life of the people as it is lived while they were there with them, or do they instead describe life as it was previously lived some years or decades earlier, from the memories of elderly informants? (4) What sorts of systematic checks on native statements did the ethnographers use? Did they systematically ask a number of informants the same questions to see if their answers agreed? Did they use psychological tests? Did they take a formal census or a household sample survey? (5) How many earlier publications by other ethnographers describing these same people did the ethnographers use or cite?

The extent to which the control factor method solves the problem of data accuracy in a holocultural study is directly related to the extent to which all plausible sources of systematic error have been examined by it. Additional strategies for detecting and controlling comparativist error will be discussed in the section on special problems in conceptualization, classification, and coding. For further discussion of data accuracy in holocultural studies and the control factor method, see Naroll (1962, 1970a). For further discussion of data accuracy in holonational studies, see Rummel (1970) and Janda (1970).

Regional Variation

The problem of regional variation is the problem of variation among major geographical regions—variation in the magnitude of the associations among variables being examined in a holocultural study. The worldwide associations do not reflect such possible variations and therefore may not be representative of the actual relationships in each of the regions. Several measures of association have varied widely when computed region by region. In failing to examine this possibility, some holocultural investigators have erroneously interpreted their results as reflecting worldwide tendencies (Sawyer & LeVine, 1966, pp. 719-27; Driver & Schuessler, 1957, pp. 336-47; Bourguignon & Greenbaum, 1973; Chaney & Ruiz Revilla, 1969, pp. 168-25).

To see if the correlation is truly worldwide, the investigator should recompute associations separately for each geographical region and determine if any of them manifests significant variation among the regions. Computer program PARTAU (Naroll & Michik, 1975; Naroll, Griffiths, Michik, & Naroll, 1975) can perform the regional recomputations of the associations and their significance levels. The significance of variations in the magnitude of an association among the regions may be determined by measuring the significance of the difference between the largest and smallest of the regional associations. If that difference is not significant, the association based on all the units in the sample may be considered to reflect a worldwide tendency. Such a worldwide tendency would seem especially clear if all the associations in every region not only have the same sign, but also range upward in absolute value from 0.20 (phi, tau b, or r) or 0.30 (gamma, Yule's Q).

Significant regional variation may indicate that the theory in question omits some relevant factors. However, it is possible that the regional variations could reasonably be explained in terms of the methodological variables involved in the holocultural study. This possibility could be examined by considering each region as a separate sample and testing for sampling bias, errors in data generation, and Galton's Problem. This has yet to be done in a holocultural study.

Conceptualization, Classification, and Coding

This section is concerned with the comparability of phenomena among cultures—with the translation of written reports on the units of study into statistics. Defining the theoretical concepts in such a way that they will be useful in explaining the characteristics of all human cultures is a basic problem in hologeistic research. The approach advocated here distinguishes between emic, etic, and theoric concepts; it is derived from linguistics (Goodenough, 1970, Chapter 4).

As Goodenough (1956, p. 37) pointed out, the definition of a variable may differ depending on whether it explains the characteristics of *one* particular culture or of *all* human cultures. In an explanation of Norwegian culture, the concept of *cannibalism* could be defined as eating human flesh and approving of the practice. It involves two distinctions: eating or not eating human flesh, and approving or not approving of the practice; these distinctions are sufficient to describe cannibalism as it relates to the rest of Norwegian culture, and would be an emic definition of cannibalism. However, when a larger number of cultures is considered, additional distinctions must be examined if the concept is to be helpful in explaining the relationships between cannibalism and the rest of the culture for all of the cultures being studied. For example, in Fiji (ca. 1850), it was important to distinguish *whom* you ate (it was a great triumph to eat your enemies). In other cultures, human flesh may be eaten to gain some quality of the victim: eat a brave man's heart to gain courage; eat a baby to regain youth. It is reasonable to suppose that in the Mbau language of Fiji, there is a word that means "eating the flesh of one's enemy;" likewise to suppose that in some language there is a word that specifically means "eating a brave man's heart to gain courage;" and again to suppose that in some language there is a word that means "eating a baby to regain youth." If in fact such distinctions are made in *any* human language, then they involve an etic concept. (Color terms and kinship terms are the only known domains of meaning where thorough etic analysis has been worldwide.) Etic concepts are abstractions generated by social scientists from the analysis of emic definitions.

In order to define an emic concept adequately, it is necessary to be aware of all its relevant etic components. The set of all the distinctions that are made in any culture concerning the significance of eating human flesh is equivalent to the universe of etic concepts of cannibalism. Each of these etic concepts describes a distinction that is relevant to explaining the relationships between consuming human flesh and other aspects of existence in at least one culture. Surprisingly enough, the etic universe needed to define all emic concepts of a specific aspect of existence may be rather small. Only eight etic distinctions describe all emic definitions of kinship terms, for example (Goodenough, 1970, Chapter 4).

This discussion of emic and etic concepts has been aimed at developing comparability among diverse systems of classifications of phenomena in different cultures. The great danger in making such comparisons is in attempting to use the emic concepts of one culture to explain characteristics of another culture. For example, early investigators were distressed to learn that Hawaiians did not know their own parents: they called all their uncles, father; and all their aunts, mother. The application of etic analysis to Hawaiian kin terms shows that in one sense this is true, but that in another sense it is absurd. The Hawaiians distinguish relatives by sex of alter (the relative being referred to) and by generation, but not by collaterality. Hawaiian has no words for father, mother, uncle, or aunt as such. Their kin term system is functional in their extended bilateral households. Each system teaches young children in the prevalent household system to classify relatives according to their social roles in the life of the child.

When anthropologists perceived how kin term systems operated, they predicted that these kin systems would be related to social structure—to rules of descent and residence. In order to test this prediction of the relationship between kin terms and social structure, kin term systems were classified according to one crucial diagnostic feature: the term a male used to refer to his female cross-cousins (see Murdock, 1949). This term was compared with the terms used to refer to sister, aunts, nieces, and female parallel cousins. For example, in the Eskimo type, female cross-cousins are referred to by the same term as female parallel cousins, but not by the same terms as sisters, aunts, and nieces;[2] in the Hawaiian type, female cross-cousins are referred to by the same term as sisters and parallel cousins, but not by the same terms as aunts and nieces; in the Iroquois type, female cross-cousins are referred to by different terms from all other female relatives, and so on.

Each of these types—six of them in all—constitutes a theoric concept and is defined in terms of a specific set of etic concepts. The usefulness of a theoric concept is established by demonstrating that it is related to other variables in explaining some universal characteristics of human culture.

These theoric kin term concepts have demonstrated their usefulness as variables in the explanation of cross-cultural variation in kinship terminology (see Naroll, 1973).

The anthropologists who developed these theoric concepts began their theoric work with a clear grasp of both the emics and the etics of kinship terminology. They understood the native kin categories from the native viewpoint for scores of kin term systems. They analyzed each in terms of etic kinship concepts and generated useful variables (theoric concepts).

In summary, emic concepts are those used in a specific culture by its natives to classify a given semantic domain. Etic concepts are those used by social scientists to analyze the conceptual distinctions made by emic systems. There are hundreds of different kinds of kin terms, but all can be defined in terms of the eight etic concepts listed by Goodenough (1970). Theoric concepts are those used by social scientists to explain variations in human cultures.

Among the variations to be explained are variations in emic systems. If it is assumed that a science of human behavior is possible, it must be assumed that much variation in emic systems is related as cause or effect to variation in other aspects of human culture. Consequently, if the range of variation of emic systems is not understood, then the theoretical problems have not been adequately defined. Development of an etic universe is the most parsimonious way of defining and describing the range of variation of emic systems. But that development is not enough. There is no reason to suppose that the etic concepts are otherwise likely to be powerful in constructing theories. The development of useful theoric concepts is a necessary step in generating sufficient explanations of characteristics of human culture. Much light on this development has been shed by papers on conceptualization in hologeistic studies (see Ford, 1967; Moore, 1969; R. Cohen & Naroll, 1970; Tatje, 1970; Ember, 1970; LeBar, 1970).

A theory which seeks to explain some characteristics of human culture may be viewed as a set of variables (theoric concepts), combined with statements of the nature of the relationships among those variables. Each of the variables may be considered as a category which encompasses some specified set of phenomena. In a holocultural survey, the universe of phenomena studied is defined by the written reports on all the cultures in the sample—what reporters say about the cultures—rather than by the cultures themselves. (The problem of inconsistencies between what the reporters say and the actual characteristics of the cultures has been dealt with in the section on data accuracy.)

The variables in a holocultural study, then, must be defined so that they can be measured by examining the reports on the units of study. Such definitions are descriptions of indicators (or coding rules) that provide information about the variables. If the reports contain quantified data (e.g., average rainfall, census reports) on the variables of interest, the coding rules are easy to design. However, holocultural investigators are often forced to deal with more impressionistic statements about their variables of interest.

Where the data are not quantified in the reports, the investigator should develop a set of coding rules to yield a ranking of the units of study on the variables of interest. A set of coding rules developed by Raoul Naroll to measure frequency of witchcraft attribution provides an illustrative example: one reporter says that among the Kapauku, witchcraft is the most common form of revenge against an enemy of another political unit; another reports that some bands among the Hottentot practice witchcraft openly, others secretly. A comparison of these two statements fails to provide convincing evidence that the true frequency of witchcraft attribution among the Kapauku is actually greater than that among the Hottentot. However, there is a frequency statement made about the Kapauku, namely that certain kinds of witchcraft are more "common"; but none about the Hottentot. It is possible that among the Hottentot all sorts of witchcraft are rare; it is not possible among the Kapauku—according to the reports at hand. For this variable, the task was to rank the reports in terms of degree of commitment of the reporter about the relative frequency of witchcraft attribution.

Naroll first ranked the reports intuitively and then analyzed that intuitive ranking to identify the element of the reports that had influenced the rank decisions. The following set of coding rules resulted.

Group I:	All deaths and illnesses are believed by the natives to be results of witchcraft.
Group II:	All deaths are believed by the natives to be the results of witchcraft.
Group III:	All illnesses are believed by the natives to be the results of witchcraft. (Illness attributions ranked after death attributions, because presumably the latter are more infuriating to survivors. On the other hand, one might have argued for the reverse order, on the grounds that illnesses are presumably more frequent than deaths.)
Group IV:	All deaths except those due to old age are believed to be the result of witchcraft.
Group V:	All deaths except those due to warfare are believed to be the results of witchcraft.
Group VI:	All deaths except those due to old age and warfare are believed to be the results of witchcraft.
Group VII:	Words are used by the reporter implying that, in general, witchcraft attributions are "common" or "not infrequent" (might be broken down into two groups).
Group VIII:	Words are used implying that in certain specified circumstances witchcraft attributions are "common" or "not infrequent" (might be broken down into two groups).
Group IX:	Witchcraft is alluded to, without any commitment by the reporter about its frequency or rarity. N.B.: Where words are used implying that witchcraft attribution is rare, except in specified circumstances, such language implies that in the specified circumstances the attribution is not infrequent (as in Group VIII).
Group X:	Witchcraft attribution is stated to be uncommon, or words to that effect (adjective unmodified by intensive adverb).
Group XI:	Witchcraft attribution is stated to be extremely uncommon (adjective modified by intensive adverb).
Group XII:	Witchcraft attribution is denied by the reporter.

The coding rules and the reports for each unit of study were then given to coders who had no knowledge of the theory being tested. By examining the reporter's statements, the coders (1) determined which group each unit of study was to be considered a member of, and (2) placed each unit in the lowest numbered group for which the reporter had made the necessary statements. This process produced an ordinal measure of the frequency of witchcraft attribution for the units in the sample.

The operational definitions of the variables, then, are the coding rules as interpreted by the coders. The immediate question concerns the reliability of the measurement process. Can it be assumed that if different coders applied the same coding rules to the same reports, they would generate the same data? If not, it must be concluded that the data reflect, at least in part, the characteristics of the coders, rather than simply the theoretical variables. Explicit coding rules reduce coding error—the coders are less likely to be able to exercise their own judgment in measuring the variables. However, it must be remembered that the coding rules constitute, in effect, the bibliographic restrictions on sample selection. If they are too restrictive, it may not be possible to obtain an adequate sample of cultures, one for which the available information is sufficient to allow for measurement of the variables.

The solution advocated here for the problem of coding reliability is (1) to make the coding rules as explicit as possible, given the nature of the data base; and (2) to measure the reliability of the coding process and assess the extent to which the coding rules are responsible for the data generated. The reliability of the coding process can be estimated by having two or more coders measure the same variables from the same materials, according to the same coding rules. At least one of the coders should be completely naive, i.e., entirely ignorant of the purposes of the study—of the theory being tested. The coders must not discuss the codings with each other at all until a third person has compared their work; nor must either coder know the codings of the other. Intercoder reliability may be determined by measuring the extent to which the coders produce equivalent data with an appropriate measure of association—for example, Kendall's coefficient of concordance (Siegel, 1956, pp. 229–38). These intercoder reliability coefficients may be interpreted as the maximum extent to which the coding rules constitute the operational definitions of the variables. Since holocultural studies do not seek to measure the characteristics of the coders in order to test theories, the reliability coefficients should be high, so that it is plausible to assume that the data are relatively free of coder bias. If the reliability coefficients are less than 0.80, the coding rules are unsatisfactory and should be refined. The effectiveness of intercoder reliability coefficients for measuring coder error in the data is directly related to the number of independent coders used in the study and the extent to which they form a heterogeneous population.

The validity of the data generated is also a concern. Do those data actually reflect the characteristics of the theoretical variables in the units of study? If the measures of association support the relationships predicted by the theory, there is reason to have some confidence in the validity of the data. A stronger presumption of validity may be created by comparing the data produced by different groups of coders, using different coding rules to measure the variable (see Campbell & Fiske, 1959). The strongest possible presumption in favor of the validity of the data is created when different researchers, using different coding rules, examine the same theoretical variables in different samples, and find similar relationships among the variables. While reliability does not imply validity, validity does imply reliability; reliability is a necessary, but not a sufficient, condition for validity.

It should be stressed that the variables examined in a hologeistic study are operationally defined according to the phenomena by which they were measured; an assertion that those variables represent anything else must be evaluated on the strength of the presumption that the data are valid measures of the variables. A problem occurs when some, but not all, of the phenomena that define the variables can be measured from the reports on the units of study. For example, anxiety is theoretically defined by suicide frequency and frequency of mental illness, but is operationally defined by only suicide frequency. Stress is theoretically defined by population density and difficulty in obtaining food, but is operationally defined by only population density. In a holocultural study, then, it is questionable whether the assertion that a significant association between those two variables—as they were operationally defined—can be interpreted as indicating a significant association between mental illness frequency and difficulty in obtaining food. For further discussion of strategies for dealing with the problems of reliability and validity, see Cronbach and Meehl (1955); Campbell and Fiske (1959); Baggaley (1964, pp. 60–90). For further discussion of the problems involved in conceptualization, classification, and coding in various contexts, see Ford (1967); Moore (1969); Berry (1969); R. Cohen and Naroll (1970); Tatje (1970); Ember (1970); LeBar (1970); Osgood (1971); Chaney (1971); Durbin (1972); Otterbein (1972); and Thomas and Weigert (1972).

Data Paucity

The problem of data paucity arises when reports on the units of study do not contain adequate direct information on the variables of interest. Holocultural tests of theory depend on these reports to yield the data necessary for measuring the theoretical variables. When topical coverage of these reports is uneven, it is not possible to test explanations of some characteristics of human culture in enough societies to form an adequate sample.

Where a variable cannot be measured directly, it must be measured indirectly (Webb et al., 1966; R. Cohen & Naroll, 1970). An indirect measure (or proxy) may be defined as a measurement of some variable which is associated with the variable of interest. While it may not be possible to measure the variable of interest directly, the characteristics of that variable may be inferred from measurements of the proxy, on the basis of its association with the variable of interest.

It is necessary to establish that the proxy is, in fact, associated with the variable of interest—that the proxy is valid as a measure of the variable of interest. This can be done by providing evidence that the proxy is significantly associated with the variable of interest in some specified manner; better still, by providing evidence that the association between the proxy and the variable of interest can be reasonably estimated as being of some specific magnitude and direction. Such evidence may be provided by a holocultural study or by a study using some other methodology (e.g., smaller scale cross-cultural studies using more complete, more precise data bases).

Naroll (1969) shows how he dealt with a presumption that a proxy was associated in some specified manner with a variable of interest—suicide frequency. Nearly all the units in Naroll's study lacked adequate data on suicide rates. The proxy was the amount of attention given to suicide by the reporter, as measured by the percentage of words about suicide in the report. Naroll found that the proxy was highly associated with divorce rules, marriage negotiation rules, drunken brawling, warfare, homicide frequency, and wife beating. The most reasonable and parsimonious explanation of this pattern of associations was that more attention was given to suicide where there was more suicide to attract attention. Thus, in the absence of plausible alternative explanations of the associations, it is reasonable to assume that the proxy has a significant positive association with the variable of interest.

Holocultural studies yield coefficients of association between variables. These associations are estimates of the reliability of measuring one variable indirectly through measurement of the other variable. Bacon, Barry, and Child (1965) found an association between instrumental dependence in adulthood and frequency of drunkenness. Thus, frequency of drunkenness, for example, may be used as a proxy for instrumental dependence. The validity of this procedure relies on the assumption that the association found by Bacon et al. reflects an actual association in the universe of cultures being studied and may be evaluated by examining their methods. The ingenuity of researchers in developing and validating proxies is a significant determinant of what variables can or cannot be measured with the available information. The process of developing and validating proxies has the effect of increasing the applicability of the holocultural method and reducing the bibliographic restrictions on sample selection.

The ideal solution to the problem of data paucity in the literature would be to collect whatever data are lacking in the field. There have been some efforts in this direction (Whiting, Child, Lambert, & Whiting, 1963; Minturn & Lambert, 1964; Campbell & LeVine, 1970). While these efforts have been difficult to carry out and have been limited to small numbers of societies, they do pave the way for improvements in methodology. Although such efforts help, they cannot be expected to solve the problem directly; most of the culture areas in the universe of all known culture areas no longer exist and therefore, cannot be reexamined. However, such studies can be crucial in validating proxies.

Causal Analysis

This section examines whether the results of a hologeistic study reflect specific causal relationships among the variables involved. Theories of human culture often predict that a particular pattern of associations will appear among certain variables because these variables are causally related in some specified way. What is meant by *causally related?* For example, variable A is a *cause* and variable B is its *effect* and their relationship is a *causal* one, if and only if it is true that control of variable A tends to give control of variable B. The concept of control in turn is best understood in terms of a servomechanism (Naroll, 1976b).

The notion of control itself fits well with the servomechanical model of human behavior offered by Powers (1973). Such a model supposes the existence of mental goals (reference signals = desires, instincts, drives), which in turn define desired states of psychological sensations (perceptual signals = feedback). The actual sensations are compared with the goals: discrepancies (complaints = error signals) are linked to appropriate responses (efforts = output quantities) by the organism. If the situation is under control, the responses by the organism tend to be followed by a change in the status being controlled (the input quantity), that in turn is followed by a change in the feedback (perceptual signal) monitoring that status, a change that reduces the complaint (error signal).

Human infants spend much of their time learning to control their own bodies, learning to make appropriate muscular efforts in order to achieve elementary purposes—to walk, or to grasp and wield a stick or a rattle, or to speak the language of their elders. When one control process has been mastered, it can be used as an effort (output quantity) to control some other process. Thus people control their wrists, hands, and arms in order to control the position of a steering wheel, in order to control the front wheels of an automobile, in order to control the course of the automobile, in order to get themselves to their place of work, in order to earn money, in order to buy food, in order to eat. Each link in this chain is a cause-effect link. Causes are associated with effects; changes in causes precede changes in effects; changes in causes permit control of changes in effects by diminishing the discrepancies between feedback and goals (i.e., between perceptual signals and reference signals). Associated with every link in this chain is a mental goal, and an apparatus, comparing the feedback with the goal. Human behavior is commonly managed through a hierarchy of servomechanisms, such as Powers (1973) posits.

Operationally, the crucial distinction is between two types of lagged correlations. The first, or spurious, lagged correlation reflects a regularity in the process but not in a potential control. There is a perfect lagged correlation between the fall of autumn leaves at Niagara Falls and the freezing of the ice bridge: the first lets the second be predicted infallibly. But you cannot freeze a pond of water in San Diego by knocking the leaves off the trees around it. *Acquiring control of the leaves does not help you acquire control of the water.*

If you are thinking about the possibility of controlling the water state (whether liquid or solid), you know better than to waste your time planning to acquire control of the leaves—even though in much of the North Temperate Zone there is a high lagged correlation between leaf fall and water state. But, on the other hand, if you lower the temperature of the water in your San Diego pond, and lower it enough, you will freeze the pond. Acquiring control of the water temperature, as measured by a thermometer, gives control of the water state, as measured by your ability to walk on it without getting wet. Operationally, the second or true type of lagged correlation is one which leads to *accurate predictions about the complaint (error signal) in the monitoring servo.* Cause and effect, then, means association plus goal relevance. Formal controlled experiments always embody all three elements: a correlation between treatment and result; priority of treatment over result; and relationship between result and experimental purpose.

Theories of human culture often predict that a particular pattern of associations will appear among certain variables because these variables are causally related in some specified way. Hologeistic studies commonly test these theories merely by looking for patterns of association. If the predicted patterns of association are not found, it may be concluded that the hypothesized causal relationships do not exist. If the predicted pattern is found, a presumption in favor of the existence of the hypothesized causal relationship is created.

There will, of course, still be plausible alternatives to the hypothesized causal explanation of the pattern of relationships. For example, a significant association between variable A and variable B may occur because: A causes B; B causes A; or both variables have been influenced by some other variable or variables. The salience of these alternative explanations is demonstrated by the fact that causal explanations of the association yielded by some hologeistic studies have been demonstrated to be false. Young (1962), for example, showed that the associations on which Whiting, Kluckhohn, and Anthony (1958) based their explanations of initiation rites were attributable to the influence of another variable. While it is never possible to rule out *all* possible alternatives to a hypothesized causal explanation empirically, there are statistical techniques by which *some* of those alternatives can be demonstrated to be less plausible than the explanation posited by the theory. The more rival explanations that are shown to be less plausible than the main theory, the stronger the presumption that the hypothesized causal relationships do, in fact, exist.

These statistical techniques discriminate between groups of mathematically possible causal explanations of the relationships among the variables on the basis of their relative plausibility; they analyze the relationships among the association coefficients between all possible pairs of variables involved in the causal model (see Rozelle & Campbell, 1969; Naroll, Griffiths, Michik, & Naroll, 1975). If the hypothesized explanation falls within the group that has been determined to be most plausible, a strong presumption is created in favor of its validity. If some or all of the other possible explanations can be ruled out on logical grounds, an even stronger presumption is created for the validity of the theoretical explanation; for example, if agricultural techniques are associated with average rainfall, it is reasonable to reject the hypothesis that agricultural techniques are a cause of rainfall. If the hypothesized explanation does not fall in the most plausible group of explanations and it is impossible to rule out *all* the explanations in the more plausible groups, then the hypothesized explanation is untenable. Examination of the explanations demonstrated to be more plausible than the hypothesized explanation may be very useful in correcting the theory, but such an altered theory cannot be considered to have been tested by the hologeistic study that prompted its generation; the probability of obtaining some specific pattern of relationships in a hologeistic study, after the relationships have been obtained from it, is equal to one. The new theory must be tested with different data, preferably using a different sample of cultures. Statistical methods of causal analysis can deal only with one-way causality; if A is a cause of B and B is a cause of A, the algebraic sum of the two relationships will be dealt with.

Statistical techniques of causal analysis can usefully be divided into two categories: synchronic, if they require data from one point in time, or diachronic, if they require data from two or more points in time. Synchronic techniques can be applied in any situation where there are at least three variables involved. Boudon (1970) has provided a powerful method of synchronic causal analysis that may be applied when parametric measures of association have been used (see also Land, 1969; Tanter, 1970; Gurr, 1972). Techniques of synchronic causal analysis, whether for parametric or nonparametric measures of association, are discussed in Blalock (1964); Boudon, Degenne, and Isambert (1967); Naroll (1970a, pp. 108–10).

A convenient tool for synchronic causal analysis is HRAFLIB Program TRIADS (Naroll, Griffiths, Michik, & Naroll, 1975), the work of Griffiths. The program deals with the causal relationships among three variables (and only three). There are twelve logically possible patterns of causal analysis among three variables. By studying the pattern of intercorrelations, the program reduces these possible patterns considerably. In some circumstances, it can pinpoint a single one of the twelve possibilities as the one most consistent with the correlation pattern. In other circumstances, it can report that none of the twelve possibilities is plausible; such a report implies that some fourth variable needs to be considered (or that the variables are not causally related). Most commonly, the program singles out a group of three of the twelve possibilities; each of these three is reported as equally consistent with the correlation pattern; but the other nine logical possibilities are dismissed as less consistent with the correlation pattern. Program TRIADS also states the confidence with which it reaches its conclusions. All of its conclusions, however, depend upon the assumption that any fourth (lurking) variable creates results completely unrelated to that created by any of the inside variables (Blalock, 1964, p. 46). They depend further upon the assumption that any outside variable is not affecting more than one of the three inside variables (Blalock, 1964, p. 48). Given these restrictions, program TRIADS is useful in narrowing the possible causal relationships among three variables.

Diachronic techniques of causal analysis are more powerful than synchronic techniques and may be applied whenever there are at least two variables. Their main disadvantage is a practical one; they require data on each of the units of study for at least two points in time, restricting the sample selection bibliographically. Their main advantage is clear enough. Suppose variable A is not merely *correlated* with variable B, but usually precedes it (changes first). Clearly such a state of affairs supports the hypothesis that A is cause and B is effect more strongly than mere correlation would. True, as economists have long known, lagged correlations may simply reflect stages in a single underlying process (see Croxton & Cowden, 1955, pp. 579–85, for example). But there are fewer underlying processes in this world than there are raw variables. A rival hypothesis on an unknown (lurking), underlying process is inherently far less plausible than a rival hypothesis or an unknown, underlying simple variable. In other words, the verification of sequence alongside correlation reduces the lurking variable problem to the lurking process problem. Such a reduction is substantial. It is worth considerable trouble and expense. In practice, for most social science hypotheses, it constitutes the strongest test open to an investigator.

The potential power of diachronic analysis may be illustrated from some doctoral dissertation research at the State University of New York at Buffalo. In a preliminary, prize-winning paper, Divale (1974a) set forth a theory of the origin of matrilocal residence. That theory saw patrilocal residence as the normal type among primitive peoples. It postulated matrilocal residence as a special adjustment to migration: matrilocal residence breaks up fraternal interest groups and thus discourages internal warfare (feuding). Peoples who have recently migrated into new territories commonly have serious external war problems with the earlier inhabitants. Thus matrilocal residence is seen as adaptive; it enables the new migrants to concentrate their military attention on their external enemies. Divale (1974a) tested his theory with simple correlations.

Divale's doctoral dissertation (1974b) used ethnohistorical studies to date the entry of each society in his holocultural sample into their present territory. Divale's theory involves a whole chain or sequence of changes—a process. His theory sees migration by a patrilocal-patrilineal people leading to a cycle of changes in their kinship systems: (1) first to uxorilocal-patrilineal; (2) next to uxorilocal-bilateral; (3) then to matrilocal-matrilineal; (4) then to avunculocal-matrilineal; and (5) finally, back to patrilineal-patrilocal. His theory predicts that on the average, patrilocal-patrilineal peoples would be longest in their present homes, avunculocal-matrilineal next longest, and so on. In his dissertation, Divale (1974b) confirms these expectations. Other techniques of diachronic analysis are discussed in Pelz and Andrews (1964), and in Rozelle and Campbell (1969); while the authors discuss diachronic techniques only in terms of parametric data, their techniques can also be used with nonparametric data, although less efficiently (Naroll, 1974b).

The techniques of causal analysis discussed cannot deal with the possibility that some unconsidered, unmeasured variable has influenced the pattern of associations. It must be assumed that the factors not included in the causal analysis—random errors, for example—are not producing changes in the pattern of coefficients of association. The danger of this assumption has been demonstrated by Barrett and Franke (1970); they showed that a previous causal explanation of rates of aggressive and inhibitive deaths, which was supported by diachronic causal analysis, was wrong; not all the relevant variables had been examined. Causal analysis can never demonstrate causality. It can only create a basis for presuming that some causal relationships exist; that presumption is always subject to disproof on the basis of further evidence.

Deviant Cases

A deviant case is a "miss," a unit of study that does not conform to the theoretically predicted relationship among the variables. This section is concerned with how such deviant cases may be explained. For a theory to constitute a sufficient explanation of culture, it must explain the variations in value of its variables among the units of study. Theoretical explanations of these variations are generally in the form of statements such as: variable B, *slavery*, manifests a specific pattern of variation because variable A, *availability of resources*, manifests a specific pattern of variation. The variation in some of the variables (the dependent variables) is explained by variation in other variables (the independent variables). In a hologeistic study, the extent to which a theory explains the variations of its variables is measured by computing coefficients of association that describe the relationships among the variables. Squaring each of these coefficients roughly estimates the percentage of variation of one variable that may reasonably be explained by variation of the other variable. When a number of variables are involved, factor analysis can determine the extent to which the variables change as a result of their interrelationships (Baggaley, 1964, pp. 91–168).

If a hologeistic study yields results that indicate the theory does not explain all the variation of the variables, there must have been some cultures that did not manifest the predicted theoretical relationships. By printing out the name of each culture in the appropriate cell, HRAFLIB program ORDMAT (Naroll, Griffiths, Michik, & Naroll, 1975) can reproduce the ordinal matrix from which each coefficient of association was computed, making it easy to determine which cases deviate from the predicted relationships. If a sufficient explanation is desired, these deviant cases must be accounted for.

Can deviant cases be explained in terms of the methodological variables—sampling error, errors in data generation, random error? If an investigator wishes to explain deviant cases arising from a test of Nieboer's (1910) hypothesis, "Where slavery, there open resources," the absolute value of the difference of each unit's ratings on the two variables may be computed. The hypothesis predicts that the ratings on the two variables will be equal for each unit. Thus, the computations are a measure of the extent to which each unit is responsible for the failure of the theory to explain the variation of the variables. This measure can be labeled *deviance*; if its variation can be reasonably explained by variation in the methodological variables, the hypothesis provides an adequate explanation of the variation of its variables—that the deviant cases could be reasonably explained as artifacts produced by the method of study. In evaluating whether the deviance is accounted for, multivariate analysis of the relationships among the methodological variables and deviance would be helpful.

If the deviant cases cannot be reasonably explained in terms of the methodological variables, the theory does not deal with *all* the factors that are relevant to a *sufficient* explanation of the characteristics of human culture that it purports to explain. The investigator then selects particular deviant cases for further study—particular societies where slavery is present, but open resources are absent, or, contrariwise, particular societies where slavery is absent but open resources are present. The ethnographic literature on each deviant case is studied thoroughly, seeking any of the six following possible explanations, suggested by Köbben (1967), for the cause of the discrepancy:

1. Investigators seek indications of multicausality (the Boolean conjunction). Do open resources make for slavery only if there is also some other condition present?
2. They seek indications of parallel causality (the Boolean disjunction). Can slavery alternatively be brought about by some other condition unrelated to open resources?
3. They seek functional equivalents of slavery. Is there some other mechanism which supplies an alternate response to open resources?
4. They seek an intervening variable. Do open resources lead to slavery only by way of some third intervening variable (for example, warfare) that would prevent the expected result when interfered with?
5. They seek signs of cultural lag. Have open resources been so recently introduced that they have not yet had time to produce slavery as their effect? Perhaps several generations are required.
6. They seek some unusual individual leader. Has some charismatic person, who opposes slavery for personal emotional reasons, interfered with the normal or usual cause-effect relationship in the situation?

Any one of these questions, positively answered, supplies in effect a revised theory. However, the revised theory cannot be considered to have been tested by the study that prompted its generation. It must be tested by a new, independent, hologeistic study.

From all that has been said, it must be clear that a trustworthy holocultural theory test is a difficult and demanding task. Such tests are usually less sensitive and less accurate than other kinds of cross-cultural research. Hence, in agreement with Rohner (1975), it is preferable to test a general theory many ways. But, any general theory about variations in human culture or culturally influenced behavior cannot be trusted unless one of these ways is the holocultural way.

Notes

1. This paper is an extensive revision of Naroll, Michik and Naroll 1974 ("Hologeistic theory testing," in Joseph G. Jorgensen, Ed., *Comparative Studies by Harold E. Driver and Essays in His Honor*, New Haven, HRAF Press, pp. 121–48).

2. First cousins are classed as either parallel cousins or cross-cousins, depending on the sex of the two linking relatives. Parallel cousins are linked by relatives of the same sex; cross-cousins are linked by relatives of the opposite sex. In many kinship systems, these differences are crucially important. For example, a man's female parallel cousins may be sexually taboo, like sisters, while at the same time his female cross-cousins are considered desirable brides for him.

References

ADAIR, J., & VOGT, E. Z. Navaho and Zuni veterans: a study of contrasting modes of culture change. *American Anthropologist*, 1949, *51*, 547–61.

ASUNI, T. Suicide in western Nigeria. *British Medical Journal*, 1962, *2*, 1091–97. Reprinted in *International Journal of Psychiatry*, 1965, *1*, 52–61.

BACON, M. K., BARRY, H., III, & CHILD, I. L. A cross-cultural study of drinking, II: relations to other features of the culture. *Quarterly Journal of Studies on Alcohol*, Supplement 3, 1965, 29–48.

BAGGALEY, A. R. *Intermediate correlational methods*. New York: Wiley, 1964.

BANKS, A. S., & TEXTOR, R. B. *A cross-polity survey*. Cambridge, Mass.: MIT Press, 1963.

BARNES, J. A. *Three styles in the study of kinship*. Los Angeles: University of California Press, 1971.

BARRETT, G. V., & FRANKE, R. H. "Psychogenic" death: a reappraisal. *Science*, 1970, *167*, 304–06.

BARTH, F. (Ed.), *Ethnic groups and boundaries: the social organization of culture difference*. London: Allen & Unwin, 1969.

BERRY, J. W. On cross-cultural comparability. *International Journal of Psychology*, 1969, *4*, 119–28.

BLALOCK, H. M., JR. *Causal inferences in nonexperimental research*. Chapel Hill: University of North Carolina Press, 1964.

————. *Social statistics*, 2d ed. New York: McGraw-Hill, 1972.

BOUDON, R. A method of linear causal analysis—dependence analysis. In R. Naroll & R. Cohen (Eds.), *A handbook of method in cultural anthropology*. New York: Natural History Press, 1970. (Reprinted New York: Columbia University Press, 1973; pp. 99–108.)

BOUDON, R., DEGENNE, A., & ISAMBERT, F. Mathématique et causalité en sociologie. *Revue Française de Sociologie*, 1967, *8*, 367–402.

BOURGUIGNON, E., & GREENBAUM, L. *Diversity and homogeneity in world societies*. New Haven: HRAF Press, 1973.

BREWER, M. B., CAMPBELL, D. T., & CRANO, W. D. Testing a single-factor model as an alternative to the misuse of partial correlations in hypothesis-testing research. *Sociometry*, 1970, *33*, 1–11.

CAMPBELL, D. T., & FISKE, D. W. Convergent and discriminant validation by the multitrait-multimethod matrix. *Psychological Bulletin*, 1959, *56*, 81–105.

CAMPBELL, D. T., & LeVINE, R. A. Field-manual anthropology. In R. Naroll & R. Cohen (Eds.), *A handbook of method in cultural anthropology*. New York: Natural History Press, 1970. (Reprinted New York: Columbia University Press, 1973, pp. 366–87.)

CAMPBELL, D. T., & NAROLL, R. The mutual methodological relevance of anthropology and psychology. In F. L. K. Hsu (Ed.), *Psychological anthropology*, rev. ed. Cambridge, Mass.: Schenkman, 1972, pp. 435–63.

CAPELL, A. *A linguistic survey of the south-western Pacific*, new and rev. ed. Nouméa: South Pacific Commission, 1962.

CHANEY, R. P. Typology and patterning: Spiro's sample re-examined. *American Anthropologist*, 1966, *68*, 1965–70.

―――. Conceptual contention: a reply. *American Anthropologist*, 1970, *72*, 1956–61.

―――. *On the intertwined problems of sampling, data patterning and conceptual organization in cross-cultural research*. Unpublished doctoral dissertation. Indiana University, 1971.

CHANEY, R. P., & RUIZ REVILLA, R. Sampling methods and interpretation of correlation: a comparative analysis of seven cross-cultural samples. *American Anthropologist*, 1969, *71*, 597–633.

CLIGNET, R. A critical evaluation of concomitant variation studies. In R. Naroll & R. Cohen (Eds.), *A handbook of method in cultural anthropology*. New York: Natural History Press, 1970. (Reprinted New York: Columbia University Press, 1973, pp. 597–619.)

COHEN, R., & NAROLL, R. Method in cultural anthropology. In R. Naroll & R. Cohen (Eds.), *A handbook of method in cultural anthropology*. New York: Natural History Press, 1970. (Reprinted New York: Columbia University Press, 1973, pp. 3–24.)

COHEN, Y. A. Macroethnology: large-scale comparative studies. In J. A. Clifton (Ed.), *Introduction to cultural anthropology: essays in the scope and methods of the science of man*. Boston: Houghton Mifflin, 1968, pp. 402–49.

CRONBACH, L. J., & MEEHL, P. E. Construct validity in psychological tests. *Psychological Bulletin*, 1955, *52*, 281–302.

CROXTON, F. E., & COWDEN, D. J. *Applied general statistics*, 3d ed. Englewood Cliffs, N.J.: Prentice-Hall, 1955.

DAWSON, J. L. M. Theory and research in cross-cultural psychology. *Bulletin of the British Psychological Society*, 1971, *24*, 291–306.

DIVALE, W. T. Migration, external warfare and matrilocal residence. *Behavior Science Research*, 1974a, *9*, 75–134.

―――. *The causes of matrilocal residence: a cross-ethnohistorical survey*. Ann Arbor, Mich.: University Microfilm No. 75-7742, 1974b.

DIXON, W. J., & MASSEY, F. J., JR. *Introduction to statistical analysis*, 3d ed. New York: McGraw-Hill, 1969.

DRIVER, H. E., & SCHUESSLER, K. F. Factor analysis of ethnographic data. *American Anthropologist*, 1957, *59*, 655–63.

DURBIN, M. Basic terms—off color? *Semiotica*, 1972, *6*, 257–78.

DURKHEIM, E. *Suicide: a study in sociology.* Glencoe, Ill.: Free Press (English translation), 1951. (First publication: *Le suicide*, Paris: F. Alcan, 1897.)

EMBER, M. Taxonomy in comparative studies. In R. Naroll & R. Cohen (Eds.), *A handbook of method in cultural anthropology.* New York: Natural History Press, 1970. (Reprinted New York: Columbia University Press, 1973, pp. 697–706.)

ERICKSON, E. E. Galton's worst: a note on Ember's reflection. In J. M. Schaefer (Ed.), *Studies in cultural diffusion: Galton's problem.* New Haven: Human Relations Area Files, HRAFlex Books, W6–002, 1974, pp. 62–83.

FERNANDEZ, J. W. *Redistribution and ritual reintegration in Fang.* Doctoral dissertation. Northwestern University, 1963.

FORD, C. S. (Ed.), *Cross-cultural approaches: readings in comparative research.* New Haven: HRAF Press, 1967.

FREUND, J. E. *Modern elementary statistics*, 3d ed. Englewood Cliffs, N.J.: Prentice-Hall, 1967.

GILLESPIE, J. V., & NESVOLD, B. A. (Eds.), *Macro-quantitative analysis: conflict development and democratization.* Beverly Hills: Sage, 1971.

GOODENOUGH, W. Residence rules. *Southwestern Journal of Anthropology*, 1956, *12*, 22–37.

———. *Description and comparison in cultural anthropology.* Chicago: Aldine, 1970.

GREENWAY, J. *Bibliography of the Australian aborigines and the native people of Torres Strait to 1959.* Sydney: Angus and Robertson, 1963.

GURR, T. R. *Politimetrics: an introduction to quantitative macropolitics.* Englewood Cliffs, N.J.: Prentice-Hall, 1972.

GUTHRIE, G. M. Unexpected correlations and the cross-cultural method. *Journal of, Cross-cultural Psychology*, 1971, *2*, 315–24.

HAEKEL, J. Source criticism in anthropology. (T. A. Tatje & E. M. Schepers, trans.) In R. Naroll & R. Cohen (Eds.), *A handbook of method in cultural anthropology.* New York: Natural History Press, 1970. (Reprinted New York: Columbia University Press, 1973, pp. 147–64.)

HAUSER, P. M. Cultural and personal obstacles to economic influence in the less developed areas. *Human Organization*, 1959, *18*, 78–80.

HELM, J. (Ed.), *Essays on the problem of tribe.* Proceedings, American Ethnological Society, 1967.

HOLMBERG, A. R. *Nomads of the long bow: the Siriono of eastern Bolivia.* Smithsonian Institution, Institute of Social Anthropology, Publication 10. Washington, D.C.: Government Printing Office, 1950.

HOLT, R. T., & TURNER, J. E., (Eds.), *The methodology of comparative research.* New York: Free Press, 1970.

HYMES, D. Linguistic problems in defining the problem of "tribe." In J. Helm (Ed.), *Essays on the problem of tribe.* Proceedings, American Ethnological Society, 1967, pp. 23–48.

JANDA, K. Data quality control and library research on political parties. In R. Naroll & R. Cohen (Eds.), *A handbook of method in cultural anthropology.* New York: Natural History Press, 1970. (Reprinted New York: Columbia University Press, 1973, pp. 962–73.)

JORGENSEN, J. G. Salish language and culture: a statistical analysis of internal relationships, history and evolution. *Indiana University Publications, Language Science Monographs 3*, 1969.

KENNEY, J. F., & KEEPING, E. S. *Mathematics of statistics*, 2d ed. (2 vols.) Princeton, N.J.: Van Nostrand, 1951.

KÖBBEN, A. J. F. New ways of presenting an old idea: the statistical method in social anthropology. *Journal of the Royal Anthropological Institute of Great Britain and Ireland*, 1952, *82*, 129–46. (Reprinted in Moore, 1966, pp. 166–92.)

————. Why exceptions? The logic of cross-cultural analysis. *Current Anthropology*, 1967, *8*, 3–19.

————. Cause and intention. In R. Naroll & R. Cohen (Eds.), *A handbook of method in cultural anthropology*. New York: Natural History Press, 1970. (Reprinted New York: Columbia University Press, 1973, pp. 89–98.)

LAND, K. C. Principles of path analysis. *Sociological Methodology*, 1969, *1*, 3–37.

LEBAR, F. M. Coding ethnographic materials. In R. Naroll & R. Cohen (Eds.), *A handbook of method in cultural anthropology*. New York: Natural History Press, 1970. (Reprinted New York: Columbia University, 1973, pp. 707–20.)

LEWIS, O. Comparisons in cultural anthropology. In W. L. Thomas (Ed.), *Current anthropology: a supplement to anthropology today*. Chicago: University of Chicago Press, 1956, pp. 259–92.

LOFTIN, C. Galton's problem as spatial autocorrelation: comments on Ember's empirical test. *Ethnology*, 1972, *11*, 425–35.

LOFTIN, C., & HILL, R. A comparison of alignment procedures for tests of Galton's problem. In J. M. Schaefer (Ed.), *Studies in cultural diffusion: Galton's problem*. New Haven: Human Relations Area Files, HRAFlex Books, W6–002, 1974, pp. 23–61.

LOFTIN, C., HILL, R. H., NAROLL R., & MARGOLIS, E. Mudock-White interdependence alignment of *Ethnographic Atlas* culture clusters. *Behavior Science Research*, 1976, *11*, 213–26.

LOFTIN, C., & WARD, S. K. An evaluation of Wirsing's adjustment procedure for the effects of Galton's problem. *Behavior Science Research*, in press.

MALEFIJT, A. DE W. *The Javanese of Surinam*. Assen: Van Gorcum, 1963.

McEWEN, W. Forms and problems of validation in social anthropology. *Current Anthropology*, 1963, *64*, 165–83.

MINTURN, L., & LAMBERT, W. W. *Mothers of six cultures: antecedents of child rearing*. New York: Wiley, 1964.

MOOD, A. *Introduction to the theory of statistics*. New York: McGraw-Hill, 1950.

MOORE, F. W. (Ed.), *Readings in cross-cultural methodology*. New Haven: HRAF Press, 1966.

————. Codes and coding. *Behavior Science Notes*, 1969, *4*, 247–66.

MURDOCK, G. P. *Social structure*. New York: Macmillan, 1949.

————. The processing of anthropological materials. In A. L. Kroeber (Ed.), *Anthropology today: an encyclopedic inventory*. Chicago: University of Chicago Press, 1953, pp. 476–87.

————. World ethnographic sample. *American Anthropologist*, 1957, *59*, 644–87.

————. *Outline of world cultures*, 5th ed., (revised). New Haven: Human Relations Area Files, 1975.

MURDOCK, G. P., & WHITE, D. R. Standard cross-cultural sample. *Ethnology*, 1969, *8*, 329–69.

NAROLL, R. *Data quality control—a new research technique: prolegomena to a cross-cultural study of culture stress.* New York: Free Press, 1962.

————. On ethnic unit classification. *Current Anthropology*, 1964, *5*, 283–312.

————. Cultural determinants and the concept of the sick society. In S. C. Plog & R. F. Edgerton (Eds.), *Changing perspectives in mental illness.* New York: Holt, Rinehart and Winston, 1969, pp. 128–55.

————. Influence analysis—an appendix; the culture-bearing unit in cross-cultural surveys; cross-cultural sampling; data quality control in cross-cultural surveys; and Galton's problem. In R. Naroll & R. Cohen (Eds.), *A handbook of method in cultural anthropology.* New York: Natural History Press, 1970a. (Reprinted New York: Columbia University Press, 1973, pp. 108–10, 721–65, 899–926, 927–45.

————. Chaney and Ruiz Revilla: sampling methods. *American Anthropologist*, 1970b, *72*, 1451–52.

————. The double language boundary in cross-cultural surveys. *Behavior Science Notes*, 1971a, *6*, 95–102.

————. Review of *The significance test controversy: a reader*, by D. E. Morrison & R. E. Henkel (Eds.). *American Anthropologist*, 1971b, *73*, 1437–39.

————. Holocultural theory tests. In R. Naroll & F. Naroll (Eds.), *Main currents in cultural anthropology.* New York: Appleton-Century-Crofts, 1973, pp. 309–384.

————. An exact test of significance for Goodman's and Kruskal's gamma. *Behavior Science Research*, 1974a, *9*, 27–40.

————. The use of ordinal statistics in causal analysis of correlations. *Social Forces*, 1974b, *53*, 251–53.

————. Galton's problem and HRAF. *Behavior Science Research*, 1976a, *11*, 123–48.

————. Cause and effect as servo elements. Paper read at the 5th annual meeting of the Society for Cross-Cultural Research, New York City, 1976b.

NAROLL, R., BULLOUGH, V. R., & NAROLL, F. *Military deterrence in history.* Albany: State University of New York Press, 1974.

NAROLL, R., & COHEN, R. (Eds.), *A handbook of method in cultural anthropology.* New York: Natural History Press, 1970. (Reprinted New York: Columbia University Press, 1973.)

NAROLL, R., GRIFFITHS, D., MICHIK, G. L., & NAROLL, F. *HRAFLIB: HRAF hologeistic computer program library, part one.* New Haven: Human Relations Area Files, 1975.

————. *HRAFLIB: HRAF hologeistic computer program library, part two.* New Haven: Human Relations Area Files, 1977.

NAROLL, R., & MICHIK, G. L. HRAFLIB: a computer program library for hologeistic research. *Behavior Science Research*, 1975, *10*, 283–96.

NAROLL, R., MICHIK, G. L., & NAROLL, F. Hologeistic theory testing. In J. G. Jorgensen (Ed.), *Comparative studies by H. E. Driver and essays in his honor.* New Haven: HRAF Press, 1974, pp. 121–48.

————. *Worldwide theory testing.* New Haven: Human Relations Area Files, 1976.

NAROLL, R., & NAROLL, F. (Eds.), *Main currents in cultural anthropology.* New York: Appleton-Century-Crofts, 1973.

NEEDHAM, R. Siriono and Penan: a test of some hypotheses. *Southwestern Journal of Anthropology*, 1954, *10*, 228–32.

NIEBOER, H. *Slavery as an industrial system: ethnological researches*, 2d rev. ed. The Hague: Martinus Nijoff, 1910.

OSGOOD, C. E. Exploration in semantic space: a personal diary. *Journal of Social Issues*, 1971, *5*, 5–64.

ORCUTT, G. H., & JAMES, S. F. Testing the significance of correlation between time series. *Biometrica*, 1948, *35*, 307–413.

OTTERBEIN, K. F. Basic steps in conducting a cross-cultural survey. *Behavior Science Notes*, 1969, *4*, 221–36.

―――. *Comparative cultural analysis: an introduction to anthropology*. New York: Holt, Rinehart and Winston, 1972.

―――. Sampling and samples in cross-cultural studies. *Behavior Science Research*, 1976, *11*, 107–22.

PELTO, P. J. *Anthropological research: the structure of inquiry*. New York: Harper & Row, 1970.

PELZ, D. C., & ANDREWS, F. M. Causal priorities in panel study data. *American Sociological Review*, 1964, *29*, 836–47.

PIERCE, A. *Fundamentals of nonparametric statistics*. Belmont, Calif.: Dickenson, 1970.

POWERS, W. T. *Behavior: the control of perception*. Chicago: Aldine, 1973.

PRYOR, F. L. The diffusion possibility method. *American Ethnologist*, 1978, *5*, in press.

PRZEWORSKI, A., & TEUNE, H. *The logic of comparative social inquiry*. New York: Wiley-Interscience, 1970.

RAULIN, H. *Problèmes fonciers dans les régions de Gagnoa et Daloa*. Paris: Office de la Recherche Scientifique et Technique Outre-Mer, 1959.

ROHNER, R. P. *They love me, they love me not: a worldwide study of the effects of parental acceptance and rejection*. New Haven: HRAF Press, 1975.

ROHNER, R. P., DEWALT, B. R., & NESS, R. C. Ethnographer bias in cross-cultural research: an empirical study. *Behavior Science Research*, 1973, *8*, 275–318.

ROHNER, R. P., & PELTO, P. J. Sampling methods: Chaney and Ruiz Revilla, comment 2. *American Anthropologist*, 1970, *72*, 1452–56.

ROKKAN, S. Cross-cultural, cross-societal and cross-national research. In *Main trends in the social and human sciences. Part one: social sciences, UNESCO*. The Hague: Mouton/UNESCO, 1970.

ROSS, M. H., & HOMER, E. L. Galton's problem in cross-national research. *World Politics*, 1976, *29*, 1–28.

ROZELLE, R. M., & CAMPBELL, D. T. More plausible rival hypotheses in the cross-lagged panel correlation technique. *Psychological Bulletin*, 1969, *71*, 74–80.

RUMMEL, R. J. Dimensions of error in cross-national data. In R. Naroll & R. Cohen (Eds.), *A handbook of method in cultural anthropology*. New York: Natural History Press, 1970. (Reprinted New York: Columbia University Press, 1973, pp. 946–61.)

SAWYER, J., & LEVINE, R. A. Cultural dimensions: a factor analysis of the world ethnographic sample. *American Anthropologist*, 1966, *68*, 708–31.

SCHAEFER, J. M. Linked pair alignments for the HRAF quality control sample universe. *Behavior Science Notes,* 1969, 4, 299–320.

――――. *A hologeistic study of family structure and sentiment, supernatural beliefs and drunkenness.* Ann Arbor, Mich.: University Microfilm, 1973, No. 73–29, 131.

―――― (Ed.), *Studies in cultural diffusion: Galton's problem.* New Haven: Human Relations Area Files, HRAFlex Books, W6–002, 1974.

SCHAPERA, I. Some comments on comparative method in social anthropology. *American Anthropologist,* 1953, 55, 353–61.

SCHWEIZER, R. *Methodenprobleme des Interkulturellen Verleichs.* Doctoral dissertation, University of Cologne, 1975.

SIEGEL, S. *Nonparametric statistics for the behavioral sciences.* New York: McGraw-Hill, 1956.

SIMONTON, D. K. Galton's problem, autocorrelation and diffusion coefficients. *Behavior Science Research,* 1975, 10, 239–48.

SIMMONS, L. W. *The role of the aged in primitive society.* New Haven: Yale University Press, 1945.

SIPES, R. G. Rating hologeistic method. *Behavior Science Notes,* 1972, 7, 157–98.

SPIRO, M. E. A typology of social structure and the patterning of social institutions: a cross-cultural study. *American Anthropologist,* 1965, 67, 1097–1119.

――――. A reply to Chaney. *American Anthropologist,* 1966, 68, 1471–74.

STRAUSS, D. J., & ORANS, M. Mighty sifts: a critical appraisal of solutions to Galton's problem. *Current Anthropology,* 1975, 16, 573–94.

TANTER, R. Toward a theory of political development. In R. Naroll & R. Cohen (Eds.), *A handbook of method in cultural anthropology.* New York: Natural History Press, 1970. (Reprinted New York: Columbia University Press, 1973, pp. 111–27.)

TATJE, T. A. Problems of concept definition for comparative studies. In R. Naroll & R. Cohen (Eds.), *A handbook of method in cultural anthropology.* New York: Natural History Press, 1970. (Reprinted New York: Columbia University Press, 1973, pp. 689–96.)

TATJE, T. A., NAROLL, R., & TEXTOR, R. B. The methodological findings of the cross-cultural summary. In R. Naroll & R. Cohen (Eds.), *A handbook of method in cultural anthropology.* New York: Natural History Press, 1970. (Reprinted New York: Columbia University Press, 1973, pp. 649–75.)

TEXTOR, R. B. *A cross-cultural summary.* New Haven: HRAF Press, 1967.

THOMAS, D. L., & WEIGERT, A. J. Determining nonequivalent measurement in cross-cultural family research. *Journal of Marriage and the Family,* 1972, 34, 116–77.

TRIANDIS, H. Cultural influences upon cognitive processes. *Advances in Experimental Social Psychology,* 1964, 1, 1–48.

WEBB, E. J., CAMPBELL, D. T., SCHWARTZ, R. D., & SECHREST, L. *Unobtrusive measures: nonreactive research in the social sciences.* Chicago: Rand McNally, 1966.

WHITING, B. B., CHILD, I. L., LAMBERT, W. W., & WHITING, J. W. M. *Six cultures: studies of child rearing.* New York: Wiley, 1963.

WHITING, J. W. M. The cross-cultural method. In G. Lindzey (Ed.), *Handbook of social psychology 1.* Reading, Mass.: Addison-Wesley, 1954, pp. 523–31.

————. Method and problems in cross-cultural research. In G. Lindzey & E. Aronson (Eds.), *Handbook of social psychology*, 2d ed. Reading, Mass.: Addison-Wesley, 1968, pp. 693–728.

WHITING, J. W. M., KLUCKHOHN, R., & ANTHONY, A. S. The function of male initiation ceremonies at puberty. In E. E. Maccoby, T. M. Newcomb, & E. L. Hartley (Eds.), *Readings in social psychology*, 3d ed. New York: Holt, Rinehart and Winston, 1958, pp. 359–70.

WINCH, R. F., & CAMPBELL, D. T. Proof? No. Evidence? Yes. The significance of tests of significance. *American Sociologist*, 1969, 4, 140–43.

WIRSING, R. *Matrix methods: new ways of measuring diffusion.* Ann Arbor, Mich.: University Microfilms No. 75-1, 531, 1974.

————. Second order partials as a means to control for diffusion. *Behavior Science Research*, 1975, 10, 143, 159.

————. Probleme des interkulturellen Vergleichs in der Ethnologie. *Sociologus*, 1975, 25: 97–126.

YOUNG, F. W. The function of male initiation ceremonies: a cross-cultural test of an alternative hypothesis. *American Journal of Sociology*, 1962, 67, 379–96.

ZUCKER, H. G. The standardized diffusion test. *Behavior Science Research*, 1976, 11, 71–102.

Name Index

Subject Index

Achievement:
  need for, 392, 413
Achievement imagery, 396
Achievement motivation:
  analysis of folktales, 404–405
  criteria for story, 258
  measurement, 258–260
Action research, 331, 362–364
Activity, 38
  analysis of activities, 41
  features of, 39
  flow diagrams, 40–41
  identifying activities, 38–39
  motivations, 41–42
  outcomes, 40
  recurring patterns, 39–40
Actor intention, 102–103
Adaptability, 17
Affiliation:
  need for, 392
African Bushmen study, 193, 202, 207
Ambiguous stimuli, 246
American Psychological Association, 49, 412
Anthropological cognition (ANC), 188–190, 192
  gap between anthropological and psychological approaches, 189
  stimulus generality, 189
  studies of Bushmen, 193, 202, 207
Anthropological literature, 394, 395
Anthropologists, 47, 412, 413
  cultural, 248
  folktale study, 413–415, 419
Anthropology, 12
Association patterns, 508–509, 511
  coefficients of association, 488, 506, 511
Attitudes, 231–232, 425
  attitude-behavior gap, 330–331, 333, 334, 340, 344–345
  investigators' attitude, 136, 143
  racial, 227
  scales, 425–426
  Sherif's definition, 233
  social change and, 227–229
  technique for attitude measurement, 231
Audiotape recordings, 89–92
  two-channel, 92–93
Authenticity, 128
Autocorrelation approach, 489–492

Behavior in naturalistic settings:
  data collection (*see also* Data analysis), 72–82
    coding systems, 96–109
      back translation, 103–104
      bases, 98–99
      behavioral boundaries as units, 97–98
      breadth and detail of coverage, 99–100
      coder reliability, 106–109
      coding and coder errors, 105–106
      cross-cultural equivalency test, 103
      inference, 101–103
      time intervals, 97
    data recording systems, 57–58, 82–96
      behavioral descriptions, 84
      behavioral replicas vs. transformations, 84–85
      event recording, 78
      observer-guided recording, 92–94
      recording mechanisms and instruments, 85–87
      recording motor behavior, 87–88, 91
      recording reliability, 95–96
      recording vocal behavior, 89–91
      representation of phenomena, 82–84
      subject reactivity, 94–95
      subject-recorder distortion, 94
    observation of, 57–126
      costs, 61–62
      definition of method, 59–61
      history, 58
      period of observation, 77–78
      phenomena to be studied, 62–72, 75–77, 82
      problems, 109, 113
      sampling strategies, 73–82
Behavior universals, 370
Behavioral sciences:
  contribution, 329
  research needed, 370
  scientists' tasks, 31
  unobtrusive research of, 324
Behaviorism, 230
Bias problem, 17–18, 30, 194, 207, 208, 293, 308, 324–325, 403, 493
  methodological, 229, 486
  in reporting, 307–308
Bibliographic error, 493–494, 496
Biesheuvel's General Adaptability Battery (GAB), 198, 201–203, 205–206

537